# TWENTIETH-CENTURY SHAPERS OF AMERICAN POPULAR RELIGION

# Twentieth-Century Shapers of American Popular Religion

Edited by CHARLES H. LIPPY

GREENWOOD PRESS
New York • Westport, Connecticut • London

**Library of Congress Cataloging-in-Publication Data**

Twentieth-century shapers of American popular religion / edited by
   Charles H. Lippy.
          p.     cm.
      Bibliography: p.
      Includes index.
      ISBN 0–313–25356–0 (lib. bdg. : alk. paper)
      1. United States—Religion—20th century.   2. Religious biography—
   United States.   I. Lippy, Charles H.
   BL2525.T84   1989
   291′.092′2—dc19
      [B]                                                           88–15487

British Library Cataloguing in Publication Data is available.

Library of Congress Catalog Card Number: 88–15487
ISBN: 0–313–25356–0

First published in 1989

Greenwood Press, Inc.
88 Post Road West, Westport, Connecticut   06881

Printed in the United States of America

∞™

The paper used in this book complies with the
Permanent Paper Standard issued by the National
Information Standards Organization (Z39.48–1984).

10   9   8   7   6   5   4   3   2   1

For Joe,
who brought me into the computer age

# Contents

# Preface

Religious broadcasters on virtually every television channel, evangelists seeking public office, religiously oriented "self-help" books available at supermarket checkouts and touted on late-night television commercials, sacred texts such as the King James Version of the Bible put on computer diskettes, board games and toys with religious themes, resorts and tourist attractions with a religious flavor—all are signs that in North America a popular religion not only exists but flourishes alongside church, temple, and synagogue. Although it is impossible to escape the presence of these manifestations of the religiosity of the masses, scholars have been reluctant to treat them as seriously as established religious institutions, if they have paid them careful attention at all. This book represents an effort to end that neglect by offering scholarly examination of the lives and careers of more than sixty individuals who have, thanks largely to the media, shaped popular religious sentiment in twentieth-century North America.

The book includes representative "princes of the pulpit" whose audiences extended well beyond their individual congregations. Ralph W. Sockman, for forty years pastor of Manhattan's Christ Church (United Methodist), was so well known from his radio preaching that at the peak of his career in the 1950s he reportedly received 30,000 letters annually from listeners across the continent. Writers of popular religious literature and music are also covered. Hal Lindsey, for example, has made best seller lists with works such as *The Late Great Planet Earth,* and the music of Bill and Gloria Gaither has become widely known among Americans of all religious faiths through recordings and concert tours. Novelists such as Lloyd C. Douglas and Morris West, whose works treat religious themes and have frequently provided the basis for Hollywood extravaganzas, also foster popular religion and hence merit inclusion. Additionally, the book examines representative figures whose impact on the popular religious mind has come about through effective use of a variety of media—figures like Robert Schuller, Oral Roberts, Billy Graham, Pat Robertson, and Jim and Tammy

Bakker. What all of these have in common is the nature of their audiences, which cut across denominations and faith traditions to include ordinary men and women of every religious affiliation and of no affiliation at all.

Even with these broad guidelines, selecting figures for inclusion was no easy task. An initial list of possibilities was more than twice as long as the list of those finally chosen. An effort was made to include men and women whose own backgrounds spanned the major religious "families" of Protestantism, Catholicism, and Judaism. In addition, care was given to have some balance between individuals whose impact still continues and those whose work lay in earlier decades of the century. In some cases, figures have been omitted because of the inaccessibility of reliable information about them and in a few cases because individuals still alive denied scholars' requests for necessary material. Others worthy of inclusion were dropped from the final list for exactly the opposite reason—material is readily available in such works as Henry Warner Bowden's *Dictionary of American Religious Biography,* J. Gordon Melton's *Biographical Dictionary of American Cult and Sect Leaders,* or other standard biographical reference works. In other words, the subjects of this study do not compose an exhaustive list of those who have shaped American popular religion in the twentieth century; rather they are suggestive of the types and range of individuals who have left an enduring mark on popular religious consciousness. If anything, the omission of figures who likewise influenced popular religion points to the need for further scholarly work in this area.

Contributing scholars developed their essays to a uniform format. Each essay begins with a biographical statement about its subject(s) and then offers a critical appraisal of the contribution of the subject(s). A survey of whatever secondary literature has been written about the subject(s) follows. Each essay concludes with a bibliography of selected works by and about the subject(s), where such exist. The essays do reflect the work of their authors, however. Consequently each emphasizes those biographical elements, analytical points, and critical studies that the scholar writing the essay thought best provided an accurate portrayal and interpretation of the subject(s).

Asterisks in the text following the mention of a particular person indicate that this individual is also the subject of a separate essay. Readers can use this cross-reference system to gain a more complete understanding of the work of any one individual as well as a sense of the interconnections among those whose work gives substance to twentieth-century popular religion in America.

An introductory essay by the editor discusses the character of popular religion, its vital role in American religious life, and critical tools for interpreting and understanding it. The volume concludes with a comprehensive index.

Work on this book has benefited from the help and counsel provided by many individuals. More than forty scholars from across the continent contributed to its creation by writing the individual essays; several were also associated with me in preparing *Religious Periodicals of the United States: Academic and Scholarly Journals* for Greenwood Press. Many contributors made valuable suggestions about precisely which figures finally to include. I am indebted to Professor Emeritus Robert T. Handy, Union Theological Seminary, New York; Professor William R. Hutchison, Harvard University; Professor Martin E. Marty, University of Chicago; Professor James H. Moorhead, Princeton Theological Seminary; Professor Russell E. Richey, Duke University; Professor John F. Wilson, Princeton University; and many others for suggesting possible contributors. Ginny Usher and especially Tricia Herring provided admirable secretarial assistance. Marian Withington of the Clemson University Library once again helped track down many technical details. I am also grateful for the support and guidance of Marilyn Brownstein at Greenwood Press.

Charles H. Lippy

# Introduction

Scholars have for many years recognized that it is not always a simple task to locate religion within a society or to isolate religious forces from other elements making up a culture. Witness the following hypothetical examples:

1. A female senior adult has been a devout Southern Baptist for more than half a century. Daily she reads her Bible, but she also watches numerous religious telecasts that feature personnel who are from different religious orientations. She sends money to, say, half a dozen of them as well as contributing to her local church. She also subscribes to several religious magazines, none of which is published under Baptist auspices. She draws on all of these sources for her own way of making sense out of her life and the world in which she lives. What is her religion? Is it Southern Baptist? Is it the religion of the television preachers she follows? Is it found primarily in the literature she reads? Or is it an idiosyncratic fusion of elements drawn from them all?

2. During the holiday season, a business entrepreneur sets up a temporary display in a shopping mall where he sells board games, puzzles, and video games. Many of them have religious or biblical themes. In conversation, he reveals that purchasers of religious games occasionally talk to him about their own religion. They include Catholics, Baptists, Pentecostals, Methodists, and a host of others. Are the games themselves part of what it means to be a Catholic, a Baptist, a Pentecostal, or a Methodist? Is the religious content of the games always in harmony with the formal doctrine of these groups? Do purchasers see any potential conflict between the views inculcated by the games and their individual religious identities? Do they somehow combine them to create their own religious world view?

3. A family includes a Jewish father and a Presbyterian mother. In the home, they celebrate religious festivals from both traditions, and they instruct their children in the teachings of both. At the same time, when they attend formal religious services, they gravitate toward the local Unitarian fellowship, for it offers a rational approach to religion that seems to them to transcend the particularities

of their own separate traditions. When Pope John Paul II visited a nearby city, they took their children to see him and brought back souvenirs that now adorn the walls of their children's bedrooms. What is their religion and that of their children? Is it any one of these traditions? Is it a mix of them all? Have they fashioned their own private religious identity even if they are unable to articulate precisely what it is?

In all of these hypothetical cases, it is not easy to define religion in conventional terms. Rather, religion seems elusive, something so individual and personal that it cannot be contained in formal religious institutions alone. And the individualized beliefs seem to defy simple denominational doctrinal labels. There is a richness to religion that the casual observer might miss by limiting religion to formal doctrines and fixed beliefs, to church, synagogue, and temple.

Sociologists call attention to this multiform dimension of religion when they distinguish between *substantive* and *functional* definitions, though both have some common assumptions. The most important of these assumptions is that religion provides some overarching framework of meaning to human life, that it deals with the "why" of human experience. A substantive understanding of religion locates this meaning primarily in such phenomena as particular belief systems (usually involving some sense of the supernatural), religious organizations like churches and synagogues, and the work of religious professionals such as priests and theologians. For those who follow this approach, there must be some specific content or character that distinguishes religion from all other components of a society. A functional understanding, however, looks more at what for a given individual or given culture actually works to provide some coherent meaning to the motley events and experiences in human life. Some of that meaning may derive from the beliefs or institutions that have the substance of religion; some of it may derive from other sources. For the functionalist, whatever provides this sense of meaning is classified as religion, even if it lacks the formal content or character that one following a substantive understanding might demand. Because a functionalist approach casts its net more widely than a substantive one, it is more likely to catch the ways in which ordinary people go about creating a coherent universe of meaning. In other words, it is apt to recognize that many, if not most, individuals draw on a variety of phenomena to organize and interpret their experience, not all of which may carry the substance of religion. And it is precisely this individual mix that constitutes "popular" religion.

At the same time, students of religion are acutely aware that even when there is an array of formal religious belief systems and institutions in a society, a gap remains between the way religious professionals and those with a more sophisticated intellectual consciousness understand the substance of religion and the way the masses do. In *Peasant Society and Culture* (1956), sociologist Robert Redfield gave a classic construction to this differentiation between levels of understanding and to the accompanying alternative ways of being religious. Redfield distinguished between the "great tradition" of the professionals, intellectuals, and elite and the "little tradition" of the people. Popular religion in this context is clearly akin to the "little tradition."

Examples of this divergent religious sensibility are multitudinous. In ancient India, to cite one, the distinction is reflected in the emergence of the caste system, with members of each caste having responsibilities or obligations (dharma) appropriate to its location in the social order. Only those in the upper castes were in a position to devote themselves to the religious pursuits that might bring release from the rebirth that all sought. But that did not mean the absence of a rich religious life for the masses. To the contrary, ordinary folk excluded from the upper reaches of formal religion developed a host of rituals, many centered in the home and some reserved for women (whose religious status was technically dependent on that of their husbands), to give expression to their religious sensibilities. Later this "religion of the people" combined with an emphasis on simple devotion to a Lord such as Krishna to lend order and meaning to the life experience of millions. For millennia, a popular religion, a "little tradition," has flourished alongside the "great tradition" in India and has functioned to provide meaning in life for the masses.

Even in contemporary Western societies the same sort of distinction endures. Religious leaders and organized denominational bodies issue pronouncements and take positions on a host of religious and social issues while theologians and philosophers pen weighty tomes expounding on the intricacies of doctrine and belief. But there is little evidence that such actions have a direct impact on the way religious followers act and believe. One illustration may suffice. The Roman Catholic castigation of artificial means of birth control is well known, but polls indicate that a majority of American Catholics see nothing morally wrong with using them and indeed do use contraceptive devices in roughly the same proportion as the total U.S. population. Clearly there is a gap between the "great tradition" of Rome and the "little tradition" of the people, between the substance of Roman Catholic life as perceived by the professionals and the popular religion of the people who call themselves Catholic.

Sociologist Thomas Luckmann, in *The Invisible Religion* (1967), approached this same general problem as it emerged in complex urban, industrialized societies, not in the peasant cultures that had caught Redfield's attention. Luckmann argues simply that in a society such as that of the United States, religion in its organized, institutional form—religion seen as the Southern Baptist Convention, the Roman Catholic Church, the United Methodist Church, and the like—has ceased to be the primary locus of popular religiosity. Tacit allegiance to a religious body, which may or may not include formal membership in the group, may be the source of some of one's beliefs, values, and personal meaning system, but only some. Luckmann suggests that individuals derive their own beliefs and values from a much wider range of human associations and groups—political parties, fraternal organizations, bridge clubs, athletic contests, the media—as well as from the more obviously religious ones, to formulate a personal, intensely private world view. It is this privatization of religion as it operates in the lives of ordinary people from day to day that renders it "invisible." Such "invisible religion" is also at the heart of popular religion.

Curiously, popular religion has until recently received scant attention among scholars. There are numerous reasons for this neglect. Popular religion rarely expresses itself in the artifacts of "high culture"—archival documents, great works of art and literature, intellectual treatises—that have been the scholars' stock-in-trade for generations. Instead the sources of popular religion that do exist have frequently been ridiculed by intellectuals, as if what fed the masses was hardly adequate to satisfy the appetite of scholars. Then too the sources of popular religion that do exist are often more difficult to locate perhaps precisely because they have long been seen as having little enduring value. But they exist in abundance in such materials as popular novels, devotional magazines, religious icons for the home, vernacular architecture, religious souvenirs, television programs, gospel rock music, and best-selling recordings of religious musicians. The cavalier treatment of such sources is evidenced by the failure of most of the conventional repositories—libraries, museums, archives—to include them in collections. Libraries may preserve complete runs of journals and magazines carrying scholarly articles or works oriented to the intelligentsia, but precious few preserve copies of mass circulation magazines. Yet it is in them that students will find one form of the public expression of the "invisible religion" of the "little tradition." Collections of folk art and other artifacts of folk culture may be one of the rare exceptions, but even in this context, all too often the word *folk* carries the pejorative sense that what is found here is not of the same elite quality as that of work found in a museum or a collection devoted to expressions of high culture; folk artifacts are more a curiosity than something to be treated with seriousness and appreciation.

The only sustained treatment of this phenomenon in the United States is Peter Williams' *Popular Religion in America: Symbolic Change and the Modernization Process in Historical Perspective* (1980). Though Williams acknowledges the influence of Redfield's categories on his own thinking, he also emphasizes the role of social change and social conflict in generating full-scale movements that reflect popular religious sentiment. Some emerge, according to Williams, when people who have been relatively isolated come into contact with aggressive outside cultures that seek to dominate or transform them. Also, during times of rapid social change the familiar, established patterns of understanding the world are in transition. The resulting dislocation often results in efforts to reach out for a fresh orientation, one that combines remnants of the familiar with the new so that individual and corporate life again fit into a coherent whole. Much of this change and conflict Williams associates with the process of modernization, in which the traditional yields to the rational, the diffuse to the compartmentalized, the sacred to the secular.

Whereas modernization may have accelerated the emergence of popular religious movements, particularly in Western cultures, strains of popular religion can be found at virtually any time and any place. In early medieval Europe, for example, Christianity on a local level frequently absorbed dimensions of popular belief and practice; in time, some of these syncretistic elements made their way into the mainstream of religious life. The fusing of Christmas with winter solstice celebrations is but one example. *Religion and the People, 800–1700,* edited by James Obelkevich, contains numerous essays showing how pilgrimages to holy shrines, intrigue with relics of the saints, personal beliefs, and even witchcraft represent expressions of a popular piety that sometimes had only a tangential relationship with the official religion of Christendom.

In the North American context, the diaries kept by numerous Puritans reveal a rich religious life that coexisted with the formalities of public religious expression and often exhibited an idiosyncrasy that challenged the Calvinism of the day. These works, as many have noted, were spiritual autobiographies that charted individuals' private quests for meaning in life. So too the famous Salem witch trials of 1692 may have had their genesis in a popular reaction to social change that was undermining the established Puritan order. The revivals of the eighteenth century, known collectively as the Great Awakening, made socially acceptable the public manifestation of intensely personal religious experience in a way that had manifold consequences. On the one hand, the awakening legitimated popular religious movements that later coalesced into Baptist and Methodist bodies. On the other hand, the emphasis of the revivals on personal experience enhanced the role of the individual as the final authority in religious matters, paving the way for the development of the private, individual world views characteristic of popular religion. At the same time, those who opposed the emotional excesses of the awakening, figures such as Charles Chauncy and Jonathan Mayhew, nevertheless argued for what the eighteenth century called the right of private judgment in matters of religion. This position also had as an unintended consequence the elevation of the individual as the final authority in things religious.

In the nineteenth century, numerous religious bodies and many groups whose membership crossed denominational lines began to publish a range of materials that fostered individual development of a private religious perspective. The devotional materials that began to issue from presses, the magazines of missionary societies and other groups oriented to social reform, and the many newspapers and kindred publications published in the native languages of immigrant peoples all helped to perpetuate the sense that individuals could construct a private religious world that complemented whatever formal religious groups offered. Sometimes the individual pursuit of a meaningful world took shape in movements that originated outside the structures of the denominations. Camp meetings, though perhaps most fully developed among Methodists, drew participants from a host of religious backgrounds (or none at all) and also influenced a distinctive style of vernacular architecture, according to historian of architecture Ellen Weiss. The holiness movement owes at least some of its beginnings to the quest of Phoebe Palmer and others for a more satisfying religious life than was found in the confines of the churches, although this one, like many others, in time gave birth to more-formalized organizations (many of which are now respected denominations themselves). The same holds true for much of the nineteenth-century fascination with spiritualism, millennialism, and communitarianism. The popular religion that flowered in tandem with organized religion also had more subtle manifestations. Colleen McDannell, for example, has shown how popular religion among both Catholics and Protestants during the Victorian era influenced not only the architectural structure of the ideal home but also the images for the proper parental roles for both men and women.

But it is in the twentieth century that popular religion in North America has had its most obvious manifestations. These are directly related to technological advances, especially in the media. Television, radio, and film have brought to the masses the voices and images of countless preachers, evangelists, and other religious personalities. The media have provided the opportunity for all sorts of persons to make a pitch for their personal religious perspectives and styles. Often the audience is unaware of the formal religious affiliation, if any, of a particular media preacher. Rather, there is the assumption that because each speaks with a ring of authority and because each has the imprimatur of a particular network or station, what is said must contain elements of religious truth. And what can be more individualized and private than viewing or listening to a religious teacher in one's own home? In this context the "invisible" character of popular religion is epitomized, for members of a television or radio audience are free to absorb whatever they wish and to combine it with elements of a recognized belief system to fashion a completely individualized, private world view. The Catholic Fulton J. Sheen, Baptist Billy Graham, former Assemblies of God Jim and Tammy Bakker, and Pentecostal Holiness turned Methodist Oral Roberts have all entered the homes of millions, directly or indirectly influencing the ways those millions are religious.

The explosion of the print media in the twentieth century has also left its mark on popular religion. Novels with religious themes, such as those of Lloyd C. Douglas, not only have sold millions of copies but also have frequently provided the basis for feature-length films. And although the novels may not evince great literary quality, they may have greater impact on the religious consciousness of individuals than do sacred texts or theological treatises expounding the doctrines of particular religious traditions. Magazines as well are part of the story. *Guideposts,* for example, has brought the "positive thinking" of Norman Vincent Peale to the masses with its "true life" short stories of the triumph of faith over any obstacles. Newspaper advice columns, such as Billy Graham's "My Answer," subtly direct the ways readers establish personal values and make sense out of many situations that threaten to unravel whatever meaning they find in life. Similar purposes are served by the growing number of religiously oriented self-help books that join their secular counterparts on book racks in airports, supermarkets, and drugstores.

The mobility of twentieth-century American society with the rise of the automobile has helped create new places of religious pilgrimage. A family on vacation can now easily attend a taping of the PTL (*Praise The Lord* or *People That Love*) Club at its studios near Charlotte, North Carolina, can spend a few days at a "Christian" resort, or can visit a Bible theme park. The news media reported anticipated traffic jams in all of the cities Pope John Paul II was to visit on his 1987 tour of the United States as hundreds of thousands were expected to travel to the places on the itinerary just to catch a glimpse of the Roman Catholic Pontiff and perhaps to attend an outdoor Mass or prayer service. Papal visits and the popular religious shrines of the automobile age have also given birth to a new style of religious relic—the souvenir or memento with a religious theme that one carries home as a reminder of the occasion.

Even such a perennial religious event as death has been transformed by the popular religiosity of the twentieth century. In articles published elsewhere, I have demonstrated how the practice of sending sympathy cards on the occasion of a death reveals how the masses cope with the fact of death and endure the grief process. Indeed the growth of sales of all genres of greeting cards with religious themes reveals the pervasiveness of popular religion, for on careful examination one will find that their specific religious content is minimal. Rather, manufacturers attempt to present a simple, somewhat vague religious message that leaves itself open to individual interpretation on the part of both sender and receiver. One can read such a message through whatever personal, private religious perspective one has created.

The point in all these examples is that the highly individualized, private, invisible religion that they represent in no way competes with formal religious organizations and institutions. Rather, they are all ways ordinary people draw on a vast array of resources to construct an understanding of their own life experience and the world in which they live. Neither is the influence of popular religion confined to members of any one religious group. It is not only Baptists who attend a Billy Graham crusade, read his "My Answer" column, or watch his services on television. It is not only Pentecostals who follow the PTL Club. It is not only Catholics who buy souvenirs of papal visits. All these phenomena cut across traditional denominational lines because they speak directly to the perceived religious needs and sensibilities of individuals, whatever their formal religious affiliation might be. They are all thus instrumental in nurturing popular religion in America.

Popular religion has no doubt existed in some form as long as human beings have engaged in the process of making sense out of life. But in the twentieth century, the resources at the disposal of ordinary people have mushroomed. Hence popular religion, that "little tradition" with an almost invisible character that flourishes alongside established religious traditions, deserves the attention of scholars who seek to understand the multitude of ways men and women go about the business of being religious. The following biographical sketches and appraisals of some of the individuals who have been most influential in this century in shaping popular religion represent an effort to promote just such scholarly scrutiny.

## Bibliography

Anker, Roy. "Popular Religion and Theories of Self-Help." In *Handbook of American Popular Culture,* edited by Thomas Inge, vol. 2. Westport: Greenwood Press, 1980.

Armstrong, Ben. *The Electric Church.* Nashville: Thomas Nelson, 1979.

Bellah, Robert, et al. *Habits of the Heart: Individualism and Commitment in American Life.* Berkeley: University of California Press, 1985.

Chase, Elise. *Healing Faith: An Annotated Bibliography of Christian Self-Help Books.* Westport: Greenwood Press, 1985.

Elzey, Wayne. "Liminality and Symbiosis in Popular American Protestantism." *Journal of the American Academy of Religion* 43 (1975): 741–56.

————. "The Most Unforgettable Magazine I've Ever Read: Religion and Social Hygiene in *The Reader's Digest.*" *Journal of Popular Culture* 10 (1976): 181–90.

————. "Popular Culture." In *Encyclopedia of the American Religious Experience,* edited by Charles H. Lippy and Peter W. Williams, 3:1727–41. New York: Charles Scribner's Sons, 1988.

Hadden, Jeffrey K., and Charles E. Swann. *Prime Time Preachers.* Reading, Mass.: Addison Wesley, 1981.

Lippy, Charles H. "Sympathy Cards and Death." *Theology Today* 34 (1977): 167–77.

————. "Sympathy Cards and the Grief Process." *Journal of Popular Culture* 17 (1983): 98–108.

Luckmann, Thomas. *The Invisible Religion.* New York: Macmillan, 1967.

McDannell, Colleen. *The Christian Home in Victorian America, 1840–1900.* Bloomington: Indiana University Press, 1986.

Martin, William. "Mass Communications." In *Encyclopedia of the American Religious Experience,* edited by Charles H. Lippy and Peter W. Williams, 3:1711–26. New York: Charles Scribner's Sons, 1988.

Marty, Martin E. "The Religious Press." In *Encyclopedia of the American Religious Experience,* edited by Charles H. Lippy and Peter W. Williams, 3:1697–709. New York: Charles Scribner's Sons, 1988.

————. *The Religious Press in America.* New York: Holt, Rinehart, and Winston, 1963.

Meyer, Donald. *The Positive Thinkers.* Garden City, N.Y.: Doubleday, 1965.

Obelkevich, James, ed. *Religion and the People, 800–1700.* Chapel Hill: University of North Carolina Press, 1979.

Owens, Virginia Stem. *The Total Image, or Selling Jesus in the Modern Age.* Grand Rapids: Eerdmans, 1980.

*Profile of the Christian Marketplace.* Newport Beach, Calif.: American Research Corp., 1980.

Redfield, Robert. *Peasant Society and Culture.* Chicago: University of Chicago Press, 1956.

Roof, Wade Clark, and William McKinney. *American Mainline Religion: Its Changing Shape and Future.* New Brunswick, N.J.: Rutgers University Press, 1987.

Schneider, Louis, and Sanford M. Dornbusch. *Popular Religion: Inspirational Books in America.* Chicago: University of Chicago Press, 1958.

Turner, Victor, and Edith Turner. *Image and Pilgrimage in Christian Culture.* New York: Columbia University Press, 1978.

*The Unchurched American.* Princeton: Gallup Opinion Research Corp., 1978.

Weiss, Ellen. *City in the Woods: The Life and Design of an American Camp Meeting on Martha's Vineyard*. New York: Oxford University Press, 1987.
Williams, Peter W. *Popular Religion in America: Symbolic Change and the Modernization Process in Historical Perspective*. Englewood Cliffs, N.J.: Prentice-Hall, 1980.

# William Aberhart

William Aberhart (1878–1943) has received a great deal of scrutiny from historians, sociologists, economists, and political scientists because he founded a political party during the Depression that dominated the legislature of the province of Alberta for a generation after his death and that dominated British Columbian politics for decades after that. But before Aberhart was a successful politician, he was a successful preacher and a pioneer of religious broadcasting in western Canada. His prominence in the latter role gave him the platform to enter the former. Yet Aberhart's unorthodox theology, strong sectarianism, egocentricity, and political career would separate him from the mainstream of Canadian evangelicalism.

## Biography

William Aberhart was born on 30 December 1878 in southwestern Ontario, the son of a German father and an English mother. He studied to become a public school teacher and principal, graduating from programs in several schools in geometry, drawing, and business. With difficulty he eventually graduated from Queen's University, Kingston, through a correspondence course. As a child he had walked to the Presbyterian Sunday School nearby and as a school principal was heavily involved in the Presbyterian Church.

Somewhere in the course of these studies, Aberhart encountered the higher criticism of the Bible, the application of scientific and literary interpretive techniques to biblical texts. Higher criticism deeply challenged Aberhart's faith, and he rejoiced in 1900 or 1901 to find answers in a correspondence course written by C. I. Scofield*, author of the well-known study Bible. These lessons moved Aberhart from Reformed theology to dispensationalism, the idea that history is divided into epochs, or dispensations, culminating in the millennial reign of Christ. He began to teach, while still a Presbyterian elder, that the true church could not produce a Christian society but should rather add converts and wait for the rapture, a central feature of dispensationalist thought.

Aberhart approached the Presbyterian Church for sponsorship to help him attend Knox College to prepare for pastoral ministry. He was turned down on the ground that the denomination could not afford to support married men with children—Aberhart had two by this time, having married in 1902 and having had two daughters shortly thereafter.

Aberhart in 1905 received an offer to preside over a high school in Calgary. Over the next decade, he served a number of schools and churches in Calgary, eventually teaching at Crescent Heights High School and preaching at West-bourne Baptist Church. This move to a Baptist Church (by way of time in both a Presbyterian and a Methodist congregation) did not seem to indicate any theological difficulties with Presbyterianism. Rather, Aberhart simply sought a place in which he could preach regularly, and Westbourne furnished him this opportunity. Westbourne could do so because it was a poor, struggling church with large debts—a mission, really, shored up by the denomination. Aberhart filled in as pastor without pay, and with an increase of numbers and funds under his leadership, the church retired its debt a year and a half later.

In the custom of many churches at the time, Aberhart had held a Bible class on Sunday afternoons in the two previous churches and continued to do so at Westbourne. Under the charismatic leadership of the tall, heavy man with the piercing blue eyes, the classes had drawn so many that by late 1917 Aberhart had begun a Thursday evening class as well. This class, open to all Christians, attracted persons from several denominations, and once it moved to Westbourne it continued to attract many non-Baptists, including some from his earlier Pres-byterian and Methodist classes.

Aberhart attracted people by his preaching of dispensationalism, especially its explanations of the "end times" or "last days" before the second coming of Christ—which Aberhart thought to be quite near. From this emphasis the class received the name "Prophetic Bible Conference." Aberhart, however, like many dispensational preachers, did not focus on the interpretation of prophecy as mere prediction of the future; rather, he constantly emphasized the shortness of time before the Lord's return so as to prompt soul-searching, repentance, and con-version.

Westbourne, having made good on its debts, petitioned the Home Mission Board of the Baptist Union of Western Canada for funds to hire a full-time pastor. The union told them to remove Aberhart and his class first. This opposition to Aberhart, never explicitly justified, may have arisen out of concern over an influential teacher who was not formally a Baptist and not ordained. It may also have arisen out of concern over some of Aberhart's theological emphases—whether dispensationalism itself or some of his increasingly eccentric ideas, like the use of Matthew 5:18 to support the inerrancy of the King James Version

(KJV) of the Bible. And one cannot discount the possibility of simple jealousy over the success of a man who taught members of other pastors' churches. Westbourne didn't care what the reason was: the church countered by making Aberhart unofficial pastor, letting him retain his principalship.

Aberhart continued to enjoy success in his Bible classes, ultimately having to move them to the Grand Theatre to accommodate the crowd. Here he used a dispensational chart he had painted on a piece of cloth measuring six by twenty-one feet. He welcomed audience response and would take questions at the end of his lectures, the answers to which he would prepare while the audience sang a hymn. Well known for his ability to remember people's names, he also could identify chapter-and-verse references for most passages of Scripture and prefaced his answers with the authoritative phrase "The Bible says," long before Billy Graham* would do so.

Aberhart adopted other media for his message as well. October 1924 saw a first issue of the *Prophetic Voice,* the official organ of the Calgary Prophetic Bible Conference, of which Aberhart was the editor and to which he made almost all the contributions. It took a stand squarely in the fundamentalist camp, its subtitle declaring it to be "A Monthly Journal for the Cause of Evangelical Christianity and the Faith Once for All Delivered unto the Saints." "We are fundamentalists in the actual sense of the word," Aberhart declared in the *Prophetic Voice* in 1924.

> We believe that the final court of appeal is the infallible verbally inspired Word of God. We believe it all, and knowing that the original manuscripts have long ago been lost, we have no confidence in those individuals, here and there, who claim such superior wisdom in the Greek and Hebrew that they attempt to correct what the Lord Jesus pronounced infallible and adamantine.

In the autumn of 1925 Aberhart began a somewhat more formal sort of Bible instruction, an evening school known as the Calgary Prophetic Bible Institute. Aberhart hoped that students, once graduated from this school, would be placed in empty rural pulpits and would withstand the menace of the new United Church of Canada (founded that year), which he saw to be the very incarnation of modernism.

Aberhart also began the Radio Sunday School correspondence course in 1926. At first, lessons by U.S. writers were used, but Aberhart later prepared the lessons himself. Question sheets were attached, and successful students were awarded prizes. The lessons were provided free, and adults were encouraged to sponsor a student for fifty cents a year. The peak year of 1938–39 saw over 9,000 students enrolled. Members not only of evangelical denominations but also of the United Church and other mainline groups enrolled in these radio classes and in the Bible Institute.

Aberhart continued to use the radio, in 1929 broadcasting the popular Prophetic Bible Conference from the Grand Theatre over Calgary's station, CFCN. By

1935 Aberhart was broadcasting five hours every Sunday over several Alberta stations, with a radio audience estimated at 350,000.

The Bible Institute too had continued to grow, and Aberhart raised money for a permanent structure for it by encouraging supporters to purchase "sods" (units of the lot) for $100, bricks for twenty-five cents, and rafters for another price. Subscribers received the added bonus of having their names read over the radio, a bonus not to be despised among rural folk whose contact with the larger world came largely through the radio. This and other fund-raising schemes paid off, and William Bell Riley, well-known American fundamentalist, preached at the grand opening of the building in October 1927.

The 1920s, which saw so much apparent success for Aberhart, saw also the emergence of several characteristics of his ministry that would alienate him from the general evangelical community. First, in this period Aberhart began to teach things well beyond the usual range of evangelical theology. Perhaps the least unusual teaching was Aberhart's defense of the inerrancy of the Authorized, or King James, Version of the Bible. True to the mentality of one trained in geometry and business, Aberhart looked for and found in the Bible straightforward truth. With the dispensational scheme to "rightly divide the Word of truth," Aberhart had found the key and needed no study of the languages behind his infallible translation. He buttressed this idea with the contention that the Textus Receptus, on which the KJV was based, had been preserved by God in the Swiss Alps, free from Roman Catholic contamination.

Second, early in this decade he made friends with H. McAllister, a "Jesus only" Pentecostal pastor of a new church in northeast Calgary. Under this man's influence, in 1922 Aberhart began to teach that believer's baptism not only declared one's faith in Christ and introduced one formally into the church, as believer's churches of most sorts assert, but also was the occasion in which the believer received the Holy Spirit. Moreover, Aberhart taught, baptism should be performed in the name of Jesus only (hence the name of the Pentecostal group), presumably following Acts 8:14–17 and 19:1–6. With these ideas came emphasis on each believer's using his or her spiritual gifts in the life of the congregation, although Aberhart encouraged the church to value prophecy, faith, teaching, and exhortation above other gifts normally emphasized in Pentecostal gatherings, specifically those of tongues and healing. These teachings would have been enough to separate Aberhart from most evangelicals of the time, who would not have had fellowship with Pentecostals of any stripe, and enough even to separate him from many Pentecostals, who would see the "Jesus only" baptism as connected with the "Jesus only" unitarian heresy current in some Pentecostal circles.

Aberhart's new theology embraced more than ordinance and worship, however. Westbourne had hired a new pastor at last, Ernest Hansell, but Aberhart retained both his job as school principal and his role as leader of the church. At first he used the title "Moderator," but later, as part of his unusual interpretation of the New Testament's teaching regarding the church, he assumed the title

"Apostle," since spiritual gifts could be received, he said, only directly as by the original apostles at Pentecost or by the laying on of an apostle's hands subsequent to baptism.

With these unorthodox teachings came an increased sectarianism. Aberhart originally had intended the Prophetic Bible Conference to bring Christians of many denominations together. But by 1922 he forced members of other churches to break either with him or with their own group and brought control of the conference directly under Westbourne. In 1926 Hansell resigned. Some acquainted with the situation cited several reasons: Hansell had difficulty defining his pastoral role vis-à-vis Aberhart's "apostleship"; Hansell could not accept several of Aberhart's teachings; Hansell had personal troubles of his own, culminating in a divorce; and, according to at least one well-placed source, Hansell had discovered Aberhart at a typewriter composing letters to himself to read over the air. Hansell left in October that year and took a number of members with him.

Perhaps with this incident in mind, Aberhart and the deacons of the church acted to secure control of the new building. They placed the building funds in the name of the institute, and then obtained tax-free status by forming the Calgary Prophetic Bible Institute Church, which was comprised only of the deacons and those they appointed. Westbourne, then, would rent the facilities of this "church."

Aberhart, by mid-decade, began to denounce other Canadian denominations. He referred to the United Church as the Sardis and to the Baptists as the Ephesus of Revelation 2 and 3, and in 1927 he pulled Westbourne out of the Baptist Union of Western Canada over alleged heresy at its college in Brandon, Manitoba, and formed an independent church.

Aberhart began advertising the church as "extreme fundamentalist." He drew up a new creed for the church that distinguished between "general" members (those who had been converted and baptized) and "active" members (those who had been baptized by the Holy Spirit and possessed spiritual gifts). Most Christian theology, of course, has not made this distinction, seeing those truly converted and baptized as necessarily possessing the Spirit and the gifts of the Spirit. More unusually, the creed also lifted Aberhart to an even higher ecclesiastical eminence, as it set out only two church offices: apostle and deacon. Pastors, who in a creed written by Aberhart in 1923 were to be ordained by other Baptist clergy, were no longer even mentioned, and the ordinances of the church were now to be administered by the apostle.

The strain of these innovations soon cost Aberhart a majority of his congregation. Having moved into the new institute buildings, 65 percent of the congregation withdrew in 1929 to return to Westbourne. And whatever support his unusual doctrine, sectarianism, and personal arrogance had not cost him among evangelicals Aberhart would lose through his foray into politics.

The story has been told at considerable length elsewhere of Aberhart's discovery of the Douglas system of economics during the early years of the Great

Depression. For those born since those times it is hard to sympathize fully with the plight of destitute farmers—victims of financial powers in Ottawa, Toronto, Washington, and New York that they could neither understand nor influence and victims of drought and pestilence, the solution to which would have taxed the compassion and wisdom of the best of governments. William Aberhart had a pastor's concern for his people, and he was thrilled to find a little book promoting Major C. H. Douglas' ideas as the solution to everyone's problems, Maurice Colbourne's *Unemployment or War* (1928).

In 1932 Aberhart began a series of lectures on "the Bible and modern economics" at the Calgary Prophetic Bible Institute. He wrote his first secular book, a little outline of *The Douglas System of Economics,* in 1933. He increasingly used radio time to teach his version of Social Credit ideas—that a relatively few financial powers in the big cities were squeezing the farmers and that with governmental rearrangement of the credit system, plus a monthly dividend of $25 paid to each citizen of the province to prime the pump of the economy, things would improve dramatically. These ideas, apparently zany in their simplicity, bore a distinct relationship to the contemporary ideas of Lord Keynes and to those behind the New Deal of Franklin D. Roosevelt and the later policies of Canadian Prime Minister W.L.M. King.

The governing party, the United Farmers of Alberta, refused to listen to Aberhart's ideas. When sexual scandals emerged involving leaders of the party, however, and when the socialistic Cooperative Commonwealth Federation appeared on the political horizon, Aberhart formed a new political party to contest the 1935 election. His party sang "O God, Our Help in Ages Past" as its anthem and set forth Social Credit as "an economic movement from God himself."

Aberhart's party won the election with fifty-seven of sixty-three seats and 54 percent of the popular vote, and Aberhart thereby became the province's premier. The Social Credit party won again in 1940, although by a much smaller margin. The Supreme Court of Canada declared most of their distinctive Social Credit legislation *ultra vires,* but Aberhart did accomplish considerable good for the province, among which was a reform of the educational system and the protection of at least some farms from foreclosure through debt legislation. He died in office in 1943, but his Social Credit party, under the leadership of a graduate of the Bible Institute's first class, E. C. Manning, dominated Albertan politics for a generation.

Aberhart's political success came at considerable religious cost. Back in the 1930s, Aberhart's church went through several pastors, pastors who had been hired to take some of the load off Aberhart so that he could promote Social Credit. The last one, Ralph C. Crouse, was so incensed when church leaders would not listen to him that he took his complaints in 1939 to the *Calgary Herald.* The newspaper then ran a three-week series of articles charging Aberhart with lending money at high interest while denouncing banks for doing the same and with running the agencies and programs surrounding the institute like a dictator. About 130 members left with Crouse to form a new church.

Aberhart lost friends in the wider fellowship of evangelicalism as well. A small battle was fought in letters and over the radio between Aberhart and leaders of the rapidly growing Prairie Bible Institute in rural Three Hills, Alberta, over Aberhart's espousal of political solutions to the Depression. Like most evangelicals, the Prairie Bible Institute people believed the Depression to be a divine judgment on a civilization that had rejected God. Christians should vote intelligently and prayerfully, to be sure, they said, but Christians had no business trying directly to bring about social reform. The real problem was personal sinfulness, and the real solution was evangelism. Aberhart's proposed solution, said a Prairie Bible Institute spokesman, smacked of "materialism, lawlessness, and communism" (Aberhart, no Communist, had drawn liberally from the *Communist Manifesto* for his first tract and for many ideas afterwards).

Aberhart was also guilty by association. He himself had recognized the affinity between himself and others working for social justice, the others being no friends of evangelicals, like the Pope and Father Charles E. Coughlin. United Church pastors and even Mormons were running as Social Credit candidates. And Aberhart had hosted the notorious Hewlett Johnson, Dean of Canterbury, to speak at the institute—the socialist who became known as the "Red Dean."

Aberhart came on the air to declare these critics "bad sinners" for defaming one who "went to eat with the sinners." The differences were clear: Aberhart would welcome to his cause people of any religious persuasion because the cause was, at least immediately, political. However, he would justify it in his own religious terms to himself and his congregation. Most evangelicals, however, believed with the Prairie Bible Institute leaders that Aberhart offered nothing distinctly Christian and that he compromised for the sake of vain politics the supreme evangelical commitment to evangelism (which was, it is worth pointing out again, the basic evangelical solution to the temporal as well as the spiritual problems of humankind, since many evangelicals have seen temporal evils as the result of spiritual evils). Far from leading an evangelical political crusade, therefore, Aberhart gained support from evangelicals for Social Credit only in the same proportion as he did voters at large in the province.

## Appraisal

The career of William Aberhart, known to many as "Bible Bill," has proven perennially fascinating to Canadians: he has been the subject of at least two documentaries and two plays on Canadian radio and television. His pioneering of religious broadcasting set the pace for a number who would follow in Alberta and throughout Canada. His Bible lectures gave many their first exposure to disciplined Bible study methods and to dispensational theology in particular, which would become very influential among Canadian and American evangelicals in this century. He also joined others in articulating a broadly supported alternative theology and ecclesiology to the social gospel and United Church–brand of ecumenism prominent in that region at the time.

As important a religious figure as he was on the Canadian and northwestern American prairies in the 1920s and early 1930s, Aberhart's biggest impact on Canadian life came from his "baptized" political experiment with Social Credit, unique in the Western world in the political success of its combination of unusual political ideas with evangelical fervor. Indeed, even after Social Credit gave way to the Progressive Conservative party in Alberta in 1971 after thirty-six years in power, it became the most powerful party in neighboring British Columbia in the two decades that followed.

But at the same time that William Aberhart made that political impact, he moved away from the common pattern of evangelicalism in this and other respects. As "Apostle" and "Premier" Aberhart grew in prominence, "Bible Bill" lost his influence in Canadian popular religion.

## Survey of Criticism

Although a few popular and adulatory works about Aberhart have been written, most of the scholarly studies of Aberhart have been conducted by sociologists and have been of the "How could it happen?" variety. That is, most students of Aberhart and of Social Credit in general have not been sympathetic with him, with his ideas, or with the political movement he founded, and they have attempted to explain how such an eccentric fellow and program could have dominated Albertan and British Columbian politics for so much of this century. S. D. Clark's *Church and Sect in Canada* and the later study by his student, W. E. Mann, *Sect, Cult, and Church in Alberta,* set the pattern for a large body of sociological research to follow.

The more recent studies of David R. Elliott and Donald A. Goertz have examined Aberhart directly as a religious figure. Elliott has posited a fundamental contradiction between Aberhart's dispensationalism and his political ideas and program (a thesis that has touched off a small but lively debate); Goertz has followed up on an idea in Elliott's work that sees Aberhart as not, in fact, representing the mainstream of Albertan evangelicalism but rather as a broadcasting pioneer who increasingly departed from the center of that fellowship.

A treatment of Aberhart remains to be done that attends fully to both Aberhart's religious and political careers and that explains both him and his prominence in Albertan religion and culture.

## Bibliography

### Books by William Aberhart

1922   *God's Great Prophecies*. Calgary: Calgary Prophetic Bible Institute.
1924   *Ecclesiastes: The Wisdom under the Sun*. Calgary: Calgary Prophetic Bible Conference.
1924   *An Introduction to the Study of Revelation*. Calgary: Calgary Prophetic Bible Conference.
1933   *The Douglas System of Economics*. N.P.
1935   *Social Credit Manual*. Calgary: Western Printing and Litho.

1941(?) *National Monetary Reform*. Edmonton: Today and Tomorrow.

1942 *Post-War Reconstruction*. First Series. Edmonton: Today and Tomorrow.

1943 *Post-War Reconstruction*. Second Series. Edmonton: Today and Tomorrow.

### Selected Studies about William Aberhart

Boudreau, Joseph Amedee. *Alberta, Aberhart, and Social Credit*. Toronto: Holt, Rinehart and Winston of Canada, 1975.

Clark, S. D. *Church and Sect in Canada*. Toronto: University of Toronto Press, 1948.

Elliott, David R. "Antithetical Elements in William Aberhart's Theology and Political Ideology." *Canadian Historical Review* 59:1 (1978): 38–58.

———. "The Dispensational Theology and Political Ideology of William Aberhart." Master's thesis, University of Calgary, 1975.

———, and Iris Miller. *Bible Bill: A Biography of William Aberhart*. Edmonton, Alberta, Canada: Reidmore Books, 1987.

Flanagan, Thomas. "Social Credit in Alberta: A Canadian Cargo Cult." *Archives de Sociologie des Religions* 34 (1972): 39–48.

Giles, Mabel C. *A Tribute to William Aberhart*. Calgary: Calgary Prophetic Bible Institute, 1943.

Goertz, Donald Aaron. "The Development of a Bible Belt: The Socio-Religious Interaction in Alberta between 1925 and 1938." Master's thesis, Regent College, Vancouver, 1980.

Hiller, Harry H. "A Critical Analysis of the Role of Religion in a Canadian Populist Movement: The Emergence and Dominance of the Social Credit Party in Alberta." Ph.D. diss., McMaster University, 1972.

Irving, John A. *The Social Credit Movement in Alberta*. Toronto: University of Toronto Press, 1954.

Johnson, L.P.N., and Ola MacNutt. *Aberhart of Alberta*. Edmonton: Institute of Applied Art, 1970.

Mallory, J. R. "The Prophet in Politics: William Aberhart." *Canadian Forum* 30 (1951): 274–76.

Mann, W. E. *Sect, Cult, and Church in Alberta*. Toronto: University of Toronto Press, 1955.

Neatby, Blair H. *The Politics of Chaos*. Toronto: Macmillan of Canada, 1972.

Schultz, Harold J. "William Aberhart and the Social Credit Party: A Political Biography." Ph.D. diss., Duke University, 1959.

Stackhouse, John G., Jr. "Proclaiming the Word: Canadian Evangelicalism since World War I." Ph.D. diss., University of Chicago, 1987.

JOHN G. STACKHOUSE, JR.

# Herbert W. Armstrong

Since the time of the Puritans there has always been a strand of American religion devoted to obedience to God and to an ardent biblicism. This movement has often included such ideas as the observance of the Saturday Sabbath. Until the 1940s the movement claimed only a tiny fraction of Americans. Herbert W. Armstrong changed the character of popular religion by establishing the Worldwide Church of God as an important presence among religious bodies not only in the United States but also around the world. His radio and television broadcasts have reached millions of people, and his publications are issued regularly in many languages. At the time of his death in 1986, Armstrong's church claimed some 80,000 members and many more adherents.

### Biography

Herbert W. Armstrong was born on 31 July 1892 to Horace and Eva Armstrong in Des Moines, Iowa. The Armstrongs were an unremarkable family, and by his own account, Herbert's early life did not distinguish him. Raised in traditional churches, young Herbert stopped attending in his late teens. A self-educated man, he turned to advertising, where he enjoyed unusual success. In 1917 he married Loma Dillon, and the couple soon had two daughters, Beverly and Dorothy.

Herbert Armstrong's conversion began not with his own inquiry, but with his wife's. Studying under the guidance of a friend, she became convinced that she had been disobeying God by observing the Sabbath on Sunday. She confided her fears to her husband, who tried to dismiss the idea. But Loma would not be deterred, and to keep peace, Herbert set out to prove to her from the Scriptures that she was wrong. Instead, he became convinced that she was right and that the vast majority of the churches were wrong. This discovery, in 1927, marked the beginning of a period of intense study during which, according to Herbert Armstrong, God revealed the secrets of the Bible to him. Herbert and Loma soon associated themselves with the Church of God near Eugene, Oregon, where they had moved for business reasons. They joined this group because of its observance of the Saturday Sabbath and because Herbert believed that it alone preserved the biblical name for the church. During the same period Herbert began to write articles for the *Bible Advocate,* a periodical issued by the Church of God from its Stanberry, Missouri, publishing house. The same period saw the birth of two sons to the couple, Richard David in 1928 and Garner Ted in 1930.

By 1930, Herbert Armstrong's place in the Church of God seemed clear. He had begun to lead evangelistic meetings for local groups and in 1931 was ordained in the Oregon Conference. Nonetheless, the seeds of his later ministry were already visible. In 1933 he began another series of evangelistic meetings at a schoolhouse outside of Eugene. The Armstrongs always identified these meetings as the beginning of the Worldwide Church of God. The meetings also marked Armstrong's break from the Church of God and the beginning of his independent ministry. In the same year, Herbert began a mimeographed newsletter that would become *Plain Truth,* the magazine voice of Herbert Armstrong's ministry. The next year saw the beginning of his radio ministry on a local radio station. The broadcast, at first called the Radio Church of God, expanded into a growing network two years later under the name "The World Tomorrow." The evan-

gelistic meetings had established a congregation that grew rapidly and that supported the increasingly diverse activities of Herbert W. Armstrong.

The character of the ministry changed dramatically in the mid-1940s. Armstrong's church in Eugene opened a publishing plant in 1946, and the radio
ministry expanded to large, regional stations. The same year saw the first of
Armstrong's speaking tours, which in time would take him to virtually every
corner of the globe. Armstrong also conceived the idea for Ambassador College,
an institution dedicated, at first, to training young men and women for Christian
witness. The college opened on 8 October 1947 in Pasadena, California. Despite
the limited vision of its founding, Armstrong soon pressed to make it a genuine
institution of higher education, although he fought to preserve its special religious
mission. In 1952 Armstrong ordained the first graduates of Ambassador College
into the ministry of the Worldwide Church of God. What had been a local church
ministry was now truly international in scope.

In the 1950s the Worldwide Church of God became more and more interested
in its international mission. Herbert Armstrong began another series of tours,
beginning in 1954, which took him into countries around the world. By 1957
his radio audience numbered between four and five million people weekly, and
*Plain Truth* magazine enjoyed a circulation of 175,000. Armstrong's followers
contributed millions in tithes to the organization. Armstrong's message continued
to attract adherents with its emphasis on obedience to Bible commands and the
unraveling of biblical mysteries. Armstrong described himself as God's ''Chosen
Apostle'' and insisted that he had penetrated mysteries of Scripture undeciphered
since the first century. He urged his followers to deny the Trinity, avoid divorce,
refuse most medical care, and prepare for the imminent return of Christ. Two
prevalent themes in his preaching were a strong emphasis on the Old Testament,
and Anglo-Israelism, a message that garnered him strong support in Great Britain.

The period of Armstrong's success was marred by growing tensions in the
ministry. Outsiders charged Armstrong and his aides with financial improprieties.
Some suggested that the leaders of the church lived in luxury while appealing
to the membership for sacrificial giving. Some insiders began to complain of
Armstrong's autocratic rule in doctrinal matters. These complaints led to a serious
crisis in 1972, when a group of dissidents first tried to take control of the church
and then left it altogether.

Perhaps the most serious crisis concerned the place in the organization of
Herbert's son Garner Ted Armstrong, who had become its official voice in 1963.
Marital difficulties and charges of infidelity led to his banishment twice in 1971
and a third time in 1972. Each time, after due repentance, the son was restored
by the father. Continuing difficulties and an apparent effort to wrest control of
the organization from his father led to Garner Ted's excommunication by his
father in 1978. The younger Armstrong formed the Church of God International,
in competition with his father, and may have played an important part in promoting charges against the ministry and its financial operations in early 1979.
As a result of a suit filed in California by some dissident members of the

organization, the church and Ambassador College were forced into receivership. The state seized all assets of the organization and took control of its operations. A prolonged court struggle eventually returned control to Herbert Armstrong and his associates, including Stanley Rader, longtime legal counsel for the Worldwide Church of God. All charges in the case were dropped, but not before the church organization had suffered traumatic disruption.

Recent years have brought fewer crises to the organization. His authority secure, Armstrong retained his role as Pastor General. The death of his wife, Loma, led to a crisis when, in 1976, he repealed his decree against remarriage for divorced people. A year later Armstrong married his secretary, Ramona, who had been divorced. (Further tension ensued when Armstrong divorced her in 1984.) He continued to write and speak, despite ill health and a heart attack in 1977. After his recovery, many of the members believed he had been resurrected and would not die before the return of Christ. His death in 1986, at the age of ninety-three, left the Worldwide Church of God under the leadership of Joseph Tkach and a twelve-member Council of Elders. Garner Ted Armstrong, once the heir apparent, said his father had rebuffed all efforts at reconciliation and vowed not to return to the church. His organization, the Church of God International, claims more than 5,000 members and annual revenues in excess of $2 million.

**Appraisal**

By any measure, Herbert W. Armstrong's career was impressive. From humble origins he built an imposing empire of religious and educational enterprises. His control of the organization remained virtually uncontested throughout his life. When dissidents sought control, they did so on the supposition that because of his age Armstrong was unable to continue his leadership. In each case, a vigorous response by the Pastor General was sufficient to end the challenge.

Uncharitable reporters have often attributed Armstrong's success to lessons learned during his early career in advertising. Certainly these skills contributed to his ability to reach the masses, but other factors seem more important. Armstrong's message has, from the beginning, touched a chord close to the heart of American religion. His emphasis on the Bible as the answer to all mystery evokes the biblicism of America's Puritan founders. Armstrong always insisted that the Bible contains all the answers to questions about the past and the future. His message, with its promise of decoding mysteries long misunderstood, appeals to those dissatisfied with the preaching of the mainline churches. At the same time, he tapped springs of millennialist sentiment with his insistence on the imminent return of Christ.

Surveys have shown that the majority of the members of Armstrong's church come from the lower middle class. They tend not to be highly educated, and with surprising frequency they have left other fairly conservative Protestant denominations. Many seem to be attracted by Armstrong's certainty about the correct interpretation of the Bible as well as his persistent criticism of traditional understandings of Scripture. Others are drawn to his promise of God's blessings for those who are obedient. Followers accept Armstrong's authority over doctrine without question. They regard him as a prophet sent by God to bring the truth in the last days. Armstrong's message provided the appeal that generated his ecclesiastical empire.

Armstrong's personal strengths suggest possible difficulties for the movement now that he is dead. The only figure who has shared something of his charisma is his son Garner Ted Armstrong. Garner Ted's excommunication has effectively ended his influence, and there seems to be no one else to fill the leadership role. Continuing debates about matters of doctrine can no longer be resolved by decree from Armstrong, suggesting the possibility of growing dissension. Although the Worldwide Church of God is far from collapse, it will sorely miss its founder.

## Survey of Criticism

There is no lack of literature about Armstrong and the Worldwide Church of God. The popular press has issued a steady stream of reports about the inner workings of the church, especially during the crises of recent years. *Time* and *Newsweek* have reported on Armstrong extensively, and *Christianity Today,* reflecting its mainline evangelical perspective, has run dozens of articles in the last twenty years, most of them critical.

Indeed, other literature reflects the difference of opinion about Armstrong and his empire. Many treatments of the movement are, at best, unflattering. Marion McNair's *Armstrongism: Religion or Rip-Off?* is a clear example of this approach. William Hinson's *The Broadway to Armageddon* is a bit more evenhanded, as is Joseph Martin Hopkins' *Armstrong Empire.*

More-favorable accounts come from within the movement itself, including many sections of Herbert Armstrong's own books that tell parts of his story. Perhaps the most flattering view of Armstrong and his movement is Stanley R. Rader's *Against the Gates of Hell,* which offers his account of the crisis created when the church was forced into receivership. Rader's eloquent defense provides extensive background in the history of the church and the lives of the Armstrongs.

Bibliographies and copies of works by and about the Armstrongs and other leaders of the church can be obtained from Ambassador College, Pasadena, California 91123, or from the Worldwide Church of God, also headquartered in Pasadena.

## Bibliography

### Books by Herbert W. Armstrong

1964   *The Missing Dimension in Sex.* Pasadena: Worldwide Church of God.
1967   *The Autobiography of Herbert W. Armstrong.* Pasadena: Worldwide Church of God.
1967   *The United States and British Commonwealth in Prophecy.* Pasadena: Worldwide Church of God.
1978   *Incredible Human Potential.* Pasadena: Worldwide Church of God.

1979  *The Wonderful World Tomorrow*. Pasadena: Worldwide Church of God.
1981  *The Seven Laws of Success*. Pasadena: Worldwide Church of God.
1985  *Mystery of the Ages*. Pasadena: Worldwide Church of God.

**Selected Studies about Herbert W. Armstrong**

Chandler, Russell. "The Armstrong Empire: Revolution and Revelations." *Christianity
    Today* 18 (15 March 1974): 701–3.
Hinson, William. *The Broadway to Armageddon*. Nashville, Tenn.: Religion in the News,
    1977.
Hopkins, Joseph Martin. *The Armstrong Empire*. Grand Rapids, Mich.: Eerdmans, 1974.
McNair, Marion. *Armstrongism: Religion or Rip-Off?* Orlando Fla.: Pacific Charters,
    1977.
Rader, Stanley R. *Against the Gates of Hell*. New York: Everest House, 1980.

MICHAEL R. McCOY

# Jim and Tammy Bakker

In the technological heyday of the late 1980s, televangelism has claimed a viewing audience far beyond the dreams of its pioneers. No longer is this religious programming, often known as the electronic church, a simple rehash of Sunday morning worship. Like the charismatic renewal, it has cut the ropes of American denominationalism to embrace a diverse viewing audience. Breaking the constraints of its early pulpit-parson-potted-plant format, it has produced highly technical and remarkably sophisticated programming.

Scholars continue to debate the effectiveness and the impact of TV religion, but the televangelists remain largely unruffled by their critics. The sex scandal that toppled Jim Bakker in March 1987 from the pinnacle of power in his PTL empire drummed up a host of pleas for greater accountability in teleministries' fund-raising. Several televangelists quickly sought to distance themselves from the scandal. Others pledged to be more accountable in how they raised money and to open their books to the press and public. Still, the contributions continue to come in. They keep the television preachers on the air and in the living rooms of the faithful. They maintain this important parameter of a Christian subculture unlike, and far afield from, the traditional American concept of church. Among the most embattled and successful of the televangelists are James Orson and Tamara Faye LaValley Bakker, simply "Jim and Tammy" to their followers. The diminutive pair were the architects of the 2,300-acre Pentecostal Christian Disneyland called Heritage USA in Fort Mill, South Carolina.

## Biography

Born on 2 January 1940 in Muskegon, Michigan, Jim Bakker was the fourth son in a family of five children. Of Dutch descent, his father, Raleigh, was a tool-and-die maker. His mother, Furnia, was a homemaker. Tammy LaValley was born 7 March 1942 in International Falls, Minnesota. When she was a preschooler, her mother and father divorced. Her mother later remarried. Tammy and her brother, Donny, grew up with the six other children their mother bore to her second husband. Tammy Bakker attended an Assembly of God church for most of her childhood.

As an adolescent, Jim Bakker was shy and ill-at-ease. Photography captured his imagination, as did public speaking after his parents bought him a reel-to-reel tape recorder. His first successful stand-up performances were as a disc jockey who emceed high school dances. Though he attended Central Assembly of God Church in Muskegon throughout his childhood, Bakker said he did not really know God until one night in 1958. He was out driving with his girlfriend, Sandy, in his father's 1952 Cadillac. He ran over a little boy in his church's parking lot. The child survived the accident, but Bakker said the spiritual searching he went through over the incident led him to feel called to preach.

In September 1959 he enrolled in North Central Bible College in Minneapolis, Minnesota, where he met Tammy LaValley, who was attending classes at the college with hopes of becoming an evangelistic missionary. Because the college forbade students to marry, the Bakkers dropped out and became husband and wife on 1 April 1961. Their union produced two children, Tammy Sue Bakker Chapman (1970) and Jamie Charles Bakker (1975). After leaving college, the Bakkers began their marriage as itinerant evangelists, preaching in small churches in textile towns in North Carolina. Their first revival was in Burlington, North Carolina. In 1965, they went to Portsmouth, Virginia, to work with M. G. "Pat" Robertson's* Christian Broadcasting Network.

On 28 November 1966, Jim Bakker launched the televangelical career that would record his sweetest victories and his most bitter defeats. On that date, Bakker began what was probably the first Christian talk show, under Robertson's mentorship in Portsmouth. Not quite six years later, Bakker said, God told him: "I want you to resign your job at CBN *today*." The moment is recorded in Bakker's autobiography, *Move That Mountain* (1976). Shortly thereafter, Bakker formed Trinity Broadcasting Systems in Santa Ana, California, with Paul Crouch, who had been assistant pastor of Bakker's home church in Muskegon. In November 1973, Bakker resigned from Trinity after a dispute with Crouch. Half the staff followed Bakker to Charlotte, North Carolina, in January 1974. In November, Bakker took over as host of a talk show on WRET-TV and named the show "The PTL Club" for "Praise the Lord" or "People That Love."

Bakker soon leased a furniture showroom on East Independence Boulevard in Charlotte, using it as a studio until July 1976, when he moved his headquarters to Park Road. There Bakker converted a posh, restored colonial mansion and its twenty-five acres into Heritage Village. The theme was colonial, and staff members often dressed in old-fashioned costumes. That property was later sold to Forest Hills Presbyterian Church in Charlotte in 1986. In 1978, Bakker broke ground for what he billed a "Total Learning Center" at an estimated cost of $100 million on a site in Fort Mill, South Carolina, a few miles south of Charlotte. Today that property is Heritage USA, estimated to be worth more than $150 million. The complex includes a 504-room hotel, campsites, a mini-shopping mall, a $10 million water park, a pyramid-shaped executive office building, a state-of-the-art television studio, condominiums, and adjacent developments of private homes. In 1986, more than six million people visited Heritage USA. As attendance grew, so did the Bakkers' dreams. Before Jim Bakker resigned, he had talked of building a multiacre recreation of Old Jerusalem with drama, bazaar, and lodging areas; a 30,000-seat "PTL Ministry Center" patterned after London's famed Crystal Palace; and "Farmland USA," designed to include an indoor, all-weather country fair.

As before, Bakker probably would have realized those dreams had a 1980 sexual encounter with former church secretary Jessica Hahn not caught up with him. Bakker always differed from other Bible-thumping Pentecostals. When he so chose, he could be a dynamic preacher. But friends and foes alike say dreaming and building, not preaching, were his greatest gifts. Bakker's sermons always emphasized God's love and generosity more than hellfire and damnation. His television messages, from the simplest interview with a Christian author guesting on "The PTL Club" to the exegesis of a favorite Scripture text, sounded the twin cymbals of salvation and prosperity. To him, those are the fruits of the Christian life. Undergirding it all was Bakker's sincere, almost simplistic, Christian faith. His was—and is—a vision that thrived on crisis. In fact, some predict his latest downfall might someday be the platform on which he will build a new ministry. Neither of the Bakkers has ruled out that possibility, in spite of Jim Bakker's defrocking by the Assemblies of God.

Since their ministry began, Tammy Bakker has played the fool to Jim Bakker's straight man. She has been the more approachable, the more public partner of the Bakker union. When Jim Bakker was away writing books or fretting over PTL's finances, Tammy Bakker would host "The PTL Club" alone. Ridiculed by critics, including newspaper columnists and college professors, she nevertheless transformed the traditional role of the shy, demure preacher's wife into a casting of equal billing. A full partner since the beginning of the Bakkers' ministry, Tammy Bakker also became a gospel recording artist, the author of two books, and a role model for many of the women who invested thousands of dollars in Heritage USA. If one spends a few hours at the theme park and talks to the women on the grounds, one finds many whose makeup parrots the heavy mascara and eyeliner for which Tammy Bakker is famous. It is even easier to find women who will talk about how her televised testimony about her faith or her talk at a workshop led them to Jesus Christ out of lives broken by divorce, alcohol, and drug problems.

With his wife at his side, Jim Bakker is the only televangelist who had a hand in building the three largest Christian cable networks—the Christian Broadcasting Network, Trinity Broadcasting Network, and the PTL Television Network, or the Inspirational Network. Yet in summer 1987, PTL teetered on a precipice of disaster. The ministry's new leaders, headed by Jerry Falwell* of Lynchburg, Virginia, had sought relief from PTL's creditors—hundreds of television stations, construction firms, lending institutions, and others to which the ministry owed some $68 million. Seeking protection under Chapter 11 of the United States Bankruptcy Code, PTL's leaders sought to chart a recovery course while the ministry continued to operate. As Falwell begged for contributions on "The PTL Club," the Bakkers were almost back where they had begun, loading their belongings into a moving truck to leave their home in Palm Desert, California (near Palm Springs). They put the California estate on the market and moved to another of their homes in Gatlinburg, Tennessee. But within several months, Falwell had withdrawn from PTL, plans for financial reorganization had appeared to give contributors some voice in the overall operation, and Jim Bakker had been ordained by a small midwestern Pentecostal denomination. Thus the Bakkers' story is far from complete.

### Appraisal

What unusual qualities catapulted Jim and Tammy Bakker to such fame? What was it about them that engendered such loyalty and devotion in their followers? How did a pair of small-town Bible college dropouts end up at the center of a hurricane of controversy?

About a week before he resigned as head of PTL on 19 March 1987, Jim Bakker videotaped a special segment for "The PTL Club" from his home in California. It was the beginning of the end and provides an example of both Bakker's unflagging faith and his petulant feelings of persecution.

> I have over the years worried over my enemies. Over the years, I've had people who've vowed to destroy me and vowed to destroy PTL in their anger. But the Lord laughs over the plotting.
>
> I've watched those who have plotted against our ministry. I've watched those who have plotted against other ministries and other churches, and other men and women of God. . . . I've watched them disappear. . . . This is God's promise to you. The devil's tried to tear you down. . . . The Bible says you've fallen, you've made a mistake. But it isn't fatal, for the Lord holds you in his hand.

About three months later, Tammy Bakker talked with reporters, expressing similar sentiments.

> I know what it's like to be hunted like a little scared animal and to be running all the time. Not to be able to get in your car and go anywhere without the cameras pressing up against the car.
>
> . . . we will do whatever the Lord speaks to our hearts to do, and so far he has told us to wait. He just told us to be still and wait and that's the hardest thing to do. There's a verse that says, 'They that wait upon the Lord shall renew their strength,' and I've got the new Tammy version, but maybe I shouldn't say it. Maybe I will. They that wait upon the Lord suffer a lot and it does hurt to wait. Because Jim and I are action people. We're 'doing' people, you know, and it's hard to wait.

The Bakkers also are survivors. Time after time, they've rebounded from controversy and disgrace. A good example is PTL's 1979 tangle with the Federal Communications Commission. In 1979, the commission investigated claims that PTL had diverted or delayed spending money raised for overseas mission projects. The commission did not rule on the purported misuse of funds. Instead, it approved PTL's sale of a television station in Canton, Ohio. That ended the commission's jurisdiction over PTL. Whether the Bakkers will rebound from leaving their ministry on the verge of bankruptcy, from charges that Jim Bakker is a homosexual (which he repeatedly has denied), and from claims that they solicited funds on the airwaves for one purpose and spent them for another, will be settled by an assortment of court battles and government investigations under way in summer 1987. But the larger questions of the long-range impact the Bakkers will have had on Pentecostalism, televangelism, and Christianity in general will be harder to answer.

Theirs was and is a "you can make it" philosophy. Jim Bakker honed that message to a mesmerizing linguistic art on camera. But he also preached it, taught it, and lived it. His words brought hope to the gloomy lives of millions. Even as PTL staggered from one financial disaster to another, it continued to grow. PTL's cable network alone reached an estimated weekly cumulative viewing audience of 3.8 million with twenty-four-hour Christian programming. Jim and Tammy Bakker tearfully pleaded for money, then blessed Jesus when it poured in. Along the way, they acquired a taste for the finer things, owning at one time or another a Rolls Royce, a Mercedes Benz, a houseboat, and other riches. Through the Bakkers, PTL supporters enjoyed fame and luxury vicariously, rubbing elbows with celebrities and basking in a reflected glamor they could never afford themselves.

Such a gospel of prosperity shocked socially conscious Christians, disturbed more sedate, old-line Pentecostals, and provided first-quality fodder for a stable of Bakker critics. But the Bakkers' fans loved it. An estimated 120,000 to 160,000 people believed so deeply in the Bakkers' bigger-than-life dreams for the "21st Century Christian retreat center," which became Heritage USA, that they were willing to contribute $1,000 or more to become "Lifetime Partners" of PTL. Each $1,000 contribution, Jim Bakker promised, earned the donor three free nights' stay per year for the rest of his or her life at Heritage USA. Whether that claim will hold is a matter to be settled by the bankruptcy court.

### Survey of Criticism

Literature about Jim and Tammy Bakker has been scarce, though the scandal over Jim Bakker's 1980 sexual encounter with Jessica Hahn and the resulting controversy is expected to spawn a series of books and in-depth articles. Until the Hahn debacle, Jim Bakker usually received only a mention or two in books on televangelism or in volumes on the New Christian Right. Most scholars found him noteworthy for one of four reasons: his apolitical posture, his lavish lifestyle, his tearful television fund-raising, or his early association with Pat Robertson and Robertson's network.

In her book, *Redemptorama,* Carol Flake discusses Bakker mainly in relation to Robertson and to fund-raising. One of the most famous "last-hour" appeals for money by televangelists was made by Bakker shortly after he went to work for Robertson, she says. "Bakker appeared on camera and announced, 'We're on the verge of bankruptcy and just don't have the money to pay our bills,' and proceeded to break down and cry. As the tears splattered on the station floor, the camera remained fixed on Bakker's face, and phones began to ring. Bakker managed to raise over $100,000 in less than four hours and earned himself the title of Jack Paar of the Preachers."

Unlike Falwell, whose gospel is laced with sociopolitical messages, Bakker preaches a gospel of a different cast. Razelle Frankl, in *Televangelism: The Marketing of Popular Religion,* writes: "The programs of Bakker, Swaggart*, and Schuller* emphasize personal redemption and social change through religious conversions. The born-again experience is far more important than ethnocentric or political remedies. Thus, these teleministers do not use the charismatic leadership appeal. Rather, Bakker, Swaggart, and Schuller preach in the tradition of Dwight Moody, who converted individual sinners with a simple and positive gospel message."

Some of the most insightful commentary on Bakker is found in the pages of newspapers and magazines. His colorful career and ministerial controversies have been followed closely by a stream of reporters for the *Charlotte Observor,* the local newspaper in Charlotte, North Carolina. One of those reporters, Frye Gaillard, writes that even Jim Bakker's most intimate friends recognize the war going on inside the man, noting the contrast between Bakker the pastor—a persona characterized by compassion—and Bakker the builder—a man intent on raising big money to build big buildings. Gaillard writes in *Race, Rock & Religion:*

> Bakker's closest friends tend to see him that way, as a child at heart, but maybe also as a peculiar adolescent—caught in the crossfire of his competing inclinations.
>
> He is petty, insecure, self-absorbed and materialistic—deeply entrapped by worldly measures of success. And, yet, somehow, he is also decent—a sensitive, humane and self-effacing little man, who has developed an affinity for the compassion of Jesus.

## Bibliography

### Books by Jim Bakker

1976  *Move That Mountain.* Charlotte: PTL Television Network.
1980  *Survival: Unite to Live.* Harrison, Ark.: New Leaf Press.
1986  *Showers of Blessings.* Charlotte: PTL Television Network.

### Books by Tammy Bakker

1978  *Run To The Roar.* Harrison, Ark.: New Leaf Press.
1978  *I Gotta Be Me.* Harrison, Ark.: New Leaf Press.

*Selected Studies about Jim and Tammy Bakker*

Conway, Flo, and Jim Siegelman. *Holy Terror*. New York: Dell Publishing Company, 1984.

Flake, Carol. *Redemptorama: Culture, Politics and the New Evangelicalism*. Garden City, N.Y.: Anchor Press, 1984.

Fore, William F. *Television and Religion*. Minneapolis: Augsburg Publishing House, 1987.

Frankl, Razelle. *Televangelism: The Marketing of Popular Religion*. Carbondale and Edwardsville: Southern Illinois University Press, 1987.

Gaillard, Frye. "The Extravagant, Childlike Faith of Jim Bakker." *Race, Rock & Religion*. Charlotte N.C.: East Woods Press, 1982.

McLendon, Mary Adams. "Jim Bakker: Seen by Millions, Known by Few." *Saturday Evening Post* 253 (April 1981): 50–53.

Watson, Russell, et al. "Holy War: Heaven Can Wait." *Newsweek* 109 (8 June 1987): 58–62.

White, Cecile Holmes, and Sue Robinson. *Greensboro News and Record*, 3 June 1986, pp. A1, A6, and A7.

Yancey, Philip. "The Ironies and Impact of PTL." *Christianity Today* 23 (21 September 1979): 28–33.

CECILE HOLMES WHITE

# Bruce Barton

Small-town Tennessee, 1925, and the battle for America: two parties, fundamentalists and modernists, were engaged in a historic conflict. Each group had a particular vision of America, and each saw the other as threat and foe. The fundamentalists were champions of traditional, evangelical America; the modernists were boosters of progressive, educated America. Clarence Darrow lost the trial but won the battle. William Jennings Bryan and his fundamentalist followers left the town disgraced and defeated. In the eyes of many Americans, they symbolized provincial, narrow-minded, mean-spirited America. They represented a tradition that needed to be buried in an unmarked grave.

During the 1920s Americans witnessed a series of clashes between parties that defended different visions of America. The Scopes trial, perhaps the most familiar event of the 1920s to us now, was only one of many such conflicts then. Historian Arthur Mann suggests that the 1920s were characterized by a number of competing "fundamentalisms." The Sacco-Vanzetti trial, for example, pitted left-wing radicals against anti-Communists. Prohibition forced Bohemians to square off against teetotalers. Isolationists passed laws that kept immigrant groups out of America. Members of the Ku Klux Klan made it clear that America was the land of opportunity for old stock Americans, not for blacks or Jews or Catholics. The Depression of the 1930s did not eliminate but only mitigated these conflicts. After 1929 most Americans were too busy with surviving to wage war against competing parties and ideologies.

Bruce Barton lived during these decades of conflict. Like many other Americans, he engaged himself in battle against more than one enemy; but he also attempted, sometimes successfully, sometimes not, to reconcile these conflicts in American culture, both for his own peace of mind and for the larger public.

## Biography

Bruce Fairfield Barton was born on 5 August 1886 to William E. and Esther Treat (Bushnell) Barton. Bruce Barton's father was literally a self-made man. William Barton had left home early, wandered and worked throughout the Midwest for two years, and then attended Berea College. On graduation he entered the ministry, a profession in which he achieved modest fame. He served Congregational churches in Robbins, Tennessee, and then in Oberlin, Ohio, where he also attended seminary. From there he moved to Boston. He finally accepted a call to a church in Oak Park, Illinois, a suburb of Chicago. He remained there for twenty-five years, until his retirement. The Barton household valued learning and service. Besides their own five children (Bruce was their first), William and Esther cared for two others, both black. The family read often and carried on lively conversations around the dinner table. The Bartons entertained many guests, from the destitute to the famous. In such company Bruce learned at a young age to think carefully and to esteem people who had achieved position and success in life.

His father was no religious conservative. He decided early on to accommodate his theology to the new learning—higher criticism, liberal theology, and progressive thought. If Bruce Barton's books show signs of liberal theology, he was only reflecting what he had learned from his father. William Barton became a denominational leader while serving in Oak Park. He also wrote several books, the most notable being a biography of Abraham Lincoln. Barton admitted on many occasions that his father had set a lofty example for him.

Perhaps it was his father's enormous influence that motivated Barton to spend a lifetime striving for success. Always serious and sober, he recoiled from mediocrity. During high school he started his own small business; he also wrote stories for and later edited the student newspaper. Though he planned to attend Amherst College, his father insisted that he attend Berea for one year so that he would learn to sympathize with students who had to struggle to get through college. It was at Berea that he first worked in a printing office. He thus added technical knowledge to his experience in editing. Such skills served him well later on when he worked as an editor of magazines and then as an advertising executive.

Barton transferred to Amherst for his final three years of college. If he was one of the wealthiest and ablest students at Berea, he was one of many average students at Amherst. Or so he thought. He felt dwarfed by the abilities and accomplishments of others and thought himself to be inferior, a peculiar notion considering his many successes there. He eventually became president of the Senior Society, the Student Council, the YMCA, and his fraternity. He was also on the debate team and was elected to membership in Phi Beta Kappa. At his graduation, he was voted the most likely to succeed. He wrote later that his many successes gave him an overwhelming sense of responsibility. He shouldered that feeling for the rest of his life.

Graduation from Amherst in 1907 precipitated the first of several crises in Barton's life. He suffered from anxiety and insomnia. He was tortured by his lack of confidence and purpose. Religious doubts plagued him. He soon took a job as a timekeeper at a railroad construction camp in Montana. The distance from home and the relative isolation from culture allowed him to settle in his own mind what he believed and where he wanted to go with his life. Though he felt an obligation to be a minister, he realized that he was not suited for such work. His experience in Montana helped him to reconcile his emerging passion—business—with his religious values. If commercial activity was to be his vocation, he would insert his religious values into it. He would become a religious idealist in the secular world of business.

On returning to Chicago, he started work as an ad solicitor for the *Home Herald*. Within a short time, he became managing editor of the *Home Herald* and two other magazines. In 1909 he was hired to work for a Presbyterian journal, *The Continent*. He had to move to New York to take the job, which he gladly did. It was at this time that he began to write in earnest, and during the next several years he published many articles and editorials in magazines like *The Continent, Congregationalist and Christian World, American Magazine, Collier's Weekly, Red Book,* and *Farm and Fireside*. In 1910 he left *The Continent* to become managing editor for *The Housekeeper*. When it failed in 1912, he went to work for Collier's in order to market *Collier's Weekly* and Collier's books, including the Harvard Classics, a series of books being promoted by Charles William Eliot, former president of Harvard University. Barton had flirted with advertising before, but his first big success came when he promoted this shelf of books. His ad promised "the essentials of a liberal education in only fifteen minutes a day." However misleading, it was an enormous success.

While visiting his family in Oak Park one summer he met Esther Randall, whose sturdy health and adaptability impressed him. She too had distinguished herself during her years in college. They were married on 2 October 1913. They had three children together: Randall, Betsy Alice, and Bruce, Jr. Esther died in November 1951.

In 1914 Barton wrote his first major book, *A Young Man's Jesus,* which he dedicated to his father. The book, anticipating Barton's more extensive treatment of religious themes during the 1920s, presented a Jesus who was anything but meek, mild, frail, and weak. He was a "young man's Jesus," an outdoors type whose strength, courage, and power gave him the kind of authority to cast the money changers out of the temple and made him the most popular dinner guest in Jerusalem. "It is to present this truer portrait—of a young man glowing with physical strength and the joy of living, athrill with the protest of youth against oppression and intolerance, yet radiating a spiritual power that has transformed the world—that this little book is written,'' he wrote in the preface. "That men should have failed to remember how strong He was seems strange indeed, when you think of the thirty years in a carpenter shop, and the rough usage of His three years of public life. Much of the time He had nowhere to lay His head: His couch was a nest of boughs under the open sky. A fine physique glories in exposure of that sort, but weakness breaks down under it.'' Barton tried to sketch a picture of Jesus in rich, earthy colors to attract to Christianity the kind of people whose feet were placed firmly in the world. His portrait of Jesus was for the young and idealistic.

From 1914 to 1918 Barton was the editor of *Every Week,* a new publication that resembled *Saturday Evening Post.* During its short lifetime it achieved a circulation of 600,000. Barton's practical and pithy editorials reached a wide circulation. Later they were reprinted in a series of books. The first, *More Power to You,* appeared in 1917, followed by *It's a Good Old World* (1920), *Better Days* (1924), and *On the Up and Up* (1929). These collections of editorials reveal Barton's basic philosophy of life. They also disclose the tension in Barton's life and thought. To us they may appear disarmingly simple; in style they resemble advertising copy. Under the surface, however, they show Barton struggling to unify business and material success with the impulse that guided his life. He appears, on the one hand, to be obsessed with the stories of powerful men who had achieved fame and fortune through business. They were the models that he wanted to imitate. Their interests and goals promised prosperity for all Americans. Yet on the other hand, he appears to be completely loyal to the ideal of cultivating Christian character. He thus embraced service over accumulation, humility over arrogance, unselfconscious goodness over ambition. In short, he wanted to sanctify business by making the example of Jesus relevant to the modern world, of which business was its greatest symbol. He wanted to make worldly concern a servant to spiritual life, and vice versa. His attempt to unify these two commitments made him both creative and ambivalent. Though essentially an optimist, he had a faint question mark about himself, his ideals, and America hovering in the back of his mind. He was confident, to be sure. But his confidence in the American experiment depended on national luck, the goodness of people, and the success of business. None of these, of course, could be completely taken for granted.

*Every Week* failed in 1918. Barton once again wondered whether he would ever succeed in journalism. So he decided, a year later, to try his hand in advertising, an endeavor that he had begun in earnest during the First World War for the war effort. Joining forces with two other friends, he formed Barton, Durstine and Osborn. Nine years later they added another associate to form Batten, Barton, Durstine & Osborn (better known as BBDO). By the time of Barton's retirement, it had become the third largest advertising agency in the United States.

Barton became master of the trade. He knew how to write good, crisp, catchy copy. For example, to title an article about the Salvation Army for *American*

*Magazine,* he scribbled across the top of the title page, "A man may be down but he's never out," a slogan that became the byword for the Salvation Army in later years. To attract young men to enroll in a correspondence school, he suggested that it was "a wonderful two years' trip at full pay, but only men with imagination can take it." To sell the public on the merits of electrical appliances he argued, "Any woman who is doing any household task that a little electric motor can do is working for three cents an hour; human life is too precious to be sold at a price of three cents an hour." BBDO also handled much of the advertising for Republican presidential candidates Calvin Coolidge and Herbert Hoover. Barton became the personal friend of both, wrote speeches for them, and helped them to project images of themselves that would win votes. This was Barton's first foray into politics; it was also his first serious attempt to use the media to sell a presidential candidate.

Barton achieved national fame when he published four religious books in rapid succession: *The Man Nobody Knows* (1925), *The Book Nobody Knows* (1926), *What Can a Man Believe?* (1927), and *He Upset the World* (1931), the first being a life of Jesus and the last a life of the Apostle Paul. Though many critics attacked the books for their superficiality, distortion of orthodoxy, and accommodation to the ethos of the business world, the public liked the books enough to make *The Man Nobody Knows* a best seller two years running. Barton did not present an orthodox version of the Christian faith and therefore could hardly be labeled a fundamentalist. He made no mention of the virgin birth or of the bodily resurrection of Christ. He explicitly rejected the substitutionary atonement and chose to gloss over the divinity of Christ. He wanted to present, as he had done once before in *A Young Man's Jesus,* a human Christ whose boundless energy, strength of body, toughness of mind, courage, and popularity would attract modern people, challenge them to do their best, and engage them in service to humanity.

Barton's Jesus mirrored the concerns of the social gospel, only presented in a guise more favorable to corporate capitalism than to socialism. Barton stressed Jesus' personal magnetism, love for ordinary people, unending patience, and ability to organize. His Jesus was strong enough to attract women, live outdoors, and heal the sick. He was a man of steely nerves and winsome personality. He was a religious genius. His religion "conquered not because there was any demand for another religion but because Jesus knew how, and taught His followers how, to catch the attention of the indifferent, and translate a great spiritual conception into terms of practical self-concern" (p. 71). He knew how to speak in the language of the people, how to make a point quickly, how to capture and hold their interest. He also knew how to express the essence of religion, in both word and deed: serve instead of enslave, give instead of receive, work twice as hard as everyone else. In Jesus' mind, as portrayed by Barton, there was no difference between secular work and religious work. All activity, however worldly, could be done with religious purpose and conviction. Though Barton expressed his life of Jesus in terms understandable to the business world (for which he was criticized), his real goal was to update and humanize the story of Jesus for people who did not, or could not, believe in traditional religious formulas but who still wanted or needed religion in their lives. His manly Jesus did that. If *The Man Nobody Knows* buttressed the myth of Christian capitalism, it also challenged business people to follow the example of Jesus.

However idealistic and grandiose his vision, Barton was not spared from personal problems and pain. During a period of several years, beginning in 1928, Barton's world teetered and almost fell. He suffered from insomnia, depression, and anxiety to such an extent that he committed himself to a sanitarium for a month in 1928. His confidence in capitalism was shaken by the Depression that began in 1929. His father, William, his best friend and hero, died in 1930. His party leader and good friend Herbert Hoover lost to Franklin Roosevelt in the presidential election of 1932. He had an affair that finally became public knowledge and resulted in a blackmail trial in 1932–33 which, though it caused him and his family considerable embarrassment, he eventually won. And his daughter Betsy became paralyzed in 1935. These problems had a subtle effect on his view of culture and on his theology. In fact, after 1931 he did not publish another religious or self-help book.

To find relief from his troubles Barton went on a cruise around the world. The diary he kept during this period reveals uncertainty about himself, capitalism, and even advertising. That old question mark, which had sometimes cast a faint shadow over him during his earlier years, began to loom larger in his mind. He wondered what the purpose of life was and whether his optimism about life was reasonable.

During the 1930s Barton devoted himself to advertising and politics. Two causes in particular dominated his time. First, he helped corporations to advertise not only their products but also themselves, as institutions. His concern for the tarnished reputation of business in post–World War I and later in Depression America led him to exploit the public relations power of advertising. He began to use advertising as a tool to define the ideal toward which business should strive. Once again, Barton attempted to infuse religious principles into the business world. His purpose was not simply to sell the benevolent role of business to the public, although that was certainly not far from his mind; it was also to make business a servant to the public. He did not realize, however, that such institutional advertising might deceive the mind of the public more than it changed the goals of the corporation. Whereas such institutional advertising showed business being supportive of traditional American values (e.g., the family), it tended in practice to undermine the very values it ostensibly supported. Macy's, Marshall Field & Company, General Motors, Standard Oil, General Electric, Du Pont, and United States Steel were a few of the many corporate clients of BBDO that benefited from Barton's philosophy.

The Depression did not change Barton's mind about business, but it did sober him. He altered his philosophy of benevolent business just enough to include government as a junior partner in the task of solving the nation's problems. He also began to see that the real problem was no longer simply a matter of production but of distribution. He urged cooperation, spiritual renewal, and corporate responsibility to heal the nation's ills. He even applauded Roosevelt's early New Deal initiatives. His commitment to America's success made him generous enough to recognize merit in the schemes of those whose political ideology differed from his own.

Second, Barton entered the arena of politics. He served two terms as a United States Representative from New York City (1937–41). At first he was considered competent and friendly, a liberal, open-minded Republican. But political and economic developments during the later years of the Depression made him increasingly hostile toward the New Deal. He expressed concern over what he identified as a major shift in American cultural values. People were less eager, he thought, to fulfill responsibilities and more eager to claim rights. He was alarmed at the spectre of mass culture, a culture that he himself helped to create, and he resisted the internationalism that was drawing the nation's attention away from domestic problems. His idealism, however fiercely held, was beginning to waver. That made his politics more reactionary than innovative. In 1940 Barton deferred to Wendell Willkie's request that he run for a Senate seat against popular incumbent James M. Mead. Willkie argued that Barton's candidacy would strengthen the party ticket. Barton lost by 800,000 votes.

Though Barton retired from political life, he did not stop thinking about political and economic issues. He remained committed to corporate capitalism as the philosophy that held the greatest potential for making America prosperous. He also continued to be a noninterventionist. He thus opposed the Korean War and the foreign policy of the Cold War. Until a stroke attenuated his energies in 1957, he worked at BBDO, either as president or as chairman of the board. He became a friend of President Eisenhower's and enjoyed the company of many other influential people. He died in 1967.

## Appraisal

It is too simplistic to argue that Bruce Barton's essential struggle was in trying to reconcile traditional religious belief with modern culture. His father was not a theological conservative; if anything, he passed on to his son a tradition of progressive thinking in religion. Barton fought many religious battles, to be sure. But conservative resistance and eventual capitulation to modern thought was not one of them. Nor can we assume that Barton was simply using his religious faith to buttress the values and goals of the business world. It is true that he was devoted to business, but he was no simpleton or fanatic. His private papers more than his books demonstrate that he possessed a measure of self-transcendence and could be critical of business, businessmen, and the free enterprise system. We cannot say, then, that his life's story was essentially a struggle of adjusting traditional faith to modern thought or of using religious belief to justify capitalism.

Early in his life Barton faced the dilemma of choosing between the ministry or business. He discovered, and his early essays and editorials prove, that he could do both at the same time. His religious faith assured him of success in business, without ethical compromise, if he followed the example of Jesus. Business became a tool in the hands of religion to shape life according to the lofty ideals of Christianity. Though Barton craved success, he hated its hideous effects: ambition, materialism, arrogance, selfishness. The ethics of Jesus kept him from being corrupted by his business interests. Such was the genius of his thought and the positive contribution he made to American culture.

Here we can also observe the irony of Barton's life. Though Barton's ideas achieved a great deal of popularity, he also had to face their unintended consequences. The perfect image of success in Barton's mind was the humble, wise, reliable, courageous man of the world (usually but not always a businessman) who knew what he wanted in life and worked hard enough to achieve it. He esteemed businessmen like Henry Ford and leaders like Abraham Lincoln, whom he was fond of quoting. Yet his corporate advertising, which helped to create mass culture and to disguise the brute reality of profits and poverty, greed and control, cultivated a cultural ethos that made it increasingly difficult to be the kind of person Barton valued. Barton's "ideal person," as independent and savvy as he was, would never have believed his advertising. That Barton was so successful in advertising only shows how destructive his profession was to his ideal. As Warren Susman argues, Barton's picture of the ideal man fit best in a producer-oriented society; his advertising, however, helped to build a consumer-oriented society. Ironically, he lamented the kind of person the capitalist consumer had become.

Further, Barton's Jesus, so attractive to those who were rising to the top, did not seem sufficient to help the very same people who, like himself, had to face the problem of being at the top, to say nothing about the millions of people who would never have a chance even to begin to climb toward the top. A human Jesus could help a young idealist. But could he help wealthy men who had become casualties of the Depression? Or famous men whose marriages were disintegrating? Or powerful men who did not know what to do with the power they had? Or blacks, women, the poor—those whom society had assigned to remain permanently in the underclass? Barton's religion provided a human example to follow, not a divine being to trust. It was adequate for his younger years. Yet there is reason to wonder how useful it was when Barton reached middle age.

Barton became more cautious in his optimism and contentious in his style after 1940. Changes in culture and problems in his own life forced him to work overtime to make religion, business, and idealism work. The Depression and World War II raised questions about the benevolent role of business and challenged the reliability of his religion. When his religious idealism was threatened, he returned by instinct, like a homing pigeon, to the ideas and institutions he

trusted most: business, Americanism, conservatism, ethical religion. He opposed
the legislation and spirit of the New Deal; he spoke out against internationalism
and socialism. He became increasingly uncomfortable in the culture that he had
helped to shape.

### Survey of Criticism

Frederick Lewis Allen's interpretation of Barton in his popular book *Only
Yesterday,* in which Barton is depicted as using religion to justify the exploits
of corporate capitalism, lodged itself in the popular mind, until scholars began
to look at Barton's life more carefully. His private papers were made available
to the public only in 1964. The articles and dissertations that appeared after this
period merit our careful attention. Of these, a few stand out. Warren Susman's
article in *Men, Women, and Issues in American History* argues that Barton's
ideas enabled Americans to shift from a traditional producer-oriented to a modern
consumer-oriented society. He suggests that Barton's secular religion enabled
Americans to make the transition without thinking they had become irreligious.
James A. Neuchterlein's ''Bruce Barton and the Business Ethos of the 1920's''
posits that Barton's idealist notion of business was the conservative counterpart
to the social gospel. Barton applied the ethic of Jesus to business; he advocated
''reform capitalism.''

Edrene Stephens Montgomery's Ph.D. dissertation on Barton is most helpful
in providing information on Barton's background. It is obvious that she thoroughly combed the sources, both primary and secondary. Although her interpretation suffers from too much reliance on popular notions of ''autonomy'' and
''self-esteem,'' both of which, in her mind, Barton lacked, it does treat Barton
as a complex figure and shows how his thought evolved and changed through
the years. In her mind, Barton's religious ideas enabled people to overcome
feelings of powerlessness; his advertising, on the other hand, contributed to the
growing ''menace of unreality'' in America. She argues further, and James
Ferreira in ''Only Yesterday and the Two Christs of the Twenties'' agrees, that
Barton's religious books were not intended to be a naive defense of capitalism.
Barton was not trying to establish a religion of business. Montgomery proves
that Barton's books were popular not because people were hoping to find a
religious justification of capitalism but because they wanted to believe in a ''real''
Jesus. Ferreira compares Barton's *The Man Nobody Knows* with another best
seller, Giovanni Papini's *Life of Christ,* to prove the same point.

Finally, Leo Ribuffo, in ''Jesus Christ as Business Statesman,'' attempts to
give a comprehensive interpretation of Barton's life. Though he regards Barton
as less complex than does Montgomery, he too sees Barton as applying Christianity to business through the ideal of service. Moreover, he suggests that Barton
was an important transitional figure in the development of positive thinking.
Barton was significant because he adapted his religion to capitalism and helped
Americans to adjust to their loss of autonomy.

## Bibliography

### Books by Bruce Barton

1912  *The Resurrection of the Soul*. Boston: Pilgrim Press.
1914  *The Woman Who Came at Night*. New York: Pilgrim Press.
1914  *A Young Man's Jesus*. Boston: Pilgrim Press.
1917  *More Power to You*. New York: Century Company.
1918  *The Making of George Groton*. Garden City, N.Y.: Doubleday, Page and Company.
1920  *It's a Good Old World*. New York: Century Company.
1924  *Better Days*. New York: Century Company.
1925  *The Man Nobody Knows*. Indianapolis: Bobbs-Merrill.
1926  *The Book Nobody Knows*. Indianapolis: Bobbs-Merrill.
1927  *What Can a Man Believe?* Indianapolis: Bobbs-Merrill.
1929  *On the Up and Up*. Indianapolis: Bobbs-Merrill.
1931  *He Upset the World*. Indianapolis: Bobbs-Merrill.

### Selected Studies about Bruce Barton

Bishop, Robert L. "Bruce Barton—Presidential Stage Manager." *Journalism Quarterly* 43 (1966): 85–89.

Boorstin, Daniel. *The Image: or What Happened to the American Dream?* New York: Atheneum, 1962.

Ferreira, James M. "Only Yesterday and the Two Christs of the Twenties." *South Atlantic Quarterly* 80 (1981): 77–83.

Hollitz, John E. "Eisenhower and the Admen: The Television 'Spot' Campaign of 1952." *Wisconsin Magazine of History* 66 (1982): 25–39.

Meyer, Donald. *The Positive Thinkers: Religion as Pop Psychology from Mary Baker Eddy to Oral Roberts*. New York: Pantheon Books, 1980.

Montgomery, Edrene Stephens. "Bruce Barton and the Twentieth Century Menace of Unreality." Ph.D. diss., University of Arkansas, 1984.

Neuchterlein, James A. "Bruce Barton and the Business Ethos of the 1920's." *South Atlantic Quarterly* 76 (1977): 293–308.

Ribuffo, Leo P. "Jesus Christ as Business Statesman: Bruce Barton and the Selling of Corporate Capitalism." *American Quarterly* 33 (1981): 206–31.

Shapiro, Stephen Richard. "The Big Sell: Attitudes of Advertising Writers About Their Craft in the 1920's and 1930's." Ph.D. diss., University of Wisconsin, 1969.

Susman, Warren. "Piety, Profits, and Play: The 1920's." In *Men, Women, and Issues in American History*, edited by Howard H. Quint and Milton Cantor, 2:191–216. Homewood, Ill.: Dorsey Press, 1975.

Szasz, Ferenc Marton. *The Divided Mind of Protestant America, 1880–1930*. University: University of Alabama Press, 1982.

Tedlow, Richard S. *Keeping the Corporate Image: Public Relations and Business, 1900–1950*. Greenwich, Conn.: JAI Press, 1979.

Wiebe, Robert H. *The Search for Order*. New York: Hill and Wang, 1967.

Wyllie, Irvin. *The Self-Made Man in America*. New Brunswick, N.J.: Rutgers University Press, 1954.

GERALD L. SITTSER

# Daniel and Philip Berrigan

On 17 May 1968, seven men and nine women invaded the offices of Local Board 33 on the second floor of the Knights of Columbus Hall in the Baltimore suburb of Catonsville. They dumped three hundred draft files into trash baskets and burned them with homemade napalm in the adjacent parking lot. Prayers over the flames were led by two of the nine, Jesuit priest Daniel Berrigan and his brother Philip, a Josephite priest. As television cameras recorded the event, the American public was introduced in dramatic fashion to Catholic radicalism.

The Catonsville action, including the trial and imprisonment that followed, was the centerpiece of a series of protests and works of poetry and prose by which the Berrigan brothers followed a trajectory of civil disobedience, from peaceful dissent to active, militant resistance against the racism and imperialism they believed to be infecting American society. In so doing, claimed Edward Duff, S.J., in an essay in *The Berrigans* (edited by William Van Etten Casey and Philip Nobile), the brothers "challenged in the public mind the automatic identification of American Catholicism with the status quo, its alliance with prevailing patriotic causes, its ambition to be accepted, not so much as an alien value-system adjusting to a politically neutral environment, but as a group of citizens 'just like everybody else.' "

## Biography

Daniel and Philip were the youngest of six boys born to Thomas and Frieda Berrigan. Daniel was born on 9 May 1921; Philip followed on 5 October 1923. Both parents influenced their sons' social consciences. After losing a railroad job in Minnesota because of his ties with the Socialist party, their father, Tom, moved the family back to Syracuse, New York, where he founded the Electrical Workers Union and started a Catholic Interracial Council. Daniel later recalled that his mother's simple Christian compassion transformed the family farm into a type of Catholic Worker Hospitality House during the Depression, as the unemployed and homeless found refuge and food within its walls. Whereas Philip excelled in athletics, Daniel nurtured a love of literature and poetry, read the Bible, the *Catholic Worker,* and *Commonweal,* and pondered the plight of the suffering. In 1939 Daniel's sense of vocation prompted him to investigate various religious orders of priests. He settled on the Jesuits, the one society that "didn't seem to want us." But the choice was appropriate: in the figure of Ignatius of Loyola, a sixteenth-century Spanish soldier who renounced arms and channeled his revolutionary energy into building a spiritual militia for Christ, Daniel Berrigan found a model for his own priesthood. He entered the Jesuit seminary near Poughkeepsie and did not return home for seven years.

In 1941, after graduating from high school and working for a year, Philip entered St. Michael's College, Toronto, only to be drafted in January 1943. Boot camp in the South was his first experience with the oppression of blacks in that region, and it affected him deeply. A supreme irony of his later life as radical pacifist lay in the fact that his experience in World War II proved Philip to be an exceptional warrior, one who, in the words of a compatriot, could "kill men enthusiastically." On returning from the war, Philip resumed his education at Holy Cross College in Worcester, Massachusetts, and graduated with a degree in English in 1950. In that year he joined his brother Jerry in the seminary for the Society of Saint Joseph, a missionary band of priests dedicated to work among American blacks.

These years of college and seminary education exposed both Daniel and Philip to various, often conflicting, schools of philosophical and theological thought. On one hand, the seminaries of the day promoted dualism, which separated the world into distinct spheres of good and evil, emphasizing the realm of contemplation and spiritual values as the proper milieu of the priest. The righteous zeal and fundamentalism of the brothers' later days as social prophets owed something to the spiritual certainties fostered by this semimonastic tradition. On the other hand, both men were deeply influenced by the liturgical renewal and incarnational theology promoted by French, Belgian, and Dutch Catholic participation in the Resistance movement against Hitler. As Francine du Plessix Gray points out in *Divine Disobedience,* the brothers' heroes were men like Emmanuel Cardinal Suhard, of the Mission de France and the worker-priest movement, and Jesuit Father Henri Perrin, who became a factory worker himself after his return from German concentration camps. These men had preached, in Suhard's words, "a fearless involvement in the temporal and social spheres," and Daniel and Philip met on weekends in the late forties (while Philip was at Holy Cross and Daniel at the Jesuit school of theology in Weston, Massachusetts) to discuss this central lesson that "their task was not to convert the world to the Church, but, rather, the Church to the world."

This lesson was brought home vividly to Daniel in 1953, the year after his ordination. His Jesuit superiors sent the young priest for pastoral work and study to a town near Lyons, France. There he met the worker-priests whose militance in the French underground and imprisonment in German camps became his models for later theories of civil disobedience. The socialistic, anticolonial perspectives of the worker-priests transformed Berrigan's understanding of history. As Francine du Plessix Gray quoted him in *Divine Disobedience:*

> The worker-priests radicalized me like nothing had before. They gave me, for the first time, a practical vision of the Church as she should be. They also transformed me politically in a historic year. The French had just lost Dien Bien Phu and were forced out of Indo-China, and my French friends woke me up to the evils of colonialism. To make it all the more traumatic, I saw this worker-priest movement, which I so admired, squashed before my very eyes . . . our icebox Pope, Pius XII, had the movement dissolved in one swift stroke. . . . Earlier, he had issued that shameful document *Humani Generis,* which was directed against many of the great French theologians who had nourished me for years. Teilhard de Chardin, Henri du Lubac, Yves Congar were condemned for deviation from doctrine. . . . I saw at

close hand intellectual excellence crushed in a wave of orthodoxy, like a big Stalinist purge. It hit me directly, it made me suffer deeply, it filled me with determination to carry on the work of the men who had been silenced.

Back in New York in 1954 for a three-year assignment teaching French and theology at the Jesuits' Brooklyn Preparatory School, Berrigan began to implement the vision he had acquired in France. He chaplained the Young Christian Workers, introduced students to members of the Catholic Worker movement on the Lower East Side, helped to organize the black and Puerto Rican communities of East Harlem, and promoted greater lay participation in the church through the Walter Ferrell Guild. He continued in this vein at LeMoyne College in Syracuse, where he taught theology until 1963, promoted pacifism and civil rights, and founded International House, "a pre-Peace Corps scene to desegregate the Catholic ghetto," which trained students for social work in underdeveloped countries. But the innovation that likely forced the hand of his opponents on the faculty centered on liturgical renewal. Two years before the Second Vatican Council approved such changes, Berrigan turned the altar around to face the congregation and said parts of the mass in English. In the spirit of Dorothy Day* and the Catholic Worker movement, he insisted on the inherent link between the community gathered for sacramental bread and wine and that community's work to redeem the world from political and social injustice. He dealt with this theme in the first of many books of poetry, *Time Without Number* (1957), which won the Lamont Poetry Award, and in his first work of theology, *The Bride: Essays in the Church* (1959).

Meanwhile, Philip, ordained a Josephite priest in 1955, battled racial discrimination in a Washington ghetto parish (1955–56) and while teaching in an all-black high school in New Orleans (1957–62). Active in such groups as the Urban League and the Congress of Racial Equality (CORE), Philip went on "freedom rides" in the South in the early sixties to lend Christian witness to the fight for racial justice. Public action of this type was at times interpreted as "grandstanding" or self-promotion; however, the brothers sought the spotlight not for themselves but for the causes they championed, causes they believed to be in the service of gospel values. As Philip expressed this point in his 1965 book on racial justice, *No More Strangers*:

> sciences and other modes of thought are valid in themselves, but they necessarily imply a limitation of concept, terminology, and action. . . . They can deal adequately with aspects of being, or say something about its appearances and manifestations, but they cannot announce the inner substance of history or point the direction of its term. Only Christians can do this. The relationship of man to Christ must therefore be dramatized before the world by fervent, intelligent believers, who are men of their times, skilled in their vocation within the Church, men who live habitually and instinctively according to the mind of Christ. Such Christians are, by definition, mediators between their Lord and their world.

After Philip's six controversial years in New Orleans, the Josephites transferred him to their seminary in Newburgh, New York, where he was to teach English.

Immediately he founded a social center modeled on Catholic Worker Houses, and he organized the seminarians, dispatching them, ward by ward, to every ramshackle dwelling in town to document building code violations.

The year of 1964 was a watershed for the brothers: it marked their final rejection of liberalism; hope for institutional reform gave way to the revolutionary discourse of radicalism. That summer Daniel returned from a sabbatical in France (ordered by his superiors at LeMoyne) during which he had toured Hungary, Russia, and Czechoslovakia and had worked with Roman Catholic families who daily jeopardized their jobs by the practice of their faith. As his friend Jim Forest reported in his essay in *The Berrigans,* the experience "de-parochialized" Daniel, transformed him into a "joyful ascetic," and confirmed him in the "kenosis (self-emptying) theology" of the French school that took for its ecclesiological model the radical pacifism and protest of the early church of the martyrs. The growing civil rights movement in the United States, dramatized by the march of Selma in the fall of 1964 and the escalation of the war in Vietnam in 1965, provided the political context for the brothers' own self-emptying commitment to the poor and oppressed in America. Philip won for himself another transfer, this time from Newburgh to a ghetto parish in Baltimore, because of his eloquent articulation, in articles and books and on the campus lecture circuit, of the connection he perceived between American military policy in southeast Asia and racism at home. The war was waged, he claimed, with the lives of black Americans who could not escape conscription and was paid for by funds siphoned from programs of social welfare. After founding the Catholic Peace Fellowship, Daniel "earned" his own transfer at the hands of an agitated superior when his attendance at the first major public demonstrations against the war and his signature on "A Declaration of Conscience" pledging civil disobedience against American policies (1965) provoked Francis Cardinal Spellman to pressure the Jesuit provincial of New York to "remove" the troublemaker.

Spellman was upset by a series of Berrigan initiatives. In August 1965, Daniel had joined a rabbi and a Lutheran pastor in forming "Clergy Concerned About Vietnam," an ecumenical antiwar group that eventually became the most powerful peace fellowship in the United States. That October, a former student of Berrigan's named David Miller burned his draft card in protest of the war. In November, a young Catholic Worker named Roger Laporte immolated himself in an act of prophecy. Delivering the eulogy at Laporte's funeral, Daniel said that "his death was offered so that others may live." Incensed, Spellman arranged for Daniel's transfer to Latin America, a move that incited 10,000 priests, nuns, seminarians, and lay Catholics to sign a full-page ad in the *New York Times* demanding the return of their hero from exile. Embarrassed, Spellman relented.

The Berrigans' relationship to the Catholic Church during these days of protest was complex. From the Second Vatican Council's emphasis on religious freedom and liberty of conscience and from Pope Paul VI's ringing condemnation of war before the United Nations in 1965, the brothers derived consolation and inspiration for their work. At the same time, both men frequently lashed out at the church's silence on Vietnam and its role as, in Philip's words as quoted by Gray, "one of the staunchest allies of nationalism . . . and militarism that nationalism demands." Nourished by the sacramental and mystical resources of the Catholic tradition, the brothers remained loyal but cynical sons of the church. "The Church is a sinner," Daniel admitted, "but She's my mother." Philip once said, "Staying in the Church gives you the chance to use the institution against itself."

The next two years witnessed an increase in the brothers' individual and united efforts in behalf of civil rights and the antiwar movement. Daniel did not return to LeMoyne but served for three years as editor of *Jesuit Missions;* became further disillusioned with liberalism by teaching in the Upward Bound program in Pueblo, Colorado, for the Office of Economic Opportunity (Gray quoted him: "Neither in Pueblo or anywhere else in the country had I seen a poverty program whose leadership were part of the community of the poor"); and finally accepted a leadership role in United Religious Work of Cornell University. There he organized a group of pacifists and in 1967 was arrested with them at an antiwar demonstration at the Pentagon. In Baltimore, Philip and other members of the Baltimore Interfaith Peace Mission began in 1966 to hold vigils on the front lawns of homes of congressmen who supported the Vietnam War. On 27 October 1967, he and three others, later known as "the Baltimore Four," raided a draft board in that city and poured blood over the files. Six months later, Daniel again made headlines by traveling with historian Howard Zinn to Hanoi in a successful attempt to negotiate the release of three captured American pilots, an adventure chronicled in his book *Night Flight to Hanoi* (1968).

This activity culminated in the famous (or infamous) raid of the Catonsville Nine. Characteristically, the Berrigans planned the event with an eye toward public exposure of their views. Daniel's play dramatizing the trial was staged around the country and adapted for film; his defense of the action, *No Bars to Manhood* (1970), suggested that "we were helping to create a new Church and a new Order." But a sizable portion of Catholics who had previously supported the Berrigans' acts of civil disobedience (which recalled a hallowed American tradition represented by Henry David Thoreau and Martin Luther King, Jr.*, among others) balked, David J. O'Brien has argued in his essay in *The Berrigans,* when the brothers "moved beyond a simple pacifism of protest to active, militant resistance."

The following five years found the Berrigans in and out of prison. Philip and Tom Lewis, his partner in both draft board raids, were sentenced to six years and denied bail during appeal, making Philip perhaps the first priest confined by the U.S. government for crimes against the state. Eventually he served thirty-nine months of the sentence. Although Daniel was incarcerated from July 1970 to February 1972, he infuriated J. Edgar Hoover by refusing to report to federal marshals and by cleverly eluding FBI agents for four months, even as he lectured and made provocative public appearances. As if in retaliation, Hoover accused the Berrigans and others in 1970 of plotting to kidnap Henry Kissinger and to bomb heating tunnels of certain government facilities in Washington, D.C.; in

1971, Philip and religious sister Elizabeth McAlister were indicted on charges of conspiracy, and Daniel was named as an unindicted coconspirator. Both men denied Hoover's accusations but called themselves "anarchists."

A number of significant publications resulted from the years of imprisonment. Philip published *Prison Journals of a Priest Revolutionary* (1970), a collection of essays and interviews descriptive of his confinement and of the response of former friends and supporters to his new militance, and *Widen the Prison Gates* (1973), his response to Hoover's charges of conspiracy. Daniel won the National Book Award in 1971 for his exposition of the exigencies of radical religion and prophecy, *The Dark Night of Resistance,* and authored a number of books of poetry and a diary about his time in Danbury Federal Penitentiary and his new objective of "resistance to the evil policies of the government." These works enjoyed sufficient popularity to warrant publication of an anthology of his poems in 1973.

After his release from prison in 1973, Philip Berrigan announced his marriage to Elizabeth McAlister, and with her he established Jonah House, a commune in Baltimore. Both continued to write and lecture into the 1980s, turning their attention increasingly to such issues as Christian feminism, nuclear proliferation, and the building of authentic Christian communities. Daniel remained a Jesuit; his writing and teaching have explored a variety of concerns from ecumenical dialogue and joint reflection on conscience and religious consciousness with a Buddist monk to spirituality and personal morality in a secular age.

**Appraisal**

Although the Berrigans continue to influence opinion to this day, their most significant period of leadership lasted from the mid-1960s to the early seventies. Their impact endures in at least two regards. First, by their eloquent words and highly symbolic rituals of protest, the brothers made their fellow American Catholics aware of the pluralism of the Catholic tradition on questions of social action. In spite of the examples of Dorothy Day and Thomas Merton*, both of whom profoundly influenced the Berrigans, most Catholics as late as 1968 believed that Cardinal Spellman spoke with almost infallible authority when he proclaimed, "My country—right or wrong." Surprisingly, Daniel reported in *No Bars to Manhood,* "my 'no' was being heard despite the sound of his immensely more powerful and permeating 'yes.' " Second, in moving beyond liberalism the Berrigans exposed the weaknesses of accepting the presuppositions of an economic and political system (be it capitalism or communism) that was not rooted in gospel values. In so doing they lent a certain prestige to yet another option in American Catholicism, the role of radical pacifist and social revolutionary. Scores of urban priests and nuns were emboldened by their example and began to refashion Catholic ministry in sometimes dramatic, sometimes subtle ways.

Perhaps John Cogley explained the Berrigans' impact most accurately in the concluding passage of his *Catholic America:*

The brothers Berrigan—secure enough in their Americanness to speak out as Americans and at the same time secure enough in their faith to speak in the name of Catholicism—may have provided an example of the duty that before long will fall upon all Catholics who do not give up on either their country or their faith.

The Berrigans (however one may criticize their practical judgment or style) have pointed out that, while Catholicism can exist very well with separation of church and state, its best representatives will always refuse to separate religion and life. And that makes all the difference.

## Survey of Criticism

Francine du Plessix Gray has published the most thorough biographies of the Berrigans in the *New Yorker* "Profiles" and in *Divine Disobedience: Profiles in Radical Catholicism,* a journalistic account of the events leading up to and including the trial of the Catonsville Nine. Among the more insightful and analytical of other secondary sources are the works of Anne Klejment. Her doctoral thesis, "In the Lion's Den: The Social Catholicism of Daniel and Philip Berrigan," positions the brothers in the Catholic Left and in the context of both the American civil rights movement and American anti-intellectualism (partially responsible for resentment of the Berrigans, she argues). It also includes an interesting investigation of the Berrigans's rather traditional attitudes on women, the family, and domestic life as reflective of the dualistic theology retained from their seminary training. "As in a Vast School Without Walls: Race in the Social Thought of the Berrigans," by the same author, explores the relationship in the Berrigans' social thought between racial justice and antiwar activism in the 1960s.

A significant number of critical essays evaluating the impact of the Berrigans on American political sensibilities and religious self-understanding have appeared in the last twenty years. *The Berrigans,* edited by William Van Etten Casey, S. J., and Philip Nobile, is a comprehensive collection of the earliest and best of these. It includes copies of documents pertinent to the various indictments and trials weathered by the Berrigans. William O'Rourke, *The Harrisburg 7 and the New Catholic Left,* contains lengthy quotations from the confiscated letters of Philip Berrigan and Elizabeth McAlister.

A significant debate about the Berrigans was conducted in various periodicals in the sixties and seventies. The following articles are representative of the range of criticism: Garry Wills, "Love on Trial: The Berrigan Case Reconsidered"; Dale Vree, " 'Stripped Clean': The Berrigans and the Politics of Guilt and Martyrdom"; and Robert A. Ludwig, "The Theology of Daniel Berrigan."

## Bibliography

### Books by Daniel Berrigan, S.J.

1957   *Time Without Number.* New York: Macmillan.
1959   *The Bride: Essays in the Church.* New York: Macmillan.
1961   *The Bow in the Clouds: Man's Covenant with God.* New York: Coward-McCann.
1962   *The World for Wedding Ring.* New York: Macmillan.

1966  *They Call Us Dead Men: Reflections on Life and Conscience.* New York: Macmillan.
1967  *Consequences: Truth And. . . .* New York: Macmillan.
1968  *Love, Love at the End.* New York: Macmillan.
1968  *Night Flight to Hanoi.* New York: Macmillan.
1970  *No Bars to Manhood.* Garden City, N.Y.: Doubleday.
1970  *The Trial of the Catonsville Nine.* Boston: Beacon Press.
1971  *The Dark Night of Resistance.* Garden City, N.Y.: Doubleday.
1973  *Selected and New Poems.* Garden City, N.Y.: Doubleday.
1974  *Lights on in the House of the Dead: A Prison Diary.* Garden City, N.Y.: Doubleday.
1977  *A Book of Parables.* New York: Seabury.

### Books by Philip Berrigan

1965  *No More Strangers.* New York: Macmillan.
1969  *A Punishment for Peace.* New York: Macmillan.
1970  *Prison Journals of a Priest Revolutionary.* New York: Holt, Rinehart and Winston.
1973  *Widen the Prison Gates: Writings from Jails, April 1970–December 1972.* New York: Simon and Schuster.
1979  *Of Beasts and Beastly Images: Essays Under the Bomb.* Portland, Oreg.: Sunburst Press.

### Selected Studies about the Berrigans

Casey, William Van Etten, S.J., and Philip Nobile, eds. *The Berrigans.* New York: Avon Books, 1971.
Gray, Francine du Plessix. *Divine Disobedience: Profiles in Radical Catholicism.* New York: Alfred A. Knopf, 1970.
———. "Profiles." *New Yorker* 46 (14 March 1970): 44–46[+].
Klejment, Anne. "As in a Vast School Without Walls: Race in the Social Thought of the Berrigans." Cushwa Center for the Study of American Catholicism *Working Paper Series* 10:1 (Fall 1981).
———. *The Berrigans: A Bibliography of Published Works.* New York: Garland, 1979.
———. "In the Lion's Den: The Social Catholicism of Daniel and Philip Berrigan, 1955–1965." Ph.D. diss., State University of New York at Binghamton, 1981.
Ludwig, Robert A. "The Theology of Daniel Berrigan." *Listening* 6 (Spring 1971): 127–37.
O'Rourke, William. *The Harrisburg 7 and the New Catholic Life.* New York: Thomas Y. Crowell, 1962.
Vree, Dale. " 'Stripped Clean': The Berrigans and the Politics of Guilt and Martyrdom." *Ethics* 85 (July 1975): 281–87.
Wills, Garry. "Love on Trail: The Berrigan Case Reconsidered." *Harper's* 245 (July 1972): 63–71.

R. SCOTT APPLEBY

# Harold A. Bosley

The preaching ministry of Harold A. Bosley spanned fifty years. Nurtured at the height of the modernist-fundamentalist controversy, Harold rejected the fundamentalism he had learned in rural Nebraska and embraced the heritage of social activism and theological liberalism. The apex of his ministry came during the 1950s and 1960s while the United States was facing an uncertain peace in the Cold War and social upheavals resulting from the national debate over the Vietnam War. He sought to proclaim an intellectually creditable faith that a person of reason would find inspiring and to promote a socially responsible ethic that a person of conscience would find challenging. Harold Bosley never achieved great fame in the popular press, but he was held in high esteem by colleagues and was in great demand as preacher and lecturer in both church and university settings.

## Biography

Harold Augustus Bosley was born on 19 February 1907 in Burchard, Nebraska, the son of Augustus and Effie (Sinclair) Bosley. He met the young woman, Margaret Marie Dahlstrom, who would become his wife while he was a young preacher in a small rural church in Nebraska. They were married on 21 July 1928 and became the parents of four sons, Paul, Sidney, Norman, and David, and one daughter, Diane. The young family mourned the passing of Sidney at the age of twelve in 1945.

Following the granting of a local preacher's license by the Nebraska Annual Conference of the Methodist Episcopal Church when Harold was only seventeen, he went on to earn the A.B. degree from Nebraska Wesleyan in 1930; the B.D. from the University of Chicago in 1932, and the Ph.D. also from Chicago in 1933. He was ordained an elder in the Nebraska Conference in 1933 and then served as Director of Religious Activities at Iowa State Teachers' College until he became pastor of the Mount Vernon Place Methodist Church, Baltimore, Maryland, in 1938. After a pastorate of nine years, he was called to be dean of the Divinity School of Duke University at Durham, North Carolina, in 1947. His two most distinguished pastorates were at the First Methodist Church, Evanston, Illinois, 1950–62 and at Christ Church, Methodist, New York City, 1962–74. Within one year of his retirement, he died on 20 January 1975 in Beach Haven Terrace, New Jersey.

Harold Bosley will be remembered above all as a preacher. He preached in three of the most distinguished pulpits in Methodism; many of his books were sermons that had been preached for those congregations; and his many invitations to lecture on college campuses resulted from his reputation as a preacher. His preaching, grounded in a liberal theology, demonstrated intellectual rigor, a passion for social justice, and commitment to the ecumenical movement. In a significant autobiographical essay appearing in *Christian Ministry* shortly after his death, Bosley conceived his duty "to be teacher, interpreter, and proclaimer of the Word of God spoken in history 1) in Jesus Christ and committed to the church as Gospel; 2) in the several religious traditions of the world. I have not been able to separate the teaching and preaching aspects of the ministry. My sermons (as best I could make them) have been both biblical and contemporary, personal and social, evangelistic and prophetic" ("The Climb of Faith to Faith,"

6). Bishop Dwight Loder of the United Methodist Church gave testimony to the intellectual discipline of Bosley in a memoir written for the *Journal of the New York Annual Conference:* "He developed a preaching style and a rigorous pattern of self-disciplined study, which he maintained through the years of his ministry. He insisted that mind contact with a congregation was far more important than eye contact" (1975, 1257).

Insight into Bosley's theological system must be derived from his published sermons. Whereas his early books are philosophical in content, his sermons reveal his theology. He never wrote a systematic theology, but his liberalism is clear nonetheless. His turning to liberal theology resulted from what he perceived to be the inadequacies of the fundamentalism he had been taught in Nebraska. He wrote in "The Climb of Faith to Faith": "I was born and matured in what Mencken labelled 'the Bible Belt' and entered the ministry as a troubled fundamentalist. Troubled, because so many questions about the Bible, the Church, the Ministry, and other problems that beset me seemed to have no answers in the framework of faith in which I was reared—at least answers that made sense." College challenged him with the problem of finding a new framework or leaving the ministry. The years at the Divinity School of the University of Chicago "provided the intellectual spur that has kept me trying to climb ever since." Studying under Henry Nelson Wieman, Charles Morris, Edward Scribner Ames, and Charles Hartshorne, Bosley was introduced to the thought of Alfred North Whitehead and thus set into place "lines of thought" from which he never departed. Bosley described these years as "the climb of faith to faith—the faith of childhood to one of maturity." He spent the rest of his life trying to help others make that same climb. Liberalism provided him the content and methodology for a reasonable faith. He wrote, "The most important discovery in student days was the possibility of a reasonable faith" (4–7).

When liberalism came under attack from fundamentalists, Bosley never backed off from describing himself as a liberal. Across the years he dedicated books to Shailer Mathews, Edward Scribner Ames, Harry Emerson Fosdick, Francis J. McConnell, G. Bromley Oxnam, and Ernest Fremont Tittle. In *Main Issues Confronting Christendom* he described himself as an "unashamed liberal" (90). Bosley claimed that liberalism "was looking and moving in the right direction . . . that the spirit and objective of historic liberalism made no major blunders in thought and policy, . . . that the spirit and objective of historic liberalism were and are, in the main, right and that any age which thinks and acts otherwise will pay for its error in the 'blood, sweat and tears' of ordinary people everywhere." He fully acknowledged the opposition to such ideas. "Fundamentalism, orthodoxy, and neo-orthodoxy agree, so far as I can see, in just one thing: their scorn of liberalism. . . . And a surprising number of books are being written which assume that the matter is now closed, that liberalism is dead and awaiting only a decent public burial" (91). Two years later, in *A Firm Faith for Today*, Bosley held that "a theology that emphasizes 'faith' as superior to 'reason' is not only irrational in method and conclusion, it seeks to affirm the fundamental irrationality of all efforts to know, to understand this divinely created universe'' (11). Dewitte Holland, in *Preaching in American History,* found Bosley to be an illustration of those preachers who enter into debate with neoorthodoxy as Bosley did in his *Sermons on Genesis* when he pleaded for the liberalism that had come under attack from the proponents of neo-orthodoxy.

Bosley's liberal theology can be adequately illustrated through the single example of his treatment of the person and work of Jesus Christ. He clearly affirmed his belief in Jesus Christ in *A Firm Faith for Today.* He made the following affirmations: ''1) We believe that he was a historical figure; 2) He was one of the greatest, if not the greatest, teacher of ethical religion the world has ever known; 3) We can believe that he is our clearest revelation of the will of God for the life of men; 4) He is God's supreme effort to save the world.'' Missing from this was the Johannine understanding of the incarnation or the orthodox notion of the death of Jesus as atonement. His three books of sermons on Jesus (*The Mind of Christ, The Character of Christ,* and *The Deeds of Christ*) sought to instill greater devotion and loyalty to Jesus but in no way corrected a liberal understanding of the person and work of Jesus.

The sermons of Harold Bosley are replete with references and illustrations drawn from the important problems of society. *Preaching on Controversial Issues: A Free Pulpit in a Free Society* was his most complete treatment of the issues then confronting the church that had grown out of society as a whole. Bosley never backed away from the difficult issues of race relations, world peace, or economic justice. At retirement he wrote, ''My years in the ministry have seen the church accept responsibility for social concerns as an essential part of her mission. Though the bone of contention at all time, there is no turning back for the church now on this matter. She is committed to the cause of being an articulate and obedient instrument, in the redemption of this world, here and now'' (''The Climb of Faith to Faith''). Bishop Dwight Loder wrote, ''Harold Bosley was a prophet and fearless but sensitive advocate of religious freedom, social justice, human rights, pacifism, and amnesty.'' Bishop Ralph Ward, in a memorial address for Bosley, spoke of his passion for world peace. ''War was for him the ultimate tragedy in the human community. To build a community of nations, to lead mankind to learn war no more was an undying passion with him. . . . To this end he endeavored to build bridges between the east and the west, between the capitalist and the communist. Whenever and wherever possible he lifted up the concept of the United Nations.''

In spite of the daily demands on an active pastor and preacher in large churches, Bosley never ceased to be the scholar and academician. He was a frequent lecturer in colleges and church conferences, including the Earl Foundation of the Pacific School of Religion in 1942; the Ayer Foundation at Rochester Colgate Divinity School in 1944; the Russell Foundation at Tufts College in 1948; the Carnahan Seminary and schools in Latin America in 1951; lecturer in Japan and Korea in 1955; Mendenhall lecturer at Depauw University in 1957; and the Willson lecturer at McMurray College, Abilene, Texas, in 1959. This close association with the academic community and the respect that accompanies this association resulted in numerous honorary degrees, including Nebraska Wesleyan, D.D., 1942; Northwestern, D.D., 1950; Ripon College, S.T.D., 1953; Cornell College, L.H.D., 1953; Manchester College, D.D., 1964; Simpson College, Litt. D., 1970; Central Methodist College, D.D., 1970; and Bucknell, D.D., 1972. While pastoring in Evanston, Bosley taught preaching, philosophy, and Christian ethics at Garrett Theological Seminary.

A prolific writer, Bosley published sixteen books, numerous articles and book reviews in *Religion in Life,* and other articles, most notably "The Climb of Faith to Faith" in *Christian Ministry* in March 1975, published within two months of his death. His first two books reflect his scholarly interest in philosophy, whereas most of his later books were compilations of his sermons. He was an active member of the editorial board of *Religion in Life* between 1961 and 1974.

The Methodist Church and the wider ecumenical community were the recipients of Bosley's creative energy and leadership. He was a delegate to every General and Jurisdictional Conference of the Methodist Church from 1948 until his retirement. He chaired the important legislative committee on Christian Social Concerns at the General Conferences of 1968 and 1970, demonstrating both his deep concern for social ethics and the respect accorded him by his peers. Bosley traveled widely in his efforts to enhance the possibilities for greater understanding among people. He went to South Vietnam in 1965 under the auspices of the Fellowship of Reconciliation. The Appeal of Conscience Foundation of New York City enabled Bosley to travel to the Soviet Union in 1966, 1967, and 1971 and to Spain in 1967. Bosley was instrumental in the formation of the National Council of Churches of Christ in the U.S.A. and served on its governing board. He was a delegate to three assemblies of the World Council of Churches: the Second Assembly in Evanston, 1954; the Third Assembly in New Delhi, 1961; and the Fourth Assembly in Uppsala, 1967. Most of the worship services for the Second Assembly were held in the church he pastored in Evanston. His ecumenical vision was often heard through his preaching, as he defended the work of the councils in many of his sermons. In addition to participating in the life of the councils, in 1955 he wrote a popular commentary on the message promulgated by the Second Assembly of the World Council entitled *What Did the World Council Say to You?* It was an effort to make available to a broad segment of the church a statement that was usually relegated to a library shelf without ever impacting the wider life of Christendom. Bosley himself claimed that "the ecumenical movement has been one of the great facts and factors of my ministry" ("The Climb of Faith to Faith").

### Appraisal

An analysis of Harold Bosley's influence and significance must distinguish between the respect accorded him during his lifetime, the eulogies offered at the time of his death, and his ongoing significance for later generations. His significance as a church leader and preacher during his lifetime is formidable. His

significance for later generations is more problematic. Yet even during his lifetime his work seemed to reflect the groundbreaking work of others more than it
demonstrated fresh insights into the Christian faith. He may be more a representation of a passing era than a transmitter of a socially conscious liberal
theology to a new generation. A reviewer of *The Mind of Christ,* writing in
*Religion in Life,* acknowledged that it was the "work of one of the most widely
respected preachers of our day" and at the same time conceded that "one has
the feeling that they [these sermon] could have been written 30 years ago"
(1966, 486).

During the 1950s and 1960s Harold Bosley was one of the most widely known
and respected preachers. He served two of the most distinguished pulpits in
Methodism. The fact that he preached eleven times at the Chicago Sunday
Evening Club between 1940 and 1974 speaks to both his popularity and his
longevity as pulpit giant. He undoubtedly reached a large audience through his
ministry as preacher, scholar, writer, and church leader. Yet his leadership
seemed confined to the life of the church. Congregations, college audiences,
pastors' schools, church conferences, and ecumenical assemblies were the arenas
of his influence. His influence was expanded by other preachers who bought and
read and referred to his books of sermons. There is little evidence that his work
reached far beyond the life of the church into society as a whole.

The esteem of his contemporaries was clearly expressed in memorial writings
at the time of his death. These are limited as historical judgments but are valuable
as expressions of affection for a beloved church leader. Bishop Loder claimed
that "his influence upon the life and shape of The United Methodist Church was
profound and lasting" (1975). Bishop Ward suggested that "any listing of the
names of the great preachers of the twentieth century would include that of
Harold. . . . A preacher's preacher, he spoke with compelling power to lay persons." Upon Bosley's death, David James Randolph, successor to Bosley at
Christ Church wrote in the 2 February 1975 church newsletter: "The world has
lost a prophet and the church has lost a champion. The loss we feel must be
measured against the greatness of the contribution of Harold A. Bosley which
will long endure."

In spite of Bosley's leadership during his lifetime, it seems safe to say that
his significance will be limited and his influence short-lived. His sermons are
dated with the issues of his day, which may be the mark of great preaching, but
they have little lasting relevance. He has not set the course for the church in the
decade since his death. The conservative right has risen in power and has eclipsed
the liberal agenda both in theology and social concerns. Denominational leadership does not carry with it broader influence in the world or lasting influence
even within church life.

### Survey of Criticism

No critical reviews or full-length studies of Bosley's life and work were found
by this writer. This lacuna may be indicative of the limited duration of Bosley's

influence. It seems unlikely that this will be corrected as historical perspectives lengthen. However, a more detailed study of Bosley's life, work, and thought in the context of the erosion of classical mainline Protestantism would be welcomed. The Protestant hegemony in which the mainline Protestant church dominated the American church scene either as individual denominations or together in ecumenical councils has given way to a fragmented Protestant community dominated popularly by evangelicals and fundamentalists. For the liberal churches, the optimism and growth of the 1950s gave way to uncertainty and numerical decline by the 1970s. Harold Bosley's career spanned these transitions, and his lasting influence has been mitigated by them.

## Bibliography

### Selected Works by Harold A. Bosley

1939 *The Quest for Religious Certainty*. Chicago: Willett, Clark and Company.
1944 *The Philosophical Heritage of the Christian Faith*. Chicago: Willett, Clark and Company.
1946 *On Final Ground*. New York: Harper and Brothers.
1948 *Main Issues Confronting Christendom*. New York: Harper and Brothers.
1950 *A Firm Faith for Today*. New York: Harper and Brothers.
1952 *The Church Militant*. New York: Harper and Brothers.
1953 "The Communication of the Gospel to the Modern World." *Religion in Life* 22: 483–91.
1953 *Preaching on Controversial Issues: A Free Pulpit in a Free Society*. New York: Harper and Brothers.
1955 *What Did the World Council Say to You?* New York and Nashville: Abingdon Press.
1956 *Sermons on the Psalms*. New York and Nashville: Abingdon Press.
1958 *Doing What is Christian*. Nashville: Graded Press.
1958 *Sermons on Genesis*. New York: Harper and Brothers.
1963 *He Spoke to Them in Parables*. New York: Harper and Row.
1965 "What is the Parish Church?" *Religion in Life* 34: 170–80.
1966 *The Mind of Christ*. Nashville: Abingdon Press.
1967 *The Character of Christ*. Nashville: Abingdon Press.
1968 "The Churches, the World and Uppsala." *Religion in Life* 37: 454–62.
1969 *The Deeds of Christ*. Nashville: Abingdon Press.
1972 *Men Who Build Churches: Interpretations of the Life of Paul*. Nashville: Abingdon Press.
1975 "The Climb of Faith to Faith." *Christian Ministry* 6: 4–7.

### Studies about Harold A. Bosley

Harmon, Nolan B., ed. *Encyclopedia of World Methodism*. Vol. 1: 302. Nashville: United Methodist Publishing House, 1974.
Holland, DeWitte. *Preaching in American History*, 282–83. Nashville: Abingdon Press, 1969.
Loder, Dwight. "Memoir." In *Journal of the New York Annual Conference, 1975*, 1257–58. N.p.: New York Annual Conference of the United Methodist Church, 1975.

ROBERT J. WILLIAMS

# William Branham

Following the spiritual drought of World War II, two major national revivals
burst forth upon the American scene: the evangelical revival, represented by
Billy Graham*, and the healing revival, symbolized by William Branham and
Oral Roberts*. The healing revival was, according to David E. Harrell, "a signs-
gifts-healing, salvation-deliverance, Holy Ghost miracle revival." This revival
was responsible for the unexpected growth of Pentecostalism in modern America
following the war years. By reaching across denominational lines and socioeconomic levels, the healing revival gave birth to the modern charismatic movement
in the late fifties and early sixties. David Barrett in his *World Christian Encyclopedia* documents that the charismatic movement with its 277 million followers
worldwide is the fastest-growing religious movement in the world today.

The person universally acknowledged as "the father" and "pacesetter" of
the healing revival is William Branham. The sudden appearance of his miraculous
healing campaigns in 1946 set off a spiritual explosion in the American Christian
subculture, moving to mainstreet USA by the fifties and giving birth in the sixties
to the broader charismatic movement that presently affects almost every denomination in the nation.

### Biography

The life of William Marrion Branham, according to respected Pentecostal
leader Gordon Lindsey, "is so . . . beyond the ordinary that were there not available a host of infallible proofs which document and attest its authenticity, one
might well be excused from considering it farfetched and incredible." Branham
was born to his fifteen-year-old mother on 6 April 1909 in a small, dirt-floored
log cabin near Burkesville, Kentucky. When he was very young, the family
moved to a farm near Jeffersonville, Indiana, where the lad was reared in deep
poverty and received only a marginal education. His family was the "poorest
of the poor," and this abject poverty was fueled by his father's alcoholism.

In pursuit of a better life, Branham moved to Phoenix at age nineteen and
started a successful professional boxing career. On the death of his brother,
Branham returned to Jeffersonville for the funeral, and there began a search to
"find God." His early life had been filled with many mystical experiences, yet
he had no religious training in his background. Within six months of beginning
his religious quest, he felt called to preach and shortly thereafter was ordained
an independent Baptist minister. Being supplied a tent in 1933, he launched his
evangelistic career with impressive results.

The first major revival was conducted in Jeffersonville, and more than 3,000
persons attended in a single night. On the heels of the revival, his supporters
built the Branham Tabernacle as a permanent meeting place, and in the following
years the church flourished. The pivotal point of Branham's career came on 7
May 1946 when, as he related to his congregation, he experienced an angelic

visitation in which he was promised to receive the gift of healing and to preach before thousands.

Following this visitation, he was summoned to St. Louis to pray for Pastor Robert Daugherty's dying daughter. He complied, and the girl was healed. In the revival that followed, the praying for the sick was highlighted. So successful was this ministry that his reputation quickly spread. Branham followed the St. Louis visit with a revival in the Bible Hour Tabernacle in Jonesboro, Arkansas, pastored by Rex Humbard's father. More than 25,000 people from twenty-eight states attended the meetings. Branham had struck into the heartland of fervent Pentecostalism, one starved for the message of old-time miracle power. With these meetings, the post–World War II American healing revival was born.

As testimonies of incredible healings increased, Branham's fame and ministry grew. Within months he had assembled an able management team of Jack Moore, Gordon Lindsey, and W. J. Ern Baxter. Lindsey initiated the *Voice of Healing* magazine to publicize Branham's ministry, although after several years it became the voice of dozens of healing evangelists. In May 1948 Branham discontinued his crusades for five months because of physical exhaustion, but when he resumed the campaigns, he added famed pentecostal evangelist F. F. Bosworth to his team. Bosworth added enormous prestige to Branham's ministry.

In the dramatic and important campaign held in Houston, Texas, in 1950, Bosworth debated the Reverend W. E. Best, pastor of the Houston Tabernacle Baptist Church, on the doctrine of divine healing, and the debate received national press coverage. In the same year, Branham's team conducted the first campaign tour of Europe made by a major healing revivalist. Branham's success in Scandinavia was startling and brought international publicity to the emerging phenomenon of healing revivals. Renowned church historian W. J. Hollenweger reported in *The Pentecostals* that "Branham filled the largest stadiums and meeting halls in the world." The European campaign also won Branham the endorsement of the internationally respected Pentecostal leader Donald Gee, editor of the *Pentecost,* the voice of international Pentecostalism.

The most famous healing in the history of the revival was effected by Branham on William Upshaw, a U.S. congressman from California who had been crippled from birth. This healing in 1951 made Branham's healing power a worldwide legend. Branham's ministry continued to grow until the mid-fifties, when it encountered severe financial difficulties. When the healing revival was transformed into the broader charismatic revival in the late fifties, Branham could not readily adapt. Although he continued to engage in healing campaigns, the thrust of his ministry shifted from healing to doctrinal teaching.

Encouraged by a devoted group of disciples, Branham began teaching doctrines that made him increasingly controversial: denial of an eternal hell, acceptance of divorce, doctrine of the serpent's seed, fierce antidenominationalism, a "Christ against culture" approach to society, predestination, and the like. In December 1965 Branham was killed in a fatal car accident. His days of prominence had faded with the heyday of the healing revival, but his significance as the father and pacesetter of the twentieth-century healing revival remains monumental. Today more than 100,000 Christians continue to follow his doctrinal teachings.

## Appraisal

William Branham's ministry made a significant impact on American Christianity in the last half of the twentieth century. As the initiator of the post–World War II healing revival he set into motion forces that were to have a profound influence on American religious culture, but because of his own limitations and lack of sophistication, he was left in the backwash of the movement he had inspired. The great healing crusades that Branham initiated in the late forties were to revitalize the American Pentecostal movement and were to popularize the doctrine of divine healing in America as never before. As the healing revival attracted hundreds of thousands of Americans from all denominational and cultural backgrounds, the charismatic movement was born. However, Branham's emphasis on holiness of life and separation from the "world" made him an outdated figure to the modish charismatic movement. He was unable to adapt to its needs or to its culture and was unable to compete with his imitators' powerful organizations for funds.

As the pacesetter of the healing revival, Branham was the primary source of inspiration in the development of other healing ministries. He inspired literally hundreds of ministers to enter the healing ministry, and a multitude of evangelists have paid tribute to him for the impact he had on their work. As early as 1950, more than a thousand healing evangelists gathered at a *Voice of Healing* convention to acknowledge the profound influence of Branham on American religious culture. Even Oral Roberts, who would surpass Branham as the most powerful and popular healing evangelist, did not venture forth into large healing crusades until after meeting with Branham. Roberts has acknowledged that Branham's ministry "certainly impacted my life for good." T. L. Osborn, one of Branham's most famous imitators, believed God had sent Branham to awaken the world to the supernatural and the miracle-oriented nature of the gospel.

## Survey of Criticism

Scholarly research on Branham is not extensive; the most serious and objective study of his significance is David E. Harrell's *All Things Are Possible: The Healing and Charismatic Revivals in Modern America*. Harrell elucidates Branham's role as the pacesetter of the post–World War II healing revival. Douglas Weaver's Ph.D. dissertation, "William Marrion Branham . . . A Paradigm of the Prophetic in American Pentecostalism," is the only critical analysis of Branham's theology. This work also identifies the theological tenets that after 1958 were to make Branham a controversial figure even in Pentecostal/charismatic circles.

The single most popular book written about Branham is Gordon Lindsey's *William Branham: A Man Sent from God*. Together with the *Voice of Healing* magazine (1947–58), this volume provides the most complete account of Branham's early life and ministry. Another important description of his early work is found in Julius Stadsklev's *William Branham: A Prophet Visits South Africa*. The best sources of information about Branham's later years are Pearry Green's *The Acts of the Prophet*, and the *Herald of Faith* magazine (1922–70), published by the esteemed Pentecostal leader Joseph Mattsson-Boze. Green's volume is written from an apologetic and hagiographical perspective, as is also Lee Vayle's *Twentieth Century Prophet*.

Standard Pentecostal histories—such as W. J. Hollenweger's *The Pentecostals*, Nils Bloch-Hoell's *The Pentecostal Movement*, and John Thomas Nichol's *Pentecostalism*—deal positively with Branham. Recent efforts to analyze the charismatic movement—such as Prudencio Damboriena's *Tongues as of Fire: Pentecostalism in Contemporary Christianity* and Steve Durasoff's *Bright Wind of the Spirit: Pentecostalism Today*—are strongly sympathetic to Branham and his leadership role in the healing revival.

Several recent publications have been quite negative in their evaluation of Branham. Carl Dyck's *William Branham: The Man and His Message* and Cal Beisner's *William Branham* present, with apologetic fervor, theological critiques of Branham's distinctives and warn of errors in them. Bob Larson, in his *Book of Cults*, identifies present-day followers of Branham's teachings as a "personality cult." Several authors who maintain the presupposition that the practice of faith healing is not acceptable within orthodox Christianity dismiss Branham as being associated with the demonic. Kurt Koch, in his work *Between Christ and Satan*, is representative of this view.

The most current source of materials relating to Branham, and especially of secondary articles, is Weaver's forty-page bibliography in his dissertation. In addition, David Mamalis' *Subject Encyclopedia of Sermons by Rev. William M. Branham* provides a means of using the 1,100-plus collection of Branham's taped sermons.

## Bibliography

### Books by William Branham

1953  *Israel and the Church*. Jeffersonville, Ind.: Spoken Word.
1960  *Adoption*. Jeffersonville, Ind.: Spoken Word.
1960  *The William Branham Sermons: How God Called Me to Africa*. Dallas: Voice of Healing.
1961  *The Godhead Explained*. Jeffersonville, Ind.: Spoken Word.
1963  *Revelation of the Seven Seals*. Jeffersonville, Ind.: Spoken Word.
1965  *The Laodicean Church Age*. Jeffersonville, Ind.: Spoken Word.
1970  *An Exposition of the Seven Church Ages*. Jeffersonville, Ind.: Spoken Word.
1970  *Gleanings from the Spoken Word*. Maniyotchi, India: Ashram Tirunelveli.
1972  *An Exposition of . . . Hebrews*. Jeffersonville, Ind.: Spoken Word.
1973  *Conduct, Order, Doctrine of the Church*. Jeffersonville, Ind.: Spoken Word.
1975  *Footprints on the Sands of Time: The Autobiography of William Marrion Branham*. Jeffersonville, Ind.: Spoken Word.

### Studies about William Branham

Beisner, Cal. *William Branham*. San Juan Capistrano, Calif.: Christian Research Institute, 1982.

Bloch-Hoell, Nils. *The Pentecostal Movement*. Stockholm: Scandinavian University Books, 1964.

Damboriena, Prudencio. *Tongues as of Fire: Pentecostalism in Contemporary Christianity*. Washington, D.C.: Corpus Books, 1969.

Durasoff, Steve. *Bright Wind of the Spirit: Pentecostalism Today*. Englewood Cliffs, N.J.: Prentice-Hall, 1972.

Dyck, Carl. *William Branham: The Man and His Message*. Saskatoon, Canada: Western Tract Mission, 1984.

Green, Pearry. *The Acts of the Prophet*. Tucson: Tucson Tabernacle Books, n.d.

Harrell, David E., Jr. *All Things Are Possible: The Healing and Charismatic Revivals in Modern America*. Bloomington: Indiana University Press, 1975.

Hollenweger, Walter J. *The Pentecostals*. London: SCM Press, 1972.

Koch, Kurt. *Between Christ and Satan*. Grand Rapids: Kregel Publishers, 1972.

Larson, Bob. *Larson's Book of Cults*. Wheaton, Ill.: Tyndale House, 1982.

Lindsey, Gordon. *William Branham: A Man Sent from God*. Jeffersonville, Ind.: Spoken Word, 1950.

Mamalis, David. *Subject Encyclopedia of Sermons by Rev. William M. Branham*. Mesa, Ariz.: William Branham Library, 1978.

Nichol, John Thomas. *Pentecostalism*. New York: Harper and Row, 1966.

Stadsklev, Julius. *William Branham: A Prophet Visits South Africa*. Minneapolis: Stadsklev, 1952.

Thom, Robert. *You and Your Ministry, William Branham*. Seapoint, Cape Province, Republic of South Africa: n.p., n.d.

Vayle, Lee. *Twentieth Century Prophet*. Jeffersonville, Ind.: Spoken Word, 1965.

Weaver, C. Douglas. *The Healer-Prophet, William Marrion Branham: A Study in American Pentecostalism*. Macon, Ga.: Mercer University Press, 1987.

PAUL G. CHAPPELL

# Bill Bright

In 1953 Billy Graham* began one of his short "Hour of Decision" television programs by introducing the lineman of the year from the UCLA football squad. Don Moomaw did not talk about winning football games, but about winning converts to Christ. He told how he had sluffed off religion in his youth and had been determined to make a final break with the constraints of church life when he went off to college. But once there he discovered Campus Crusade, where he met Christ—and Bill Bright.

Bill Bright is synonymous with Campus Crusade for Christ. Begun as a fledgling college witness team in 1951, Campus Crusade is a well-managed worldwide evangelistic organization in its fourth decade of expansion, determined to saturate every continent in seeking "decisions for Christ." It emphasizes a simplified package of the biblical scheme of salvation and a step-by-step approach to conversion through a time-tested and copyrighted tool called the "Four Spiritual Laws."

Contemporary with Billy Graham, Bright emerged in the evangelical revival of the 1950s, convinced that personal religious renewal among the young was needed to counter the rising secularism at home and the forces of atheistic communism abroad. He is in a long tradition of American revivalism that has often linked Protestant evangelical conversion with moral reform and renewal of America's redemptive role. Revivalists like Charles Finney, Dwight Moody, and Billy Sunday* all believed the essence of America to be her Protestant heritage; the striking success of individual liberty and free-market capitalism were signs of her faithfulness in spreading Christianity and democracy. Personal conversion was promoted as the key to producing moral individuals, loyal citizens, and a strong national covenant of continued favor under God. Yet by the Second World War this vision had been severely battered. The fundamentalist-modernist controversy of the early twentieth century provoked a split in the old evangelical empire. Strident biblical inerrantists retreated into a private subculture. Liberal Protestants made an uneasy truce with various aspects of modernity. Evangelicals were no longer the custodians of the moral rudder of the republic.

Cold War anxiety in the 1950s and civil turmoil in the 1960s proved to many evangelicals that secularism's brand of modernity was bankrupt. A postwar religious revival gave renewed hope. Graham preached the old-time gospel to thousands in his tent crusades in Los Angeles. Billy James Hargis*, who shares Oklahoma roots with Bright, enlisted thousands as his Christian Crusade fought to keep the Bible in the school and communism out of the hemisphere. The nation yearned to reclaim its mythic past as a "Christian nation." "God" was written into the Pledge of Allegiance. Hollywood made biblical spectaculars. Denominational differences paled, as Will Herberg argued that Catholics, Protestants, and Jews all agreed to invest the "American Way of Life" with religious ultimacy.

This evangelical resurgence had a more civil tone, a mood that Bill Bright would skillfully appropriate. The doctrines of biblical inerrancy, blood atonement, and a willful personal commitment to Jesus remained, as did belief in miracles and the physical second coming of Christ. But the vociferous fundamentalist attack on all things worldly was gone. Billy Graham set the tone. He wrote to Harold Lindsell in 1955 encouraging a new evangelical publication (*Christianity Today*) that would appeal to "popular jargon" and would never "villify, criticize and beat." "Fundamentalism has failed miserably with the *big stick* approach, now it is time to take the *big love* approach," Graham counseled. Bill Bright fully agreed and built his Campus Crusade on this advice. He would build one of the most effective evangelistic organizations in modern times, putting emphasis on simple personal conversion while easily adapting to the protean cultural blessings of American materialism and technology.

50 BILL BRIGHT

## Biography

William Rohl Bright was born in Coweta, Oklahoma, on 19 October 1921.
He was early influenced by the gentle piety of his mother, whose conversion at
sixteen perhaps exposed him to elements of Methodist holiness. Yet Bright was
also interested in worldly success, claiming to be mildly agnostic throughout his
early adult life. A high achiever, he gained notoriety at college; he edited the
yearbook and was elected to "Who's Who" and chosen student body president.
After college and a short teaching stint, he went west to seek his fortune,
establishing "Bright's California Confections." He was a gifted and aggressive
salesman, blessed with a strong ego and striking good looks. A photo from this
period reflects a dashing "Clark Gable" image.

He was drawn into the orbit of the Hollywood Presbyterian Church through
the influence of Dawson Trotman, originator of the Navigators, and Dan Fuller,
son of radio preacher and seminary founder Charles E. Fuller*. The evangelistic
emphasis at Hollywood Presbyterian often mixed witnessing with social enjoy-
ment, with groups frequently meeting at the homes of the wealthy and influential.
Here Bright found people who were successful and loved Christ and who could
have a good time without carousing and getting drunk. He recalled, as Richard
Quebedeaux reports, one gathering at the mansion of a developer in Bel Air,
where "we would eat his delicious food, swim in his pool, and listen to conversations about Jesus Christ."

He experienced a quiet, prayerful conversion in response to the teaching of
Henrietta Mears, whose phenomenal evangelistic success at Hollywood Presbyterian led to the founding of Gospel Light Publishing House. "There is no
magic in small plans," she encouraged, and her use of "deputation teams,"
Bible-study witnessing fellowships, and prominent celebrities suggested techniques of organization that Bright would adopt for Campus Crusade.

He entered Princeton Seminary in 1946 but transferred to Fuller in Pasadena,
California, the following year. He married a hometown sweetheart, Vonette
Zachary, in 1948, with whom he had two sons, Zachary and Bradley. Vonette
shared Bill's early enthusiasm for Campus Crusade and continued in an active
role. The vision for Campus Crusade came to Bill while he was studying for a
Greek exam in his final year of seminary. In a 1986 interview, he recalled the
event as an "intoxicating experience" as God came to him at midnight. "I
received his commission to go into all the world and make disciples of all
nations—to help fulfill the great commission." He would soon add the phrase
"in this generation" to this oft-repeated call. He quit seminary, sold his business,
and rented a house near the UCLA campus. Within months, 250 students had
committed their lives to Christ.

By the early 1960s, Campus Crusade was expanding on colleges throughout
the country. The key to success was the use of a simple formula for witnessing,
a small portable booklet describing the "how to's" of salvation called *Have You
Heard of the Four Spiritual Laws?* Bright's genius was to combine sales and

marketing skills with the empirical language of science, treating the Bible and God's teachings as verifiable, rational facts. "Just as there are physical laws which govern the physical universe, so are there spiritual laws which govern your relationship with God." (1) Gods loves you and has a plan for your life; (2) sin separates us from God; (3) Jesus is the only provision for man's sin; (4) we must individually *receive* Christ as savior. The booklet closes with an invitation, "You can receive Christ right now through prayer," and a sample is offered. Bright's approach is strikingly reminiscent of the nineteenth-century lawyer-turned-revivalist Charles Finney, who also emphasized technique and human willpower. Finney's 1835 *Lectures on Revivals of Religion* further argued that conversions were neither miraculous nor unpredictable but purely the philosophical result of the right use of means. For forty years Bill Bright has counseled strict adherence to his own time-tested method. As he commented in *Transferable Concepts Series,* vol. 6, "When you share the Four Spiritual Laws, do not elaborate with personal illustrations, which often confuse the one to whom you are speaking. Simply read through the booklet!"

Campus Crusade staff are encouraged to make as many as fifteen witnesses each week, with the first phase, *penetration,* designed to gain campus leaders who have a "heart for God and a teachable attitude." Three more phases—*concentration, saturation,* and *continuation*—are pursued until no one on campus can be found who has not heard of the Four Spiritual Laws. Staff members are typically young (mid to late twenties) and reflect the values and personality of those who recruit them. They are energetic and optimistic, with a pleasing personality and willingness to adhere to Crusade's conservative doctrinal statement and "chain-of-command" authority structure. They are also aggressive and goal-centered and find renewal and encouragement by attending annual training seminars at Campus Crusade headquarters at Arrowhead Springs, a historic resort hotel nestled in the San Bernardino, California, foothills. Arrowhead, purchased in 1961 for $2 million, is also the site of the Lay Institutes for Evangelism, the Executive Seminars, and the recently established International Christian Graduate University.

Bright has displayed a masterful ability to adapt his techniques to the changing mood swings in American life while preserving his simple, conservative message. In the 1950s he appropriated the popularity of Billy Graham, having him appear at numerous campus rallies. "Athletes in Action" was formed in timely response to the growing media attention given to sports in the mid-1960s. The AIA basketball squad consists of championship athletes who have given up lucrative professional contracts to compete hard, win, and witness to their personal faith at half time. When student activism erupted in the late 1960s, Bright adopted phrases like "revolution now" and was quoted in defense of student radicals, claiming "we need dissent in our society." Campus Crusade developed a "Berkeley blitz" for Christ and promoted its own folk-rock singing group through the use of popular singers like Paul Stookey and Johnny Cash.

Yet beneath all of Bright's apparent accommodation to a changing culture, he is deeply committed to the preservation of conservative piety and traditional middle-class values. He has also nurtured an expanding network of financial supporters from the business community, appealing to a conservative philanthropist like Herbert J. Taylor to help promote his Executive Seminars as a way to counter "radical revolutionaries bent on destroying the American Way of Life." The seminar program, often led by famous lay Christians from the world of finance, sports, or entertainment, might feature speakers such as entertainer Dale Evans, financier Ross Perot, or Craig Baynham of the Chicago Bears. The presentations (often separate for male and female) reinforce a linkage between personal Christian evangelism and a constellation of traditional American values such as personal initiative, a work ethic tied to private moral rigor, optimistic "Horatio Alger" hopes for success and wealth, and the assumption that the free enterprise capitalistic system is biblically ordained as the core engine of democracy.

In a similar way, Bright has carefully and effectively planned for his "Explo" events, first held in 1972. These are massive public rallies designed to excite young high school and college age students to adopt the simple Campus Crusade techniques for their homes, churches, and schools. Bright envisions new Explo converts as an evangelistic army that will saturate all areas of life in the quest for worldwide Christian conversions. But the rallies also made a contrasting statement to the counterculture of the late 1960s and early 1970s. The agenda for the clean-cut youth attending the "Explo '72" rally in Dallas was discreetly orchestrated in its mix of personal evangelism and uncritical patriotism. The 85,000 participants were carefully shielded from any dissent surrounding United States Vietnam policy or the civil rights movement. Two years later, Bright took "Explo '74" to South Korea, where 300,000 massed to promote Campus Crusade's evangelism while Bright naively endorsed president Park Chung Hee's autocratic brand of "democracy." Bright received a public rebuke from Billy Graham for defending the repressive Park's imprisonment of religious and political dissidents. "When I read what Bright said over there, it sickened me," Graham was quoted in the 6 September 1976 *Newsweek*.

Bright's movement continued to expand overseas. "Explo '85" was a worldwide evangelistic rally and training event that linked ninety-four sites through sophisticated telecommunications satellites and simultaneous live television coverage. More than 300,000 were trained in the techniques and message of the Four Spiritual Laws. Bright claims that the "Jesus" film has been shown to 270 million people in 104 languages, and the "Agape movement" is an attempt to evangelize third world countries. Bright edits a sophisticated monthly magazine, *Worldwide Challenge*. In an in-house interview in *Worldwide Challenge* (November-December 1986), Bright enthusiastically proclaimed the "Explo '90" goal of training five million for witnessing in his pursuit of fulfilling the Great Commission. "All we need is to mobilize the resources—money, manpower, and technology." Campus Crusade claimed that its 1987 budget would exceed $120 million.

## Appraisal

Some staff members from within the movement complain that the structure of Campus Crusade is rigid and that Bright is an authoritarian father-figure. He is indeed a relentless achiever who prizes efficiency and pragmatic results. His sympathetic biographer, Richard Quebedeaux, admits that though key players in the organization behave as a tight-knit family, Bright is in firm control. Women are obvious by their absence, especially in more prominent positions. The promotion of male athletes and businessmen as winners and achievers reinforces a traditional conservative view that women should defer to male authority and be supportive as helpmates. In 1972 Edward Fiske of the *New York Times* noted the impressive "respect factor" commanded by the men of Athletes in Action. Their gymnastic performance was given background support by girls in blue skirts, white blouses, and red scarves who looked like "American Airline Stewardesses." Again Quebedeaux admits, "Campus Crusade tends to be a family of dominant brothers and submissive sisters."

Some have left the movement because dissent or probing questions are not easily tolerated. Others become frustrated with the relentless emphasis on goals and production, disillusioned that "decisions for Christ" are indistinguishable from "expanding marketing share." Hal Lindsey*, author of *The Late Great Planet Earth,* left because Bright rejected his premillennial stance. Top leaders like Jon Braun, Pete Gilquist, and Robert Andrews quit to form what became the Evangelical Orthodox Church, seeking deeper commitment and nurture on the model of a first-century church.

Those outside the movement deplore Bright's heavy reliance on sophisticated management techniques and his high dependence on wealthy conservatives from the business world. Business leaders come "by invitation only" to his Executive Seminars at Arrowhead Springs, where the amenities are most comfortable. Bright defends his tie to the wealthy. He was quoted in Quebedeaux's biography: "They lead more people to Christ, they give more generously of their funds, and are less 'worldly' than some I know who really don't have anything." Here again Bright stands in a familiar tradition. The wedding of conversion and capitalism is as old as the Businessman's Revival of 1857–58. Dwight Moody enlisted the support of Cyrus McCormick and J. P. Morgan; Billy Sunday was promoted by Andrew Carnegie; and in 1925 Bruce Barton* described Jesus as the first great advertising executive. Just as Billy Graham was pushed by William Randolph Hearst, Bill Bright has an avid supporter in Nelson Bunker Hunt.

Church leaders criticize Bright for paying lip service to the local church and manipulating volunteers in Crusade's singular goal to gain numerous and rapid converts. Kenneth Chafin, a Southern Baptist pastor, complained in the 16 June 1980 *Newsweek*, "When people need help they find that Bright's groups are not there—they're out making more money." Denominational campus pastors find

Bright and Campus Crusade theologically simplistic and intellectually shallow. They question the "plastic smiles" of Crusaders and tag the Four Spiritual Laws as a "seventy-seven word crash course in Christianity" deceptively proselytized under the guise of doing a "religious survey."

Bright and his staff defend their aggressive approach because it gains results. They also note that no one else is doing the job. Bright has attempted to add intellectual credibility to Campus Crusade through the establishment of a Christian graduate school. Readers of his monthly column are repeatedly reminded that Bright "did graduate work at Princeton and Fuller Theological Seminaries" and has "several honorary degrees, including doctor of laws, doctor of divinity and doctor of letters." Yet evangelical historian Nathan Hatch groups Bright with Oral Roberts*, Jerry Falwell*, and Jim Bakker* as representative of the failure of conservative evangelicals to sustain serious intellectual life. They suffer from the schizophrenia of saving souls and losing minds. "Small wonder," Hatch has written in his essay in *Evangelicalism and Modern America* (edited by George M. Marsden), "that evangelical thinking which once was razor-sharp and genuinely profound, now seems dull, rusty, even banal."

Bright shows little interest in scholarly thinking or theological investigation. His piety finds renewal in what he calls "spiritual breathing." George Marsden has correctly noted that this is a contemporary expression of ideas formulated by Andrew Murray of the Keswick holiness movement from the turn of the century. Confessed sin is "breathed out" while Christ's spiritual presence is "breathed in," providing one with power to overcome one's carnal nature. This state of holiness requires constant maintenance of renewal, which for Bright is translated into active evangelism.

Such spirituality is also without a strong mechanism for self-criticism, since sin, corruption, and pride seem easily overcome. Bright is not always aware that his equation of conversion with American success provokes a tension that has historically plagued evangelicalism—the fear of being taken captive by the very culture they desire to transform. As one AIA athlete put it, according to Carol Frake, "It's important for us to win, not because God wants winners, but because Americans do."

### Survey of Criticism

The literature about Bill Bright is scanty, especially that of a scholarly nature. Since the mid-1960s *Christianity Today* has featured Bright and Campus Crusade on more than twenty occasions, usually from a sympathetic posture. In the same period the *Christian Century* published a number of critical pieces. Aubrey B. Haines questioned the sincerity of Campus Crusade's social concern in "The 'New' Face of 'Campus Crusade.' " J. Randolph Taylor offered a perceptive critique of the Atlanta "Here's Life" effort in "Here's Bright America." Jim Wallis* and Wes Michaelson accused Bright of equating evangelical Christianity with right-wing politics in "The Plan to Save America" in *Sojourners. Chris-*

*tianity Today* gave Bright a chance to reply in an interview, "Yoking Politics and Proclamation—Can It Be Done?"

The only biographical treatment is Richard Quebedeaux's *I Found It!* It is highly sympathetic in its heroic portrait of Bright. James D. Hunter's *American Evangelicalism* is a lucid sociological study that argues that evangelicals refuse to be restricted to the private sphere by creating their own subculture of "parallel institutions," from Christian colleges to motorcycle clubs. He evaluates Bright's use of the "grammar of empiricism" commodity. Carol Flake's *Redemptorama* is a witty, yet sometimes uneven, literary treatment that discusses Bright as part of evangelicalism's creation of a "Christian Disneyland," a fantasy world protected from the harsh realities of pluralist culture.

Several historians of American religion offer cogent assessments of the larger cultural context of Bright's evangelical style. Martin E. Marty's chapter, "Evangelicalism and Fundamentalism," in *A Nation of Behavers* argues that although evangelicals are a cognitive minority, they are adroit at building coalitions and behaving as a sociocultural majority. Robert T. Handy has written a new chapter, "Variant Attitudes Toward New Realities (1940–1980)," tracing the attempt of evangelicals to reclaim the vision of a Christian America. William McLoughlin's final chapter in *Revivals, Awakenings, and Reform* is a provocative essay treating evangelicalism in the larger context of "revitalization movements," adapting a formation from anthropologist Anthony F. C. Wallace. Bill Bright fits McLoughlin's larger thesis that Protestant American history is one long millenarian movement, with freedom and piety combining to perfect the individual, nation, and world. A fine collection of essays that includes the best of recent evangelical scholarship is *Evangelicalism and Modern America*, edited by George Marsden.

## Bibliography

### Works by Bill Bright

1959   *Letter to Dr. Randolph Van Dusen.* San Bernardino: Campus Crusade.
1963   *Paul Brown Letter.* San Bernardino: Campus Crusade.
1965   *Have You Heard of the Four Spiritual Laws?* San Bernardino: Campus Crusade.
1966   *Have You Made the Wonderful Discovery of the Spirit-Filled Life?* San Bernardino: Campus Crusade.
1968   *Ten Basic Steps Toward Christian Maturity.* 10 vols. Rev. ed. San Bernardino: Campus Crusade.
1969   *Revolution Now.* San Bernardino: Campus Crusade.
1970   *Come Help Change the World.* Old Tappan, N.J.: Revell Co.
1977   *A Movement of Miracles.* Old Tappan, N.J.: Revell Co.
1979   *Believing God for the Impossible.* San Bernardino: Campus Crusade
1979   *Come Help Change Our World.* San Bernardino: Campus Crusade.
1980   *The Holy Spirit, the Key to Supernatural Living.* San Bernardino: Campus Crusade.
1981   *Handbook for Christian Maturity.* San Bernardino: Campus Crusade.
1981   *Handbook of Concepts for Living.* San Bernardino: Campus Crusade.
1981   *Transferable Concepts Series.* 9 vols. San Bernardino: Campus Crusade.

1983   *Promises: A Daily Guide to Supernatural Living.* San Bernardino: Campus Cru-
       sade.

*Selected Studies about Bill Bright and the Context of Contemporary
Evangelicalism*

"The Children of Bright." *Newsweek* 95 (16 June 1980): 55.
"Door Interview: Bill Bright." *Wittenberg Door* (February–March 1977): 6–23, 26.
Flake, Carol. *Redemptorama: Culture, Politics, and the New Evangelicalism.* New York:
       Penguin, 1985.
Haines, Aubrey B. "The 'New' Face of 'Campus Crusade.' " *Christian Century* 86
       (1969): 1650–51.
Handy, Robert T. *A Christian America.* 2nd ed. New York: Oxford University Press,
       1984.
Hunter, James D. *American Evangelicalism: Conservative Religion and the Quandary of
       Modernity.* New Brunswick, N.J.: Rutgers University Press, 1983.
McLoughlin, William G. *Revivals, Awakenings, and Reform.* Chicago: University of
       Chicago Press, 1977.
Marsden, George M., ed. *Evangelicalism and Modern America.* Grand Rapids: Eerdmans,
       1984.
Marty, Martin E. *A Nation of Behavers.* Chicago: University of Chicago Press, 1976.
Quebedeaux, Richard. *I Found It! The Story of Bill Bright and Campus Crusade.* San
       Francisco: Harper and Row, 1979.
Sweet, Leonard I., ed. *The Evangelical Tradition in America.* Macon, Ga.: Mercer
       University Press, 1984.
Taylor, J. Randolph. "Here's Bright America." *Christian Century* 93 (1976): 1030–32.
Wallis, Jim, and Wes Michaelson. "The Plan to Save America." *Sojourners* 5 (1976):
       4–12.
Wells, David F., and John D. Woodbridge, eds. *The Evangelicals: What They Believe,
       Who They Are, Where They Are Changing.* Rev. ed. Grand Rapids: Baker Book
       House, 1977.
White, James W., and John G. Hallsten. "Campus Crusade Goes Suburban." *Christian
       Century* 89 (1972): 549–51.
World Christian Federation. "Bright's Blitz: Group Research Report to the World Student
       Christian Federation." 25 June 1980.
"Yoking Politics and Proclamation—Can It Be Done?" *Christianity Today* 20: 20–22.
                                                              JOEL SHERER


# William Jennings Bryan

William Jennings Bryan was one of many Americans dislocated between the
verities of Victorian America and the uncertainties of modernity. Theologians
who tried to span the gulf between the small-town religion they cherished and
the urbanity they wished to reach; philosophers who respected simple faith and
constructed a towering skepticism; Woodrow Wilson, the president Bryan served,
caught between old-fashioned vision and a new-fashioned war; Bryan's opponent

at Dayton, Clarence Darrow, who undermined one nineteenth-century faith with another—all shared this most uncomfortable place.

## Biography

Bryan was born on 19 March 1860 in Salem, Illinois. He was the eldest living son of Silas and Mariah Bryan. His mother was from an established local family—the Jennings. His father was Scotch-Irish and had moved west from Virginia to seek place and fortune. As a circuit court judge, gentleman farmer, and Democratic politician, he found a modicum of each. Diligently, he and Mariah prepared their son to gain more. This preparation reflected the educational, religious, political, and cultural values of the parents.

Bryan's education was basic. His mother taught him first with the omnipresent McGuffey *Reader*. He continued in the local public schools until he enrolled in Whipple Academy in Jacksonville, a preparatory institution for Illinois College. In his two years at Whipple and his four at Illinois, Bryan pursued learning diligently, earning the distinction of college valedictorian. But he was most at home in the student societies that nurtured his talent for the spoken word. Bryan pursued learning to pursue public speaking, and he pursued public speaking to pursue politics.

On graduation in 1881, Bryan entered Union Law School in Chicago. His father's connections placed him under the tutelage of distinguished lawyer Lyman Trumbull. His own effort carried him through the required study while earning a modest keep. He worked as a clerk in Trumbull's office, lived in a working-class neighborhood, and walked the four miles to school. His grades were good, though he was an indifferent reader, more apt to learn by observing Trumbull and others around him. In 1883, Bryan completed his study of law, the practice of which would advance his political goals.

His career was not the sole beneficence of Silas Bryan. He also left William a legacy of faith. The elder Bryan was a staunch Christian of slight Baptist coloration. He opened sessions of the circuit court with prayer, and he admonished lawyers on moral as well as legal points. Mariah exhibited a Methodist hue. Their son attended both parents' Sunday Schools. When converted at age fourteen, he in turn joined the local Cumberland Presbyterian Church.

This phenomenon of nearly interchangeable churches remained a facet of William Bryan's life. His faith was an irenic, mildly evangelical Protestantism. Coming between the denominationalization of the early nineteenth century and the fundamentalist-modernist fissure of the early twentieth, this style of Christianity was a hiatus in the fractious faith common to much of American religious history. Despite association with the fundamentalist side of the twentieth-century controversy, Bryan breathed a faith in many ways as protoliberal as it was protoconservative, one interested in practice more than doctrine.

One important element in that faith—more liberal than conservative in expression—was a thoroughgoing optimism. Bryan was convinced that humanity was on a gradual upward course—uncertain, capable of setback and sidetrack, but noticeable to any impartial observer. This quality he shared with many Americans of his day. When Bryan cried out, "Justice should be done; justice must be done; justice shall be done!" folk who applauded matched the speaker's faith that such was the logical sequence for a virtue both they and he well understood. As Bryan prepared to enter law practice in Jacksonville, Illinois, he was well equipped both by law school and Sunday School for his life's work.

Bryan would need such equipment. Jacksonville was lightened only by his marriage to Mary Elizabeth Baird in 1884. His legal practice was restricted largely to debt collection and insurance sales. If central Illinois was fine soil for education, it was poor for a budding lawyer and it was abysmal for a budding Democratic politician. For one who valued character above all, bending with any wind was unconscionable. For the son of Silas Bryan, one time Jacksonian Democratic congressional candidate, bending to a Republican wind was unthinkable. For one reinforced by the antiwealth, antimonopoly thinking of Trumbull, the Republican party was a pox on the body politic. And for one with ambitions to inhabit the White House, remaining stifled in Jacksonville was death itself. He decided on a move to Lincoln, Nebraska, in 1887.

His law practice in Nebraska differed little from that in Illinois. Major cases still eluded him. However, the Democratic strength in Nebraska opened new political opportunities for Bryan—but not without price. The Nebraska party differed from that of his native southern Illinois. Bryan's cultural preparation, woven in the warp and woof of both his religion and his politics, did not prepare him for the cultural and ethnic pluralism of the postwar Democratic party. The homogeneity of small-town, southern, Protestant Illinois inculcated values at odds with a vital portion of Nebraska Democrats.

If not exactly nativist, Bryan still embraced a native American view of many issues. An advocate of temperance and Sabbath-law observance, Bryan met opposition from many Democrats on these themes of WASP culture. A former farm worker who valued rural life and small-town politics, Bryan collided with ward politics and urban culture. His ardent devotion and speaking talents recommended him to Nebraska political boss J. Sterling Morton, who sought to mold this younger colleague to political reality. Once Bryan downplayed his more controversial themes and played to a reliable agenda of opposition to unrestrained wealth and monopoly, he was encouraged to pound the huskings for the party.

He complied with enthusiasm, speaking far and wide, writing glowing reviews on himself, and working his way into the party. The result surprised both Bryan and his mentor. His popularity soared. With keen powers of observation, he fitted tirades against predatory wealth and for popular government into the mounting discontent of many Nebraskans with the state of their nation. Rising Populism established Bryan in his party, as he articulated the frustrations of a region within a Jacksonian dream of democracy. More, Bryan articulated these themes with peerless eloquence. In an age that depended on the spoken word for needs that are today diffused among several media, Bryan gave form to aspirations just below the surface of many people's daily lives.

By 1890, Bryan could stand apart from Morton and win election to Congress with a combination of Democratic and Farmer's Alliance support. This combination did cause some difficulty. His attachment to the party led to embarrassment as Republican prohibitionists tarred him with the brush of alcohol and as Alliance radicals decried his unwillingness to "come out" from a tainted party. His election depended on a balance of not-so-compatible views, and Bryan demonstrated remarkable elasticity.

Bryan came to Washington in 1891 as a first-term congressman. An unprecedented seat on the Ways and Means Committee and a forceful speech on the tariff in 1892 gave him national repute. His efforts for Nebraska identified him with a reform agenda more or less Populist and arrayed him against the Democratic leadership. As a result, Bryan appealed to loyalists uneasy with the conservative policies of President Grover Cleveland. Bryan's powerful voice rallied those Democrats and Populists stirred by the Omaha Platform and the birth of the People's party. Cleveland Democrats, even in Nebraska, belittled this sentiment. Bryan did not. He forged the groundswell for popular government into a coalition that eked out a second-term victory over both Morton Democrats and Republicans and then took control of the Nebraska Democratic party. From this base, Bryan prepared to assault the 1896 Democratic National Convention. He was thirty-five.

The weapon Bryan chose was "the money question." To conservatives, the ideal was the stability of the gold standard. To western activists behind Bryan, the goal was the purchasing power of silver. Prior to the convention, Bryan became the leading speaker for silver. He also orchestrated the delegate selection process, ensuring substantial silverite representation at the convention. But Bryan's eloquence tipped the scale. The famous "Cross of Gold" speech enthralled the house and ushered Bryan into the nomination for president. It also arrayed the party on the side of reform, and there Bryan was determined that it should stay.

Bryan lost the 1896 election. He campaigned tirelessly, traveled 18,000 miles by train, visited twenty-six states, and addressed over five million people. Republican William McKinley, backed by Mark Hanna, won a disputed election. In defeat, however, Bryan emerged with a stronger hold on his party. Democratic conservatives hoped in vain that the Populism of 1896 was temporary. The nerve Bryan had touched was sore enough to carry Democrats well into the twentieth century.

Bryan also proved that this nerve had more than one synapse in the body politic. He deviled McKinley with a host of issues, including silver, the direct election of senators, labor rights, and opposition to imperialism. Shunted to Florida during service in the Spanish-American War, Bryan exchanged podium for pen. His book on the 1896 campaign and his writings for the *Omaha World-Herald* were widely read. He influenced national policy through a network of supporters in the party and in Congress. It was almost a foregone conclusion that Bryan would carry his party's banner again in 1900. It was also almost foregone that he would lose. Support had cooled, especially on silver. Further, the Republican nominee for vice-president, Theodore Roosevelt, stole some of Bryan's thunder on reform and tapped wartime patriotism. Bryan ran in vain.

The defeat of 1900 shook Democratic support for Bryan. His bolt shot with Populist passions, some accused their premiere representative of ignoring political reality. But he was still powerful. He still captured the public eye, even influencing the daily workings of Congress. He now had the role of Democratic boss and public conscience. He played the former aggressively, with a network of alliances among party regulars. He played the latter with his wonted flair, writing for his own publication, *The Commoner,* and regaling his supporters with an indefatigable schedule of speeches and Chautauqua lectures. His agenda, little changed with the years, gripped audiences bound by the power of his voice.

The frame of Bryan's thought was remarkably consistent. Small changes put peace before silver, even as Prohibition would follow peace, then antievolution, antiliquor. With a clear message, he even achieved the unexpected—a third nomination for president. This feat followed his defeat by the "reorganizers" in the 1904 convention, a blow that had seemed to end his political career. However, Roosevelt's victory and the growing Progressive movement, which embraced many of his reforms, gave new life to a Bryan candidacy. In 1908 he again carried the party banner against Taft.

And again, Bryan bore that banner to defeat. The rebel of 1896 could not win the votes of enough middle-class Progressives. Puzzled, Bryan announced that he would not seek election again. Instead, he returned to politics in Nebraska and to reform activity wherever and whenever he could write and speak. Oddly, in defeat his moral stature increased. The popularity of reforms that Bryan championed for years ensured that he would be heard, if not elected. Further, the power of new groups like the Anti-Saloon League, which advanced Bryan's temperance views, put him back in the limelight. If such issues eventually fractured the Democratic machine that he had put together in the early nineties, they also secured his influence for 1912, guaranteeing him a place in any administration of candidate Woodrow Wilson.

Wilson won a three-way campaign that year, and Bryan, who had not held office since he left the House, was named secretary of state. His tenure featured idiosyncrasy, idealistic diplomacy, and unyielding commitment to high moral standards. Bryan amused official Washington with his informal style and grape juice at the table. He bemused the same people with his conciliation treaties sealed with plowshares made from surplus swords, his high-minded attitudes toward Latin America and Mexico, and his stubborn insistence on strict neutrality in the war in Europe. He angered many with his resignation when convinced that Wilson intended a pro-Allied neutrality that would undercut any American bid to mediate peace. Despite the cost, Bryan stood by his principles. He retired to private life under a storm of criticism, determined to take his cause to the people. And the people listened. Rallying the strength of the peace and international arbitration movements, Bryan led the last-ditch fight against America's entry into war.

Whether Bryanism could have changed the events of 1914–18 is moot. America went to war. So too did Bryan. He did not follow the few radical pacifists but loyally supported Wilson even in the more stringent war measures. Bryan divided his time between advocating postwar policies (many of which found their way into Wilson's Fourteen Points) and stumping for other issues. Women's suffrage, prohibition, and antievolution took his attention in turn. He watched with pleasure as the constitution was amended to accommodate not only the first two of those reforms but also the direct election of senators and the income tax. Indeed, in a strange twist, Bryan's agenda became policy even as the man himself lost ground.

In the party councils of the twenties, Bryan was both elder statesman and tragic figure. His Populism was routinized into the ideology that would undergird Franklin D. Roosevelt's New Deal. To some in the party, however, it was unclear whether Bryan was a labor and suffrage Progressive or a prohibition and anti-evolution reactionary. The Nebraska party slipped from his control, denying him a delegate's position in 1916, but he attended the convention with press credentials. Though he won an at-large position in 1920, he knew his hold was weak. Moving to Florida in 1921, Bryan garnered a strong vote for delegate in 1924, raising hopes for a Senate seat in 1926. But the 1924 convention showed the instability of his place in the party. Bryan was jeered by delegates supporting Al Smith and was smeared for presumed association with the Ku Klux Klan. Even his supporters noted the decline.

Before he could test the Senate race, Bryan became involved in the Scopes Trial in Dayton, Tennessee. John Scopes, charged with violating a state anti-evolution law, attracted Clarence Darrow for his defense. Bryan volunteered his services to the prosecution, finally pleading a major case before the bench. He won the case, but lost the media battle. At Darrow's hands, Bryan appeared not only obscurantist, but simpleminded. The major event of the trial, Darrow's examination of the chief counsel for the prosecution, left Bryan looking befuddled. The incisive voice of the nineteenth-century faith in science, embodied in Darrow, ran down what remained of Bryan's own nineteenth-century Protestantism (which, to the consternation of many supporters, could accommodate theistic evolution) rather than the increasingly militant fundamentalism behind the Tennessee ordinance. Miscast as the champion of a movement in many ways alien to his sensibilities, Bryan suffered defeat.

The media turned the defeat into a national rout. Bryan was subjected to all manner of criticism. The "Great Commoner" did not have an opportunity to rally his yet considerable following in rebuttal, however. On 26 July 1925, less than a week after the end of the trial, Bryan died in his sleep in Dayton.

## Appraisal

Bryan was but one of many people, famous and unknown, who found the nineteenth-century world drastically changed in the second decade of the twentieth. He was but one of the host who found that change surprising. Even those who opposed the vision that he represented were often cut from the same cloth. All had high hopes for America. The outraged farmers of Populism and the muckracking journalists of Progressivism plied remedies that had more than a few overtones of utopia. The Gilded Age softened rough edges and domesticated wild ideas. The reorientation of the universe by science, the restructuring of the mind by psychology, even the rethinking of the nature of God by theology—all entered the world of ideas buffered by a gentle haze of optimism. Thus if Bryan's vision of America was among the first casualties of this century, it was certainly not the last.

Among historians at least, Bryan has come to represent the soul lost in transition, completely at home in one age, completely adrift in the next. In part, Bryan has been fated to this reputation by his own public image. To others, the unyielding integrity that Bryan saw as essential to his own humanity appeared both noble and quixotic. As a losing presidential candidate, a resigning secretary of state, a public servant seldom elected to any office, Bryan often seemed to win by losing. He early gained a moral stature that was widely applauded but seldom questioned. On the other hand, as the century turned, Bryan's voice was heard on more issues that, to many, had less and less to do with current events. Peace fell to preparedness, faith converted to an ill-mannered fundamentalism, character to the state-sponsored coercion of prohibition, economic solutions to attempts by rural America to restrain the growth of corporate America. That the economic reforms fell earliest from credibility obscured the fact that many reforms, including Bryan's cherished bimetallism, reappeared in the days of the New Deal. By this time, however, Bryan was remembered for Dayton rather than the Cross of Gold. He had become wrongheaded.

The appellation has a certain element of truth, and for more than the last years of Bryan's life. In some ways, his entire sixty-five years were spent in efforts to run against the tide. He was a Southern Democrat from Illinois, dedicated to a party smeared by the title Copperhead and divided by its own diversity. He was an ardent reformer in a Nebraska riven along ethnic lines, and a prohibitionist in a party that counted strongly on the wet urban vote. Bryan was bimetallist when the gold standard reigned supreme, anti-imperialist in the age of the glorious little war against Spain, and in favor of international arbitration as the countries of Europe found compelling reason to batter one another. Even his name was used against him, with rumors that he had changed it from O'Brian to hide an Irish past. His last acts were not at all out of character for one who held principle above all other motives for human action. They were in fact bedfellows with earlier positions that somehow found a comfortable home in the untidy thinking of the Great Commoner.

William Jennings Bryan was a divining rod. He drew into himself the faith of an age and pointed it toward its own best, and sometimes worst, conclusions. If the result was a ramshackle edifice, perhaps the fault did not lie all with the exemplar. As Paul Carter in *The Spiritual Crisis of the Gilded Age* so well pointed out, few Americans of the Gilded Age would have escaped prosecution had logical vagueness been against the law. The fact that Bryan continues to appeal today to different people for different reasons—some in grudging respect of his pacifism, others in adulation of his fundamentalism—might warn us that Carter's dictum applies closer to home.

### Survey of Criticism

Calm reflection did not replace partisan passion when Bryan died. His family published his memoirs with suitable dispatch. Mary Baird Bryan also worked to keep her husband's memory alive and in print. Wayne Williams wrote admiring biographies, including *William Jennings Bryan: A Study in Political Vindication.* Other works in the twenties continued a hagiographical approach.

On the other hand, Paxton Hibben, in *The Peerless Leader: William Jennings Bryan,* found little helpful or healthy in the Great Commoner. To Hibben, whose study was endorsed by Charles Beard, Bryan was an eloquent mass of inhibitions who stumbled onto celebrity. Endlessly, and usually pointlessly, fascinated with the female influences on Bryan, Hibben belittled his presidential stature, ignoring the fact that, if Bryan was not the best-qualified candidate, he was certainly on a par with many who have inhabited the White House. Hibben's view found important support in Richard Hofstadter's *American Political Tradition,* which dismissed Bryan as an example of the wrongheadedness endemic to the American reform impulse and all things rural.

More recently, historians have followed two paths in dealing with Bryan. Some study a particular period or issue in his life, concerning themselves with questions of change in Bryan's thought. Was he a Populist radical or a fundamentalist reactionary? Or were the two somehow linked in an untidy mind? During the sixties, Paul Glad's *Trumpet Soundeth: William Jennings Bryan and His Democracy, 1896–1912* and Lawrence Levine's *Defender of the Faith: William Jennings Bryan, The Last Decade, 1915–1925* concluded that Bryan's mind changed less than the issues he supported would seem to imply. These studies indicate that the key to understanding Bryan rests in the complexities of his personality and received culture.

Other scholars have taken the whole of Bryan's life or career. Paolo E. Coletta's three-volume *William Jennings Bryan* is the landmark study of this type, though Louis Koenig's *Bryan: A Political Biography of William Jennings Bryan* and Robert Cherny's *Righteous Cause: The Life of William Jennings Bryan* mark significant single-volume contributions. Like the studies with more limited focus, those of Coletta, Koenig, and Cherny see Bryan as a particular product of a particular setting. Small-town southern Illinois and the American Midwest; McGuffey and debating societies; Jackson, Jefferson, even Tolstoy; evangelical

Protestantism and Victorian optimism; above all, the power of the spoken word, whether from pulpit or lectern—these are the components that comprehend the Great Commoner. If Bryan's ideas were flawed by a superficial intellect and his politics by a want of realism, the former still reached the deepest desires of many people of his day, and the latter succeeded not only because of his eloquence but also because of his organizing ability.

## Bibliography

### Selected Books by William Jennings Bryan

1896   *The First Battle: A Story of the Campaign of 1896*. Chicago: W. B. Conkey.
1899   *Republic or Empire? The Philippine Question*. Chicago: Independence Co.
1900   *The Second Battle*. Chicago: n.p.
1909   *The Prince of Peace*. Chicago: Reilly and Britton.
1912   *The Forces That Make for Peace: Addresses at the Mohonk Conferences on International Arbitration*. Boston: World Peace Foundation.
1912   *A Tale of Two Conventions*. New York: Funk and Wagnalls.
1913   *Speeches of William Jennings Bryan*. 2 vols. New York: Funk and Wagnalls.
1917   *The First Commandment*. New York: Fleming H. Revell.
1917   *Heart to Heart Appeals*. New York: Fleming H. Revell.
1922   *In His Image*. New York: Fleming H. Revell.
1925   *The Memoirs of William Jennings Bryan*. Philadelphia: John C. Winston.

### Selected Studies about William Jennings Bryan

Anderson, David D. *William Jennings Bryan*. Boston: Twayne, 1981.
Cherney, Robert W. *A Righteous Cause: The Life of William Jennings Bryan*. Boston: Little, Brown and Company, 1985.
Clements, Kendrick A. *William Jennings Bryan: Missionary Isolationist*. Knoxville: University of Tennessee Press, 1982.
Coletta, Paolo E. *William Jennings Bryan—Political Evangelist, 1860–1908*. 3 vols. Lincoln: University of Nebraska Press, 1964–69.
Curti, Merle E. *Bryan and World Peace*. Northampton, Mass.: Department of History of Smith College, 1931.
Glad, Paul W. *The Trumpet Soundeth: William Jennings Bryan and His Democracy, 1896–1912*. Lincoln: University of Nebraska Press, 1960.
———, ed. *William Jennings Bryan: A Profile*. New York: Hill and Wang, 1968.
Herrick, Genevieve F., and John D. Herrick. *The Life of William Jennings Bryan*. Chicago: Buxton, 1925.
Hibben, Paxton. *The Peerless Leader: William Jennings Bryan*. New York: Farrar and Rinehart, 1929.
Hollingsworth, J. Rogers. *The Whirligig of Politics: The Democracy of Cleveland and Bryan*. Chicago: University of Chicago Press, 1963.
Koenig, Louis W. *Bryan: A Political Biography of William Jennings Bryan*. New York: Putnam, 1971.
Levine, Lawrence W. *Defender of the Faith: William Jennings Bryan, The Last Decade, 1915–1925*. New York: Oxford University Press, 1965.
Long, J. C. *Bryan: The Great Commoner*. New York: D. Appleton and Co., 1928.

Smith, Willard H. *The Social and Religious Thought of William Jennings Bryan.* Lawrence: University Press of Kansas, 1975.

Werner, M. R. *Bryan.* New York: Harcourt, Brace and Co., 1929.

Williams, Wayne C. *William Jennings Bryan: A Study in Political Vindication.* New York: Fleming H. Revell, 1923.

————. *William Jennings Bryan.* New York: G. P. Putnam's Sons, 1936.

DANIEL SWINSON

# Will D. Campbell

In its 8 May 1972 issue, *Newsweek* described Billy Graham* as the best known of the South's Baptist preachers. Second to him, the article contended, was a "bourbon-guzzling, tobacco-spitting, guitar-strumming man who rarely preaches a Sunday sermon and believes that the institutional church is perhaps the greatest barrier to the proclamation of the Gospel" (*Newsweek,* 8 May 1972, p. 84). That person was Will D. Campbell, whose rise to prominence was primarily the result of his activism in the civil rights movement. Familiarity with Will D. Campbell has perhaps increased since 1972, largely as a result of his recent memoirs and novel. He is, many suspect, the model for the Reverend Will B. Dunn of Doug Marlette's syndicated comic strip, *Kudzu.* And he remains an active gadfly to a complacent and establishment Christianity with his many articles (most often in recent years in *Christianity and Crisis*) and public addresses.

## Biography

Will Davis Campbell was born in Amite County, a poor rural community of southern Mississippi, in 1924. His father was a farmer and a Baptist who had once aspired to be a preacher and who retained the nickname "Preacher" even after the opportunity for serving in that capacity had passed. His mother was a homemaker, often sick, as was the case with Will. There were four children in the Campbell family: Lorraine, Joseph Lee, Will, and Paul Edward. The family was close-knit, the bond between Joe and Will being especially strong.

Early in his childhood Will decided he would be a preacher. Perhaps it was expected of him because of his health or intelligence. At any rate, his resolve was strong and the family was supportive of that decision. At the age of seven Campbell confessed his sins at the East Fork Baptist Church and was baptized. At the age of sixteen he began preaching in the county, and less than a year later he was ordained by his church to the gospel ministry.

Following graduation from high school, he enrolled at Louisiana College in Pineville to begin his preparation for the ministry. This first college experience was somewhat unsuccessful because of various distractions, and Campbell dropped out of college and enlisted in the military. He was stationed in New Caledonia, Guam, and Saipan, serving as a medic during World War II. It was during this period in the South Pacific, in relative isolation from blacks, that Campbell's consciousness about the civil rights of blacks began to be raised. His brother Joe, who had been hospitalized following an automobile accident, wrote him letters describing the accomplishments of blacks and urging him to read Howard Fast's *Freedom Road*. In *Brother to a Dragonfly* Campbell describes reading this work as a conversion experience for him. "I knew that the tragedy of the South would occupy the remainder of my days" (98).

After his military service he returned home to marry Brenda Fisher, a student whom he had met while at Louisiana College, and to enroll at Wake Forest College in North Carolina under the G.I. bill. Campbell graduated from Wake Forest with an A.B. degree in 1948. He then enrolled in and received a master's degree in English literature from Tulane University before graduating from Yale Divinity School in 1952.

Campbell's first pastoral call came a short time later to Taylor Baptist Church in northern Louisiana. After serving the church for two years (1952–54) he left, feeling that there was too little freedom in the pastorate. The University of Mississippi, "Ole Miss," offered him the position of Director of Religious Life at the university, and believing that there would be considerably more freedom in an academic context than in a parish, Campbell accepted the position. He started work scarcely three months after the 1954 *Brown* v. *Board of Education* Supreme Court decision, and Will Campbell's involvement in the civil rights movement soon ensued.

There were some relatively minor incidents of harassment of Campbell as a result of his commitment to civil rights early in his time at Ole Miss. Having been observed playing Ping-Pong on campus with a visiting black minister friend, Campbell found his yard covered the next morning with Ping-Pong balls, half of them painted black, half of them white. On another occasion Campbell had invited black journalist Carl Rowan to stay overnight at his home; the reprisal for that occurred at a party that Campbell's staff had prepared for new students. During the party someone placed a cup of feces in the punch bowl. Campbell's dedication to the civil rights issue while at Ole Miss is best seen in a conflict he had with the administration in 1956. Finding too little discussion of racial justice on campus, Campbell planned a Religious Emphasis Week with speakers who would address the issue. Prominent among them was Alvin Kershaw, an Episcopal priest from Ohio who had appeared on the "Sixty-four Thousand Dollar Question" game show and had devoted some of his winnings to the NAACP. The university forbade Kershaw's appearance, the other speakers cancelled, and Religious Emphasis Week consisted of an hour of silent reflection each day as spotlights shone on two empty chairs on the auditorium stage. Campbell was once and for all disabused of his belief that there was such a thing as genuine academic freedom. A short time later he resigned from his position at the university.

He was hired in 1956 for a two-year appointment as a race relations specialist in the South by the Department of Racial and Cultural Relations, National Council of Churches. He and his family moved to Nashville, where he began his work. And a busy time it was for Campbell and the civil rights movement. During those first two years with the National Council of Churches Campbell was the only white man present at the formation of the Southern Christian Leadership Conference of Dr. Martin Luther King, Jr.* He walked with the first nine black children to enter the white schools of Little Rock in 1957. He negotiated with white authorities in Montgomery, Birmingham, New Orleans, Baton Rouge, Chattanooga, Fort Worth, and Richmond. His work viewed as successful, he was rehired by the NCC and stayed in that position until 1963.

But things began to go sour with Campbell and the NCC in the early sixties. As Campbell sees it, the same stifling of freedom that he had felt in the pastorate and that he had felt at Ole Miss, he began to feel with the National Council of Churches. In speeches and interviews he suggested that the black, just like the white, was capable of doing grievous violence. He also expressed some sympathy for a Southern "redneck" sheriff. These were embarrassing to the NCC, and so he was asked not to say certain things in public and to submit all articles and speeches first to the New York office. Campbell refused and shortly thereafter resigned.

His first book, *Race and the Renewal of the Church,* was published in 1962. The book was a stinging indictment of the institutional church. The church had failed to act for racial reconciliation, and when it had acted it had acted in the wrong sort of way, merely echoing the cries of the secular world. Instead of being the reconciled body of Christ, a "third race," the church had followed the walk of society in racial matters and had made an issue of race. The cornerstone of Campbell's understanding of Christian gospel was II Corinthians 5:19, "God was in Christ reconciling the world to himself." According to Campbell, because God has accomplished this reconciliation, the church is to act as the community of the reconciled and to carry that message of reconciliation to all peoples. Instead the church had worshipped the gods of law and order as well as bought into programs of social engineering. Campbell's first book was a call for the church to be the church, and although critical of the church the book did end on a note of hopefulness for the church, a note that would become increasingly muted in future works.

In 1962 Will Campbell claims to have had his third conversion experience. Jonathan Daniel, a divinity student from the Episcopal Theological Seminary in Cambridge, Massachusetts, who had been active in Alabama registering black voters, was gunned down by an Alabama special deputy, Thomas Coleman, outside a grocery store. Will was discussing theology with his brother Joe and a gadfly Southern journalist, P. D. East, just after the shooting took place. East asked Campbell to summarize the gospel in ten words or less. Campbell's answer: "We're all bastards but God loves us anyway." East pressed Campbell to recognize Daniel as well as Coleman as a bastard and to acknowledge the forgiveness and reconciliation of both. Campbell recognized that he had taken sides, taken sides against a people—call them rednecks—who had been victimized every bit as much as the blacks. He had taken sides in a way fundamentally inconsistent with his belief that God had reconciled *all* to himself. From that moment on Campbell attempted to extend his ministry to all victimized. Hence he has befriended and ministered to, for example, members of the Ku Klux Klan, thus earning the scorn and disdain of liberal whites. But even as he has ministered to the Ku Klux Klan, his commitment to the reconciliation of blacks and whites and to justice for all has not faltered.

Following his resignation from the NCC, the next position Campbell occupied, from 1964 until its gradual dissolution in the late 1970s, was director of the Committee of Southern Churchmen. The committee was the publisher of *Katallagete* and was something of an informal gathering of those who saw things more or less as Will D. Campbell sees things, that is to say, those who "believed the Gospel has to do with poor folks, black folks, drug folks, prison folks, military deserter folks, Ku Klux Klan folks and others of God's children," as Campbell wrote in the fall-winter 1972 issue. The journal, *Katallagete,* took its name from II Corinthians 5:20, "In Christ's name, we implore you, be reconciled (katallagete) to God." It served as a clearinghouse for reflection, most of it by Southern churchmen, on what it means to be a reconciled people today. As such the journal devoted attention to prison reform, articulated opposition to the death penalty and to war, and addressed the plight of farm workers, nonunionized labor, and racial minorities as well as the victimization of the redneck.

Will Campbell's message has altered little since his conversion in the early 1960s. He continues to emphasize the universal presence of sin and, though never denying the locus of its presence in the human heart, to stress its expression in institutional form. The state, the military-industrial complex, the corporate economic structure, the academy—the public school system as well as both public and private universities—agribusiness, and the church have all been agents of oppression. All have victimized the poor and the dispossessed. Campbell thus speaks as a prophet against these institutions, warning people not to misplace allegiances, calling Christians, liberal and conservative alike, away from unholy alliances with sinful institutions and back to a life as a reconciled people. Campbell seems now to be suggesting that the model for authentic Christian practice is the community of the sixteenth-century Anabaptists.

Currently Will D. Campbell resides with his wife and a number of farm animals in Mt. Juliet, Tennessee, just outside of Nashville. There he lives on a forty-acre farm where he serves as preacher to "a pulpitless, roofless, unpropertied and uncodified church." There he has ministered to country musicians, drug addicts, Ku Klux Klansmen, draft resisters and military deserters, black radicals, and Presbyterian ministers, among others. He has counseled, married, baptized, and buried many who for one reason or another have found no home in the institutional church. These days, when he is not off on a speaking engagement or holding a service for someone whose path he has crossed along the way, he can be found at home in Mt. Juliet either baptizing or marrying someone or holding some sort of worship service or writing or whittling or playing his guitar or singing a song that he or one of his many friends in the country music world has authored. It is not the life of the typical minister, but it is, Will D. Campbell believes, his vocation.

## Appraisal

Will Campbell's career has been a multifaceted one, from civil rights activist to pastor to Ku Klux Klansmen, from university chaplain to critic of the academy; from pastor of an organized congregation to pastor of a congregationless "forty acres." He has filled many roles, but always the role of "preacher" broadly construed.

Certainly his presence in the forefront of the civil rights movement will long be remembered by students of the civil rights movement in the South. And Campbell will be remembered as an expert and moving chronicler of his own life and the life of his brother. But whether his theological message will have any lasting impact is far more disputable.

Campbell's basic theological message has long been clear. God, in the sacrifice of Jesus on the cross, redeemed and reconciled all people to himself. And part of what it means to be reconciled to God is to be reconciled to each other. Furthermore, there can be no genuine reconciliation of one person to another independent of reconciliation to God, and thus all non-"religious" attempts at solving social problems have failed. Campbell has often quoted Thomas Merton* on this point that "to reconcile man with man and not with God is to reconcile no one at all." God reconciled us to himself, and all that is left for us to do is to act as reconciled persons. The failure of Christians, Campbell suggested in *The Failure and the Hope,* lies in "seeking reconciliation through social and political action when there already is reconciliation by God's action, not ours" (9).

But what does it actually mean for Christians to live as those reconciled? What, beyond generalities, does this reconciliation look like? Campbell has offered little in the way of an answer, perhaps, in all fairness, because he thinks that if you have to ask the question you have not yet grasped adequately what it means to be reconciled. But almost two thousand years of church history indicate that it is not obvious exactly what the ramifications of that reconciliation are. When pressed, Campbell has suggested "Think Sect!" because, as he wrote in *Up to Our Steeples in Politics,* "the idols of the sects are not as secure as those of the established church" (49). What "Think Sect!" apparently means is for the church to dissolve its wealth, to return to small independent ministries to the poor and outcast, and to renounce the use of violence and reliance on the state.

In recent years Campbell has seemed to point to the Anabaptists of the sixteenth century as his model. The Anabaptist tradition by and large has satisfied these criteria. Yet the tradition has also identified aspects of the faith with which Campbell could hardly be comfortable. The emphasis on separation from all sin and worldliness, the practice of church discipline, and the submission of the individual to the Christian community are all aspects of the Anabaptist tradition with which Campbell has shown little affinity. So one wonders how seriously to take Campbell's belief that the only real Baptist is an Anabaptist. One wonders exactly what Will Campbell's brand of Anabaptism looks like and whether his ideals of freedom and independence could possibly be consistent with a tradition whose locus of authority resides in the community of the saints. A pastor whose ministry has largely been independent of the sustained common life of a Christian community is perhaps not the most credible voice for a return to the Anabaptist tradition. This is not to denigrate the validity of Campbell's call to "Think Sect!" It is to suggest that much more clarity than this imperative provides is required about exactly what the Christian community should look like.

Campbell has functioned most effectively as a social critic, a prophetic voice crying out against the unholy alliances between Christian and the state, Christian and the economic system, Christian and the academy. His messages have certainly been valuable charges to a church all too ready to make accommodations with its culture. But Campbell has stated with little clarity exactly what the Christian posture toward these institutions is to be. He acknowledges that we cannot avoid participation in these institutions, but he acknowledges no legitimate Christian involvement in them. Campbell a bit too glibly seems to suggest that Christians should participate but then should recognize that participation as sinful. Such is the tragedy of sin in our fallen world.

Campbell does well to remind Christians of the tragedy of human existence. Nevertheless, the charge could be made that Campbell does not have an adequate doctrine of creation or of redemption, that the seriousness with which he takes sin has prevented him from acknowledging both the goodness of created institutions after the fall as well as the extension of Christ's redemptive power even to corrupt institutions. The recognition of the created goodness of the state and of the extension of the redemptive activity of Christ to the state would foreclose such claims as that made in an essay in the 30 May 1984 *Christian Century:* "Our call is not to be Caesar; our call is to be in conflict with Caesar" (571). This recognition would acknowledge that in passing civil rights legislation and in working for the passage of civil rights legislation one is not cooperating with the evil one but is acknowledging Christ's defeat of the evil powers and is providing a glimpse—a glimpse not to be confused with a complete picture—of what God desires for human community. Campbell is correct to identify how easily such a view may lead to idolatry. But there is surely more to be said than that alone.

Perhaps Will D. Campbell is best taken as part prophet and social critic, part gadfly, and all preacher. His message is that God has reconciled all things to himself and that Christians ought to act as those reconciled. But his message is also that of tragedy, a tragedy created in a good creation by human usurpation of God's sovereignty. The effects of this human sin are so great that even now Christ's redemptive activity does not eradicate the tragic nature of our existence. This recognition of the tragic nature of human existence and the call to live genuinely as those reconciled by Christ have surely been much needed, even if seldom heard, in the context of a contemporary American religiosity all too comfortably "at ease in Zion."

## Survey of Criticism

Literature about Will D. Campbell tends to be descriptive rather than critical. Representative pieces are those of John Egerton and popular stories in *Newsweek* (8 May 1972, p. 84) and *People* (17 July 1978). Marshall Frady has turned a more critical eye on Campbell with an appreciative assessment in "Fighter for Forgotten Men." More successful yet is his juxtaposition of Campbell and Billy Graham in *Billy Graham: A Parable of American Righteousness* (Boston: Little, Brown and Company, 1979).

The only book-length treatment of Campbell is Thomas L. Connelly's *Will Campbell and the Soul of the South*. Connelly takes Campbell's character to be symbolic or representative in fundamental ways of Southern character, and his book attempts to develop this claim. His emphasis is on Campbell's attraction to and involvement with the world of country music. However, the work contains little new information about Campbell.

For information about and an understanding of Will D. Campbell, the best works remain his own *Brother to a Dragonfly* and *Forty Acres and a Goat*.

## Bibliography

### Books by Will D. Campbell

1962  *Race and the Renewal of the Church*. Philadelphia: Westminster.
1970  *Up to Our Steeples in Politics*. With James Y. Holloway. New York: Paulist.
1972  *The Failure and the Hope: Essays of Southern Churchmen*. Edited with James Y. Holloway. Grand Rapids: Eerdmans.
1973  " . . . and the criminals with him . . . " *Luke 23:33*. Edited with James Y. Holloway. New York: Paulist.
1975  *Callings*. Edited with James Y. Holloway. New York: Paulist.
1977  *Brother to a Dragonfly*. New York: Seabury.
1980  *An Oral History with Will Davis Campbell, Christian Preacher*. With Orley Caudill. Hattiesburg: University of Southern Mississippi.
1982  *The Glad River*. New York: Holt, Rinehart and Winston.
1983  *Cecelia's Sin*. Macon, Ga.: Mercer University.
1983  *God on Earth: The Lord's Prayer for Our Time*. With Bonnie Campbell and Will McBride. New York: Crossroad.
1986  *Forty Acres and a Goat: A Memoir*. Atlanta: Peachtree.

### Selected Studies about Will D. Campbell

Carey, John J. "Will D. Campbell." In *Encyclopedia of Religion in the South*, edited by Samuel S. Hill. Macon, Ga.: Mercer University Press, 1984.
Connelly, Thomas L. *Will Campbell and the Soul of the South*. New York: Continuum, 1982.
Egerton, John. *A Mind to Stay Here: Profiles from the South*, 15–31. New York: Macmillan, 1970.

Frady, Marshall. "Fighter for Forgotten Men," *Life* (16 June 1972): 57–68.
————. "Travels with Brother Will." In *Southerners: A Journalist's Odyssey,* 359–84.
    New York: New American Library, 1980.
Gibble, Kenneth L. "Living Out the Drama: An Interview with Will Campbell." *Christian
    Century* 101 (30 May 1984): 570–74.

THOMAS D. KENNEDY

# James Cannon, Jr.

If controversy follows influence, then Bishop James Cannon, Jr. (1864–1944), of the Methodist Episcopal Church, South, was undoubtedly an influential man. He was always surrounded by the accusations of his enemies and frequently confronted by the opposition of his friends. He advocated aggressive legislative Prohibition in a region traditionally wet and a church traditionally apolitical. Yet his name was advanced as a gubernatorial candidate in Virginia, and he was elevated to the episcopacy at the height of his involvement in the agitation for Prohibition. He always felt that his greatest talents and happiest hours were associated with a small institution dedicated to the education of young women. Yet he compulsively left that setting for causes that drained his resources and that left him, as often as not, in the midst of a maelstrom.

## Biography

Cannon was not born to such contradictions. In fact, he was born on 13 November 1864 to a family of substance and lineage in the society of the Delmarva Peninsula. His uncle, William Cannon, was governor of Delaware from 1863 to 1865. His father, James, Sr., was a successful merchant whose most radical act was to move family and business to Salisbury, Maryland, to find a climate more amenable to his strong pro-southern views. In the years following the war, this change included a shift from the local Methodist Episcopal Church to the local Methodist Episcopal Church, South. Thus, Cannon was raised in a family devoted by choice to antebellum ideals of social order. Such ideals included not only matters of race (the effects of which Cannon freely admitted) but also matters of politics. Cannon early acquired a dedication to the southern "states rights" wing of the Democratic party. Further, from his church he learned rigorously to separate the sacred and civil realms, relegating each to its "proper" sphere. For the church, this sphere was exclusive rather than inclusive, containing a personal moral and religious influence but specifically eschewing that broad political influence that Southern Methodism abhorred in its sister denomination to the north.

Thus, when Cannon succumbed simultaneously to the calls to Christian faith and to Christian ministry as a college student in Virginia, it could fairly be assumed that he would enter a vocation that would seldom, and then only formally, cross into the realm of civil discourse. However, new winds were blowing, and there was in Cannon's background enough at odds with his culture to ensure that he would feel the breeze.

First, Cannon grew up in a family with strong temperance views. His mother, Lydia Primrose Cannon, was one of Salisbury's prominent citizens who actively supported local temperance organizations. Her son, a delicate boy who showed no particular desire for public acclaim, seemed more interested in baseball and his riding horse than civics. However, he followed his mother in her uncompromising battle with the saloon. At the age of twelve, after witnessing a drunken saloonkeeper berating his mother, Cannon vowed to join her in the fight against liquor. Cannon's experience prepared him to be an ardent and public foe of the traffic in alcoholic beverages.

A second influence in Cannon's background was educational. He was a diligent student in Salisbury. He graduated from Wicomico High School at age fifteen. In 1881 he entered Randolph-Macon College, a highly regarded Methodist institution in Ashland, Virginia. In addition to a standard education, Cannon received confirmation of his temperance views. The college president, Dr. W. W. Bennett, worked politically for local option in the sale of alcoholic beverages and published a temperance paper, the *Southern Crusader*. While other students visited "legal" saloons, Cannon helped to put out Bennett's paper.

Following his graduation from Randolph-Macon College, Cannon decided to prepare for the ministry by attending seminary, not in one of the accepted schools of the South, but in Princeton, New Jersey. In so doing, he not only abandoned regional preference but also entered a theological tradition very different from his own. He formed his adult commitment to Wesleyan theology against the influence of the Princeton School at its apogee, seated under the ministrations of Francis L. Patton, Archibald Alexander Hodge (whom he respected), Benjamin B. Warfield (whom he did not), and others. In addition, he traveled extensively through the Northeast, gaining firsthand experience with a broad range of that class of evangelicals who supported Dwight L. Moody's crusades, John Wanamaker's benevolence, A. T. Pierson's missionary zeal, and the work of various "princes of the pulpit." In the period prior to the fragmentation of the nineteenth-century evangelical consensus, Cannon gained significant firsthand experience with the heirs of Harriet Beecher Stowe and Charles Grandison Finney. He formed thereby a positive opinion of the northern tradition of social benevolence, an opinion strengthened by visits to Jerry McCauley's Bowery Mission in New York. Thus Cannon gained a valuable "outside" confirmation of his own growing commitment to church-sponsored social action.

A third influence on Cannon's career was personal. Cannon grew up in the shadow of the church. His parents helped found the Methodist Episcopal Church, South, congregation in Salisbury. He recollected the plain and pointed preaching, the frequent calls to give his life to Jesus. Yet he resisted. Because he felt strongly that for him conversion to the Christian faith entailed devotion to the Christian ministry, Cannon was forced into what was both a spiritual and a vocational crisis. His fond hope during school was to pursue a legal career, with the goal of someday sitting on the U.S. Supreme Court. But because he felt that he could not consider that role as an active and committed layperson, Cannon seemed faced by a choice of pursuing ambition or faith. He nevertheless kept open the door to the former throughout his early life. Although he pleased his parents with his attitude toward drink, he also caused them alarm by steadfastly refusing to respond to appeals directed toward the benefit of his soul. He succeeded in reaching college without ever having publicly professed faith in Christ. Toward the end of his Randolph-Macon stay, under steady parental barrage, he surrendered to the call to conversion. In the process, he sublimated his prior career goal, abandoning the bar for the pulpit. Though he denied any regrets, at least some of the intensity of his social commitment might appear the consequence of his choice.

Fourth, Cannon benefited from the gradual changes overtaking his church. In the wake of the sectional division of the Methodist Episcopal Church in 1844, the Southern body responded to charges that it was proslavery by propounding a doctrine of church-state relations that forbade any interference by the church in institutions regulated by the legislative authority of the state. Though some Southern Methodists wished to take a friendlier stand toward slavery, the church maintained a generally disapproving attitude while at the same time disclaiming any power to oppose that or any legally sanctioned system. In place of such opposition, Southern Methodism gave priority to its "scriptural and spiritual" tasks of spreading salvation and sanctification to the population of the southern states. Following the cataclysm of war, amid the near destruction of both church and state, Methodists returned to these tasks with desperate fervency. Their focus was sharpened by the clumsy political efforts of Northern Methodism to subsume the membership of the Church, South, into a reunited, "loyal" church. In fending off these attempts, the Southern leadership used their apolitical vision of mission as one element in defining their opposition to Northern interference. As the church grew, attaining regional status by the turn of the century unrivaled except by Southern Baptists, the tendency to attribute the success to this formula guaranteed that it could not be opposed as a point of doctrine.

Despite the force of this position, the church did not remain apolitical. Several factors militated against complete disengagement. The simple potency of numbers meant that one of the largest denominations of the South would be courted for its possible influence on matters not strictly its own. The elevation of lay members to the highest legislative body of the church, the General Conference (an advanced position forced on the denomination by the exigencies of reorganization following the war), had the effect of supporting the progressive voices among the preachers. Finally, the ever sticky difficulty of separating the moral from the legal led to an alteration of the doctrine of separation, beginning in the 1800s, that legitimated preaching (at least) on issues that might affect public policy.

Cannon's active ministry began in 1888, following his marriage to Lura Bennett, daughter of the president of Randolph-Macon. He was first appointed to the six churches of the Charlotte Circuit in southern Virginia. The second year he moved to Newport News. In both settings he preached freely against the moral evil of intemperance. By his third appointment, at Farmville, Virginia, in 1891, he had expanded to the point of advocating local Prohibition of saloons in both pulpit and press. Thus early in his career the unyielding hostility of the Methodist Episcopal Church, South, to political involvement had altered sufficiently to allow Cannon to join with those who sought to blaze new ground. And though the doctrine of separation was not by any means dead and indeed would arise later to serve as the focus for opposition to Bishop Cannon from both within and without his own denomination, never would the church recant his efforts in the civil sphere.

These influences worked to place Cannon at the forward edge of his church and region. They fed a lifetime of work as pastor, then administrator, then editor, then Prohibition worker, then bishop, amplifying an already frenetic nature into a compulsion to achieve. The strength of this compulsion might be gauged by the fact that in each of the roles mentioned, Cannon set out to accomplish tasks that individually would have filled a lifetime. As pastor, Cannon was noted more for diligence than warmth. His determination to reach appointments on time, at the expense of horse and buggy on rutted Virginia roads, left people in awe of his strength of will. His boundless energy spilled over into sidelines that included attending not only the sessions of his own Annual Conference but also any other religious assemblage of note.

As administrator, Cannon's compulsion found expression in his work with the Blackstone Female Institute, a women's prep school barely and poorly started when Cannon was asked to take over as principal at the tender age of twenty-nine. In addition to working long hours to establish the school, Cannon sought to give it the proper moral and spiritual undergirding. Each course was geared to a presentation of learning in the context of a devout evangelical theology that stressed obedience to God and proper Christian comportment. In the midst of his labors to ensure the financial stability of the school, Cannon and his wife also kept close and personal oversight of the students. In return, a man noted by most of his friends and foes as cold and humorless was regarded by his students with consistent affection.

Commitment to education also appeared in his work as founder and director of the Southern Assembly at Lake Junaluska, North Carolina. He purchased and developed the property in behalf of the Southern church. He also organized the early programs. In these two tasks, Cannon's reputation for tireless labor was established. While at Blackstone, he averaged nineteen-hour days. Commuting to North Carolina, he would match and exceed this schedule in preparing the campground for a new season. In all of this activity, Cannon was happiest. Indeed it was for the administrative task that he considered himself best suited by temperament and education. Ironically, it was in the performance of this task that Cannon ran foul of public morality. To support both the institute and the assembly, Cannon engaged his considerable talent for speculation, forwarding deals in stocks that sounded to his church suspiciously like gambling and to his secular enemies considerably like chicanery. In all fairness, Cannon's "deals" would probably never have been noticed had he not been in the public eye as one of the premier advocates of constitutional Prohibition.

As editor, Cannon turned his experience with Bennett's *Southern Crusader* to good use. Writing first as editor of the *Methodist Recorder,* a task he took up the year he came to Blackstone, then later of the *Baltimore and Richmond Christian Advocate,* Cannon commented on most of the major issues of church and country. Further, he engaged actively in several of the most pressing controversies of both the Annual and the General Conferences, opposing the most venerable preachers in both settings. He earned enough supporters to be elected delegate to the General Conference in 1902. He also earned enough enemies to supply his editorial pen with material for years.

As a Prohibition worker, Cannon found his most public niche. The newly organized Anti-Saloon League, which styled itself "the church in action against the saloon," provided a nonpartisan vehicle for reform that combined advanced methods in business management, neutrality in political orientation, and shrewdness in public policy. As the leading southern spokesman for the league, Cannon was able to parlay its assets into unrivaled state, regional, then national influence. He worked directly with the Virginia legislature and personally with the governor to fulfill the league's agenda. He cooperated in the organization of state leagues throughout the South. He held steadily more responsible positions in the national body, made more powerful by his proximity to the capital, until, after the death of his primary rival Wayne Wheeler, Cannon emerged as the best-known regional figure in the defense of national Prohibition. A measure of that fame may be garnered from the dispute surrounding his part in the southern bolt from "wet" Democratic candidate Al Smith in the presidential elections of 1928. Whatever the reality, both friend and foe attributed a major role to Cannon. He was feted by Herbert Hoover and royally scorned by party loyalists.

In 1918, prior to his greatest influence on the league but following his emergence as its most forceful spokesman in the region, Cannon was elected bishop. In this position, he forwarded the temperance sentiment that played so great a part in his election. He chaired the Commission of Temperance and Social Service, established the same year as his elevation to the episcopacy, and wielded the moral position of bishop to the benefit of the temperance movement in Southern Methodism.

However, Cannon's episcopacy was not limited to this sphere. Picking up an early interest in missions (he had been rejected for missionary service in India because of a family history of respiratory illness), he requested and consistently received oversight of mission conferences. This passion also touched the public sphere because of Cannon's work with the Near East Advisory Committee in behalf of the Christian minorities of the Turkish Empire. He went so far in this role as to advise the secretary of state and members of the Senate to intervene militarily against the Turks during 1922. Cannon also worked in behalf of the reunification of American Methodism, serving as chair of the Commission on Church Relations and then as an episcopal member on the Joint Commission on Unification. While fulfilling the duties of bishop, Cannon took opportunity to comment on, if not participate in, most of the major undertakings of his church.

It was, however, his association with temperance-Prohibition that set Cannon apart and, eventually, adrift. His many enemies converged after the 1928 election to mount a major campaign against him. At the very time that his power seemed most secure, with presidential invitations at his pleasure, he came under attack. He was accused of being a "bucketshop gambler" (stock speculator) and was investigated by both his church and in time the U.S. Senate. When the widowed bishop had the poor judgment to marry his private secretary in 1930, his moral stock fell further. His shaky relations with traditionalist bishops like Edwin D. Mouzon deteriorated into an unseemly struggle that resulted in an unusual book-length assault on Cannon by a southern minister. In 1930 and again in 1934 his foes sought to retire him from his ecclesiastical duties. Cannon rallied his forces to the defense, and the attempt failed. However, a second attack did not. In 1934 Southern Methodism abandoned its official vehicle for reform, the Board of Temperance and Social Service, even while retaining the services of its president, Bishop Cannon.

The disintegration of his ecclesiastical career paralleled that of Prohibition. Despite the best efforts of the Anti-Saloon League and its allies, the nation rejected the noble experiment. More, the nation rejected those deemed responsible for that enterprise. The fortunes of the movement plummeted. Older partisans like Cannon, whose majority had been spent in advancing the cause, battled on. But nobody seemed to be listening anymore. Cannon continued to advocate Prohibition as well as the other ecclesiastical reforms associated with his episcopacy. He spoke widely, wrote occasionally, and dreamed on—even when by 1942 the executive branch of the Virginia Anti-Saloon League consisted solely of the bishop and a secretary. He died on 6 September 1944 in Chicago, while attending a national league meeting.

### Appraisal

The struggle to alter the way in which Americans used and abused alcohol was the struggle that established Cannon's reputation in the public sphere, as well as his influence on a generation of Protestants. The movement displayed an ability to recruit talented people, sustain them through difficulty, expend their considerable energies in remapping the political landscape of America, and distill their hopes into a dream for a country free of the bondage to intoxicants. This ability is one of the unexplored facets of one of the least understood reform movements in American history. Indeed, revisionist historians of temperance-Prohibition have concluded that it was a movement that, in another of those facets, provided access to public power for many who were disenfranchised or otherwise restricted from participation in the body politic. The fact that temperance had broad appeal, could adapt itself to the reform vocabularies of several periods in American history (from early colonial efforts to the Progressive era), and seemed capable of infinite rebirth may say as much about how power is held and shared in this country as it does about the American propensity to abuse alcohol.

Women were among the disenfranchised who found temperance an avenue to the public conscience. Much attention has been focused in recent years on the struggles of such leaders as Frances Willard to beat down opposition to many reforms with weapons forged in the temperance struggle. Clergy provide another, though less well-documented example, in this case a group with restricted access to the political arena. For Northern clergy, reform was the one viable path to such influence. The political careers of many a loyal Methodist in the Northern church were guaranteed by the considerable influence that accrued to the church by the association of such leaders as Bishops Matthew Simpson and E. R. Ames with the antislavery, pro-Union causes surrounding the Civil War. For Southern clergy like Cannon, who had an aversion to some kinds of reform (particularly those that engaged the attention of their Northern brethren), temperance became the preferred point of contact. However objectionable "political preachers" might be in relation to other issues, their voice was respected in the sphere of reform. Cannon was heir to this political fact of American life. The movement provided Cannon an intersection with public life that he might not otherwise have had.

The intersection served him well. Operating with his usual boundless energy, Cannon made his voice heard, and feared, from the capital in Richmond to the capital in Washington, D.C. In turn, Cannon gave the temperance-Prohibition movement not only his considerable energies and whatever peace of mind he valued but also his ability to frame the cause in language acceptable to the circumscribed reform sentiment of the South. Cannon was a commodity sorely needed by the largely northern leadership of such prohibitionist organizations as the Anti-Saloon League. Whereas the traditional rhetoric of temperance-Prohibition emphasized a spiritual kinship with the crusade against slavery (especially as articulated by the rival Northern Methodist), with its overtones of Republican politics and victorious Union soldiers, the crusade that Cannon articulated generated images of southern righteousness, a pure Jeffersonian Democracy, and a state's rights vision of Prohibition.

This crusade had its Janus' face. In the 1928 presidential campaign, antiforeign and anti-Catholic venom joined Cannon's more characteristic emphases in encouraging the southern bolt from Al Smith's Democratic bid. There was also a tendency to exacerbate racial attitudes common to the country (and the movement) with southern patterns of Jim Crow. Indeed, the regional sensibilities that Cannon epitomized for the temperance movement even helped to dull the once avid, almost proprietary interest that many temperance leaders had in attaining suffrage for women.

Whatever its shortcomings, the view that Cannon advanced had the power to rally considerable southern sentiment behind the effort to establish and maintain national Prohibition. That sentiment may have been in part the protest of a common run of southerners who resented the entrenched power of the elite. Certainly Cannon was ambivalent toward those of that class in his home base of Virginia. He both courted and confronted them. They in turn heeded and abused the meddlesome cleric, reaping perhaps their final revenge in Virginius Dabney's scathing biography of the bishop.

Another part of the support that catapulted Cannon to national prominence may have been in effect the revenge of the southern church upon its own region. Having demanded and received lockstep support from the churches in the bid to maintain a way of life, the South found itself confronted by a church demanding payment in the form of a quasi-moral, quasi-social, quasi-political reform that would legitimate the Protestant presumption of moral dominance in the region. Such a view would explain certain "quirks" in Cannon's ecclesiastical popularity, for the bishop was both beloved and bedeviled by his church. As long as both the person and the cause were upright, Methodist support was unflagging (even if unenthusiastic in some quarters). When Prohibition appeared not only a failure but an unprincipled failure, church support waned.

### Survey of Criticism

During his lifetime, many people evaluated Bishop James Cannon. Some defended him loyally. Most criticized him recklessly. None had either the materials or apparently the desire to come to any dispassionate conclusion. Cannon, with his penchant for controversy, his flair for defiance (he walked out on the Senate Lobby Committee in 1930—the first person so to defy a Senate investigation), and his mask of dour aloofness, only exacerbated the situation. Since his death, the matter has improved but little. Virginius Dabney's *Dry Messiah*, written within five years of the bishop's death, found little appealing in the man and less in the cause he advanced. As editor of the *Richmond Times-Dispatch* Dabney was certainly privy to much of the media coverage focused on Cannon. That the *Times-Dispatch* was a leading editorial opponent of Cannon and his crusade vitiates somewhat the value of that background. Indeed, the only other posthumous treatment came in response to some of the shortcomings that the family perceived in *Dry Messiah* and took the form of publication of Cannon's unfinished autobiography, *Bishop Cannon's Own Story: Life As I Have Seen It*. A valuable balance when taken with Dabney, the latter still has the marks of a work of justification done while the subject was under fire.

### Bibliography

*Work by James Cannon, Jr.*

1955    *Bishop Cannon's Own Story: Life As I Have Seen It*. Edited by Richard L. Watson. Durham: Duke University Press.

*Studies about James Cannon, Jr.*

Cherrington, Ernest Hurst. *Standard Encyclopedia of the Alcohol Problem*, 2: 506. Westerville, Ohio: American Issue Publishing Company, 1924.

Clark, Norman H. *Deliver Us From Evil: An Interpretation of American Prohibition.* New York: W. W. Norton and Company, 1976.

Dabney, Virginius. *Dry Messiah: The Life of Bishop James Cannon, Jr.* New York: Alfred A. Knopf, 1949.

Kerr, K. Austin. *Organized for Prohibition: A New History of the Anti-Saloon League.* New Haven: Yale University Press, 1985.

Smith, Rembert Gilman. *Politics In a Protestant Church.* Atlanta: Ruralist Press, 1930.

DANIEL SWINSON

# Russell H. Conwell

During his long lifetime, which closely paralleled the difficult period between the Civil War and World War I, Russell H. Conwell (1843–1925) was renowned not only as a journalist, lawyer, educator, and political biographer, but also, and above all, as an inspirational preacher, writer, and lecturer. While keeping the rigorous schedule for his famous lecture, "Acres of Diamonds" (which he delivered over 6,000 times), after 1890 Conwell simultaneously served as pastor of the "largest Protestant Church in America" (Grace Baptist Church in Philadelphia, also known as the Baptist Temple), founded and nurtured the growth of Temple University as well as three community hospitals, and wrote at least thirty-seven books. Because there is good reason to claim, along with several obituaries, that he "addressed more people than any man of the past century," Conwell may be viewed as a significant transitionary figure within the "success"-oriented sector of American popular religion as it entered the twentieth century.

## Biography

Russell Herman Conwell was born 15 February 1843 near Worthington, Massachusetts. Conwell's parents were staunch Methodists, and his upbringing reflects typical New England Puritan/Yankee notions of hard work yoked with devout piety. In keeping with revivalism's reform impulse before the Civil War, Conwell's father took an active part in the western Massachusetts underground railroad, transporting fugitive slaves to Canada. Through his father's contacts, Conwell boasted boyhood friendships with John Brown, Frederick Douglass, and William Cullen Bryant.

In 1857, Conwell enrolled at the Methodist Wilbraham Academy, where he was exposed to the ideas of Francis Wayland. Wayland, a Baptist minister and president of Brown University, wrote two popular textbooks on political economy and moral science that were widely disseminated by colleges and prep schools in the mid-nineteenth century. Heavily reliant on the philosophy known as Scottish common sense realism, political economy and moral science combined natural law and common sense to explain "the scope of Divine Providence" that provides unlimited opportunity, rewards diligent labor, excoriates idleness,

blesses private ownership of property, and encourages stewardship of accumulated wealth.

In 1861 Conwell began to study law at Yale, which at that time was particularly
self-conscious of its exclusivity among the well-to-do and was making a concerted
effort to provide funds for "poor boys" to attend. Despite the administration's
inclusive attitude, Conwell's egalitarian spirit was deeply wounded by what he
felt to be insulting treatment from the "rich boys"—a bitterness against the
offspring of the wealthy that remained his entire life. During these Yale years,
Conwell also adopted atheism in rebellion against his parents' piety.

Amid this humiliating encounter with New Haven, good fortune came in the
form of the Civil War, which not only gave Conwell an excuse to leave school
and enlist but also provided him with a wartime crisis conversion experience
that helped shape his own peculiar wedding of revivalistic conversion, hard
work, and success.

When the war was over, Conwell married Jennie Hayden (who later died,
leaving him with two children). After resuming the study of law and graduating
from the Albany Law School, Conwell moved his family to St. Paul/Minneapolis,
where he worked variously as a lawyer, journalist, and real estate speculator.
Also while in Minneapolis, Conwell was baptized at the First Baptist Church
and conducted noontime businessmen's prayer meetings in his law office, from
which was founded a local chapter of the YMCA. After he left Minneapolis in
1868 because of health difficulties, Conwell served a short time as an immigration
agent to Germany and for some years worked also as a correspondent for the
*Boston Traveler* and the *New York Tribune*. In 1869 Conwell relocated in Boston
and established another law practice. Among his legal clients in Boston during
the 1870s was Mary Baker Eddy, founder of Christian Science. Conwell claimed
to have been one of the first to read Eddy's *Science and Health* before its initial
publication in 1875.

For the next decade, Conwell's reputation as an orator and writer grew through
his association with the Chautauqua-oriented James Redpath lecture agency and
his "official" campaign biographies of Republican presidential candidates Ulys-
ses S. Grant, Rutherford B. Hayes, James A. Garfield, and James G. Blaine.
When not traveling, he taught a young men's Sunday School class at Boston's
Tremont Temple. At its peak, the class reached nearly 2,000 members.

Following the death of his first wife in 1872, Conwell married Sarah Sandborn
of Newton Centre, Massachusetts. He credited Sarah with helping him to recognize a long-suppressed urge to enter the ordained ministry. Conwell enrolled
at nearby Newton Theological Institute on a part-time basis, though he never
completed a degree there. Yet when a nearly abandoned church in Lexington,
Massachusetts, approached attorney Conwell to help liquidate its property and
assets, Conwell volunteered to serve as temporary pastor. After a sudden revival
sparked by his preaching produced a renovated church structure as well as a
rapidly growing membership, Conwell yielded to the church's call to become
its full-time pastor, quit his law practice, and was ordained in 1879.

News of Conwell's ecclesiastical success reached the struggling ninety-member Grace Baptist Church of Philadelphia. In 1882 Conwell accepted their call to become pastor under the condition that he be allowed to continue lecturing. By 1891 Grace Church had grown to more than 3,000 members and had completed building a new sanctuary seating over 4,000, making "the Temple" the "largest Protestant church in America." Besides a gymnasium, reading rooms, and a large Sunday School, "Temple College" was begun in 1884 when Conwell met in his church office with several young workers who desired an education but could not afford it. By 1893 the college was offering free evening education to more than 3,100 Philadelphia workers, later expanding to full university status with several graduate schools. Nearly 100,000 students had attended Temple University by the time of Conwell's death. In 1969, the Conwell School of Theology merged with the Gordon Divinity School near Boston to form the Gordon-Conwell Theological Seminary.

During the 1890s, with widening publicity over the explosive growth of the whole Temple complex, which by then also included two hospitals providing free medical care for the poor, Conwell participated in general discussions of the era on the problems of urbanization and the developing "institutional church." In this regard, Baptist Temple was considered to be an excellent example of the "modern church" through its progressive ministry to the spiritual, medical, and educational needs of the working class.

Conwell continued to lecture, write, and serve as pastor at Baptist Temple until his death in December 1925 at the age of eighty-two. Indicative of his enduring popularity and influence was Conwell's selection by the *Christian Century*'s clergy poll as one of the twenty-five most "outstanding preachers of the American pulpit today" in December 1924.

Perhaps more important than his pastoral work was Conwell's immense popularity on the lecture circuit and as an inspirational writer. As a regular speaker at the Chautauqua movement's headquarters in New York as well as its many regional centers, Conwell lectured over 10,000 times, averaging almost 175 lectures a year for all his adult life. Criss-crossing the nation's developing railway system, he reached an estimated 13 million hearers—an incredible feat in the day before electronic mass communication. In addition to his popular oratory, Conwell's many inspirational books had broad appeal. Louis Schneider and Sanford Dornbusch's classic study *Popular Religion: Inspirational Books in America* lists Conwell's book *Acres of Diamonds* among the inspirational best sellers around the turn of the century. Other Conwell books such as *The New Day; or, Fresh Opportunities, a Book for Young Men, Observation—Every Man His Own University, What You Can Do With Your Will Power*, and many more all demonstrated the Conwellian faith in success. His 1892 biography, *The Life of Charles Haddon Spurgeon, The World's Greatest Preacher*, sold 125,000 copies in its first four months.

Of course, Conwell is best remembered for "Acres of Diamonds." The lecture received its name from a story told to Conwell in his travels by an Arab guide about a man who left his home to travel the world seeking his fortune (a journey that ended in a despairing suicide). Conwell tells his audience that shortly after the man's departure, his original homestead ironically became the site of the world's richest diamond mine. He went abroad seeking fortune when there were "acres of diamonds" in his own backyard.

Conwell's corollary: in America there is the opportunity in anyone's backyard to become rich. Conwell proclaimed, contrary to what he considered a widely held misconception of faith, that it is one's Christian duty to become immensely wealthy: "I have come to tell you what in God's sight I believe to be the truth. ... I say that you ought to get rich, and it is your duty to get rich. How many of my pious brethren say to me, 'Do you, a Christian minister, spend your time going up and down the country advising young people to get rich, to get money?' 'Yes, of course I do.' They say, 'Isn't that awful! Why don't you preach the gospel instead of preaching about man's making money?' 'Because to make money honestly is to preach the gospel.' That is the reason." Poverty, Conwell believed along with evangelists Dwight L. Moody and Billy Sunday*, was the result of sinful idleness which could be overcome through conversion, hard work, and common sense.

Because this part of the message has sounded shrill and sensational to later twentieth-century interpreters, Conwell's intention is sometimes forgotten: "Money is power, and you ought to be reasonably ambitious to have it! You ought to because you can do more good with it than you could without it. Money printed your Bible, money builds your churches, money sends your missionaries, and money pays your preachers. . . . " Conwell advocated a stewardship of riches, similar to Andrew Carnegie's "Gospel of Wealth," found both in political economy (with its Scottish common sense influence) and America's Puritan heritage, stressing diligence, frugality, and faithfulness in both the "general" and "particular" callings or vocations. Unlike Carnegie's more elitist approach, however, Conwell's gospel was egalitarian, stressing the possibilities for success and stewardship for all.

Personal style and charisma had much to do with Conwell's immense popularity. He was often compared to the great orators of his day: Henry Ward Beecher, William Jennings Bryan*, and Dwight L. Moody. Contemporaries also frequently commented on Conwell's ability to adapt his messages to local needs and circumstances as well as to embellish them from a huge collection of flamboyant success stories. The local flavor and examples of success combined to give an air of factuality to his lectures. Yet as the new century progressed and Conwell persevered in meeting the demand for his lecture, "Acres of Diamonds" was in many ways becoming a classic text quite apart from Conwell's oratorical skill. The lecture was printed repeatedly and has been included within numerous speech textbooks and historical anthologies since his death.

### Appraisal

Russell Conwell's prime influence on American popular religion was as a powerful popularizer of what has been called the gospel of success. He stands midway in a long line of religionists of success stretching from early American Puritanism and its somewhat secularized version in Benjamin Franklin's *Poor Richard's Almanack,* through McGuffey's readers and the "rags-to-riches" genre of Horatio Alger and Orison Swett Marden, to twentieth-century popularizers such as Bruce Barton*, Norman Vincent Peale*, and Robert Schuller*. Many scholars, such as Donald Meyer in *The Positive Thinkers,* connect such people with New Thought figures like Phineas P. Quimby, Ralph Waldo Trine, and Mary Baker Eddy. These all share an emphasis on harmonial religious self-help, pursued through wealth, health, and uplifting positive attitudes.

Because such a lengthy and disparate list of persons and ideas spans nearly four centuries and represents massive shifts in American culture and thought, Conwell should be placed in that transitional period linking the late nineteenth to the early twentieth century. Conwell attempted to relate a traditional American popular ethos of optimism, individualistic opportunity, and the "Protestant ethic" to mammoth social and psychological changes caused by urbanization, immigration, and industrialization. Though Conwell's ideas were certainly not unique or innovative, the longevity and popularity of "Acres of Diamonds" attests to his broad resonance with enduring popular religious notions. In classic language, echoing traditional American beliefs that poverty is the result of sinful sloth and that wealth signifies rewards for honesty and hard work, Conwell's gospel of "sanctified common sense" rested on the belief that the Christian life was essentially identical to his own experience of conversion that had inspired hard work and ultimately produced success. Conwell's lectures and books, like those delivered and written by the other proponents of the positive, were filled with inspiring examples of those who had heard the message, heeded, and succeeded. In the context of these widely affirmed optimistic American attitudes, it was quite reasonable for Conwell to believe that the experience of conversion, hard work, and success was available to all who could by common sense perceive the opportunities to gather the "acres of diamonds" in their own backyard.

Yet this gospel of the Gilded Age did not merely represent continuity with the past or attempt to use religion as an opiate to quell restless workers by baptizing immoral wealth in religious respectability and poverty in disrespectability; Conwell also significantly helped to transform symbols by which turn-of-the-century Americans, experiencing massive social change, could orient themselves to new economic realities. By assuring an anxious middle America that wealth was indeed a worthy spiritual ambition if one became rich through sweat and honesty and if riches were then used wisely, Conwell helped to accommodate popular religious culture to both the new accumulation of capital and the democratic right of anyone to pursue it. However, stewardship of riches on a grand scale was the primary goal of such enterprise, symbolized in the era's huge philanthropic gestures by those such as the Carnegies, Rockefellers, and Dukes and the hundreds of lesser examples Conwell used to illustrate and "factualize" opportunities for success. Of great symbolic significance was the oft-repeated fact that Conwell gave away all the proceeds from his lecturing (an estimated $11 million) to help young "poor boys" finance their college education.

Yet "Acres of Diamonds" held together a cluster of ideas and beliefs that became increasingly difficult to justify as the dawning "Christian century" brought growing labor tension and urban poverty and as postmillennial optimism was shattered by the Great War. Though Conwell was an old man by the 1910s and in some respects showed little variance from earlier ideas of unlimited opportunity (during World War I, for instance, he wrote *How a Soldier May Succeed After the War*), at the same time many of his views began to soften. Later in his life Conwell occasionally even preached positions comparable to those who advocated "Progressive Christianity" or the "Social Gospel." In fact, because Baptist Temple was considered to be such a fine example of the progressive institutional church, Conwell shared the podium in several conferences on "Church Work in the City" with such well-known Social Gospel figures as Walter Rauschenbusch, George Herron, and Josiah Strong.

Conwell's ambivalent attitudes concerning wealth and "social Christianity" may at first seem contradictory. Yet the period in which he lived was itself characterized by a fluidity of thought that could easily hold together these seemingly incompatible beliefs about laissez-faire capitalism, fair labor practices, and unlimited financial opportunity. This fluidity of thought remained strong until the impact of two world wars, the fundamentalist-modernist controversy, and the Great Depression shattered the easy optimism of Conwell's generation. Of course, Conwell died before many of these changes were fully realized. Meanwhile, the modified Gospel of Success that grew out of changes in the 1920s has shown little evidence of waning in later twentieth-century popular belief. Therefore, Conwell may be seen primarily as one who helped shape this transition of the Gospel of Success for a new generation of symbol transformers such as Bruce Barton, Norman Vincent Peale (*The Power of Positive Thinking,*) Robert Schuller ("possibility thinking"), and a host of other entrepreneurial spirits such as Napoleon Hill (*Think and Grow Rich)* and W. Clement Stone (founder of *Success Magazine*). Yet even beyond this legacy carried forth by his spiritual ancestors, Conwell himself is still faintly heard: *Acres of Diamonds* remains in print for the public, is also available on cassette tape through W. Clement Stone's "Success Unlimited Catalogue," and is still regularly advertised in publications such as *Success Magazine*.

### Survey of Criticism

During his lifetime Conwell was the subject of five rather hagiographic biographies written by admiring coworkers or parishioners. In addition, because of Conwell's status as one among those Martin Marty has called the "celebrity clerics" (Henry Ward Beecher, Phillips Brooks, T. DeWitt Talmadge), Conwell was the subject of much "popular" press in various newspapers, magazines, and denominational publications.

Although he has received cursory treatment as a popularizer of the "Gospel of Wealth" by most major historians of American religion as well as by historians of the ideas of "success" in American thought, little extended critical study of Conwell has been made. What historian R. Laurence Moore has written about the study of "harmonial philosophy" in *Religious Outsiders and the Making of Americans,* could well include Conwell's gospel: "Manifestations of it were everywhere present in the popular culture of nineteenth-century America. We know very little about this influential current of belief, but this fact has to do with the taste of scholars rather than its importance. Harmonial philosophy was the romanticism of the unlearned, that is, of virtually everyone" (116).

This distaste with figures such as Conwell was demonstrated in the 1920s and 1930s progressive Menckenesque critique of anything smacking of "Puritanism" or popular beliefs. An excellent example was W. C. Crosby's scathing article, "Acres of Diamonds," which appeared in Mencken's *American Mercury.* Crosby caricatured Conwell as an opulent huckster who, "buttered with the authority of a Baptist pontiff," made his lecture "as standard and staple a part of the American scene as Anheuser-Busch beer, the Odd Fellows, Peruna, or William Jennings Bryan."

In the 1940s, intellectual historians Merle Curti and Ralph Henry Gabriel, in their classic studies *The Growth of American Thought* and *The Course of American Democratic Thought,* likewise accounted for Conwell and "Acres of Diamonds" in the Puritan stream of thought and as an excellent example of the "conservative reaction" to Progressive politics and religion, a sentiment echoed by Henry F. May in *Protestant Churches and Industrial America.* However, stemming from research into Conwell's involvement in the "institutional church," other historians of the period—such as Arthur M. Schlesinger, Sr., in his seminal work "A Critical Period in American Religion, 1875–1900" (1932), William Warren Sweet in his *Story of Religions in America* (1930), and Aaron I. Abell in *The Urban Impact on American Protestantism, 1865–1900* (1943)— treated Conwell as a progressive pastor without reference to "Acres of Diamonds." In 1962, Clyde K. Nelson, who had written his doctoral dissertation on Conwell's social ideas, convincingly argued in "Russell H. Conwell and the 'Gospel of Wealth' " that although Conwell certainly popularized many ideas associated with Carnegie's "Gospel of Wealth," Conwell became increasingly sensitive to economic and social inequities and began espousing what Henry May has called "progressive Christianity." Nelson admitted, "The Conwell who emerges from this larger view is difficult to understand; to some, perhaps, he is even contradictory."

Another study of Conwell growing out of a doctoral dissertation was Daniel W. Bjork's *Victorian Flight: Russell H. Conwell and the Crisis of American Individualism.* Combining psychological analysis with social and intellectual history, Bjork regarded Conwell as symbolic of a "broad cultural transition." Bjork saw a pattern in Conwell's life history that illustrated the inner tension created by transition from the rural, Victorian, nineteenth-century setting to an urban, industrial, institutionally bureaucratic twentieth-century America. In this interpretation, Conwell's restless career changes, lusty pursuit of fame, staunch Victorian defense of the "home," and controlled style of institutional management were symptoms of a societal psychological crisis. Conwell's personal "identity crisis" merely represents the general failure of society to provide meaningful boundaries for the sense of self during the tumultuous transition from Victorian America to industrial America.

Scholars interested in communication have studied Conwell as an orator, particularly Mary Louise Gehring, who completed her dissertation on Conwell's rhetorical style and wrote "Russell H. Conwell: American Orator." Joseph C. Carter, now an emeritus professor at Temple University, has written "Russell H. Conwell's 'Lectures on Oratory' " and has edited *Magnolia Journey,* a collection of Conwell's articles written shortly after the Civil War. In 1981, Carter privately published *The "Acres of Diamonds" Man,* a massive, three-volume collection of Conwell material and information available only in selected libraries.

Conwell's personal papers, along with archives from Temple Church, are housed in the Conwellana-Templana Collection at Temple University's Samuel Paley Library.

## Bibliography

### Selected Works by Russell H. Conwell

(Note: See Maurice F. Tauber, *Russell Herman Conwell, 1843–1925, A Bibliography* [Philadelphia: Temple University Library, 1935], for a complete, though not exhaustive, list of Conwell's writings.)

1872   *The Life of General U.S. Grant.* Boston: B. B. Russell.
1876   *The Life and Public Services of Gov. Rutherford B. Hayes.* Boston: B. B. Russell.
1880   *The Life, Speeches, and Public Services of Gen. James A. Garfield of Ohio.* Boston: B. B. Russell.
1884   *The Life and Public Services of James G. Blaine.* Augusta, Maine: E. C. Allen and Company.
1888   *Gleams of Grace: Eight Sermons.* Philadelphia: Businessmen's Association of Grace Baptist Church.
1892   *The Life of Charles Haddon Spurgeon, The World's Greatest Preacher.* Philadelphia: Edgewood Publishing Company.
1899   "The Church of the Future: A Forecast of the Successful Church of the Twentieth Century." *Our Day* 18 (July 1899): 205–12.
1904   *The New Day; or, Fresh Opportunities, a Book for Young Men.* Philadelphia: Griffin and Rowland Press.
1912   *How to Live the Christ Life.* New York: Fleming Revell.
1915   *Acres of Diamonds, by Russell H. Conwell, With His Life and Achievements by Robert Shackleton.* New York: Harper.
1917   *How a Soldier May Succeed After the War.* New York: Harper.
1917   *The Jolly Earthquake; or, The Power of a Cheerful Spirit.* Philadelphia: Shelley; Philadelphia: Judson Press, 1938.

1917   *Observation—Every Man His Own University*. New York: Harper.
1917   *What You Can Do With Your Will Power*. New York: Harper.
1920   *The Angel's Lily*. Philadelphia: Judson Press.
1921   *Effective Prayer*. New York: Harper and Brothers.
1922   *Sermons for the Great Days of the Year*. New York: Doran.
1922   *Unused Powers*. New York: Fleming Revell.
1922   *Why Lincoln Laughed*. New York: Harper and Brothers.
1923   *Borrowed Axes, and Other Sermons*. Philadelphia: Judson Press.
1924   *The Romantic Rise of a Great American*. New York: Harper and Brothers.
1924   *Six Nights in the Garden of Gethsemane*. New York: Fleming Revell.
1925   *Fields of Glory*. New York: Fleming Revell.

### Selected Studies about Russell H. Conwell

Barton, Bruce. "Conversation Between a Young Man and an Old Man." *American Magazine* (July 1921): 13ff.

Bjork, Daniel W. *The Victorian Flight: Russell H. Conwell and the Crisis of American Individualism*. Washington, D.C.: University Press of America, 1979.

Burdette, Robert J. *The Modern Temple and Templars: A Sketch of the Life and Work of Russell H. Conwell*. Boston: Silver, Burdette, 1894.

Burr, Agnes Rush. *Russell H. Conwell and His Work*. Philadelphia: Winston, 1926, 1943.

Carter, Joseph C. *The "Acres of Diamonds" Man*. 3 vols. Philadelphia: Privately published, 1981.

———. "Russell H. Conwell's 'Lectures on Oratory.' " *Foundations* 12 (January/March 1969): 47–65.

———, ed. *Magnolia Journey: A Union Veteran Revisits the Former Confederate States*. University: University of Alabama Press, 1974.

Crosby, W. C. "Acres of Diamonds." *American Mercury* 14 (May 1928): 104–13.

Gehring, Mary Louise. "Russell H. Conwell: American Orator." *Southern Speech Journal* 20 (Winter 1954): 117–24.

Higgins, William. *Scaling the Eagle's Nest*. Springfield, Mass.: Gill, 1889.

Nelson, Clyde K. "Russell H. Conwell and the 'Gospel of Wealth.' " *Foundations* 5 (January 1962): 39–51.

Shackleton, Robert. *Acres of Diamonds, by Russell H. Conwell, With His Life and Accomplishments by Robert H. Shackleton*. New York: Harper's, 1915.

———. "The Great Accomplisher." *Harper's Monthly Magazine* 132 (December 1915): 134–39.

Smith, Albert Hatcher. *The Life of Russell H. Conwell*. Boston: Silver, Burdett, 1899.

Wilson, Thane. "Russell H. Conwell: Who Has Helped 3,000 Young Men to Succeed." *American Magazine* 81 (April 1916): 15.

JOHN R. WIMMER

# Harvey Gallagher Cox

The children of the Great Depression years came of age during World War II. It was this generation that grew to realize how profoundly interconnected the patterns of life history and of global events had become in the modern world.

Although it was a collective experience, interpretations and social applications varied. In the United States, the postwar years were marked by the red scare of McCarthyism, the beginnings of nuclear arms buildup against an imagined threat of global Communist aggression, the resurgence of conservative religion, and a general retreat into private family life. And yet, deep strains of dissent in American culture surfaced in the lives of some who became the vanguard of peace and social justice movements in the 1960s. Harvey Cox belongs to this war generation and to its dissenting vanguard. An eminent theologian and religious activist, he has made important contributions to the changing dialogue of social conscience in the past thirty years.

## Biography

Harvey Gallagher Cox was born on 19 May 1929 in Phoenixville, Pennsylvania. He grew up in the town of Malvern in Chester County, then a small rural settlement. The Coxes were Baptists whose eclectic roots went back to early Quaker, Welsh, and Rhineland pietist immigrants. Harvey Cox's father had learned the painting and interior decorating trade from his own father and ran the family business. He was proud of his craft and independence and was humiliated when the failure of his business in 1940 almost forced him to join the ranks of factory workers at a local tubing plant. He went to work instead at a chemical plant in West Chester, seven miles away. Cox's paternal grandmother was active in church and local Republican politics. Both his father and his grandmother symbolized different aspects of the small-town mentality and basic community experience that he would later call "the tribal village."

Harvey Cox left Malvern for the first time in 1946 when he was seventeen. He spent a few months on a transatlantic horse and cattle ship, the *Robert Hart,* run by the United Nations Relief and Rehabilitation Administration and the U.S. Merchant Marine. In Europe he saw the war-torn cities of England, Germany, Poland, and Belgium. These images and the conversations he had with people brought the small world of Malvern into a global context. The next year he entered the University of Pennsylvania, where he graduated in 1951 with honors in history. From 1953 to 1954 he was the Protestant chaplain at Temple University. In 1955 he earned a B.D. from Yale Divinity School and married Nancy Neiburger. They had three children: Rachel (1959), Martin (1961), and Sarah (1964). From 1955 to 1958 Cox served as director of religious activities at Oberlin College, where he tapped into the school's radical tradition. After ordination as an American Baptist minister in 1957, he began graduate work at Harvard University in the history and philosophy of religion.

To help support himself and his family, Cox taught at Andover Newton Theological School while working for the Home Mission Society of the American Baptist Convention. Eventually he became an assistant professor. In 1962, during the tense months that followed the erection of the Berlin Wall, he was an Ecumenical Fraternal Worker in Berlin for Marxist-Christian dialogue. In 1963 he received his Ph.D. from Harvard after completing a dissertation entitled

"Religion and Technology: A Study of the Influence of Religion on Attitudes toward Technology with Special Reference to the Writings of Paul Tillich and Gabriel Marcel." Together with the influence of Dietrich Bonhoeffer and the Berlin experience in Marxist-Christian dialogue, this work on religion and technology provided the background for his first book, *The Secular City: Secularization and Urbanization in Theological Perspective* (1965). It became a cause célèbre soon after its publication and an international best seller translated into eleven languages.

Cox gave up his assistant professorship at Andover Newton for an appointment as associate professor at the Harvard Divinity School. He has been the Victor S. Thomas Professor of Divinity there since 1969. Altogether he has published eight books, has edited one, and has written numerous articles as well as introductions and prefaces to the works of others.

Harvey Cox's academic life has been inseparable from what he calls his "extracurricular causes." After his year in Berlin, he became active in the civil rights movement and in the antiwar movement of the Vietnam years. More recently he has been engaged in antinuclear peace work and in the liberation theology of Central America's political struggles. In 1963 Cox moved his family to Roxbury, Massachusetts, where they lived until 1970. He later learned that the sudden increase in drug-related crime that drove them from the neighborhood was caused by urban renewal in the South End that had pushed the dealers into adjacent Roxbury. The Roxbury years coincided with his teaching at Andover-Newton and Harvard and with his civil rights and peace work. Cox attached himself to the Blue Hill Christian Center, a congregation that also served for an educational and social action agency. It housed the first chapter of Martin Luther King, Jr.'s* Southern Christian Leadership Conference north of the Mason-Dixon line. He worked for the SCLC in Selma, St. Augustine, and Williamston, North Carolina. At Williamston, he marched in support of the local SCLC chapter and was jailed with other activists. In jail he was one of several who fasted for four days to demand desegregation of the cells. On the fourth day of the fast, Cox and three others were transferred to the black section. Soon afterward they were released. Back in Roxbury, Cox's black neighbors were approving but not overly impressed by this white liberal's brief encounter with oppression. Cox considers his years in Roxbury and his days in the Williamston jail important steps in his "faith journey."

In April 1968 came the assassination of Martin Luther King, Jr., followed by Robert Kennedy's assassination in June. Cox had worked in the Kennedy campaign in Oregon and in California. He subsequently "fled" the country for Cuernavaca, Mexico, where he taught at Ivan Iilich's Center for Intercultural Documentation. Since that time Cox's ties with Central and South America have remained strong. In 1973 Augusto Cotto, a Baptist minister from El Salvador, invited him to teach at the Seminario Bautista de Mexico, a place to which he has returned many times. In 1978 a visit to Kyoto, Japan, for an international and interreligious peace conference, and a visit to Hiroshima prompted his organizational role in the antinuclear campaign. Cox was a founder of the Traprock Peace Center in western Massachusetts. His work to get a bilateral nuclear moratorium on the ballot as a referendum question was accomplished in November 1980 in three senatorial districts of the state. As the nuclear freeze campaign spread, peace work became his highest priority.

There have have been other changes in Cox's life in recent years. Since 1982 he has been teaching a course at Harvard College on "Jesus and the Moral Life," which has the highest enrollment in the university. He has also spent some time leading an amateur band called "The Embraceables" which has entertained locally at retirement homes and other places where they are welcome. Harvey Cox and his first wife were divorced, and in 1986 he married Nina Tumarkin, a professor of Russian history at Wellesley College. They have a son, Nicholas, who was born in August 1986. Cox is currently a member of the editorial boards of the *Harvard Theological Review* and *Christianity and Crisis*.

## Appraisal

Harvey Cox has come a long way from Malvern, Pennsylvania. Yet old Malvern is representative of the base communities that he believes are essential to the health of future societies. As a theologian and religious activist, Cox anchors his social vision in biblical language and in personal faith. It is this traditional religious language that creates the sense of community for participant believers in both a global and historical context. Cox has centered his life on that simple reality, although he has struggled with its problematic meaning for a postmodern generation. Cox's own contribution to postmodern theology is rooted in historical and cross-cultural foundations. A close reading of his major works uncovers deep currents of Radical Reformation piety, Enlightenment anticlericalism, republican ideology, postmillennial perfectionism, and the fusion of Social Gospel optimism with the conscientiousness of neo-orthodoxy. His most recent works show the strong influence of Latin American Roman Catholic theology. The ability to creatively synthesize these diverse elements in American culture has enabled him to bridge a gap between theology as an academic and clerical subject, and social justice as a theological engagement in a secular world.

This interaction was basic to the new cultural patterns he discerned in *The Secular City*. This first book was an ebullient tract celebrating a collective coming-of-age in a technopolitan society. Cox's viewpoint owed much to the theologies of Karl Barth, Dietrich Bonhoeffer, and Paul Tillich. But *The Secular City* also drew on the philosophies of Nietzsche and Marx, as well as on the interdisciplinary resources of anthropology and sociology. It was a period when sociologists, historians, and politicians alike were focusing on the problems posed by the industrialized urban wilderness. The book developed out of a series of lectures Cox gave at the annual Baptist Student Conference in August 1963, just days after his participation in a March on Washington for Jobs and Freedom. These lectures were also published in 1965 with the title *God's Revolution and Man's Responsibility*. The issues of the march on Washington, together with

Cox's ecumenical work in Berlin, set the context for his theme of secularization as a global revolution "from economic and political bondage." Liberation was also the underlying theme of *The Secular City*. Cox had his finger on the pulse of a popular stream of consciousness in the early 1960s. He offered a positive response to the "death of God" in the modern world by recalling Bonhoeffer's point that religious terminology, rituals, and institutions were encrustations of the past and were therefore dead to the actuality of divine presence in secular life. For God was indeed alive in social change. Cox reassured his readers about the anonymity and mobility of urban life; the displacement of human labor by computer technology; and the separation of public and private spheres by bureaucratic organization. Even pragmatism received high marks as characteristic of John F. Kennedy's presidential style. Politics, Cox argued, had replaced metaphysics as the language of theology. Marxist-Christian dialogue had obviously not substituted a language of basic economic relationships for his inherited faith in the political process as the fundamental agent of social change. *The Secular City* was a youthful work that spoke directly to a generation that, having lived through the shock of John F. Kennedy's assassination, remained optimistic about the future in the years of the Great Society. Its core message reappeared in his later explorations of secularization. *On Not Leaving it to the Snake* (1967) was a collection of essays on the theme of religion in a postmetaphysical world. Though the term *postmodern* did not form part of the vocabulary of social change until the 1970s, it was anticipated in the idea of a historical transition under way. But the thesis of *The Secular City* was itself transformed by the course of events that followed its publication in 1965.

Cox's second major book, *The Feast of Fools: A Theological Essay on Festivity and Fantasy* (1969), was a response to the critical commentary he had received on *The Secular City*. It was also shaped by the changing world around him. This second book veered from pragmatic activism toward the inner life of religious experience. Even here Cox was arguing for a potential reciprocity between mystical awareness and political action. This historical process, he argued, would build the authentic communities of the future. *The Feast of Fools* signaled the changing mood from the mid to the late sixties. In 1968 Cox had left the United States for Cuernavaca, Mexico, deeply discouraged and disillusioned by the assassinations of Martin Luther King, Jr., and Robert Kennedy. The age of the Flower Children was in full bloom; and academics were delving into the writings of French structuralists where they were rediscovering fundamental truths in the meanings of sacred space, ritual, and play. In 1965 Cox had celebrated the deliverance of the modern psyche from metaphysical and magical controls. Now, four years later, he seemed to be saying the opposite—that the nonrational religious reality was in fact the secular city's golden thread. Yet his shifting argument had continuity with the earlier secularization theme. Cox defined play as philosophy in action and saw its potential for enlisting interdisciplinary energies toward community building. He used Nietzsche's idea of "higher history" to argue for the role of festivity in synthesizing the contradictions of modern life. It would do so by giving playful people a transcendent knowledge of how plurality and relativity were the means of revolutionary change. In an introduction to his chapter on "Fantasy and Utopia," Cox quoted Lewis Mumford, who had said that "the cities and mansions that people dream of are those in which they finally live." For Cox, Mumford's observation defined the meaning of the secular city where religion's singular contribution was its gift of structural and symbolic coherence to the politics of social revolution.

The political context of festive play also found its way into Cox's third book, *The Seduction of the Spirit: The Use and Misuse of People's Religion* (1973). It was an attack on the media with its reliance on cues, signals, and the barrage of information intended to manipulate and control the inhabitants of the secular city. Cox was now openly critical of modern society's prescribed division between faith and reason, emotion and intelligence, religion and science. In *The Secular City* he had paraphrased the Marxian dialectic in his own model of historical progression from tribe-to-town-to-technopolis. *The Seduction of the Spirit* begins with an essay on "the tribal village," which is none other than Cox's boyhood home of Malvern, Pennsylvania. Malvern becomes the psychological locus for the kind of pluralistic intimacy that ideally should thrive in the multiple social networks that make up the secular city. The city itself was the agency that could forge a new moral consensus from the shared experience of urban diversity. More specifically, it would be the religion of *homo urbanitas* that would effectually knit together the new social reality, replacing a world that was falling apart. *The Seduction of the Spirit* reflected the general disillusionment of the times, a factor that made its prescriptions for change somewhat ambiguous. Cox evinced a longing for some past commitment and consensus that Americans thought they had lost in the backwash of the Vietnam and Watergate years. In 1973 he still envisaged the secular city as the generator of authentic community relationships, but he admitted dolefully that where strong polities were most needed—at the local and global levels—they were weakest. Here, he concluded, the festive forms of popular religion might accomplish what the politics of church and state had not.

Cox further commented on the disillusionment of the sixties activists in his 1977 book, *Turning East: The Promise and Peril of New Orientalism*. He explained how Eastern philosophies challenged the Western commitment to "making history" without contemplating the meaning of history itself as a cultural creation. Cox had turned East himself and experimented with several meditative disciplines. But his interest in festivity and in the contemplative life was still not divorced from social application. The "peril" he saw in the popularity of the Eastern religions for Americans in the 1970s was the general narcissism that resulted from a misunderstanding and misapplication of Eastern ways. He observed that Americans tended to use meditation and the Eastern philosophy of detachment for the purpose of self-fulfillment in retreat from responsible social action. Nevertheless, he believed that the Eastern ways could lead disciples back to their Judaic or Christian origins where they could learn to appreciate the contemplative sources in these Western traditions. *Turning East* advocated refreshment at the wells of past experience to generate the forward movement into a revolutionary society.

In 1965 Cox had seen the shape of things to come in the urban centers of the Western world. By 1984, when he published *Religion in the Secular City: Toward a Postmodern Theology,* it had become clear to him that the center of modernity could no longer hold its own. In fact, the modern world had become a postmodern one. He now saw the impetus for change coming instead from the social margins of the American mainstream and from the global peripheries of the so-called third world countries. In this manner, his idea of a postmodern theology complements other radical commentaries that have come into the arena of public discourse in recent years. His postmodern theology is a reorientation of Western traditions with contemporary experience in the making of a collective history. Cox has said that both contemporary American fundamentalism and Latin American liberation theology are the cutting edges of this new social critique. He believes, however, that the future really belongs to the theologies of liberation that have emerged from the popular struggles in Latin America. It is there, he argues, that "the irrational dichotomies of modernity" are being overcome.

Harvey Cox has clearly revised his fledgling predictions of 1965 that modernity was the future wave of reason over premodern religion and metaphysics. Having turned East and also South, he has discovered other nonmodern truths. But he has also turned full circle in reaffirming his original belief that the roots of community must be nurtured at a home base that integrates all. From his perspective in the 1980s, the base communities of Latin American Christians, like the meditative disciplines of Eastern cultures, are models for the revitalization of North American societies. These Latin American communities seem to evoke something of his boyhood experience in Malvern, Pennsylvania. But they are not the same, he cautions. Nor can North Americans co-opt the historical reality of struggling peoples elsewhere. Even so, he sees the meaning of theology for all peoples in a global and local context anchored by the concrete relationships of community—not in retreat from the world, but in a pilgrimage of secular engagement.

## Survey of Criticism

Harvey Cox received a considerable amount of critical attention in the late 1960s following the publication of *The Secular City.* Since then the public focus has shifted toward the new evangelical and fundamentalist movements and less has been heard about the radical theologians. He has been criticized by theologians who question his positive attitude toward secularization and by Marxists who argue that his emphasis on political process naively ignores the intransigence of basic economic relationships. A collection of critical reviews and essays by theologians was published as *The Secular City Debate,* edited by Daniel Callahan (New York: Macmillan Co., 1966). Another book review of *The Secular City,* by Phyllis Clarke, written for the *Marxist Quarterly* (Spring 1966) is reprinted in *Christianity and Marxism in Dialogue*. Evaluations of Cox's theological views in general are also found in Donald G. Bloesch, *The Christian Witness in a Secular Age: An Evaluation of Nine Contemporary Theologians,* and in Lonnie Dean Kliever and John H. Hayes, *Radical Christianity: The New Theologies in Perspective.*

The international scope of Cox's work is evident from the balance of English-language critiques with others. Among these are Jourdain Bishop, *Les Théologiens de 'La mort de Dieu';* Gustave Thils, *Christianisme sans religion?*; Ferdinand Kerstiens, *Die Hoffnungsstruktur des Glaubens;* and J. H. Velema, *Nieuwe wegen oude sporen.*

Apart from criticism, Cox has also received some recognition. *The Seduction of the Spirit* was awarded the National Book Prize, and *Turning East* was an alternate for the Book-of-the-Month Club, as well as being selected by the American committee for display at the Moscow Book Fair. Cox holds honorary LL.D. degrees from Ohio Wesleyan University (1968) and Kalamazoo College (1970). He has been a visiting professor and lecturer in several universities in the United States and in Italy, Spain, India, Japan, Mexico, Peru, and Brazil. Helping to shape a global awareness in the dialogue of social justice has been Harvey Cox's most important contribution to popular religion in America.

## Bibliography

### Books by Harvey Gallagher Cox

1965   *God's Revolution and Man's Responsibility.* Valley Forge: Judson Press.
1965   *The Secular City: Secularization and Urbanization in the Theological Perspective.* New York: Macmillan.
1967   *On Not Leaving it to the Snake.* New York: Macmillan.
1968   *The Church Amid Revolution: A Selection of the Essays Prepared for the World Council of Churches Geneva Conference on Church and Society.* Edited by Cox. New York: Association Press.
1969   *The Feast of Fools: A Theological Essay on Festivity and Fantasy.* Cambridge: Harvard University.
1973   *The Seduction of the Spirit: The Use and Misuse of People's Religion.* New York: Simon and Schuster.
1977   *Turning East: The Promise and Peril of the New Orientalism.* New York: Simon and Schuster.
1983   *Just as I Am.* Knoxville, Tenn.: Abingdon Press.
1984   *Religion in the Secular City: Toward a Postmodern Theology.* New York: Simon and Schuster.

### Selected Studies about Harvey Gallagher Cox

Bishop, Jourdain: *Les Théologiens de 'La mort de Dieu.'* Paris: Editions du Cerf, 1967.
Bloesch, Donald G. *The Christian Witness in a Secular Age: An Evaluation of Nine Contemporary Theologians.* Minneapolis: Augsburg Publishing House, 1968.
Clarke, Phyllis. "Harvey Cox on the Secular City: A Review Article." In *Christianity and Marxism in Dialogue.* Toronto: Progress Books, 1966.

Kerstiens, Ferdinand. *Die Hoffnungsstruktur des Glaubens*. Mainz, West Germany: Matthias-Gruenewald-Verlag, 1969.
Kliever, Lonnie Dean, and John H. Hayes. *Radical Christianity: The New Theologies in Perspective*. Anderson, S.C.: Drake House, 1968.
Thils, Gustave. *Christianisme sans religion?* Paris: Caterman, 1968.
Velema J. H. *Nieuwe wegen oude sporen: analyse, motieven en perspective*. Apeldoorn, The Netherlands: Uitgeverij Semper Agendo, 1969.

BARBARA RITTER DAILEY

# W. A. Criswell

To meet W. A. Criswell is to be impressed, if not a bit intimidated. His physical appearance is striking. A study in character, his face is composed of a rock-strong jaw with just the right touch of dimple; a noble, political cartoonist's dream of a nose; deep-set and penetrating blue eyes clearly evidencing the keen mind operating behind them; perfectly creased forehead; and wavy, impeccably groomed silver hair. When all these features are combined with Criswell's immaculate dress and flawless carriage, any observer would have to agree that the man's demeanor offers the definitive picture of Texas-sized confidence and Scotch-Irish resolve. Pastor since 1944 of the largest Baptist church in the world, Criswell is, as C. Allyn Russell has pointed out, "a widely recognized preacher of unusual ability in a generation when giants of the pulpit are few."

## Biography

W. A. Criswell was born in Eldorado, Oklahoma, on 19 December 1909. He later took the name Wallie Amos on prompting from government immigration officials who insisted that he have a name beyond just his initials. The poverty of his early years proved to be the anvil on which the strength of his personality was forged. When he was five, his family moved to Texline, Texas, on the Texas–New Mexico border. Living in a town that offered little entertainment for a young boy, Criswell learned to thrive on the written word. His home life centered on religious piety and the activities of the little Baptist church in town. At the age of ten, he was converted by the preaching of John Hicks during a revival series held at the church. At twelve, Criswell formally dedicated his life to the Christian ministry in a service where John R. Rice, later the noted fundamentalist editor of the *Sword of the Lord* newsletter, led the music.

Criswell's mother sacrificed nobly for the education of her children. When it came time for W. A. to go to college, she left the rest of the family temporarily and moved to Waco to help finance his education and provide the home she felt he needed to meet successfully the demands of his schooling. He graduated magna cum laude from Baylor University in 1931. Throughout his Baylor years, he preached wherever he could get the opportunity, whether in the public square, in the jailhouse, or to people in his student pastorates of Devil's Bend, Pulltight,

Mound, and Marlow, Texas. According to Billy Keith, his official biographer, people around Pulltight even as late as 1973 still remembered that the voice of the preacher on a clear night carried for as far away as five miles.

After graduating from Baylor, hoping to expand his horizons Criswell traveled to Southern Baptist Seminary in Louisville, Kentucky, for his graduate work. He spent six years at Southern, earning both his Th.M. (1934) and Ph.D. (1937) degrees. Under the tutelage of solid Baptist scholars like John R. Sampey, A. T. Robertson, and W. O. Carver, Criswell grew into a student scholar of first rank. While continuing his student pastoring, Criswell met and fell in love with Betty Mae Harris, a student at a nearby college who played the piano for the Mount Washington church he served. Typifying the sentimentality for which Criswell is famous, they were married on Valentine's Day in 1935. They had one child, Mabel Ann (1939).

By the time he received his Ph.D., Criswell had already developed quite a pulpit reputation. The First Baptist Church of Chickasha, Oklahoma, extended a call, and the Criswells moved to the Southwest. During these days, according to Keith, Criswell became known as the "holy roller preacher with a Ph.D." The church at Chickasha flourished under Criswell's leadership even though he was never really very happy there.

Criswell's approach to preaching changed with his next move. The "holy roller" style remained but with a different type of sermon. He moved away from topical preaching, which had characterized his earlier years, to "preaching the Bible." Ever since those days at the First Baptist Church of Muskogee, Oklahoma (1941–44), Criswell has considered himself an expository preacher. Even though his sermons are rarely shorter than forty-five minutes, the congregation follows his every word with interest, usually with pens to paper or to Bible. A captivating speaker, Criswell exudes emotion and intense energy in every facial expression and gesture of the hand. Without a note, he delivers flawless monologues sprinkled with poetry, anecdotes, humor, historical illustrations, and usually a few tears.

He carried his newly developed expository preaching style with him in August 1944 to the First Baptist Church of Dallas when that church called him shortly after the death of the respected Texas Baptist leader George W. Truett*. Succeeding Truett, who had served the church faithfully for forty-seven years, could not have been an easy task. At thirty-four, Criswell knew that he had to earn the respect and admiration of the 7,000-member congregation. Yet, the church's response to his first sermon was overwhelming, and as the 19 November 1944 *Fort Worth Star-Telegram* reported, "It was obvious that the world's largest Baptist church would live on under his leadership."

In 1946, Criswell announced his intention to preach his way through the Bible verse by verse. Of the seventeen years he spent on the series, he preached for three years in the Old Testament, four years in the Gospels, seven years on the Acts and the Epistles (with nearly a year on the ninth chapter of Hebrews), and three years in the book of Revelation. Throughout the seventeen years of this preaching series, the church grew. In the twelve-year period from 1946 to 1958, the church experienced a 300 percent increase in annual gifts to all causes, from around $406,000 to approximately $1,303,000.

Every one of his messages during the years he has preached at the church has ended in a fervent call for commitment. As Keith has expressed it, when Criswell preaches, he "preaches for a verdict." He believes that the entire focus of every church is evangelism, and in over forty years, the invitation, often a half-hour to forty minutes in length because of congregational response, has not ended without someone coming forward. One never forgets the gentle sing-song of Criswell's voice as he sends forth the words: "In a moment we shall stand and sing our appeal and while we sing it, a family you, a couple you, or just one, somebody you, to give your heart to the Lord, to put your life in the fellowship of the church, to answer God's call, upon the first note of the first stanza come."

Success in evangelism has taken the church to soaring heights of membership. During Criswell's tenure at the church, membership has grown nearly fourfold, to a membership, on paper at least, of around 26,000. Most members drive in from the comfortable and affluent suburban areas of Dallas, with the majority of members representing the middle to upper-middle classes. Until his death, the oil billionaire H. L. Hunt, at one time described as America's richest man, was a member of the church. Distinguished members now include Billy Graham*, since 1953, and Paul Harvey, the church's 20,001st member.

Criswell has provided the necessary organizational genius to keep people driving from the suburbs to the downtown church. With fifteen nursery classes to at least nineteen different adult departments, each with classes of its own, the church's graded Sunday School program offers its more than 9,000 participants a hodgepodge of choices for education during the time period between the two morning services. Twenty-three choirs and a fifty-piece orchestra grace the church's music program. The high school Chapel Choir has given concerts all over the world. Since the 1970s, the church has gradually expanded its operation to provide a Christian day school for grades one through twelve, as well as the Criswell Center for Biblical Studies, composed of the Criswell Bible College and the Graduate School of the Bible, dedicated to the preparation of ministers.

A ten-million-dollar annual budget supports the programs of the church. On one particular Sunday in 1986, during a special appeal, the members of the church contributed $1.3 million in cash. Under Criswell's leadership, the church has changed from a rather staid downtown church catering mostly to mature adults, to a dynamic family-oriented one with a vibrant building program. Composed of eight buildings, the church plant offers two gymnasiums, a roller-skating rink, nautilus machines, a sauna, racquetball courts, bowling alleys, and a complete church restaurant. As is often true of fundamentalist churches, the church has become the center of life for most people who attend it. Its prime location includes ample parking in various multilevel garages that provide a supplementary income for the church by catering during the week to the Dallas business community.

Criswell's powerful influence extends far beyond his Dallas congregation. Every Sunday morning sermon is carried over radio and television (color broadcasts since 1970) throughout the southwestern portion of the United States. The church owns its own radio and television equipment, along with a radio station recently approved by the FCC to broadcast beginning in 1989 at 100,000 watts. For decades, the church has mailed tapes of Criswell's sermons all over the world. The minister has traveled extensively as well, taking mission trips throughout England, Scotland, Finland, Italy, Russia, Africa, and Asia. While in Italy in 1971, he received a personal invitation to visit with Pope Paul VI. This visually depicted the complete turn Criswell had taken in his views toward Catholicism. He had always been strongly anti-Catholic and during the late fifties fought the presidential election of John F. Kennedy on precisely that ground. Since then, he has preferred to expend his energies against atheists (he officially debated Madalyn Murray O'Hair in what turned out to be a well-publicized shouting match) and liberals.

The height of Criswell's influence in the Southern Baptist Convention came in 1968 when he was elected president of the convention. Another turn of a different type became widely publicized during that time period. Throughout the fifties, Criswell had been outspoken in his support for racial segregation in the South. In a long-remembered address before the South Carolina legislature, delivered at the invitation of Governor George Timmerman in 1956, Criswell spoke forcefully against racial integration. "Integration," he said, "is a thing of idiocy and foolishness." Yet, in 1968, just one week before the convention, he persuaded his deacons that the church ought to announce that all people were welcome in the church. The week following his election to the presidency, he preached a sermon entitled, "The Church of the Open Door." Critics saw it as a superficial gesture aimed at securing the election to the presidency. Supporters claim that Criswell's change of heart on the matter had nothing to do with convention politics. Though Criswell has consistently spoken against racism since 1968, his more recently published *Criswell Study Bible* still embraces the view that Genesis 9 should be interpreted as a curse placed on the African people. Despite Criswell's changed attitude since 1968, his congregation in Dallas remains basically a white congregation with only a handful of black members.

Criswell has also had considerable contact with the White House. Through the years, he has acted on numerous invitations to visit the White House for briefings on various issues. He had a genuine affection for Richard Nixon, "personally one of the finest men you could ever meet." Though he publicly criticized Betty Ford's statements about premarital sex and support of abortion, he welcomed Gerald Ford's appearance at his church in the fall of 1976 and endorsed his bid for the presidency during that visit.

Criswell has always been very vocal on political matters. His comments have grown out of his view of biblical prophecy. For him, the Bible's prophetic literature is infallibly predictive of today's events. In his view, the battle of Armageddon is close at hand and will involve both the Soviet Union and the

United States in a war centered on the Middle East, a war that will also involve both the Jews and the Arabs. His public politics have, therefore, been both staunchly anti-Communist and fervently pro-Israel. Prime Minister Menachem Begin officially recognized Criswell's strong support of Israel in 1978 when he presented the Dallas pastor with the Israeli Humanitarian Award. Criswell is the only Christian minister ever presented with the award.

### Appraisal

Criswell is a man of enormous energy. On this all observers agree. Beyond that, however, true agreement is harder to find. Both his defenders and his critics do point to his enormous success as a pastor, his masterful and charismatic presence in the pulpit, his large heart and obvious love for his congregation, his tenderness with children, his graceful humor, his disarming candor, and his overwhelming success as an evangelist of the gospel. His critics, however, want to point out other dimensions of the man and his ministry. They speak of his unbridled passion, often working to the detriment of reason, his tendency toward unsubstantiated generalization, his overzealous and often captious treatment of those with whom he disagrees, his emphasis on numbers (both in terms of finances and human beings) as the measure of who stands on the side of truth, his certainty that social applications of Christianity are mostly misguided, his uncritical commitment to American laissez-faire capitalism, and his authoritarian disposition.

Though Criswell's church staff is large, numbering over 150 individuals and assisted by almost 400 deacons, there is no question about who is in charge. Criswell firmly controls all elements of the church's life. On 9 April 1986 *The Christian Century,* in its "No Comment Department," reported Criswell's statement that "a laity-led, layman-led, deacon-led church will be a weak church anywhere on God's earth. The pastor is the ruler of the church. There is no other thing than that in the Bible." Criswell could, perhaps, best be described as a religious autocrat. Though his unquestioned rule of the church assures an unambiguous decision-making process, it does little for the development of maturity and of the qualities of leadership among the deacons and general membership of the church.

Ambiguity seemingly has no place in Criswell's vocabulary, at least where the message of his faith is concerned. His theology is as certain and unquestioned as his leadership in the church. Billy Keith, his sympathetic biographer, astutely observed that "Criswell is seldom bothered by intellectual doubts for his is a quest of soul rather than of mind." This observation characterizes the man rather well and may help to explain why some of his pronouncements sound as if they are anti-intellectual. As Russell has described it, "despite the extent of his ample education (although inbred), one wonders if Criswell has read in depth or seriously struggled with major theological currents other than his own."

Criswell's dogmatic certainty is the natural concomitant of his belief that the Bible is inerrant and infallible in the original manuscripts. Biblical authors merely transcribed what God inspired them to write. Criswell's view is most clearly set forth in his 1969 book *Why I Preach that the Bible is Literally True*. This characteristically fundamentalist view of the Bible has led Criswell and other conservative Southern Baptist leaders to launch a frontal assault on the so-called moderate wing of the convention. In the 1980s, a carefully orchestrated movement has meant that inerrantists have steadily gained control of the major committees and denominational boards within the Southern Baptist Convention. This political movement within Southern Baptist life has controlled the convention's presidency since 1979.

The center of power for this Southern Baptist inerrancy party is the Criswell Center for Biblical Studies. Southern Baptist critics of this minister's training ground see it as one of three such "inerrancy" schools, the other two being Mid-America Baptist Theological Seminary in Tennessee and Luther Rice Theological Seminary in Florida, set up to compete with the more moderate, mainline Southern Baptist seminaries. The center's president and Criswell's lieutenant, Paige Patterson, has been the most outspoken critic of the moderate party and has carefully orchestrated most of the political gains for the conservative party.

Though Criswell has not been as vocal as Patterson, many people generally assume that he stands as the real power and inspiration ("the patriarch") behind Patterson and a coterie of the superchurch pastors in the denomination, who have collectively been occasionally referred to as Criswell's "kitchen cabinet." Such an assessment is probably oversimplistic. Yet, Criswell's voice has been heard loud and clear throughout this controversy, and the goals of the inerrancy group merely reflect and build on the views Criswell has held throughout the fifty-plus years of his personal ministry. Indeed, if schism comes to the Southern Baptist Convention, it will result in no small measure from the influence of Criswell, who said, in a sermon entitled "The Curse of Modernism" preached decades ago, "Even though it breaks our hearts to part company in our institutions with the affable, personable, scholarly modernist preacher and teacher, we ought to purge out corrupting leaven wherever it appears." Though today's moderates in Southern Baptist life are a far cry from the "modernists" of the 1940s, these conservatives seem to feel sure they know "corrupting leaven" when they see it.

Criswell's personal theology, therefore, is consistent with his approach to leadership in the church. He is able to proclaim "the truth" in both areas without much of a second thought. In a time of skepticism regarding many conservative and fundamentalist ministries, Criswell's credibility is absolutely above reproach. No one, friend or foe, who knows the man could possibly doubt either the sincerity of his convictions or the integrity of his ministry. Presenting himself as the unassailable theologian and church leader, Criswell stands able to provide ideological and institutional safety and protection for anxious wayfarers seeking certainty and shelter in the storm produced by modern secular life in the late twentieth century. Though the church's membership has stabilized in recent years, and perhaps even entered a period of decline, it nevertheless remains as an example that significant numbers of people still find their religious needs met by such an approach. For others, those who have been unable or unwilling to ignore the development of modern scientific, sociological, and historical methods of intellectual inquiry and their impact on how one understands, receives, and appropriates Christian faith, Criswell represents an interesting, but rarely relevant, voice from another time and another place.

## Survey of Criticism

Not a great amount of critical material exists on W. A. Criswell. He has been the subject of countless brief articles in the religious and secular press, though most of these have had an ax of some kind or another to grind. Billy Keith's book, *W. A. Criswell: The Authorized Biography,* is to this date the only full biography of the man. It is an insider's account which unashamedly admits to being written with profound and complete sympathy for its subject. Keith clearly stands in awe of Criswell's "enigmatic and elusive genius." Yet the book is a rich source of anecdotes about the man and his ministry and sometimes, in spite of itself, reveals more content for a critical assignment than was probably intended.

Another rather sympathetic look at the man appears in *The First Baptist Church of Dallas: Centennial History (1868–1968),* a book commissioned by the church's historical committee in the mid-1960s and written by H. Leon McBeth, Professor of Church History at Southwestern Baptist Theological Seminary. Though McBeth is himself a moderate Southern Baptist opposed to the politicized inerrancy posture represented by Criswell, one will not find any critical perspective of the man in these pages. A brief and again thoroughly sympathetic chapter on Criswell can be found in Ed Gill's book *Through the Years: A History of the First Baptist Church Muskogee, Oklahoma, 1890–1965.*

There are several collections of Criswell sermons put together with brief introductory material written by various editors. One of these collections, edited by James E. Towns, is entitled *The Social Conscience of W. A. Criswell.* The book's purpose is to demonstrate that Criswell's brand of evangelicalism is not without its own social conscience. In essence, the book confirms that Criswell's social conscience is completely subsumed under his belief that personal conversion is the only foundation for social transformation.

By far the most complete and scholarly assessment of Criswell is offered in an article written by C. Allyn Russell, well-known and respected Boston University Professor of Religion. The article, entitled "W.A. Criswell: A Case Study in Fundamentalism," was published in the Southern Baptist Theological Seminary journal *Review and Expositor.* The article is written in the same format as the essays found in his well-received book *Voices of American Fundamentalism: Seven Biographical Studies* (Westminster Press, 1976). Along with his book, this article helps to dispel some of the popular notions of fundamentalism as a movement and, through its careful and systematic attention to primary sources, to clearly demonstrate that fundamentalism is multidimensional. Moreover, it reveals a good bit about the resurgence of right-wing conservatism during recent decades of American life.

## Bibliography

### Books by W. A. Criswell

1947   *The Church Library Reinforcing the Work of the Denomination.* Nashville: Baptist Sunday School Board.

1953   *These Issues We Must Face.* Grand Rapids: Zondervan.

1957   *Did Man Just Happen?* Grand Rapids: Zondervan.

1958   *Five Great Questions of the Bible.* Grand Rapids: Zondervan.

1959   *Five Great Affirmations of the Bible.* Grand Rapids: Zondervan.

1960   *The Gospel According to Moses.* Grand Rapids: Zondervan.

1961   *Expository Notes on the Gospel of Matthew.* Grand Rapids: Zondervan.

1965   *The Bible for Today's World.* Grand Rapids: Zondervan.

1966   *The Holy Spirit in Today's World.* Grand Rapids: Zondervan.

1967   *In Defense of the Faith.* Grand Rapids: Zondervan.

1969   *Expository Sermons on Revelation: Five Volumes in One.* Grand Rapids: Zondervan. Volume 1, 1962; Volume 2, 1963; Volume 3, 1964; Volume 4, 1965; Volume 5, 1966.

1969   *Fifty Years of Preaching at the Palace.* Grand Rapids: Zondervan.

1969   *Why I Preach that the Bible Is Literally True.* Nashville: Broadman.

1970   *Look Up, Brother!* Nashville: Broadman.

1970   *The Scarlet Thread Through the Bible.* Nashville: Broadman.

1972   *Christ and the Contemporary Crisis.* Dallas: Crescendo.

1973   *The Baptism, Filling, and Gifts of the Holy Spirit.* Grand Rapids: Zondervan.

1973   *Expository Sermons on Galatians.* Grand Rapids: Zondervan.

1974   *Ephesians.* Grand Rapids: Zondervan.

1975   *Christ the Savior of the World.* Dallas: Crescendo.

1975   *Expository Sermons on the Epistle of James.* Grand Rapids: Zondervan.

1975   *What To Do Until Jesus Comes Back.* Nashville: Broadman.

1976   *The Compassionate Christ.* Dallas: Crescendo.

1976   *Expository Sermons on the Book of Daniel: Four Volumes in One.* Grand Rapids: Zondervan. Volume 1, 1968; Volume 2, 1970; Volume 3, 1971; Volume 4, 1972.

1976   *Expository Sermons on the Epistle of Peter.* Grand Rapids: Zondervan.

1976   *Welcome Back Jesus!* Nashville: Broadman.

1977   *The Christ of the Cross.* Dallas: Crescendo.

1977   *Isaiah.* Grand Rapids: Zondervan.

1978   *Acts: An Exposition, Volume 1.* Grand Rapids: Zondervan.

1978   *What A Savior!* Nashville: Broadman.

1978   *With A Bible In My Hand.* Nashville: Broadman.

1979   *Acts: An Exposition, Volume II.* Grand Rapids: Zondervan.

1979   *The Criswell Study Bible.* Nashville: Thomas Nelson.

1980   *Acts: An Exposition, Volume III.* Grand Rapids: Zondervan.

1980   *Criswell's Guidebook for Pastors.* Nashville: Broadman.

1985   *Great Doctrines of the Bible.* Grand Rapids: Zondervan. Volume 1, *Bibliology,* 1982; Volume 2, *Theology Proper,* 1982; Volume 3, *Christology,* 1983; Volume 4, *Pneumatology,* 1984; Volume 5, *Soteriology,* 1985.

*Selected Studies about W. A. Criswell*

Gill, Ed. *Through the Years: A History of the First Baptist Church Muskogee, Oklahoma, 1890–1965*. Muskogee, Okla.: Hoffman Printing Co., n.d.

Keith, Billy. *W. A. Criswell: The Authorized Biography*. Old Tappan, N.J.: Revell, 1973.

McBeth, H. Leon. *The First Baptist Church of Dallas: Centennial History (1868–1968)*. Grand Rapids: Zondervan, 1968.

Russell, C. Allyn. "W.A. Criswell: A Case Study in Fundamentalism." *Review and Expositor* 81 (Winter 1984): 107–31.

Towns, James E., ed. *The Social Conscience of W. A. Criswell*. Dallas: Crescendo, 1977.

MARK G. TOULOUSE

# Dorothy Day

In the early decades of the twentieth century, the Roman Catholic Church in the United States was primarily the church of immigrants. Many so-called native Americans suspected that its members were controlled by the Pope and were therefore untrustworthy citizens. Dorothy Day was an American convert to Catholicism who brought to it her commitment to radical social ideals. With Peter Maurin, she was the founder and longtime leader of the activist, "organic, decentralized" Catholic Worker movement, which combined those ideals with conventional religion. The activities of Day and the Catholic Worker contributed to the development of American Catholicism and inspired many persons within and outside that group to an active Christianity devoted to the poor and the pursuit of peace.

## Biography

Dorothy Day, the third child of John and Grace (Satterlee) Day, was born on 8 November 1897 in Brooklyn, New York. Her father was a sports journalist from Tennessee who was actively nonreligious. First her radicalism and then her religiousness estranged Dorothy from her father. Nonetheless, she remained in contact with her mother throughout her life. Dorothy's older brothers, Sam and Donald, were also journalists; she was not close to them. Her relationship with her younger sister, Della, was close, as was that with John, born when Dorothy was fourteen. The elder John Day's career took the family from Brooklyn to Berkeley and Oakland. The San Francisco earthquake sent them back east to Chicago, where they first lived on the Southside and then moved to the Lincoln Park area.

Day early manifested her desire to learn, her sympathy for the poor, and her religious sensibility which would come to fruition in her later life. Reading Upton Sinclair stimulated her interest in the poor and prompted her to take long walks into Chicago's Westside. Day's childhood religion was episodic. As an adult she recalled reading the Bible and identified several periods of religious activity, such as participation in the activities of Methodist neighbors in California and in the life of Episcopal parishes in Chicago. Having won a Hearst scholarship, Day went to the University of Illinois, Urbana, at age sixteen.

Her two years as a student in Urbana gave Day personal acquaintance with poverty and introduced her to Socialism. The small scholarship did not cover her expenses, so Day worked in homes to earn a meager income. She was frequently hungry and cold. Her attendance at class was ruled by her desire to learn rather than by course requirements. Her few friends were made among the writers, Socialists, and Jews. She was particularly close to Rayna Simons Prohme, who would later become a Communist.

When her family returned to New York, Day followed but did not live with them. Rather, she found a job with the radical newspaper *Call* and set herself up in a room on the lower East Side. After *Call* was closed, Day worked for *Masses* and much later for Crystal Eastman's *Liberator*. In these positions she cultivated her journalistic skills and her sympathy for radical programs. Her associates included radicals like Mike Gold as well as Greenwich Village residents such as Peggy Baird and Eugene O'Neill. In 1917 Day and Baird were arrested and jailed in Washington, D.C., for their participation in a women's suffrage demonstration.

During World War I Dorothy and her sister, Della, were probationer nurses at the Kings County Hospital. Dorothy left the program to live with Lionel Moise, a journalist she had met at the hospital. The relationship ended when Day became pregnant and had an abortion. This difficult period was the basis for Day's single novel, *The Eleventh Virgin*. In the spring of 1920 Day married Barkeley Tobey, a promoter of ideas with a record of short marriages. The one with Day was no exception: it was both unsatisfactory and brief. When the marriage ended, Day spent several months in Italy. Then she returned to the United States and moved about the country doing various jobs. First she returned to Chicago, and then she and Della moved to New Orleans. With the income from the film rights to her novel, Day went back to New York where she bought a beach house on Staten Island.

Day revived friendships from her earlier years in New York and expanded her circle. Among her new acquaintances was biologist Forster Batterham. Beginning in 1925 she and Batterham shared Day's beach house. They did not marry because he was opposed to the intervention of the state into such matters and was antireligious. In *The Long Loneliness,* Day heads her discussion of this period of her life with the subtitle ''Natural Happiness.'' The birth of Tamar Teresa in the spring of 1927 was both the culmination of her happiness and the beginning of its end.

Her gradual turn to Catholicism had accelerated, and Day determined to have Tamar baptized despite Batterham's objections. All the while that she received catechetical instruction as part of the preparation for Tamar's baptism, Day struggled with her own desire to be baptized. That action would force her to lose Batterham, who refused to be married. Finally, on 28 December 1927

Dorothy Day was baptized into the Roman Catholic Church. Her conversion was inexplicable in the minds of most of her radical friends, and she fell out of touch with them.

Since she knew no lay Catholics, Day's first years as a Catholic were lived in relative isolation from the community of the church; she was, however, faithful in her participation in the sacraments. A contract with Pathe studios to write screenplays took mother and daughter to Los Angeles and provided the funds for a sojourn in Mexico. Back in New York, they shared an apartment with Day's brother John and his wife. Day pursued several free-lance jobs. She wrote for the Catholic *Commonweal,* which had printed her articles about her life in Mexico. As a reporter for *Commonweal* and the Jesuit *America,* Day went to cover a Hunger March in Washington, D.C., in 1932. Watching the demonstration, she was struck by the self-centeredness of her life since her conversion, and she prayed for a sign as to what she could do for the poor.

When she arrived home, Day found Peter Maurin waiting for her. A French peasant philosopher with a vision of a better world, he took up the task of educating Day. The outcome was the Catholic Worker movement, which gave Day her vocation and to which she gave the rest of her life. The movement's personalist base gave it an organic and fluid character not unlike the church's first decades. Its emphasis on prayer, study, and work suggests similarities to Benedictine monasticism. The program of the movement was carried out through three means: the paper, houses of hospitality, and farms.

The first issue of *Catholic Worker* appeared on May Day 1933. Its price, then as always, was one cent. The paper's circulation fluctuated; in 1980 it was estimated to be between 85,000 and 100,000. In addition to Maurin's "Easy Essays" and Day's column, "On Pilgrimage," the paper carried news reports and comments from Catholic workers. Day's writing combined homely details about life in the movement with reflections on world events and spiritual matters. She was unwavering in her commitment to labor and pacifism, even when her positions caused rifts in the movement. Nonetheless, her statement that she would stop publishing immediately if church officials told her to do so is often quoted to indicate her conventional obedience to the church.

In houses of hospitality across the nation, the Catholic Workers provided food and lodging to all who came without asking anything in return. There was no preaching, unlike the practice in rescue missions. The workers' lives, like Day's, combined voluntary poverty, works of mercy, and personal responsibility with communitarianism. The example of their austerity and commitment brought some of those to whom they ministered into the church. The work provided many faithful people with a means of expressing their faith and helped them to remain members of the church.

Similar work was carried on at a series of farms that served as vacation spots for urban residents, homes for families, and retreat centers. The farms were often the setting for conflicts. More than once Day withdrew from a location leaving it to the "opposition."

After the founding of the movement, Day's life was closely tied to it. Socially informed ascetic spiritual retreats on the model of Father Onesimus Lacouture became an essential element in Day's own life and that of the movement in the 1940s. Day spent several months away from the center of the movement in 1943; she returned refreshed, with deepened resolve and serenity. Her long-standing pacifism encouraged many people involved in the American peace movement of the 1960s and extended her influence beyond the Catholic Worker groups. Although she was disturbed by some of the results of Vatican II relative to morality and changes in religious practice, Dorothy Day provided the primary leadership for the Catholic Worker movement until her death in December 1980.

## Appraisal

In his insightful and measured obituary, David J. O'Brien judged Dorothy Day, "the most significant, interesting, and influential person in the history of American Catholicism." Any attempt to appraise her importance is complicated by the impossibility of distinguishing the person from the movement she founded and led and by the tendency of her admirers to cast her as a saint. During her lifetime she resisted this impulse. Perhaps those who lived with her in the slums and among the poor were most vividly aware that she was a strong-willed as well as loving woman; it was those who looked on from afar who could ignore her human weaknesses. Students of American religious history cannot ignore her life and work.

In some degree Day contributed to the problem. In her autobiographical writings she traced the path toward her conversion and her vocation at the Catholic Worker movement. She was reluctant to reveal the details of her prior life lest it lead other young people toward such a life. However, that prior life makes her vocation all the more believable. Day was not a do-gooder who had never known any other existence. As she has written, she only knew how to learn things the hard way.

In his 1981 introduction to *The Long Loneliness,* Daniel Berrigan* noted the direct influence of Day on the Catholic radicals of the 1960s and, perhaps more important, her indirect influence on the official positions of the Catholic Church in the United States on issues such as peace, nuclear war, and economics. Her indirect influence can also be traced to many persons, some of whom are not Catholics, who continue to be concerned with building a better world.

Day's detractors, and some of her allies, charged her with sentimentality. This was so with regard to her pacifism and, to a lesser degree, her views of community. Though it is true that Day was an idealist who expected the best from people, it is not the case that she was softheaded. To the contrary, she was a reflective thinker whose ideas were informed by Catholic theology and world literature. Her own positions were worked out as she lived in Catholic Worker houses and farms and traveled the nation by bus. Her writing reveals realism tempered by hope.

Day's influence within the Roman Catholic Church is particularly remarkable since she was female, lay, and a convert in a church made up primarily of lifelong members and led by a hierarchy of male clergymen. Although Day was firm in her commitment to the Catholic Worker as a lay movement, she held the clergy in high regard. A happy by-product of this evident respect for the clergy was protection from undue suspicion. Until his death in 1949, the presence of Peter Maurin also provided something of a shield from possible objections to leadership by a woman.

An activist, Day influenced others through the example of her life. She was not a self-conscious advocate of women's rights, and it is as an example that her significance as a female religious leader is seen. In this regard Day is an ambiguous figure. Day appears to have subscribed to conventional notions about women, whom she described in *The Long Loneliness* as "more materialistic [than men], thinking of the home, the children." Although she did not marry, Day had relished her home life with Batterham, and she was a mother. Indeed, it was motherhood that finally propelled her into the Catholic church. But home and children did not define her realm. As the founder and leader of the Catholic Worker movement, Day was a remarkable, strong woman who made her way in a male church. In so doing she brought to bear the materialism that she viewed as women's nature. Although she could be severe and demanding, she modeled an organic leadership unlike that of the church hierarchy.

The Catholic Worker has since its beginning been an ever changing movement. The number of houses and farms and the circulation of the paper fluctuates. For decades Dorothy Day was the mothering leader who visited, who encouraged, and who scolded. Since her death, the movement and the paper have continued to function and to change, an indication of her ongoing influence both within the movement and beyond it.

## Survey of Criticism

Long before her death in 1980, Dorothy Day was attracting the attention of Catholic and non-Catholic journalists and scholars. The occasion of her seventy-fifth birthday received wide press coverage. Since her death, the number of studies of Day and of the Catholic Worker movement has mushroomed. These fall into two sorts, those that begin with Day and those that begin with the movement. Anne and Alice Klejment's *Dorothy Day and The Catholic Worker* provides a comprehensive bibliographic guide to the expanding body of materials.

Dorothy Day's autobiographical writings and her columns provide access to her perception of her life. In *The Long Loneliness,* a work in the tradition of Augustine's *Confessions,* Day tells her life's story up to 1952. The plot of her account is in two parts: her journey toward conversion and her vocation in the Catholic Worker movement. She admits that she left her sins out of her earlier work *From Union Square to Rome;* although she allows some of them to creep into this volume, she does not dwell on those incidents or on the conflicts in the movement. There are major events and periods of time missing from Day's portrayals of her life prior to her conversion. Nonetheless, her writings are important, and they reveal her thoughtfulness and religiousness.

William D. Miller's biography, published two years after Day's death, provides a more comprehensive account of her life. Miller knew Day and discussed a biography with her. Although she did not officially authorize his work, she cooperated with him through conversations and by providing materials. Other materials from the Catholic Worker Collection at Marquette University were available to him. Nearly 40 percent of Miller's volume is devoted to the years prior to Day's conversion, and he included information that was previously little known, such as her abortion and marriage. Miller is well acquainted with the Catholic Worker movement, and he intertwined its story with Day's. He also gave attention to Day's relationship to her family and to Tamar and her family. The final chapters are the weakest.

Slightly different perspectives on Day are found in Dwight Macdonald's profile in *New Yorker,* Judith Nies' sketch in *Seven Women,* and Daniel Berrigan's introduction to the 1981 printing of *The Long Loneliness.* Macdonald wrote in the early 1950s and introduced Day to many of his readers. His impressionistic and visual profile is of Day in the midst of her activity. He described her as a woman who "combines mystical feeling with practicality." Nies considered Day as a daughter of the American radical tradition. She gave insufficient weight to the importance of religion in Day's life. Because of the additional information provided by Miller, Nies' value as a brief biography is reduced. Of these three, Berrigan was closest to and most directly influenced by Day. His introduction attests to her significance to religiously informed social activists.

Several scholars began with the Catholic Worker and wove Day's story into their studies of the movement she founded. Mel Piehl's *Breaking Bread* is of this sort. Piehl skillfully placed the movement in the context of American Catholicism and social movements. His consideration of Maurin's contributions and Day's adaptations is insightful. Giving less attention to the early years of Day's life and to her various relationships allowed him to devote more attention to the spread of the movement and to its later years.

Similarly, Nancy Roberts' *Dorothy Day and the Catholic Worker* focuses on the journalistic aspect of Day's work and continues beyond her death. Roberts' work is informed by women's history and benefits from her consideration of the significance of Day's having been a woman. Debra Campbell's article in the 1984 special issue of *Crosscurrents* also contributes to this topic.

Photographs by Jon Erickson complement Robert Coles' text in *A Spectacle Unto the World.* Coles' perspective is that of an admiring friend who is also a psychologist and an astute observer of American society. Without sharing all of Day's commitments, he is respectful of them, as he is of her actions. His thoughtful words appropriately place Day in the context of primitive Christianity. Erickson's photographs provide an evocative view of the life Day led and inspired others to take up.

## Bibliography

### Books by Dorothy Day

1924    *The Eleventh Virgin*. New York: Boni.
1938    *From Union Square to Rome*. Silver Spring, Md.: Preservation of the Faith Press.
1939    *Houses of Hospitality*. New York: Sheed and Ward.
1952    *The Long Loneliness*. New York: Harper.
1960    *Thérèse*. Notre Dame, Ind.: Fides Publishers.
1962    *Loaves and Fishes*. New York: Harper and Row.
1972    *On Pilgrimage in the Sixties*. New York: Curtis Paperback.
1983    *By Little and By Little: The Selected Writings of Dorothy Day*. Edited by Robert
        Ellsberg. New York: Alfred A. Knopf.

### Selected Studies about Dorothy Day

Campbell, Debra. "The Catholic Earth Mother: Dorothy Day and Women's Power in
        the Church." *Crosscurrents* 34 (Fall 1984): 270–82.
Coles, Robert. *A Spectacle Unto the World*. New York: Viking, 1973.
Klejment, Anne, and Alice Klejment. *Dorothy Day and The Catholic Worker: A Bibli-
        ography and Index*. New York: Garland Publishers, 1986.
Macdonald, Dwight. "The Foolish Things of the World." *New Yorker* 28 (4 and 11
        October 1952).
Miller, William D. *Dorothy Day: A Biography*. San Francisco: Harper and Row, 1982.
———. *A Harsh and Dreadful Love: Dorothy Day and the Catholic Worker Movement*.
        New York: Liveright, 1972.
Nies, Judith. *Seven Women: Portraits from the American Radical Tradition*. New York:
        Penguin Books, 1977.
O'Brien, David J. "The Pilgrimage of Dorothy Day." *Commonweal* 107 (19 December
        1980): 711–15.
Piehl, Mel. *Breaking Bread: The Catholic Worker and the Origin of Catholic Radicalism
        in America*. Philadelphia: Temple University Press, 1982.
Roberts, Nancy. *Dorothy Day and the Catholic Worker*. Albany: State University of New
        York Press, 1984.

L. DeANE LAGERQUIST

# Major J. (Father) Divine

As late as 1946, some ten years after he had reached the zenith of his ministry, Major Jealous Divine, founder of the Peace Mission movement, still found it necessary to identify himself: "My name is MR. MAJOR J. DIVINE as a civilian and citizen of the United States; but as a Minister of the Gospel, REVEREND MAJOR J. or M. J. DIVINE, better known as FATHER DIVINE." This repeated explanation defines the discrete social and religious identities that Divine cultivated throughout his ministry. Divine, the socially active black American who lived through much of the racism of late-nineteenth-century America, was involved in relief efforts during the Great Depression and became in the 1960s an elder statesman of the civil rights movement. Though inextricably intertwined with this social activism and serving as a guiding force for much of it, the other Divine, the reverend and the father, was somewhat detached from the social ills; he was a mystical, somewhat quixotic presence whose followers proclaimed—and he never denied—that he was a god.

For all of the effort Divine made to acquaint the curious with his two guises, one senses an air of defensiveness. He had good reason for this attitude; Divine did not exist in either role without controversy. In his man-on-the-street role, many thought that Divine was no more than a petty rogue, whereas in his spiritual patriarch role, others believed—and he at times confirmed—that he was not just any god: he was God, the Judeo-Christian one. Thus it is out of a complex matrix woven of disparate, yet complementary, images and reinforced by a personal commitment to reshape societal and religious values that Major/Father Divine emerged from near obscurity in 1932 to become a significant religious figure.

### Biography

As one might expect of a man-god, Divine's origins are for the most part untraceable. He spoke in vague terms about his birth, telling a judge in 1932, as reported in the 11 June 1932 *Baltimore Afro-American*, "I think I am 55 years old." As if to confound any attempts to reconstruct his past, Divine told an interviewer in 1935 that he was "around fifty-two . . . humanly speaking." Not to allow even this much specificity to stand, Divine made the following disclaimer during the same interview, which was carried in the 20 August 1932 *New York News*: "We have spiritually and mentally in reality, no record."

This biographical obscurity served Divine's purposes well. In the 1930s he rose to fame on the claim that all of his believers should expect of him what they would from any omnipotent god. Divine needed to be timeless, originless, placeless—in essence enshrouded in an aura of infinity—to authenticate his deification. At the same time, he needed to imply omnitemporality through his deeds. Thus he told questioners that he had married Pinninnah, his goddess wife, in 1882. (No matter that this fact would make him unborn at the time of his marriage according to the figure he gave in 1935). He told them that some time before 1914 he had traveled through the South where he miraculously escaped thirty-two "lynch mobs" while preaching his "truth."

Little evidence independent of Divine's memories remains to verify these recollections. In Valdosta, Georgia, in 1914, Joel R. Moseley, author of several inspirational works, helped obtain the release of a man from jail who had been arrested for calling himself God. When Moseley met Divine in New York in the late 1930s, he claimed that Divine was the man whom he had rescued in 1914. At a service over which Divine presided in 1937, a woman testified that she had attended "meetings" that Divine years earlier had led in Americus, Georgia, at which "people were singing and shouting and praising and worshipping . . . all day long." Divine said later that he had been in Americus and had nearly been lynched there.

At the point where documentary evidence emerges, one finds Divine already engaged in the formation of his movement. In October 1919, Divine, with a small group of believers in tow, bought a house in Sayville, Long Island. The deed shows that Pinninnah, at that time known as Mother Divine, contributed part of the $700 down payment that Divine made toward the purchase price of $2,500. The presence of Pinninnah and others indicates that Divine had been building a following and that he considered the communal setting that the house would provide integral to the movement. As much as this reason might have been important, it seemed secondary to Divine's stated purpose for moving to Sayville, as reported by biographer Kenneth Burnham: to "refrain from coming into contact, and running into collision with the other versions of GOD and other religions."

Sayville provided more than a spiritual refuge; there Divine, the activist citizen, could dole out his "Own Unadulterated LOVE." He started a free employment agency, a service he considered "a GIFT OF GOD." On Sundays, he gave sumptuous banquets that he and his followers considered Holy Communion services. But to the many underfed who could make it to his well-laid tables, Divine's meals were more than religious rituals: they were miracles served by a caring man and perhaps provided by an incredible god. Divine's man-god image grew even larger with less auspicious "services." Along with the spiritual advice he gave freely, he provided many of his closest followers with a place to live and with other material needs. Many considered their belief in him to be the "born again" experience of traditional Christianity.

Clearly, the social service aspect of Divine's ministry, more than the theistic ideology of it, brought him his first notoriety. Indeed, during the last of his years in Sayville, 1929–32 (the period of the Great Depression), powerful non-religious incentives worked to bring the general, nonbelieving public to Divine's home to find jobs, food, and general solace. By 1932 six policemen had to control the traffic and crowds around Divine's house. A local newspaper reported that he served people continuously "from early morning until midnight." Divine not only provided a seemingly endless feast but also did so for free, refusing all donations and gifts. The financial support for his charity came from his followers who devoted their earnings and personal property to Divine. Divine's radical beneficence and his means of funding it would later become two of the most distinguishing and controversial facets of his ministry.

Divine probably would have continued this unusual work had he not encountered resistance from the community. A small Long Island village, Sayville could hardly absorb the throngs who flocked to Divine's each week, crowds that were multiracial and spanned the ranges of different economic and social classes. There seemed no limit to Divine's attraction and the near bedlam that followed it. The community's resentment came to a climax in November 1931 when Divine and eighty of his followers were arrested for disturbing the peace. Residents of the city offered to drop the charges if Divine and his "cult" would move. Divine refused; he and twenty-four others were brought to trial in May 1932.

Divine's arrest and trial were responsible for his rise to national fame. Immediately after the arrest, James C. Thomas, a former assistant district attorney, agreed to defend Divine, stating that if black Divinites could be denied their rights to worship, there would be consequences not only for "every Negro man, woman and child in the United States," but for all other citizens as well. With such solid support for Divine from one of the prominent persons in New York's legal community, black leaders and black newspapers quickly came to Divine's defense. Between Thomas' announcement and the trial, thousands of persons, not all of whom were believers in Divine, attended rallies, celebrations, and speeches to protest his plight. Out of his apparent martyrdom, Divine's notoriety grew by leaps and bounds.

But it took an event at the close of the trial to gain widespread support for Divine, the god, over Major Jealous, the unjustly accused religious eccentric. The judge in the case, Lewis J. Smith, proved to be unfair, particularly when he discovered that white women were among Divine's most devoted followers. During the trial he prodded witnesses and used his presiding power to thwart the defense and to discredit Divine. Even though the jury, having found Divine guilty of disturbing the peace, had recommended leniency, Smith gave Divine the maximum sentence: one year in jail and a $500 fine. Three days later, Smith, who had no known medical problems, died suddenly. Hearing of Smith's death, Divine, with an uncharacteristic display of self-aggrandizement, was quoted as saying: "I hated to do it."

Both Divines were vindicated. Major Divine was released immediately on bond, and the conviction was overturned by the appellate division of the New York State Supreme Court in a unanimous finding of judicial prejudice. Father Divine was catapulted to a near messianic figure. The number of Divinites who formed communities modeled after the one in Sayville multiplied. Those who were unconvinced of his divinity had to reconcile themselves to the coincidence of Smith's death with the near demise of Divine's movement. Even to the most cynical, Divine was the phoenix rising out of the ashes of ill will. To his believers, his return represented the resurrection. His period of trial and his apparently self-engineered deliverance amounted to irrefutable proof that Divine was, as his followers would later proclaim from banners posted around Harlem, "GOD ALMIGHTY."

### Appraisal

If Divine was regarded as an enigmatic blend of man and god by the public, he was not so regarded by himself, at least as one can ascertain his self-perception through his religious thought. The major indication of this unity of disparate selves can be found in Divine's tendency to deflect attention away from his followers' claims of his being God. With the exception of his outbursts at various writers who attempted to malign him, or his occasional oblique reference to his control over international affairs and broad calamities, Divine for the most part avoided direct assertions of his alleged godliness. He preferred to reveal himself in vague, almost tautological statements, such as the one recorded in the 25 June 1936 *New Day*: "as real as you observe GOD to be, even so real will GOD be to thee."

Divine's purpose might not have been to obfuscate so much as it was to avoid distracting possible believers away from his real goal, which was to instill in his believers the values of primitive Christianity. As he put it in the 1 October 1942 issue of *New Day*: "But live in harmony and in keeping with MY Teaching and bring your body into subjection to the life and the teaching of JESUS as recorded in the four Gospels." Divine worked not so much to bring the would-be believer to an encounter with his metaphysical nature, but to inspire him to a new way of life. This beneficent duplicity underlies the two Divines his public saw, in contrast to the one Divine his religious idealism promoted. In essence, God Divine would lead one to a deeper involvement in the Christian experience.

This same duplicity underlies Divine's ministry from Sayville until his death in 1965. There is no clearer example of this than the communal living that Divine provided his closest followers. A Divine "heaven" was to be the modern replica of the church-communities the early Christians built. From all reports it was. Divinites gave their possessions to the movement or at least put them at its disposal. Members refused worker's compensation, social security, and other types of governmental assistance and even private gifts and tips in the belief that they had to "trust in GOD" for their well-being. Divine also required the residents of the communes to subscribe to his International Modest Code that included, as Mother Divine wrote in *The Peace Mission Movement*, "no smoking, no drinking, . . . no profanity, [and] no undue mixing of sexes [i.e., celibacy, even for married believers]."

His desire to recreate the primitive church prompted Divine to hold his well-known banquets. These were not, however, feasts for the sake of appetite. Divine meant the banquets to be the modern-day replicas of the daily communions that early Christians celebrated, and they became the main conduit through which the general public, particularly prospective members, became exposed to Divine. Since he did not allow anyone to indicate acceptance of his teachings by merely "joining" the movement, he found the banquet, the community's only public ritual, to be the most commonly used point of entry for aspiring believers. As Mother Divine recalled in *The Peace Mission Movement*, a prospective member, impressed by the "abundance and splendor, . . . order, [and] cleanliness" of the service, would logically want to learn more about Divine.

The essence of institutionalized Divinism, therefore, is the community of believers and its ritual banquet, the communion service. In the period shortly after his release from prison in 1932, during which Divine relocated his head-quarters to Harlem, the proliferation of his followers was most evident by the appearance of Divine communities throughout the United States. With an eye toward the early Christian churches, Divine never legally incorporated these communities, preferring to bind them together only through their commitment to his teachings. Today, the Peace Mission movement, as this confederation of communities became known, is still unincorporated. There are, however, incorporated "churches" throughout North and Central America, Africa, Europe, and Australia. To emulate the early Christianity, Divine insisted that no membership records of the Peace Mission movement be kept. Even today no one knows the number of adherents, although Divine stated as early as 1935 that his "deeds" had brought about the "conscious conviction of twenty odd million."

For all the obscuring of his godliness that one finds in the spiritual dimension of Divine's ministry, there is a pronounced lack of it in his social mission. It should be remembered that Divine first became widely known to the public not because of his assertion of being a god but because of the injustice that he and his religious community suffered. Thus it was racism, more so than godliness, that thrust Divine into public prominence. On the other hand, the sudden death of Judge Smith, for which Divine took responsibility, and his followers' subsequent proclamations of his godhood kept Divine, the god, from being eclipsed by Divine, the black American who had been racially violated.

This mixture of victim and god is the key to understanding why Divine would place different emphasis on his mystical being when addressing social problems than he did when promulgating his religious ideas. The authority he needed to correct the racial injustice he suffered came from his claim to be God. Virtually from the first day of his release from jail in 1932, Divine spoke on the race problem with messianic authority: "I came to establish the Kingdom of God in the hearts and minds of men. I am no race, no creed, no color, and I will not tolerate the thought of them." Race, something god-Divine considered himself to be addressing directly by residing in a black man's body, became one of the major motifs of his social message. Divine insisted that his followers live and work in totally integrated settings and forbade them even to refer to anyone by a racial title. Divine's ultimate statement on race was made with his second marriage: this Mother Divine, a Canadian, represented the return of Pinninnah in a caucasian body; she was the carnal enunciation of his tenet that divinity knows no racial boundaries.

Thus Divine, the social leader, is best defined by the social ills he saw affecting his life and by the spiritual power by which he claimed to cure them. This is demonstrated most clearly in his "Righteous Government Platform" that he proposed in January 1936. With both the Depression and racism taking their toll, Divine undertook a fundamental reshaping of the economic and political orders by calling a convention to discuss his proposals. Over 6,000 delegates, many of whom led social and political efforts not associated with the movement, helped craft the platform. To ensure that the wider public would not take his proposals as a surreptitious attempt to grab power, Divine once again avoided drawing attention to his claim of supernatural being by proclaiming that "without the true concept of CHRIST and the recognition of HIS Presence among the politicians, the world will continue to be filled with corruption." Despite Divine's attempt to focus on Christ, the final document, which bore his signature, and is reprinted in Mother Divine's *The Peace Mission Movement*, was stamped with both his religious and social idealism: "Through the Dispensation of GOD on earth in Bodily Form, we already have a Righteous Government, for Righteousness, Justice and Truth are now reigning in us where unrighteousness, injustice, and untruth once held sway."

A delicate balance between politics and political advocacy points up a certain pragmatism in Divine's social message. With the Righteous Government Platform and wide support for it, Divine could have used his position as leader of a major religious group for overt political gain; he appears, however, to have done so rarely, although he was openly courted by politicians such as Franklin D. Roosevelt. But he had no hesitancy about using the political process as a means of agitating for social change: between 1936 and 1940, for example, he worked long and hard with various congressmen for passage of a federal anti-lynching law.

## Survey of Criticism

Those who have written about Divine have been as perplexed by his two persons as has the general public. Popular biographers have tended to ignore the movement's principles, seeking instead to discredit it and Divine. Robert A. Parker's *Incredible Messiah: The Deification of Father Divine*; John Hoshor's *God in a Rolls-Royce: The Rise of Father Divine: Madman, Menace, or Messiah?*; and Sara Harris's *Father Divine: Holy Husband* are the best examples of the popular biographical studies of Divine. Their lack of documentation and their focus on the sensational cast doubt on the usefulness of these works for the scholar. Of particular note for this type of biography is the series of articles by St. Clair McKelway and A. J. Liebling in the *New Yorker* in June 1936. Having located a number of informants, one of whom—a John Hickerson— claimed to have taught Divine, McKelway and Liebling attempted to construct Divine's pre-Sayville life. Their account takes Hickerson's word that Divine worked with Hickerson in Baltimore at the turn of the century and was then called George Baker. Divine has denied this. Parker, Hoshor, and Harris each accepted Hickerson's account without personally contacting him or seeking independent documentation. Unless more reliable evidence comes to light, the researcher might want to follow the Library of Congress's Cataloguing Department's decision in 1979 to "correct" its "George Baker" heading to read "Father Divine."

The most documented and serious biography of Divine is Robert Weisbrot's *Father Divine and the Struggle for Racial Equality*. With the exception of his acceptance of the George Baker story, Weisbrot's book follows a well-laid source trail. He is the only biographer to fully assess the impact of Divine's social activism on black Americans.

A number of studies have attempted to locate Divine's Peace Mission among American religious movements. The most plentiful are "cult" studies, most of which are plagued by the wide gulf that exists between the denotive and connotive meanings of cult. Marred by questionable research methods and preconceived notions of nonmainline religious groups are Raymond Julius Jones' *Comparative Study of Religious Cult Behavior Among Negroes* and William M. Kephart's *Extraordinary Groups*. More objective sociological/anthropological studies of Divine's movement are found in Charles S. Braden's *These Also Believe* and Arthur H. Fauset's *Black Gods of the Metropolis*. Efforts to place Divine in the broader social/cultural matrix of black America are rather numerous, with Claude McKay's *Harlem: Negro Metropolis* and Roi Ottley's *'New World A-Coming': Inside Black America* among the most thorough and sensitive descriptions. In this same vein but with an effort to place Divine in black American religious history is *Black Sects and Cults* by Joseph R. Washington, Jr.

Divine studies have long lacked critical commentary on Divine's theology. This vacuum is well toward being filled by Kenneth E. Burnham's *God Comes to America*, which makes extensive use of official transcripts of Divine's sermons and talks, and Ronald Moran White's master's thesis, ''New Thought Influences on Father Divine.''

There is no evidence that Divine ever wrote or published anything, including personal documents or letters. There are, however, transcriptions (most in the form of stenographic records) and, in some instances, tape recordings of the approximately 10,000 sermons, interviews, and office talks that Divine delivered. In addition there are copies of the many pieces of correspondence he dictated. Although none of these primary sources is available to the public, excerpts from them do appear and reappear in the official news organs of the Peace Mission movement, the most prominent of which are the *New York News* (1932–34), *Spoken Word* (1934–37) and the *New Day* (1936–    ). These and other newspapers, along with many published excerpts of Divine's word, can be consulted at the movement's archives in its headquarters in Gladwyne, Pennsylvania. Also the New York Public Library's Schomberg Collection contains complete runs of the movement's two major newspapers and a large file of clippings from other publications. The only published primary account of the movement is the second Mother Divine's *Peace Mission Movement*, published in 1982.

## Bibliography

### Studies about Major J. (Father) Divine

Braden, Charles Samuel. *These Also Believe: A Study of Modern American Cults and Minority Religious Movements*. New York: Macmillan, 1949.
Burnham, Kenneth E. *God Comes to America: Father Divine and the Peace Mission Movement*. Boston: Lambeth Press, 1979.
Divine, Mrs. M. J. *The Peace Mission Movement: Founded by Reverend M. J. Divine, Better Known as Father Divine*. Philadelphia: Imperial Press, 1982.
Fauset, Arthur Huff. *Black Gods of the Metropolis: Negro Religious Cults of the Urban North*. 1944. Reprint. Philadelphia: University of Pennsylvania Press, 1971.

Harris, Sara [Drucker]. *Father Divine: Holy Husband*. Garden City, N.Y.: Doubleday
    and Company, 1953. Revised and expanded as *Father Divine*. New York: Collier
    Books, 1971.
Hoshor, John. *God in a Rolls-Royce: The Rise of Father Divine: Madman, Menace, or
    Messiah?* New York: Hillman-Curl, 1936.
Jones, Raymond Julius. *A Comparative Study of Religious Cult Behavior Among Negroes
    with Special Reference to Emotional Group Conditioning Factors*. Howard Uni-
    versity Studies in the Social Sciences, vol. 2, no. 2. Washington: Graduate School
    for the Division of the Social Sciences, Howard University, 1939.
Kephart, William M. *Extraordinary Groups: The Sociology of Unconventional Lifestyles*.
    New York: St. Martin's Press, 1976.
McKay, Claude. *Harlem: Negro Metropolis*. New York: E. P. Dutton, 1940.
McKelway, St. Clair, and A. J. Liebling. "Who Is This King of Glory?" *New Yorker*
    (13 June 1936): 21–28; (20 June 1936): 22–28; (27 June 1936): 22–37. Reprinted
    in *True Tales From the Annals of Crime and Rascality*, edited by St. Clair
    McKelway, 147–97. New York: Random House, 1950.
Ottley, Roi. *'New World A-Coming': Inside Black America*. Boston: Houghton Mifflin,
    1943.
Parker, Robert Allerton. *Incredible Messiah: The Deification of Father Divine*. Boston:
    Little, Brown and Co., 1937.
Washington, Joseph R., Jr. *Black Sects and Cults: The Power Axis in an Ethnic Ethic*.
    New York: Doubleday, 1973.
Weisbrot, Robert. *Father Divine and the Struggle for Racial Equality*. Urbana: University
    of Illinois Press, 1983.
White, Ronald Moran. "New Thought Influences on Father Divine." Master's thesis,
    Miami University, 1980.

MICHAEL HARRIS

# Lloyd Cassel Douglas

Every year at Holy Week, television viewers have the opportunity to watch an
array of Hollywood-produced religious spectacles. *The Robe,* starring Richard
Burton, Victor Mature, and Jean Simmons, has long been a staple of the lineup.
Based on the novel of the same name by Lloyd C. Douglas, the film launched
Burton's American acting career and introduced cinemascope film technology.
More important, it continues to disseminate the influence of Lloyd C. Douglas
on popular religiosity. Douglas was the largest-selling author of popular religious
fiction during the 1930s and 1940s, and his career reflects many of the changes
that U.S. Protestantism underwent during the first half of the twentieth century.

## Biography

Lloyd Cassel Douglas was born in Columbia City, Indiana, on 27 August
1877. His parents, Alexander Jackson and Sarah Douglas, dedicated the infant
Douglas to the ministry and, by all accounts, directed his childhood and adolescence. His father, a lawyer, felt a call to the ministry and spent his life as

part-time pastor of several small Lutheran churches in northern Indiana. Both father and mother loved fiction and introduced Douglas to the classics of English literature. Douglas studied at the theologically conservative Wittenburg College and Hamma Divinity School from 1894 to 1903. In the latter year he entered the parochial ministry, pastoring Lutheran churches in North Manchester (1903–5) and Lancaster (1905–9), Indiana, and the prestigious Luther Place Memorial Church in Washington, D.C. (1909–11).

Although Douglas' training at Wittenburg had emphasized orthodox Protestant theology, he was not interested in doctrine and especially not in doctrinal disputes. Rather, he wanted practicality. In his pastorates, he preached heroic sacrifice, muscular Christianity, and the power of Christian idealism to transform both the individual and society. This practical faith had to be scientific, so Douglas looked for science and pseudoscience (especially psychic healing and mind power) to work wonders. He declared that twentieth-century Christians could open more eyes of the blind in a hospital in one day than Jesus opened during all the years of his ministry. Jesus turned water into wine, but his followers could turn coal and iron into steel.

For Douglas, progress and practical idealism had a distinctively Progressive and business slant. He was always a joiner of chambers of commerce and Rotary Clubs and liked to speak to businessmen's organizations. He also organized men's Bible classes that appealed to businessmen and that brought in Russell Conwell* and other such speakers.

It was his community leadership in Lancaster, Indiana, and his growing reputation as a speaker that brought him to the pastorship of the Luther Place Memorial Church in Washington, D.C., at the young age of thirty-two years. The congregation was split between conservatives and progressives and between an older and younger generation, and Douglas' role was to be a unifier. Hence he limited his preaching to the value of vaguely defined goodwill. At the same time, he began to doubt the ability of conservative Lutheranism to adjust itself to the scientific and progressive temper of the times. Then, late in 1910, he attended a series of lectures by Shailer Matthews, professor of historical and comparative theology at the University of Chicago and a leading modernist. The following year, Douglas was offered the job of director of religious work for the YMCA at the University of Illinois. Douglas used the opportunity to resign his pastorate and his connection with Lutheranism; he became a Congregationalist minister.

Douglas' role as an active Congregationalist minister lasted from 1911 to 1933. After the Urbana YMCA (1911–14), he was pastor of Congregationalist churches in Ann Arbor, Michigan (1914–21), Akron, Ohio (1921–26), and Los Angeles, California (1926–28), and of St. James' United Church, Montreal, P.Q., Canada (1929–33). During this period as an active Congregationalist minister, he elaborated his earlier practical Christianity and began to write. At Illinois and Ann Arbor, Douglas continued to emphasize Christian belief as the source of psychological power and change, talking about "the Christ power" and "the Christ

spirit" and avoiding the miracles. He was a charter member of the Ann Arbor
Rotary Club.

Douglas embraced the First World War as an altruistic endeavor and was
prominent in Ann Arbor's many prowar rallies. He encouraged total dedication
to the war effort, for he believed that the war would release "psychic powers"
that would reconstruct the social order, cleanse U.S. politics, and assimilate
foreigners. In 1920, he was asked to head the publicity department of the Congregationalist World Movement, a denominational subsidiary of the Interchurch
World Movement. The IWM was a combined effort of about thirty U.S. denominations, designed to coordinate their budgets and fund-raising. It was proposed to raise $3.5 billion in five years, to bring together all Protestant activities
in the United States, and to complete the task of Christianizing the world. The
campaign used the ballyhoo of 1920s advertising—the fund to be collected was
known as the "Jackpot"—and Douglas enthusiastically supported it. The campaign, however, was a miserable failure. The "Jackpot" was not reached, despite
extending the deadline, the Baptists and Presbyterians withdrew, and the IWM
abandoned the campaign.

The collapse of the "Jackpot" campaign and the failure of the war to transform
society dealt sharp blows to Douglas' idealism. He accepted a call to the First
Congregational Church of Akron, Ohio. In part, he was stale; in part, he wanted
to get away from University of Michigan intellectuals and to meet practical
businessmen. His wartime Germanophobia, moreover, had alienated Ann Arbor's large German community. In Akron, Douglas emphasized ritual, arguing
that the church existed primarily for worship. Although continuing his practice
of joining community groups, he avoided campaigns and social activism. By
1926, however, he tired of Akron, of Shriners, of church administration, of teas
with ladies' guilds. As Virginia Douglas Dawson and Betty Douglas Wilson
reported in their biography of their father, Douglas also was going through
something of a midlife crisis: "I had always thought of myself as the Boy
Wonder. . . . I began to realize I was no longer a boy and not much of a wonder."
He secured a call to the First Congregational Church of Los Angeles. But he
found that the congregation was full of conservative Midwestern retirees who
disliked his blend of moderate modernism and the power of positive thinking.
Few of his flock, moreover, were community leaders. Unable to fill the role of
civic spokesman as he had in Ann Arbor and in Akron, Douglas turned to the
writing of fiction. Relations with his congregation soon soured, and he resigned
in the autumn of 1928.

After a few months of anxiety over his future, Douglas received a call from
St. James' United Church, Montreal, early in 1929. His pastorate there was
uneventful, and tired of the parochial ministry, he resigned in 1933. By then a
best-selling novelist, Douglas believed that he could bring the Christian message
to more people by writing than by preaching. Although remaining a clergyman,
he never again served a parish.

## Appraisal

Douglas' enduring impact on American popular religion is through his books and through the films made from them. His first novel, *More Than a Prophet* (1905), about John the Baptist and Jesus, "was less than a profit," in his words. Chastened by this failure, he confined himself to writing for Lutheran, Congregationalist, and Unity journals and for the *Christian Century*.

His second foray into book-length writing was *Wanted: A Congregation* (1920), which emerged from the collapse of the IWM "Jackpot" campaign. It originated as a response to an article in the *Christian Century* by the Socialist author John Spargo. (Spargo had argued that all the preaching in the United States did not improve Americans' well-being as much as the work of one farmer or one schoolmaster.) Douglas admitted that the church was failing to retain the loyalty of youth and to direct the life of the community, but he claimed that the cause was that preachers were "poor psychologists." Douglas explained that preachers could regain "pulpit power" through advertising, imaginative promotion, and an appealing religious message. In his view, the seminaries needed to train clergy in "pulpit power" by focusing on journalism, psychology, and marketing, rather than on useless academic courses such as the study of the Apocrypha.

A series of articles for the *Christian Century* appeared in book form in 1924 as *The Minister's Everyday Life,* a practical guide for young Protestant ministers. Douglas then turned to writing theology for a popular audience. *These Sayings of Mine* (1926) was an up-to-date interpretation of Jesus' ethical teachings. Attempting to strike a balance between fundamentalism and modernism, Douglas concentrated on showing how the sayings had practical value for businessmen. *Those Disturbing Miracles* (1927) continued Douglas' Modernist drift. Douglas believed that the proof of Christianity lay in the practical value of Jesus' teachings as they affected individual lives, not in the literal truth of the miracles (which he explained by naturalistic reasons). If Jesus is to be the exemplar for humans, Douglas argued, then he has to live under human conditions. However, the virgin birth, miracles, resurrection, and atonement separate Jesus from humans rather than make him an example. In Douglas' view, the true importance of Jesus was that he was in touch with the divine spirit and that he showed that humans could be too.

Although these books were well received in the pages of the *Christian Century* and made something of a name for Douglas (helping him to secure the position in Montreal, for instance), they did not sell—*Those Disturbing Miracles* sold fewer than a thousand copies. After much thought, Douglas decided that he had to return to the novel form to communicate his ideas.

Douglas had long been thinking of an incident reported in a Detroit newspaper, in which a physician died because the oxygen machine that he needed was in use to save another man's life. Using this episode as the plot, Douglas wrote *Magnificent Obsession* (1929) to show how the power of Jesus' teachings was available to all, how that power could regenerate both individual lives and society, and how Christianity had both mystery and scientific authority about it. Douglas placed the novel with the Chicago religious publishing house of Willett, Clark and Colby, after Harper Brothers, the publishers of his popular theology, had rejected it. The novel was published on 22 October 1929, in the midst of the stock market crash. Despite the inauspicious timing, it had slow but steady sales of about 400 copies per month through 1930. Then it took off, requiring eight new printings in 1931. By December 1932, it was selling 6,000 copies a month. Douglas had created a best seller.

Douglas followed quickly with *Forgive Us Our Trespasses* (1932), which Houghton Mifflin asked to publish. This too was a best seller. Its theme was that Christian forgiveness would free individuals from frustration, bitterness, hatred, and regret, thereby allowing one to attain personality transformation, personal power, and success. Both *Magnificent Obsession* and *Forgive Us Our Trespasses* offered readers the mind power and paths to success of the 1920s, without embracing the decade's cynicism and materialism. After publication of *Forgive Us Our Trespasses,* Douglas resigned his pastorate at Montreal and focused completely on his fiction.

His next two novels, *Green Light* (1935) and *White Banners* (1936), emphasized "personal peace" and adequacy in the face of the Great Depression. Their inspirational theme was that one need not worry about external problems. By following the teachings of Jesus, one could transform inner life; as one's inner life was transformed, the world also would be transformed. For good always triumphs over evil, and one can claim the power of good by attuning one's mind to positive thinking. Douglas now had two more top-selling novels.

There were cinematic possibilities in Douglas' works. The film rights to *Magnificent Obsession, Forgive Us Our Trespasses,* and *Green Light* brought in considerable money; *Magnificent Obsession* was filmed in 1935 with Robert Taylor and Irene Dunne and was remade in 1954 with Rock Hudson and Jane Wyman. Douglas thought about working in Hollywood, but he did not like the atmosphere of "this hectic, unscrupulous, kike-ridden" town, where he would have "to jump through the hoop for a lot of swarthy Israelites." But in 1936 he moved from Wellesley, Massachusetts, to the Bel Air district of Beverly Hills, for the climate and for the lifestyle.

Douglas needed to write best sellers more than ever, and he was well aware of his readers' tastes—he pushed advertisements for *Green Light* in the *Christian Century* and in the *Rotarian,* which catered to his two main audiences, liberal Protestants and businessmen. So his following novels—*Disputed Passage* (1939), *Doctor Hudson's Secret Journal* (1939), and *Invitation to Live* (1940)—stressed style, action, and sex rather more than the message.

World War II proved to be another turning point in Douglas' message, and the atmosphere of Hollywood provided the lens through which he projected it. In his novels, *The Robe* (1942) and the *The Big Fisherman* (1948), he helped his readers to face a war-torn world, in which the triumph of good was not necessarily guaranteed, by offering an unquestioning faith in a God beyond scientific examination and in a kingdom not of this world. Christianity was still presented as optimistic, but its function was to provide a spiritual anchor in a world at war rather than to offer individual self-realization. In these books, the miraculous plays a central role, and the Christian message is one of personal, internal peace.

Douglas' research for the *The Robe* consisted of reading Edward Gibbon's *The History of the Decline and Fall of the Roman Empire* and the novels *Ben Hur, Quo Vadis,* and *The Last Days of Pompeii;* it is thus perhaps not surprising that independent producer Frank Ross snapped up the film rights for $100,000, even before the book was completed. *The Robe* marked the height of Douglas' popularity and was his best-selling novel; the sales campaign for the book and the ballyhoo over preparation for its filming fed on each other. From the beginning, then, *The Robe* was destined for the silver screen. Although Douglas had dabbled in scriptwriting, working briefly on *Going My Way* and on *The Rosary,* his role in turning *The Robe* into a screen epic was that of carping. Douglas referred to producer Frank Ross as "this kike," and he believed that there were altogether "too many jews [*sic*]" involved in the film.

By 1948, when his last novel, *The Big Fisherman,* appeared, Douglas was in bad health. Perhaps for that reason, the book was pessimistic. Its theme was that the world was not ready for Jesus because conflicts between nations would continue despite the Christian message. In such a world, people should seek internal peace by means of a childlike faith in Jesus and his miracles.

Douglas died on 13 February 1951, in Los Angeles. He had married, in 1904, the former Besse Io Porch, who preceded him in death, and he was survived by two daughters.

### Survey of Criticism

Little has been written on Lloyd C. Douglas' novels or on the films made from them: most literary and cinematic critics are interested in high culture, not middebrow culture. Douglas' name cannot be found in most studies of the twentieth-century novel, the historical novel, the religious novel, or the filmed novel. Edwin M. Moseley, in his *Pseudonyms of Christ in the Modern Novel,* states explicitly that he deals only with "sincere books which enrich contemporary themes," not with "the flood of novels which attempt to recreate a facet of the Scriptures for better or for worse, such as . . . *The Robe*." Lion Feuchtwanger, in his *House of Desdemona,* dismisses *The Robe* as "a banal and sentimental though instructive story." F. W. Dillistone devotes a paragraph of *The Novelist and the Passion Story* to *The Robe*. Writing from the theological rather than the literary perspective, Dillistone acknowledges the popular appeal of both book and film but faults Douglas' focus on the magical relic and suggests that the novelist conveys an encounter with the first-century world rather than with the living Christ.

Virginia Douglas Dawson and Betty Douglas Wilson produced a filiopietistic study of their father's domestic life, *The Shape of Sunday*. Douglas' own posthumously published autobiography, *Time to Remember,* is relatively unrevealing.

Scholarly studies relevant to Douglas' career are few and mostly unpublished. For background, Edward Barkowsky's "The Popular Christian Novel in America, 1918–1953" is of some utility. It analyzes nineteen best-selling novels and seeks to show changes from the optimistic materialism of the 1930s to the conservative mysticism of the 1940s. Four studies focus on Douglas. Carl Bode's "Lloyd Douglas: Loud Voice in the Wilderness" suggests how Douglas' novels reflect the movement from liberalism to neo-orthodoxy. Richard Leon Stoppe's "Lloyd C. Douglas" is a rhetorical analysis of Douglas' preaching style. Mary Ann Russell's "Lloyd C. Douglas and His Larger Congregation" compares the novels of the 1930s with those of the 1940s.

The most comprehensive scholarly study is Raymond Arthur Detter's "Ministry to Millions." Based on all of Douglas' published works and on his private papers in the Michigan Historical Collections (Bentley Historical Library, University of Michigan, Ann Arbor), Detter's 975-page thesis is an exhaustive study that clearly analyzes its subject's career and fixes it in the context of the times.

Finally, there are the reviews of Douglas' novels and of the films made from them. These provide rich evidence to show how Douglas purveyed a mix of piety, action, sex, and (in the case of the films' cinemascope and stereophonic sound) technological discourse and how what New York- or London-based critics saw as loud vulgarity represented a moving and uplifting religious experience for ordinary people.

## Bibliography

### Books by Lloyd C. Douglas

1905  *More Than A Prophet*. Chicago: W. B. Conkey Company.
1920  *Wanted: A Congregation*. Chicago: Christian Century Press.
1924  *The Minister's Everyday Life*. New York: Charles Scribner's Sons.
1926  *These Sayings of Mine: An Interpretation of the Teachings of Jesus*. New York: Charles Scribner's Sons.
1927  *Those Disturbing Miracles*. New York: Harper and Bros.
1929  *Magnificent Obsession*. Chicago: Willett, Clark and Colby.
1932  *Forgive Us Our Trespasses*. Boston: Houghton Mifflin Company.
1933  *Precious Jeopardy*. Boston: Houghton Mifflin Company.
1935  *Green Light*. Boston: Houghton Mifflin Company.
1936  *White Banners*. Boston: Houghton Mifflin Company.
1937  *Home For Christmas*. Boston: Houghton Mifflin Company.
1939  *Disputed Passage*. Boston: Houghton Mifflin Company.
1939  *Doctor Hudson's Secret Journal*. Boston: Houghton Mifflin Company.
1940  *Invitation to Live*. Boston: Houghton Mifflin Company.
1942  *The Robe*. Boston: Houghton Mifflin Company.
1948  *The Big Fisherman*. Boston: Houghton Mifflin Company.
1951  *Time to Remember*. Boston: Houghton Mifflin Company.

### Selected Studies about Lloyd C. Douglas

Barkowsky, Edward Richard. "The Popular Christian Novel in America, 1918–1953." Ed.D. diss., Ball State University, 1975.

Bode, Carl. "Lloyd Douglas: Loud Voice in the Wilderness." *American Quarterly* 2 (1950): 340–58.

Dawson, Virginia Douglas, and Betty Douglas Wilson. *The Shape of Sunday: An Intimate Biography of Lloyd C. Douglas*. Boston: Houghton Mifflin Co., 1952.

Detter, Raymond Arthur. "A Ministry to Millions: Lloyd C. Douglas, 1877–1951." Ph.D. diss., University of Michigan, 1975.

Dillistone, F. W. *The Novelist and the Passion Story*. New York: Sheed and Ward, 1960.

Feuchtwanger, Lion. *The House of Desdemona; or, The Laurels and Limitations of Historical Fiction*. Detroit: Wayne State University Press, 1963.

Moseley, Edwin M. *The Pseudonyms of Christ in the Modern Novel: Motifs and Methods*. Pittsburgh: University of Pittsburgh Press, 1962.

Russell, Mary Ann Underwood. "Lloyd C. Douglas and His Larger Congregation: The Novels and a Reflection of Some Segments of the American Popular Mind of Two Decades." Ph.D. diss., George Peabody College for Teachers, 1970.

Stoppe, Richard Leon. "Lloyd C. Douglas." Ph.D. diss., Wayne State University, 1966.

D. G. PAZ

# John Foster Dulles

Why, one might ask, would a written portrait of John Foster Dulles be included in a book examining shapers of American popular religion? That he was a distinguished political figure is well known, but a religious figure? Incredible as it may seem, concentration on the religious dimensions of the former secretary of state's character may shed more light on his role as a significant figure in American history than a mere look at his political activities could ever hope to provide. Raised in a Presbyterian manse by parents dedicated to instilling a sincere religious sensibility in all their children, John Foster Dulles learned early to appreciate the importance of religious convictions. His life's story demonstrates he not only appreciated them but saw them as foundational for the living of his life. A brief look at that story will help to point out why Dulles may be counted as one of the most significant shapers of popular religion in America.

### Biography

Born in a city he would grow to love, John Foster Dulles entered the world without much attendant pomp and ceremony in the home of his maternal grandparents in Washington, D.C., on 25 February 1888. His father, the Reverend Allen Macy Dulles, could not even be present, as he was in the process of moving the family's belongings from Detroit, Michigan, where he had served for several years as pastor of the Trumball Avenue Church, to a parsonage in a small northern village known as Watertown in the state of New York. He had just accepted the call to serve as the new pastor of the First Presbyterian Church located amid the tranquil surroundings of that small town.

Three months after his birth, young Foster, as he was called by both family and friends, left Washington in the company of his mother to join his father in upstate New York. The next seventeen years were spent in the small-town atmosphere of Watertown. His minister father and committed Christian mother provided an intensely religious environment for Foster and his siblings, a brother and three sisters. The family ancestors, after all, included numerous ministers and several missionaries to various areas of the world. His paternal grandfather, John Wesley Dulles, dedicated his life to mission service, once traveling in an open boat for 132 days to carry the gospel to Madras.

Foster's father, a liberal Protestant minister, was greatly influenced by the theological trends of his day. Though he held what his day saw as an enlightened and literary-critical view of the Bible, the older Dulles still stressed the importance of a pious and educated commitment to its principles. Every morning around 7:30 A.M. the Dulles family gathered in the living room of the white clapboard parsonage for devotions, usually called to the assembly by the sound of Mrs. Dulles' piano playing or by the pastor's tenor voice lifted in song. Regular attendance at every church activity was not just encouraged but was expected in the Dulles household, including Monday evening youth services, Wednesday night prayer meetings, and preparatory services on Friday night whenever communion was to be served on the following Sunday.

All of this religious activity was not lost on young Foster. His mother, Esther Foster Dulles, in her personal diary, described the five-year-old Dulles as "reverential to a striking degree." Throughout his life, he devotedly read the Bible and consistently carried a small New Testament with him. At one point, as a teen, he memorized the entire Gospel of John. Even though Dulles must not be considered a theologian, the religious atmosphere of his upbringing contributed to his sincere belief that God worked in the world as a "force for good." As an adult, he often commented that the basic Christian principles he had learned at home had provided him with a sense of direction that significantly shaped his development as an individual.

Dulles entered Princeton University in the fall of 1904, at the tender age of sixteen. At first, he found the rigorous academic setting there somewhat disconcerting. Though he had read widely for his age, his problems in grammar and spelling showed up early. Dulles worked hard to compensate for his age and the deficiencies of his preparation. As a philosophy major, he experienced great success. As a junior, he was awarded the Dickinson Prize for an essay in logic. As a graduate, he earned the highest honors bestowed by the Philosophy Department. His senior thesis brought him the Chancellor Green Mental Science Fellowship, accompanied by a year of study at the Sorbonne. Even though he graduated second in his class, the school named him valedictorian at his graduation.

In the spring of 1907, Dulles' junior year was interrupted by an incident that proved highly influential in his ultimate decision to become a lawyer. His maternal grandfather, John W. Foster, former secretary of state to President Benjamin Harrison, invited the nineteen-year-old Dulles to accompany him to the Second Hague Peace Conference. Foster had been chosen by the Chinese government to serve in its behalf as a delegate to the conference. Dulles became a secretary to the Chinese delegation, a pretty heady experience for such a young man, one that made an immense impression on him as he struggled with the question of choosing a vocation. His parents, throughout his college years, assumed he was heading toward a future in the ministry. Foster himself talked about the possibility. After the Hague conference, however, he made it clear that he had made up his mind to become an international lawyer.

The fall following his year of work at the Sorbonne, where he studied briefly with the eminent philosopher Henri Bergson, Dulles entered George Washington University Law School in Washington. He completed the program in two years and took the New York State bar exam in 1911. His marriage to Janet Avery followed shortly thereafter. Taking a job as a law clerk with the prestigious Wall Street law firm of Sullivan and Cromwell, Dulles quickly worked his way up. By the time he was thirty-two, the firm had made him a full partner. Seven years later, he became the head of the firm.

Even though his job led to heavy responsibilities relating to international law and diplomatic affairs, including an appointment at Versailles after World War I, Dulles did not neglect his relationship to the church. He served as an elder in the Park Avenue Presbyterian Church and later in the Brick Presbyterian Church after the two churches merged into one. Occasionally, he even filled the pulpit, an activity that seemed to please him very much.

Dulles' presence in the church was not limited to his service as an elder in the local congregation. Throughout the early 1920s he worked as an official member of the Presbyterian General Assembly. Perhaps one of the most significant early religious activities of Dulles came through his contribution to the liberal side of the famous fundamentalist-modernist controversy as it affected the Presbyterian Church. Representing the New York Presbytery, he argued Harry Emerson Fosdick's* case before the 1924 Presbyterian General Assembly. This brought him into direct confrontation with William Jennings Bryan*.

Dulles again represented the New York Presbytery in the aftermath of the controversy surrounding the ordination of Henry Pitney Van Dusen, who later served as president of Union Theological Seminary in New York. The presbytery had ordained Van Dusen in spite of the fact he had denied the virgin birth. At issue was the right of local presbyteries to decide what candidates met ordination requirements without interference from higher church judicatories. Dulles' legal brief, presented to the Synod of New York in 1926, convinced the authorities of the Presbyterian church that the process of ordination should remain the same. In its final report, the judicial committee borrowed liberally from that brief. Henry Sloane Coffin and other influential pastors in the church praised Dulles for the "masterly way" he had presented the case before the synod.

Dulles served in ecumenical church circles as well. Accepting an invitation in 1921 from Robert E. Speer, president of the Federal Council of Churches (FCC), Dulles began a term of membership on the newly formed Federal Council

Commission on International Justice and Goodwill. His association with the FCC continued until 1946, and his service assumed a variety of forms.

Impressed by his work with the FCC, several influential religious leaders secured Dulles the opportunity to deliver a major address at the 1937 Oxford Ecumenical Church Conference. Entitled "The Problem of Peace in a Dynamic World," Dulles' address asserted his belief that Christianity could help to overcome the pride and selfishness of nations in the world by helping to create an international ethos based on its universal vision. Dulles' experience at Oxford served to remind him of the importance of trying to transform his own inherited spiritual values into practical contributions in the political sphere.

Throughout the next couple of years, he participated in numerous ecumenical conferences dealing with issues of religion and international affairs. When World War II started, Dulles, at the request of the FCC, drafted a document that succeeded in uniting church leaders at a time when divisive issues were driving them apart. Pacifists and just-war advocates both were able to affirm his unity statement, as it urged Christians to rise above the hatreds of war in order to maintain a relationship with one another on a worldwide basis. Chief among the thoughts presented was the plea that Christians recognize the need for repentance, humility, avoidance of hatred and hypocrisy, and the spiritual supremacy of God rather than the state.

In 1941 the leadership in the FCC asked Dulles to chair a newly formed commission, the Commission on a Just and Durable Peace (CJDP). His work as the chair of this commission enabled him to have enormous influence in the work of the church during the trying years of World War II. Under his leadership, the commission dedicated itself to implementing the liberal Christian version of world order, one that reminded nations of their finite status and condemned the pride and self-righteousness of human institutions.

The commission's membership included such notable church leaders as John R. Mott*, Reinhold Niebuhr, John C. Bennett, William E. Hocking, Charles Clayton Morrison, and Harry Emerson Fosdick. Nearly every one of the countless documents produced by the commission over the years originated on Dulles' yellow legal pad. The most widely distributed of the Dulles commission documents was entitled "The Six Pillars of Peace." The document called for the establishment of political mechanisms after the war that would help ensure cooperative action between the nations of the world. Widely distributed, the seventy-page study guide even reached China. Several prestigious figures in government, including Sumner Welles, Thomas Dewey, and Senator Joseph Ball, heartily endorsed the "Six Pillars." President Franklin D. Roosevelt also found the document impressive and called Dulles into the Oval Office to discuss it.

In addition to these written documents, the commission also sponsored three major study conferences on particular aspects of the postwar world. The last of these conferences occurred when Secretary of State Edward Stettinius, fellow Presbyterian and friend to Dulles, officially requested that the CJDP address the recent Dumbarton Oaks proposals on world order. These proposals emerged from a meeting at Dumbarton Oaks between American, British, and Chinese representatives and contained a tentative charter for a permanent international organization, to be called the United Nations.

The church conference called by the CJDP to deal with the Dumbarton Oaks proposals met in Cleveland, 16–19 January 1945. Four hundred eighty-one delegates representing thirty-four communions, eighteen religious bodies, and seventy city and state councils of churches attended the meeting. Dulles, chair of the conference, opened with an address entitled "America's Role in the Peace." The address, and Dulles' leadership at the conference, helped to steer the thought of the Protestant church leaders in a more realistic direction on the question of world order. The main question under consideration centered on how the churches could properly maintain the tension between what Christian principles require and what can actually be achieved in the realm of national policy without making the former concern irrelevant to the latter result.

The final "Message" of the conference stated that the Dumbarton Oaks proposals were not good enough to satisfy the churches completely but that they were good enough to serve as "an important step in the direction of world cooperation." The Cleveland Conference provides important evidence that the "Dulles Commission" effectively led the churches toward a responsible position on the subject of a future world order. President Harry Truman expressed his appreciation for this work in a letter to Dulles penned in the fall of 1945: "If today we Americans have a clearer understanding of our place in the world community—and I believe we have—it is due, in no small part, to the church's advanced position in international thinking taken by the Federal Council."

Dulles' contribution to the life of the church during these years should not be underestimated. He proved—through his administrative capabilities, his dedication to the task, and his incredible breadth of knowledge concerning international affairs—that the FCC had chosen the proper person to lead the Protestant churches to a clear and responsible position as they encountered the very difficult issues raised by World War II. There is little doubt that his diligent work for the FCC gained him a significant reputation as an international analyst and helped to make him a prime candidate for a position of leadership in the secular arena.

Thomas Dewey, governor of New York and presidential candidate in 1944 and 1948, chose Dulles as his primary foreign affairs consultant and, in all likelihood, would have named him his secretary of state had the close election of 1948 gone the other way. Dulles interrupted his work with the FCC in 1945 to work as a legal adviser to the American delegation to the United Nations Organization Conference in San Francisco. Throughout the Truman years, Dulles worked as a Republican adviser to the State Department on questions of foreign policy. For four months in 1949, he served as a member of the U.S. Senate, fulfilling the remainder of retired Senator Robert Wagner's term. In 1950–51, Truman charged Dulles with the task of negotiating the Japanese Peace Treaty.

Two years later, Dwight Eisenhower named Dulles to his cabinet as the new secretary of state, a post Dulles held until his death in 1959.

### Appraisal

Though Dulles' popular influence as a religious leader during the years he chaired the FCC Commission is unquestioned, his most significant popular religious influence may lie in yet another area. As World War II ended, most interpreters and leaders believed that the worst was over. The 1930s and, particularly, the 1940s had been difficult decades indeed. Those years seemed almost to demand a compromising spirit so that people of entirely different cultural backgrounds and political ideologies could band together to defeat the obvious evil of Fascism.

After 1945, the tension in international affairs became, if possible, even more intense. The actions of the Soviet Union were frightening. Nearly all Americans were shocked by the seemingly endless atrocities committed in Eastern Europe. Few political leaders in the West were capable of assessing the events dispassionately. Freedom was being trampled. Dulles, as he witnessed these events, reported them accurately to his friends in religious circles and to the public at large.

As the Cold War began to reach alarming proportions and as anxieties increased, the American people sought answers to the practical questions raised by Soviet behavior. Dulles also sought these answers and began an intense study of Soviet philosophy. Immersing himself in the writings of Stalin, Dulles began to unravel what he thought might provide the key to understanding Soviet actions. Ultimately, he placed the blame on the antireligious, clearly materialistic, nature of the Soviet Union. The more he studied this particular dimension of Soviet ideology, the more he became convinced that the Soviets were bent on the destruction of all religious expression. Since, for Dulles, commitment to the moral law was a religious commitment, he came to view Soviet attacks on religion as direct attacks levied against the moral law. Conversely, since the United States defended religious expression and religious freedom, he came to see American policy as a defense of the moral law.

For Dulles, in the face of the very real crises of post-1945, America assumed the role of God's redemptive agent in the world. He developed a renewed appreciation for the religious heritage of the American republic—a heritage that seemed, for many, to have resulted from the permeation of Christian principles into the democratic institutions of American government. Since Dulles viewed the American heritage in this way, he saw no contradiction in his newly developed identification between the moral law and American policies.

In an important way, the Cold War acted as a revelatory event for America. Dulles' reaction to it exemplifies its impact. He saw in its development a new incarnation of the will of God for the world. It revealed God's purposes for the nation and provided the nation with a clear mission to fulfill in much the same way as the American Revolution had. As Dulles interpreted this revelatory event, it also led him to call for American rededication to the task of fulfilling this mission from God. Soviet behavior convinced Dulles of the need to call America to a spiritual revival, a return to faith in God and in democratic institutions as instruments of God's will.

Thus, Dulles committed his activities during the late 1940s to fostering this revival of America's spiritual life. That revival came about in the so-called revival of religion during the 1950s. During the years immediately prior to his term as secretary of state, the success of the revival depended as much on John Foster Dulles' activities as it did on the activities of Billy Graham*, perhaps even more so. Dulles spoke in Protestant churches and at important civic, community, and national functions across the nation, week in and week out, calling for a "spiritual revival" that would serve to "heal the sores of the body politic." As sociologists have testified, the revival that emerged left Americans with a self-righteous confidence that God would bless their every move. The moralistic tendency to equate American activity with the will of God became a trademark of the 1950s.

Religious leaders who had worked with Dulles in the FCC, leaders like Reinhold Niebuhr and John Bennett, were very critical of the fact that Dulles adopted what seemed to them to be an all too easy division of the world into good nations and bad nations. Most Americans, on the other hand, welcomed the new Dulles' confident assurances that God stood behind America in a Cold War that seemed to have no end in sight. Indeed, Dulles' moralistic rhetoric revealed the true nature of the man behind it: a determined Calvinist who was transformed as the anxiety of events after the war led him to translate his tradition's long-held belief in the reality of a moral universe into a belief in the moral virtue of his own nation. As a result, Dulles unfortunately bequeathed to the country a "religious" legacy that is still powerfully operative in the diplomacy of our present day.

### Survey of Criticism

As one might expect, most of the literature written about John Foster Dulles concerns his activities as an international lawyer and government servant. Of the many books written about him in these areas, two works deserve comment. Townsend Hoopes' 1973 critical study of the secretary of state years, *The Devil and John Foster Dulles,* claims that Dulles' contribution to intensifying the Cold War emerged as the natural culmination of a lifelong, consistently self-righteous, character pattern. Of the 505 pages of Hoopes' book, only about 5 pages are devoted to Dulles' religious activities. In those 5 pages, Hoopes interprets the earlier years of Dulles' activity with the churches through the lens of his later activities as secretary of state. As a result, the integrity of Dulles' earlier contributions to the life of the church is not fully appreciated. In this particular approach, Hoopes depends on the interpretation offered a few years earlier by John M. Mulder, current president of Louisville Presbyterian Seminary, in an article entitled "The Moral World of John Foster Dulles." Mulder took his title from a one-page critical essay Reinhold Niebuhr had written for the *New Republic* in 1958.

Ronald Pruessen's *John Foster Dulles: The Road to Power* appeared in 1982. It offers a complete critical and scholarly evaluation of Dulles' early life. A welcome and exceedingly significant contribution to the Dulles literature, it is the first to reveal, even partially, the philosophical flexibility of Dulles' early years. The book's thesis seeks to assert that "economic preoccupations were often a dominant and initiating force in his [Dulles'] world view and thought." Written by a diplomatic historian, the book falters when it discusses Dulles' involvement in religious circles. It underestimates both the realistic trend of Protestant thought concerning international issues at the time and Dulles' sincere participation therein.

Only two book-length studies actually concentrate on Dulles' activities in religious circles. Albert Keim, in his 1971 Ohio State Ph.D. dissertation, "John Foster Dulles and the Federal Council of Churches, 1937–1949," argues that Dulles' work in the churches was "strategic rather than substantive." In his view, Dulles' ideas were not as important to the churches as were his "contacts and access to decision makers." Mark G. Toulouse's 1985 book, *The Transformation of John Foster Dulles: From Prophet of Realism to Priest of Nationalism,* takes issue with Keim on precisely this point. It argues that Dulles made his greatest contribution not through his contacts with influential people but precisely through his shaping of ideas. The book further argues that the prophetic and realistic thought characterizing the work of Dulles in the early 1940s gave way, after the Cold War began, to an overly simplistic worldview that tended to see America as God's divine agent in the world.

## Bibliography

### Selected Works by John Foster Dulles

1938    "As Seen by a Layman." *Religion in Life* 7:36–44.
1939    *War, Peace and Change*. New York: Harper and Brothers.
1940    "Churches' Contribution toward a Warless World." *Religion in Life* 9:31–40.
1942    "The American People Need Now to Be Imbued with a Righteous Faith." In *A Righteous Faith for a Just and Durable Peace,* edited by John Foster Dulles. New York: Commission to Study the Bases of a Just and Durable Peace.
1942    "A Righteous Faith." *Life* 13:49–51.
1944    "The Churches and a Just and Durable Peace." *Biennial Report of the Federal Council of Churches of Christ in America,* 22–29.
1948    "Moral Force in World Affairs." *Presbyterian Life,* 13ff.
1950    *War or Peace*. New York: Macmillan Company.
1952    "A Diplomat and His Faith." *Christian Century* 69:336–38.
1960    *The Spiritual Legacy of John Foster Dulles*. Edited by Henry P. Van Dusen. Philadelphia: Westminster Press.

### Selected Studies about John Foster Dulles

Berding, Andrew H. T. *Dulles on Diplomacy*. Princeton: Van Nostrand, 1965.
Comfort, Mildred H. *John Foster Dulles, Peacemaker*. Minneapolis: T. S. Denison, 1960.

Dulles, Eleanor Lansing. *John Foster Dulles: The Last Year*. New York: Harcourt, Brace and World, 1963.

Goold-Adams, Richard John Morton. *The Time of Power: A Reappraisal of John Foster Dulles*. New York: Appleton-Century-Crofts, 1962.

Guhin, Michael A. *John Foster Dulles: A Statesman and His Times*. New York: Columbia University Press, 1972.

Hoopes, Townsend. *The Devil and John Foster Dulles*. Boston: Little, Brown and Company, 1973.

Keim, Albert. "John Foster Dulles and the Federal Council of Churches, 1937–1949." Ph.D. diss., Ohio State University, 1971.

Mosley, Leonard. *Dulles: A Biography of Eleanor, Allen and John Foster Dulles and Their Family Network*. New York: Dial Press/James Wade, 1978.

Mulder, John M. "The Moral World of John Foster Dulles." *Journal of Presbyterian History* 49 (Summer 1971): 157–82.

Niebuhr, Reinhold. "The Moral World of John Foster Dulles." *New Republic* 139 (1 December 1958): 8.

Pruessen, Ronald W. *John Foster Dulles: The Road to Power*. New York: Free Press, 1982.

Toulouse, Mark G. *The Transformation of John Foster Dulles: From Prophet of Realism to Priest of Nationalism*. Macon, Ga.: Mercer University Press, 1985.

MARK G. TOULOUSE

# Jerry Falwell

Fundamentalist preacher and televangelist Jerry Falwell is the best-known and most widely publicized spokesperson for the "new Christian right." Falwell's creation, the Moral Majority, founded in 1979, and the Moral Majority's successor, the Liberty Federation, exemplify the broad populist reaction against the cultural and social changes of the 1960s, though neither organization claims to embrace that reaction in entirety. Speaking for those whom Falwell characterizes as "pro-life, pro-family, pro-moral and pro-American," the Moral Majority, especially, is credited with having politicized previously inactive fundamentalist and evangelical constituencies, enough to pose a significant presence in the 1980 presidential election, and with having "ecumenized" fundamentalism itself by seeking wider conservative alliances. The Christian right's actual impact on Ronald Reagan's victory is debatable, and its subsequent lobbying on behalf of "pro-family" legislation has not been notably successful. Yet the interests Jerry Falwell articulates not only tap into a deep American cultural tradition but also represent a formidable political potential.

### Biography

Jerry Falwell was born in Lynchburg, Virginia, on 11 August 1933. His father, Carey, was a self-made businessman who dropped out of school in the sixth grade and abandoned his own father's occupation of dairy farmer. Through dint of effort, the elder Falwell earned a comfortable income by managing an oil dealership, a service station, a dance hall, and a trucking company. Carey's wife, Helen, likewise came from a rural agricultural background. One of sixteen children born into a tobacco-farming family in Appomattox County, Virginia, she too dropped out of school at an early age. Despite their commonalities, however, Jerry's parents were divided as to the place of religion in the raising of their four children. Jerry's mother, whose own family held deep fundamentalist convictions, insisted on attending church regularly herself and also on encouraging the same from her reluctant children. The elder Falwell abstained, believing that church going was the duty of women. According to one account, Carey's growing drinking problem arose not only from a bitter dispute with his brother that resulted in the latter's violent death but also as a protest against Prohibition, strongly favored by his wife's family.

Jerry Falwell groped with the alternatives presented by his parents throughout his teenage years. A promising student and athlete whose ambition was to become an engineer, he nonetheless earned a reputation as a prankster. Despite his mother's best efforts, he ceased attending church with her. Yet on the other hand, his secular ambitions and his seeming rejection of religion left a void that would be filled only by his subsequent conversion at the age of eighteen and his decision to study for the ministry. Falwell's change of heart resulted partly from the subliminal appeal of Charles E. Fuller's* radio broadcast, "Old Fashioned Revival Hour," which his mother deliberately turned on to influence her children as she departed to church. Fuller's preaching created such an impression that Falwell searched around Lynchburg for a pastor like him, finally finding a close approximation in the Reverend Paul Donnelson of the fundamentalist Park Avenue Baptist Church. It was Donnelson who presided over his conversion, and it was the "Old Fashioned Revival Hour" that became the model for Falwell's "Old Time Gospel Hour." Yet equally important was the death of Jerry's father in 1948, the result of cirrhosis of the liver. The hard-driving, successful, self-reliant, and non-church-going businessman could not, as his son later understood it, realize his limits and turn to God for help with his problems. Though Falwell deeply admired his father's energy and capitalist values, those qualities lacked the sacred foundation that would bring about their fulfillment. The centrality of religious discourse and church life in the Lynchburg area provided the only complete explanation for life's high and low points.

After two years at Lynchburg College, Falwell transferred to the fundamentalist Bible Baptist College in Springfield, Missouri. At graduation, he toyed briefly with entering the ministry in Macon, Georgia, but decided to return to Lynchburg when approached by a small group of dissident parishioners from the Park Avenue Baptist Church. Dissatisfied with Donnelson's successor, they looked to Falwell to launch an alternative. The success story of the Thomas Road Baptist Church, which began in an abandoned plant of the Donald Duck Bottling Company, illustrates the consequence of charismatic preachers not only to the survival of fundamentalism but also to the very vitality of fundamentalism in the decades after its exile from the mainline denominations.

The membership of the Thomas Road Baptist Church in 1987, estimated at over 17,000, is composed predominantly of technicians, clerical workers, skilled and semiskilled factory workers, pensioners, and low-income people who reside in government-built housing projects. Though containing some black members, Thomas Road Church is mainly white. Falwell's church offers not only an extensive range of social services but also a kindergarten through college educational network consisting of Liberty Christian Academy and Liberty University. The latter has an enrollment of 7,000, including those signed up through extension courses, and a projected student population of 50,000 by the end of the century. Falwell hopes that Liberty University's fundamentalist students, trained in its undergraduate and graduate schools, will penetrate America's ruling elite. Thus, instead of criticizing the establishment from without, as fundamentalists have done in the past, this new generation will saturate it with their values from within. The proceeds from Falwell's nationally syndicated television program, "The Old Time Gospel Hour," which are rebroadcasts of Thomas Road services, are funneled back into Falwell's educational enterprises.

Notwithstanding Falwell's achievements as an evangelist, his entry into politics has generated the most national attention and controversy. In the mid-1960s, when numerous clergy joined antiwar protests, counseled draft evaders, and lobbied for civil rights, Falwell countered by stating that the churches should confine themselves to transforming individuals through the saving power of the Gospel instead of reforming institutions. His position characterized a movement whose history favored separation from "the world," in expectation of the apocalypse, rather than engagement. While fundamentalism forged its identity against the reformism of the Social Gospel clergy and the modernism of the dominant Protestant churches, its conservatism had remained latent and subordinate to personal regeneration. Falwell's subsequent repudiation of his statement as "false prophecy" ensued from his perception of an America that had fallen into a general crisis, manifestations of which included high divorce rates, the "uncloseting" of gays, agitation for the Equal Rights Amendment, the spread of pornography, public schools without prayer, military defeat in Vietnam, and especially, the Supreme Court decision permitting abortion, *Roe* v. *Wade*. Furthermore, these reflections of decay were being broadcast daily on the media into communities otherwise untouched by the changes surrounding them and were being at least tacitly encouraged by the mainline churches whose liberal priorities sat with Vietnam and civil rights. Although the language of premillennialism remained appropriate and the objects of criticism went unchanged, Falwell's strategy altered. The challenges the general crisis presented could no longer be met by unpolitical withdrawal. The formation of the Moral Majority came after Falwell's first appearance on the national stage as the organizer of a series of "I Love America" rallies to commemorate the Bicentennial.

The Moral Majority, which formed chapters and local affiliates in all fifty states, was to influence legislation at the local, state, and national levels, register conservative voters, support conservative political candidates, combat the American Civil Liberties Union through its Legal Defense Fund, and fight humanism through the courts. The money it raised from contributions financed an extensive media campaign that included replies to critics not only in major newspapers but also in its own newsletter, *Moral Majority Report*. Though its success was attributed to the publicity it received from Falwell's "Old Time Gospel Hour" and to its mass mail techniques, its growth came mostly from its linkage of conservative, mainly independent Baptist clergy into a common lobbying and voter registration drive. Though the Moral Majority's own estimates of its membership as close to four million were sharply disputed, even the most conservative rendering of 400,000 denoted significant mass appeal.

Since becoming a national figure, Jerry Falwell has modified the harshness of his earliest pronouncements, but his positions have remained essentially intact. As a premillennialist and dispensationalist, he asserts the global interconnectedness of America's domestic situation and international status. The spiritual health of the former affects the latter. The fall of the Roman Empire, he claims in *Listen America!*, ensued because "pleasure and hedonism became the rule of the day," and humanism reigned supreme. Similarly, America has approached the brink of disaster, the root cause of which is "the decay of our individual and national morals. This has resulted in the subsequent decadent state and and instability of everything else in America—including economics, politics, defense, etc. The choices we as Americans have made in moral and religious questions have determined the way America is going today." Moral decay leaves us open to invasion from without, especially from communism and its leading carrier, the Soviet Union, against which Falwell advocates a strenuous military buildup. "Communists know that in order to take over a country they must first see to it that a nation's military strength is weakened and that its morals are corrupted so that its people have no will to resist wrong. When people begin to accept perversion and immorality as ways of life, as is happening in the United States today, we must beware."

Although Falwell's speeches and writings draw from a wide spectrum of conservative opinion, the Bible is his primary source, the inerrant guide to personal morality and social structure. A return to the Bible will reaffirm America as the chosen land of God's designs in history, as the base of "world evangelization." Failure to do so, Falwell asserts prophetically, will bring about divine judgment. The Bible condemns homosexuality and pornography as sins, and abortion as murder, states that a strong military is imperative, forbids drug abuse and alcoholism, and demands education that teaches patriotism, prayer, and moral absolutes. Although both Falwell and the Moral Majority's platform deny disputing the civil rights of gays or the equal employment opportunities of women, Falwell decries the disintegration of clearly defined gender identities. He sees feminism as destructive of the family and urges the submission of women to the benevolent protection of their husbands. To accept homosexuality as an "alternative" but normal lifestyle countenances the conscious will to sin and contributes to the downfall of America.

Falwell believes a correlation exists between the breakdown of traditional morality and the erosion of respect for authority, be it that of the father in the family or that of the nation's leadership. Yet though he urges a return to that respect, he reflects a strong populist suspicion of governmental intrusion. Runaway government spending and taxation, he states, interfere with free enterprise, which is itself biblically mandated. However well-intentioned, efforts to stop child abuse interfere with the duty of the families to discipline their children. Welfare, although necessary for those who cannot care for themselves, undermines the work ethic and destroys individual initiative. In short, according to *Listen America!,* moral perversion and government intrusion have placed America at "the point of no return. There can be no doubt that the sin of America is severe. We are literally approaching the brink of national disaster. Many have exclaimed, 'If God does not judge America soon, He will have to apologize to Sodom and Gomorrah.' "

In 1986, Falwell created the "Liberty Federation" to replace the Moral Majority. Although still concerned with domestic moral issues, the new organization attends more closely to foreign policy and national defense than did its predecessor. Falwell's change of emphasis testifies to the limits of his moral crusade both in forming national policy and in affecting the outcome of the last presidential election. In recent years, in fact, Falwell has shown signs of losing his knack of delivering public statements appropriate to their probable reception. Claiming that the citizens of the Philippines enjoyed the privileges of freedom, he endorsed President Ferdinand Marcos just as the Philippine revolution threatened to overtake that dictatorship. Calling South Africa a bulwark against communism, he endorsed Pieter Botha's limited reforms and rejected economic sanctions while the South African government's piecemeal measures satisfied few blacks' demands for justice. Having designated South African Bishop Desmond Tutu a "phony" and unrepresentative of South African blacks, Falwell found himself awash in criticism. Finally, evangelist Pat Robertson's* presidential aspirations vied successfully with Falwell for media attention. Yet Falwell's assumption of the leadership of Jim and Tammy Bakker's* scandal-ridden and financially troubled evangelistic empire, PTL ("Praise the Lord" or "People that Love"), put him back in the spotlight. But amid the continuing controversy over the reorganization of PTL, Falwell resigned after a few months at its helm. Shortly thereafter he also withdraw from the leadership of the Liberty Federation, announcing his intent to abandon all political activity.

### Appraisal

Much of what Jerry Falwell expresses has resided for decades not only in the fundamentalist and evangelical constituencies but in the popular right as a whole. The Moral Majority converged loosely with a labyrinth of rightist lobbies and activist associations that came to life in the 1980s, including the National Pro-Life Political Action Committee, Christian Voice, the Roundtable, and the National Conservative Political Action Committee—groups that endeavored to make public long latent political sentiments. Falwell denied that the Moral Majority subsidized the political campaigns of approved candidates or composed "hit lists" of disapproved ones, tactics often attributed to the associations of the "new right." Nonetheless, its leadership interacted frequently with those of other groups composing the right reaction.

Yet in insisting on the ideological commonalities between his fundamentalist constituents and such traditionally suspect groups as Jews, Catholics, and blacks, Falwell contributes to the novelty of pursuing allies for fundamentalism beyond its traditionally Protestant rural and small-town base. Crediting the Catholic church for having struggled alone against abortion for so long, he invites its members to join the Moral Majority. Having disavowed segregation, to which he was accustomed in his youth, Falwell in *The Fundamentalist Phenomenon* urges equal opportunity for all and the liberation through free enterprise of "minority groups from the virtual 'prison' of the welfare system, which threatens to strangle their life and hope from generation to generation." Having emerged from a setting where anti-Semitism was at least latent, Falwell condemns it as the work of Satan. He militantly supports the state of Israel as a bastion of democracy in a region threatened with Soviet expansion, and he understands the return of the Jews to their ancient lands as the fulfillment of biblical apocalyptic prophecies. Acutely aware that "right-wingers" perpetrated the Nazi Holocaust, Falwell nonetheless pleads that his right appreciates Christianity's Jewish foundations, rejects Christian anti-Semitism as "unchristian," and loves the Jewish people as the chosen instruments of God's purposes.

Although some have suggested a Catholic Moral Majority membership of 30 percent, the evidence as a whole suggests that Falwell's efforts to diversify have met with limited success. Without denying an important component of middle-class suburbanites or the upward mobility of fundamentalists as a group, the greatest support for the Moral Majority and the New Christian Right comes from independent Protestant congregations in small towns and rural areas. It settles among those with lower levels of education in blue-collar or lower-middle-class occupations. Blacks and the upper middle classes, particularly city dwellers and holders of graduate degrees, are underrepresented. The very narrowness of that constituency might well explain the Christian right's failure to win congressional approval for an antiabortion law, tuition tax credits, or voluntary school prayer. Whether owing to the limited appeal of "family" issues or to the insurmountable differences among the groups Falwell targets, the Moral Majority's actual impact has been less than was anticipated earlier in the decade. Moreover, Falwell's appropriation of the PTL was undoubtedly undertaken to prevent the discrediting of Protestant populist religion as the next election neared.

Nevertheless, if Jerry Falwell's ambitions have not been realized, neither has his influence been negligible. His presence in the newspapers and on talk shows is not the only evidence. Despite President Reagan's unwillingness to commit his administration to its legislative platform, the religious right is a potent force within the Republican party, as indicated by Reagan's frequent appeals to its concerns. Falwell has won hearings from the White House on such foreign policy issues as aid to the Contras in Nicaragua, "constructive engagement" in South Africa, and the Strategic Defense Initiative ("Star Wars"). In fact, the Liberty Federation speaks directly to those issues that attract Falwell's most powerful audience. His impact in the future will depend not only on his ability to give voice to his constituency but also on the degree to which his convictions are supported by a broader conservative groundswell, exploited by this country's political elites and translated into law by a conservative Supreme Court.

## Survey of Criticism

Because of the prominence of the New Christian Right, scholarly, journalistic, and polemical treatments of Falwell and Falwell's place in the fundamentalist movement abound. Whereas sympathizers see him as America's salvation, liberals attack him for imposing his resolute Christian morality on a pluralistic society, obliterating the boundaries between church and state, and inventing a mythical American past to justify his commitments. Richard Pierard's "The New Religious Right in American Politics," included in George Marsden's volume *Evangelicalism and Modern America,* ably summarizes the vast literature that accumulated up to 1984. Since then, several new works of note have appeared. The conservative journalist Dinesh D'Souza defends the evangelist against liberal misrepresentations in his biography, *Falwell: Before the Millennium.* Merill Simon's interview, *Jerry Falwell and the Jews,* probes Falwell's support of Israel and his espoused philosemitism. The author's point of departure is the question raised often by Falwell's opponents: does Jerry Falwell really respect the integrity of Judaism, or does he merely see Jews as supporting actors in an apocalyptic drama in which only true Christians triumph? Grace Halsell's *Prophecy and Politics* attacks Falwell's Middle East positions from a different angle. She charges him with insensitivity to the rights of the Palestinian Arabs and terms his millenarianism a surefire recipe for nuclear war.

Frances Fitzgerald's excellent journalistic work, *Cities on a Hill,* includes a lengthy essay on Falwell that appeared originally in the *New Yorker.* Supplementing that piece with a short follow-up analysis, she discusses Falwell's solutions to a familiar fundamentalist dilemma: how to juxtapose political involvement in the world while standing apart from the world's corruptions. Finally, Erling Jorstad's *The New Christian Right, 1981–1988* suggests that Falwell has recently lost some of his political surefootedness with his ill-timed support of Ferdinand Marcos and his equally ill-timed attack on Bishop Desmond Tutu.

Perhaps the most stimulating analysis of Falwell can be found in a short piece generally unknown to Falwell observers. In his essay "America's Civil Religion," the political scientist Sheldon Wolin places the evangelist within the republican tradition of civil religion, the great theorist of which was Machiavelli. Republics, notoriously susceptible to the decay of civic spirit, according to Machiavelli, required a means of promoting the popular fulfillment of the obligations of citizenship while legitimating the hegemony of a socioeconomic elite. For Wolin, the Puritan heritage, transformed by the Great Awakening, became the vehicle of populist pressure but not of populist rule. Jerry Falwell now employs that heritage to effect a reawakening of American spiritual values while avoiding a direct challenge to the legitimacy of this nation's economic and social leadership.

## Bibliography

### Books by Jerry Falwell

1980   *Listen America!* New York: Doubleday.
1981   *The Fundamentalist Phenomenon: The Resurgence of Conservative Christianity.* With Ed Dobson and Ed Hinson. New York: Doubleday.

### Selected Studies about Jerry Falwell

Bromley, David G., and Anson Shupe, eds. *New Christian Politics.* Macon, Ga.: Mercer University Press, 1984.

Cooper, John Charles. *Religious Pied Pipers: A Critique of Radical Right-Wing Religion.* Valley Forge, Pa.: Judson Press, 1981.

D'Souza, Dinesh. *Falwell: Before the Millennium. A Critical Biography.* Chicago: Regnery Gateway, 1984.

"Evangelicals Fight Over Both Body and Soul." *New York Times,* 31 May 1987.

Fitzgerald, Frances. *Cities on a Hill: A Journey through Contemporary American Cultures.* New York: Simon and Schuster, 1986.

Hadden, Jeffrey K., and Charles E. Swann. *Prime-Time Preachers: The Rising Power of Televangelism.* Reading, Mass.: Addison-Wesley Publishing Co., 1981.

Halsell, Grace. *Prophecy and Politics: Militant Evangelists on the Road to Nuclear War.* Westport, Conn.: Lawrence Hill and Company, 1986.

"Heaven Can Wait While the Holy War Heats Up." *Newsweek* 107 (8 June 1987): 58–72.

Hill, Samuel S., and Dennis E. Owen. *The New Religious Political Right in America.* Nashville: Abingdon, 1982.

"An Interview with the Lone Ranger of American Fundamentalism." *Christianity Today* 25 (4 September 1981): 22–27.

Jorstad, Erling. *Evangelicals in the White House: The Cultural Maturation of Born Again Christianity, 1960–1981.* New York and Toronto: Edwin Mellen Press, 1981.

————. *The New Christian Right, 1981–1988: Prospects for the Post-Reagan Decade.* Lewiston, N.Y.: Edwin Mellen Press, 1987.

Kater, John L., Jr. *Christians on the Right: The Moral Majority in Perspective.* New York: Seabury Press, 1982.

Liebman, Robert C., and Robert Wuthnow. *The New Christian Right: Mobilization and Legitimation.* New York: Aldine Publishing Co., 1983.

Marsden, George M., ed. *Evangelicalism and Modern America.* Grand Rapids: Eerdmans, 1984.

Noll, Mark A., Nathan O. Hatch, and George M. Marsden. *The Search for Christian America.* Westchester, Ill.: Crossway Books, 1983.

Pingry, Patricia. *Jerry Falwell: Man of Vision.* Milwaukee: Ideals Publishing Corporation, 1980.

Selvidge, Marla J. *Fundamentalism Today: What Makes It So Attractive?* Elgin, Ill.: Brethren Press, 1984.

Shriver, Peggy L. *The Bible Vote: Religion and the New Right.* New York: Pilgrim Press, 1981.

Shupe, Anson, and William A. Stacey. *Born Again Politics and the Moral Majority: What Social Surveys Really Show.* New York and Toronto: Edwin Mellen Press, 1982.

Simon, Merill. *Jerry Falwell and the Jews.* Middle Village, N.Y.: Jonathan David Publishers, 1984.

Wolin, Sheldon S. "America's Civil Religion." *Democracy* 2 (April 1982): 7–17.

Zwier, Robert. *Born-Again Politics: The New Christian Right in America.* Downers Grove, Ill.: InterVarsity Press, 1982.

SHELLEY BARANOWSKI

# Harry Emerson Fosdick

Albert C. Outler once described the story of the life of Harry Emerson Fosdick as "the biopsy of an epoch." Indeed, the Baptist preacher, known as "modernism's Moses" to his fundamentalist opponents and as "the most celebrated preacher of the day" to his admirers, enjoyed a long and successful career that in many ways mirrored the major developments and controversies of American Protestantism during the decades in which the United States emerged as a powerful nation-state. Fosdick's active ministry spanned two world wars; in retirement, he lived to see and comment on the conflict in Korea and the war in Vietnam. During this long and eventful life (1878–1969), Fosdick established himself as the pre-eminent apologist for liberal Christianity through nearly fifty books and a thousand printed sermons and articles, through forty years of teaching at Union Theological Seminary and preaching in various Baptist and Presbyterian churches and on national radio, and through his championship of the Social Gospel and civil liberties. A pioneer as well in psychological pastoral counseling, Fosdick comforted millions of troubled souls as a popularizer and interpreter of what he considered the richest spiritual resources of the Christian tradition. Ralph W. Sockman*, a contemporary, rightly judged him "the most influential interpreter of religion in his generation" (as quoted in Robert Moats Miller's biography).

## Biography

Born on 24 May 1878 to Frank Sheldon and Amie Weaver Fosdick, Harry had "a definite experience of conversion" at age seven, described in his autobiography, *The Living of These Days,* as "being born again." Likely he was also caught up in the enthusiasm accompanying John R. Mott's* much-publicized challenge to youth to "evangelize the world in this generation." Fosdick's family raised him in the Baptist tradition, nurturing in him a spirit of individualism, personal liberty, and freedom of conscience. Early in life, he rejected the Calvinist ethos and theology that produced "a God who is a devil" and relied instead on the authority he found in his personal experience of the divine. These distinct experiences, which his biographer Robert Moats Miller terms "mystical," were occasioned by crises in the family, including his mother's, his father's, and, eventually, his own nervous breakdown. Accordingly, he found himself in many ways in greater sympathy with the Quaker fellowship than with certain of his Baptist, Methodist, and Presbyterian friends. The Lord was to be found in living experience, not at the end of a creedal proposition.

Accordingly, his high school and college years found Harry crafting a persona as "the Jesse James of the theological world," a rebel against creedal sectarianism. Later in life he boasted that he had never repeated the Apostles' Creed. At the same time, he felt called to Christian ministry and preaching, and at Buffalo High School and especially at Colgate University, he honed his natural talent for public speaking and writing by studying debate, logic, rhetoric, and homiletics. His mentor and "spiritual godfather" at Colgate, the great American Ritschlian William Newton Clarke, bequeathed to this gifted orator of photographic memory the approach to religion detailed in his classic *Outline of Christian Theology*. Under Clarke's tutelage, Fosdick grasped the all-important distinction between religious experience and the philosophical, theological, and cultural forms by which it is expressed. These experiences, which precede particular doctrinal formulations, could and should be interpreted in the light of changing cultural conditions and advancing knowledge. Fosdick epitomized this lesson in an oft-repeated slogan: "We must distinguish between abiding experience and changing categories."

In 1901 Fosdick entered Union Theological Seminary in New York City and embarked on a three-year period of turmoil that Miller judges to be the most decisive period in his life. During the first year at Union, Harry also took classes at Columbia University in philosophy and epistemology, experienced the underside of American society in his ministry to the Bowery bums of the city, and preached in a rural and a downtown church. Within eighteen months he was in Gleason Sanitarium in Elmira, New York, the victim of a nervous breakdown, "a severe neurotic reactive depression" (Miller), probably caused by intense anxiety. Later in life, after recovery and return to Union, Fosdick saw the breakdown as a turning point in that it confirmed his desire to preach and "get at people with problems," heightened his interest in and aptitude for pastoral counseling of others similarly troubled, and most important, demonstrated the redemptive power of personal prayer, which he relied on heavily during his ordeal.

At that time Union Theological Seminary was at the center of the fundamentalist-modernist controversy plaguing American Protestantism. Fosdick was influenced there by the New Theology and higher criticism of the Bible, by the emphasis on divine immanence (Arthur Cushman McGiffert and Adolf von Harnack), American Idealism (Josiah Royce and William Ernest Hocking), and Pragmatism (William James). Borden Parker Bowne's *Personalism* (1908) and

James' *The Varieties of Religious Experience* (1902) lent theological and psychological substance to Fosdick's interest in the human subject as the arena for God's continuing self-disclosure. On 18 November 1903 Fosdick was ordained at the Madison Avenue Baptist Church, committed, in words quoted by Miller, "not [to] the exaltation of the Baptist Faith but [to] the promotion of Christianity on the broadest and best lines."

In 1911 he joined the faculty of Union and accepted the pastorate of the First Baptist Church of Montclair, New Jersey, where he served until 1915. During these years the young preacher made a reputation for himself locally and began to develop a national audience for his ideas as well, primarily through the publication of six devotional books which eventually sold millions of copies. Herein lay one of Fosdick's great talents. For the rest of his writing career, stretching into the 1950s, he continued to turn out books like the classics *The Meaning of Faith, The Meaning of Prayer, The Meaning of Service, The Second Mile, The Manhood of the Master,* and *The Assurance of Immortality.* Excerpts from his books and articles appeared throughout the first half of the century in *Harper's, Ladies Home Journal, Atlantic Monthly, Reader's Digest,* and other popular publications. These writings were an extension of the kind of pastoral ministry Fosdick first established in Montclair: Christian service open to all people regardless of denomination or creed, buoyant in tone, uplifting in outlook, optimistic about the possibilities of human nature which, as revealed in Christ, carried within itself something of the divine.

This liberal optimism Fosdick at first wedded to a vibrant patriotism. As America considered entry into the war ravaging Europe in 1917, Fosdick, retired from the pastorate in Montclair, penned *The Challenge of the Present Crisis,* an interventionist tract urging the United States to arms. But a six-month tour of the front in 1918 affected Fosdick significantly. As he preached to and encouraged the American and British (Fosdick was a lifelong Anglophile) soldiers, he confronted the sordid moral, physical, and emotional results of war. This experience deepened his sense of human sinfulness and contingency, and he returned to New York's First Presbyterian Church to described Europe as "an insane asylum and a butcher's stall." By 1922 his shift toward the conditional pacifism that would characterize his later life was evident in *Christianity and Progress,* the published Cole Lectures at Vanderbilt. He supported the League of Nations and began to see internationalism as the only path to lasting world peace.

On the domestic front, Fosdick found himself in a somewhat anomalous position from 1918 to 1925—Baptist minister of a New York Presbyterian congregation. By the time he mounted the pulpit of First Presbyterian, Fosdick's eloquence as preacher and effectiveness as apologist for modernism had earned him a reputation among evangelicals, liberal and conservative alike. According to Miller, J. Gresham Machen, a fundamentalist scholar and promoter of the five articles of Presbyterian faith, suggested that "the question is not whether Dr. Fosdick is winning men, but whether the thing to which he is winning them is Christianity.'' On 21 May 1922, Fosdick answered with an epoch-making sermon, ''Shall the Fundamentalists Win?'' in which, from a Presbyterian pulpit, he declared belief in the virgin birth of Christ nonessential, the inerrancy of the Scriptures incredible, and the doctrine of the Second Coming of Christ freighted with outmoded imagery. Evangelical Christianity, he warned, was threatened by ''bitterly intolerant'' fundamentalists who insisted that their version of orthodoxy was binding on all true believers. Fosdick demurred, but closed on a note of reconciliation. Ivy Lee, the publicist for John D. Rockefeller, Jr., whose fancy Fosdick had captured, distributed copies of the sermon to every ordained Protestant clergyman in the United States—some 130,000 in number. The battle between fundamentalists and modernists was joined.

William Jennings Bryan* was particularly offended by Fosdick's espousal of theistic evolution and launched a campaign before the New York Presbytery and the General Assembly to expose his ''utter agnosticism'' and ''meretricious rhetoric.'' When both ecclesiastical bodies deemed it appropriate to investigate the situation at First Presbyterian, the debate raged at the national level, with prominent periodicals such as the *Christian Century* and the *Presbyterian* taking up the polemics. In a conciliatory message to the General Assembly, Fosdick defined himself as an evangelical Christian having ''no patience with an emasculated Christianity that denudes the Gospel of its superhuman elements, its redeeming power and its eternal hopes.'' In a public broadcast cited by Miller, he professed his faith in the following terms:

> I believe in the personal God revealed in Christ, in his omnipresent activity and endless resources to achieve his purposes for us and for all men; I believe in Christ, his sacrificial saviorhood, his resurrected and triumphant life, his rightful Lordship, and the indispensableness of his message to mankind. In the indwelling Spirit I believe . . . in the redeemed and victorious life . . . and life everlasting. This faith I find in the Scriptures and the objective of my ministry is to lead men to the Scriptures as the standard and norm of religious experience—the progressive self-revelation of God in the history of a unique people, culminating in Christ.

But he refused to adopt the five points or to become Presbyterian in order to retain his position at the church, which he resigned in 1924. He firmly believed that insistence on creedal uniformity militated against the final aim of Christian religion, namely, to reproduce in its adherents that same experience of God narrated in Scripture.

The fundamentalist-modernist controversy followed Fosdick back into the Baptist fold. There, the conservatives stewed at such Fosdick-approved actions as Baptist membership in the Interchurch World Movement and the adoption of a unified budget for the Northern Baptist Convention. Equally alarming was Fosdick's 1925 alliance with the wealthiest layman in the nation, John D. Rockefeller, Jr., who, to the chagrin of the fundamentalists, found the preacher's nondenominational, world-embracing evangelicalism congenial to his own notion of an efficiently operated, rationalized church emphasizing good works rather than creed and ritual. In May of that year Fosdick accepted a call to Park Avenue Baptist Church, a temporary way station on the road to the glorious structure Rockefeller was building on Morningside Heights to contain Fosdick and congregation. A modern Gothic cathedral seating over 2,300 worshippers, the Riverside Church was Fosdick's spiritual home during his pastorate from 1930 to 1946 and for the twenty-three years of his retirement from full-time ministry, during which he continued to write and preach occasionally.

Although a developed ecclesiology was notably absent from Fosdick's writings, Riverside became a model for his ecclesiology-in-practice. Incorporated as Baptist and affiliated with the Northern Baptist Convention, the church was nonetheless open to all evangelical Christians of every denomination. To accommodate various preferences, the public worship varied in style from the high ritual of eucharistic celebration to the unadorned simplicity characteristic of Quaker prayer meetings (although Fosdick admitted his own inclination for the latter). As a center of community activity, Riverside boasted a staff of seventy permanent workers and over one hundred part-timers. Fosdick believed in a collegiate approach to ministry and delegated responsibility for management and education-recreation to two "co-pastors" while he focused on worship and preaching. Riverside became a base from which its members could affect local, national, and even international reform; for its pastor, the church provided a platform from which he could pronounce on leading questions of the day, from Zionism and the movement to establish an independent Jewish state in the 1920s and 1930s (Fosdick was accused, rightly, of anti-Zionism, but he was in no way anti-Semitic) to Prohibition (he was opposed to the law if not to the activity it restricted) to American intervention in World War II (he was adamantly opposed).

## Appraisal

Harry Emerson Fosdick was perhaps the most important and influential evangelical liberal in American Protestantism in the first half of the twentieth century. Because he was highly visible, popular, and articulate his opinions both reflected the mood of sizable segments of the church-going population and set the tone for popular religious thought. When Fosdick spoke, Protestants listened, whether friend or foe. For example, in 1935, Fosdick "dropped an unexpected depth charge into the sea of theology," Miller reported that theologian William Hordern said, in a sermon preached at Riverside entitled "The Church Must Go Beyond Modernism." Although many theological minds had already been changed by the neo-orthodoxy of Karl Barth, Emil Brunner, Reinhold Niebuhr, and others, it was only with Fosdick's sermon, broadcast over national radio and reprinted in mainstream religious publications such as the *Christian Century,* that the American public stood up and took notice. Without fully relinquishing his affirmation of divine immanence and the nobility of human nature, Fosdick critiqued modernism's capitulating to transient cultural norms, softening the reality of God, and watering down the traditional Christian awareness of personal and social sin. Into his rhetorical arsenal he introduced a Christ standing in defiant judgment of many trends in American society and religion. In so doing, Fosdick helped transform the face of American Protestantism in the interwar years.

Fosdick's métier was the sermon, and he is best remembered for his stirring orations preached from the pulpit and, after 1927, broadcast weekly as the "National Vespers Hour" to between two and three million listeners (a 1946 *New York Times* estimate) from Boston to Chicago. The content of his sermons was also disseminated through book-length collections and periodicals, and his methodology of preaching found a receptive audience in a generation of Union Seminary students who took his course in homiletics. Fosdick defined preaching as "personal counseling on a group scale"; his critics contended that he was more a clinical psychologist, less a proclaimer of the Christian kerygma. Yet Fosdick incorporated into his homilies, which he prepared painstakingly for hours every morning, the best elements of biblical criticism, contemporary theology, and evangelical confessions of faith. Still, he saw preaching and pastoral counseling as the two indispensable offices of the same vocational task—the task of the preacher, he wrote in *The Living of These Days,* was "to produce in the lives of the congregation . . . the supreme experience of the Bible: the response in contrition and faith of the disciples to Jesus." In *The Meaning of Faith,* he recognized true religion in the moment "when God outwardly argued is inwardly experienced." If the right quote or rhetorical flourish or practical example furthered this end in this congregation—he would conclude sermons with "I want everyone here to make a choice about this now"—he deemed it appropriate for his presentation.

Coincident, therefore, to his preaching was an emphasis on personal counseling. Fosdick was a pioneer in clinical-pastoral education; one of his Union Students, Anton Boisen, is acknowledged as father of that field. Much of Fosdick's ministry was given to comforting and advising the troubled; his methods and suggestions were quoted widely and are contained in large part in his 1943 work, *On Being a Real Person.* Fosdick read Sigmund Freud and Carl Jung but was influenced more by his own family and personal experiences of emotional difficulty. He also drew great strength from his wife, Florence Whitney, and two daughters. His appeal lay in a common-sense approach informed by gospel values. To this day popular advice columnist Ann Landers quotes his simple, courageous affirmation of life in a definition of success that reads in part: "to find the best in others; to leave the world a bit better, whether by a healthy child, a garden patch or a redeemed social condition; to know even one life has breathed easier because you lived."

Fosdick was more than a popularizer, however. He produced two scholarly works on the Bible that demonstrated a knowledge of the most sophisticated methods of historical, literary, and textual analysis of the day. His life was also devoted to extraecclesial concerns that he perceived as an aspect of the Social Gospel promoted by his friend Walter Rauschenbusch. In the 1940s and 1950s, he was a champion of civil liberties, inviting blacks to preach from his pulpit, raising funds for the NAACP, and urging Congress to pass civil rights legislation.

Several of his social positions were quite radical; for example, a devotee of eugenics and family planning, he supported voluntary sterilization. And he caucused and worked with pacifists of various stripes to prevent American entry into World War II. Failing that, in 1941 he accepted an invitation to serve on the Federal Council of Churches' Commission on a Just and Durable Peace, under the chairmanship of John Foster Dulles*. To these and other concerns too numerous to mention here, he brought, in Miller's words, "a faith that could not be shaken."

## Survey of Criticism

The definitive biography of Fosdick is by Robert Moats Miller. *Harry Emerson Fosdick: Preacher, Pastor, Prophet* is a massive work of scholarship, impressive in detail and scope. It situates Fosdick in the larger crises and movements of American history as well as religious history. Miller considers his subject to be the most prominent American Protestant minister of the past century; to support that contention, he devoted over a decade of his life to collecting every conceivable source about Fosdick's life, from personal interviews of those who knew him to everything written by or about him. Although a careful reading of Miller will not substitute for reading even one complete sermon of Fosdick's, it will provide the reader with as much (and at times more) information as one might desire. The most significant weakness of the book lies in the regrettable fact that the author eschewed footnotes and conventional documentation of his sources, substituting instead a series of brief bibliographic essays after his 570-page narrative.

No other secondary work on Fosdick compares to Miller's, but two or three are worth consulting for a different, succinct perspective. Indispensable are chapters in William Hutchison's *Modernist Impulse in American Protestantism* and Kenneth Cauthen's *Impact of American Religious Liberalism,* both of which situate Fosdick in the context of Protestant religious thought at the turn of the century and beyond. A dissertation written by Harry Beverly, Jr., for the University of Basel, on the preaching of Fosdick, published as *Harry Emerson Fosdick's Predigtweise, Its Significance (for America), Its Overcoming* is an effective critique of his subject's notion of preaching as "personal counseling on a group scale." Beverly claims that this approach at times leaves little room for the proclamation of the kerygma, reducing the gospel message to the immediate context of the needs of the contemporary audience. Roger Shinn's study of Fosdick as religious reformer is incisive and is found in *The Riverside Preachers,* edited by Paul Sherry.

## Biography

### Books by Harry Emerson Fosdick

1908   *The Second Mile.* New York: Association Press.
1913   *The Manhood of the Master.* New York: Association Press.
1915   *The Meaning of Prayer.* New York: Association Press.

1917   *The Challenge of the Present Crisis.* New York: Association Press.
1917   *The Meaning of Faith.* New York: Association Press.
1918   *The Assurance of Immortality.* London: James Clarke.
1920   *The Meaning of Service.* New York: Association Press.
1922   *Christianity and Progress.* New York: Fleming H. Revell.
1923   *Twelve Tests of Character.* New York: Association Press.
1924   *The Modern Use of the Bible.* New York: Macmillan.
1927   *A Pilgrimage to Palestine.* New York: Macmillan.
1932   *As I See Religion.* New York: Harper and Brothers.
1933   *The Hope of the World: Twenty-five Sermons on Christianity Today.* New York: Harper and Brothers.
1938   *A Guide to Understanding the Bible.* New York: Harper and Brothers.
1943   *On Being a Real Person.* New York: Harper and Brothers.
1944   *A Great Time to be Alive: Sermons on Christianity in Wartime.* New York: Harper and Brothers.
1956   *The Living of These Days.* New York: Harper and Row.

**Selected Studies about Harry Emerson Fosdick**

Abbot, E. H. "Dr. Fosdick's Religion." *Outlook* 51 (11 March 1925): 364–65.
Beverly, Harry, Jr. *Harry Emerson Fosdick's Predigtweise, Its Significance (for America), Its Limits, Its Overcoming.* Winterthur, Switzerland: P. G. Keller, 1965.
Cauthen, Kenneth. *The Impact of American Religious Liberalism.* New York: Harper and Row, 1962. Chap. 4.
Crocker, Lionel, ed. *Harry Emerson Fosdick's Art of Preaching.* Springfield, Ill.: Thomas, 1971.
Hutchison, William. *The Modernist Impulse in American Protestantism.* Cambridge, Mass.: Harvard University Press, 1976.
Miller, Robert Moats. *Harry Emerson Fosdick: Preacher, Pastor, Prophet.* New York: Oxford University Press, 1985.
Shinn, Roger. "Harry Emerson Fosdick, Religious Reformer." In *The Riverside Preachers,* edited by Paul Sherry. New York: Pilgrim Press, 1978.

R. SCOTT APPLEBY

# Charles E. Fuller

The first of the electronic marvels of mass communication, radio revolutionized popular culture in the United States in the twentieth century. Ministers and evangelists, quick to see the advantages of the new medium, took to the air with a wide range of approaches to reach the American public. But the greatest impact of religious broadcasting came from a few who developed an appealing format and who linked up with a national network. One of these was Charles Edward Fuller.

## Biography

Born the youngest of three sons of an aspiring Los Angeles farmer-businessman on 25 April 1887, young Charles enjoyed a childhood in the family orange groves near Redlands on the eastern edge of the Southern California basin. His parents were devout Methodists, his father becoming affluent enough to take two trips around the world to assess missionary needs and eventually to support, in full or in part, scores of Christian workers around the world. Charles, though, displayed little interest in spiritual things and was so shy that his father thought his destiny was to finish high school and simply be a foreman on the family ranch. His mother countered this by insisting that he go to nearby Pomona College, where he played football, participated in debating, and graduated *cum laude* in chemistry in 1910. The next year he married his high school sweetheart, Grace Payton, and seemed to fulfill his father's prophecy by settling down nearby to grow his own orange trees. A disastrous freeze in 1913 forced him to move forty miles west to Placentia to serve as the manager of an orange growers' cooperative packing plant. But his business savvy in buying and selling orange groves, leasing land for oil drilling, and even launching a trucking company gradually brought him a prosperity that he would never entirely lose.

While active members of the Placentia Presbyterian Church, Grace and Charles were introduced to Protestant fundamentalist teaching through a friend. Charles underwent a dramatic spiritual experience in 1916 under the preaching of Paul Rader, pastor of Chicago's Moody Church, and began teaching an adult Sunday School class in his own church. Increasingly dissatisfied with his secular work, Charles resigned his job in 1919 to train for vocational religious work at the Bible Institute of Los Angeles (BIOLA). There he was grounded in premillennial fundamentalist teaching and biblical interpretation by such teachers as Reuben A. Torrey, dean of the school.

After graduation in 1921 he worked as the president of Orange County Christian Endeavor while supported by income from his orange grove. His main energies, though, were expended on his Sunday School class, which became so large and so at odds with the congregation that it broke away and formed itself into the independent Calvary Church in 1925. Fuller became its pastor after seeking ordination from a group of Baptist churches associated with the fundamentalist Baptist Bible Union.

Not content to settle down to traditional pastoral work, Fuller held evangelistic meetings along the West Coast and became deeply involved as trustee and later as chairman of the board of BIOLA. His most auspicious work beyond pastoral duties, however, was with radio. Fuller had tinkered with electrical devices as a boy and since 1924 had preached occasionally on local radio stations. But in 1929, after enthusiastic response to his radio preaching in Indianapolis while on an evangelistic tour, he decided that he could make a major contribution to the gospel cause as a radio evangelist. He began broadcasting his church's worship services and a Bible study program the next year over area radio stations. Eventually his congregation became disgruntled over his consuming interest in radio and his evangelistic travels. In turn, he was impatient with their lack of vision to evangelize the world and felt drained by church members whose demands for attention from their pastor seemed insatiable. In 1933 he finally resigned the pastorate to form the nonprofit Gospel Broadcasting Association to sponsor his full-time radio and evangelistic ministry.

The Depression and the bankruptcy of a business partner made it an inauspicious time to get a fledgling radio ministry off the ground. Despite the hardships, Fuller was encouraged by public response to his programs and seized opportunities to expand his radio ministry by committing to several powerful stations and regional networks that enabled him to reach most of the West Coast and eastward as far as the Mississippi River. At one point, he was broadcasting two half-hour programs on 50,000-watt stations, in addition to two hour-long programs on a Long Beach Station. The programs bore a variety of titles: "Radio Bible Class," "The Voice of Hollywood," "The Prophetic Lamp Hour," "Sunday School Hour," "Heart to Heart Hour." In 1934 he settled on the format of a Sunday evening revival service before a live studio audience—which he would keep for almost thirty-five years—and called it "Radio Revival Hour." He continued one other program, "Pilgrim's Hour," on a local station on Sunday mornings until 1947. With the help of his wife he published *Heart to Heart Talk,* a promotional sheet that bound listeners to him and helped to raise funds to pay for the broadcasts.

His move to national network broadcasting was accomplished with the help of some good fortune. One crucial station had dropped him when it joined CBS, whose policy was to prohibit paid religious programming. In his scramble to locate several others to take its place, he contracted with a station that in 1937 became part of the Mutual Broadcasting Network, which permitted paid religious programs. As the young network expanded its stations and standardized its programming nationwide, it repeatedly presented Fuller with the choice of accepting the increased costs of more stations or giving up his prime Sunday evening time slot. In each case, he decided to go with the network and sought funds from listeners to defray the costs. On 14 MBS stations in 1937, his program by 1942 was on 456. His renamed revival service, "Old Fashioned Revival Hour" (OFRH), became so popular that it reached more listeners than such well-known secular shows as those of Bob Hope or Charlie McCarthy.

Why this expansion? In part it was the result of Fuller's aggressive approach to revivalistic evangelism. He boldly took risks to expand his radio ministry and showed little patience with those more cautious than he. Also, he held to the traditional practice of conducting evangelistic meetings in tandem with his radio ministry. Each supported and complemented the other. He preached all over the country to some sizable audiences: 40,000 for a 1938 Easter Sunrise Service in Chicago's Soldier Field, twice in one day to overflow crowds in New York's Carnegie Hall in 1939 during the World's Fair, and two packed services in Boston Garden in 1941. But even more frequently, he was in medium-sized cities, broadcasting his OFRH from these locations on Sunday evenings.

Another reason for his radio success was the cooperation and endorsements he secured from a growing network of fundamentalist leaders and institutions. Not the least of these were Charles Trumbull, influential editor of the fundamentalist *Sunday School Times*; J. Elwin Wright, who spearheaded the formation of the National Association of Evangelicals in 1942; and Dawson Troutman, whose Navigators group utilized Fuller's radio program to do evangelistic work among American sailors on ships and in ports all over the world.

Finally, the times contributed to the growth of Fuller's radio ministry. The effects of the Depression and the anxieties attending World War II led people to seek spiritual certainties and cosmic answers to nagging human questions. Fuller's traditional evangelical message of a Christ sent from heaven to save a lost world helped to meet these inner needs.

The popularity of OFRH peaked during the war years. The program, carried on short-wave radio and powerful foreign stations in Luxembourg, Ecuador, Ceylon, and the Philippines, was heard by servicemen and English-speaking people all over the Americas, Europe, and Asia.

A crisis occurred in 1944 when Mutual followed the other networks in dropping all paid religious programming except on Sunday morning because of the negative impact of political religious demogogues like Father Charles Coughlin and the financial chicanery of some unscrupulous radio evangelists. Since the Federal Council of Churches strongly supported the action, fundamentalists were convinced it was a high-handed move by the liberal establishment to eliminate programs other than those featuring its own free-time liberal preachers.

Cut off from a national network, Fuller's agent plunged into the task of lining up independent stations who would carry delayed transcriptions of the program. In addition, Fuller moved the broadcast from a small studio to the 5,000-seat Municipal Auditorium in Long Beach, allowing a rally atmosphere to infuse fresh enthusiasm into the services. The result sustained the program into the postwar period, with listeners worldwide estimated at twenty million. Eventually, a new network, ABC, picked up the program and aired it live beginning in 1949.

The explosive growth of television, however, helped to bring about a long decline for the program. Fuller sensed the new medium was the wave of the future, but his six-month experiment with it in 1950 was a failure. In his sixties, Fuller simply did not make the transition to television. ABC forced the program, along with other religious programs, to pare down to a half hour in 1958 and eventually forced it off the network in 1963.

Despite the fact that the postwar era saw a gradual decline in Fuller's position as a popular religious leader, his most enduring influence on American religion was achieved during this period, through education.

His vision of founding a "Christ-centered, Spirit-directed training school" went back to 1939, and in 1942 he established the Fuller Evangelistic Foundation (later Association) to administer and supplement a fund his father had set up to train and support foreign missionaries. Property was purchased in Pasadena, where his GBA was located, but Fuller vacillated over what kind of school he wanted—whether a seminary or some type of college. He also struggled to find a younger, energetic leader to put together a faculty and academic program. The man he eventually persuaded to organize the school, Harold Ockenga, pastor of

Boston's evangelical and mission-oriented Park Street Church, also solved the first problem by convincing Fuller of the need for a postgraduate institution. The school, named Fuller Theological Seminary for his father, was legally an arm of the foundation until the early fifties.

Ockenga gathered an impressive faculty, and the doors of the new school opened in 1947. The Fullers became deeply involved with the school. They invited students to their home; Mrs. Fuller took a personal interest in the physical appearance of the grounds; and Charles always spoke in a fall chapel. Most important, he controlled the purse strings of the foundation that bought the property, constructed the buildings, and contributed $150,000 annually from oil wells to keep the seminary afloat in the early years. And his word was final on selections of faculty and administration.

Yet it would be mistaken to conclude that he shaped the school in his own image. He was a premillennial fundamentalist who simply wanted a training school to supply missionaries and evangelists to the other branch of the foundation, a department of evangelism that coordinated missions and evangelistic work. Although sympathetic with this goal, Ockenga and the faculty had another agenda: to use the institution to help reshape a narrow, separatist fundamentalism into a broadly based evangelicalism that could measure up intellectually to the best of the Ivy League seminaries and could make a credible defense of the evangelical faith.

This additional purpose created a tension between Fuller and his institution in its first two decades. Controversies swirled over the school's general approval of the Revised Standard Version translation of the Bible, generally condemned by fundamentalists as a liberal work, and over the move away from fundamentalist positions supporting a premillennial view of Christ's second coming, the inerrancy of Scripture, and lifestyle matters generally approved by pious evangelicals. Exasperated, Fuller estimated at one point that such controversies cost him 40 percent of his support for his radio program.

Why he allowed the school to develop as it did can be attributed to two factors: Fuller's own irenic spirit and the influence of his only child, Dan Fuller. Charles never engaged in acrimonious battles between fundamentalists and liberals, choosing instead to concentrate on proclaiming the gospel. And he not only had great hopes that his son would succeed him either as a radio speaker or as a leader in the seminary but also depended on him for evaluations of school issues. Dan had been educated at Princeton Seminary and had studied at Basel under Karl Barth before returning to the new school to take up a position of leadership. His progressive views carried the day with his parents, even though they personally were uneasy about them.

Charles, never comfortable with an academic institution, felt vindicated when the seminary started a school of missions in 1965. But even here the head of the new school, Donald McGavran, put more emphasis on the notion of "discipling" whole nations, an approach that mystified Fuller, than on the typically evangelical Protestant strategy of converting individuals.

But at least the aging evangelist had his beloved radio program. Off a national network, he lined up independent stations and preached nearly to the time of his death on 18 March 1968. The program continued with David Hubbard, president of the seminary, as speaker under the new name "The Joyful Sound."

### Appraisal

Charles Fuller was the most popular American revivalist between Billy Sunday* and Billy Graham*. Like all revivalists before and after him, he held series of evangelistic services all over the country, preaching a basic evangelical message of individual salvation through the atoning work of Christ. What made Fuller such an influential figure was his use of the communication technology of his day—radio. For this he was in the right place at the right time. Southern California was already the motion picture capital, and radio developed quickly there. But even more strategic was the formation of the national networks in the late twenties and thirties. Fuller took advantage of opportunities to expand with them as they established a national programming schedule.

But Fuller's good fortune and risk taking only partially explains why he, and no other revivalist radio preachers of the period, became so well known. A fuller explanation must take account of the team and the program he put together. The music was especially attractive, consisting of hymns and gospel songs with which most Protestants were familiar. But unlike in many of their churches, it was done with a slick professionalism worthy of Hollywood, where Fuller did much of his broadcasting in early years. The mixture of pleasant sounds from the choir, the mellow voices of the quartet, and background runs by pianist Rudy Atwood and organist George Broadbent provided a sentimental, congenial atmosphere for the listener.

One member of the team was crucial—his wife. On each program Grace read letters from listeners telling their stories of how the program or other circumstances had been used by God to bring about their personal transformations or improvements in their life situations. These letters came from all over the world and gave the listener the feeling of being part of a worldwide movement. Not incidentally, both Charles and Grace had excellent radio voices, especially Grace, whose precise diction and lilting tones riveted listeners to their seats.

The folksy mannerisms of Charles himself proved to be disarming to listeners. Every service on the radio included the airy chorus of "Heavenly Sunshine," with mistakenly created lyrics by Fuller from the gospel hymn "Heavenly Sunlight," during the singing of which he encouraged people to turn around and shake hands with their neighbors. At the end of sermons, he would ask for hands to be raised before prayer and told his radio audience that an "altar service" would ensue beyond the radio time. He introduced Grace's segment with the affectionate "Go ahead, Honey." He came across as one at ease with the microphone, someone who was able to be himself before a national audience. As he said on the program aired 8 June 1952, "If everything seems informal, just remember it's the 'Old Fashioned Revival Hour.' " In sum, he seemed like the firm, relaxed father, and Grace the soft, efficient mother.

In his preaching, Fuller used directness and simple analogies to communicate effectively. He always imagined he was talking to a miner alone in a cabin or to a housewife in a humble dwelling. With transparent earnestness he would exhort, "Listen to me!" and then proceed to make his point. He evoked images of physical objects or everyday events to illustrate biblical and spiritual truths, utilizing a homiletical approach that appealed to the common person.

Not only in style, but also in substance, his message was effective. Fuller's simple evangelical message was well known to many of his listeners from their past and was appealing to others who were seeking spiritual help in times of uncertainty. This is perhaps the best explanation of what separated Fuller and the other major radio preacher of the day, Walter A. Maier* of "The Lutheran Hour," from better-connected and better-educated radio preachers such as Harry Emerson Fosdick*, S. Parks Cadman, and Ralph Sockman*. On the other hand, what separated Fuller and Maier from their conservative brethren who clogged the airwaves was a positive emphasis on a basic evangelical faith that avoided divisive and rancorous controversies and that focused almost exclusively on meeting pressing spiritual needs of people.

Because of this approach, Fuller was in a unique position to be the bridge from the militant fundamentalism of the twenties to the accommodating neoevangelicalism of the postwar period. He started by being a schismatic who felt his moderate Presbyterian congregation was too liberal. Yet by the forties he had moved beyond separatism and was collaborating with other evangelical leaders in the establishment of organizations designed to transform American culture in accordance with the evangelical vision. In this his school, eventually the largest nondenominational seminary in the country, filled a crucial role of leadership even though Fuller's own convictions were often at odds with the positions of the institution.

Yet the impact of the radio program continues with fundamentalists who concur with Fuller's personal beliefs and evangelistic approach but who look askance at the "compromising" developments in his seminary. Jerry Falwell*, leading fundamentalist leader who emerged in the seventies, credits his hearing the OFRH as a crucial event in his own religious conversion. It is perhaps Falwell's tribute to Fuller that he calls his own television program "The Old Time Gospel Hour."

## Survey of Criticism

Only three major works make up the literature on Fuller, all of them sympathetic. J. Elwin Wright's *The Old Fashioned Revival Hour and the Broadcasters* is a laudatory account of the Fullers and their program up to 1940, with the latter half of the book consisting of collections of letters from listeners grouped around various needs expressed. Wilbur Smith, one of the original faculty of the seminary, updated Wright's work to the beginnings of the seminary in *A Voice for God: The Life of Charles E. Fuller*. The third and most important work builds on the other two and offers the only complete biography of Fuller. In *Give the Winds a Mighty Voice: The Story of Charles E. Fuller,* Daniel P. Fuller contributes the unique perspective that only a son can give. Though it is more critical than the first two, it still reflects an admiring son's viewpoint of a dominant figure in his life.

Although not a biography as such, George Marsden's *Reforming Fundamentalism: Fuller Seminary and the New Evangelicalism* explains Fuller's involvement in the beginnings and development of the influential school that is his main legacy. Marsden details the personal conflicts and theological disputes, many involving Fuller, that surrounded the first twenty years.

## Bibliography

### *Works by Charles E. Fuller*

There are no works by Fuller. Documents he left consist of issues of *Heart to Heart Talk,* various Bible study guides sent to his listeners and supporters, and sermon manuscripts in the Fuller Archives, Fuller Theological Seminary, Pasadena, California. In addition, a series of five programs of the "Old Fashioned Revival Hour" is available on cassette tape from the Charles E. Fuller Institute on Evangelism and Church Growth in Pasadena.

### *Studies about Charles E. Fuller*

Armstrong, Ben. *The Electric Church.* Nashville: Thomas Nelson, 1979.

Atwood, Rudy. *The Rudy Atwood Story.* Old Tappan, N.J.: Fleming H. Revell, 1970.

Fuller, Mrs. Charles E. *Heavenly Sunshine: Letters to the "Old-Fashioned Revival Hour."* Westwood, N.J.: Fleming H. Revell, 1956.

Fuller, Daniel P. *Give the Winds a Mighty Voice: The Story of Charles E. Fuller.* Waco, Tex.: Word, 1972.

Marsden, George M. *Reforming Fundamentalism: Fuller Seminary and the New Evangelicalism.* Grand Rapids: Eerdmans, 1987.

Parker, Everett C., et al. *The Television-Radio Audience and Religion.* New York: Harper and Brothers, 1955.

Smith, Wilbur M. *A Voice for God: The Life of Charles E. Fuller, Originator of the Old Fashioned Revival Hour.* Boston: W. A. Wilde, 1949.

Wright, J. Elwin. *The Old Fashioned Revival Hour and the Broadcasters.* Boston: Fellowship Press, 1940.

L. DAVID LEWIS

# Bill and Gloria Gaither

In 1963 an unknown songwriter from a small midwestern town published what was to be the first of many songs that would influence thousands upon thousands of Christians. With "He Touched Me," the career of William J. ("Bill") Gaither began an ascent that continues a quarter of a century later. After publishing some 400 songs, the names of Bill and Gloria Gaither are some of the best known in the world of gospel music.

## Biography

Born on 28 March 1936 in Alexandria, Indiana, Bill wanted to be in gospel music as far back as he can remember. As a youngster he would run home after school to see if the latest gospel quartet record had arrived in the mail. This interest in music continued throughout his years at Anderson (Indiana) College, where he received his bachelor's degree in 1959. He completed a master of arts degree in guidance at Ball State University in 1961 and in 1973 was awarded an honorary doctor of music degree from his alma mater, Anderson College. If asked his occupation, Bill might reply, "Composer, Songwriter, Teacher, Businessman, Producer, Father—though not necessarily in that order." Bill began his career as a high school English teacher in his hometown, but during his six years at that occupation, Bill spent much of his spare time on his real love, writing songs. He and Gloria, whom Bill believes God provided as his life's companion, were married in 1962 and began singing Bill's songs, with the help of Bill's brother Danny, at churches near their home in Alexandria. Bill's first song, "I've Been to Calvary," was published in 1960, when contemporary gospel music was beginning to become popular. Since that time the music of the Gaithers, which has been described as middle-of-the-road contemporary, has become a standard in the gospel music industry. With the publication of "He Touched Me" in 1963, the Gaithers' popularity soared. The initial idea for that song came from a conversation with Doug Oldham and Doug's father after a revival meeting led by the Oldhams at a town near Bill's home. As the three men rode in a car and talked about the miraculous things God had done in their lives, the elder Oldham mentioned the phrase "he touched me" and suggested that Bill write a song with that theme. The next Sunday morning before going to church, Bill wrote the song in less than 45 minutes. "He Touched Me" was to become one of Bill's most popular songs. Throughout the 1960s the Gaithers became nationally known through the publication of songs such as "The Longer I Serve Him" (1965), "It Will Be Worth It All" (1966), "Something Worth Living For" (1967) [written with Doug Oldham], "I Believe in a Hill Called Mt. Calvary" (1968), and "Thanks to Calvary: I Don't Live Here Anymore" (1969). During the 1970s, the Bill Gaither Trio was deluged with concert requests but because of family considerations chose to travel only on weekends (with the exception of January, which they designated "flu month"), and they appeared in major auditoriums throughout the United States. During the last several years, the traveling schedule has been altered to two annual tours of three or four weeks during the spring and fall. It was also in the 1970s that the Gaithers became internationally known and acclaimed. In 1972, Bill was given an international award as the American composer with the greatest international exposure for "He Touched Me." This song has been recorded by artists ranging from traditional gospel singers like George Beverly Shea to secular artists such as Elvis Presley, Kate Smith, and Lawrence Welk. For the years 1969–70 and 1972–77 Bill was named songwriter of the year by the Gospel Music Association and received a special award of merit for "his contribution to the world of gospel music." In 1974, "Because He Lives" was named the gospel song of the year. Some other well-known songs from the Gaithers' pens during the seventies include "The Old Rugged Cross Made The Difference" (1970), "Something Beautiful" (1971), "Get All Excited" (1972), "Let's Just Praise the Lord" (1972), "I Just Feel Like Something Good Is About To Happen" (1974), "Jesus, I Heard You Had A Big House" (1974), "I Lost It All To Find Everything" (1976), and "It Is Finished" (1976), a song that took the Gaithers a year full of "prayer, inspiration and discussion" to write. "Jesus, I Heard You Had A Big House," one of the Gaithers' most popular children's songs, was inspired by a ride through a Philadelphia ghetto. Bill "ached for those kids" living in squalor and playing in the streets, and he wondered if there was any hope for them. Their hope, as that of all people, Bill believed to be in Jesus Christ, but how could that message be expressed to them in words they would understand? They could not relate to heaven as a place with streets of gold and gates of pearls, but, as Bill was quoted in *Christian Life* in 1978, "they could relate to having their own room and a big yard to play in, food, and lots of love," as the song says.

The eighties continue to witness the popularity and productivity of the Gaithers. In 1982 Bill was inducted into the Gospel Music Association Hall of Fame, and the album *I've Just Seen Jesus* was named Album of the Year in the category of Worship and Praise by the Gospel Music Association. The Gaithers' writing and publishing has continued unabated with such notable songs as "Then Came The Morning" (1982) [written with Chris Christian], "Upon This Rock" (1983) [written with Dony McGuire], "Unshakable Kingdom" (1985) [written with Michael W. Smith], and "I've Just Seen Jesus" (1987) [written with Danny Daniels]. Bill and Gloria's eldest daughter, Suzanne, assisted with the lyrics to "I Just Can't Make It By Myself" (1986).

In 1981, Bill expanded his involvement in music ministry with the formation of the New Gaither Vocal Band. With three other male singers (Gary McSpadden, Larnell Harris, and Mike English) joining Bill, the band performs a wide variety of musical styles ranging from the traditional male quartet music style loved by Bill as a youngster, to more contemporary vocal arrangements. The group has recorded four albums and was nominated for Grammy awards for its album *New Point Of View* in 1985 and for the song "No Other Name But Jesus" in 1984. They have also received nominations for the Gospel Music Association's Dove Award in three consecutive years for their albums *The New Gaither Vocal Band* (1983), *Passin' The Faith Along* (1984), and *New Point Of View* (1985).

Bill is also deeply involved in the business of music publishing and distribution. He serves as chief executive officer of the Gaither Music Company, his publishing concern, and Alexandria House, a major Christian music distribution firm. He is also interested in a number of smaller companies that have evolved with the growth of the former businesses. Through these avenues, seen as extensions of ministry, Bill tries to provide means for increasing the quality of music in all areas of Christian life, from that of other touring artists to local church choirs.

Gloria Gaither plays an essential part in the ministry of this husband-and-wife team. She has been described as the "principal lyricist" for the 400 songs they have written and has coauthored an additional 100. Born on 4 March 1942 in Michigan, Gloria grew up as the daughter of a minister and a writer. She attributes her own interest and facility with lyrics and prose to this lifelong association with a family of communicators. Gloria received a bachelor's degree from Anderson College in 1963 with majors in English, French, and sociology, and in 1983 she was awarded an honorary doctor of arts degree from Warner Southern (Florida) College. Gloria has authored five books: *Make Warm Noises* (1971), *Rainbows Live at Easter* (1974), *Because He Lives* (1977), *Decisions: A Christian's Approach to Making Right Choices* (1982), and *Fully Alive* (1984). In addition, she coauthored with Shirley Dobson *Let's Make A Memory* in 1983 and recorded a solo album, *Let's Talk About . . . Something Beautiful* in 1969. In 1982, she was presented the Woman of Distinction Award from the East Central Indiana Professional Chapter of Women in Communication and in 1983 was one of the invitees to a "Briefing for Evangelical Women Christian Leaders" at the White House with President Ronald Reagan. In 1985, she received the Gospel Music Association's Dove Award as lyricist for song of the year for "Upon This Rock" and in 1986 was given the Dove Award as songwriter of the year. The Gaithers have three children, Suzanne Renée (1964), Amy Michelle (1969), and William Benjamin (Benjy) (1970).

From performing as a family trio early in their careers, the Gaithers have seen their presentation evolve into a complete concert including Christian singers, musicians, and actors. They regularly draw crowds that range from 3,000 to 15,000 people. The keystone of the presentation remains the Bill Gaither Trio. The original trio included Bill, his sister Mary Ann, and brother Danny. Danny continued to sing with Bill and Gloria from the time of their marriage until 1977, when Gary McSpadden joined the group. At present Bill, Gloria, and McSpadden are accompanied by four backup singers and eight band members. The trio has recorded thirty-five albums, including five that were written specifically for children. In all, some four million albums have been produced. In 1969, the group was nominated for a Grammy award for their album *He Touched Me* and again in 1974 for *Thanks For Sunshine*. They received Grammys in 1973 for *Let's Just Praise The Lord* and again in 1975 for *Jesus, We Just Want To Thank You*. In 1977, the Recording Industry Association of America certified their *Alleluia, A Praise Gathering For Believers* as the first Christian album to reach gold status. The Gospel Music Association named the trio mixed group of the year in 1975 and 1980. *Jesus, We Just Want To Thank You* was named inspirational album of the year by that organization in 1976, and *Pilgrims' Progress* received that award in 1978. In 1981 *The Very Best Of The Very Best For Kids* was named children's music album of the year by the Gospel Music Association and in 1985 the trio recorded *Ten New Songs With Kids . . . For Kids About Life*, whose producer, Ron Griffin, received that honor.

## Appraisal

Although the evaluation of journalist Casey Banas that the Gaithers might be "God's man and woman for America in the 1970s and perhaps into the 1980s," as Billy Graham* was God's man in the 1950s and 1960s, might be overstated, it is a fact that Bill and Gloria Gaither have exerted a tremendous influence on thousands of people throughout the world. Estimates ranged from 300,000 to 500,000 people per year who attended Gaither concerts when the group traveled most extensively. Currently, with their abbreviated touring schedule, it is estimated that some 175,000 people attend their concerts each year, not to mention the millions who own their recordings.

A key to the Gaithers' appeal is their emphasis on communication. As Gloria put it in "Gloria Gaither: A Brief Biography," "God is not complex. He speaks to us in ultimate simplicity." It is through the lyrics of their songs that they attempt to convey their simple, but profound, message. "The music," said Bill in *Family Life Today* in 1985, "is neither here nor there. It's just a tool God gives us to use. The only thing that makes gospel music different from any other music is the lyrics." Gloria agrees: "We use different musical styles to communicate our message," she commented in "A Matter of Heart." "We want to take the message to as many ears as we can attract."According to composer and arranger Ronn Huff, the Gaithers are able to take a simple song title with a profound message and unite it with a simple tune of the type that will remain in one's mind and on one's lips throughout the day. Indeed, the Gaithers have a knack for convincingly relating the message of the gospel to seemingly ordinary events in everyday life.

Their musical style has not always been readily accepted in the Christian community, however. Early in their careers, some condemned their music because of its supposed similarity with increasingly popular "rock and roll" and other secular styles. Even after they had gained a broad base of support in Christian circles, they found that the continuing development of their musical style brought stinging criticisms. Bill defends this evolution of style, against charges that the Gaithers "used to be spiritual" but now use all kinds of "worldly" instruments, with a reference to the psalmist's instructions to praise God with all manner of musical instruments.

The Gaithers are deeply committed to consistent improvement in the quality of their music and Christian music in general. Bill states that one of their aims is to prepare their records with as much quality as would any secular group. "God demands our best," he was quoted in the *Saturday Evening Post* in 1977. In producing an album, for example, they insist on the best equipment, the finest technicians, and "as many takes as it takes" to get the songs just right.

Through their music they are able to cross denominational and ideological barriers that tend to isolate many others with beliefs comparable to theirs. An explicit example of this desire for unity among Christians was a concert in the 1970s in Chicago. Bill asked each person to state out loud his denominational affiliation. After experiencing the incoherent and unpleasant sound made by the mixture of denominational names, he had them all repeat the name of Jesus. Softer and softer they repeated the name that emphasized their oneness as Christians. The Gaithers are also deeply concerned with "humanism and the secularization of our society," and they openly promote what they see as traditional values of home, family, and morality. They denounce American culture as a "cesspool" and decry the role of secular music, films, and television in lowering the standards of society. Yet they come off as less offensive and threatening to those with differing beliefs than do many who say similar things. Their message is basically positive, celebrating the lordship of Christ, his resurrection, and the fact that he is living in the lives of people. But, said Bill in *Christian Life* in 1978, they also want to "prick some consciences about value systems without heavy preaching." Thus, much of their music is thought-provoking without being confrontational.

One avenue of spreading their message that the Gaithers see as vital is that of children's music. Their goal is to offer an attractively packaged alternative to the destructive influences they see at work in society. That alternative emphasizes, they were quoted in *Eternity* in 1979, "discovering who we are in Jesus and being happy with who we are and what God has given us to work with, and then digging in and doing something about it." Their children's songs affirm the goodness of children as God's creations and stress the possibilities of each individual life. They also teach traditional moral and ethical values in an active and fun way.

Although their audiences are primarily made up of Christians who would describe themselves as "born again," the Gaithers insist that a number of non-Christians also attend each gathering. According to letters they receive, many people bring non-Christian friends who would not normally attend regular church services. Thus, the Gaithers try to be sensitive to evangelism as well as to edification of those who are already Christian. Far from being merely passive observers, audiences are regularly involved in Gaither concerts. They clap their hands to the beat of the music and sing along, and sometimes people from the audience give personal testimonies. The mood of the concert is upbeat. There is no reason, the Gaithers believe, that celebration should not be fun and uplifting. Rather than dwell on guilt and fear, they emphasize God's love and his desire to provide help and salvation.

The Gaithers seem refreshingly unaffected by their popularity and success. Their modest Alexandria home exudes the feeling of average, midwestern, small-town family life. They have emphasized throughout their singing careers that "serving the Lord as good parents" is their first priority. During the years that the group traveled on weekends, they insisted on returning home for Sunday church services with their children. And at one point they regularly turned down nine out of every ten invitations to sing in order to maintain priorities of family life. Bill has been known to put off important recording and publishing work to attend his children's activities. Concerning their popularity, Bill insists that because they are involved in ministry they do not have the "luxury" of thinking about their success for even a moment. The only reason there is any success, he says, is because God has chosen to bless their ministry. Though that phrase sounds too much like the common justification for all manner of extravagance, coming from Bill Gaither it is quite believable. The numbers of records or copies of sheet music are far less important to the Gaithers than the knowledge that those numbers in some way represent particular persons who are being helped through their music. In harmony with the upbeat message of their music, Bill is looking forward to the future. "I'm about one-third of the way through life," he says. "This is only the beginning."

Bill and Gloria Gaither are sincere, talented, dedicated, and quite admirable people. They are convinced of what they believe and are determined to spread their message, and yet they are not overbearing in its presentation. In this age of scepticism—too often justified—about those in high-profile Christian ministries, it is refreshing to find two people who are as successful as the Gaithers but who maintain their integrity in an industry that is not always known for such consistency of character.

## Survey of Criticism

Literature about the Gaithers is very scarce. There have been a few interviews, mostly in evangelical Christian magazines such as *Moody Monthly, Christian Life, Family Life Today,* and *Christianity Today.* Articles describing the Gaithers' music include Casey Banas, "Bill and Gloria Gaither: They Sing The Way You Feel," which gives a brief biographical sketch of Bill and Gloria and includes descriptions of particular concerts; Samuel B. Walton, "People Like Honest Sounds," which focuses on the simplicity of the Gaithers' message and its widespread appeal; and Lois Shaw, "How Bill and Gloria Gaither Write for Kids," which describes the Gaithers' development of children's musicals as an important teaching resource.

## Bibliography

### Books by Gloria Gaither

1971  *Make Warm Noises*. Nashville: Impact Books.
1974  *Rainbows Live at Easter*. Nashville: Impact Books.
1977  *Because He Lives*. Old Tappan, N.J.: Fleming H. Revell.
1982  *Decisions: A Christian's Approach to Making Right Choices*. Waco, Tex.: Word.
1983  *Let's Make a Memory*. With Shirley Dobson. Waco, Tex.: Word.
1984  *Fully Alive*. Nashville: Thomas Nelson Publishers.

Gloria has also written articles for magazines such as the *Saturday Evening Post, Moody Monthly, Today's Christian Woman, Charisma,* and *Christian Life.*

The Bill Gaither Trio has recorded thirty-five albums, Bill and Gloria Gaither have written seven musicals that have been recorded, Gloria recorded one solo album, and the New Gaither Vocal Band has recorded four albums.

*Selected Studies about Bill and Gloria Gaither*

Banas, Casey. "Bill and Gloria Gaither: They Sing the Way You Feel." *Christian Life* 40 (August 1978): 34–35, 51–52.

"Gloria Gaither: A Brief Biography." Available from Gloria Gaither, P.O. Box 300, Alexandria, IN 46001.

Jenkins, Jerry B. "Bill Gaither's Real Trio." *Moody Monthly* 75 (February 1975): 25–27.

"A Matter of Heart." *Family Life Today* (December 1985): 14–15.

Shaw, Lois. "How Bill and Gloria Gaither Write for Kids." *Eternity* 30 (March 1979): 27–29, 40–41.

Struck, Jane L. "Bards and Fellow Strugglers." *Christian Life* 43 (November 1981): 66–67.

Walton, Samuel B. "People Like Honest Sounds." *Saturday Evening Post* (April 1977): 46–47, 99–100.

STEPHEN R. GRAHAM

# Marcus Garvey

Afro-Americans after World War I were by and large disillusioned with their leadership and with the United States. The experience of discrimination, poverty, and racial violence in the North undercut Afro-American hopes that the North was a "promised land" of redemption from the suffering they had experienced in the South. Afro-American leaders were not offering directives that attracted popular support. Booker T. Washington was dead, and the "Great Migration" of Afro-Americans from the South to the North after 1916 can be viewed as a popular rejection of his self-help philosophy to stay in the South and accommodate to the interests of southern planters. Discrimination made W.E.B. Du Bois' wartime advocacy of patriotism and integration questionable, whereas socialists declared the imminence of workers' solidarity despite the fact that the vast majority of labor unions excluded blacks. Marcus Garvey, a Jamaican black nationalist, emerged in 1916 as a public figure in the Afro-American community who drew popular support by refocusing the hope for redemption onto a future black homeland in an "Africa for Africans."

## Biography

Born on 17 August 1887 in St. Ann's Bay, Jamaica, to Sarah and Marcus Garvey, Sr., Marcus Garvey, Jr., entered a family descended from the Maroons of Jamaica, an eighteenth-century community of ex-slaves who won independence from the British through armed struggle. Unlike most Afro-Jamaicans, descendants from the Maroons were tradesmen when they integrated into post-emancipation Jamaican society in 1838. Marcus Garvey, Sr., was a master stonemason who provided his family with a comfortable life until his properties were confiscated because of a legal dispute over an unpaid debt. Young Marcus was forced to drop out of school at the age of fourteen to find work. Apprenticed to a pair of uncles, he learned the printer's trade which provided him with the skills to become a foreman with Jamaica's largest printing firm at the age of nineteen.

Despite his occupational success, Garvey became increasingly dissatisfied during his teenage years. Living mostly in Kingston, he became concerned with the poverty of Afro-Jamaicans and developed the sense of a spiritual link with black people because of their sufferings. He wrote in *The Philosophy and Opinions of Marcus Garvey,* "I saw the injustices done to my race because it was black and I became dissatisfied." He became enmeshed in Kingston's vibrant street culture and its political debates. Impressed by the power of the spoken word, Garvey searched for a way to redeem his people from their sufferings by listening to Kingston's preachers and street orators.

Gradually, Garvey became conscious of a political dimension to Afro-Jamaican poverty. In 1907, he was the only management person to actively support a strike by workers at his place of employment. Blacklisted throughout Jamaica for his support of the workers, Garvey began to see politics as a calling. He founded the National Club and the *Watchman* paper in 1910. Both of these institutions represented attempts to persuade Jamaica's white and mulatto power brokers to labor reforms on behalf of black workers.

Discouraged by the lack of response to his activism in Jamaica, Garvey continued his mission on behalf of the black working poor by establishing papers in Costa Rica, Panama, Ecuador, Nicaragua, Spanish Honduras, Colombia, and Venezuela without any tangible success. In 1912, he returned to Jamaica, but months later he moved to London to push for reform of labor conditions at an international level. The indifference of British officials awakened a new level of racial consciousness in Garvey, since their indifference toward black workers in Jamaica and Latin America coincided with an era of government-instituted labor reform in England. While in London, discussions with Africans and Afro–West Indians added to Garvey's suspicion that the British government was unconcerned with the problems of blacks. As a result, he began to envision a future black nation as the source of hope for blacks.

Apparently, Garvey's reading of Booker T. Washington was a key influence that helped convince him of a calling to become a black nationalist leader. As he put it in *The Philosophy and Opinions of Marcus Garvey,* "I read 'Up From Slavery' . . . and then my doom of being a race leader dawned on me. . . . I asked where is the black man's Government? Where is his President, his country, and his ambassador, his army, his navy . . . I said, I will help to make them." Booker T. Washington also provided Garvey with the directives for reaching the envisioned black homeland. Self-help, through hard work and thrifty business ventures, became an almost covenantal practice for Garvey, one that promised to lift black peoples out of poverty and into a prosperous black nation. "God helps those who help themselves," he concluded.

Believing he had clarified his mission in life, Garvey returned to Jamaica, where he founded the Universal Negro Improvement and Conservation Association and African Communities League on 1 August 1914. It later became known as the Universal Negro Improvement Association (UNIA). The UNIA was to establish industrial colleges and farms as springboards to "conduct worldwide commercial intercourse." Garvey believed that blacks were about to change the face of world politics by becoming thrifty in their use of existing resources and by developing for themselves the institutions that constitute a nation. As recorded in John Henrik Clarke's *Marcus Garvey and the Vision of Africa,* he declared that blacks "will found an Empire on which the sun shall shine ceaselessly as it shines on the Empire of the North today." Britain, not Africa, seemed to serve as his model for the imminent black nation as he talked of "Empire" and of taking "civilization" (Western science) to the "backward tribes of Africa." Although sure that his model for the future was right, Garvey was not able to secure the finances and popular support necessary to maintain the UNIA. Once again he turned to Booker T. Washington for directives, but Washington died in November 1915 before Garvey could visit him. Determined to find an answer to his misfortune in the United States, Garvey arrived in New York on 23 March 1916 to embark on a countrywide lecture tour.

Two years of traveling throughout Afro-America and studying socioeconomic conditions convinced Garvey to become a militant advocate of separatism as the foundation of his commitment to self-help. In 1918, he established the New York chapter of the UNIA and began a second countrywide lecture tour to organize support. He argued that racial discrimination and racial violence prevented institutions controlled by whites from developing legitimate solutions to problems in the black community. These institutions can serve the interests only of whites, Garvey reasoned. He concluded that Afro-American leaders like civil rights advocate W.E.B. Du Bois and socialist A. Philip Randolph were "mere opportunists" with "no program" other than accommodation to the interests of whites. Garvey believed that Afro-Americans possessed the economic resources to build separate institutions powerful enough to force whites into recognition of blacks as equals.

Garvey articulated a theology of land that viewed the possession of a homeland as inseparable from black redemption. In the 3 August 1920 *New York Times* he was quoted as saying, "It is time for the 400,000,000 Negroes to claim Africa for themselves. . . . Africa must be redeemed and all of us pledge our manhood and our blood to this sacred cause." He preached that blacks must think of "race first" and become single-minded about building a separate nation on African soil, since the United States was the "white man's country." Garvey's message included a theology of labor that envisioned hard work as the way to the redemptive homeland. "One God, one aim, one destiny," Garvey exhorted in *The Philosophy and Opinions of Marcus Garvey,* "forward to the redemption of a great country."

Garvey's sermons attracted a massive following. By 1920, the UNIA consisted of 700 local branches in the United States alone and a membership that scholars have estimated at between 100,000 and two million. The association's weekly,

*Negro World,* reached a clientele of 200,000, and the Black Star Shipping Line, created in 1919 as the UNIA's primary business venture, sold $610,000 of stock in three months. In 1920, tens of thousands lined the streets as President General Marcus Garvey led the UNIA's Provisional Government of Africa through Harlem to open the first International Convention of the Negro Peoples of the World. The parade included the UNIA's army of African Legionnaires, the Black Cross Nurses, officials of the African Orthodox Church, and executives from the Negro Factories Corporation. After the procession, Garvey stepped to the podium and announced the consummation of an agreement with Liberia to build a UNIA headquarters, a residential community for Afro-American immigrants, and a UNIA industrial park in Liberia. The black nation Garvey envisioned in control of Africa had begun to take shape in the midst of Harlem.

Garvey's popularity declined sharply during the latter part of 1921. Black Star stock did not sell, and UNIA membership fees for 1921 yielded only $4,000, in contrast to more than $25,000 collected during 1920. Scores of Black Star officers and workers resigned as the Black Star Line was on the verge of bankruptcy. By 1922, the remaining Black Star workers were on strike and UNIA leaders accused each other of ill faith. An exodus of leaders followed. Sensing Garvey's demise, critics and opponents took to the offensive.

After two years of keeping Garvey under surveillance as a suspected Communist, the FBI indicted Garvey and the UNIA on charges of mail fraud in 1922. Afro-American leaders undertook a "Garvey must go" campaign that called for the deportation of Garvey as a swindler. Liberia, under pressure from England, France, and the United States, cut off its plans with the UNIA and banned the UNIA as a "seditious" organization with designs to overthrow the Liberian government. To top off the onslaught, Garvey was convicted on the mail fraud charges by a federal court in 1923 despite scanty evidence and the acquittal of the three other defendants from the UNIA.

Seeing himself as a martyr for the causes of truth and justice, Garvey did not think critically about UNIA institutions or creeds: "Let them crucify me and the UNIA shall succeed the more." He declared that the UNIA's troubles were solely the result of the corruption of employees and the sabotage of outsiders. Confronted by the specter that his separate institutions were deteriorating, Garvey preached more fervently the gospel of self-help and separatism while the promise of a homeland faded from his message. In 1922, he negotiated with Ku Klux Klan officials to stress the compatibility of the separatist social views of both groups. Opposing labor reforms as illusory hopes in the United States, Garvey exhorted black workers to "work for a lower wage than white union workers . . . since the white capitalist is the only true friend of the Negro in America." He became more and more critical of the black poor, arguing: "We [blacks] are the most careless and indifferent people in the world. We are shiftless and irresponsible." Though Garvey's social views remained essentially consistent with the principles of self-help and separatism, he sounded more and more like an apologist for white power brokers, and his views lost their popularity.

On imprisonment in 1925, after the failure of court appeals to overturn his mail fraud conviction, Garvey's view of himself as a martyr evolved into the consciousness of a ''suffering servant'' who would rise again as a world leader: ''I lay down my life for the cause of my people . . . for in new life I shall rise with God's grace to lead the millions up the heights of triumph.'' While in prison, Garvey republished a lengthier, revised version of *The Philosophy and Opinions of Marcus Garvey* (1923) and wrote weekly exhortations in the *Negro World* in an attempt to regain popular support. President Calvin Coolidge pardoned Garvey in 1927 under an agreement with the FBI to deport him immediately. In December 1927, he was taken to New Orleans, where a crowd of hundreds gathered to hear his final words on U.S. soil.

Garvey returned to Jamaica, where he was given a hero's welcome, but his efforts to reestablish former programs and policies failed. Consequently, he endorsed political action for economic reform and won a seat in the Kingston city legislature in 1930. Fearing the potential for the poor's support of Garvey, political opponents were able to disqualify Garvey's election through a court ruling that his campaign had been ''libelous.'' Once again, Garvey moved his base of operations to London, finalizing the move in 1935. There he established the *Blackman* paper, scrapped his endorsement of political activism, and began a campaign of apology for the old UNIA program of self-help, separate development, and black nationalism. But Garvey could barely attract crowds of one hundred. Overworked for an ignored message, he suffered a heart attack in January 1940 and died on 10 June 1940, never having set foot on the redemptive soil of Africa.

## Appraisal

Marcus Garvey's primary significance lies in the fact that he led the first mass movement of Afro-Americans. Since the vast majority of Afro-Americans were poor, an Afro-American mass movement was by definition a movement based in the black poor. Consequently, assessments of Garvey have been mostly concerned with explanations for the rise and decline of his support among the black poor. Some analysts say Garvey's popularity was based on continuity between Garvey's social views and Afro-American intellectual traditions. Garvey's emphases on self-help, the work ethic, separate development, and the colonization of Africa are correctly linked to influential Afro-American thinkers like Booker T. Washington, Henry McNeal Turner, and Martin Delany. Nevertheless, there is little evidence that any one of these thinkers was ever popular with the black poor. It is unclear why their ideas would suddenly become popular with the black poor in 1919–20. Other analysts see Garvey as harmonious with Afro-American folk culture. Garvey did build on Afro-American folk traditions like local fraternal societies and the concept of God as black. Yet it is not apparent that Garvey was sympathetic toward the revivalistic Protestantism and the artistic traditions valued by most Afro-Americans. Garvey was a practicing Catholic who encouraged the Reverend George McGuire to found the African Orthodox

Church, modeled on Eastern Orthodoxy, as a Christian complement to the UNIA. Additionally, *Negro World* editor William Ferris, handpicked by Garvey, sought to promote black celebration of "classical values" in music and art while rejecting "jubilee" traditions (Afro-American folk arts) as part of a shameful past that should be forgotten.

Other assessments of Garvey's popularity emphasize his promises of empowerment. Critics have claimed that Garvey represented empowerment only for artisans or professionals. But Garvey did attract the black poor's support en masse. His emphasis on race was relevant to black poverty, since the black poor were by and large restricted to unskilled, low-paying jobs because of their race. Advocates have claimed that Garvey represented empowerment for all blacks, regardless of their class. But the fact that the black poor were his base of popular support indicates that something was distinctive about Garvey's appeal to the poor vis-à-vis artisans or professionals. It is possible the black poor were especially attracted to Garvey's theology of land. A theology of land that sees God's redemptive activity as related to the possession of land can be directly linked to a tradition of the Afro-American poor. This tradition reaches back through the "promised land" imagery of the "Great Migration," to the "forty acres and a mule" creed of freedpersons during Reconstruction, and even further to slave Christianity's interpretation of Jesus' redemptive activity as related to a return to Africa. Additionally, Garvey's sudden appearance as a leader who promised liberation may have been viewed by the black poor as the possible fulfillment of a traditional belief that expected liberation from an outsider. This tradition of the black poor can also be traced back to slave Christianity with its hope in the coming of Jesus as a second Moses.

Historically, the land and liberation theologies of the Afro-American poor have been at odds with the ideology of most Afro-American leaders and professionals, who have been more concerned with self-help, the work ethic, civil rights, and the issue of integration versus segregation. This class conflict may have been involved in Garvey's sudden decline from popularity when the black poor shifted from support of Garvey to indifference. Garvey's increased emphasis on self-help and separate development, to the detriment of his advocacy for appropriation of land and liberation, was simultaneous with the decline of his popularity.

From a socioeconomic perspective, Garvey seemed to preach the infallibility of self-help and separate development long after it became evident that the black poor lacked the resources for self-development. The black poor were by and large workers whose wages barely enabled them to subsist. The expectation that they could finance businesses, like the Black Star Shipping Line, to successfully compete with multinational corporations was unrealistic. Garvey assumed the black poor possessed the independence to accumulate sufficient wealth to accomplish self-development goals. This ignored the fact that the black poor were not separate from white society but were already integrated into a political economy where they were dependent on the price, job, and wage controls of

wealthy whites. Garvey's expectation that liberation of the black poor was possible without changes in white society and without empowering the black poor
economically was fanciful.

In the last analysis, prophets who promise redemption have been held accountable to historical verification. Perhaps Garvey's failure to deliver land and
resources led the black poor to reassess their support for him. Nevertheless,
Garvey made several important contributions. Living in a society pervaded by
the imagery of white heroes and the power of European civilization, Garvey
emphasized that black people had been as heroic as whites and that Africa
possessed civilizations before Europe. He was a pioneer among influential Afro-
American leaders in his belief that it was no more ridiculous to think of God or
Jesus as black than to think of them as white. Whereas many Afro-American
leaders and professionals were defensive about their racial identity, Garvey
celebrated blackness. He was one of the most vocal and influential critics of
colonialism, acknowledged by African nationalist leaders of the fifties, like
Kwame Nkrumah and Jomo Kenyatta, as a monumental influence. Perhaps even
more important were the subtle ways Garvey reinterpreted into an international
context African religious traditions long submerged in the black poor of Western
civilization. Ultimately, these traditional elements—such as a theology of land,
faith in the Divine as a liberating power who breaks into history, and communal
moral values—may have constituted both his uniqueness as an Afro-American
leader and his most significant contribution to U.S. religious thought as a whole.

## Survey of Criticism

Literature about Marcus Garvey is sparse, though scholarly. Len Nembhard's
*Trials and Triumphs of Marcus Garvey* initiated literary assessments with a
sympathetic and uncritical view from an insider. Similarly uncritical were the
early appraisals by Roi Ottley in *New World A-Coming* and by Amy Jacques
Garvey in *Garvey and Garveyism*. John Hope Franklin broke the ice for scholarly
critical interpretations in *From Slavery to Freedom* by arguing that Garvey offered
little besides a psychology of self-esteem for the black poor. Franklin rightly
discerns Garvey's significance as the first leader of an Afro-American mass
movement, although his emphasis on the psychological dimension of the black
poor's support is reductionistic. E. David Cronon popularized Franklin's interpretation in *Black Moses: The Story of Marcus Garvey and the Universal Negro
Improvement Association*. Cronon's work remains the best chronology of Garvey
and the UNIA, but it repeats Franklin's overdrawn characterization of Garvey
as a reactionary.

The revival of black nationalism during the sixties brought forth a new gen-
eration of scholars who effected a shift in the literature on Garvey. Theodore
G. Vincent's *Black Power and the Garvey Movement* and Tony Martin's *Race
First: the Organizational and Ideological Struggles of Marcus Garvey and the
Universal Negro Improvement Association* led the way in reconstructing the
portrait of Garvey in a hero's mold. Their reinterpretation of Garvey as one who

was ahead of the times is overstated, and it neglects a critical appraisal of Garvey. Tony Martin has since expanded the scope of his scholarship on Garvey with a five-volume study entitled *The New Marcus Garvey Library* which includes a biography, studies of Garvey's aesthetic sensibilities, a study of Garvey's first wife, Amy Ashwood, and an interpretation of Garvey's religiosity.

A second shift in literature about Garvey has occurred during the eighties through a variety of efforts that depart from the hero's mold of the seventies. James C. Boyd's "Garvey and Garveyites, 1887–1930: Primitives on the Move" echoes the Franklin-Cronon interpretations by characterizing Garvey as a "pre-modern racist" and a "primitive" who attracted followers through his ability to command a mass psychology of paranoia among the black poor. Lawrence Levine's "Marcus Garvey: The Politics of Revitalization" utilizes Anthony F. C. Wallace's cultural revitalization thesis to argue for the cultural appeal of the Garvey movement for the black poor. Most helpful is Levine's historical and social contextualization of Garvey's popularity, though he fails to achieve an equivalent contextualization of Garvey's decline. Judith Stein's *The World of Marcus Garvey: Race and Class in Modern Society* sees the Garvey movement as one exclusively for upwardly mobile black artisans displaced by twentieth-century capitalism. She argues persuasively, though with some exaggeration, that Garvey's racial consciousness was an outdated interpretation of society, given the class dynamic of twentieth-century capitalism.

Also noteworthy are more-specialized studies of the Garvey movement. Randall Burkett's *Garveyism as a Religious Movement* captures the religious dimension of Garvey's popularity but fails to confront adequately the points of conflict between the movement and the black poor. Emory Tolbert's *The UNIA and Black Los Angeles* is an account of the Los Angeles UNIA during the twenties which provides a useful introduction to the issues of unity and conflict between Garvey and his U.S. followers.

## Bibliography

### Writings by Marcus Garvey

1918–1933  *Negro World*. New York: U.N.I.A.
1923  *The Philosophy and Opinions of Marcus Garvey*. Edited by Amy Jacques Garvey. Reprint. New York: Atheneum, 1969.
1927  *The Tragedy of White Injustice*. Reprint. New York: Haskell House Publishers, 1972.
1983  *The Marcus Garvey and Universal Negro Improvement Association Papers*. Edited by Robert A. Hill. Berkeley: University of California Press.
1986  *Message to the People: The Course of African Philosophy*. Edited by Tony Martin. Dover, Mass.: Majority Press.

### Selected Studies about Marcus Garvey

Boyd, James C. "Garvey and Garveyites, 1887–1930: Primitives on the Move." Ph.D. diss., University of Southern California, 1983.

Burkett, Randall K. *Garveyism as a Religious Movement: The Institutionalization of a Black Civil Religion*. Metuchen, N.J.: Scarecrow Press, 1978.

Clarke, John Henrik. *Marcus Garvey and the Vision of Africa*. New York: Vintage Books, 1974.

Cronon, Edmund David. *Black Moses: The Story of Marcus Garvey and the Universal Negro Improvement Association*. Madison: University of Wisconsin Press, 1955.

Davis, Lenwood, and Janet L. Sims, eds. *Marcus Garvey: An Annotated Bibliography*. Westport, Conn.: Greenwood Press, 1980.

Franklin, John Hope. *From Slavery to Freedom: A History of American Negroes*. New York: Alfred A. Knopf, 1967.

Garvey, Amy Jacques. *Garvey and Garveyism*. Kingston, Jamaica: Collier Books, 1970.

————. *United States of America vs. Marcus Garvey: Was Justice Defeated?* New York: n.p., 1925.

Levine, Lawrence. "Marcus Garvey: The Politics of Revitalization." In *Black Leaders of the Twentieth Century*, edited by John Hope Franklin and August Meier. Urbana: University of Illinois Press, 1982.

Martin, Tony. *Race First: The Organizational and Ideological Struggles of Marcus Garvey and the Universal Negro Improvement Association*. Westport, Conn.: Greenwood Press, 1976.

————. *The New Marcus Garvey Library*. Dover, Mass.: Majority Press, 1983.

Nembhard, Len. *Trials and Triumphs of Marcus Garvey*. Millwood, N.Y.: Kraus Reprint Co., 1978.

Ottley, Roi. *New World A-Coming*. Cleveland: World Publishing Co., 1943.

Stein, Judith. *The World of Marcus Garvey: Race and Class in Modern Society*. Baton Rouge: Louisiana State University Press, 1986.

Tolbert, Emory J. *The UNIA and Black Los Angeles: Ideology and Community in the American Garvey Movement*. Los Angeles: Center for Afro-American Studies, University of California, 1980.

Vincent, Theodore G. *Black Power and the Garvey Movement*. New York: Ramparts Press, 1971.

CRAIG A. FORNEY

# Charles Manuel "Sweet Daddy" Grace

With the close of the First World War in 1919, blacks in the United States looked forward to enjoying the rights and privileges of all first-class citizens. But white Americans seemed equally determined that the fruits of liberty should be reserved for themselves and their heirs. Although the National Association for the Advancement of Colored People had scored some impressive victories for blacks in the courts, the organization was ill-equipped to address the deep spiritual yearning felt by blacks, especially those on the lower end of the economic scale. The mainline black denominations achieved some success but failed to speak to the total needs of black Americans. The time seemed ripe for Marcus Garvey* and other charismatic leaders who attempted to address at once the economic and spiritual problems facing black Americans. One of the most significant of these messiahs was Charles M. Grace, better known to his followers as "Sweet Daddy."

## Biography

Charles Manuel "Sweet Daddy" Grace, the charismatic and flamboyant founder and leader of the United House of Prayer for All People on the Rock of the Apostolic Faith, was born Marcelino Manoel de Graca on 25 January 1881 in Brava, Cape Verde Islands, a Portuguese territory off the West African coast. Of African and Portuguese ancestry, he was one of ten children born to Delomba and Emmanuel de Graca, a Portuguese stonecutter. Grace came to the United States around 1903 and worked, at various times, as a cook and grocer in New Bedford, Massachusetts, a Portuguese settlement. Some time after arriving in this country, he changed his name to Charles M. Grace and began his career as a holiness preacher. According to a niece, in a 1960 interview with Kays Gary of the *Charlotte Observer*, Grace had once been married and had had a son (who died at a young age). The marriage ended in divorce because the wife "didn't want a spiritual life." The wife, whom the niece declined to identify, was no doubt Jennie J. Lombard of New Bedford, whom Grace reportedly married on 2 February 1909.

Charles Grace established his first House of Prayer in West Wareham, Massachusetts, in 1924 and began preaching around 1925 in tents throughout the Southeast. The bishop, a title he assumed early in his ministry as head of the House of Prayer, quickly established a number of Houses along the eastern seaboard from as far south as Tampa to as far north as Buffalo. But the greatest number of Houses were established in the southeastern states of Georgia, North Carolina, and South Carolina. These Houses were almost always built in a blighted area of the city, giving some credence to the opinion held by a black minister in Charlotte, North Carolina, according to Rufus Wells, that Daddy Grace "took a rock no one else would use and made it the cornerstone of his church."

Grace and his followers seldom spoke of these establishments as churches and frowned on outsiders who insisted on doing so. They preferred the term "Houses of Prayer," based on Isaiah 56:7: "These I will bring to my holy mountain, and make them joyful in my house of prayer; their burnt offerings will be accepted on my altar; for my house shall be called a house of prayer for all peoples." The tendency in the organization to follow a literal interpretation of Scripture is seen here, as well as in the reference to the altar as the "holy mountain," a designation that holds to this day.

Daddy Grace, in establishing his religious empire, was beset by obstacles from every quarter. But each new setback, far from diminishing the bishop's power and authority, actually seemed to support the claim of his invincibility made by many of his followers. An elder in the Grace organization who had been a member of one of the first Houses of Prayer in Charlotte recounted the following incident to Rufus Wells of the *Washington Afro-American* in February 1960.

> Once when Sweet Daddy was on trial for preaching false doctrine, he said there would be a sign from heaven to prove that he was a spiritual man. While the court was in recess, a ball of fire came down from heaven and knocked a huge limb from a tree in the courtyard. Lots of people were standing in the yard, but no one was hurt. This was the sign he had predicted. The court dismissed the case against him.

To outsiders the incident was a mere chance occurrence, but to the faithful it was evidence of Grace's divine powers.

In 1934, Grace faced a Mann Act charge in Brooklyn, New York, for allegedly transporting a young woman across state lines for immoral purposes. The twenty-year-old woman, a pianist in the Grace organization, said they lived together as man and wife. After a three-day trial, Grace was found guilty and was sentenced to a year and a day in jail. After posting a $7,500 bond and appealing the case, he was acquitted. During the same year the government filed a lawsuit against him for tax evasion, beginning a series of such litigations against Grace and his organization. The government claimed that he owed back taxes in the amount of $15,000 for the years 1927–32, a period during which it was shown that he had paid only $41 in income tax. This suit was later dismissed, as Grace successfully argued that his "income" consisted of free-will donations to the church that were not taxable.

Later, in 1957, a most trying year for the now aging cleric, Grace was hauled into court on at least two occasions. Mrs. Louvenia Royster, a schoolteacher from Waycross, Georgia, filed a suit claiming she had married Grace on 26 September 1923 in New York City, when he was known as John H. Royster. This suit was dismissed, as Grace showed documents proving that he had been out of the country when the marriage was said to have taken place. In the second case, Grace was arrested on a charge of striking a fourteen-year-old girl at the House of Prayer in Richmond, Virginia. According to Wells, the girl claimed that she had resisted his efforts when it appeared that "he was trying to feel my legs, way up high." As in the previous cases, he was cleared of the charges. Through all of these trials, his followers remained faithful, claiming that Daddy could not sin. And in those cases involving women, it seemed as if the female members of his organization provided the greatest support.

The air of invincibility was carefully cultivated by Daddy Grace himself. With his long flowing hair, two-inch fingernails (painted red, white, and blue), cutaway coat, and chauffeured limousines, the bishop struck an impressive if not awesome figure. He was an unquestioned leader and enjoyed total control of the affairs of his organization. Although there was a General Council, this body served at the pleasure of the bishop and was clearly only advisory. Daddy Grace had the last word in all matters involving this organization. According to anthropologist Arthur Fauset in *Black Gods of the Metropolis,* Grace often boasted that he would not have a minister serve under him whom he considered smart enough to question his undisputed authority.

Although Grace established his first House of Prayer in West Wareham, not far from his home in New Bedford, he achieved his greatest success in Charlotte, North Carolina, a city in which the group today claims a membership that rivals that of the traditional denominational churches. This congregation, at least during the 1960s, occupied the largest single black church structure in the city. The first House in Charlotte began when Grace visited that city in 1926 and set up a tent located at 3rd and South Caldwell streets. Here Grace preached and baptized a number of converts in a small lake.

Some of the older members who remember Grace's first visit to Charlotte suggest that part of Grace's power and magnetism lay in the physical resemblance he bore, for some at least, to Jesus. The *Charlotte Observer* of 13 January 1960 carried the following testimony of one of the oldest members:

> I know he seemed different from any man; so one day I ask him, "ain't you Jesus?" And he said, "Look upon me and what you see then that is what I am." Then I came to know that while Jesus was dead, he was carrying Christ in him and he was the last prophet. There ain't going to be no more.

Grace, in fact, unlike his rival Father Divine*, never claimed to be God. But it is also fair to say that he never attempted to dispel the impression of those of his followers who insisted that he occupied a station alongside the Trinity. The terms that Grace himself preferred were ''God's representative'' or ''God's chief angel.'' He saw himself as undertaking a powerful mediating role, as is evidenced by an often-quoted passage, where he plays on the name as ''Grace.'' He would admonish his followers, according to Arthur Fauset in *Black Gods of the Metropolis:* ''Never mind about God. Salvation is by Grace. . . . Grace has given God a vacation, and since God is on His vacation, don't worry him. . . . If you sin against God, Grace can save you, but if you sin against Grace, God cannot save you.''

The House of Prayer for All People, as its name implies, is open to all, regardless of race, color, or creed. Many of the first members of the organization were from lower-economic backgrounds. And though this particular group still accounts for the majority of the organization's membership, there is an ever increasing number of well-educated middle-class blacks. According to a recent issue of *Truth and Facts,* the membership today claims individuals from all economic levels, including doctors, lawyers, and teachers. Although there are some whites and members of other ethnic groups in the various Houses, the membership is predominantly black. Those whites who join tend to be young and liberal and are attracted to the organization's commitment to a worship service free of the bias and prejudice of the color bar so often associated with the mainline denominations.

The House of Prayer emphasizes conversion, sanctification, divine healing, and the gift of the Holy Spirit manifested through speaking in tongues and thus belongs to the group of churches commonly called Pentecostal. Like most of these churches, the House of Prayer is fundamentalist in its teachings. It stresses the inerrancy of biblical Scripture and prohibits drinking, profanity, adultery, fornication, and interfaith marriages. Although there is an unwritten dress code, it does not appear to be applied as strictly as in a number of the other holiness churches.

From God's White House, the organization's headquarters located at 601 M Street in the nation's capital, to the smaller missions, the "churches" exhibit a remarkable degree of uniformity, even to the point of the predominant color scheme of red, white, and blue that is found both inside and outside the structures. Services at each of the Houses are held nightly, beginning around 7:30 or 8:00 P.M., and throughout the day on Sundays. They are often spontaneous affairs, punctuated by singing, blaring trombones, ecstatic shouting, and testimonies to the healing powers of Grace or of one of his numerous products, which are sold at each of the services. Although there is preaching, it does not occupy center stage, as it does for example in the traditional Baptist church. Grace, in fact, was not considered a dynamic speaker.

The single most important event occurs each year during convocation, a kind of convention that attracts members from across the nation. These convocations are held in late summer and early fall in locations where there are Mother Houses with sufficient seating to accommodate the vast numbers who regularly attend. The appearance of the bishop (the title was assumed by Walter McCollough in 1962) near the end of the week is the central attraction. There are programs in his honor on Friday and Saturday evening; and on Sunday morning, there is a large baptism, followed by a parade through the neighborhood.

The House of Prayer's emphasis on fund-raising is clear and unmistakable, leading some to consider this aspect as a rite in itself. Indeed, the *General Council Laws of the United House of Prayer for All People* contains numerous references to the proper conduct of the members and pastors regarding the collection and disposition of funds. Various "laws" forbid the local pastor from handling money yet require him to be knowledgeable of "every penny raised and spent." Another law mandates that "each House must have representative a man besides the pastor to take note of everything and accompany the pastor at the time of checking." Further checks on the handling of funds are accomplished through the establishment of two important committees: a banking committee and a bills-paying committee. At least two of the members of the banking committee must go to deposit all funds before they are eventually sent to the headquarters in Washington. All bills are to be paid by check. Whereas the local pastors are bound by stringent rules of accountability, the bishop himself enjoys the widest latitude in all financial matters. Rule #40, often referred to as the Golden Rule, states: "All pastors must see to it that each member pays his convocation fee and substantial rallies put on for the upbuilding of the Kingdom of Heaven and this is to be put in the hands of our General Builder to build as he sees fit without bounds." One night per week, usually on Tuesday or Wednesday, the local pastor is permitted to keep for himself the money collected.

Much of the organization's revenue is raised through numerous clubs and groups that vie with each other in efforts to achieve the "victory," accorded to the individual or group that raises the largest sum of money. The financial report from the Charlotte Mother House for 7 February 1971 lists over thirty such groups, including the Elder Board, Grace Soldiers, Literature Club, String Band, Home Lovers, Female Scouts, Senior Queens, Female Royal Guards, Willing Workers, Soul Hunters, and Junior Nurses. Whatever other responsibilities these organizations have, their chief duty seems to be that of fund-raising.

Additional revenue is generated through the sale of a line of products bearing the leader's name, all of which carry rather fantastic claims. Grace soap and Grace cold cream can cleanse the body and promote healing; Grace writing paper is helpful in composing a good letter; and Grace coffee beans brew the best cup of coffee.

The most important of these products is *Grace Magazine,* a monthly reportedly published since the late 1920s. Inside the front cover of each issue is a picture of Daddy Grace with the caption: "Daddy Grace, the Last Prophet." The contents page includes the magazine's statement of purpose: "[T]o unfold the Hidden truth of the gospel; to Magnify the life of Christ; to Teach, to appreciate the Gift of God; to Testify of the Present Blessing Received by the Thousands, and Healing by the Millions." Testimonies regarding healing are a central emphasis of the magazine, taking up more than half of an average issue. The magazine not only serves as the official organ for proclaiming the healing powers of Grace and of the various products but also is believed to have healing powers itself. Interviews conducted with several of the older members of the Charlotte House disclosed that many in the organization, usually women, regularly wear pieces of the magazine on their bodies to ward off illness and ill fortune. One woman claimed that after applying a small piece of the magazine to a corn on her toe, the pain ceased and the corn went away. Another credited the magazine with healing a bone ailment, and still another wrote of the power of the magazine when used in conjunction with some other Grace product. She said:

> On June 15, 1944, I was doing some work in my garden, and a snake bit me. . . .
> I then took some of the Grace Hair Grower and put it on a piece of *Grace Magazine*
> and made a plaster and applied it to the place where I had been bitten and it was
> healed, and I am still well. I had faith in the God of Daddy Grace. I thank God
> for Sweet Daddy Grace and all the Grace products.

These statements, representative of the type of testimonies that can be found in each issue, point to the central role that divine healing occupies in the religion.

Before his death of a heart attack in Los Angeles on 12 January 1960, Charles Grace could claim a following of over three million in well over one hundred Houses and financial holdings estimated at over $25 million. But the House of Prayer itself seemed to be in great turmoil. The organization had lost not only its spiritual leader and "boyfriend to the world" but a skilled businessman and tactician who had been able to keep the government and other detractors at bay. The IRS greeted the news of his death with a tax suit of nearly $6 million on the Grace estate. Lawyers for the House of Prayer maintained that the properties did not belong to Grace personally but to the church and therefore should enjoy the tax-exempt status commonly afforded such property. Indeed, Grace left only $70,000 to his relatives; the rest was willed to the organization. After a lengthy court battle, U.S. District Court Judge George L. Hart, Jr., ordered, in March 1963, that assets of over $4.6 million be turned over to the House of Prayer.

The House of Prayer also had to contend with internal problems. The constitution, for example, did not clearly provide for a successor to Daddy Grace. There were several pretenders to the throne, each claiming in some way to have been appointed by Grace himself. Elder Walter McCollough, a native of Great Falls, South Carolina, and the owner of a dry cleaning establishment in Washington, prevailed after a long, bitter struggle that eventually had to be handled by the courts. The court ordered a new election between the major candidates when a group of dissident elders questioned the legitimacy of the first election and therefore McCollough's claim to leadership. Capturing 410 of the 462 delegates' votes, McCollough assumed his office on a permanent basis on 8 April 1962.

McCollough's greatest task still lay before him: he had to heal the wounds caused by the protracted legal battle as well as to justify his status as Daddy Grace's successor. This was no easy matter, as Grace had been considered the "Last Prophet," after whom there would be no other. To make as smooth a transition as possible and to dispel any impression that his actions were motivated by self-interest, McCollough for the first few years of his administration tried to keep the organizational structure as it had been under Grace's leadership. He considered himself Grace's son and, for a while, called himself "Sweet Daddy Grace" McCollough. A man of fair complexion, he allowed his hair and fingernails to grow, so that even casual observers could see a striking physical resemblance between the two men. Gradually, over a period of twenty-five years, he seems to have built the organization in his own image. The Grace products have now given way to McCollough shampoo, McCollough soap, and various other McCollough products, including *McCollough Magazine*. Moreover, as the official successor to Daddy Grace, McCollough assumed the title of bishop, which had been reserved exclusively for Daddy Grace. When several members of the Mother House in Charlotte were asked about the differences between McCollough and Grace, most of the respondents faithful to McCollough claimed that there is no essential difference, only that the work is now greater. They pointed to the number of new Houses that are cropping up throughout the nation in cities that heretofore had no Houses. A major reason for this expansion is that McCollough tells his followers that they should not live in a city where there is no House of Prayer. If one is not there, they should build one. These kinds of efforts have kept the organization vibrant and flourishing; today it is one of the largest of the independent Christian communities in the United States and is a major force in the spiritual lives of thousands of black Americans.

## Appraisal

Despite bits of biographical information that can be found here and there, Bishop Charles Manuel Grace remains something of an enigma to us. This, of course, is owing largely to the bishop himself, who, it is reported, often spoke in riddles or parables when he felt pushed or pinned down on a fine point. Added to this are questions regarding his intellectual prowess. Some have claimed that Grace could speak several languages, whereas others insist just as vigorously that he had great problems reading and writing.

Grace never delved into the arcanae of theological or religious thought. His belief system, as he himself once suggested, was based on faith rather than religion. As God's intermediary, he promised his followers spiritual as well as material rewards that they could have in the present. Grace never emphasized the compensatory, otherworldly doctrines that Benjamin Mays and Joseph Nicholson found to characterize much of the preaching in the black church during the 1930s. For members of the House of Prayer, the Word was made flesh in the embodiment of Grace himself.

There are those, of course, who consider Grace to have been more of a businessman than a spiritual leader. They have fallen just short of agreeing with Joseph Washington's assessment: "The movement was a profit-making venture by a black entrepreneur who succeeded by manipulating spiritual hunger into a system of self-aggrandizement." Although Grace certainly lived comfortably, perhaps extravagantly, reports of his personal wealth are no doubt exaggerated. Most of the money seemed to have been ploughed back into the organization in the form of larger and better-appointed sanctuaries, apartment buildings, and other properties that belonged to the House of Prayer and not to Grace personally.

Mays and Nicholson, in their book *The Negro's Church* (1933), conclude, "It is characteristic of the Negro church that the Negro owns it and that it is largely the product of his hand and brain." The statement is perhaps even more relevant in regard to the House of Prayer, for the members not only own the titles to the various sanctuaries but the deeds as well. It had always been the policy of Grace (and now McCollough) to complete payment of the building before it was dedicated as a House of Prayer. Those members of the congregation who may not own their own homes can point with pride to their partial ownership in the House of Prayer.

The House of Prayer, which prides itself on being open to all, regardless of color or creed, may be vulnerable to charges of sexism. Although women in most of the Houses outnumber men two or three to one, they are forbidden (based on Scripture) from advancing in the church's hierarchy to positions of minister or elder. Although there appear to be no insurgent voices among the women at this time, one wonders how long this silence will continue in light of the protests by women in the mainline churches.

**Survey of Criticism**

There have not been many scholarly studies of Charles Grace or the United House of Prayer. The classic study remains Arthur H. Fauset's *Black Gods of the Metropolis,* in which he discusses four other black groups of the urban North in addition to the House of Prayer. Though Fauset's study was done over forty years ago, it still provides very useful information, since there have been few changes in ritual and organization. A more sustained treatment of the House of Prayer may be found in Albert Whiting's dissertation, "The United House of Prayer for All People: A Case Study of a Charismatic Sect." Whiting lived among the members of the Augusta, Georgia, House for a month in order to get a firsthand look at its religious practices. The study includes fascinating interviews with the members, but the effort to determine personality characteristics from such information is less successful. A more recent study is John W. Robinson's essay "A Song, a Shout, and a Prayer," which updates Fauset's materials and provides useful information on the transition from Grace to McCollough. There are also several news series that appeared shortly after Grace's death, in such dailies as the *Washington Post,* the *Afro-American,* and the *Charlotte Observer.* Of these, Phil Casey's seven-part series, appearing in March 1960, provides the most detailed data.

Further research on Bishop Charles Grace and the United House of Prayer is necessary to correct certain negative and unfounded generalizations, such as the view held by Sydney Ahlstrom in *A Religious History of the American People* (1972). He asserts that adherents are from "depressed elements of the black communities" with deep insecurities, anxieties, and psychic needs. It is questionable whether those individuals who join the House of Prayer differ radically from those who join the more orthodox groups. What appears to be the case is that the House of Prayer and similar organizations have been more imaginative and resourceful in addressing the full gamut of needs of their followers. There seems to be little doubt that the United House of Prayer will continue to flourish in its own right, not merely as an alternative to the mainline churches.

**Bibliography**

*Studies about Charles Manuel "Sweet Daddy" Grace*
Casey, Phil. "The Enigma of Daddy Grace." *Washington Post,* 6–13 March 1960.
Fauset, Arthur H. *Black Gods of the Metropolis: Negro Religious Cults in the Urban North.* Philadelphia: University of Pennsylvania Press, 1944.
Gary, Kays. "Spiritual Life Not for Wife, So Daddy's Marriage Ended." *Charlotte Observer,* 13 January 1960, p. 2A.
Gaultney, Judy. "House of Prayer Got Its Start in Downtown Tent." *Charlotte News,* 17 February 1979, p. 5A.
*General Council Laws of the United House of Prayer for All People.* Washington, D.C.: United House of Prayer, 1938.
LaFarge, John. "The Incredible Daddy Grace." *America* 103 (2 April 1960): 5.

McCollough, Walter. *The Truth and Facts: United House of Prayer*. Washington: House of Prayer, 1986.
MacDonald, Donald. "Daddy Grace Coming Sept. 7 to Dedicate His New Church." *Charlotte News*, 14 August 1954, section 2, p. 1.
Oberdorfer, Don. "Daddy Grace Profited by Being a Prophet." *Charlotte Observer*, 3–4 February 1960.
Robinson, John W. "A Song, a Shout, and a Prayer." In *The Black Experience in Religion*, edited by C. Eric Lincoln. Garden City, N.Y.: Doubleday, Anchor Books, 1974.
Washington, Joseph R., Jr. *Black Sects and Cults*. Garden City, N.Y.: Doubleday, 1972.
Wells, Rufus. "Secrets of Daddy Grace." *Washington Afro-American*, 12 February–5 March 1960, magazine section.
Whiting, Albert N. "The United House of Prayer for All People: A Case Study of a Charismatic Sect." Ph.D. diss., American University, 1952.
York, John. "The Spiritual Empire of Sweet Daddy Grace." *Charlotte Observer*, 20 February 1983, pp. 1E, 7E.

JOHN O. HODGES

# Billy Graham

The United States after World War II was not the nation it had been before. Gone was the naive liberalism that earlier in the twentieth century had dominated much of American thought, including religious thought. The dawn of the Cold War and the dread of communism brought a stark realism to American life. The time was ripe for an evangelical upsurge in religion, one with a convincing interpretation of the postwar world and a ready resolution for its problems. It came in the so-called revival of religion of the 1950s. At the center of that revival one person loomed larger than life in the popular mind: Billy Graham.

### Biography

Born near Charlotte, North Carolina, on 7 November 1918, William Franklin Graham, by all accounts, enjoyed a typical rural childhood. A passion for things religious developed only after Graham's conversion in 1934 at a revival led by Mordecai Ham. Following a summer selling Fuller Brush products in South Carolina, Graham enrolled at Bob Jones College, then in Cleveland, Tennessee. Discontent with the restrictive environment there, he transferred to Florida Bible Institute near Tampa. While there, Graham became a Southern Baptist and had his first experiences preaching. Aware of the power of the preached word and sensing a personal inadequacy, Graham reportedly practiced his sermons while walking around the campus. Even then, Graham exhibited an extraordinary pulpit presence and a compelling, if somewhat frenzied, fast-paced preaching style.

After graduation, Graham entered Wheaton College, near Chicago, majoring in anthropology. At Wheaton, he met Ruth McCue Bell, daughter of medical missionaries to China. They were married on 13 August 1943, shortly after completing their degrees. Five children issued from the marriage: Virginia (1945), Anne (1948), Bunny (1950), William Franklin, Jr. (1952), and Nelson (1958). After marriage, Graham became pastor of a struggling church in Chicago, eschewing going to seminary because of a compulsion to preach. Graham has often lamented his lack of theological education, although he reads widely and avidly. In 1986 he was quoted by *Inside the American Religious Scene* as saying, "If I had to do it over again, I would speak less and study more."

Chicago introduced Graham to radio evangelism when he and his congregation accepted a challenge to sponsor "Songs in the Night," a weekly program with Graham preaching. Graham soon joined the staff of Youth for Christ, leading evangelistic campaigns targeted at adolescents and young adults in the United States and Europe. In 1947 he accepted the presidency of the Northwestern Schools, a post he retained for over four years, despite his increasing commitment to a career as an evangelist.

Graham was catapulted into national attention in 1949 when the response and publicity given to a campaign in Los Angeles led to its extension from three weeks to two months. Graham's confidence that a personal decision to accept Christ as Savior resolved all problems, his cry for fresh national commitment to morality, his conviction that the United States had a God-ordained role in human affairs, and his biting condemnation of communism struck home. His preaching made the realities of postwar life understandable and offered hope for the future. The Los Angeles revival made Graham a celebrity. With an increase in invitations to hold evangelistic meetings, Graham made a concerted effort to avoid traditional pitfalls and criticisms of popular revivals by maintaining rigorous financial integrity and by instituting a system to provide later contact with persons recording conversions. The latter have characterized the Graham enterprise since. In 1950, Graham first used "crusade" to identify his campaign in Columbia, South Carolina. The attendance of South Carolina Governor Strom Thurmond at one service and his endorsement of Graham began a long association with prominent political figures that enhanced Graham's image, until Graham's involvement with President Richard Nixon brought concern when scandal forced Nixon's resignation.

Also in 1950, a new radio ministry emerged when Walter A. Maier*, preacher on the popular "Lutheran Hour" radio series, died. Forming the Billy Graham Evangelistic Association (BGEA) to oversee the expanding work, Graham began his "Hour of Decision" broadcasts that November. So wide was the broadcast audience that by 1952 Graham was receiving more than 1,000 letters a day. BGEA's staff expanded to handle the increased demands of the ministry. In 1951 Graham also added another dimension to his work when his organization released the feature-length film "Mr. Texas." Since then several films have been released over the years for evangelistic use in churches, and "The Hiding Place" (1974) was released commercially. Graham introduced "My Answer," a question-and-answer daily newspaper column, in 1952. Inspired by Eleanor Roosevelt's popular "My Day" column, Graham's attained a circulation in excess of twenty-two million within twenty years. *Peace with God,* Graham's first major book, appeared in 1953, joining kindred works such as *Peace of Soul* by Rabbi Joshua Liebman and *Peace of Mind* by Roman Catholic Fulton J. Sheen* as religious best sellers of the decade after the war. The common theme obviously marks an attempt to respond to the perceived religious needs of Cold War culture. In 1955, Billy Graham, his father-in-law, and other staunchly orthodox Protestants helped launch *Christianity Today,* a popular religious and political commentary designed as an evangelical alternative to the more liberal *Christian Century.* By 1984, its biweekly circulation exceeded 180,000. "Hour of Decision" telecasts began with the New York crusade of 1957; since then selected services from most major crusades have been televised, usually by videotape, weeks or months later.

Establishing auxiliary ministries did not diminish commitment to evangelism. Graham's reputation as a revivalist who inspired record numbers of conversions was growing. International recognition came with a crusade in 1954 in London, which was still recovering from the war. The response to his preaching convinced Graham and his associates that the work was both blessed by God and a fitting response to the crisis of the age. International crusades remain integral to Graham's evangelism. By 1960, he had held crusades on every continent except Antarctica, including well-received preaching missions in countries controlled by Communists, against whose ideology Graham once railed and whose rise he once saw as a sign of the nearness of the apocalypse, that final showdown between Christ (good) and Antichrist (evil). A crusade in New York City in 1957 saw Madison Square Garden filled for four months, with thousands registering decisions for Christ or recommitments to religious faith. Crusades since have taken the Graham team to virtually every major U.S. city and a number of smaller urban centers. President Richard Nixon's speaking at a crusade in Knoxville, Tennessee, in 1970 testified to Graham's stature as the premier figure in popular American evangelism.

Graham has actively promoted the evangelical perspective through sponsoring and/or attending conferences on evangelism. In 1960, for example, he convened a conference on world evangelism in Montreaux, Switzerland. A World Congress on Evangelism in Berlin in 1966 paved the way for regional congresses in Asia, Latin America, and Europe during the next five years and for the Congress on World Evangelization in Lausanne, Switzerland, in 1974 with more than 4,000 participants from some 150 nations attending. The BGEA has subsidized these conferences, which reflect Graham's conviction that evangelism should be ongoing, guided by indigenous leaders, and not just the province of itinerant evangelists. Graham's belief that many Christian bodies, particularly those identified with the World Council of Churches, had allowed radical theology and political action to supersede the call for salvation also spurred his desire to support international evangelical activities. Inspiring local evangelism also demonstrates Graham's recognition that advancing years will limit his personal appearances and will require planning for continuation of the BGEA after his death.

Frequently plagued by ill health, Graham has curtailed the number and length of his crusades in recent years. Yet he has also expanded the scope of his work. In 1977, construction of the Billy Graham Center on the Wheaton College campus marked one new avenue: providing for the scholarly study of evangelicalism and the Billy Graham Archives. Land near Montreat, North Carolina, Graham's home since the 1950s, was targeted for an institute to train laity for urban ministry. The media ministry continues to flourish.

Graham's irenic evangelicalism, retreat from association with political figures, and increasing awareness of the complexity of late-twentieth-century social problems, along with the rise of a more strident fundamentalism, have muted, but not silenced, his presence. The emergence of televangelists like Jim Bakker* and Pat Robertson* and fundamentalists like Jerry Falwell*, who urge political action, has given popular evangelicalism an uncompromising, more conservative cast. But Billy Graham, who has preached to more persons than any other individual, remains the voice of midcentury evangelicalism.

## Appraisal

Billy Graham stands in a tradition of American revivalism reaching to Jonathan Edwards in the eighteenth century and including figures like Charles Grandison Finney and Dwight L. Moody in the nineteenth and Billy Sunday* in the early twentieth. Graham has mastered techniques developed by his predecessors: use of a large hall or arena for public meetings (usually space not ordinarily associated with religious causes), careful advance planning, sponsorship across denominational lines, extending a campaign over several weeks or months, training local personnel to serve as counselors, holding prayer meetings and auxiliary services before and during a crusade, enriching services with musical presentations and singing, direct appeals to make a religious commitment, and extensive efforts to follow through on conversions. Graham attributes the success of his crusades to divine sanction; analysts recognize the human element in the apparatus of a crusade and argue that careful orchestration guarantees results. Questions about the emotional dimension of appeals for decision have been common to revivals since the eighteenth century. The spectacle of the crusade and the drama of preaching, rather than reasoned choice, may prompt response to the invitation. Students of crusades have also noted that a majority of those registering conversion are adolescents and young adults who may lack the maturity to make lasting commitments. The age of converts surprises no one familiar with William James' *The Varieties of Religious Experience* (1902), which demonstrated that adolescents and young adults constitute the group most likely to undergo intensive personal religious experience. Crusade analysts have found as well that a significant percentage of those making a decision for Christ already have formal religious affiliation or former involvement with a religious institution. Thus, the number of converts recorded may exaggerate the number of those making an initial religious commitment. Supporters counter that age matters less than the experience and that renewed commitment is as vital as initial commitment.

Graham's theology stands solidly in the conservative wing of orthodox Protestant thought. Primary is the conviction that all are sinners needing salvation, a gift from God in Jesus Christ proclaimed in a verbally inspired Bible. Until individuals recognize their need for salvation, they are without hope for eternal life. As long as there are sinners, evil will mark the society they create. The more sin prevails, the closer the world comes to the apocalypse. Hence the present is a time of crisis, resolved only through commitment to Christ. As well, social reform, apart from conversion, solves nothing, whether the problem be juvenile delinquency or the spread of communism. Morality, an individual phenomenon, has social consequences only because individuals comprise society. Critics have castigated Graham's approach as theologically and sociologically simplistic, though one can discern increasing appreciation of the complex nature of social problems in Graham's published writings.

Advocates herald Graham's early policy to end segregated seating at crusades as a sign of social concern, especially in the area of civil rights, and his establishment of funds earmarked for social welfare causes as evidence of social commitment. Further, Graham has shifted from near exclusive references to personal immorality and the dangers of communism in sermon illustrations to include calls for human justice and dignity. But Graham still views personal conversion as the sine qua non for societal transformation.

Graham's long association with political leaders has brought criticism, for the popular mind could misconstrue such as endorsement of particular political positions. Graham has been perceived as equating evangelical morality with an American civic piety that minimizes religion's role as social critic. Marshall Frady subtitled his biography of Graham "A Parable of American Righteousness" to emphasize this point. Graham's early assault on a monolithic communism may also reflect uncritical support for American policy, creating the impression that criticism of governmental policy equals lack of genuine religious commitment.

Compared with someone like Jerry Falwell, Graham hardly seems a rabid fundamentalist locked into a rigid religious or political perspective. The fairest assessment is that Graham's views have grown with the years, though remaining rooted in orthodox Protestant evangelicalism.

## Survey of Criticism

Literature about Billy Graham is voluminous, much of it in popular format. For example, in the two decades after the 1954 London crusade, *Newsweek* alone featured more than fifty stories on Graham and his work. More than 300 books in part or in whole treat Graham's life and ministry; several uncritically recount stories of particular crusades. A listing, revised frequently, may be obtained from the Billy Graham Center Library, Wheaton, Illinois. Commentary on selected secondary literature is found in chapter 15 of Charles H. Lippy, *A Bibliography of Religion in the South* (Macon, Ga.: Mercer University Press, 1985).

John Pollock has written two "insider" studies: *Billy Graham: The Authorized Biography* and *Billy Graham: Evangelist to the World*. Pollock fills both with facts, clearly admires Graham, and attributes Graham's success to God. Stanley High's *Billy Graham: The Personal Story of the Man, His Message, and His Mission*, now long outdated, is an uncritical, sympathetic study of the early years of Graham's ministry. Hagiographic in tone is *Billy Graham: The Making of a Crusader* by Curtis Mitchell.

Of academic studies, William G. McLoughlin's *Billy Graham: Revivalist in a Secular Age* remains among the most carefully researched. Quite critical of Graham, it argues that Graham mirrors the simplistic piety of the postwar revival of religion, and it somewhat inaccurately forecasts limited influence for Graham. Marshall Frady's *Billy Graham: A Parable of American Righteousness*, though overwritten, locates Graham in the broader context of southern religion. Frady is particularly sensitive to how Graham fuses religious and national values to create a guide to what one should think and do to be a moral citizen. Reinhold Niebuhr's "Liberalism, Individualism, and Billy Graham" criticizes Graham's understanding of sin and conversion for neglecting the corporate, social nature of sin.

The most provocative studies are by sociologists. Ronald C. Wimberly, et al., "Conversion in a Billy Graham Crusade: Spontaneous Event or Ritual Performance," argue for the latter. Weldon T. Johnson, in "The Religious Crusade: Revival or Ritual?" also notes the reliance on fixed patterns. Donald A. Clelland, et al., "In the Company of the Converted: Characteristics of a Billy Graham Crusade Audience," based on the campaign in Knoxville, shows that those attending have higher incomes, more formal education, and more prestigious jobs than do the average residents of a region where a crusade is held. This study also documents a higher degree of involvement in religious activities and a more conservative political stance among those attending. It argues that converts have little observable change in religious activity a year later. Also noteworthy is James L. McAllister's unpublished essay of an early crusade, "Greensboro and Billy Graham."

## Bibliography

### Books by Billy Graham

1947   *Calling Youth to Christ*. Grand Rapids: Zondervan.
1950   *Revival in Our Time*. Wheaton, Ill.: VanKampen Press.
1951   *America's Hour of Decision*. Wheaton, Ill.: VanKampen Press.
1953   *Peace with God*. Rev. ed. Waco, Tex.: Word Books, 1984.
1955   *Freedom from the Seven Deadly Sins*. Grand Rapids: Zondervan. Published as *Find Freedom* (1971).
1955   *Helping Others Find Christ*. Chicago: Moody Press.
1955   *The Secret of Happiness*. Garden City, N.Y.: Doubleday.
1960   *My Answer*. Garden City, N.Y.: Doubleday.
1965   *World Aflame*. Garden City, N.Y.: Doubleday.

1969    *The Challenge: Sermons from Madison Square Garden*. Garden City, N.Y.: Doubleday.
1971    *The Jesus Generation*. Grand Rapids: Zondervan.
1975    *Angels: God's Secret Agents*. New York: Doubleday.
1977    *How to Be Born Again*. Waco, Tex.: Word Books.
1981    *Till Armageddon*. Waco, Tex.: Word Books.
1983    *Approaching Hoofbeats: The Four Horsemen of the Apocalypse*. Waco, Tex.: Word Books.

### Selected Studies about Billy Graham

Ashman, Chuck. *The Gospel According to Billy*. Secaucus, N.J.: Lyle Stuart, 1977.

Barnhart, Joe E. *The Billy Graham Religion*. Philadelphia: United Church Press, 1972.

Burnham, George. *Billy Graham: A Mission Accomplished*. Westwood, N.J.: Fleming H. Revell, 1955.

————. *To the Far Corners: With Billy Graham in Asia*. Westwood, N.J.: Fleming H. Revell, 1956.

————, and Lee Fisher. *Billy Graham and the New York Crusade*. Grand Rapids: Zondervan, 1957.

Clelland, Donald A., et al. "In the Company of the Converted: Characteristics of a Billy Graham Crusade Audience." *Sociological Analysis* 35 (1974): 45–56.

Colquhoun, Frank. *Harringay Story: The Official Record of the Billy Graham Greater London Crusade, 1954*. London: Hodder and Stoughton, 1955.

Corry, John. "God, Country, and Billy Graham." *Harper's* 248 (February 1969): 33–39.

Frady, Marshall. *Billy Graham: A Parable of American Righteousness*. Boston: Little, Brown, 1979.

High, Stanley. *Billy Graham: The Personal Story of the Man, His Message, and His Mission*. New York: McGraw-Hill, 1956.

Houston, Neil. "Billy Graham." *Holiday* 23 (1958): 62–65, 80–81.

Johnson, Weldon T. "The Religious Crusade: Revival or Ritual?" *American Journal of Sociology* 76 (1971): 873–90.

Lippy, Charles H. "Billy Graham's 'My Answer': Agenda for the Faithful." *Studies in Popular Culture* 5 (1982): 27–34.

McAllister, James L. "Evangelical Faith and Billy Graham." *Social Action* 19 (March 1953): 3–36.

————. "Greensboro and Billy Graham." Manuscript. Yale Divinity School, 1952.

McLoughlin, William G. *Billy Graham: Revivalist in a Secular Age*. New York: Ronald Press, 1960.

Meyer, Donald. "Billy Graham and Success." *New Republic* (22 August 1955): 8–10.

Mitchell, Curtis. *Billy Graham: The Making of a Crusader*. Philadelphia: Chilton Books, 1966.

Niebuhr, Reinhold. "Liberalism, Individualism, and Billy Graham." *Christian Century* 73 (1956): 640–42.

Pierard, Richard V. "Billy Graham and the U.S. Presidency." *Journal of Church and State* 22 (1980): 107–27.

Pollock, John. *Billy Graham: Evangelist to the World*. New York: Harper and Row, 1978.

————. *Billy Graham: The Authorized Biography*. New York: McGraw-Hill, 1966.

Whitam, Frederick L. "Revivalism as Institutionalized Behavior: An Analysis of the
    Social Base of a Billy Graham Crusade." *Social Science Quarterly* 49 (1968):
    115–27.
Wimberly, Ronald C., et al. "Conversion in a Billy Graham Crusade: Spontaneous Event
    or Ritual Performance." *Sociological Quarterly* 16 (1975): 162–70.
                                                                CHARLES H. LIPPY

# Kenneth Hagin, Sr.

The expansive landscape of American Christianity has continuously produced
new religious movements and traditions. One of the most popular and influential
movements birthed in twentieth-century American Christianity has been the charismatic movement. From out of the healing revival of the post–World War II
period and from a resurgent Pentecostalism, this movement was born in the late
1950s and early 1960s. David Barrett, author of the *World Christian Encyclopedia,* reports that the charismatic movement has grown to a worldwide following
of 277 million and is the fastest growing religious movement both in America
and the world today. It has tripled in size during the past ten years.

The charismatic movement encompasses various theological traditions but is
unified by the common belief that the supernatural gifts of the New Testament
are operative today. This movement is composed of two major groups. The
Charismatic Renewal is made up of those who accept the operation of the
charismata (gifts) as normative today and who have remained within the traditional denominations. The other group is the Charismatic Independents, the
fastest growing part of the movement.

A prominent part of this latter group is commonly referred to as the Faith
movement or the Word movement. The Faith movement began as a grass-roots,
parachurch movement consisting of a mixture of evangelistic revivalism, fundamentalist literalism, and Pentecostal experientialism. The acknowledged father
of the Faith movement is Kenneth Hagin. The national religious press has acclaimed him as "the grandaddy of the Faith teachers." Without question, every
major faith ministry in America has been influenced by his teachings.

### Biography

Born prematurely on 20 August 1917 in McKinney, Texas, Kenneth Erwin
Hagin was given up to die by the attending physician. The less-than-two-pound
infant survived, but only to experience a tragic childhood. Because of his frail
physical condition, which continued throughout his early life, young Hagin was
unable to experience a normal childhood. Compounding the situation was the
desertion of the family by his father when the boy was only six and his mother's
subsequent nervous breakdown. This resulted in the boy's being reared by his
discipline-oriented grandparents.

At the age of fifteen, Hagin's health worsened, and for sixteen months he lay bedridden, partially paralyzed, with his six-foot frame slowly emaciating to a mere 89 pounds. During this time he experienced a religious awakening that changed his life and resulted in his physical healing. Hagin was able to return to school and graduated from McKinney's Boyd High School. Shortly after graduation, he was accepted as a pastor at a local community church with a Baptist tradition in Roland, Texas, just eight miles from his hometown. Being young and inexperienced and having no formal Bible or theological training, Hagin memorized the sermons of Charles Spurgeon and others and preached them verbatim.

While pastoring in Roland, Hagin began frequenting Pentecostal circles because they taught the doctrine of divine healing. By 1937 he so identified with the Pentecostals that he resigned his church and was licensed by the Assemblies of God. For the next twelve years, Hagin pastored small Assemblies of God churches in such east Texas towns as Tom Bean, Farmersville, Talco, Greggton, and Van. While pastoring in Tom Bean, he met Oretha Rooker and married her on 25 November 1938. These first years of ministry were characterized by both unusual spiritual experiences and confrontation with parishioners over his teachings. In *The Authority of the Believer,* Hagin later characterized himself during these times as being "so ignorant of the Bible it was a wonder that the deacons did not have to pull [me] out of the rain."

In February 1949, Hagin entered the second phase of his ministry by joining the expanding ranks of itinerant healing evangelists. As such he ministered in the circles of William Branham*, Oral Roberts*, A. A. Allen, Jack Coe, and T. L. Osborn, although his outreach during these early years was more limited than theirs and most of his engagements were in small-town churches in the Southwest and California. His contribution to the healing revival was not so much as a healer, for he was considerably outclassed by others, but rather as a teacher. He had developed into an able teacher with a homey and humorous Texas style, but he was surpassed by many as a platform performer. Overall, the years from 1950 to 1959 were survival years for the Hagin ministry. His healing ministry was minimally successful, and these were, by his estimates, lean years of growing debts and dwindling crowds.

By the early sixties, Hagin's ministry had begun to turn around. In 1960 he published his first book, *Redeemed from Poverty, Sickness and Death.* He also became a popular speaker for the Full Gospel Businessmen's Fellowship International. Beginning in 1966, he made several crucial decisions that resulted in explosive growth for his ministry. In that year he moved his offices to Tulsa, Oklahoma, purchasing T. L. Osborn's former headquarters. He also began his "Faith Seminar of the Air," a daily fifteen-minute radio program that is syndicated today to approximately 180 radio stations. This was followed two years later with the publication of a monthly magazine, *Word of Faith,* which has a present circulation of over 190,000. In 1973 Hagin began holding an annual old-fashioned camp meeting in Tulsa with his supporters coming from across the nation to participate. By 1987 attendance was averaging 24,000. In 1974 he inaugurated a correspondence school and a residential training center. The Rhema Bible Training Center is located on a $20 million, eighty-acre campus in a suburb of Tulsa. Its two-year program has an average enrollment of 2,000. Together these two programs have graduated more than 16,000 students. Hagin also extends his ministry through his television program "Faith That Lives." In addition, since 1960 he has published over thirty-three million copies of the 126 books he has written. It is presently estimated that over 20,000 teaching tapes are distributed monthly. As a result of these outreaches, Hagin's ministry has become one of the largest in the nation, with a mailing list of over 200,000 supporters to whom 4.2 million pieces of mail were sent in 1986 and from whom $14 million a year in contributions are received. At seventy years of age, Hagin remains extremely active as a traveling preacher, writer, and teacher at his Bible training center. He speaks publicly twice daily on approximately 250 days a year.

### Appraisal

Kenneth Hagin has been a strong force in the expansive landscape of American popular religion for the past two decades, and his influence is assured for the rest of this century. His teachings on faith, prosperity, and healing have birthed a movement, and through his thousands of disciples and imitators these teachings have reached millions of Americans in grass-roots Christianity. His teachings have been foundational for every major minister in the Faith movement, many of whom have large television/radio ministries. Among the most prominent imitators are Kenneth Copeland, who has one of the top ten syndicated religious television programs in America according to Arbitron ratings; Fred Price, also in the top ten Arbitron ratings and with the largest black audience of any syndicated religious television program in the country; Jerry Savelle; Charles Capps; Norvel Hayes; John Osteen; Marilyn Hickey; Ken Stewart; Ray Hicks; Don Gossett; Lester Sumrall; and Robert Tilton. In addition, a veritable army of graduates have come forth from his training center, and tens of millions of pieces of literature and tapes have been distributed.

Apart from the prime-time televangelists, it would be difficult to name any independent ministry that has grown more rapidly in the 1970s and 1980s than that of Kenneth Hagin. His influence in the charismatic movement has been significant. The 10 July 1987 *Christianity Today* recently proclaimed that his Faith movement is becoming "increasingly popular," and quoted Vinson Synan, the acclaimed Pentecostal historian and director of the North American Congress on the Holy Spirit and World Evangelization, "Faith teachers are enjoying increasing acceptance and prestige outside their own ranks."

Hagin's theology is a unique blend of evangelical orthodoxy, biblical fundamentalism, charismatic theology, and metaphysical thought. He is well schooled in the teachings of early Pentecostal leaders (such as F. F. Bosworth, Smith Wigglesworth, John G. Lake, and Aimee Semple McPherson*), the post–

World War II healing evangelists, and the metaphysical teachings of New Thought/Christian Science as presented by E. W. Kenyon. Hagin has been significantly influenced by and dependent on the writings of E. W. Kenyon for a number of his basic theological presuppositions. His theology is, however, inexplicable apart from the visions and personal visitations of Jesus that he claims in a number of his books.

His faith message has characteristics similar to other teachings that have been given prominence in twentieth-century America. His emphases that divine healing is in the atonement and that believers have the authority to bind demonic powers in the name of Jesus echo the teachings of Pentecostals. His belief in the present-day operation of the spiritual gifts of the New Testament and in glossolalia is similar to that of all charismatics. His ideas on positive thinking have some parallel with those of Norman Vincent Peale* and Robert Schuller*. His prosperity message is close to that of Pat Robertson*, Oral Roberts, and Zig Ziglar.

Because Hagin's theology is a unique blend or synthesis of several theological/ philosophical influences some Christian groups, such as the Christian Research Institute in San Juan Capistrano, California, regard Hagin's teachings as "aberrational." This is a term the institute uses for groups that, as Bruce Barron wrote in *Christianity Today,* "affirm the basic essentials of the faith, then make statements that seriously compromise this position." Five of Hagin's major doctrines in which he employs this synthesis present areas of concern for many. These are his doctrines of identification, faith, prosperity, healing, and revelation knowledge. As Dan McConnell points out in his volume *A Different Gospel,* there are several points of Hagin's teachings that cause major concerns for orthodox Protestant thought: Hagin's teachings of a deistic view of God where man seems to be able to manipulate spiritual laws; a demonic view of Christ wherein he had to be "born again" in hell; a gnostic view of revelation that denies the physical senses; and a metaphysical view of salvation that deifies man and spiritualizes the atonement. In addition, there are three practices in Hagin's teaching that, when used together, have caused alarm in the Christian community because of their numerous tragic results. They are the use of positive confession, sensory denial (particularly as it relates to physical symptoms of illness), and implicit rejection of medical science.

It is a fair assessment to state that Hagin's influence and that of his imitators are continuing to spread rapidly. At the same time, not all of those being influenced are adopting the theology or practices in total; in fact, most seem to be ignorant of the total theological package.

**Survey of Criticism**

Significant criticism toward Hagin and the Faith movement did not develop until the late 1970s and 1980s. The most challenging criticism came from scholars within the charismatic community. In 1979 Charles Farah, Ph.D., professor of theology at Oral Roberts University, in his book *From the Pinnacle of the Temple,* strongly attacked Hagin's teachings. He particularly condemned the "confess it and possess it" teaching that did not count the cost, meet the conditions, or take into account the larger purpose of the sovereignty of God. He characterized Hagin's teachings as a "faith-formula" that was a presumption on the grace and sovereignty of God and that was directly responsible for numerous tragedies and deaths.

In the spring of the same year, Gordon Fee, Ph.D., professor of New Testament literature at Gordon Conwell Seminary and an ordained Assemblies of God minister, published a series of articles for *Agora* magazine, entitled "Some Reflections on a Current Disease." He denounced the "cult of prosperity" as nonbiblical and rejected the idea that healing was in the atonement the same way as salvation and the forgiveness of sins. He strongly denied that healing was automatically given by God in direct response to the believer's confession and appropriation of the atonement.

Criticism began to intensify in 1980 with the appearance of several new antifaith publications. The first of these was Larry Parker's *We Let Our Son Die,* which told the story of how the Parkers withheld insulin from their diabetic son while confessing his healing. As a result the son died. Because of the growing influence of Hagin's teachings in Pentecostal churches the General Presbytery of the Assemblies of God issued an official statement entitled "The Believer and Positive Confession." This statement called attention to the conflicts between this teaching and the Bible and to the excesses of the doctrine. Several years later the Presbyterian and Reformed Renewal Ministries issued a stronger statement, written by John Fickett, in their *Confess It, Possess It: Faith's Formulas?*

In November 1980, Charles Farah used the scholarly forum of the annual conference of the Society for Pentecostal Studies meeting at Oral Roberts University to deliver the strongest criticism to date against Hagin's teachings. In his paper "A Critical Analysis: The 'Roots and Fruits' of Faith-Formula Theology," Farah called Hagin's teachings "charismatic humanism," "the new gnosticism," and "a burgeoning heresy." *Christianity Today,* the major evangelical publication, in a 12 December 1980 article entitled "Faith Formula Fuels Charismatic Controversy," referred to Farah's paper as a "declaration of war on the faith-formula teachings." *Charisma,* America's leading charismatic publication, declared that the theological faculty of Oral Roberts University was attacking the teachings of Hagin's ministry.

The war against Hagin's teachings quickly escalated when internationally known Assemblies of God evangelist Jimmy Swaggart* published a series of articles in his *Evangelist* magazine under the title "The Balanced Faith Life." He acknowledged that he had once accepted the "utopian claims made for the power of positive confession" but now saw the errors of such teachings. He followed these articles with a book entitled *Hyper-Faith: A New Gnosticism,* based on a manuscript by Judith Matta and later revised and published as *The Born-Again Jesus of the Word-Faith Teaching.* In 1985 Dave Hunt and T. A. McMahon's volume *The Seduction of Christianity* and later Hunt's *Beyond Se-*

*duction* charged Hagin's teachings with being a revival of New Thought and a new Science of the Mind cult.

Scholarly analysis of the sources and influences on Hagin in the writing of his theology has raised questions regarding intellectual honesty. Dan McConnell, in his 1982 master's thesis, "The Kenyon Connection," documented that Hagin heavily plagiarized the works of E. W. Kenyon in his own writings. McConnell expanded his investigative work in his 1988 volume *A Different Gospel: The Cultic Nature of the Modern Faith Movement*. In 1985 Dale H. Simmons, in his master's thesis, "A Theological and Historical Analysis of . . . Hagin's Claim to Be a Prophet," revealed massive plagiarism. Simmons documented more expansive plagiarism from Kenyon and discovered additional major plagiarism from Finis Jennings Dake and John A. MacMillan. One of Hagin's foundational volumes, *The Authority of the Believer*, was found to be 75 percent plagiarized from MacMillan's 1928 work by the same title.

Interestingly, the extensive criticism of Hagin's teachings and the major discovery of plagiarism have done little to abate the growing influence of his ministry and teachings. The influence of Hagin and his imitators among grass-roots Christianity continues to grow, especially among the independent charismatic movement and the black community.

### Bibliography

*Selected Books by Kenneth Hagin, Sr.*

(All volumes are published by Hagin's Faith Library Publications in Tulsa, Oklahoma, unless otherwise indicated.)

1960  *The Ministry of a Prophet*
1960  *Redeemed from Poverty, Sickness and Death*
1965  *The Authority of the Believer*
1966  *Right and Wrong Thinking*
1966  *What Faith Is*
1967  *Prayer Secrets*
1968  *Demons and How to Deal with Them*
1969  *Ministering to the Oppressed*
1971  *The Interceding Christian*
1972  *I Believe in Visions*. Old Tappan, N.J.: Fleming H. Revell.
1972  *New Thresholds of Faith*
1972  *Seven Steps to Reaching the Holy Spirit*
1973  *Exceedingly Growing Faith*
1973  *The Human Spirit*
1973  *Prevailing Prayer to Peace*
1974  *Concerning Spiritual Gifts*
1974  *The Holy Spirit and His Gifts*
1975  *Understanding Our Confessions*
1975  *Why Tongues?*
1975  *The Woman Question*
1976  *Growing Up Spiritually*

1977  *God's Medicine*
1977  *Key to Spiritual Healing*
1978  *How You Can Be Led by The Spirit of God*
1978  *Praying to Get Results*
1979  *How to Write Your Own Ticket with God*
1979  *The Name of Jesus*
1979  *Seven Things You Should Know About Divine Healing*
1979  *You Can Have What You Say*
1980  *The Art of Intercession*
1980  *El Shaddai*
1980  *Having Faith in Your Faith*
1980  *Healing Belongs to Us*
1981  *A Better Covenant*
1981  *Turning Hopeless Situations Around*
1981  *Zoe: The God-Kind of Life*
1982  *Godliness is Profitable*
1982  *Must Christians Suffer?*
1982  *Seven Steps for Judging Prophecy*
1983  *His Name Shall Be Called Wonderful*
1983  *Paul's Revelation*
1983  *Understanding the Anointing*
1984  *The Believer's Authority*
1984  *Love Never Fails*
1984  *The Precious Blood of Jesus*
1985  *The Coming Restoration*
1985  *The Gifts and Calling of God*
1985  *Signs of the Times*
1986  *Hear and Be Healed*
1986  *Learning to Flow With the Spirit*
1986  *Ministering to Your Family*
1987  *Understanding . . . Good Fight of Faith*

### Selected Studies about Kenneth Hagin, Sr.

Barron, Bruce. *The Health and Wealth Gospel.* Downers Grove, Ill.: InterVarsity, 1987.

Farah, Charles. *From the Pinnacle of the Temple.* Plainfield, N.J.: Logos, 1979.

———. "A Critical Analysis: The 'Roots and Fruits' of Faith-Formula Theology." Society for Pentecostal Studies, November 1980.

Fee, Gordon. *The Disease of the Health and Wealth Gospels.* Costa Mesa, Calif.: Word for Today, 1979.

Fickett, John. *Confess It, Possess It: Faith's Formulas?* Oklahoma City: Presbyterian and Reformed Renewal, 1984.

Hagin, Kenneth, Jr. *Kenneth E. Hagin's 50 Years in the Ministry: 1934–1984.* Tulsa: Faith Library, 1984.

———. "Trend Toward Faith Movement." *Charisma* (August 1985).

McConnell, Daniel R. *A Different Gospel: The Cultic Nature of the Modern Faith Movement.* Peabody, Mass.: Hendrickson Publishers, 1988.

McMillan, Kevin. "Kenneth Hagin: Anthropology, Soteriology, and Major Dynamics of Divine Healing." Master's thesis, Oral Roberts University, 1984.

Matta, Judith A. *The Born-Again Jesus of the Word-Faith Teaching*. Fullerton, Calif.: Spirit of Truth, 1984.

Neuman, H. Terris. "An Analysis of 'Positive Confession.' " Master's thesis, Wheaton Graduate School, 1980.

Simmons, Dale H. "Hagin—Heretic or Herald of God? A Theological and Historical Analysis of Kenneth E. Hagin's Claim to be a Prophet." Master's thesis, Oral Roberts University, 1985.

PAUL G. CHAPPELL

# Billy James Hargis

After World War II the United States was convulsed by a wave of fear about communism. New awareness of the growing Communist movement in Europe sparked consternation and dread in America. The Cold War and the McCarthy hearings seemed to provide all the evidence needed to convince many of the looming danger. The American way of life seemed overshadowed by threats at every hand. This sense of threat gave rise to the far right in American politics, a movement that has always combined the concerns of American civil religion about traditional morality, patriotism, and broad piety. There is perhaps no better representative of the mingling of politics and religion on the far right than Billy James Hargis.

### Biography

Born on 3 August 1925 in Texarkana, Texas, Billy James Hargis learned fundamentalism during the depths of the Depression. He turned to religion early and was ordained to the ministry by Rose Hill Christian Church (Disciples) in 1943. In 1948, after a series of pastorates in Arkansas, Missouri, and Oklahoma, Hargis founded Christian Echoes National Ministry in Tulsa to fight "Communism and its godless allies." By 1950, Hargis had given his full-time commitment to the work.

His work soon attracted attention, especially from others of similar persuasion. Never an ardent student, Hargis had little formal education. Indeed, it was limited to less than two years at Ozark Bible College. He received an honorary doctorate in divinity from the Defender Seminary in Puerto Rico in 1954 and a second from Bob Jones University in 1961. Hargis also has B.A. and B.Theo. degrees from Burton College and Seminary and an LL.D. degree from Belin Memorial University, two schools that have appeared on a list of "degree mills" issued by the federal Department of Education in Washington, D.C.

Hargis proclaimed a message directed against the enemies of his society. He numbered among the enemies of America communism, liberalism, socialism, the national press, the National Council of Churches, the United Nations, and a variety of individuals including the Reuther brothers, the Kennedys, Lyndon Johnson, and Martin Luther King, Jr.* He often preached against communism, pornography, homosexuality and sexual indiscretion, and modernism in religion. In the 1950s Hargis began a program to launch balloons carrying Bible verses across the borders of Iron Curtain countries. An Air Force manual for noncommissioned officers cited Hargis as an expert on communism in the late 1950s.

In 1966 Hargis left the Disciples of Christ and founded the Church of the Christian Crusade in Tulsa as an independent ministry. Hargis also sponsored a series of rallies and mass meetings of the Christian Crusade ministry in which he relied heavily on the talents and appeal of well-known retired military and political leaders, including General Edward Walker. These gatherings, along with Hargis's *Christian Crusade* magazine, demonstrated his impressive ability to raise funds, a talent he also exercised through the sale of patent medicines and vitamins in the early 1960s.

Hargis' ministry was always controversial, if only because of his willingness to accuse by name those he regarded as enemies of America. He continued to assert the Communist connections of leading religious and political leaders. His charges were so blatantly political that, in 1964, Hargis' organization lost its tax-exempt status.

Hargis' ministry continued to expand, however, and in 1970, he founded American Christian College to teach "anti-Communist patriotic Americanism." The next year he founded Americans for Life, an antiabortion group. Controversy engulfed Hargis when, in 1974, several students from his college accused him of sexual misconduct. Confronted by other leaders in the college, Hargis retired from public life, ostensibly because of ill health. His retirement lasted less than a year, ending when Hargis returned to Tulsa from his private farm and sought to regain control of his ministries. He managed to gain control of several groups, including the David Livingstone Missionary Foundation and Christian Crusade, but could not recover his position as president of the college. Without Hargis' fund-raising abilities, American Christian College closed in 1977. Hargis continued to promote his ministry and founded the Billy James Hargis Evangelistic Association in 1975. His effort to renew his ministry after the scandal also led to the founding of his Good Samaritan Children's Foundation.

In recent years Hargis has found it difficult to get his message on radio and television. In 1981 he obtained a license to own and operate a UHF television station. His radio network has dwindled to less than twenty stations, mostly located in the South Central states. He continues to write and direct the ministry from its headquarters in Tulsa.

**Appraisal**

The ministry of Billy James Hargis has always been closely tied to the political mood of the country. He has been most successful during those years when the country turned toward conservatism. Indeed, Hargis' greatest popularity came during a time of intense fear of communism. When more moderate or liberal politics prevail, Hargis has always found it more difficult to raise money and to sustain his radio network. This pattern explains the modest resurgence of his ministry in the mid-1980s, despite the scandals of the previous decade.

It is important to note that this ministry, like so many in twentieth-century America, depends heavily on its founder. American Christian College could not survive the scandal and departure of Hargis. The evangelist himself, however, has managed to perpetuate a viable, if smaller, ministry in spite of his difficulties. As long as Hargis is able to continue preaching his message of the far right, he will find a constituency.

Hargis' ministry can also be regarded as part of the larger movement usually called the religious right. Whereas Hargis was recognized as a leader in this circle in the 1960s, he has lost much of his eminence since that time. His uncompromisingly strident message, combined with the embarrassments of his sale of vitamins and patent medicines and the scandal at American Christian College, stripped away his aura of respectability for many former admirers. Though Hargis' ministry may struggle, the broader phenomenon of the religious right is still strong. The movement as a whole, however, has moderated considerably from Hargis' extreme.

## Survey of Criticism

Billy James Hargis has not attracted a great deal of attention from scholars. Biographical works are limited to brief treatments in other contexts and his own autobiography, *My Great Mistake,* published in 1986. There are many discussions of his career in works that examine the American religious right. The most reliable examination of Hargis in the religious right is John Harold Redekop, *The American Far Right: A Case Study of Billy James Hargis and Christian Crusade.* Unfortunately, this work makes use of Hargis' career to illustrate other principles and does not undertake a systematic biography.

Several other books have devoted chapters to Hargis, often in service to their criticism of the religious right. Most strident among these critics of Hargis is *Danger on the Right,* by Arnold Forster and Benjamin Epstein. More moderate treatments include *The Far Right,* by Donald Janson and Bernard Eismann, and Richard Dudman's *Men of the Far Right.* It is noteworthy that all of these treatments, and indeed most of the polemic works against Hargis, come from the middle and late 1960s, when Hargis was most influential.

If Hargis has been largely ignored by scholars, he has attracted more attention in the popular press. *Time* and *Newsweek* magazines have devoted several articles to Hargis and his ministry over the years. These articles, along with a number of critical pieces in *Christian Century* and a scattering of other magazines, have tended to appear either in the mid-1960s or in response to the scandals that beset Hargis in the early 1970s. Such negative press has been balanced, in some measure, by glowing reports in Hargis' own *Christian Crusade* magazine and in the staunchly conservative *American Mercury.*

### Bibliography

*Books by Billy James Hargis*

1960  *Communist America—Must It Be?* Tulsa: Christian Crusade.
1961  *Communism, The Total Lie.* Tulsa: Christian Crusade.
1962  *Facts About Communism and the Churches.* Tulsa: Christian Crusade.
1964  *The Real Extremists—The Far Left.* Tulsa: Christian Crusade.
1965  *Distortion By Design.* Tulsa: Christian Crusade.
1968  *Is the School House the Proper Place to Teach Raw Sex?* Tulsa: Christian Crusade.
1974  *Why I Fight for a Christian America.* Tulsa: Christian Crusade.
1977  *The Depth Principle.* Tulsa: Christian Crusade.
1977  *Thou Shalt Not Kill My Babies.* Tulsa: Christian Crusade.
1978  *The Disaster File.* Tulsa: Christian Crusade.
1978  *Riches and Prosperity Through Christ.* Tulsa: Christian Crusade.
1980  *The National News Media.* Tulsa: Christian Crusade.
1982  *Abortion on Trial.* Tulsa: Christian Crusade.
1982  *The Cross and the Sickle—Super Church.* Tulsa: Christian Crusade.
1985  *The Federal Reserve Scandal.* Tulsa: Christian Crusade.
1986  *My Great Mistake.* Tulsa: Christian Crusade.

*Selected Studies about Billy James Hargis*

Dudman, Richard. *Men of the Far Right.* New York: Pyramid Books, 1962.
Forster, Arnold, and Benjamin Epstein. *Danger on the Right.* New York: Random House, 1964.
Janson, Donald, and Bernard Eismann. *The Far Right.* New York: McGraw-Hill, 1963.
Redekop, John Harold. *The American Far Right: A Case Study of Billy James Hargis and Christian Crusade.* Grand Rapids: Eerdmans, 1968.

MICHAEL R. McCOY

# Bob Jones, Sr., Jr., and III

To a great extent, one of the major issues in twentieth-century religion has been the conflict between fundamentalism and modernism. In this battle, few have been as consistent in their commitment to the cause of fundamentalism as have been Bob Jones, his son, and his grandson. For over ninety years they have formed an unbroken line of resistance to anything that, to them, smacks of deviation from the true word of Scripture. During this time they have gained for themselves a place in the history of American fundamentalism and American religion.

### Biography

Bob Jones, Sr., was born on 30 October 1883 in Skipperville, Alabama, to William Alexander Jones and Georgia Creal Jones. He was their eleventh child. His parents were farmers who struggled to feed their large family. For someone who lived as long and full a life as he did, his beginnings were inauspicious, for he was weak and sickly as a child. Bob received an early introduction to public speaking at the prodding of his father who insisted that Bob memorize inspirational and patriotic pieces clipped from newspapers and magazines. Bob was then later required to recite them whenever company came. Though such an experience must have been frightening to one so young, it gave Jones an exposure to public speaking of which he made good use.

This training showed early results in the young Bob Jones. He gave his first public oration at the age of twelve, when he spoke at a rally for the Populist party, and he was soon speaking at meetings of the Farmer's Alliance throughout the region. Political speaking, however, was not to be the direction in which the young man was led. The year before his first speech for the Populist party, Bob Jones had been converted in the Methodist Church attended by his family. His biographer tells us that even at that young age, Bob Jones was aware that he was sick in his soul and that hell was his certain destination without the saving grace of Jesus. The ability of this grace to heal his sickness was manifest in a sermon preached from Mark 2:4 where a cripple is lowered from the roof to Jesus' feet by his friends and his physical illnesses are cured. For Bob Jones the awareness that Jesus could cure the physically ill illustrated that he could also cure his soul's sickness. This young man took his conversion to heart and immediately turned his speaking gifts to the Lord's work. He preached his first revival at the age of twelve, and by thirteen he had a brush arbor church with fifty-four members. The Alabama Conference of the Methodist Episcopal Church, South, licensed him to preach at the age of fifteen and made him a circuit rider the following year.

His early life, however, did not consist solely of preaching. Since Bob was their youngest child and one with obvious gifts and talents, William and Georgia Jones saw to it that he received an education. In southern Alabama in the late nineteenth century this was more difficult than it sounded. Many of the schools in the area had only a three-month school year. In fact, at one time Bob Jones was attending a public school in a neighboring town during its three-month session and when that was completed attended a different school in a different community for another three months. A family friend, recognizing the child's talents, offered a better solution. J. C. Hammett, who was principal of a school with a nine-month term, felt that Bob Jones needed the extra education available there and offered to allow him to move in with his family. While he was attending this school, fate dealt the teenager two cruel blows. His mother died shortly after he left home, and his father died before Bob graduated from high school. At the age of seventeen, the young preacher was an orphan.

In December 1900, four months after his father's death, Bob Jones entered Southern University in Greensboro, Alabama. During his time there he continued his active preaching and evangelizing schedule, working weekend revivals and filling empty pulpits. During the summer months he traveled throughout the South, leading longer, protracted meetings.

After two years at Southern University, Bob Jones embarked on a career as a full-time evangelist. He spoke throughout the state of Alabama and the South as a whole. During this time he also became terribly ill and was diagnosed with tuberculosis of the throat. His physician recommended that he go out West for his health but doubted the young man would see another year.

While recuperating in Texas the young man began to attend the sessions of a medium. Although he was skeptical, something about the sessions intrigued him, and he continued to return. Soon the "spirit" of his mother began to appear and speak to him. After several of these sessions, Bob Jones began to question the spirit, asking "his mother" why she never spoke of Jesus and heaven. The spirit responded that Jesus was only a great medium, no different than the one he dealt with. This was all he needed to hear to convince him that spiritualism was the work of demons, for he knew that his mother would never speak like that. He stormed out of the room convinced of his belief that the devil was indeed at work in the world trying to seduce the innocent and naive.

The West's dry weather evidently did the young evangelist some good, for when he returned to Alabama he was pronounced cured. On his return Bob Jones resumed his work as an evangelist traveling about winning souls to Christ. One on these souls was to become his wife.

Mary Gaston Stollenwerk was descended from a fairly distinguished Alabama family. She had all the graces and culture that the young evangelist lacked. When Bob Jones arrived in Uniontown to preach a revival, the young woman soon came to his attention. She not only was converted under his preaching but also found herself courted by the fiery young preacher. They were married in June of 1908. Mary Gaston provided a great deal to the successes of Bob Jones' evangelistic career. In the early days she traveled with him, leading the women in Bible study and prayer meetings. Her husband's evangelistic schedule, which demanded constant travel, also meant that she had the major responsibility for the rearing of their son, Bob Jones, Jr., who was born in October 1911.

Bob Jones' life was filled with evangelistic meetings. He traveled throughout the United States, evangelizing not only in the South but also in Ohio, Pennsylvania, Indiana, New York, Illinois, and other states. Many rated him second only to Billy Sunday* as an evangelist of his day. His evangelistic work slowed after 1926 as Bob Jones University took up more of his time and energy. He was active in the World's Christian Fundamentals Association as well as in the fundamentalist-run Winona Lake Bible Conference. He also served as a member of the faculty of Moody Bible Institute's continuing education department. Bob Jones' connections with American fundamentalism were long and deep, lasting until his death in 1968. This commitment to fundamentalism was passed on to his son Bob Jones, Jr., and his grandson, Bob Jones III (1939–). His fundamentalist position and his refusal to be yoked with those who held unscriptural doctrine resulted in his decision to leave the Methodists, a denomination that he felt was overrun with modernists and liberals. This position, mandated as he thought by the scriptural warrant of II John 9–11, was to lead to a much publicized conflict with Billy Graham* in the 1960s.

## Appraisal

Perhaps the most important endeavor of Bob Jones was the founding of the school that bears his name, Bob Jones University of Greenville, South Carolina. The school originally founded by Bob Jones, Sr., at College Point, Florida, in 1926 was a victim of the crash of 1929. The Depression resulted in a loss of thousands of dollars to the school. This, along with the collapse of the Florida real estate market, necessitated that the school relocate, which it did, to Cleveland, Tennessee, in 1933. Here the school remained until 1946, when its success caused it to outgrow all its available space and required a move to a larger campus. In 1947 the school moved again, this time to its present home in Greenville, South Carolina.

The school was founded as an explicitly fundamentalist institution with a commitment to the "Christian religion and the ethics revealed in the Holy Scriptures; combatting all atheistic, agnostic, pagan and so-called scientific adulteration of the gospel," as the school's creed put it. The school, which has strict rules regulating the behavior of its students, faculty, and staff, has grown into the largest fundamentalist institution of higher education in the United States and has trained many of the leaders of American fundamentalism.

The three Bob Joneses have come close to establishing a religious dynasty. The presidency of the university has passed from father to son to grandson. All three have established reputations as evangelists and as staunch fundamentalists. There have been may evangelists, but few have maintained the staunch attitude of separatism of these three, and none have had the impact that they have had as a result of their school, Bob Jones University. And although there are several schools with an outlook similar to that of Bob Jones University, none can match it for size (about 6,000 students in 1984) or longevity.

The fundamentalism of the Bob Joneses extends beyond a commitment to a rigid Christian orthodoxy that accepts as literal the virgin birth, the resurrection, and God's creation of Adam. The Bob Joneses also have been committed to a political conservatism that is strongly anti-Communist and that for years defended racial segregation as scripturally mandated. Although Bob Jones University is now racially integrated, its position on race has caused trouble with the federal government, leading to a revocation of its tax-exempt status.

Their interpretation of Scripture has also led the Joneses to identify the whore of Babylon in the Book of Revelation with the Roman Catholic Church, and they are staunchly anti-Roman Catholic. This stance, along with their shared fundamentalism, has brought them into close contact with Ian Paisley of Northern Ireland. Bob Jones, Jr., even wrote the foreword to Paisley's exposition of the *Epistle to the Romans*.

What basically sets the Bob Joneses apart, however, is their commitment to separation from unbelievers, those who preach false doctrine, and those who associate with either. This separatism led them to join with Carl McIntire* in forming the American Council of Christian Churches as an opposition force to both the National Council of Churches and the National Association of Evangelicals. This commitment to separatism also led to a conflict with Billy Graham during the 1950s and 1960s. Graham, who attended Bob Jones University for a semester, erred greatly—according to the Joneses—by including nonfundamentalist congregations and ministers in his local crusades and by failing to channel his converts into fundamentalist churches. Graham not only worked with modernists and liberals and failed to attack Roman Catholicism but also accepted the Revised Standard Version of the Bible. Because of his willingness to join with preachers of false doctrine Graham himself became anathema to Bob Jones, Sr. This animosity reached its peak in 1966 when Graham held a crusade in Greenville, South Carolina, the home of Bob Jones University. In the 1 April 1966 issue of *Christianity Today* Bob Jones, Jr., labeled Graham as one "doing more harm to the cause of Jesus Christ than any living man."

Although Bob Jones, Jr., and his son Bob Jones III have maintained the strict orthodoxy of their father and grandfather, they were overshadowed by more politically active fundamentalists, such as Jerry Falwell*, during the 1970s and 1980s. These fundamentalists, who found it useful to put aside separatism for political goals, have discovered a much wider audience in the nation as a whole. By doing so, however, these preachers become partners of the middle-of-the-road compromise that Bob Jones detested and against which he, his son, and grandson have struggled for so long.

### Survey of Criticism

There has been little in the way of critical study on any of the three Bob Joneses. The standard source of biographical information is *Builder of Bridges* by R. K. Johnson, who was the business manager at Bob Jones University for many years. Though it is a fiercely partisan piece of writing, it does provide a good source of biographical information, primarily on Bob Jones, Sr., but also on his son and grandson. Another important text is *A History of Fundamentalism in America* written by George Dollar, a professor of church history at Bob Jones University. Its scope is wider than the Bob Joneses, and it provides a good background on all three men and locates them within the context of American fundamentalism. Finally there are two histories of the university itself: *Fortress of Faith* by Melton Wright and *Bob Jones University* by Margaret Tice. Again, these are unabashedly favorable books written by committed believers, but they provide a good deal of basic information regarding the school that promotes itself as the "world's most unusual university."

The books by the three Bob Joneses are primarily collections of sermons, although Bob Jones, Jr., has written a series of commentaries on the books of the Old Testament. He has also written several novels and plays illustrating Christian themes and has directed and acted in several movies produced by the University, including an award-winning production of *Macbeth*. All of this work, however, is ancillary to the task of the gospel, and the movies and plays revolve around inspirational and religious themes.

Perhaps the most important source for understanding the thought of the Bob Joneses is *Spectrum of Protestant Beliefs,* edited by Robert Campbell. This book examines the beliefs held along the Protestant spectrum from the radical death of God theology to militant fundamentalism. Bob Jones, Jr., represents the latter, and the topically arranged book allows one to gain an insight into the belief system of this man and the fundamentalist movement of which he is a prime exemplar.

## Bibliography

### Books by Bob Jones, Sr.

1911   *Bob Jones' Sermons.* Montgomery: Paragon Press.
1923   *The Modern Woman: A Sermon to Women.* Chicago: Glad Tidings.
1923   *Two Sermons to Men: Sowing and Reaping, and You Can't Beat the Game.* Chicago: Glad Tidings.
1942   *Comments on Here and Hereafter.* New York: Loizeaux Bros.
1944   *Things I Have Learned: Chapel Talks at Bob Jones College.* New York: L. B. Printing Co.
1948   *Bob Jones' Revival Sermon.* Wheaton, Ill.: Sword of the Lord.
1973   *Heritage of Faith.* Greenville, S.C.: Bob Jones University Press.
1983   *Bob Jones' Sermons.* Greenville, S.C.: Bob Jones University Press.
1983   *My Friends.* Greenville, S.C.: Bob Jones University Press.

### Books by Bob Jones, Jr.

1945   *"As the Small Rain."* Grand Rapids: Zondervan.
1945   *How to Improve Your Preaching.* New York: Fleming H. Revell.
1946   *Inspirational and Devotional Verse.* Grand Rapids: Zondervan.
1950   *Wine of Morning, A Novel of the First Century.* Wheaton, Ill.: Van Kampen Press.
1951   *Shower Upon the Grass.* Grand Rapids: Zondervan.
1960   *How to Improve Your Preaching.* New ed. Grand Rapids: Kregl.
1963   *Ancient Truth for Modern Days: Sermons on the Old Testament Subjects that Particularly Apply to Our Times.* Murfreesboro, Tenn.: Sword of the Lord Publishers.
1968   *Prologue: A Drama of John Hus.* Greenville, S.C.: Bob Jones University Press.
1971   *All Fullness Dwells.* Greenville, S.C.: Bob Jones University Press.
1973   *Historical Books.* Greenville, S.C.: Bob Jones University Press.
1973   *Job Through Isaiah.* Greenville, S.C.: Bob Jones University Press.
1973   *More from the Prophets.* Greenville, S.C.: Bob Jones University Press.
1973   *Old Testament Sermons.* Greenville, S.C.: Bob Jones University Press.
1973   *The Pentateuch.* Greenville, S.C.: Bob Jones University Press.
1981   *Rhyme & Reason.* Greenville, S.C.: Bob Jones University Press.
1984   *Daniel of Babylon.* Greenville, S.C.: Bob Jones University Press.
1985   *Cornbread and Caviar.* Greenville, S.C.: Bob Jones University Press.

### Books by Bob Jones III

1980   *A Sermon a Day Keeps the Devil Away.* Greenville, S.C.: Bob Jones University Press.
1981   *Biblical Answers to Bothersome Questions.* Greenville, S.C.: Bob Jones University Press.

*Selected Studies about the Bob Joneses*

Campbell, Robert, ed. *Spectrum of Protestant Beliefs*. Milwaukee: Bruce Publishing Co.,
      1968.
Dollar, George. *A History of Fundamentalism in America*. Greenville, S.C.: Bob Jones
      University Press, 1973.
Johnson, R. K. *Builder of Bridges*. Murfreesboro, Tenn.: Sword of the Lord, 1969.
Tice, Margaret Beall. *Bob Jones University*. Greenville, S.C.: Bob Jones University
      Press, 1976.
Wright, Melton. *Fortress of Faith*. Grand Rapids: Eerdmans, 1960.

                                                                    EDWARD L. QUEEN II

# E. Stanley Jones

The life of E. Stanley Jones (1884–1973) still awaits a full-length, critical biography. Missionary extraordinary, influential spokesman for American Protestantism, author of twenty-eight books and hundreds of articles, Jones has as
yet eluded the fine-meshed scholarly net that such a work would provide. As a
result, evaluations depend on his published works, his quasi-autobiographical
*Song of Ascents,* and a small body of dissertations and secondary works. The
most significant of the latter share with Jones' own work an overriding emphasis
on the thought rather than the life of the man. Thus, at present, any treatment
of Jones is largely a treatment of his thought.

## Biography

Eli Stanley Jones, who preferred to be called by his middle name, was born
on 3 January 1884 in Clarksville, Maryland. His father was a sometime farmer,
clerk, and patronage worker in the city of Baltimore, to which the family moved
when Jones was quite young. His mother was a public school teacher. She was
also the primary influence in the upbringing of her children. Recalling these
early years, Jones remembered his mother as a strict disciplinarian, a religious
legalist who kept him from youthful temptation until he discovered the joys of
religion through conversion. Of his father or other family members, he shared
little. An apparently major reversal in the family fortunes and ensuing hard times
brought only indirect comment. Instead, a struggle between expectations and
freedom, between the high moral tone of his mother and his own search for
meaning in life, held center stage.

Typically, this struggle intensified in his youth—which, Jones states, was
given over to foolish and potentially destructive pursuits. The glimmers show a
group of "chums," all connected with Memorial Methodist Episcopal Church,
South, Baltimore, involved in cursing, cards, and other unnamed acts of rebellion
against the strict code of his mother. Little else surfaces from the period he
dismissed as B.C.—Before Christ. The picture clears only at about the time of
Jones' conversion. At age seventeen—still in church, still with the same

"chums" and the same lifestyle—Jones heard evangelist Robert J. Bateman. A converted alcoholic and straightforward speaker, Bateman provided clarity of example. Jones wanted what Bateman had and labored in prayer at the altar until he found it.

What Jones found he then described in terms that could have been used by any number of others touched by the tradition of revivalism. E. Stanley Jones was deeply, soundly, classically converted. From periods of deep despair, hopeless rage, and listless depression through the experience of hope, light, and peace, to a settled sense of new life as a committed Christian, Jones duplicated the pattern central to the revivalist expression of Christian faith. For Jones, conversion was the occasion for deep and lasting change. It also became a pattern for crisis points in his later life and ministry. The direct voice of God through experience would prove crucial in guiding the choices of his varied career.

This pattern took shape as Jones struggled with the issue of vocation. Should he continue with earlier plans to follow a legal career, only now with a Christian commitment, or should he follow the urgings of family and friends to enter the ministry? Jones had learned to articulate his faith confidently in the intense setting of a Methodist class meeting. However, when encouraged to preach, he experienced failure. He found that he was comfortable sharing conversationally with groups of any size but that the homiletic confines of classical sermon preparation left him confused and voiceless. These potential conflicts were resolved by close attention to his developing sense of God's guidance, and the not inconsiderable influence of southern evangelist Henry Clay Morrison. Turning aside doubt, Jones entered Asbury College in Wilmore, Kentucky, an independent college embued by Morrison and his colleagues with their own holiness version of Wesleyan doctrine.

Asbury suited both the diligent moral tone and the fervent experiential bent of the young student. It provided the setting for a particular spiritual refinement unique to Jones. Overcoming a disdain for the "shouting religion" of his classmates, yet keeping a distance from the insistent holiness theology of Morrison and his associates, Jones found a middle ground. During 1905, when Asbury was touched by a spontaneous outpouring of spiritual enthusiasm, Jones awakened dramatically to the direct intervention of the Holy Spirit. However, the aspect of that awakening that had the greatest influence on him was not the exercises of the Pentecostals or the intense excitement of the majority of his fellow students, but the sense of infinite quiet, the holy calm that still impressed its subject over sixty years later. This calm made Jones both observer and participant in the scene about him. As he tiptoed under its influence through the remaining days of religious excitement and the remaining years of college, Jones found in this attitude of inner calm a source for religious expression that was both remarkably assured and at the same time remarkably irenic.

This attitude, assured of God's direct guidance yet open to the very human voices surrounding the struggling saint, became Jones' middle ground. With it, he managed to impress people on opposite sides of the vexed holiness issue. On graduation in 1907, Jones was invited to conduct evangelistic services in the United States, to remain at Asbury and teach, or to go to India as a Methodist missionary. The last invitation was striking in that it was issued by the Mission Board of Northern Methodism, rather than his own Methodist Episcopal Church, South. Confused by conflicting voices, Jones retired to prayer to listen for the voice. What he heard, briefly and clearly, was India.

After a perfunctory examination by the mission board, Jones was given, he recalled in *A Song of Ascents,* "a Hindustani grammer, forty pounds in British gold, a ticket to Bombay via Britain, a handshake, and sent off." He received no training, no evaluation, not even a physical. He arrived in Bombay, India, on 13 November 1907, a stranger to everything Indian. He found his way to the station at Lucknow, where he was appointed pastor of the Lal Bagh Church, a large mixed congregation of Indians, Anglo-Indians, and Europeans. Preaching regular services in the morning and evangelistic services in the evening, Jones soon found himself, despite serious lack of experience, the popular pastor of a growing congregation. He served the Lucknow Church for four years, during which time he moved primarily along the colonial strata of Indian society, among the English and the anglicized. Since Lucknow was the administrative center of Methodist missions in India, Jones was situated to continue in a comfortable and successful ministry.

He was not satisfied, however. Jones felt himself cut off from the real India, which he identified with neither the multiform indigenous culture nor the British imperial administration but with the growing movement for Indian independence. The vital currents of Indian nationalism stood in contrast, for Jones, to either the enforced unity of British rule or the fragmentation of traditional society. He desired to be out and about, evangelizing across the boundaries of Indian society. So, after marrying Mabel Lossing, a missionary teacher at the Isabella Thoburn College of Lucknow (first women's college in Asia), Jones moved to Sitphar, a city of 27,000, fifty miles northwest of Lucknow. He was placed in charge of evangelistic work among the million people of the Sitphar District. Jones worked diligently, visiting from house to house and organizing to reach every household in his district. Again he was successful. His presence was recognized and appreciated by the people of his district and later of the Lucknow, Hardoi, and Rae Bareilli districts, which were added to his charge. Supervision of the 500 workers of these districts, along with the local agency of the Methodist Publishing House, was entrusted to a thirty-year-old first-term missionary, still without formal training for most of the work he performed.

Yet Stanley Jones was still not satisfied. Expectations had been met and surpassed, but he had not achieved the freedom of his lifework. He also began to suffer physically. A ruptured appendix, followed by a nearly fatal case of tetanus, broke a frayed constitution. Physical collapse was followed by nervous collapse. After eight and one-half years of service, Jones was furloughed home. Before he left, however, he caught a glimpse of a possible new ministry. In an encounter with members of the Hindu professional class, who were curious about the missionary concentration on work with the outcastes, Jones was encouraged to bring Christ to the Indian intelligentsia "in the right way." He began to consider ministry to those at the fore of the struggle for independence.

Jones returned to India after furlough still weak physically and spiritually. Thwarted by ill health and mental distress and on the verge of quitting, he experienced another crisis and resolution. Discovering a new level of personal surrender to God, Jones renewed his commitment to missions. His work was not to follow traditional lines, however. The challenge to reach the intelligentsia of Indian society set him on course to new methods and new outlooks that freed him from the strictures of his self-denominated religious conservatism. He no longer defended the whole of christendom—or even those cultural or doctrinal parts that had nurtured Jones himself. Speaking of Christ alone, "disentangled" from Western Christianity, he built an influential ministry. Although he spoke of Christ at great length, he steadfastly refused to engage in other controversies. Jones chose his ground. He abandoned the sanctuary, the compound, and the denomination as appropriate tools of missions. Henceforth, he was an interdenominational, itinerant teacher-evangelist.

Jones developed the programmatic aspects of this ministry over the two decades following his return to India in 1918. He began with series of public meetings. Held on neutral ground (any ground but a church), chaired by prominent non-Christian citizens, with a topic of religious interest upheld by Jones' unique skills in communication, and closed by question-and-answer periods, these meetings proved exceptionally popular. The current national ferment and intellectual stirring were peculiarly suited to his method. His "disentangled Christ," a person-centered faith unconcerned with the traditional forms and doctrines of Christianity, surprised many of his Hindu hearers, especially as Jones incorporated insights from Indian religions to advocate an "Indian road" of Christ. The ministry blossomed. Jones itinerated widely.

As a second step, Jones added "Round Table" discussions to concentrate on invited guests, select individuals from the intelligentsia. These talks were free and open. They not only presented Christ in a winsome way to cultured Indians but also opened Jones himself to the influence of others. By far the most powerful such influence came in 1919 when Jones first met Mahatma Gandhi. He found in the Indian leader a nearly pure expression of the virtue of the very Christ whom he presented in his ministry. He never confused the two, but Jones did find a certain embodiment in Gandhi that gave him hope for an authentic Indian Christianity.

Under Gandhi's influence and that of Rabindranath Tagore and Charles Andrews, whose ashram "Shantineketan" (The House of Peace) advanced ideals of simplicity and peace in a traditional Indian format, Jones undertook the third step in his program. In 1930 he established his Christian ashram "Sat Tal" (Seven Lakes) in the foothills of the Himalayas. A simple lifestyle nurtured an intense spiritual quest in prayer, study, and discussion. The ashram was an Indian form that Jones found amenable to Christian use. Without identifying too

closely with specific doctrines of Hinduism, the ashram provided a setting for
Christian renewal. The ashram also included a communal lifestyle that supported
Jones' growing concept of the Kingdom of God, a society where love found
expression in a life of other-directed service. Jones experimented with urban
settings to combine the qualities of retreat and active service. However, the rural
setting and the emphasis on personal spiritual renewal marked the popular ashram
exported to other countries.

As Jones' ministry grew, so did his stature as a Christian leader. He carried
his program around the world. He published books from the experience of his
meetings, round tables, and ashrams that have had an enduring popularity. He
interpreted Gandhi, India, and in time the whole of Asia to a Western audience.
He was called to confer with British authorities on their negotiations with Gandhi.
As early as 1924, when he attended the quadrennial meeting of the Methodist
General Conference as a delegate, Jones' fame was such as to make him a
candidate for bishop. Though he withdrew, in 1928 he was elected on one ballot.
This precipitated a crisis for Jones that he resolved, under the guidance of his
inner voice, by resigning. He toured America as a missionary leader and advocate
of church unity, peace, racial understanding, Gandhi's nonviolent noncoopera-
tion, his own cooperative understanding of the Kingdom of God, and devotional
spirituality. His name recognition over continents was such that when the peace
party in the Japanese embassy in Washington sought a confidential avenue to
the U.S. government in the tense days before World War II, they approached
Jones. At the urging of the Japanese, he recommended that President Roosevelt
send a personal telegram to Emperor Hirohito, which may have averted or delayed
hostilities.

Jones continued his peripatetic ministry for several decades. Few matters of
inportance in the church passed his notice or comment. Jones was controverted
in both his actions and ideas, but his fame was as durable as his own confident
spirituality. He was indefatigable in traveling, speaking, and writing until late
in his life. His autobiography was written as he passed eighty. His thought,
honed over many years of public interaction, remained compelling even in its
latest expression. India remained in his heart, even as Sitphar remained his home
base. But he shared his message with the world.

### Appraisal

In his *Religious History of the American People* (1972), Sydney Ahlstrom
included Jones in his discussion of "harmonial religion." An optimistic religion
of rapport with the cosmos, this rubric covers a disparate lot—from Christian
Science, through New Thought, to positive thinking. For Ahlstrom, Jones stood
within the last school. In his devotional writings, Jones shared with Harry Emerson Fosdick* the distinction of a careful, liberal positive thinking approach. On
the other hand, when evaluated from the perspective of his work in India, he
appears a creative, even brilliant missiologist. The secondary works done on
Jones by Indian writers often border on veneration. So also, if taken on the basis

of his racial, social, or ecumenical thought, Jones is different yet again. In some ways, the significance of E. Stanley Jones depends on which part of his varied career receives the focus.

For that matter, Jones' significance also varies depending on which part of the theological spectrum he occupies. To Ahlstrom, he stood in the tradition of Protestant liberalism. To others, the focus is the evangelical tendencies of his devotional thought or even the near fundamentalism of his image of Christ. As a major shaper of popular American religion, Jones remains remarkably difficult to pin down.

Perhaps part of Jones' influence rests in this very elusiveness. He simply ignored the tribal taxonomists, not only of American religion but also of world religions, finding in his confident inner calm the strength to form provisional "middle grounds" across the boundaries on which others insisted. In this regard, the habit of mind that appeared as early as Asbury functioned throughout Jones' life to pull what others would define as opposites into some sort of pacific dialogue. Whatever specific problems might appear with this or that combination in his thought, Jones somehow matched the integrity of several great ideals (the disentangled Christ, the Kingdom of God, the federal union of the churches, etc.) with the ability to feather the rough edges of countervailing opinion.

Such an evaluation might seem to relegate E. Stanley Jones to the position of the hopeless romantic and his influence to the vestigial appeal of those habits of thought to one part of the modern mind. In this light, Jones' popularity would rest in a defect in one cog of modernity. However, since most "great shapers" seem to share something of the same ability to bypass the instinct to categorize diverse views of the world into exclusivity, Jones may in fact embody a rare and powerful quality somehow slighted by other parts of the same modern mind. Though sloppy and eclectic, he may indeed deserve the designation of creative thinker. If the heartfelt popular response that he generated even in the camps of his most ardent detractors bears any claim as evidence, such a designation may be appropriate.

Certainly Jones had a widespread appeal. Though his theology would seem dated in either its liberal or evangelical tint and his approach to other cultures out of step with current endeavors to appreciate each expression within its own context, Jones may yet find an audience. If the official position of his own Methodist denomination is sympathetic to only those parts of his thought that speak to peace and racial issues, there remains a broad lay constituency that would feel very much at home with his other, more characteristic ideals. If those who have maintained the popularity of his devotional books move beyond them to his other writings, there may yet be a renaissance of interest in Jones.

## Survey of Criticism

Jones was involved in several controversies during his life. Critical appraisals of his thought appear primarily in the context of these debates rather than, at present, in the cooler atmosphere of scholarly investigation. During his active ministry, discussions of Jones turned on one issue of identity and three of thought. The issue of identity queried whether Jones was a theological liberal or conservative. This issue was most often raised on the Christian right, where empathy with his Christology was nearly always countered by questions regarding other areas of his theology. Whereas Jones' view of Christ and his emphasis on evangelism were all that the evangelical community could ask for, his sympathy for other religions, his view of the Old Testament as "pre-Christian and sub-Christian," and his pronounced ecumenical opinions all gave editors pause. Though Jones liked to dismiss such concern by calling himself a man with a modernist mind but a fundamentalist soul, conservative Christians were not mollified. From the *Princeton Theological Review* to the *Sunday School Times*, writers raised and then variously answered the question of Jones' status in the theological community.

The issues of Jones' thought regarded his politics, his ecumenicity, and his devotional theology, derived in turn from his concepts of the Kingdom of God, the federal plan of church union, and the place of the historical Jesus. Impressed by the dedication to the revolution that he saw during his travels through Russia in 1935 and struck by the Depression-era failure of capitalism, Jones advocated a concept of the Kingdom of God that depended heavily on an exegesis of the communal lifestyle in the early part of the Book of Acts. The resulting strong tinge of socialism brought Jones under considerable fire. A milder critic, Reinhold Niebuhr, in his *Interpretation of Christian Ethics* judged Jones' ideas "the most perfect swan song of liberal politics." The later, less charitable House Committee on Un-American Activities simply found him Red. Though Jones modified his understanding of both communism and capitalism, he continued to draw fire on his political orientation.

As a missionary, Jones was scandalized by the continued divisions of Christianity. His attempt to address the issue by advancing a federal plan for church union placed him in the middle of ecumenical discussions. His vague ideal of a church of root and branches, or an American system of a federated governing body over denominational "states," drew an immense popular response but an equally critical reading among ecumenists and denominational officials. From the Madras Missionary Conference of 1939, where Jones advocated the Kingdom of God as a priority over church union (only to be rejected as the Conference opted for the latter), to later interchanges in the ecumenical format of the *Christian Century,* Jones found himself fighting an uphill battle against what he characterized as the "hierarchy" of the ecumenical movement.

In the third area of his thought, on the nature of the historical Jesus, Jones confronted the impact of higher critical study on the central tenet of his ministry. The disentangled Christ of his proclamation arose from a conservative, noncritical reading of the Gospels. Jones' Jesus was the Jesus of evangelism. Late in life, Jones became aware that this view was controverted by scholars working from the very tradition and with the very tools that he had accepted when used to qualify the status of the Old Testament. If his rejection of neo-orthodox thought indicates the "modernist mind" of Jones' brand of positive thinking, his rejection of scholarship on the historical Jesus certainly indicates the "fundamentalist soul" of his disentangled Christ. In turn, the criticisms leveled at Jones' rather fuzzy understanding of biblical scholarship undergirded the evaluation of contemporaries like Ahlstrom who were preparing to damn Jones' status as a Christian figure with the faint praise that he achieved it despite ephemeral habits of thought from the center out.

## Bibliography

### Books by E. Stanley Jones

1925   *The Christ of the Indian Road*. New York: Abingdon Press.
1928   *Christ at the Round Table*. New York: Abingdon Press.
1930   *The Christ of Every Round*. New York: Abingdon Press.
1931   *The Christ of the Mount*. New York: Abingdon Press.
1933   *Christ and Human Suffering*. New York: Abingdon Press.
1935   *Christ's Alternative to Communism*. New York: Abingdon Press.
1936   *Victorious Living*. New York: Abingdon Press.
1937   *The Choice Before Us*. New York: Abingdon Press.
1939   *Along the Indian Road*. New York: Abingdon Press.
1940   *Is The Kingdom of God Realism?* New York: Abingdon Press.
1942   *Abundant Living*. Nashville: Abingdon-Cokesbury Press.
1944   *The Christ of the American Road*. Nashville: Abingdon-Cokesbury Press.
1946   *The Way*. Nashville: Abingdon-Cokesbury Press.
1948   *Mahatma Gandhi: An Interpretation*. Nashville: Abingdon-Cokesbury Press.
1949   *The Way to Power and Poise*. Nashville: Abingdon-Cokesbury Press.
1951   *How to be a Transformed Person*. Nashville: Abingdon-Cokesbury Press.
1953   *Growing Spiritually*. Nashville: Abingdon-Cokesbury Press.
1955   *Mastery: The Art of Mastering Life*. Nashville: Abingdon Press.
1957   *Christian Maturity*. Nashville: Abingdon Press.
1959   *Conversion*. Nashville: Abingdon Press.
1961   *In Christ*. Nashville: Abingdon Press.
1963   *The Word Became Flesh*. Nashville: Abingdon Press.
1966   *Victory Through Surrender*. Nashville: Abingdon Press.
1968   *A Song of Ascents*. Nashville: Abingdon Press.
1970   *Reconstruction of the Church: On What Pattern?* Nashville: Abingdon Press.
1972   *The Unshakable Kingdom and the Unchanging Person*. Nashville: Abingdon Press.

### Studies about E. Stanley Jones

Johnson, Martin Ross. "The Christian Vision of E. Stanley Jones: Missionary Evangelist, Prophet, and Statesman." Ph.D. diss., Florida State University, 1978.

Paranjoti, Violet. *An Evangelist on the Indian Scene: Dr. E. Stanley Jones*. Bombay, India: Bombay Tract and Book Society, 1970.

Taylor, Richard W. *The Contribution of E. Stanley Jones*. Confessing the Faith in India Series, No. 9. Madras, India: Christian Literature Society for the Christian Institute for the Study of Religion and Society, 1973.

Thomas, C. Chacko. "The Work and Thought of Eli Stanley Jones with Special Reference
    to India." Ph.D. diss., State University of Iowa, 1955.
Thompson, Kenneth Ralph. "The Ethics of Eli Stanley Jones." Ph.D. diss., Southwestern
    Baptist Theological Seminary, 1960.

DANIEL SWINSON

# Mordecai M. Kaplan

The death of Mordecai Menachem Kaplan in November 1983 at the age of 102 represented the conclusion of a career that was remarkable both for its duration and for the range of interests it represented. The time during which he worked out a vocation as a rabbi, seminary professor, and insightful analyst of Jewish experience in America spanned a period during which Judaism in its different manifestations was assimilated as an established feature of the American religious landscape. During this same period, Judaism in the United States, as Nathan Glazer and others have pointed out, began to develop into Reform, Conservative, and Orthodox families, based on the degrees of accommodation with intellectual and cultural patterns of American religious life.

### Biography

Born in Lithuania in 1881, Kaplan was exposed from an early age to the tenets and practices of Orthodoxy and at the same time to a need to accommodate sensibilities characteristic of modern critical approaches. Kaplan's father, Israel, a Talmudic scholar, devoted himself to study while his mother, Anna, supported the family by managing a small business. Israel Kaplan's views about most matters were traditional; however, he did come to believe strongly in the importance of Jewish education for womem, a view that Mordecai himself took up in his later popularization of the practice of encouraging girls to become *bat mitzvah* ("daughters of the commandment"), just as boys became *bar mitzvah*.

In 1889, the Kaplan family immigrated to New York City so that Israel Kaplan could accept an appointment in the office of the chief rabbi of New York. Here, Kaplan's simultaneous encounter with American Judaism and American culture commenced. Kaplan's education in the public schools of the city and as a student of his father and his father's rabbinical colleagues highlighted the tensions between the two "civilizations." This experience caused him to feel deeply the problem of being Jewish while becoming American. This tension is constitutive for his subsequent development.

By this time, the Reform movement had already made significant inroads among the American descendants of Western European Jewry, the *Ashkenazim*. The waves of Orthodox Jews emigrating from Eastern Europe had already begun to challenge the compromise with American ways symbolized by the Pittsburgh Platform (1885), the "creed of Reform Judaism." For Kaplan, this accommodation with American sensibilities, based on a deemphasis of ritual, anti-Zionism,

and an emphasis on individualism, represented a deformation—not a reformation—of Jewish tradition that the Historical or Conservative movement would
seek subsequently to redress. The Conservative movement would assert the
compatibility of modern conventions of critical intellection with ritual observance, commitment to Torah study, and an American Jewish identity developed
in relation to the Jewish community.

In 1893, at the age of twelve, Kaplan enrolled in the preparatory class at the
Jewish Theological Seminary of America, the institution that subsequently developed as the principal institution for educating the Conservative rabbinate. In
1895, he also enrolled as a "sub-freshman" at the College of the City of New
York, from which he received a bachelor's degree in 1900. In 1902, he graduated
from the Jewish Theological Seminary Association, was ordained as a Conservative rabbi, and earned the degree of master of arts in philosophy at Columbia
University.

Thus, from 1889 until 1902, Kaplan's education was a product of the two
"civilizations" he would devote the remainder of his career to reconciling. The
tensions between these worlds and his involvement in both secular and religious
study at a time when the identity of Judaism as an American phenomenon was
shifting encouraged him to construct a distinctive American form of Judaism
respectful of both Jewish tradition and the need for evolution of that tradition.
He sought to shape an approach in which a Jewish world view could be accommodated to Western thinking. Kaplan commented that while his education "deepened his Jewish consciousness," it also "troubled his Jewish conscience."

Although not an Orthodox rabbi, Kaplan was called in 1903 to serve as a
spiritual leader of *Kehilath Jeshurun,* a leading New York Orthodox congregation
whose people were willing to forgo traditional ordination in order to have an
English-speaking rabbi. Kaplan reported later that he had accepted this position
for two reasons: first, despite his own doubts and questions about supernaturalistic
interpretations of religion, he strictly conformed to Jewish ritual practice; second,
he was not expected to address fundamental theological problems. Rather, his
task was to interpret texts on the basis of which his congregation could better
understand their ritual obligations. Kaplan also indicated that his avoidance of
theological issues, such as the nature of God, the Mosaic authorship of the
Pentateuch, and the historicity of miracles, was facilitated by his regular emphasis
on the origin, character, hopes, and frustrations of the Jewish people.

Characteristically, Kaplan emphasized the communal, rather than the dogmatic, significance of Jewish experience. The rationale of ritual observance was
to enhance consciousness of the social, human, and vulnerable community of
which every Jew was a part. Thus, Kaplan set himself to the task of constructing
a program whereby traditional Judaism might be adjusted to a non-Jewish environment by stressing, following sociologist Émile Durkheim, the social basis
and purpose of Jewish religious experience. He found himself in difficulty with
members of his congregation when he suggested that the demands of the American workplace made it all but impossible for the average Jew to refuse to work

on the Sabbath. As a practical consequence of this view, he argued that, in a year when Yom Kippur fell on the Sabbath, the day could be partially observed if a "Sabbath spirit" were cultivated. Kaplan viewed this pastoral advice as a necessary accommodation of the "modern environment."

As he wrote in an autobiographical sketch, "The Way I Have Come," found in Ira Eisenstein and Eugene Kohn's *Mordecai M. Kaplan: An Evaluation,* this incident convinced him that "as long as Jews adhered to the traditional conception of Torah as supernaturally revealed, they would not be amenable to any constructive adjustment of Judaism that was needed to render it viable in a non-Jewish environment." It was to the task of defining such a "constructive adjustment" that Kaplan subsequently devoted himself as a religious leader and seminary professor. In Kaplan's view, Orthodox Judaism based on the dogma of *Torah min ha-shamayim* ("supernatural origin of the Torah") could not withstand the scrutiny of modern critical thought about the Bible.

At this early point in his ministry, Kaplan was in search of a different compass to orient himself in relation to Jewish tradition. Having used Durkheim as an aid for understanding the centrality of the social context of religious experience, Kaplan found in Matthew Arnold an elucidation of an alternative to conceptions of God based on miracles or metaphysics. Arnold's stress on experience complemented Durkheim's stress on social structure to help round out an approach whereby Kaplan could recover his faith in the Bible. "All of this," he wrote in the autobiographical essay, "was a source of great relief to me, because it convinced me, that despite the chasm that divided my conception of God and the Bible from my congregants, I was in a position to imbue them with a love for both as a means of winning and holding their loyalty to the Jewish people. The notion of having them love God and the Bible as a means of saving their own souls did not even occur to me."

Kaplan, oriented finally by notions of community and experience, turned to the Russian writer Ahad Ha'am (the pseudonym of Asher Ginzberg), the proponent of spiritual Zionism, whose ideas provided a countervailing approach to the political Zionism of Theodor Herzl. Ahad Ha'am emphasized that the Jewish people were a living organism, animated by what Kaplan termed "an irresistible will to live." In this conception, he found both "spiritual anchorage" and a basis subsequently for distinguishing his interpretation of Judaism from Reform Judaism's anti-Zionism.

The substance of this recognition, which Kaplan termed nothing less than a Copernican revolution, was that the people of Israel were the central reality in Judaism. The meaning of God or the significance of the Torah could be properly understood only in relation to that center. The main concern of Judaism was, therefore, the origin, vicissitudes, and destiny of the Jewish people. In this interpretation, the significance of an ontological or metaphysical understanding of the nature of God was far less important than what God meant in moral, social, economic, and political terms to Israel's spiritual leadership. Kaplan's own summary of his approach, in "The Way I Have Come," makes clear the

terms of his frame of reference, as well as the extent to which he was influenced
by the empiricism of the American thinkers William James and John Dewey:

> To find plausible the view, which is supported by an unbiased and preconceptionless
> survey of the Jewish heritage, I had to fit it into the general character of human
> thought and behavior. Thus, I arrived by way of a clearer awareness of Judaism's
> universe of discourse, of what I soon recognized to be pragmatism, the philosophical
> method which insists upon rendering thought . . . relevant to man's needs. Any
> idea, to have meaning, must be seen in a context of natural conditions and human
> relations. The function of belief in God is to make us aware of the moral and
> spiritual context of our conduct, so that we come to move within the orbit of the
> "Power that makes for righteousness." Judaism uses the belief in God to make
> Jews aware of the natural conditions that have to be established and the human
> relations that have to be maintained for the Jewish people, if it is to achieve salvation
> collectively and individually.

Kaplan set forth these ideas emphasizing community, social responsibility,
and evolution—which parallel empirically oriented theological developments in
American Protestantism—in a speech at an annual meeting of the Rabbinical
Assembly in 1909. Among those who listened was Solomon Schechter, the
distinguished Talmudic scholar and rabbi who had been called from Cambridge
University earlier in the decade to lead the Jewish Theological Seminary. Schechter invited Kaplan, whose views continued to evolve away from the sensibilities
of his congregation, to head the newly organized Teachers Institute at the seminary. Thus began an association with the Jewish Theological Seminary that
would span more than half a century. In 1910, Kaplan took on the additional
post of professor of homiletics in the rabbinical school. He retained these two
positions until 1946, when he gave up the deanship of the Teachers Institute.
He remained a professor at the seminary until "retiring" in 1963 at the age of
eighty-two.

In 1915, while serving at the Jewish Theological Seminary, Kaplan was again
called to lead an Orthodox congregation, this time on New York's West Side.
In 1921, after a dispute within the congregation, he resigned this post and formed
the Society for the Advancement of Judaism, with a small congregation dedicated
to his interpretation of Judaism and to the reconstruction of Jewish life. Kaplan's
relationship with the Conservative movement was not always easy, but by and
large he felt that he could be more effective in the "left wing" of Conservative
Judaism than as the leader of a separate movement. In his 1963 letter of resignation, addressed to Louis Finkelstein, the president of the Jewish Theological
Seminary, Kaplan acknowledged that Reconstructionism had not achieved its
potential within the Conservative movement:

> The reason I wish to be relieved of my duties at the Seminary is that I wish to
> devote the rest of my life to the cause of Reconstructionism. I would like to
> concentrate all my energies on promulgating it on as large a scale as possible. I
> have by this time become passionately convinced that the Reconstructionist ap-
> proach to Judaism is the only one that is likely to stop the stampede of our Jewish

intellectuals from Judaism, though it by no means claims to be the only authentic approach to Judaism as such.

The preamble to the platform of the Reconstructionist movement, which until the 1960s sustained itself as a "branch" of Conservatism, strongly emphasized its identity as an American movement. "As American Jews, we give first place in our lives to the American civilization which we share in common with our fellow Americans, and we seek to develop our Jewish heritage to the maximum degree consonant with the best in American life." The platform emphasized the necessity of reinterpreting traditional beliefs and ritual practices, the need for a Jewish homeland in Palestine, and the importance of social action directed toward the elimination of economic injustice and the development of a "cooperative society" based on elimination of the profit system and public ownership of natural resources and basic industries.

Reconstructionism, whose central theses were given initial systematic expression in Kaplan's *Judaism as a Civilization* (1934), attracted a small number of adherents who identified themselves formally with the movement and a somewhat larger number of individuals who maintained interest in Kaplan's work. Although precise numbers of adherents are not available, the *Reconstructionist,* the periodical organ of the movement, had a circulation of 6,000 in 1970, two years after the founding of the Reconstructionist Rabbinical College in Philadelphia. According to the 12 November 1983 *New York Times,* at the time of Kaplan's death, the movement claimed 50,000 followers.

### Appraisal

Kaplan's influence, however, cannot be understood merely as a function of these numbers. He exercised wide influence as a maverick at the Jewish Theological Seminary, insisting that an eternal revelation was not a static thing. In so doing, he challenged generations of Jewish religious professionals to think about the renewal and transformation of the Jewish community.

Whereas many in the Conservative movement believed that Kaplan had simplistically reduced theological concerns to questions of community and ethics, Kaplan believed that he was responding to the forces that had fundamentally shaped the theological task. Although his theology was constructed in social terms, it continued to be based on what he described late in his life as an "unchanging relationship between God and Israel." The character and terms of that relationship did not in all times and places for Kaplan take the same form. The vocation of Judaism—reconstructed and evolving—was, as always, to be a light to others while, as he himself had been, enlightened by others. One of Kaplan's prayers, found in virtually all Reconstructionist prayer books, gives expression to his faith in a God who continues to act:

God is in the faith
By which we overcome
The fear of loneliness and helplessness,

Of failure and death.
God is in the hope
Which, like a shaft of light,
Cleaves the dark abysms
Of sin, of suffering and of despair.
God is in the love
Which Creates, protects, forgives.
He is the spirit
Which broods upon the chaos men have wrought
Disturbing its static wrongs,
And stirring into life the formless beginnings
Of the new and better world.

## Survey of Criticism

The first significant effort to assess Kaplan's contribution is the 1952 volume *Mordecai M. Kaplan: An Evaluation*. This sympathetic account, edited by Kaplan's son-in-law and colleague, Ira Eisenstein, along with Eugene Kohn, includes fifteen articles, as well as the very useful retrospective, "The Way I Have Come," that Kaplan prepared as a concluding chapter. Of particular interest is the chapter "Idea of God," written by the University of Chicago theologian Henry N. Wieman, in which he discusses Kaplan's understanding of the "God-concept." The book also includes discussion of Kaplan's contributions to liturgical reform, as well as his promotion of the Jewish Center, an analogue to the institutional church in which social and religious activities undertaken on behalf of the community complemented the traditional emphasis on prayer and liturgy. An adumbration of the more recent discussion about civil religion is found in Joseph Blau's article, characterizing Kaplan as a "Philosopher of Democracy."

The sociologist Charles S. Liebman prepared a useful and highly suggestive article, "Reconstructionism in American Jewish Life," for the 1970 *American Jewish Year Book*. On the basis of a close reading of the Reconstructionist corpus, as well as interviews with Kaplan and his colleagues, Liebman argued that Reconstructionism was a "second-generation" American Jewish phenomenon, the study of which "opens the door to an understanding of American Judaism" of the period. Liebman also emphasized Kaplan's role at the Jewish Theological Seminary, where he attracted a "significant proportion of the most talented and idealistic students at the Seminary." Liebman notes that whereas many of the students did not formally associate themselves with Reconstructionist-oriented institutions, Reconstructionism represented an important stage in the development of their vocations as rabbis. Liebman also notes the particular appeal that Kaplan had for Jewish educators and activists who were seeking to reconcile tradition-oriented sensibility with secular vocations.

Finally, Liebman argued that though Reconstructionism appealed to and conformed to attitudes widely prevalent among American Jews, it was still "numerically and institutionally insignificant":

Its core institution, the Reconstructionist Foundation, commands the support of fewer individuals than does any one of a dozen hasidic *rebbes*. There are a number of synagogues in the United States each of which has a larger paid membership than the Reconstructionist Foundation. . . . The disparity between the acceptance of Reconstructionist ideas and the failure of the organized movement is striking. Exploring the reasons for this disparity helps shed light on the nature of American Judaism, and on the relationship between the ideologies and the institutions of American Jews.

A clue to this paradox may be found in Herbert Parzen's *Architects of Conservative Judaism,* where Parzen noted that though it was true that Kaplan had "incalculably enriched the content and program of the Conservative movement . . . the impact of his theology has not been significant and is suspected by many who have adopted the rest of his program." Liebman also observed, characterizing Reconstructionism as "the folk religion of American Jews," that the effort to systematize it philosophically exposed its inadequacy as a religious program, making it less appealing to the very group who at other levels was attracted to its practical and service-oriented dimensions. The implication of Liebman's analysis is that Reconstructionism might have fared better if Kaplan and his followers had taken less trouble to spell out the critical implications of their creed. This observation raises the question of whether Reconstructionism finally gave too little attention to the numinous and the symbolic aspects of Jewish experience.

The latter point is taken up in *The Chosen People in America* by Arnold M. Eisen, who concentrated on Kaplan's critique of the idea of election of Jews as a chosen people and his conversion of election as chosenness to election as vocation. In repudiating the idea that Jews were a special people, Kaplan gave up a formative aspect of the tradition that bound the Jewish people. Eisen's conclusion reinforces this point:

> Religiously identified American Jews . . . would be an ethnic group that retained the consciousness of being something more and lay claim to a calling different from all others, even if they could not explain, justify, or account for it. They would act like Reconstructionists, and at one level, even believe like them, but would reserve space for symbolic affirmation that Kaplan's literalness in the matter of chosenness denied them. Through Reform and other movements, they would retain chosenness precisely as a symbol which gripped through the power of its resonances and not as a concept expounded coherently.

The fact that Kaplan could not accept the idea of chosenness meant that his system might not finally appeal to the emotions of faith and loyalty and therefore could not appeal to the deep sensibility—the need for symbolic identification with the divine mystery—that continued to affect a large number of American Jews.

The most recent study, Richard Libowitz's *Mordecai M. Kaplan and the Development of Reconstructionism,* provides a useful framework for understanding Kaplan's development as a religious thinker up to the publication of *Judaism as a Civilization*. Libowitz exposes and delineates Kaplan's intellectual debt to Arnold, Durkheim, James, and Dewey and emphasizes Kaplan's distinctive fusion of Jewish and Western intellectual sources.

## Bibliography

### Books by Mordecai M. Kaplan

1934  *Judaism as a Civilization*. New York: Macmillan.
1936  *Judaism in Transition*. New York: Covici, Friede.
1936  *Mesillat Yesharim: The Path of the Upright*. By Moses Hayyim Luzzato. Philadelphia: Jewish Publication Society. Edited and translated by Kaplan.
1937  *The Meaning of God in Modern Jewish Religion*. New York: Behrman's Jewish Book House.
1948  *The Future of the American Jew*. New York: Macmillan.
1955  *A New Zionism*. New York: Theodor Herzl Foundation.
1956  *Questions Jews Ask*. New York: Reconstructionist Press.
1958  *Judaism Without Supernaturalism*. New York: Reconstructionist Press.
1960  *The Greater Judaism in the Making*. New York: Reconstructionist Press.
1964  *The Purpose and Meaning of Jewish Existence*. Philadelphia: Jewish Publication Society.
1970  *The Religion of Ethical Nationhood*. New York: Macmillan.

### Selected Studies about Mordecai M. Kaplan

Breslauer, S. Daniel. *The Ecumenical Perspective and the Modernization of Jewish Religion*. Missoula: Scholars Press, 1978.
Eisen, Arnold M. *The Chosen People in America*. Bloomington: Indiana University Press, 1983.
Eisenstein, Ira, and Eugene Kohn, editors. *Mordecai M. Kaplan: An Evaluation*. New York: Jewish Reconstructionist Foundation, 1952.
Glazer, Nathan. *American Judaism*. Chicago: University of Chicago Press, 1972.
Libowitz, Richard. *Mordecai M. Kaplan and the Development of Reconstructionism*. New York: Edwin Mellen Press, 1984.
Liebman, Charles. "Reconstructionism in American Jewish Life." In *American Jewish Year Book, 1970*, pp. 3–99. New York: American Jewish Committee.
Nadelman, Ludwig. "Mordecai M. Kaplan (1881–1983)." In *American Jewish Year Book, 1985*, pp. 404–11. New York: American Jewish Committee.
Parzen, Herbert. *Architects of Conservative Judaism*. New York: Jonathan David, 1964.
Rudavsky, David. *Modern Jewish Movements*. New York: Behrman House, 1979.
Sklare, Marshall. *Conservative Judaism: An American Religious Movement*. Lanham, Md.: University Press of America, 1985.

EUGENE Y. LOWE, JR.

# Martin Luther King, Jr.

The Montgomery bus boycott of 1955 and 1956 thrust Martin Luther King, Jr., to the fore as the most powerful spokesman for social justice in mid-twentieth-century America. Drawing on his roots in the faith and style of the southern

black church, King was influenced by the social gospel of Walter Rauschenbusch, the Boston school of theological personalism, the tempered political
radicalism of Reinhold Niebuhr, and Mahatma Gandhi's tactics of nonviolent
social protest. Until his assassination in 1968, the young black Southern
Baptist preacher challenged the nation with the values of its biblical religion
and liberal political heritage.

## Biography

Born on 15 January 1929, in Atlanta, Georgia, the son and grandson of pastors
of the city's Ebenezer Baptist Church, Martin Luther King, Jr., was educated
in local schools for black youth. Having skipped several grades, he entered
Morehouse College at fifteen and matured under the influence of President Benjamin Mays. Young King was ordained at Ebenezer and graduated from Morehouse in 1948. At nineteen, he entered Crozer Theological Seminary at Chester,
Pennsylvania. King was deeply engaged by the liberal evangelical theology of
Crozer's faculty, served as president of the student body in his senior year, and
graduated with highest honors in 1951. Entering Boston University for graduate
study in theology later that year, he absorbed the school's insistence on the
sacred worth of human personality as the immanent manifestation of the transcendent Person. On 18 June 1953, King married Coretta Scott, a student at the
Boston Conservatory of Music. They had four children: Yolanda Denise (1955),
Martin Luther III (1957), Dexter Scott (1961), and Bernice Albertine (1963).

In September 1954, the Kings moved to Montgomery, Alabama, where he
became the pastor of Dexter Avenue Baptist Church. After Mrs. Rosa Parks was
arrested for refusing to give up her seat on a Montgomery bus to a white man
on 1 December 1955, the city's black leadership organized the Montgomery
Improvement Association (MIA) and chose the young clergyman to lead a massive bus boycott. When negotiations broke down, the black community prepared
for a lengthy protest, and the city retaliated with a "get tough" policy. On 30
January King's home was bombed, and with eighty-eight others, he was indicted
for conspiracy to organize an illegal boycott on 21 February 1956. Although
King was found guilty of conspiracy on 21 March, a federal court found that
laws requiring segregation in public transportation were unconstitutional. On 13
November the U.S. Supreme Court confirmed the lower court's decision, and
six weeks later King and others brought the boycott to an end by boarding a
desegregated bus. Within two days, King's home was fired on, and in the next
month four other homes, four black churches, and a business establishment were
also attacked.

Following the organization of the Southern Christian Leadership Conference
(SCLC) at Atlanta's Ebenezer Baptist Church on 10 January 1957, King was
chosen as its first president. Four months later, SCLC joined other civil rights
organizations in a Prayer Pilgrimage to Washington, where King stressed the
importance of school desegregation and the franchise for black Southerners. In
September 1958, while autographing copies of *Stride Toward Freedom,* his

account of the Montgomery bus boycott, King was stabbed by a woman who was later judged insane. On trips to Africa in March 1957 and to India in February 1959, Martin Luther King, Jr., affirmed the solidarity of the American civil rights movement with the African struggle against imperialism and deepened his own commitment to Gandhian nonviolent resistance to oppression.

In January 1960 King became copastor of Atlanta's Ebenezer Baptist Church. He supported the sit-in movement that began in February, and he convened a meeting of student activists at Raleigh, North Carolina, in April that led to the formation of the Student Nonviolent Coordinating Committee (SNCC). When King was given a four-month prison sentence for violating probation on a charge of driving without a Georgia driver's license, Democratic presidential candidate John F. Kennedy intervened to win his release on bail. Kennedy's action may have substantially increased black support for his candidacy in the closely con- tested race with Richard M. Nixon. But when Freedom Riders sponsored by the Congress of Racial Equality (CORE) were greeted by violent white mobs in Birmingham and Montgomery, King rejected Attorney-General Robert Kenne- dy's call for a cooling-off period. He went to Albany, Georgia, in December 1961 to give leadership to the civil rights movement in the southwest Georgia city. Although the demonstrations continued through the summer of 1962, King and the movement won no concessions from the city's white leadership. By the end of the year, Albany was considered a clear defeat for Martin Luther King.

In 1963, King launched a boycott of businesses and demonstrations at seg- regated lunch counters in Birmingham, Alabama. Arrested on Good Friday, 12 April, he wrote his "Letter from a Birmingham Jail" to local white clergymen, outlining their lack of leadership in race relations, the grievances of the black community, and his nonviolent protest for social change. Although King was found guilty of criminal contempt, the Birmingham campaign reached a climax when children began demonstrating in large numbers and Commissioner of Public Safety Eugene "Bull" Connor ended a period of restraint. On 2 May, 900 children were arrested, and as demonstrators prepared to march the next day, they were attacked by police dogs and policemen wielding clubs and fire hoses. As the media reported the story, public opinion shifted in King's favor, and the Kennedy administration sought to intervene. When police attacks provoked sev- eral thousand blacks to riot, Birmingham's black and white leadership reached a settlement. Although bombings led to another riot, the agreement survived, only to be narrowly interpreted by the city's white leadership. But Birmingham was a turning point, as President Kennedy called for new civil rights legislation on public accommodations, desegregation, and employment.

His position of leadership in the movement restored, King joined other civil rights leaders in addressing 250,000 followers at the March on Washington in August 1963. His "I Have a Dream" oration repeated biblical and democratic themes underlying many of his earlier sermons and speeches. When a bomb exploded in a black church in Birmingham on 15 September 1963, killing four young black girls, Martin Luther King demanded federal intervention to prevent a "racial holocaust." In March 1964 his attention turned to St. Augustine, Florida, where demonstrators were attacked by white mobs. Five months later, public facilities in St. Augustine were desegregated by federal court order. During the summer, King toured Mississippi to encourage black people there to support the Mississippi Freedom Democratic Party (MFDP) and to support the MFDP's challenge to the all-white regular Mississippi delegation at the Democratic National Convention.

Shortly after the announcement that Martin Luther King, Jr., was to receive the Nobel Peace Prize, FBI Director J. Edgar Hoover attacked him as "the most notorious liar in the country" for suggesting that the FBI had been ineffective in protecting the civil rights of black people in the South. Although King avoided public confrontations with Hoover, the federal agency had been taping his telephone and hotel room conversations for two years. After he received the Nobel Prize, on 10 December 1964, King and his wife received a tape recording purporting to reveal his infidelity to her and a letter strongly suggesting that the only way to avoid public humiliation was to commit suicide. They rightly suspected that the tape and the letter had come from the FBI.

In January 1965 King's attention turned to Alabama, where civil rights leaders sought a march on Montgomery to protest the brutality in Selma. On 7 March, a mounted posse of white volunteers and state troopers led by Colonel Al Lingo and Sheriff James Clark stopped a column of 500 demonstrators led by SCLC's Hosea Williams and SNCC's John Lewis at Selma's Edmund Pettis Bridge. Then they charged the line of marchers with cattle prods, clubs, and tear gas. Despite a federal court injunction and pressure from the Johnson administration, King led a similar march two days later. When confronted by troopers, he knelt with his marchers in prayer and then turned the line back toward Selma. Though this gesture was widely criticized by black militants, President Johnson addressed a joint session of Congress on 15 March, denouncing the violence in Selma, calling for passage of a voting rights bill, and concluding that "We Shall Overcome." Two days later, a federal court authorized the march, and on 25 March 1965 Martin Luther King led 25,000 demonstrators into Montgomery and up Dexter Avenue to the state capitol. Six months later, he met other civil rights leaders at the White House where President Johnson signed the voting rights act into law.

In 1966 when he attacked discrimination in Chicago, King met the indifference of Mayor Richard Daley's regime and hostile white mobs. The campaign was interrupted when James Meredith was shot on a march from Memphis to Jackson, Mississippi. When King joined SNCC's Stokely Carmichael and CORE's Floyd McKissick to complete the march with a closing rally at Jackson, divisions in the movement came to the surface. The NAACP's Roy Wilkins and the Urban League's Whitney Young refused to subscribe to SNCC's "massive public indictment" of American society. Although King signed SNCC's statement, he balked at Stokely Carmichael's intonation of "black power." Returning to Chicago, King led demonstrations at city hall and met with Mayor Daley. After a three-day riot in the city's West Side ghetto, his marches into Chicago's white neighborhoods to protest housing discrimination attracted hostile counter-demonstrators. Two days before a march into Cicero, King reached an agreement with the city's establishment, halting the demonstrations. Although it was only a pledge by the white leadership to curb discrimination, King was increasingly aware of the tenacity of social problems in the urban ghetto and outspoken about the need for radical change in the social order.

After the Montgomery march, Martin Luther King was increasingly critical of the U.S. role in the Vietnam War and called for greater attention to the plight of the urban poor. The war not only offended his nonviolence but also diverted important resources from domestic needs. Yet his criticism of American foreign policy alienated King from the Johnson administration and from other civil rights leaders. Though he continued to argue that nonviolent methods could produce genuine social change, he was less optimistic in his expectations of white America. By late 1966, the strain of internal dissension and a new agenda that attacked the Vietnam War as well as poverty and racial discrimination in the urban North had begun to undermine the civil rights coalition for which King spoke.

When in 1967 the U.S. Supreme Court upheld a contempt of court conviction stemming from the 1963 Birmingham demonstrations, Martin Luther King spent his prison sentence planning for an interracial coalition of poor people to press for new antipoverty legislation. Plans completed in February 1968 called on poor white, black, Indian, and Hispanic Americans to march on Washington and demonstrate for federal legislation to guarantee jobs and a viable income for the poor and to end discrimination in education and housing. The campaign faced strong opposition from the Johnson administration and won little support from other civil rights groups. In March, King took time away from planning the Poor People's Campaign to go to Memphis to lead a mass march in support of the city's striking sanitation workers. The demonstration was marred when some protesters began smashing windows and looting stores, but King returned to Memphis to lead a second march a month later. At 6:00 P.M. on 4 April while he was standing on the balcony of his motel, Martin Luther King was shot in the head and died almost instantly. Two months later, James Earle Ray was arrested in London, and in March 1969, after being charged with King's murder, Ray pleaded guilty.

## Appraisal

Critical reflection on the life and thought of Martin Luther King, Jr., is likely to suggest that he was a far more complex figure than the public knew in his own lifetime or than his biographers have yet seen. Current scholarship, for example, is likely to emphasize the importance of his nurture in a black family, a black church, and black schools. Yet, precisely what the "blackness" of King's roots and background means for understanding his later career is much less certain because all of the biographers' attention has been given to his later public career. King's years of study at Crozer Theological Seminary and at Boston

University were undoubtedly important for his remarkable capacity to communicate with white northern audiences, but even those years are given relatively slight attention in the biographies. It is as if he were a tree without roots. Once the roots are more fully examined, we may begin to appreciate the tree itself in an entirely new way.

Similarly, the whole of King's intellectual and religious development needs careful re-examination. We know entirely too little about his religious background, which he later characteristically dismissed as "fundamentalist," to evaluate its influence on his development. We know all too little about his youthful experience at Morehouse College, where Benjamin Mays, Walter Chivers, George D. Kelsey, Lucius Tobin, and Samuel Williams introduced him to a world of ideas and served as important role models of the black male as intellectual. Only once these influences have been explored will we be prepared to appreciate his confrontations with Marx and Nietzsche, as well as his appropriations of Crozer's evangelical liberalism and Boston's theological personalism.

Finally, whereas the exploration of King's background and early life is likely to reshape our understanding of his public career, evaluation of that career is also tied inextricably to changing attitudes toward the movement with which he was so closely identified. The end of the first reconstruction was followed by a half century of negative historiography. Although Martin Luther King has recently been officially enshrined as a national hero and the central achievements of the second reconstruction are rarely directly challenged, there are signs that we are entering a similar period of negative retrospection.

### Survey of Criticism

The first generation of writing about Martin Luther King, Jr., was dominated by authors closely associated with their subject. Beginning in 1959 with the first biography, *Crusader Without Violence* by Lawrence D. Reddick, a civil rights activist who taught history at Alabama State College while King served as pastor at Dexter Avenue Baptist Church, these works include *What Manner of Man* by Lerone Bennett, who studied at Morehouse while King was there; William Robert Miller's *Martin Luther King, Jr.,* whose author knew King through the Fellowship of Reconciliation's interest in the Montgomery bus boycott; Coretta Scott King's *My Life With Martin Luther King, Jr.,* the autobiographical reflections of an often misunderstood widow and mother; and *Daddy King,* the autobiographical reflections of a bereaved widower and father. Whereas they often include both important biographical information and personal insights, these works characteristically lack a critical emotional distance from a life so intimately intertwined with that of the authors.

Critical reflection "on the role of Martin Luther King" began, however, with August Meier's article of that title, written during King's own lifetime, and it continued, shortly after the assassination, with David Lewis' *King,* the first critical biography. Critical works now dominate the second generation of writings about Martin Luther King, in the widely researched and sometimes sensational books by David Garrow, *Protest at Selma* and *The FBI and Martin Luther King, Jr.* Although Stephen B. Oates' *Let the Trumpet Sound* is a lyrical tribute to the spirit of the civil rights movement, by comparison with the work of Lewis and Garrow it is strangely weak on specific information. More recently, however, the publication of Garrow's Pulitzer Prize–winning *Bearing the Cross* and Adam Fairclough's *To Redeem the Soul of America* marks the culmination of the second, critical generation's reflections on the life and work of Martin Luther King, Jr.

There are now many studies of Martin Luther King's thought. John Rathbun's "Martin Luther King: The Theology of Social Action" and Warren Steinkraus' "Martin Luther King's Personalism and Nonviolence" were pioneering studies in the field. Stephen Oates' "The Intellectual Odyssey of Martin Luther King" is more satisfactory than his later biography of King. The studies of important dimensions of King's thought, however, are scarcely adequate. Both Hanes Walton's *Political Philosophy of Martin Luther King, Jr.* and Ervin Smith's *The Ethics of Martin Luther King, Jr.* need to be replaced by more careful studies in their fields. Still the most important intellectual biography of King is Kenneth Smith and Ira Zepp's *Search for the Beloved Community*. Although it makes some important contributions, John Ansbro's *Martin Luther King, Jr.: The Making of a Mind* threatened to reduce its subject to a set of abstractions produced by white influences. Fred Downing's *To See the Promised Land* offers a more helpful approach by interpreting King's life and thought largely in terms of James W. Fowler's "stages of faith" approach to religious development. But a *Union Seminary Quarterly Review* symposium in 1986, which included James Cone's "The Theology of Martin Luther King, Jr.," Garrow's "The Intellectual Development of Martin Luther King, Jr.," and Vincent Harding's "Recalling the Inconvenient Hero," offers important correctives to all previous studies.

In *A Testament of Hope,* an important sourcebook of King texts, Union Theological Seminary's James Washington offered a harbinger of the third generation of work on the life and thought of Martin Luther King, likely to be dominated and nurtured by the publication of the Martin Luther King Papers. Edited by Stanford University's Clayborne Carson, the King Papers Project expects to publish twelve volumes of primary sources, beginning in 1990. For the first time, it will make a massive amount of documentary evidence on King's life and thought widely available to the public. Students of King's role in the civil rights movement should also be aware of three outstanding audio-visual treatments of the subject, available on videotape. "Martin Luther King: From Montgomery to Memphis" is a three-hour documentary of news film clips graphically depicting King's career from 1955 to 1968; "In Remembrance of Martin" is a one-hour commemoration of the first national holiday celebration of Dr. King's birthday conducted through interviews with family members, friends, and associates; and "Eyes on the Prize" is a six-hour documentary history of the movement.

## Bibliography

### Books by Martin Luther King, Jr.

1958  *Stride Toward Freedom: The Montgomery Story*. New York: Harper and Brothers.
1959  *The Measure of a Man*. Philadelphia: Christian Education Press.
1963  *Strength to Love*. New York: Harper and Row.
1964  *Why We Can't Wait*. New York: Harper and Row.
1967  *Where Do We Go From Here: Chaos or Community?* New York: Harper and Row.
1968  *The Trumpet of Conscience*. New York: Harper and Row.

### Selected Studies about Martin Luther King, Jr.

Ansbro, John J. *Martin Luther King, Jr.: The Making of a Mind*. Maryknoll, N.Y.: Orbis Books, 1982.

Bennett, Lerone, Jr. *What Manner of Man: A Biography of Martin Luther King, Jr.* Chicago: Johnson Publishing Co., 1968.

Cone, James H. "The Theology of Martin Luther King, Jr." *Union Seminary Quarterly Review* 40 (January 1986): 21–39.

Downing, Fred L. *To See the Promised Land: The Faith Pilgrimage of Martin Luther King, Jr.* Macon, Ga.: Mercer University Press, 1986.

Fairclough, Adam. *To Redeem the Soul of America: The Southern Christian Leadership Conference and Martin Luther King, Jr.* Athens: University of Georgia Press, 1987.

Garrow, David J. *Bearing the Cross: Martin Luther King, Jr., and the Southern Christian Leadership Conference, A Personal Portrait*. New York: William Morrow and Co., 1986.

————. *The FBI and Martin Luther King, Jr.: From 'Solo' to Memphis*. New York: W. W. Norton, 1981.

————. "The Intellectual Development of Martin Luther King, Jr.: Influences and Commentaries." *Union Seminary Quarterly Review* 40 (January 1986): 5–20.

————. *Protest at Selma: Martin Luther King, Jr., and the Voting Rights Act of 1965*. New Haven: Yale University Press, 1978.

Harding, Vincent. "Recalling the Inconvenient Hero: Reflections on the Last Years of Martin Luther King, Jr." *Union Seminary Quarterly Review* 40 (January 1986): 53–68.

King, Coretta Scott. *My Life With Martin Luther King, Jr.* New York: Holt, Rinehart and Winston, 1969.

King, Martin Luther, Sr. *Daddy King: An Autobiography*. New York: William Morrow, 1980.

Lewis, David L. *King: A Critical Biography*. New York: Praeger, 1970.

Meier, August. "On the Role of Martin Luther King." *New Politics* 4 (Winter 1965): 52–59.

Miller, William R. *Martin Luther King, Jr.* New York: Weybright and Talley, 1968.

Oates, Stephen B. "The Intellectual Odyssey of Martin Luther King." *Massachusetts Review* 22 (Summer 1981): 301–20.

————. *Let the Trumpet Sound: The Life of Martin Luther King, Jr.* New York: Harper and Row, 1982.

Rathbun, John W. "Martin Luther King: The Theology of Social Action." *American Quarterly* 20 (Spring 1968): 38–53.

Reddick, Lawrence D. *Crusader Without Violence: A Biography of Martin Luther King, Jr.* New York: Harper and Brothers, 1959.

Smith, Ervin. *The Ethics of Martin Luther King, Jr.* Lewiston, N.Y.: Edwin Mellen Press, 1981.

Smith, Kenneth L., and Ira G. Zepp, Jr. *Search for the Beloved Community: The Thinking of Martin Luther King, Jr.* Valley Forge, Pa.: Judson Press, 1974.

Steinkraus, Warren E. "Martin Luther King's Personalism and Nonviolence." *Journal of the History of Ideas* 34 (January-March 1973): 97–111.

Walton, Hanes, Jr. *The Political Philosophy of Martin Luther King, Jr.* Westport, Conn.: Greenwood Publishing Co., 1971.

Washington, James M., ed. *A Testament of Hope: The Essential Writings of Martin Luther King, Jr.* San Francisco: Harper and Row, 1986.

RALPH E. LUKER

# Kathryn Kuhlman

Perhaps no single statement better summarizes Kathryn Kuhlman's understanding of her healing ministry than the one she made in *Christianity Today* in 1973 in the only full-length verbatim interview with her ever published:

> I resent very much being called a faith healer, because I am not the healer. I have no healing virtue. I have no healing power. I have never healed anyone. I am absolutely dependent upon the power of the Holy Spirit. When I see a sick child, in a moment like that I sense in a special way how dependent I really am. And it's just like that.

Kuhlman's rejection of the term *faith healer* and of personal healing power, her consistent theological focus on the Holy Spirit rather than on healing per se, even her trademark phrase, "And it's just like that," were as much characteristics of her healing ministry when it began in April 1947 as when this interview was recorded. By the time of her death in early 1976, Kuhlman was the best-known deliverance evangelist in the nation, on a par with Oral Roberts*. This recognition came only during the last decade of her life. Because of this Kuhlman seemed to many to be a latecomer to the healing and charismatic revivals of post–World War II, known as deliverance revivals because they offered to deliver the soul from sin and the body from sickness. But her full-time and uninterrupted evangelistic career began in 1923, the same year that Aimee Semple McPherson* dedicated her Angelus Temple in Los Angeles, a remarkable fact given that Kuhlman was only sixty-eight when she died more than fifty years later. Other than both being women and successful preachers, the comparison between Kuhlman and McPherson stops there—although many would make that comparison throughout Kuhlman's career. By the time of her death, Kathryn Kuhlman was credited by many within and outside the post–World War II deliverance revivals of rekindling interest in the Holy Spirit and in all the biblical gifts of the Spirit, especially in the mainline churches caught up in the charismatic movement beginning in the late 1950s and 1960s. She was also credited with helping to promote ecumenism, especially between Protestants and Catholics, by means of her miracle services.

### Biography

Kuhlman's paternal grandparents came from Germany, settling in the United States in 1853 in Concordia, a German-speaking community 90 percent Lutheran in the central Missouri farmlands. On 9 May 1907, Kathryn Kuhlman was born near Concordia on a 160-acre farm to Emma Walkenhorst Kuhlman (1872–1958) and Joseph Adolph Kuhlman (1866–1934). Four years later, her parents moved their family to the small town of 1,200 people, where her father would soon become its wealthiest citizen and mayor. Emma was a Methodist, as was her father, and Joe was a nominal Baptist with a distaste for preachers. Kathryn grew up attending both churches, placing membership with her father's Baptist church after her conversion in 1921 at age fourteen. Two years later, Kuhlman left Concordia to begin a lifetime of evangelistic work, itinerating for the next ten years.

Schooling in Concordia went only to the tenth grade, and so by the summer of 1923 Kuhlman had completed all the formal education she would ever have. She and her sister Myrtle, fifteen years Kathryn's senior, persuaded their parents to allow Kathryn to travel with the Parrott Tent Revival. Myrtle in 1913 had married evangelist Everett B. Parrott, who had studied at the Moody Bible Institute in Chicago. During the summer of 1923, Kathryn's apprenticeship was launched as she traveled to Oregon with her sister and brother-in-law in order to study under Charles S. Price. Price was one of the persons who most directly influenced the post–World War II healing revivalists. He held citywide auditorium meetings, emphasized the baptism of the Holy Spirit, taught a great deal on the power of God, and had an impressive healing ministry. People were "slain in the Spirit" at his meetings. During the 1930s he would sustain his ministry by appealing especially to non-Pentecostal Christians. Kuhlman's own ministry would be known for all of these same features. Kuhlman's sister Myrtle recounted that her younger sister seemed to experience her "call to preach" after one of Price's meetings that first summer. Kuhlman herself never made mention of this event, except obliquely in her 1973 interview: "If everybody in the world told me that as a woman I have no right to preach the Gospel, it would have no effect upon me whatsoever, because my call to the ministry was as definite as my conversion." During this time Kuhlman studied the Bible on her own, later saying that the Holy Spirit was the only teacher she ever had.

In Boise, Idaho, Kuhlman became an independent itinerant evangelist beginning at age twenty-one in 1928. Helen Gulliford joined her as her accompanist and confidant for the next eleven years. Gulliford had been a pianist for Charles S. Price and then for the Parrott Tent Revival. Gulliford was the first of a small handful of women who formed a close bond with Kuhlman and became key elements in her worship services and in the administration of her ministry. Later,

Marguerite (Maggie) Hartner would become Kuhlman's closest friend for over thirty years. Like Gulliford, she too roamed the aisles of Kuhlman's services in search of individuals who put up their hands to come forward, this time not just for prayer, but to claim healings and to testify. For the next five years Kuhlman and Gulliford traveled throughout the Northwest, billing themselves as "God's Girls." In the early 1930s, Kuhlman held a meeting in Joliet, Illinois, where members of the Evangelical Church Alliance (then known as the Fundamental Ministerial Association) persuaded her that ministerial credentials would give her more credibility. Kuhlman held papers with the Alliance until her death, the only ministerial authorization she ever received.

Kuhlman began a six-month meeting in downtown Denver, Colorado, on 27 August 1933. She told her Depression audience, "We're saints, not beggars," and they believed her. The crowds flocked to her services by the hundreds, and her congregation persuaded her to stay, promising to build her a tabernacle. In 1934 the Kuhlman Revival Tabernacle opened in a paper warehouse and almost instantaneously became one of the fastest-growing assemblies in the West. Guest evangelists such as Phil Kerr, who had a nationwide radio ministry, appeared at the Tabernacle for campaigns, oftentimes preaching on healing and holding healing services. In May 1935 the Denver Revival Tabernacle was dedicated in new quarters. Harry D. Clarke, who had worked as Billy Sunday's* advance man, and Raymond T. Richey, one of the pioneers in the techniques of healing revivalism during the 1920s, appeared at the Tabernacle. At this time Kuhlman made her first entry into religious broadcasting by appearing live over a Denver radio station at the close of each service.

Evangelist Burroughs A. Waltrip from Texas preached a two-month campaign at the Tabernacle in 1937. The following year, on 18 October 1938, Kuhlman married Waltrip, who had divorced his wife and left their two children to marry her. Helen Gulliford resigned immediately, thus ending their eleven-year relationship. Kuhlman's congregation dispersed quickly because of the scandal. Kuhlman failed to see that her rebellion against the mores of her congregation destroyed her Denver ministry. For the next eight years Kuhlman suffered her "Midian desert." She and Waltrip traveled the sawdust trail throughout the West and finally wound up in Los Angeles. The story of their scandal followed them everywhere. Kuhlman began to despair of her ability ever to meet her call to preach under these conditions.

Kuhlman experienced her baptism of the Holy Spirit on a dead-end street in Los Angeles in early 1944 when she and the Holy Spirit "made each other promises." She chose her relationship with the Holy Spirit, which she understood in explicit husband-wife concepts (according to Katherine Leisering she once said, "It's like some things you know that are so personal between a husband and wife. You just don't display them out in public."), over her relationship with Waltrip. Three days later Kuhlman left Waltrip, never to return, and traveled alone the next two years, evangelizing first in Franklin, Pennsylvania, then through Ohio, Illinois, Indiana, West Virginia, Virginia, the Carolinas, and

Georgia. Wherever she went, news of her scandal followed, and her evangelizing was frequently cut short.

In February 1946, Kuhlman returned to the Gospel Revival Tabernacle in Franklin, just north of Pittsburgh. Her success was immediate, much as it had been in Denver. By spring she decided to stay rather than travel on and began daily half-hour radio broadcasts. On occasion Kuhlman held her own healing lines at the end of services. Shortly after deciding to remain near Pittsburgh, Kuhlman attended incognito the revival of a noted healing evangelist to learn more about divine healing. Instead, she was appalled by what she witnessed—"fanaticism" (ecstatic worship), healing power attributed to the touch and prayer of the evangelist, people told that their failure to receive healing was the result of their lack of faith, and commercialism. Kuhlman's concept of God as a God of mercy and compassion was negated by the experience. Kuhlman spent the rest of 1946 and on into 1947 studying her Bible to see what it teaches about divine healing. She concluded that Christ's redemptive work brings healing to both body and soul and that the Holy Spirit carries on Christ's work today—and that the Spirit supplies healing power. This perspective fit well with Kuhlman's view of holiness. She would say on more than one occasion, "The baptism of the Spirit is given for one purpose only: power for service." Her view coincided with that of the Keswick holiness movement in England in the late nineteenth century, which strongly influenced the holiness revivals in the United States. Keswickian holiness saw the baptism of the Holy Spirit as an anointing with "enduement of power" for service separate from the sanctification process, not as an instantaneous cleansing from sin identical with the sanctification event.

On Sunday, 27 April 1947, Kuhlman began a preaching series on the Holy Spirit. As she preached with more focus and insight than she had ever had before, a woman was healed spontaneously of a tumor and came back the next night to testify, after getting her doctor's confirmation. The following week, while Kuhlman preached on the Holy Spirit, a man was healed of a blind eye and came back two days later to testify. There were no healing lines, no individual prayers from the evangelist, no anointed "touch." Kuhlman's healing ministry had begun.

Because of her large Pittsburgh constituency, Kuhlman held her first service in Pittsburgh at Carnegie Auditorium in July 1948. She now called her meetings "miracle services" and distributed her first tract called "The Lord's Healing Touch." Friday morning miracle services lasting four to five hours at Carnegie Auditorium, a Sunday service in Youngstown, Ohio, at Stambaugh Auditorium, Tuesday Bible studies at First Presbyterian Church in Pittsburgh, and an expanded radio ministry were all added to Kuhlman's schedule and remained her basic schedule until her death. In 1950 she moved her ministry permanently to Pittsburgh. Local ministers picketed her services during 1951, protesting that Kuhlman took people away from their churches.

During a crusade in Akron, Ohio, in 1952, Rex and Maude Aimee Humbard invited Kuhlman to hold miracle services. She accepted and was viciously attacked for being a woman preacher and a "faith healer" by Dallas Billington, a prominent local Baptist minister who had been part of the ultraconservative Baptist Bible Union along with J. Frank Norris* and John R. Rice (author of *Bobbed Hair, Bossy Wives and Women Preachers,* 1941). Kuhlman stood her ground, and the conflict, now on the front pages of Akron newspapers, ended in a draw.

At a time when many evangelists of the healing revival (ca. 1947–58) were beginning to lose financial support, Kuhlman established the Kathryn Kuhlman Foundation in 1957 to manage and distribute the unsolicited funds that kept coming in. The foundation would support more than twenty overseas missions, as well as scholarship and student loan funds, local needs (food, clothing, assistance), special projects, the radio and later the TV ministry. Unlike other successful deliverance evangelists, Kuhlman never published a magazine or newsletter, never established a financial partners' program or membership organization to provide regular support, supplied no giveaways, and rarely solicited funds except for one collection at the miracle services. Her ministry remained small-time and solvent, even when it became nationwide.

Kuhlman's first book, *I Believe in Miracles,* was published in 1962 and became a national best seller. She was soon persuaded by several people, especially by a prominent local evangelist in California, Ralph Wilkerson, to begin monthly services in California, her first foray outside of the Pittsburgh–eastern Ohio area since her arrival nearly twenty years earlier. Kuhlman held her first California service in early 1965 and by early 1966 had moved her monthly services to the larger Shrine Auditorium in Los Angeles.

Kuhlman began her television ministry at CBS studios in California around 1967. Dick Ross, producer of several Billy Graham* films, signed on as Kuhlman's producer. By the time of her death, Kuhlman had taped 500 half-hour programs. With the addition of the TV series, carried by sixty stations, Kuhlman's fame exploded nationally. The cost of the TV ministry grew along with her fame, and by the early 1970s Kuhlman had to be on the road continuously to support it. She began to hold miracle services throughout the United States and traveled overseas. Kuhlman also published several more books during this time to help support the ministry.

"I knew that Kathryn Kuhlman was God's anointed vessel, and I thrilled because as I sat there I saw things that God hadn't done through me. I saw things God hadn't done through anybody I had seen. . . . I looked up on the platform and saw all those Catholic priests and Protestant ministers and a Jewish rabbi. I had never seen that group coming together before." So said Oral Roberts after he attended incognito his first Kuhlman miracle service in Los Angeles in 1971. Kuhlman and Roberts recognized each other as the leaders of the charismatic revival, just as Roberts and William Branham* had recognized each other as the leaders of the healing revival back in the late 1940s. In 1973 Oral Roberts University awarded its first honorary doctorate to Kuhlman: "The one person in the world who epitomized all we believe in was Kathryn Kuhlman."

In the last two years of her life, Kuhlman's health began to fail rapidly. Suffering from an enlarged heart diagnosed twenty years before, by the summer of 1974 she learned that it was radically enlarged. Still, Kuhlman increased her pace rather than slackening it. In November 1975, three days after her return from the Second World Conference on the Holy Spirit held in Israel, Kuhlman held her last miracle service in Los Angeles. A week later she was hospitalized in Tulsa, Oklahoma, and on 27 December she had heart surgery. On 20 February 1976, Kathryn Kuhlman died in Tulsa of "pulmonary hypertension" after complications overtook her. She was buried at Forest Lawn Memorial Park in Glendale, California, where her surviving relatives live nearby, including Myrtle Parrott. The cemetery's privacy (admission by key only) helps to ensure that her gravesite is not turned into a shrine.

## Appraisal

Although Kuhlman herself was never a part of the network that organized, promoted, and dominated the post–World War II healing revival based around the *Voice of Healing* magazine, her participation nonetheless went directly back to the earliest weeks and months of the revival, just as her very earliest training and work in the 1920s and 1930s led directly into the revival. No later than 1950 did Kuhlman begin to use the "word of knowledge" or the gift of discerning people's illnesses by calling out their healings simultaneously as they occurred. This was the part of the service where the preaching stopped and the miracles began. It is not known how soon after April 1947 Kuhlman began to use this technique or how it came about. The technique was very similar to that of William Branham, also of Baptist background and the pioneer of the healing revival whose work *Voice of Healing* was founded to promote. Not until 1949 did Branham receive the gift of the "word of knowledge," and not until the early 1950s did Branham rely exclusively on that gift in his meetings, much as Kuhlman already did in hers.

During the miracle services, Kuhlman's intense quiet and stillness were offset by her dramatic stage techniques, but she was never flamboyant in the popular deliverance evangelist, usually Pentecostal, style. Kuhlman often eschewed what she called "fanaticism," which she associated with the excesses of Pentecostal worship practices. Nonetheless, the feature most compelling to many who came to her services was the phenomenon of being slain in the Spirit (which Kuhlman called "going under the Power"), a regular feature of many Pentecostal services. Kuhlman brought this phenomenon—a feature of all the awakenings and revivals in American religious history—to a broadly based, middle-class, interdenominational, neo-Pentecostal audience during the charismatic movement in the 1960s and 1970s and made it part of the worship experience, much as Charles Grandison Finney made revivalism a part of the urban, middle-class church experience during the latter phase of the Great Revival in the 1820s and 1830s.

Kuhlman never understood herself to be a faith healer because she believed that only the sick needed and received the gift of healing. She understood her gifts to be the "faith" to believe in divine healing and the "word of knowledge" to recognize healings as they happened. Her preaching consistently intertwined three topics—the Holy Spirit, faith, and healing. Calling her a "veritable one-woman shrine of Lourdes," *Time* magazine observed in 1970 that "Kathryn preaches no theology of healing" and teaches primarily on the Holy Spirit. One observer described her later sermons as a "valentine" to the Holy Spirit. By the late 1960s, upwards of 60 percent of the audiences at her miracle services were Roman Catholic. Kuhlman always had an interdenominational cross-section of clergy sit on the platform during services, as well as physicians from institutions such as the Johns Hopkins and Stanford University medical schools, to confirm healings. Kuhlman worked more closely with medical professionals than any other evangelist with a prominent healing ministry.

By 1970, Kuhlman was the oldest deliverance evangelist of her stature with an active ministry. Her roots in the revival, in terms of the span of her career, also went back farther than those of any other evangelist in the field. Just as Oral Roberts and William Branham were the two best-known leaders of the healing revival beginning in the late 1940s, so Oral Roberts and Kathryn Kuhlman were the two leaders most recognized at the height of the charismatic revival.

## Survey of Criticism

Materials other than newspaper articles are sparse on Kathryn Kuhlman. Except for entries in biographical dictionaries, one doctoral dissertation, and a master's thesis, no critical work has been written on her. Katherine Leisering's dissertation adds little to the biographical information already available, but her analysis of over one hundred Kuhlman radio sermons, her transcription of Kuhlman's popular recording *I Believe in Miracles,* and her viewing of the only four films ever made of Kuhlman's miracle services have allowed her to offer a content analysis of Kuhlman's teachings and a communications analysis of her preaching style otherwise not available.

The books published under Kuhlman's name were all ghostwritten, the first by Emily Gardiner Neal, who also wrote the first article to give Kuhlman national attention in 1950, and the rest by Jamie Buckingham. These books recount nothing about Kuhlman herself; instead they are case studies of healings that have taken place under her ministry. Two physicians published their assessments of Kuhlman's "miracle healings," one pro (H. Richard Casdorph) and one con (William A. Nolen). Kuhlman never allowed a book of her sermons to be published during her lifetime. The only published record of her teachings are the two pamphlets listed below and *A Glimpse into Glory,* gleaned after her death from transcripts of her radio broadcasts (other transcripts have been made since then and are available from the Kathryn Kuhlman Foundation).

Two "insider" biographies have been written about Kuhlman. Helen Hosier's provides many names from Kuhlman's earliest years, but her piece is almost hagiographic. Jamie Buckingham's *Daughter of Destiny* provides the most accurate and complete chronology; Kuhlman had selected Buckingham to be her biographer. The title of Allen Spraggett's work, *Kathryn Kuhlman: The Woman Who Believes in Miracles,* makes it sound like a biography, but it looks at Kuhlman's ministry from the standpoint of psychic phenomena and provides little biographical information but much praise.

## Bibliography

### Works by Kathryn Kuhlman

1962   *I Believe in Miracles.* Englewood Cliffs, N.J.: Prentice-Hall.
1969   *God Can Do It Again.* Englewood Cliffs, N.J.: Prentice-Hall.
1971   "My First Healing." *Guideposts* (June): 10–12.
1973   *Captain Le Vrier Believes in Miracles.* Minneapolis: Bethany Fellowship.
1973   "Healing in the Spirit." *Christianity Today* (20 July): 4–10.
1974   *How Big Is God?* Minneapolis: Bethany Fellowship.
1974   *Nothing Is Impossible with God.* Englewood Cliffs, N.J.: Prentice-Hall.
1974   *10,000 Miles for A Miracle.* Minneapolis: Bethany Fellowship.
1975   *Never Too Late.* Minneapolis: Bethany Fellowship.
1975   *Standing Tall.* Minneapolis: Bethany Fellowship.
1979   *A Glimpse into Glory.* With Jamie Buckingham. Plainfield, N.J.: Logos International.
n.d.   *I Believe in Miracles.* Logos International Recording. Recorded ca. early 1970s.
n.d.   "The Lord's Healing Touch." Pittsburgh: Kathryn Kuhlman Foundation. Pamphlet. Orig. pub. ca. 1948.
n.d.   "These That Thou Hast Given Unto Me." Pittsburgh: Kathryn Kuhlman Foundation. Pamphlet. Orig. pub. ca. 1975.

### Selected Studies about Kathryn Kuhlman

Armstrong, Lois. "Kathryn Kuhlman Heals by Faith—Maybe, Doctors Say." *People* (9 December 1974): 52–55.
Blau, Eleanor. "Faith Healer Draws the Sick and Anguished." *New York Times,* 20 October 1972, p. 36.
Buckingham, Jamie. *Daughter of Destiny: Kathryn Kuhlman . . . Her Story.* Plainfield, N.J.: Logos International, 1976.
Butler, Ann. "A Friend to the End . . . And Then Some." *Pittsburgh Press Sunday Roto,* 16 March 1980, pp. 30–31, 35–39.
————."She Believes in Miracles." *Pittsburgh Press Sunday Roto,* 3 February 1974, pp. 18–23.
Casdorph, H. Richard. *The Miracles.* Plainfield, N.J.: Logos International, 1976.
Farr, Louise. "The Divine Ms K." *MS* (July 1975): 12–15.
Hart, Alberta Sophia. "Kathryn Kuhlman: An Analysis of Communicative Ritual in the Great Miracle Service." Master's thesis, California State University at Los Angeles, 1974.
Hosier, Helen Kooiman. *Kathryn Kuhlman: The Life She Led, the Legacy She Left.* Old Tappan, N.J.: Fleming H. Revell Co., 1976.
"I Believe." *Bulletin Index* (6 November 1948): 8–10.
Kathryn Kuhlman Foundation. *From Medicine to Miracles.* Minneapolis: Bethany Fellowship, 1978.
Keatley, Vivien B. "Siren of the Sawdust Trail." *Coronet* (August 1957): 52–58.

Leisering, Katherine Jane. "An Historical and Critical Study of the Pittsburgh Preaching Career of Kathryn Kuhlman." Ph.D. diss., Ohio University, 1981.

Mattsson-Boze, Joseph. "Miss Kuhlman's Ministry in Sweden." *Herald of Faith* (July/ August 1969): 3, 5–6.

"Miracle Woman." *Time* (14 September 1970): 62–63.

Morris, James. "Kathryn Kuhlman." In *The Preachers*, 235–52, 400–401. New York: St. Martin's Press, 1973.

Neal, Emily Gardiner. "Can Faith in God Heal the Sick?" *Redbook* (November 1950): 28–31, 93–96.

———."Kathryn Kuhlman (Evangelist)." In *God Can Heal You Now,* 201–5. Englewood Cliffs, N.J.: Prentice-Hall, 1958.

Nolen, William A. "Kathryn Kuhlman." In *Healing: A Doctor in Search of a Miracle,* 41–102. New York: Random House, 1974.

Roberts, Oral. "A Tribute to Kathryn Kuhlman." *Abundant Life* (May 1976): 2–5.

Spraggett, Allen. *Kathryn Kuhlman: The Woman Who Believes in Miracles.* New York: World Publishing Co., 1970.

                                                    DEBORAH VANSAU McCAULEY

# Tim and Beverly LaHaye

After suffering a loss in several key denominational, institutional, and legal controversies in the early 1920s, fundamentalist Christianity slipped from the national limelight during the Depression years and the decade of World War II, all the while expanding its grass-roots constituency. After the war, neoevangelicalism burst onto the scene in the early fifties with a less strident posture than its predecessor, but uncompromising fundamentalism never went away. Throughout the fifties and sixties it quietly grew. Then in the seventies it began to demand national attention by asserting its influence through the new televangelists, rapidly growing Christian Colleges, conservative political action groups, and a vigorous call for conservative moral reform in America. The common enemy of the New Right was tagged "secular humanism." The man and woman most responsible for identifying this villain and popularizing the fundamentalist crusade against it were Tim and Beverly LaHaye.

## Biography

Tim LaHaye was born the eldest of three children in Detroit, Michigan, on 27 April 1926. His father, Francis T. LaHaye, was an electrician who died when Tim was nine years old. His young mother, Margaret Palmer LaHaye, with the help of relatives, worked evenings to support her family. Tim was raised in a devout and conservative Baptist home: his mother was a fellowship director in their local Baptist church, and his uncle E. W. Palmer was a Baptist preacher.

Detroit made national headlines in 1943 when the city was shaken by racial riots, polarizing much of the populace into black and white factions. It was Tim's senior year in high school. There is no record of whether the LaHayes were affected by the discord, but after a brief stint in the U.S. Army Air Force, in which Tim attained the rank of sergeant, he headed south to Bob Jones University in Greenville, South Carolina, one of America's last bastions of traditional values, conservative morality, and racial segregation.

It was 1946, and Tim LaHaye was a twenty-year-old freshman. That year he met Bob Jones University coed Beverly Jean Ratcliffe. The two held several things in common. Besides sharing Tim's conservative Christian faith, Beverly's father had also died when she was young, and though her mother later remarried, the family had been forced to move several times, living in Missouri and Michigan before Beverly went away to college. Like Tim, she had early experienced family instability stemming from the loss of a male parent. Doubtless this was a contributing factor to why the two of them would later spend much of their lives crusading for a strong patriarchal model both for the church and the family. The two were married on 5 July 1947. The marriage produced four children: Linda (Mrs. Gerald Murphy), Larry, Lee, and Lori. Beverly dropped out of school after marriage to Tim, exchanging her role as student for that of homemaker and pastor's wife, as Tim spent his final two years at Bob Jones University pastoring a small Baptist church in Pickens, South Carolina.

On Tim's graduation with a bachelor of arts degree in 1950, he moved his family north to Minnesota where he spent the next six years pastoring a Baptist church in Minneapolis. In 1956, the LaHayes joined much of the nation's population in moving west to the Sun Belt. Settling in El Cajon, California, an eastern suburb of San Diego, LaHaye began a pastorate at Scott Memorial Baptist Church that would last for the next quarter century.

The basis for most of the LaHayes' career developed out of a primary focus on marriage and family ministry. Beginning in 1956, the couple appeared weekly on a thirty-minute television program called "LaHayes on Family Life." The program was later nationally syndicated and ran for three years. During the same period, the two expanded their family ministry through the publication of articles and books and a national lecture series called "Family Life Seminars" that began in 1972.

Dissatisfied with "humanist" influences in the local school system, in 1965 LaHaye founded the Christian High School of San Diego, which later grew into the Christian Unified School System, consisting of two high schools, an elementary school, and, since 1970, Christian Heritage College, of which LaHaye served as president until 1976. One of the cofounders of the college was Dr. Henry Morris, a Ph.D. in hydraulics, who formerly headed the civil engineering department at Virginia Polytechnic Institute. Despite a lack of formal training in science, LaHaye later teamed up again with Morris to found the Institute for Creation Research, which pioneered the renascent creation-evolution textbook controversy in public school systems across the country.

The first of Tim LaHaye's many pop Christian psychology works, *Spirit-Controlled Temperament,* was written in 1966 and met with phenomenal success. After a decade, it had undergone twenty-five printings, with over 500,000 copies sold. Spin-off titles included *Transformed Temperaments* (1971), *Spirit-Controlled Woman* (1976), *Understanding the Male Temperament* (1977), and *Spirit-Controlled Family Living* (1978).

Although Bob Jones University had awarded him an honorary doctorate of divinity in 1962, LaHaye felt the need for further formal education to accompany his college presidency and growing national exposure. In 1977, he completed his doctorate of ministry degree at Western Conservative Baptist Seminary in Portland, Oregon. Throughout the seventies, the LaHayes continued to jointly write works on marriage and family while also producing several self-help books on biblical interpretation and Christian pop psychology.

By the end of the seventies, the LaHayes were approaching a new career direction, one that, when combined with the emerging power of the New Christian Right, would send tremors across the country. In 1976, Tim resigned from the presidency of Christian Heritage College and spent the next two years traveling with his wife, carrying their Family Life Seminar to more than fifty cities across America and into several foreign countries. While preaching traditional conservative family values, LaHaye was also increasingly pointing out the dangers of secular humanism.

LaHaye's thoughts on secular humanism were crystallized in his 1980 work *The Battle for the Mind,* a polemical treatise that took the fundamentalist world by storm. LaHaye's book caught the momentum of a wave that had swept the country at the close of the seventies, ushering Jimmy Carter out of and Ronald Reagan into the White House. *Battle for the Mind* was widely read and praised by the nation's fundamentalist leaders and televangelists. From the time of its publication, secular humanism became the new focal point of the fundamentalist assault. Over the next few years, LaHaye followed the book's success with two sequels, *The Battle for the Family* in 1982 and *The Battle for the Public Schools* the following year.

Having established a national audience, the LaHayes began taking an increased interest and involvement in national politics. By the end of the seventies, Tim had already organized and served on committees such as the Coalition for Religious Freedom, formed to help elect conservative Christians to public office and lobby for government noninterference in religious affairs. In 1979, Beverly contributed to the effort by organizing women into a national body called Concerned Women for America, dedicated to such popular right-wing causes as antigay rights, anti-ERA, antiabortion, and proprayer in public schools. By 1984, Concerned Women boasted a membership of more than 500,000 and held its first annual convention in Washington, D.C., with more than 2,000 participants.

Sensing the growing conservative momentum across the nation, Tim rallied together the bulk of the Christian Right's leaders into his own political lobby organization called the American Coalition for Traditional Values. ACTV's executive committee and board reads like a "Who's Who" in popular American Christianity: televangelists Jerry Falwell*, Jimmy Swaggart*, Jim Bakker*, Rex Humbard, Robert Tilton, James Robison, and Kenneth Copeland; Campus Crusade for Christ founder and head Bill Bright*; James Kennedy, pastor of the largest Presbyterian church in the country; Jimmy Draper, Charles Stanley, and Adrian Rogers, all former presidents of the Southern Baptist Convention; Bob Dugan, director of the National Association of Evangelicals' Washington office; and Thomas Zimmerman, general superintendent of the Assemblies of God. In 1984, Tim and Beverly left their San Diego ministry and relocated in Washington, D.C., to head the national offices of their new organizations.

Even before the New Christian Right could enjoy the 1984 Republican presidential landslide, however, trouble was brewing over alliances between LaHaye and the politically conservative Unification Church. Sun Myung Moon, embattled millionaire-messiah of the Unification Church, had long been an advocate of right-wing American causes and considered nothing so valuable as the possibility of attaining respectability within the American religious community. Ironically, these two interests came together in 1982 when Moon was convicted of tax evasion, fined, and imprisoned. In 1984, LaHaye's Coalition for Religious Freedom, a precursor to ACTV, found itself on the side of Sun Myung Moon and his followers, protesting the interference of the federal government in the free expression of religion. In July 1984, LaHaye's Coalition hosted a "Pageant for Religious Freedom," a lavish event that brought together pastors from all over the country to emphasize the need for active resistance to government intrusion into religious affairs. When pastors and fundamentalist church members learned that the cost of the pageant had been underwritten by the Unification Church, a storm of protest ensued. LaHaye responded by reaffirming the principle of the pageant while attempting to divorce himself from the doctrines of Moon. Before the year was out, however, he had resigned from the Coalition for Religious Freedom and had begun plans to set up the more ambitious ACTV.

Relations with the Unification Church, however, did not end with the dissolution of the Coalition for Religious Freedom. Citing unanticipated expenses in establishing a Washington office for ACTV, LaHaye admitted in January 1986 that he had accepted financial assistance from Bo Hi Pak, top aide to Unification Church leader Sun Myung Moon.

In an atmosphere that has recently seen the demise of several of the New Christian Right's leading figures, Tim and Beverly LaHaye's intense resistance to federal auditing of religious institutions may not continue to be tolerated. However, by 1986, along with his national speaking engagements, syndicated television commentary, and ACTV presidency, LaHaye joined the staff of Prestonwood Baptist Church, an affluent north Dallas congregation that is purportedly "the fastest growing church in the history of Southern Baptists." In 1987, seven million copies of his twenty-three books were in print, hammering away at secular humanism while bolstering traditional family values. Meanwhile, Beverly LaHaye continued to direct Concerned Women for America while adding to her list of seven widely read books. Given this range of influence the LaHayes' contribution to popular religion in America seems well established.

## Appraisal

Tim and Beverly LaHaye offer a striking parallel to the classic fundamentalism of the 1920s. Tim LaHaye's antihumanist diatribes have all the fervor and sting of liberal-bashing Billy Sunday* at his best. The LaHayes' moralistic prescriptions compare satisfactorily with those of Bob Jones, Sr.,* whereas their Creation Research Institute promises countless recastings of the 1925 Scopes Monkey Trial. The twist in this contemporary drama is that in the 1920s it was mainline Protestantism, with its liberal social agenda and nationally recognized pulpiteers, that wrote the script for a Christian America. Today, the limelight goes to the fundamentalists, and it is the Christian Right that sits in the director's chair.

The character of the LaHayes' work demonstrates once again that the indispensable element separating fundamentalism from mere conservative biblicism is the presence of an aggressive enemy, either real or perceived. For Greshem Machen and the Princeton fundamentalists of the twenties, the enemy was modernity-embracing liberalism espoused by the likes of Harry Emerson Fosdick* and Shailer Matthews. For the LaHayes, it is an insidious secular humanism pervading the nation through institutions such as the ACLU, the NCCC, the UN, SIECUS (Sex Information and Education Council of the United States), and NOW (National Organization for Women).

Like their fundamentalist forebears, the LaHayes carry an exclusive ideology, which differs, however, in its crusade for moralistic purity as opposed to the strict doctrinalism of the twenties fundamentalism. Unlike their predecessors, the LaHayes appear less resistant to the religious pluralism of the modern period. Instead, Tim has shown an eagerness to align with Catholics, Jews, Mormons, and even Unificationists for the cause of "morality" against the common enemy of secular humanism.

The willingness to cross over confessional lines for the sake of national and moral issues that transcend creedal particularities raises the question of whether the LaHayes themselves have transcended a "correct" positioning within the ranks of conservative Christianity. Tim LaHaye's rejection of professed Christian politicians Mark Hatfield, Paul Simon, and Jimmy Carter is well within the bounds of traditional fundamentalist behavior, but his conservative coalition with Mormon Orin Hatch and Unificationist Bo Hi Pak is something new.

Despite the couple's strong ties to the vast majority of the Christian Right's national leaders, the realpolitik of the eighties has revealed in the LaHayes current activities a more accurate location outside the perimeters of traditional Christianity. If it is accurate, as Tim LaHaye claims, to refer to secular humanism as a religion, then the LaHayes must concede that they too have taken up residence in another religion, that of moralistic American conservatism. Only within this framework can one explain the LaHayes' high prioritizing of such extrabiblical issues as opposition to the Equal Rights Amendment, resistance to the UN and NCCC, and support for increased national defense spending. The strongest evidence, however, for this new religious entity is seen in the unorthodox alignment of the most exclusive sectors of American society for the sake of a common conservative political agenda.

A critical analysis of the LaHayes' thought reveals that much of the LaHayes' reasoning is deductive in nature, deriving specific applications from fundamental principles or absolute values. By identifying and isolating these fundamental values, one can better understand the subsequent activities of the LaHayes. Three values are predominant: Bible, family, and country.

Tim LaHaye described his own hermeneutical principle in *The Beginning of the End:* "When the plain sense of scripture makes common sense, seek no other sense, but take every word at its primary, literal meaning unless the facts of the immediate context clearly indicate otherwise." LaHaye's rigid adherence to the literal sense of Scripture is most noticeable in his understanding of the first and last books of the Bible. In 1976, he coauthored with John David Morris a serious inquiry into the present-day location of Noah's ark, entitled *The Ark on Ararat.* His conclusion was that the vessel may rest today beneath glacial ice in the mountains of Turkey.

Theologian Paul Tillich once noted that the best way to study a religion is to examine its conception of the end times. Tim LaHaye's eschatology is particularly revealing. In his 1972 work *The Beginning of the End,* Tim echoed the imminent apocalyptic predictions that proved so popular in Hal Lindsey's* *The Late Great Planet Earth.* LaHaye's guide to the apocalypse equated world communal efforts such as the United Nations and the World Council of Churches with the nefarious apocalyptic symbols of the beast and scarlet whore. LaHaye also agreed with the premillennial notion that the world is headed irrevocably toward a nuclear Armageddon that will destroy all except Christians who will be divinely snatched from tribulation by an extraterrestrial "rapture." The implications of the La-Hayes' interpretation of the end time for world peace is quite disturbing, especially since, as he implies in the book title, "the beginning of the end" has arrived.

More than any other topic, the family has dominated the public and literary efforts of the LaHayes. The familial model embraced by the LaHayes is the traditional nuclear family consisting of male provider, female homemaker, and children. As a fundamental value, anything that threatens the family unit comes under harsh attack. The "radical feminist movement" is one of those threats because it tends to draw the mother away from the home, leading to the neglect of child rearing and marriage maintenance. A second evil because of its presumed threat to fundamental family values is the gay liberation movement. Since homosexuality, for the LaHayes, poses an alternative to the traditional nuclear family, it qualifies as a satanic forgery of God's ideal. In *The Unhappy Gays* (1978), Tim LaHaye united his biblical hermeneutic with a defense of the family to condemn the gay liberation movement as a modern-day Sodom and Gomorrah.

Involvement in national politics came as a natural outgrowth of the LaHayes' involvement in Bible and family ministry. The conduit for their political engagement was the public educational system. After withdrawing their children from the local school system in San Diego, the LaHayes developed a private educational network. While thousands of conservative white Americans were removing their children from public schools in the integrationist sixties, it was LaHaye who identified the real enemy not as ethnic minorities but as secular humanism.

Secular humanism is, in fact, less a national conspiracy than a heuristic device invented by LaHaye to cover all the liberal developments that have infiltrated the public school system since the close of World War II. When the LaHayes found it a successful tool to use in their attack on the public schools, they projected their secular humanist model onto the national and international arenas and found it to be equally useful there.

In a 1980 interview in *Wittenburg Door,* Tim LaHaye was quoted as saying, "If I have a writing gift, I have the gift of simplicity where I can put things down so the common man can understand." Beverly LaHaye shares this gift, along with her husband's remarkable organizational skills. The LaHayes' gift of literary and oratorical simplicity can be credited with stirring previously quietist American fundamentalists into the mainstream of national politics. Unfortunately, simplicity does not readily lend itself to managing the complexities and nuances of modern pluralist America. This being so, for the forseeable future the battle for the public mind will continue.

## Survey of Criticism

No biography, critical or otherwise, of the LaHayes has been written. Likewise, virtually no journal treatment of their lives is in existence. The major reason for this omission would seem to be that the academic world has dismissed them as fringe figures who, despite an immense popular following, offer little to the wider scholarly community and therefore should not be taken seriously; thus, the academic community will no doubt continue to ignore them, since all of their books have targeted lay Christian audiences and critical scholarships, until the agenda of the Christian Right, with many of the LaHayes' ideals, has become adopted national policy.

In 1980, the Christian parody magazine *Wittenburg Door* interviewed Tim LaHaye, but no other periodicals followed. Though Tim was also written about in *Contemporary Authors,* Beverly, despite her best-selling books and her induction into the National League of American Pen Women, was excluded.

## Bibliography

### Books by Beverly LaHaye

1976   *The Spirit-Controlled Woman.* Irvine, Calif.: Harvest House.
1977   *How to Develop Your Child's Temperament.* Irvine, Calif.: Harvest House.
1978   *Spirit-Controlled Family Living.* Old Tappan, N.J.: F. H. Revell.
1980   *I Am a Woman by God's Design.* Old Tappan, N.J.: F. H. Revell.
1984   *The Restless Woman.* Grand Rapids: Zondervan.

1984   *What Lovemaking Means to a Woman*. Grand Rapids: Zondervan.
1984   *Who But a Woman?* Nashville: Nelson Publishers.

### Books by Tim LaHaye

1966   *Spirit-Controlled Temperament*. Wheaton, Ill.: Tyndale House.
1971   *Transformed Temperaments*. Wheaton Ill.: Tyndale House.
1972   *The Beginning of the End*. Wheaton, Ill.: Tyndale House.
1973   *Revelation Illustrated and Made Plain*. Grand Rapids: Zondervan.
1974   *Sex Education Is for the Family*. Grand Rapids: Zondervan.
1974   *Ten Steps to Victory Over Depression*. Grand Rapids: Zondervan.
1976   *The Ark on Ararat*. With John David Morris. Nashville: Thomas Nelson Publishers.
1976   *The Bible's Influence on American History*. San Diego: Master Books.
1976   *How to Study the Bible for Yourself*. Irvine, Calif.: Harvest House.
1977   *Understanding the Male Temperament*. Old Tappan, N.J. F. H. Revell.
1978   *The Unhappy Gays*. Wheaton, Ill.: Tyndale House.
1980   *The Battle for the Mind*. Old Tappan, N.J.: F. H. Revell.
1982   *Anger Is a Choice*. Grand Rapids: Zondervan.
1982   *The Battle for the Family*. Old Tappan, N.J.: F. H. Revell.
1983   *The Battle for the Public Schools*. Old Tappan: F. H. Revell.
1983   *How to Manage Pressure Before Pressure Manages You*. Grand Rapids: Zondervan.
1984   *The Coming Peace in the Middle East*. Grand Rapids: Zondervan.
1984   *The Hidden Censors*. Old Tappan, N.J.: F. H. Revell.
1984   *What Lovemaking Means to a Man*. Grand Rapids: Zondervan.

### Jointly Authored Book

1976   *The Act of Marriage*. Grand Rapids: Zondervan.

### Works about Tim and Beverly LaHaye

Clouse, R. G. "The New Christian Right, America and the Kingdom of God." *Christian Scholar's Review* 12 (1983): 3–16.
Colwell, W. E. Review of "How to Win Over Depression." *Journal of Psychology and Theology* 2 (1974): 149–50.
Evory, Ann, and Linda Metzger, eds. *Contemporary Authors*. New rev. ser., 9:321. Detroit: Gale Research Co., 1981.
Johnston, Robert K. Review of "The Unhappy Gays." *Christianity Today* 23 (20 July 1979): 28–30.
Minnery, T. Review of "Battle for the Mind." *Christianity Today* 26 (7 May 1982): 60–61.
"Tim LaHaye—DOOR Interview." *Wittenburg Door* 55 (June/July 1980): 8–12.
Spring, Beth. "Magazine Says Tim LaHaye Received Help from Unification Church." *Christianity Today* 30 (17 January 1986): 40–41.

DAVID GARRISON

# Sinclair Lewis

Sinclair Lewis made his indelible mark on popular religion in jazz-age America with *Elmer Gantry,* his novel about a morally bankrupt Protestant preacher. The book sold a record 175,000 copies in six weeks and, to put it mildly, agitated the ranks of traditional Christian believers. The book was immediately banned in Boston, and for a time Sinclair Lewis was the pre-eminent infidel in America. In the course of his career, Lewis wrote twenty-one other novels, and most of them made some comment on twentieth-century American popular religion. He was best known as a satiric debunker of religious hypocrisy and obscurantism, but there was also a more benevolent impulse toward religion in Lewis' writing that drew on romanticism, emphasized the importance of a spiritual quest, encouraged identification with the oppressed and minorities, and advocated the appreciation of natural and designed beauty.

## Biography

Harry Sinclair Lewis was born the youngest of three sons of a Sauk Centre, Minnesota, physician in February 1885. According to his biographer, Mark Schorer, the boy was a lonely one, inept at the usual social skills of midwestern village youths and prone to more solitary pursuits such as reading, writing in his diary, playing imaginative games, or participating in the life of the local Congregational church, of which his father and stepmother (his mother died when he was six) were members. In his early teens, Lewis developed an extraordinary personal curiosity about religion. He attended his own Sunday School and worship regularly and even frequented the other Sauk Centre churches, favoring the Roman Catholic and Episcopalian services particularly.

In 1902, after entering Oberlin Academy to prepare for the Yale entrance exams, Lewis' curiosity about religion turned to zeal when he was converted at a YMCA meeting. He vowed to become a missionary, held prayer meetings in his dormitory room, taught Sunday School at a rural church, and generally annoyed his fellow students with his proselytism. As the young Lewis dramatically said in his diary: "This day of my profession of Christ is surely one of the most important of my life." He began to draft a volume of verse, "In Praise of God," which he later burned.

Shortly after reaching Yale, however, Lewis began a gradual process of disenchantment with Christianity. By the end of his second year, he could write in his diary, under the heading "My Religion": "If there be saints—they are Voltaire—as well as Christ; Shelley as well as St. Paul." He began to publish verse and short stories in the *Yale Literary Magazine* and the *Yale Courant* and determined to pursue a literary career. An early short story, "The Heart of Pope Innocent," was a study of religious pretension identical in spirit to the later *Elmer Gantry.* And as editor of the "Lit" in 1906, Lewis took the opportunity to extol "that new religion, whose trinity is cosmic emotion, beauty-worship, and public service." The missionary impulse was fashionably sublimated, but hardly lost.

In November 1906 Lewis left Yale to join socialist Upton Sinclair's "Helicon Hall" commune, at which he lasted about a month. He eventually graduated from Yale in the spring of 1908. After graduation, he traveled to California and elsewhere across the states, finally settling in New York City in 1910. There he took a variety of editorial, advertising, and reviewer positions while also writing verse and short stories for children's magazines. He was occasionally published by more substantial popular or literary magazines, but generally he wrote to sell. In 1914 Lewis married Grace Livingstone Hegger, a New York socialite, and published his first novel, *Our Mr. Wrenn.*

From 1915 to 1920 Lewis wrote four more novels, traveled across the country by car with his wife, and produced his first play, *Hobohemia.* Religion figures centrally in neither the novels nor the play, although in the second novel, *The Trail of the Hawk* (1915), Lewis gained a measure of revenge on his Oberlin semester by portraying "Plato College" as a stultifying evangelical school run by third-rate scholars.

The twenties were as giddy for Lewis as for the country at large. 1920 saw the publication of *Main Street,* originally entitled "The Village Virus," and this work established Lewis as an important novelist and social critic. It was also a best seller, and Lewis used the royalties to travel to Europe, where he spent most of 1921 writing *Babbitt*—a satire of the average American businessman and perhaps Lewis' best pure novel. *Arrowsmith,* Lewis' most heroic work about the "religion of the scientist," was published in 1925 and garnered him an offer of a Pulitzer Prize, which he dramatically declined as corrupting.

Throughout most of 1926 Lewis lived in Kansas City while researching *Elmer Gantry.* He attended a variety of religious services, met with ministers and rabbis formally and informally, kept copious notes, and gained wild notoriety when he stood up in a Kansas City pulpit one Sunday and dared the fundamentalists' vindictive God to strike him dead as an infidel. Lewis survived the challenge, and the book was a huge popular success. It called forth denunciations from nearly every prominent Christian leader, including the evangelist Billy Sunday*, who labeled Lewis "Satan's cohort," and the fundamentalist Dr. John Roach Straton, whose view of the novel's merit was succinctly expressed by the word "putrid."

Two more books rounded out the Lewis work for the decade, which must rank among the most productive and profitable in early twentieth-century American literary history. *The Man Who Knew Coolidge* was a rambling satiric monologue that was a critical failure. With *Dodsworth* Lewis returned to the theme of the American businessman and his lack of spiritual perception. To cap the decade, Lewis became the first American to be offered the Nobel Prize for literature, on 5 November 1930. He did not refuse this one.

By all accounts, Lewis' career declined thereafter. Signs had been present before. He had divorced in 1928 and married journalist Dorothy Thompson the same year. The relationship was notoriously unstable, ending also in divorce in 1942. Lewis drank heavily, especially during Prohibition, and the effects of this habit contributed to his deterioration. He traveled almost incessantly, tried his hand at acting, and even taught college for two years. The ten novels he wrote between 1930 and his death in 1951 often reworked themes from the twenties, with the exception of *It Can't Happen Here* (1935), a nightmare about a total-itarian regime in the United States, and *Kingsblood Royal* (1947), which ad-dressed the irrationality of racism. Lewis planned throughout this period to write what he called his "labor novel," which was to feature a Christ-figure modeled after Eugene Debs. The book was never written, and although Lewis continued to be a best seller, the critics had largely dismissed him. He died in Rome of heart disease on 10 January 1951.

### Appraisal

It is helpful to distinguish Sinclair Lewis' public religious role from his literary contribution to American popular religion. His role was as "the infidel" in American culture. Vernon L. Parrington was the first to call Lewis "Our Di-ogenes," but parallels much closer to home can be found in the careers of Thomas Paine, Robert Ingersoll, Mark Twain, and H. L. Mencken. Lewis clearly enjoyed this role, undoubtedly under the influence of his close friend Mencken, to whom *Elmer Gantry* is dedicated.

But unlike Mencken, Lewis was not religiously tone-deaf, and in fact his literary work can be read for its contributions to the shaping of an American popular religion. Three points seem particularly obvious. The first is his pre-sentation of the virtue of a spiritual quest. Martin E. Marty has used the metaphor of "pilgrims" to describe the American popular faith, and Lewis' characters are often pioneers, restless, experimenters, adventuresome, or "seekers." Glen A. Love has called this romantic representation of pioneering "a basic belief" of Lewis', and the terminology is apt. Carol Kennicott, the protagonist of *Main Street,* is constantly testing the limits of conventional village life in Gopher Prairie, Minnesota; and indeed throughout Lewis' novels, early and late, good and bad, what he called in *Main Street* "our comfortable and sure faith" is precisely that which we need to transcend.

The epitome of this anticonventional, mildly skeptical questing spirit among Lewis' cast of characters is undoubtedly Martin Arrowsmith. Arrowsmith, who is trained in bacteriology and medicine, passes through a series of trials or temptations in the course of the novel. He must choose at each juncture between comfort, success, wealth, and security on the one hand and purity of intellect and practice on the other. At the end of the novel, Arrowsmith has renounced society to practice pure bacteriology at a laboratory tucked away in the woods. This "ascetic" motif can be identified in almost all of Lewis' heroes. It reaches an apotheosis in *The God-Seeker* (1949), where Lewis portrays Aaron Gadd as a Christian missionary converted to carpentry. This essentially romantic con-ception of life possessed enormous appeal to the American populace, and it formed the positive foundation of Lewis' critique of denominational religion as stagnant and stultifying.

A second, more ambivalent part of Lewis' contribution to American popular religion might be called his pressing of the aesthetic question. Lewis crafted almost exclusively crass, vulgar religious characters, of which Gantry is the paradigm, but when he did infrequently depict a religious figure favorably, that character was often an aesthete, or "high church." In other words, institutional religion was generally dull or irrelevant to Lewis' most heroic characters, or, less often, religious folk were depicted as commonly insensitive to what Carol Kennicott described as "the holiness" of "making a beautiful thing." By setting up this conflict between a crass "reality" and a more aesthetically pleasing ideal, Lewis may have raised the artistic consciousness among certain of the religious in America. He may also have contributed to a cult of the aesthetic, although Lewis was generally scornful of artistic pretension. He advocated art as a means to an end rather than as an end in itself, and it is thus not surprising that the question of whether Lewis himself deserved the title "artist" was and is a topic of significant debate.

Third, what is clear is that the "end" served by Lewis' art was the perpetuation of a restless spiritual questing in the interest of critical social improvement or "public service." Regarding the latter, several of Lewis' novels attempt to present heroically minorities and the traditionally powerless in America or to depict antiheroically "establishment" figures. *Elmer Gantry* once again represents the latter; *Ann Vickers,* Lewis' portrait of a woman college graduate who breaks with conventional sexual roles and morality to become a prison reformer, is an example of the former. The antiheroic figures are undoubtedly the more memorable, because better done, and this makes discerning the positive values underlying Lewis' satire a difficult interpretive pursuit. The "labor novel" was to be Lewis' definitive heroic work: its absence from the corpus suggests a corresponding absence of coherence to the religious vision of Sinclair Lewis.

But the strands are there. Lewis' ideological sympathy with socialism and his ability to find spiritual meanings immanent in the civil struggles of labor, women, blacks, or even in carpentry made for natural affinities between Lewis, the Social Gospel movement, and liberal Christianity more generally. It is one of the ironies of his career, as Walter Lipmann first pointed out in his review of *Elmer Gantry,* that Lewis could not recognize or articulate more clearly this affinity. We have suggested that the key to unlocking this irony might be found in the distinction between Lewis' role as infidel and his literary contribution to American popular religion. For underneath the overt criticism of institutional religion in Lewis' writings can be found a subtle ideal of an American popular religion, with beauty-worship, public service, and a vital spiritual quest as its basis.

## Survey of Criticism

General critical studies of Lewis' career are of course plentiful. Mark Schorer's mammoth 800-page biography, *Sinclair Lewis: An American Life,* plays down the role of religion somewhat in favor of attention to broader, if less deep, social factors. Schorer has been criticized for portraying Lewis too melodramatically, especially by James Lundquist in *Sinclair Lewis*. Nevertheless, Schorer's book remains indispensable, particularly if supplemented by the much briefer and more appreciative work of Sheldon Norman Grebstein, *Sinclair Lewis*. D. J. Dooley, *The Art of Sinclair Lewis*, is an apology against the claims that Lewis was simply a publicist writing fiction or was an artless vulgarian mimic. Martin Light emphasizes in *The Quixotic Vision of Sinclair Lewis* the importance to Lewis of what we called a "spiritual quest," while also stressing the quest's diffuseness, ironies, and even contradictions. Two anthologies of criticism make available the finest contemporary and posthumous evaluations of Lewis' career: *Sinclair Lewis: A Collection of Critical Essays,* edited by Schorer in 1962, and *Critical Essays on Sinclair Lewis,* edited by Martin Bucco in 1986. Finally, for further general criticism, see Robert E. Fleming and Esther Fleming, eds., *Sinclair Lewis: A Reference Guide*.

Criticism directed to the religious aspect of Lewis' writing has focused almost exclusively on his satirical hostility to institutional religion. Wilfried Edener, *Die Religionskritik in den Romanen von Sinclair Lewis,* is typical in this respect but still very useful for setting Lewis in the line of previous "infidels" in American religious history. To his credit, Edener also finds some constructive religiosity in Lewis' novels and stresses in this light especially the author's "religious agnosticism," rationalism, socialism, mysticism, and ambivalent connection to any number of historic Protestant doctrines. Edener's is the only full-length monograph addressing Lewis and religion, to my knowledge.

Among journal articles and reviews, Edward Shillito's " 'Elmer Gantry' and the Church in America" gives a typical ecclesiastical response to Lewis by a contemporary, and Rebecca West's review, "Sinclair Lewis Introduces *Elmer Gantry,*" is an oft-cited critique of the novel for its lack of depth. Walter Lippmann's section on Lewis in *Men of Destiny* treats Lewis' religious satire as a part of a broader reaction to Puritan civilization and raises the question of Lewis' inability to find virtue in liberal Christianity. Sheldon Grebstein's "Education of a Rebel: Sinclair Lewis at Yale," illustrates nicely Lewis' transition from Christian convert to critic, as does John Borrego, "If There Be Saints: Faith in the Novels of Sinclair Lewis." Borrego in particular hints at defining "a secular, this-worldly faith" undergirding Lewis' satire.

Two articles not specifically addressing religion are nonetheless helpful in identifying Lewis' values: "Martin Arrowsmith: The Scientist as Hero," by Charles E. Rosenberg, points out how Lewis portrayed Arrowsmith as a "hero ... of the spirit," and Glen A. Love stresses the pilgrim faith of many of Lewis' characters in "New Pioneering on the Prairies: Nature, Progress and the Individual in the Novels of Sinclair Lewis."

Nearly all of Lewis' twenty-two novels have some bearing on popular religion. Those cited in the bibliography below seem particularly pertinent.

## Bibliography

### Books by Sinclair Lewis

1915  *The Trail of the Hawk. A Comedy of the Seriousness of Life*. New York: Harper.
1920  *Main Street: The Story of Carol Kennicott*. New York: Harcourt, Brace and Howe.
1922  *Babbitt*. New York: Harcourt, Brace.
1925  *Arrowsmith*. New York: Harcourt, Brace.
1927  *Elmer Gantry*. New York: Harcourt, Brace.
1928  *The Man Who Knew Coolidge: Being the Soul of Lowell Schmaltz, Constructive and Nordic Citizen*. New York: Harcourt, Brace.
1929  *Dodsworth*. New York: Harcourt, Brace.
1933  *Ann Vickers*. Garden City, N.Y.: Doubleday, Doran.
1935  *It Can't Happen Here*. Garden City, N.Y.: Doubleday, Doran.
1935  *Selected Short Stories*. Garden City, N.Y.: Doubleday, Doran.
1947  *Kingsblood Royal*. New York: Random House.
1949  *The God-Seeker*. New York: Random House.
1953  *The Man from Main Street: A Sinclair Lewis Reader. Selected Essays and Other Writings, 1904–1950*. Edited by Harry E. Maule and Melville H. Cane. New York: Random House.

### Selected Studies about Sinclair Lewis

Birkhead, L. M. *Is Elmer Gantry True?* Girard, Kans.: Haldeman-Julius, 1928. Pamphlet.
Borrego, John E. "If There Be Saints: Faith in the Novels of Sinclair Lewis." *Historical Magazine of the Protestant Episcopal Church* 47 (1978): 463–72.
Bucco, Martin, ed. *Critical Essays on Sinclair Lewis*. Boston: G. K. Hall, 1986.
Chiel, Arthur A. "Sinclair Lewis—A Pro-Jewish Stance." *American Jewish Historical Quarterly* 64 (March 1975): 258–67.
Dooley, D. J. *The Art of Sinclair Lewis*. Lincoln: University of Nebraska Press, 1967.
Edener, Wilfried. *Die Religionskritik in den Romanen von Sinclair Lewis*. (Beihefte zum Jahrbuch für Amerikastudien, 10.Heft.) Heidelberg: Carl Winter, 1963.
Fleming, Robert E., and Esther Fleming, eds. *Sinclair Lewis: A Reference Guide*. Boston: G. K. Hall, 1980.
Grebstein, Sheldon Norman. "Education of a Rebel: Sinclair Lewis at Yale." *New England Quarterly* 28 (September 1955): 372–82.
———. *Sinclair Lewis*. New York: Twayne, 1962.
Hilfer, Anthony Channell. *The Revolt from the Village*. Chapel Hill: University of North Carolina Press, 1969.
Light, Martin. *The Quixotic Vision of Sinclair Lewis*. West Lafayette, Ind.: Purdue University Press, 1975.
———, ed. "Special Issue: Sinclair Lewis." *Modern Fiction Studies* 31 (Autumn 1985): 479–546.
Lippmann, Walter. *Men of Destiny*. New York: Macmillan, 1927.
Love, Glen A. "New Pioneering on the Prairies: Nature, Progress and the Individual in the Novels of Sinclair Lewis." *American Quarterly* 25 (December 1973): 558–77.
Lundquist, James. *Sinclair Lewis*. New York: Ungar, 1973.
Marty, Martin E. *Pilgrims in Their Own Land*. Boston: Little, Brown, 1984.
Parrington, Vernon L. *Our Own Diogenes*. Seattle: University of Washington Press, 1927.

Rogal, Samuel J. "The Hymns and Gospel-Songs in *Elmer Gantry*." *Sinclair Lewis Newsletter* 4 (Spring 1972): 4–8.

Rosenberg, Charles E. "Martin Arrowsmith: The Scientist As Hero." *American Quarterly* 15 (Fall 1963): 447–58.

Schorer, Mark. *Sinclair Lewis: An American Life.* New York: McGraw-Hill, 1961.

———, ed. *Sinclair Lewis: A Collection of Critical Essays.* Englewood Cliffs, N.J.: Prentice-Hall, 1962.

Shillito, Edward. " 'Elmer Gantry' and the Church in America." *Nineteenth-Century and After* 101 (May 1927): 739–48.

Silhol, Robert. *Les Tyrans Tragiques. Un Témoin Pathétique de Notre Temps: Sinclair Lewis.* Paris: Presses Universitaires de France, 1969.

"Storm over Elmer Gantry." *Literary Digest* 93 (April 16, 1927): 28–29.

West, Rebecca. "Sinclair Lewis Introduces *Elmer Gantry*." In *Sinclair Lewis: A Collection of Critical Essays.* Edited by Mark Schorer, 39–46. Englewood Cliffs, N.J.: Prentice-Hall, 1962.

JON PAHL

# Hal Lindsey

How does one go from being a tugboat captain to a best-selling author of Christian books? From an agnostic to a believer so convinced of his interpretation of biblical prophecy and current events as to be willing to take on all comers in debate? From a person terrified with the very thought of speaking in front of a group to one of the most sought-after lecturers in America? From a person without hope and contemplating suicide to one who sees the future with clarity and assurance that encompass all contingencies of history and certify personal salvation even though the greatest catastrophes of all time are at hand? Perhaps the answer to those questions goes beyond the scope of historical explanation, but an example of just those changes is to be found in the life of Hal Lindsey.

### Biography

Lindsey was born in Houston, Texas, in 1930. His early life was characterized by vacillations in the level of his Christian commitment. In fact, he was baptized on three different occasions. His ambivalence toward religion eventually led him to agnosticism. "Religion made me feel guilty," he said in *Publishers Weekly* in 1977, "and so I just kissed it off." He spent two years as a business major at the University of Houston before enlisting in the Coast Guard during the Korean War. Following his stint in the Coast Guard he worked as a tugboat captain on the Mississippi River. After the breakup of his first marriage and anxiety about the world that led him to the point of contemplating suicide, Lindsey was led to become a Christian through reading a Gideon New Testament which had been given to him as a small boy. He describes his conversion as "like taking a dare." If what the Gospels said was true about spiritual rebirth, then he was willing to say to God, "Go ahead and do whatever you want with my life." It was under the immediate direction of the Holy Spirit, not any particular Christian mentor or group, that Lindsey feels he became converted. During the first year of his new-found faith, he taught himself to read Greek, and he read the Bible secretively for nearly eight hours per day, but remained apart from any fellowship with other Christians. In fact, the first association he had with other Christians was a decidedly negative influence on him, for some of them insisted, he recalled in *Christian Life* in 1982, that "the Bible was filled with errors, it wasn't historical, and I couldn't believe in it."

This kind of advice filled Lindsey with renewed doubts about his faith and caused him to flounder spiritually. It was not until 1956, when he attended a meeting in which a young minister named Jack Blackwell talked about biblical prophecy, that Lindsey knew he had found a firm foundation for his faith. According to Lindsey, at the meeting, "a fire was kindled within me then that has never gone out." After listening for two and one-half hours to this speaker, Lindsey recalled in *The Rapture*, he was so excited he could "hardly sleep for a week." Following that experience, Lindsey says he became an avid student of the Bible, especially prophetic sections. In fact, it was his conviction that current events dovetailed with prophetic statements of the Bible made thousands of years earlier that caused him finally to believe that the Bible was indeed the word of God. He cites the book of Ezekiel, chapters 36 through 38, as being particularly meaningful and relevant in his early interest in prophetic literature. These passages contain mention of the restoration of Israel as a nation and the threat to the new nation of a powerful enemy from the "uttermost north." Identifying this enemy with the Soviet Union enabled Lindsey to place these prophecies at the center of current world events. These prophecies and Lindsey's belief that they were being fulfilled before his eyes became the firm cornerstone of his growing faith. As these situations came clearer to Lindsey, he began intensive study of the Bible to see if other world situations were mentioned. He speaks of ecstatic experiences of the Holy Spirit during this search in which he physically felt the love of God moving over him. Lindsey continues to identify prophecy as the primary force that keeps him zealous in his personal Christianity and impels him to put into action things that he has learned.

Following his exposure to prophecy, Lindsey attended Dallas Theological Seminary (1958–62), where he earned a master's degree in theology, with major emphasis in New Testament and early Greek literature and a minor in Hebrew. He highly values that experience and cites his studies of the Greek and Hebrew languages as being the most helpful for his later career. While at Dallas, Lindsey met and married his second wife, Jan. For ten years following Hal's graduation from seminary, he and Jan served as domestic missionaries for Campus Crusade for Christ, lecturing to college students in the United States, Canada, and Mexico. They preached to raucous student gatherings during the sixties at turbulent institutions such as Berkeley and San Francisco State. It was during this period that Lindsey polished his style and learned how to communicate with the youth culture. He was continually challenged to discard traditional theological language and to try to make Christianity accessible in the common parlance of the day. In the early 1970s, Lindsey left Campus Crusade and channeled his energies into a campus ministry at UCLA with the catchy name of "The Jesus Christ Light and Power Company."

In 1969 Lindsey began to gather his Campus Crusade notes into a book that was to vault him into worldwide prominence. Lindsey, with the help of Carole C. Carlson—a free-lance religious writer who has also done work with Corrie ten Boom and Billy Graham*—wrote what was to become a best seller, *The Late Great Planet Earth,* based on sermons Lindsey had preached during his campus ministry days. Published in 1970, the book is purported to have sold twenty million copies around the world in fifty-two languages and was named by the *New York Times* as the number one best-selling nonfiction book of the 1970s.

The main point of *The Late Great Planet Earth,* according to Lindsey, is that there is a pattern of events happening in our time (1970s) that was predicted hundreds of years ago. The key event was the restoration of Israel as a nation to the land of Palestine in 1948, and since 1967, Jewish control of old Jerusalem. Other events that have been prophesied, according to Lindsey, include the alignment of Arab and Black African states against Israel, the rise in power of the U.S.S.R. as the northern nation mentioned in Ezekiel chapter 38, the emergence of Communist China with a possible army of 200 million soldiers, the possibility of a revived "Roman empire" in the form of the European Economic Community, the movement toward a one-world government and a single world church, an increase in the number and scope of wars, and an increase in natural calamities such as earthquakes, famines, and strange diseases. These circumstances will lead to the final apocalyptic warning, the emergence of the Antichrist, who will lead the world into seven years of disaster called the "Great Tribulation" after his rise as the world's savior. This person will have recovered from a fatal head wound through the power of Satan, will rebuild the Jewish Temple on its original site—necessitating the removal or destruction of the Moslem Dome of the Rock—and will then precipitate the world-ending battle of Armageddon.

In all of this future gloom and doom, one's only hope is to be a Christian— and, one assumes, a Christian of the fundamentalist Protestant variety—and be taken out of the world before this period of tribulation through an event called the "rapture." Lindsey teaches that true Christians will be removed from the world through "the ultimate trip" to heaven. Such teaching has led to arrangements by some believers for their less fortunate brethren to succeed them as legal heirs to church property and, in one instance, occasioned a rider on an insurance policy that guarantees the raptured the same status as deceased clients, thus providing the benefits of their policy to the next named beneficiary.

A film version of the book was released in 1978, with narrations by Lindsey, Orson Welles, and a host of other "knowledgeable" spokesmen. A graphic portrayal of the contents of the book, it has received many of the same criticisms; it has been called biased, manipulative, lacking in integrity, and dangerous. These charges are based on the apparent assumption by Lindsey that if one does not believe his interpretation of the Bible, then one does not believe the Bible, period. Critics also question the expertise of Lindsey's witnesses and his citation of seemingly minor historical events as having deep significance in prophetic history. For example, skin cancer, cloning, and the killer bees of Brazil are cited as irrefutable signs of fulfilled prophecy and the end-times.

The most fundamental and important criticism of the book and film is that the whole structure is based on the premise that the world must end within one generation of the founding of the state of Israel. As mentioned earlier, this is the assumption identified by Lindsey as the key to his entire prophetic structure. If this one assumption is granted, the rest of the system falls into place—at least it does with a little imagination and some squeezing of a few round pegs into square holes. According to Lindsey, even though Christian prophets have predicted the end of the world during their lifetimes ever since the first generation of Christians, there was "nothing really relevant" to Christ's second coming before Israel was reborn as a nation. When this key piece to the jigsaw puzzle of biblical prophecy was found, the rest of the pieces fell harmoniously into place. In fact, there is only one event that would shake Lindsey's faith in his own reading of prophecy, and that is the destruction of the nation of Israel. This would not lead him to question the truthfulness of the Bible, he insists, but it would convince him that his interpretation was in error.

In 1972, Lindsey and Carlson again collaborated on a book called *Satan Is Alive and Well on Planet Earth*. This book, also a huge seller, expands on a topic introduced in *The Late Great Planet Earth,* that of the progression of the work of Satan in the modern world. Lindsey is fully conscious of the risks faced by the author of such a book because, as he puts it in the introduction, as work was progressing on the book, "we all discovered the reality of our adversary." The book is dedicated to the memory of Carole Carlson's son, who was killed in a plane crash on the very day that the book was being completed. Though not explicitly stated, the inference is certainly possible that Lindsey saw this tragedy as an evidence of the attacks of Satan on those who dare expose the evil plans. Lindsey documents the rise of interest in America and Europe in supernatural powers and the association of that interest with the drug culture, along with the alarming departure from the truth of historic Christianity by the churches. He ranges from discussions of witchcraft to demon possession, from Jeane Dixon to B. F. Skinner, from the phenomenon of speaking in tongues to the philosophies of Immanuel Kant, Georg F. Hegel, and Karl Marx. The book ends with instructions for Christians on how to avoid Satanic influence and with an affirmation of the ultimate victory of Christ over all evil.

Lindsey wrote three books in the early 1970s. In 1973, he wrote *There's A New World Coming,* an in-depth analysis of the book of the Revelation of St. John, in which Lindsey identifies modern weapons such as helicopters and nuclear bombs as fulfillments of prophecies from that book. An updated version of the book, which takes into account advances in technology and changes in world circumstances, appeared in 1984. In 1974, both *The Liberation of Planet Earth* and *The Promise* were written. Lindsey speaks with obvious relish of the fact that *There's A New World Coming* and *The Liberation of Planet Earth* made the *New York Times'* best-seller list at the same time. He insists that this accomplishment took place in spite of the prejudice against religious books that was evident in the seeming reluctance of the *Times* to put *The Late Great Planet Earth* on the list, even though it outsold nearly every other book. Lindsey was ultimately to become one of the few authors to see three of his books on the *Times'* best-seller list at the same time.

In 1976, Lindsey again worked with Carole C. Carlson in writing *The Terminal Generation*. In spite of the ominous sound of the title, the first line of the introduction declares, "This is a book about hope" The book expands on the theme introduced in *The Late Great Planet Earth* that since Israel has been reestablished as a nation, this will be the final generation of the world. Lindsey avoids the mistake made by some prophecy experts of the past of setting a precise date for the end of the world. He sets the length of a generation at between forty and one hundred years (based on his understanding of uses of the term in the Bible); as Israel was founded in 1948, the end could indeed be very soon.

During the last years of the 1970s, Lindsey experienced a period of personal difficulty during which his writing career was put on hold and he suffered through his second divorce. In 1980, however, he returned to writing with a book that served as an update of *The Late Great Planet Earth* called *The 1980's: Countdown to Armageddon*. This book recounts prophecies that have been fulfilled since the former book was published, such as the addition of members to the European Common Market to reach the prophetically required number of ten (the number is now twelve, however, because of the addition of Spain and Portugal in 1986), the surpassing of the United States by the Soviet Union in military power, the fall of the Shah of Iran, and the Soviet invasion of Afghanistan, which Lindsey sees as a prelude to the Soviet takeover of Iran. Included are charts that show the overwhelming strength of the Soviet military in relation to that of the United States and that list the growing numbers of nations under Communist influence. A significant change in this book, as compared to *The Late Great Planet Earth,* is Lindsey's open espousal of particular political positions quite separate from a foundation in biblical prophecy. For example, in *The Late Great Planet Earth* Lindsey insisted that the United States would necessarily fade as a power on the world scene because it is not mentioned in prophetic scriptures. In *The 1980's: Countdown to Armageddon,* however, Lindsey insists that America can maintain its position, but only if it resists the spread of communism through military strength externally and returns to traditional capitalist political values and resists socialistic tendencies internally.

Lindsey's next book, *The Rapture: Truth or Consequences* (1983), is another expansion on a topic introduced in *The Late Great Planet Earth* but is of a quite different character than his earlier books. This book is an explicit defense of the dispensationalist system, a view that sees history divided into set periods (dispensations) leading to the end. This type of biblical interpretation is definitely present in Lindsey's earlier books but remained always in the background in his quest to avoid what he calls theological jargon. In *The Rapture,* on the other hand, Lindsey takes on various posttribulation and midtribulation positions with much more complex and detailed arguments than are found in his earlier books. Written in Lindsey's popular style, the book deals with complex arguments about interpretation of specific biblical words and phrases, and carries on a lengthy dialogue with Stanley Gundry's *The Church and the Tribulation* (Zondervan, 1976). Though of all-consuming importance for readers of the dispensationalist and premillennialist schools, the arguments are definitely of an "in-house" character and are uninteresting, if not unintelligible, for people outside those camps. Also appearing in 1983 was *A Prophetical Walk Through The Holy Land,* a pictorial journal of one of Lindsey's many tours of sites in Palestine that play a central role in his prophetic scheme.

*Combat Faith,* released in 1986, also made best-seller lists. Lindsey again trumpets the threat of communism and a newer danger that he calls the "New Age Movement." This movement, Lindsey notes, is being used by the devil as a universal substitute religion which feeds on the disillusionment that grew out of the 1960s and 1970s. Included in the movement, according to Lindsey, are everything from the physical fitness fad to Eastern religions. The answer to these threats is a kind of faith that is tough, uncompromising, and ready to do battle.

Lindsey has established a personal management firm, the Generation Company, that oversees Hal Lindsey Ministries, itself a charitable foundation that supports campus ministries, Christian youth programs, and various training ventures. He is host of "Saturdays With Hal Lindsey," a radio news commentary and call-in talk show that is heard in over 200 American cities. Lindsey lives in Rolling Hills Estates, California, with his third wife, Kim, and serves as pastor of the Palos Verdes Community Church there.

### Appraisal

The astounding popularity of Lindsey's books results in part from his demand that they be published in hard-cover and paperback simultaneously. Insisting that he has never coveted the hardback market, Lindsey says that his audience is primarily young people, from fourteen to twenty-five years of age. In his writing he imagines that he is sitting across a table from a young, cynical, irreligious person, trying to convince that person of the truth of Bible prophecies. If that kind of person is convinced, says Lindsey, then others who are not in the "religious club" will find the arguments compelling also. Lindsey speaks of his "passion for simplicity." Not because of ignorance or an inability to use "theological jargon"—which he maintains his education at Dallas Theological Seminary would enable him to do—Lindsey keeps his writings simple in order to reach "the common man," both the ordinary Christian and the nonreligious.

Lindsey insists that his message is not novel. Rather, it is the restatement of what has been believed by a number of "fine Bible students" for at least one hundred years (earlier he had put the figure at 300 years). His goal in writing is to place the teachings of the Bible about events happening in the present day into the frame of reference of modern secular people. Prophecy, therefore, becomes "the message for today." It is the message that arrests the attention of "the secular man, the irreligious man, the man who normally wouldn't be attracted by any other thing the Bible has to say," he said in *Christian Life* in 1973.

As a result, Lindsey maintains that thousands of people have been converted to his brand of Christianity through his writings. His proof for this comes from the "hundreds" of letters he receives. A specific example given by Lindsey is the conversion of an irreligious air force colonel who was given a copy of *The Late Great Planet Earth,* found himself unable to put it down, and told Lindsey later that "it scared the hell out of me." The reason the colonel gave for the book's impact on him was that top-secret air force intelligence to which he had access exactly confirmed Lindsey's pattern of events. This led him to follow Lindsey's advice in the book and "accept Christ." Lindsey maintains that re-sponders to his message and call for acceptance of Christ include many Jews, people from liberal churches, and primarily youth. Sources for Lindsey's infor-mation, besides the Bible and daily news reports, include contacts "in Wash-ington, the Pentagon, everywhere," and a retired U.S. intelligence officer, whom he called in a 1982 *Christian Life* article "one of the best intelligence information gatherers I've ever seen."

Some have criticized Lindsey for enjoying too much the wealth that his best sellers have brought him. Lindsey makes no apologies for his wealth, however (reports of which he claims are greatly exaggerated). "I've made my money legitimately," he insisted in *Publishers Weekly* in 1977. "I don't know any other profession where you're constantly asked for a financial report simply because you've been successful." It is ironic, to say the least, that the writer of book after book proclaiming the soon-coming end of the world should sink a substantial portion of those book royalties into long-term real estate invest-ments. Lindsey bristles at constant questions about his finances, has "come close to punching a few guys" for their persistence, and defends his investments as insuring the continuance of his ministry. This raises another irony because when asked in an interview what effect it would have if the churches really believed that this was the "terminal generation," Lindsey urged that they might sell a few buildings and properties, get out of the building and land business, and get into the business of reaching people for Christ.

Lindsey's message was not new; world conditions were not obviously more desperate than those of past generations; his writing was a folksy style. But the time in 1970 was ripe, the man was totally convinced and full of zeal, and events fit the pattern with enough plausibility to create a following numbering in the millions. And the following continues to grow.

## Survey of Criticism

Critical studies of Lindsey's life and work are surprisingly few when one considers the astounding numbers of books he has sold. At present there are no book-length evaluations of the Lindsey phenomenon, and only a very limited number of articles and chapters in books have been written. Interviews with Lindsey were published in *Christian Life* magazine in January 1973 and February 1982 and in the January 1977 edition of *Eternity*. More deeply probing articles are Kenneth Woodward's "The Boom in Doom" and Russel Chandler's "Profits of Doom." These articles deal with the current fascination with the message of coming catastrophe and place Lindsey at the forefront of a widespread popular interest in apocalypticism. Lindsey's relationships with various publishers is outlined in a brief article by Ray Walters in "Paperback Talk." Jonathan Kirsch of *Publishers Weekly* interviewed Lindsey in 1977 and dealt with the phenomenal success of Lindsey's books and the way Lindsey's lifestyle reflects his handling of that success. Stanley D. Walters, in "Hal Lindsey: Recalculating the Second Coming," sketches Lindsey's second thoughts about the time of the second coming because of the approach of his originally projected possible date of 1988; Walters maintains that in other areas, Lindsey's assertions have become bolder and less qualified. In "Why Biblical Criticism by Scholars Is Imperative," Maxine Negri takes Lindsey to task for limiting questions and responses at a talk given at UCLA to university students and for refusing to allow scholarly participants from a concurrent conference on "Armageddon and Biblical Apocalyptic: Are We Living in the Last Days?" to interrogate him. Negri insists that it is only through scholarly biblical criticism that assertions by interpreters like Lindsey can be refuted. A scathing review of Lindsey's film version of *The Late Great Planet Earth* is "The Doomsday Chic," written by Gary Wilburn.

A lengthier treatment is Dale Moody, "The Eschatology of Hal Lindsey," in which Moody critically reviews Lindsey's dispensational hermeneutic and faults him for assumptions of the infallibility of that method of biblical interpretation. Chapters on Lindsey by Marlin L. Jeschke, "Pop Eschatology: Hal Lindsey and Evangelical Theology," and J. W. Nelson, "The Apocalyptic Vision in American Popular Culture," place Lindsey within a tradition of American apocalypticism and attempt sociological and theological explanations of the general phenomenon and Lindsey's leading role in its contemporary manifestation. Timothy Weber includes a brief but insightful discussion of Lindsey's writings in the revised version of his *Living in the Shadow of the Second Coming*.

## Bibliography

### Books by Hal Lindsey

1970   *The Late Great Planet Earth*. With C. C. Carlson. Grand Rapids: Zondervan.
1972   *Satan Is Alive and Well On Planet Earth*. With C. C. Carlson. Grand Rapids: Zondervan.
1973   *The Guilt Trip*. With C. C. Carlson. Grand Rapids: Zondervan.

1973   *There's A New World Coming*. Santa Ana, Calif.: Vision House. Updated version, 1984, Eugene, Oreg.: Harvest House.
1974   *The Liberation of Planet Earth*. Grand Rapids: Zondervan.
1974   *The Promise*. Eugene, Oreg.: Harvest House.
1976   *The Terminal Generation*. With C. C. Carlson. Old Tappan, N.J.: Fleming H. Revell.
1976   *The World's Final Hour: Evacuation or Extinction?* Grand Rapids: Zondervan.
1980   *The 1980's: Countdown To Armageddon*. New York: Bantam.
1982   *The Promise*. Eugene, Oreg.: Harvest House.
1983   *The Rapture: Truth or Consequences*. New York: Bantam.
1986   *Combat Faith*. New York: Bantam.

### Selected Studies about Hal Lindsey

Board, Stephen. "The Great Cosmic Countdown: Hal Lindsey on the Future." *Eternity* 28 (January 1977): 19–21, 80–81.

Chandler, Russel. "Profits of Doom." *Baptist Reformation Review* 10 (1981): 19–22. Reprinted from the *Roanoke Times,* 18 May 1981.

Clark, Stephen. "The Last Days According to Hal Lindsey." *Christian Life* 43 (February 1982): 44–47.

Jeschke, Marlin L. "Pop Eschatology: Hal Lindsey and Evangelical Theology." In C. Norman Kraus, ed., *Evangelicalism and Anabaptism*. Scottsdale, Pa.: Herald Press, 1979.

Kirsch, Jonathan. "PW Interviews." *Publishers Weekly,* 14 March 1977, pp. 30–32.

Moody, Dale. "The Eschatology of Hal Lindsey." *Review and Expositor* 72 (Summer 1975): 271–78.

Negri, Maxine. "Why Biblical Criticism by Scholars Is Imperative." *Humanist* 44 (May/June 1984): 27–28.

Nelson, J. W. "The Apocalyptic Vision in American Popular Culture." In Lois P. Zamora, ed., *The Apocalyptic Vision in America: Interdisciplinary Essays on Myth and Culture*. Bowling Green, Ohio: Bowling Green State University Press, 1982.

Walters, Ray. "Paperback Talk." *New York Times Book Review,* 12 March 1978, pp. 45–46.

Walters, Stanley D. "Hal Lindsey: Recalculating the Second Coming." *Christian Century* 96 (12 September 1979): 839–40.

Weber, Timothy P. *Living in the Shadow of the Second Coming: American Premillennialism, 1875–1982*. Enlarged ed. Grand Rapids: Zondervan, 1983.

"When Is Christ Coming?" *Christian Life* 34 (January 1973): 37, 40–42.

Wilburn, Gary. "The Doomsday Chic." *Christianity Today* 22 (27 January 1978): 22–23.

Woodward, Kenneth L., et al. "The Boom in Doom." *Newsweek,* 10 January 1977, pp. 49, 51.

STEPHEN R. GRAHAM

# Carl McIntire

Dissident Presbyterian minister Carl McIntire emerged earlier this century as a powerful symbol of fundamentalist separatism. Adamantly refusing fellowship with the "modernists" and "apostates" he saw infecting the mainline churches, including his own denomination, he established his own counter organizations to challenge ecumenism, higher biblical criticism, and clerical social activism. In the 1950s, as the Cold War produced a wider audience for his vociferous mix of laissez-faire ideology, superpatriotism, and apocalyptic anticommunism, McIntire's influence spread beyond his limited base among Protestant religious circles. Not a few of McIntire's supporters maintained that his political outreach severely compromised his separatist principles, and as a consequence, many deserted him. Yet McIntire's explicit intertwining of fundamentalism and right radicalism foreshadowed the explosion of the "religious right" in the 1980s.

## Biography

Carl McIntire was born on 17 May 1906 in Ypsilanti, Michigan, into a Presbyterian family of Scotch-Irish ancestry. Shortly after his birth, his parents moved to Oklahoma, where Carl reached adulthood. After receiving a teaching certificate from Southeastern State Teachers College in Oklahoma and a B.A. from Park College in Missouri, he elected to study for the ministry. In 1927, he enrolled at Princeton Theological Seminary. There McIntire became embroiled in the fundamentalist-liberal controversies that not only troubled Princeton but also ultimately split several Protestant denominations by the end of that decade. He fell under the influence of the prominent New Testament scholar J. Gresham Machen, whose best-known work, *Christianity and Liberalism*, demanded that the Presbyterian Church U.S.A. purge liberals from the seminary's board of trustees and faculty and deny ordination to liberal divinity students. Machen's affirmation of fundamentalist positions, including the inerrancy of Scripture and the virgin birth and the bodily resurrection of Jesus, was so complete that he even rejected the label "fundamentalist." The use of that term, he believed, implied the existence of more than one kind of Christian, when for Machen, either one was or one was not.

Although McIntire eventually broke with his teacher, he never deviated from the separatism Machen articulated. Several decades later in his book *Twentieth Century Reformation,* the very title of which demonstrated McIntire's commitment to restoring and purifying Protestantism's proper theological roots, he referred to the fundamentalist-modernist controversy. "One is said to be a modernist Christian and another is said to be a fundamentalist Christian," he noted. "Here is where the terminology is so disastrous. A man who calls himself a modernist is not a Christian. He cannot be. The things he believes and teaches deny the very essentials of the Christian faith.... The fundamentalist is the Christian, and to call a man a fundamentalist Christian implies that there is some other kind of Christian, which there is not. The modernist is not a Christian." In fact, where Machen was known to remain personally charitable toward modernists, McIntire refused all association—perhaps a reflection of the latter's stark premillennial convictions. As the End neared, the true church had to remain pure.

Machen's exclusionary efforts, however, failed to persuade the leadership of the Presbyterian Church U.S.A., which wanted to reduce conflict through conciliation. In 1929, Machen left Princeton to found Westminster Seminary, taking his student with him. As McIntire completed his studies and won ordination, he joined with Machen in an all-out assault on both the denominational leadership and the ecumenical Federal Council of Churches, accusing them of encouraging their missionaries to spread communism. The Westminster faction formed the Independent Board of Foreign Missions as a rival to the Presbyterians' own constituted body, an act of rebellion that, in 1936, resulted in Machen's and McIntire's ouster from the church. In short order the two and their supporters formed the Presbyterian Church of America, claiming to be the "true" church, the only one faithful to the Westminster Confession.

Despite that act of defiance, the new church soon succumbed to bitter conflicts that arose from within its ranks—conflicts that placed McIntire at loggerheads with his mentor. Disputes occurred in regard to not only the language of the church constitution and the private use of alcohol but also the troublesome relationship between premillennialism and dispensationalism on the one hand and fundamentalism on the other. Where Machen and his supporters reluctantly accepted premillennialism but rejected dispensationalism as biblically unsound, McIntire urged full acceptance of both. In 1937, Machen died, after McIntire's faction had prevented his reelection as president of the Independent Missions Board. The Presbyterian Church of America, just one year after its birth, divided into two irreconcilable bodies: the Orthodox Presbyterian Church, incorporating most of Machen's Westminster group, and McIntire's Bible Presbyterian Church. McIntire's group came to include its own Faith Theological Seminary; two small colleges, Shelton in Cape May, New Jersey, and Highland in Pasadena, California; a radio program, "The Twentieth Century Reformation Hour," first aired in 1955; a newspaper, the *Christian Beacon,* which achieved a circulation of 250,000; and the Christian Beacon Press. McIntire's 1,200-member congregation, the Bible Presbyterian Church of Collingswood, New Jersey, has been an important source of contributions and the home base for McIntire's other enterprises.

McIntire, however, did not rest with establishing an alternative Presbyterian Church. He went on to challenge the very principle of liberal ecumenical cooperation among the denominations embodied first in the Federal Council of Churches and later in the National Council of Churches. For him, the ecumenical movement smacked not only of socialist internationalism but also of modernist inclusivism of the sort that could only dilute the historic creeds on which all

Protestant denominations were based. As he put it in *Twentieth Century Reformation:*

> Let the Baptists be Baptists. Let the Presbyterians be Presbyterians. Let the Lutherans be Lutherans. Let the Methodists be Methodists. Let us all be what we are, and in the strength of our individual convictions we shall be stronger Christians, and shall hold more tenaciously to the great Christian doctrines that unite the Lord's people.

McIntire was particularly disturbed by ecumenical overtures to Jews and Roman Catholics as though Protestantism, Catholicism, and Judaism stood in perfect harmony. With regard to Roman Catholicism specifically, McIntire insisted: "The historic Protestant faith would never admit for one moment that the Roman Catholic testimony is Christian." Although McIntire eventually admitted that some Catholic dogmatic commitments, especially the virgin birth, suggested some common ground between the church and fundamentalism, he never deviated from assuming the Protestant character of American culture.

In 1941, largely at McIntire's initiative, the American Council of Christian Churches was founded to provide fundamentalist congregations with an alternative to the Federal Council of Churches. The ACCC's goals ranged from awakening "Bible-loyal Protestants everywhere to a Twentieth Century Reformation," to projecting "a united stand against religious modernism," to displaying "prominent leadership in opposing Communism and all ideologies which would destroy political, economic and religious freedom in the United States." The ACCC insisted on total separation from any agency, church, or individual associated with the Federal Council, thus parting company even with the most conservative Protestants who countered apostasy from within the Federal Council's member churches. In 1948, also at McIntire's behest, the International Council of Christian Churches was established in direct reaction to the creation of the World Council of Churches. To dissipate the impact of the latter's first meeting in Amsterdam, McIntire arranged a simultaneous session that spelled out guiding principles for the ICCC—terms that closely resembled those of the ACCC.

McIntire's rightist political views grew naturally from his hostility toward Protestant modernism and particularly from the harsh apocalyptic distinction he drew between the redeemed church and unredeemed world. He accused the Federal Council of Churches of having fostered pacifism during the interwar years and after, the inevitable outcome of its belief in the brotherhood of man but to McIntire an impossible option given a world ruled by sin and governed by force. Pacifism not only permitted Germany to rearm and Russia to run rampant, but also denied the reality of Christ's resurrection as the cosmic triumph over Satan by preaching nonresistance. McIntire's antagonism toward the Soviet Union evidenced itself well before the Cold War dampened allied dreams of a peaceful postwar world order. As he argued in 1944 in *Twentieth Century Reformation,* "Stalin is just as much a dictator as Hitler and Tojo ever were. The battle between Stalin and Hitler is one dictator versus another dictator, and there is no use deceiving ourselves in this matter. We are glad to help Stalin beat Hitler, but we must be exceedingly careful to see that Stalin does not destroy us in the bargain." After the war was over, McIntire decried the idea of co-existence with Russia. The Soviet Union's atheism and alternative social system represented such satanic power that the only solution was its elimination. Better that the United States use the atomic bomb first against Russia, McIntire suggested in his *"Author of Liberty,"* than allow Russia to strike first against the United States. Nuclear war, he pointed out some years later, was to be feared less than the wrath of God at the end of history. True believers would escape the devastation of both at Christ's return.

If Russia epitomized evil for McIntire, the United States represented its opposite, though prophetic warnings were frequently necessary to keep America from succumbing to the demonic influences of creeping socialism and social engineering. Unregulated free enterprise, private property, liberty, and individualism not only made America great but were biblically sanctioned as well. Christ's teaching and deeds, McIntire explained in *"Author of Liberty,"* supported "our American system of freedom—private enterprise, individual initiative, personal responsibility, competition, and what we call the capitalistic system. Of course, He does not approve or sanction its abuses and perversions . . . but the capitalistic system, in its ideal and essential ingredients, comes from no other person than the Lord Jesus Christ." Although not opposed to labor unions or to collective bargaining, McIntire attacked proposals allowing for collective management between business and labor as communistic, and strongly affirmed the open shop as consistent with individual conscience. McIntire condemned the welfare state as containing the seeds of totalitarian collectivism. If left unchecked, such a state by its demands for total loyalty and its octopus-like intrusions into every aspect of life would suppress individual initiative, destroy personal liberty, and, in misguided fashion, eliminate the distinctions between rich and poor:

> Men are not always rich because they have been greedy. Men are not always poor because they have had their wages kept back. There are many, many other factors that enter into the relationship between riches and poverty. The attempt to eliminate this distinction by the collectivistic ordering of society enslaves men. Men must be free to be either poor or rich.

McIntire strongly endorsed the separation of church and state as preserving the core of American individualism, one's freedom of conscience.

McIntire's emergence after World War II as a noteworthy exponent of the radical right paralleled the growing awareness of the Soviet Union as a rival superpower and the Cold War that resulted from U.S.-Soviet conflict. As Senator Joseph McCarthy's investigations of Communist infiltration picked up support, ACCC and ICCC leaders cooperated with McCarthy's staff in exposing the "Communist" inspirations behind leading ecumenical leaders and the new Revised Standard Version of the Bible. The ICCC attempted to eliminate communism from behind the "iron curtain" by launching "truth" balloons emblazoned with biblical quotations into eastern Europe. Opposition to the Revised Standard Bible, especially, illustrated the convergence of McIntire's fundamentalist beliefs and political convictions. To him, the translation denied the virgin birth and the pre-existence of Jesus—the end product of biblical scholars who, McIntire charged, belonged to Communist-affiliated organizations. McIntire's direct political involvement inspired other fundamentalists, most notably Billy James Hargis* and Edgar C. Bundy, to seek both a national audience through the use of radio and, however tentatively, alliances with secular right-wing organizations.

Despite McCarthy's subsequent censure and the decline of the most extreme forms of anti-Soviet hysteria since the death of Stalin, McIntire remained active in numerous religiously inspired political crusades, even involving his organizations in Barry Goldwater's 1964 presidential campaign. His intense anticommunism, far from waning, surfaced repeatedly in his attacks on the civil rights movement and on Vietnam War protests, both of which he saw as manipulated by Moscow. Civil rights legislation not only entailed a loss of freedom because it interfered with property rights but also was doomed to failure because of man's sinful nature. Goodness could not be legislated. The Vietnam War was nothing less than "a holy righteous crusade" against atheistic communism. By the late 1970s, the ICCC was attacking the United Nations–sponsored "Year of the Child" for "inciting children to rebel against their parents"; the ICCC was also condemning liberation theology, criticizing America's diplomatic recognition of the People's Republic of China, and denouncing the Strategic Arms Limitation agreements.

In recent years, however, McIntire's visibility has waned in favor of such younger fundamentalist preachers as Jerry Falwell* and Pat Robertson*, who have built a substantially larger religiously conservative mass base. McIntire has instead been left to fight repeated legal and financial battles to preserve his small Bible Presbyterian denomination. These have included the loss of the license of his radio station, WUXR in Media, Pennsylvania, for violating the Fairness Doctrine; difficulties in paying back taxes on church-held properties in Cape May, New Jersey; the parlous financial condition, declining enrollment, and subsequent division of Faith Theological Seminary; and finally, Shelton College's loss of accreditation, a decision of the New Jersey Department of Higher Education upheld by the Supreme Court in early 1985.

**Appraisal**

Carl McIntire's fervent commitment to separatism respresents an extreme fundamentalism's denial of theological and secular modernism. Although McIntire has often claimed substantial memberships in his organizations, most observers see his appeal as small in comparison to the more moderate evangelical organizations and the mainline denominations themselves. The ACCC, whose fluctuating enrollment consisted of predominantly independent Methodist and Baptist churches, numbered at most 250,000, roughly one half of 1 percent of all American Protestants. Like the ACCC, the ICCC's exact membership figures have been hard to come by. In the early 1970s, the organization claimed to embrace 122 churches that supported extensive missionary work, especially in Asia, Africa, and Latin America. Yet even accepting the accuracy of that total, most of the ICCC's churches are considered numerically insignificant. Finally, the Bible Presbyterians, as of the mid 1970s, included scarcely more than 8,000 members. None of McIntire's organizations has been immune to dissension or schism, owing in large measure to McIntire's uncompromising leadership—certainly a logical consequence of his separatism.

Yet McIntire's significance goes beyond what he represents to the history of fundamentalism as a protest movement within American Protestantism. It arises from the explicit connections he drew between fundamentalism and right-wing politics. Although he never formed active political organizations, his efforts on behalf of McCarthy's investigations, Goldwater's presidential campaign, and the war in Vietnam showed enough potential to merit attention from many commentators who now see him as a forerunner to the politically charged fundamentalism of the 1980s. Once ridiculed as an ignorant subculture residing at the fringes of American society, fundamentalism now asserts its vision of America all the way to the White House. At bottom was McIntire's militant anticommunism and passionate free-marketeering. Though like his separatism, his political ideology was and is considered extreme, it nonetheless sharply underscores in its broadest outlines a world view shared by a society that permits no alternative to capitalism or to anticommunism even as it allows for their modification.

### Survey of Criticism

One leading historian, William R. Hutchison, in *The Modernist Impulse in American Protestantism,* argues that the great reactions against Protestant modernism, fundamentalism, and neo-orthodoxy agreed on the necessity of a clear choice between Christianity and no Christianity at all, even if they converged on little else. Thus, in retrospect, McIntire's "either/or" position was by no means unusual. Yet not a few of McIntire's supporters came to challenge his political commitments as severely compromising his separatism because they brought him into association with nonbelievers. In the late 1960s, McIntire was removed from the ACCC's executive committee, and the organization as a whole voted to leave the ICCC because, it was claimed, McIntire violated his principles. The tension between political involvement and separation from the "world" was unresolved not only in McIntire's case; it has grown more obvious in the 1980s, as the leadership of the religious right has moved conspicuously in leading political circles whose composition is anything but exclusively fundamentalist.

Criticism of McIntire has centered also on the degree to which his categorical attitudes affected not only his leadership of the organizations he founded but also his reception outside fundamentalist circles. If some supporters saw his separatism compromised by political involvement, others saw it as encouraging high-handedness, authoritarianism, and intolerance. In addition to the Bible Presbyterians themselves splitting in 1956 amid complaints of McIntire's "undemocratic" leadership, the ACCC's own decision late the following decade arose, in part, from similar charges. A significant number of fundamentalist churches had, in fact, refused to join the ACCC all along, accusing McIntire of uncharitable criticism of opponents, irresponsible public political statements, and arbitrary leadership. In the political realm, McIntire has been accused of sowing hate, dissension, authoritarianism, and extremism—perhaps the logical consequence of his intolerant fundamentalism, but directly at odds with the American way he has claimed to defend.

Despite McIntire's numerous published works and his propensity for controversy, he has not attracted the kind of sustained attention given to such figures as Billy Graham* or Jerry Falwell. The great majority of recent works on fundamentalism and evangelicalism, though they acknowledge McIntire as a significant forerunner to the movement of the 1980s, mention him only in passing. In fact, it is a West German scholar, Jutta Reich, who has provided, in her *Amerikanischer Fundamentalismus: Geschichte und Erscheinung der Bewegung um Carl McIntire,* the only full account of McIntire's life, theology, and political beliefs. George Dollar's *A History of Fundamentalism in America* commends McIntire for having the courage of his convictions. Gary Clabaugh's *Thunder on the Right* and Ralph Lord Roy's *Apostles of Discord* frequently mention McIntire as representative of a larger movement dangerously situated outside the mainstream of American politics. Erling Jorstad's less polemical but equally critical account of fundamentalist radicalism, *The Politics of Doomsday,* provides perhaps the best means of understanding McIntire's career. He sees McIntire as highlighting not so much the tension between separatism and politicism as their amalgamation in a variant of civil religion. The most serious problem raised by McIntire and others like him, notes Jorstad, is that of equating American values and citizenship with Christianity itself. Thus, the nation's need for transcendent standards of judgment, repentance, and self-examination are ignored in the process. Whether one agrees with Jorstad or not, that issue continues to inform not only discussions of McIntire's successors on the religious right but also the larger questions of business, coexistence, and confrontation with the "evil empire."

## Bibliography

### Books by Carl McIntire

1944   *Twentieth Century Reformation.* Collingswood, N.J.: Christian Beacon Press.
1945   *The Rise of the Tyrant.* Collingswood, N.J.: Christian Beacon Press.
1946   *"Author of Liberty."* Collingswood, N.J.: Christian Beacon Press.
1946   *For Such a Time as This.* Collingswood, N.J.: Christian Beacon Press.
1950   *The Struggle for South America.* Collingswood, N.J.: Christian Beacon Press.
1953   *The New Bible, Revised Standard Version: Why Christians Should Not Accept It.* Collingswood, N.J.: Christian Beacon Press.

1954  *The Wall of Jerusalem also Is Broken Down.* Collingswood, N.J.: Christian Beacon Press.
1955  *Servants of Apostasy.* Collingswood, N.J.: Christian Beacon Press.
1958  *The Epistle of the Apostasy: The Book of Jude.* Collingswood, N.J.: Christian Beacon Press.
1967  *The Death of a Church.* Collingswood, N.J.: Christian Beacon Press.

### Selected Studies about Carl McIntire

"Carl McIntire: On the Move from Cape to Cape." *Christianity Today* 23 (17 August 1979): 45–46.

Clabaugh, Gary K. *Thunder on the Right: The Protestant Fundamentalists,* 69–97. Chicago: Nelson-Hall, 1974.

Dollar, George W. *A History of Fundamentalism in America,* 237–40. Greenville, S.C.: Bob Jones University Press, 1973.

Hutchison, William R. *The Modernist Impulse in American Protestantism.* Cambridge, Mass.: Harvard University Press, 1976.

"Jersey Upheld on Regulating Degrees of Religious Colleges." *New York Times,* 13 January 1985.

Jorstad, Erling. *The Politics of Doomsday: Fundamentalists of the Far Right.* Nashville: Abingdon Press, 1970.

Liebman, Robert C., and Robert Wuthnow. *The New Christian Right: Mobilization and Legitimation.* New York: Aldine Publishing Company, 1983.

Marsden, George M. *Fundamentalism and American Culture: The Shaping of Twentieth-Century Evangelism, 1870–1925.* New York: Oxford University Press, 1980.

"On the Beach, On the Brink." *Christianity Today* 21 (23 September 1977): 49–50.

Reich, Jutta. *Amerikanischer Fundamentalismus: Geschichte und Erscheinung der Bewegung um Carl McIntire.* 2nd ed. Hildesheim: Verlag Dr. H. A. Gerstenberg, 1972.

Ribuffo, Leo P. *The Old Christian Right from the Great Depression to the Cold War.* Philadelphia: Temple University Press, 1983.

Roy, Ralph Lord. *Apostles of Discord: A Study of Organized Bigotry and Disruption on the Fringes of Protestantism.* Boston: Beacon Press, 1953.

Sandeen, Ernest R. *The Roots of Fundamentalism: British and American Millenarianism, 1800–1930.* Chicago: University of Chicago Press, 1970.

SHELLEY BARANOWSKI

# Aimee Semple McPherson

The Pentecostal Azusa Street Revival of 1906 and the Scopes Trial of 1925 are just two evidences that the early decades of the twentieth century were characterized by both religious enthusiasms and religious conflicts. Aimee Semple McPherson's life and career displayed both characteristics. Following a brief period of adolescent skepticism fed by Darwinian theory, she experienced a Pentecostal conversion. As a sensational evangelist, McPherson made use of the most "up-to-date" methods and was the subject of a highly publicized scandal.

Her legacy to American religion includes an established denomination, the International Church of the Foursquare Gospel.

## Biography

Aimee (Kennedy) Semple McPherson was born in rural Ontario, Canada, near Ingersoll on 9 October 1890. She was the only child of James Morgan Kennedy and Mildred "Minnie" (Pearce) Kennedy. Her parents were both active churchfolk. James Kennedy was a successful farmer who was also a leader in the local Methodist congregation. Minnie Pearce was his second wife. An orphan, she had been raised by a Salvation Army family. She had come to Kennedy's farm to nurse his first wife. After the first Mrs. Kennedy died, Minnie married James.

A mere six weeks after Aimee's birth, her mother dedicated infant "Beth" (as Aimee was then called) to the Lord's service at a Salvation Army meeting in nearby Salford. Throughout her childhood Aimee was exposed to the enthusiasm of the Salvation Army and along with her mother was an active participant. Aimee held meetings for her dolls and led her classmates around the schoolyard in parade accompanied by rousing hymns. She won prizes from the Women's Christian Temperance Union for her orations. As she matured, however, Aimee moved away from the Army into her father's more sedate Methodist congregation.

As a high school student, Aimee expanded her activities to include dances and novel reading as well as participation in the school's dramatic productions. Her class work exposed her to scientific theories that she took as proofs against her earlier religious positions. Neither her schoolteacher nor the Methodist minister provided the young skeptic with any other solution to her dilemma. Efforts by the Salvation Army officers to dissuade her were unsuccessful.

Aimee's way back to faith was through the Pentecostal movement and the preaching of Irish-born evangelist Robert Semple. In December 1907 she persuaded her father to stop in at a revival. She was drawn to both the message and the person of the man who seemed to speak directly to her. In the following days Aimee skipped school to take part in prayer meetings held in the home of local Pentecostal believers. She was converted. Her mother's objections to the particular sort of Christianity Aimee had embraced were overcome when a study of the Bible revealed no indication that the spiritual gifts had been withdrawn.

Within a year Aimee and Robert had married (12 August 1908) and had launched a promising career as evangelists. Among the places in which they conducted meetings were Toronto, Chicago, and Findlay, Ohio. Robert was the major preacher, and Aimee gave support in a variety of ways. She encountered various manifestations of the Holy Spirit: her ankle was healed by faith, and she demonstrated a gift for interpreting tongues. At a Full Gospel Assembly in 1909, Aimee Semple was constituted a preacher. This was her only official call; she was never ordained by any other church.

In answer to Robert's call, the young couple traveled via Ireland to Hong Kong to take up the task of evangelism among the Chinese. In her autobiographies

Aimee revealed a romantic view of the Chinese as potential converts but little sympathy for them as individuals. Her contacts with the Chinese were limited by the briefness of her stay, first in Hong Kong and then in Macao, and by her condition. During 1910, the Semples' partial year of residence, she was pregnant and sick. Before the year was out, Robert died, very likely of typhoid, and Aimee gave birth to a daughter, Roberta Star Semple. The significance of these months for Aimee seems to have been less in the missionary work than in the loss of her beloved husband.

Financial help, which came solicited from Minnie Kennedy and unsolicited from other supporters of the Semples' work, allowed Aimee to return to the United States. The next six years were unhappy ones in which Aimee displayed little of the spunk and energy that had been characteristic of her until then. She went first to Chicago and then to New York where her mother was working for the Salvation Army. The young widow's loss of direction and purpose was evident in her movement back and forth between these two cities.

In early 1912, in Chicago, she married Harold Stewart McPherson. For a time the McPhersons lived in Providence, Rhode Island. Unlike Aimee's first one, this marriage was unhappy, and she did not recover her earlier energy or purpose. Following the birth of Rolf Kennedy McPherson in 1913, she became quite ill and had surgery which prevented her from having other children. By her own account, Aimee was struggling with God, who had called her to again take up the task of evangelism. Finally, in the spring of 1915 she left McPherson and took her two children with her to her parents' home in Canada.

As a repentant sinner, Aimee attended a revival in Kitchener (then Berlin) and did whatever tasks needed to be done. She took her turn washing dishes, serving meals, and playing the piano. She also met Mrs. Elizabeth Sharp, who invited Aimee to hold a series of meetings in Mount Forest, Ontario. The success of those meetings launched Aimee's evangelistic career. It also provided for a temporary reconciliation with Harold McPherson, who accompanied her on her tours until 1918.

Aimee Semple McPherson traveled from Maine to Florida in the next three years conducting revivals in her own tent or in local churches and halls. When Harold McPherson left, her mother capably assumed responsibility for the business end of the work. In these early campaigns McPherson already showed the sort of inventiveness that would typify her style and she began practices that would remain a part of her work. During the revival in Corona, New York, a young Roman Catholic woman was healed; in Washburn, Maine, the parable of the wise and foolish virgins was dramatized. The *Bridal Call*, her movement's magazine, was first published in June 1917. Offerings were used to purchase the "Gospel Auto" which McPherson decorated with evangelistic slogans and on one occasion drove in a Mardi Gras parade. She and her mother adopted a nurse's white dress and blue cape as their uniforms. In modified form, McPherson continued to wear this uniform throughout her life.

The fall of 1918 saw the Gospel Auto on its way to Los Angeles. There McPherson established a permanent base, although she continued to travel widely and held over three dozen well-attended revivals in cities such as Boston, Denver, and San Diego between 1918 and 1923. She held a campaign in Australia in 1922 just before Angelus Temple was completed. This pie-shaped white building overlooking Echo Park became the center of McPherson's work and the head-quarters of the International Church of the Foursquare Gospel.

When Angelus Temple was opened on 1 January 1923, McPherson did not intend to establish a denomination. Her vision of the foursquare gospel had come to her the previous year as she preached from Ezekiel. She had seen the four faces of the cherubim (a man, a lion, an ox, and an eagle) as the four faces of Christ: the only Savior, the Mighty Baptizer with the Holy Spirit, the Great Physician, and the Coming King. This was not a doctrinal innovation. Mc-Pherson's innovations were more in method than in doctrine.

The programs of Angelus Temple continued McPherson's willingness to make use of whatever would appeal to the people. Services included a brass band, an orchestra, and robed choirs in addition to her own dramatized sermons. One evening service per week was devoted to healing. The Temple's 500-watt station, KFSG, was the first religious radio station in the nation. A twenty-four hour prayer watch was kept in the Temple's tower. The physical needs of humanity were also met through the commissary and an employment service. In 1926 the Lighthouse of International Foursquare Evangelism (LIFE) was dedicated to house McPherson's Bible College.

The scandal of McPherson's alleged kidnapping in May 1926 expanded her notoriety. McPherson appeared to drown in the ocean one afternoon. When she resurfaced several weeks later, McPherson charged that she had been kidnapped. The press, and others, contended that she had run away with Kenneth G. Ormiston, the former operator of KFSG. After months of publicity, the Los Angeles County courts dropped the charges of conspiracy to obstruct justice and subornation of perjury.

By 1930 Angelus Temple had 12,000 members. Its programs and those of the worldwide organization of the Church of the Foursquare Gospel continued to grow in the 1930s and 1940s. However, the final years of McPherson's life were marked by personal conflicts. Her third marriage to David L. Hutton in 1931 was brief and unsatisfactory; they were divorced in 1935. Her long partnership with her mother came to an unpleasant end in 1928, and she was similarly estranged from her daughter in 1936. Aimee Semple McPherson died on 27 September 1944 in Oakland from what was declared to be an accidental overdose of sleeping pills.

### Appraisal

Aimee Semple McPherson was in her lifetime well known as a personality and a religious figure. Whereas her several autobiographies provide the student with a vivid impression of her self-evaluation, further study suggests that her significance in the history of American religion can be considered in three over-lapping categories: as an evangelist, as a religious founder, and as a female religious leader.

As an evangelist McPherson was remarkable in her willingness to adopt new and untried methods to achieve her goals. She was not, of course, unique in this characteristic. Her contemporary Billy Sunday* was also known for his flam-boyance. Other evangelists conducted healing services. However, it is worth noting that McPherson made early and effective use of the media. In 1922 she was the first woman to deliver a sermon over the radio, and not long after that, Angelus Temple established the first religious radio station. Early in her career McPherson also made good use of the printed word (specifically the *Bridal Call*) to consolidate her following.

Services at Angelus Temple had a distinctly theatrical character, and Mc-Pherson's self-presentation and her trademark white dress, blue cape, and red roses suggest that had she continued in her adolescent resolve to be an actress, she might have met with some success. Her startling actions, such as entering the Temple on a motorcycle, were in keeping with her design for the building with its pie shape, huge organ, and dramatic windows. There were, no doubt, many who came to McPherson's services for the show; many others heard a message of hope from this woman who "saw the sunshine."

During her lifetime the charitable works carried out by Angelus Temple suggest that McPherson may have absorbed some of the concerns of the Salvation Army or of the Social Gospel movement. However, she wrote little about these two influences in her several autobiographies.

Although the initial attraction of the Foursquare Gospel may have been heavily dependent on McPherson's personal style and leadership, the institutions (Angelus Temple, LIFE, and the denomination) she founded survived the test of her alleged kidnapping and her death. When she died, there were some 22,000 members of the International Church of the Foursquare Gospel. Under the leadership of her son, Rolf McPherson, the denomination continued to grow. In 1970 there were 1,796 churches with a membership of 186,782 in twenty-seven countries.

McPherson's achievements as an evangelist and a founder were remarkable particularly when it is recognized that she was relatively uneducated and did not have the backing of any previously organized group. That she was a woman makes these accomplishments so much the more notable. Throughout most of her career McPherson was divorced, hardly a state designed for good public relations in the second quarter of the century. Nonetheless, she was able to draw on her own style, the business talents of her mother, and the power of her message to attract a large following and to build a stable denomination.

In doing this McPherson was in the fluid tradition of that strand of Christianity that bases authority in spiritual gifts. Like earlier Holiness preachers Phoebe Palmer and Amanda Berry Smith, McPherson's call to ministry came directly from God; it was not mediated through an established church. It has been suggested that McPherson was directly influenced by the example of Salvation Army leader Evangeline Booth, who served as commander of U.S. forces from 1904 to 1934 and as international general from 1934 to 1939. Certainly McPherson must have known of Booth, and it is likely that Booth's example may have encouraged her, but there is little evidence that it had specific effects.

The coincidence of McPherson's career and a gradual opening of opportunities for women in American society may have compounded the advantages of her location in the Holiness/Pentecostal camp. She placed more emphasis on her motherhood than on her independence as a single woman, but there was little attention to either topic in her autobiographical writings. Neither did she make much of her gender or of women's rights, so it is difficult to argue that she viewed her religious work in a feminist way. Nor do the programs of the Foursquare Gospel appear to have any distinctly feminist concerns.

Although McPherson left her second husband to resume her career, she had begun it while Robert Semple was alive. Throughout her life she carried a strong affection for her first husband. What direction her life would have taken if he had lived can, of course, not be known. However, the role of her ill-fated relationships with other men in her life has not yet been adequately studied. The intertwining of her personal desire for male companionship and her commitment to the ministry of Angelus Temple appears to be crucial to an interpretation of her supposed kidnapping.

McPherson was a remarkable evangelist who made creative use of a variety of methods in her work, she was a successful founder of a denomination, and she was an exceptional woman who created her own career. William G. McLoughlin, in "Aimee Semple McPherson: 'Your Sister in the King's Glad Service,' " has suggested that McPherson "may stand as one of the more engaging and authentic products of America as a civilization." He further noted that McPherson herself provided the phrase that describes her best, "Your sister in the King's glad service." Certainly, she cannot be understood without serious attention to her own evaluation of her career as a response to God's call.

### Survey of Criticism

In contrast to the notoriety Aimee Semple McPherson attained during her lifetime, little scholarly attention has been given to her career. The primary sources for her biography are her several autobiographies; however, these neglect significant positions of her life. Secondary works by Nancy Mavity and Lately Thomas which are concerned primarily with the alleged kidnapping of 1926 are helpful. Other contemporary reports and reactions to McPherson are available; Robert Bahr lists many of these in his bibliography. As he notes, there is an official version of McPherson's story that is guarded by the leaders of the Church of the Foursquare Gospel. Consequently, access to the church's archives is sometimes limited.

Bahr's popular biography is, by his own design and statement, a speculative work. He takes the position that McPherson ran away with Kenneth Ormiston in 1926. Throughout his volume, Bahr has taken other liberties with facts, such as the location of events, and has supplied dialogue. Thus his biography must be regarded as a fictionalization that is not adequate for scholarly study.

David Clark's article is useful for placing McPherson in the context of early-twentieth-century Los Angeles and for his observations about her bridging "the gap between two historic styles of religious dramatization." The work of Barbara Brown Zikmund and of Letha Dawson Scanzoni and Susan Setta considers McPherson in the tradition of female leaders in the Holiness and Pentecostal movements. The most insightful treatment of McPherson is to be found in William G. McLoughlin's 1967 article in the *Journal of Popular Culture*. McLoughlin brings to bear his vast knowledge of American revivalism and provides a sympathetic analysis of McPherson's work and its importance in American religious history.

## Bibliography

### Books by Aimee Semple McPherson

1919 *This Is That: Personal Experiences, Sermons, and Writings*. Los Angeles: Bridal Call Publishing Co.
1921 *Divine Healing Sermons*. N.p.
1923 *This is That: Personal Experiences, Sermons, and Writings*. Rev. ed. Los Angeles: Echo Park Evangelistic Association.
1927 *In the Service of the King: The Story of My Life*. New York: Boni and Liveright.
1936 *Give Me My Own God*. New York: H. C. Kinsey.
1951 *The Story of My Life*. Edited by Raymond W. Becker. Hollywood: International Correspondent's Publication.
1969 *Fire from on High*. [Los Angeles]: California Heritage Committee.
1969 *The Foursquare Gospel*. Compiled by Raymond L. Cox. [Los Angeles]: California Heritage Committee.
1973 *The Story of My Life*. Waco, Texas: Word Books.
n.d. *The Foursquare Hymnal*. Los Angeles: International Church of the Foursquare Gospel.
n.d. *Lost and Restored*. Los Angeles: Foursquare Publications.
n.d. *Personal Testimony*. Los Angeles: Foursquare Publications.
n.d. *Songs of the Crimson Road*. Los Angeles: International Church of the Foursquare Gospel.

### Selected Studies about Aimee Semple McPherson

Bahr, Robert. *Least of All Saints: The Story of Aimee Semple McPherson*. Englewood Cliffs, N.J.: Prentice-Hall, 1979.
Clark, David L. "Miracles for a Dime: From Chautauqua Tent to Radio Station with Sister Aimee." *California History* 57 (1978–79): 355–63.
McLoughlin, William G. "Aimee Semple McPherson: 'Your Sister in the King's Glad Service.'" *Journal of Popular Culture* 1 (1967): 193–217.
Mavity, Nancy Barr. *Sister Aimee*. New York: Doubleday, 1931.
*Notable American Women: A Biographical Dictionary*, 1971, s.v. "McPherson, Aimee Semple," by William G. McLoughlin.

Scanzoni, Letha Dawson, and Susan Setta. "Women in Evangelical, Holiness and Pentecostal Traditions." In *Women and Religion in America,* edited by Rosemary Radford Ruether and Rosemary Skinner Keller, 3: 223–35. San Francisco: Harper and Row, Publishers, 1986.

Thomas, Lately [pseud.]. *The Vanishing Evangelist.* New York: Viking, 1959.

Zikmund, Barbara Brown. "The Feminist Thrust of Sectarian Christianity." In *Women of Spirit: Female Leadership in the Jewish and Christian Traditions,* edited by Rosemary Ruether and Eleanor McLaughlin, 206–24. New York: Simon and Schuster, 1979.

L. DeANE LAGERQUIST

# Walter A. Maier

The 1920s ushered in an age of mass popular culture for Americans through the media of film and radio. Even those who had not personally followed the demographic shift from farm to city were included in this cultural migration of the people. Popular cultural dominance and impact was no longer determined solely by the old factors of WASP social hegemony. For immigrant religious communities such as Lutheranism, the new age of radio offered an escape from life on the cultural periphery as well as evangelistic access to the cultural mainstream. Among the most particularist of the American Lutheran groups was the Evangelical Lutheran Synod of Missouri, Ohio and Other States, the so-called "Missouri Synod," which began a painful linguistic transition from German to English only in 1917. In 1924, this branch of the old Lutheran free church tradition, a tradition that had consistently distanced itself from all forms of American revivalism, made a surprise entrance on the stage of American popular religion with a national radio broadcast that would come to be known as "The Lutheran Hour." The broadcast's founder and preacher for its first seventeen seasons was Harvard Ph.D. and Concordia Seminary professor Walter A. Maier.

### Biography

Walter Arthur Maier was born to German immigrant parents in Boston, Massachussetts, on 4 October 1893. Educated at Cotton Mather Public School in Boston-Dorchester and at Concordia Collegiate Institute, Bronxville, New York, Maier received his B.A. degree from Boston University in 1913. In the context of a warm family piety and an upbringing in Zion Evangelical Lutheran Church in Boston, "Wam," as he was known to his student friends, felt drawn to the ordained ministry. He received his B.D. degree from Concordia Seminary, St. Louis, Missouri, in 1916. In that year, Maier returned to Boston to serve as vicar at Zion Church and to undertake further theological studies made possible by a scholarship to the Harvard Divinity School. He was ordained to the ministerium of the Missouri Synod and installed as assistant pastor of Zion Church in 1917. Admitted to the Harvard Graduate School in 1918, Maier earned the

M.A. degree in 1920. He was subsequently admitted to the doctoral program at Harvard in the field of Semitic studies.

Pastoral responsibilities and other churchly involvements prolonged but never entirely interrupted Maier's doctoral studies. He served as U.S. Army chaplain to German prisoners of war along the eastern seaboard during World War I. In 1920, Maier accepted a call to be the first executive secretary of the Walther League, the youth auxiliary of the Missouri Synod. During his two years of service in this capacity, he expanded the Walther League's involvement in home and overseas missions and in diaconal work. Maier served also as editor-in-chief of the youth auxiliary's organ, the *Walther League Messenger,* which continued to increase its circulation in the tens of thousands until his resignation in 1945. As *Messenger* editor, Maier contributed hundreds of editorials and other articles of social, political, and religious commentary.

In 1922, Maier reluctantly accepted a full professorship at Concordia Seminary, the chair of Old Testament Interpretation and History. He felt unworthy of the dignity of the title, since he had not yet completed the Harvard doctorate. This was not seen as a deficit from the perspective of the Missouri Synod. Concordia Professor Theodore Graebner, in particular, stood vehemently opposed to orthodox Lutheran professors accepting advanced degrees from heterodox institutions such as Harvard. Maier's appointment bears witness to an alternative outlook at Concordia at a time of tremendous institutional expansion and corporate self-confidence for that flagship of Old Lutheranism in North America. Maier charged into his teaching responsibilities with characteristic gusto. His marriage to schoolteacher Hulda Eickhoff in 1924 added to the joy of a ministry and a career on the ascendant. The sustaining friendship and home life of Maier's lifetime partner helped him to maintain his focus on personal goals that were not necessarily shared by colleagues or church. In 1929 he received one of the very few doctorates conferred by Harvard in Semitics up until that time.

Though he thus covered himself with academic glory, he would be remembered as a preacher rather than as a scholar and teacher. He first came to public notice as a preacher to mass audiences in 1917. In August of that year, Maier addressed a mission day rally in Clinton, Massachussetts. He returned to Clinton in October to preach a Reformation Day sermon on the 400th anniversary of the posting of Luther's Ninety-five Theses. Both sermons received notice in the Boston press. As Walther League secretary, Maier had many occasions to address mass rallies. In his capacity as *Messenger* editor, the Concordia professor maintained a constant focus on a mass, unseen audience. His decision in 1924 to experiment with the infant medium of radio as an evangelistic tool flowed naturally out of his already established mass preaching and communication ministry.

The national broadcast of the Cox-Harding presidential returns in 1920 had intrigued Maier. The possibilities of radio to combine and extend the ministry of preaching and timely comment seemed boundless to him and to others. Religious radio programming in the United States had begun in January 1921 with the broadcast of an Epiphany service conducted by the Reverend Edwin Jan van Etten, rector of Calvary Episcopal Church, Pittsburgh, Pennsylvania, over station KDKA, Pittsburgh. The "Radio Pulpit of the Air" was begun soon thereafter as the first national religious broadcast series. In 1924, Maier approached Concordia with the proposal that the seminary establish its own radio station. With financial backing from the Walther League, station KFUO, "The Gospel Voice," went on the air for the first time at 9:15 P.M., 14 December 1924. The studio was in an attic. The speaker was Professor Walter A. Maier.

Original weekly features of Radio KFUO included a "Sunday Vespers" series and "Views on the News," commentary on major news stories of the week from a political, social, and religious perspective. Occasionally, services from the Concordia chapel were broadcast. The programming produced a vigorous mail response and newspaper commentary from the St. Louis press. The Lutheran Laymen's League soon added its backing to the project. A radio committee of the seminary that included Maier and the seminary dean, John Henry Charles Fritz, was formed. The St. Louis Lutheran Publicity Organization attempted to provide an annual sum for station operation, enabling KFUO to extend its programming from two hours per week in 1924 to thirty hours per week in 1927. In that year, the station moved from its attic housing on South Jefferson Avenue to the newly constructed and dedicated seminary plant on De Mun Avenue in suburban Clayton. New facilities for the station, built at a cost of $50,000 from Laymen's League contributions, were given to the Missouri Synod in a service of dedication on 27 May 1927.

Maier's radio commentary on current events was paralleled by his new column in the *Messenger,* "Turret of the Times." The Lutheran radio preacher offered social criticism of jazz-age libertinism and materialism, and he launched especially pointed and sustained attacks on the religious expression of liberal theology, "modernism," with its emphasis on the social and psychological dimension of Christianity at the expense of the supernatural and classical theological themes. Maier surprised the news media with his constructive comment on contemporary youth and his decidedly nonpietistic stance on such burning issues of the day as temperance, bobbed hair, and the use of cosmetics. He differed sharply and openly with other 1920s evangelists on and off radio in his criticism of the call for a return to the good old days of American religiosity. For Maier, that was a time which never was. Listener mail response soared, as did subscriptions to the *Messenger.* Under Maier's editorship, the Lutheran youth magazine's circulation went from 7,000 to 80,000.

The 1929 crash meant financial belt-tightening for all religious denominations. The Missouri Synod could no longer sustain the Maier broadcasts as before. In 1930, the Laymen's League assumed this burden. The decision under Maier's leadership, even at such a dark hour, was to move forward. "The Lutheran Hour" was born through an arrangement with CBS. The Hour's first broadcast originated from station WHK in Cleveland, Ohio, on 2 October 1930. It was a Thursday evening program following "The Shadow." In its first year of broadcasting, the Hour received more mail than any other religious radio program in the United States. Every fourth program was devoted to youth, "The Young People's Lutheran Hour," with the Walther League underwriting the cost.

Underwriting sufficient to meet the prohibitive costs of network broadcasting continued to be a problem that plagued Maier throughout the "Lutheran Hour's" second season. CBS executives threatened more than once to drop the program; funding was provided in some instances only hours before air time. Maier determined that the Hour should not be continued on such a basis. Broadcasts were interrupted beginning in June 1931 and would not be resumed until a sure financial basis could be arranged.

The three-year hiatus in "Lutheran Hour" broadcasting that followed provoked a public reaction. Plaudits for the Hour and for Maier's preaching came from every quarter of American religion, including the American Jewish community. The Roman Catholic press, in particular the pages of *Our Sunday Visitor,* carried praise for Maier's attacks on religious modernism and his defense of high Christology and the divine inspiration of Scripture. The secular press too was curious about what was to become of the Hour and its widely respected preacher. Maier declined to be interviewed by the *St. Louis Globe-Democrat* in 1932. He gave in to requests for an interview from a reporter for the Hearst Corporation's Sunday supplement, as part of a review of his book *For Better, Not for Worse: A Manual of Christian Matrimony.* Maier was repaid for his one-time concession to celebrity status by a distorted reportage of the interview and book in both prose and cartoon.

With underwriting from Barney Knudsen, the Lutheran president of GM's Chevrolet division, the "Lutheran Hour" began its second series with the Mutual Broadcasting System in 1935. Transcription broadcasts began with the Hour's seventh season in 1939, together with shortwave transmission. An international radio ministry in many languages now had its beginning.

The new series of "Lutheran Hour" broadcasts provided Maier with a new means to devote his energies to preaching without undue financial worry. Private underwriting, Walther League and Laymen's League support, and listener contributions enabled the Old Testament professor and his largely volunteer staff to carry on, week after week, and to plan for future expansion. The early decades of the Hour's new series were not without conflict, however. There was a prolonged dispute with the Federal Council of Churches, which sought at one point to have all paid religious broadcasting banned by the Federal Communications Commission. Ultimately, the FCC permitted the Hour to remain on the air, but the networks never granted the free or reduced-cost air time for which Maier had long hoped.

Early on, Maier adopted a radio preaching format that remained constant throughout his broadcast ministry. Introduced by announcer R. W. Janetzke as "Professor of Old Testament Interpretation and History, Dr. Maier," Maier would launch into the twenty-minute address with a prayer but without further salutation to the listener. A story or item from current events would follow.

After a lead-in paragraph in which the biblical theme and text were announced, the body of the sermon would typically revolved around a problem-solution/law-gospel outline in two, three, or (rarely) four parts. A conclusion with a summary of the message and an invitation to accept Christ was followed by an intercessory prayer for the listener. The sense of urgency and conviction in each Maier broadcast and the strong biblical content were the most frequently admired characteristics of his preaching, judging from listener mail. His machine-gun delivery, necessitated in part by the limitations of air time, was Maier's signature. His *Seelsorge,* his genuine spiritual care for the listener, was what came through the verbal torrent loud and clear.

Listener mail had to be handled by a small army of volunteer and paid staff. Form responses were sent to those writing to register support, but Maier responded personally to each "problem" letter, dictating a word of counsel to his stenographers. The burden of teaching, the radio ministry that developed into a television ministry in Maier's last year, and the scores of mass rallies at which he preached was borne at great cost in no way offset by monetary compensation beyond his professor's salary and travel expenses paid by the Lutheran Laymen's League. When the opportunity for a long-overdue sabbatical presented itself, some members of the seminary board of control sought to evict the Maier family from faculty housing on the grounds that the professor was devoting too little time to teaching. A grateful Missouri Synod responded firmly to this shortsightedness. Until his death from a heart attack in 1950, Maier was affirmed by his church in the ministry that had taken its message far beyond the ethnic cultural confines of German-American Old Lutheranism.

### Appraisal

As one of the founders of American mass-media evangelism, Walter A. Maier made a distinctive mark on the world of American popular religion, though his precise impact is difficult if not impossible to gauge. As a public figure who entered the arena of civil discourse through his social and political commentary, as a Lutheran theologian of Old Lutheran stamp, and as a radio preacher, Maier and the ministry he began stand out in sharp relief against the backdrop of the radio evangelism of his own day and the "electric church" of the present.

As a public figure, Maier was unabashedly patriotic, a Jeffersonian democrat to the core, consistently opposed to racial and ethnic bigotry in both its religious and social manifestations. His membership in an ethnic minority that was suspect during World War I made it impossible for Maier to indulge in the WASP chauvinism and warmongering of the religious era in which he grew up. He expressly opposed the racism and fascism of the likes of Father Charles Coughlin while being himself accused of Nazi sympathies because of his sympathetic attitude toward Hitler's social and economic program in the mid 1930s and because of his consistent opposition to atheistic communism. Maier was later openly critical of the Nazi regime and especially of its policy toward European Jewry, whereas the official organ of his church, the *Lutheran Witness,* remained completely silent on this issue throughout World War II. Maier upheld American democratic values as ideals for Christian youth while avoiding the moralism of a fictitious "return" to a Christian American.

As a theologian, Maier never deviated a hair's breadth from the official teaching of the Missouri Synod or the Lutheran orthodoxy he had been taught at Concordia Seminary under Franz Pieper's presidency. His personal investment in the Lutheran theological traditional and his Harvard education insured that Maier's basic attitude could never be that of an anti-intellectual. His repeated attacks on radio and in the pages of the *Walther League Messenger* on so-called modernism and "the classroom atheist" are to be interpreted in light of his high regard for academia, the life of the mind, and the scholarly research that his preaching ministry prevented him from pursuing beyond the doctoral dissertation. Within the fundamentalist-modernist controversy of the twenties and thirties Maier did, without doubt, open a door to those with fundamentalist predilections to the classical tradition of Reformation theology and Lutheran church doctrine and practice. In identifying himself in early broadcasts and articles as a "fundamentalist," only later qualifying his use of this term and preferring the label "fundamental," Maier may have lent Lutheran respectability to the American fundamentalism that helped to facilitate his denomination's shift in that direction and its sharp turn away from union with other Lutheran bodies in the mid 1970s. As a public exponent of Protestant orthodoxy at precisely the time in which neo-orthodoxy was making inroads in America, Maier may indeed have aided in the postwar religious revival by making historic, doctrinal Protestantism an option worth considering in the American popular religious supermarket. The Lutheran Hour and its founding preacher raised the public profile of all of American Lutheranism immeasurably.

On the American scene, Maier was distinctive as a radio evangelist. He was neither a prophet of doom nor a guru of positive thinking. The structure and much of the content of his preaching provide an enduring homiletical model. His vision of radio evangelism seems ironic in view of the contemporary development of the "electric church." The radio, Maier hoped, would prevent any cult of the preacher's personality, for it would conceal the messenger and reveal only the message. Parish clergy were constantly referred to as workers in the Lutheran Hour ministry, and listeners were urged to make contact with them or to send in their names for referral to the Missouri Synod Lutheran pastor nearest them. Despite this self-effacing attitude toward his work, Maier's death left a void that was never completely filled by any of his successors on the program.

Lawrence Acker stepped into the breach in 1950, followed by Armin Oldsen in 1951 and, after a two-year interruption in broadcasting, Oswald Hoffman in 1955.

## Survey of Criticism

The voluminous literature specifically treating Walter A. Maier is mostly testimonial in nature or related to Maier's position on specific issues. A comprehensive bibliography of secondary sources is provided in the biography by Maier's younger son, Paul L. Maier, *A Man Spoke, A World Listened: The Story of Walter A. Maier and the Lutheran Hour*. Paul Maier surveys every phase of his father's life and career in rich and memorable detail. He sees "Wam" in his variegated ministry as quite definitely a part of the post–World War II religious revival and as at least a peripheral influence on the grass-roots impact of neo-orthodoxy. Paul Maier calls attention to the "Lutheran Hour's" role in extending the mission and vision of the Missouri Synod, much to the chagrin of arch-confessionalists who accused Dr. Maier of elitism and theological "unionism" as evidenced by his willingness not only to preach to but also to pray with non-Missourians and even non-Lutherans. Paul Maier regrets his father's failure to draw a sufficiently distinct line between his own orthodox Lutheranism and fundamentalism.

Missouri Synod theologian Milton L. Rudnick gives an extensive treatment of Maier in his published doctoral dissertation, *Fundamentalism and the Missouri Synod: A Historical Study of Their Interaction and Mutual Influence*. Rudnick, like Paul Maier, sees Walter A. Maier as doctrinally orthodox and biblical in the inerrantist tradition of the Missouri Synod but not as a pure biblicist in the ahistorical, nondoctrinal sense of American fundamentalism. Rudnick points to the "Lutheran Hour" as a refuge for many from the extreme dispensationalist preaching of the fundamentalist churches and as a bridge over which many of these Christians crossed into the Missouri Synod fold. Rudnick dubs Maier the sole Lutheran "ambassador" to American fundamentalism.

Two master's theses, L. E. Zeitler's "An Investigation of the Factors of Persuasion in the Sermons of Dr. Walter A. Maier" and Michael C. Wolfram's "Dr. Walter A. Maier's Use of Preventative Group Therapy in His Preaching Against Divorce," attempt critical assessments of Maier's preaching while viewing him very definitely as one of the authoritative fathers of the Missouri Synod. Walter A. Maier has yet to be thoroughly studied as an individual American theologian. The twenty volumes of Lutheran Hour sermons edited by him, together with his monographs and several volumes of devotional booklets, provide ample source material for future study.

## Bibliography

### Books by Walter A. Maier

1931   *The Lutheran Hour*. St. Louis: Concordia.
1935   *Christ for Every Crisis*. St. Louis: Concordia.
1935   *For Better, Not for Worse: A Manual of Christian Matrimony*. St. Louis: Concordia. First of three editions.
1936   *Christ for the Nation*. St. Louis: Concordia.
1937   *Fourth Lutheran Hour*. St. Louis: Concordia.
1938   *The Cross from Coast to Coast*. St. Louis: Concordia.
1939   *The Radio for Christ*. St. Louis: Concordia.
1940   *Peace through Christ*. St. Louis: Concordia.

1941   *Courage in Christ.* St. Louis: Concordia.
1942   *For Christ and Country.* St. Louis: Concordia.
1943   *Victory through Christ.* St. Louis: Concordia.
1944   *America, Turn to Christ!* St. Louis: Concordia.
1945   *Beautiful Savior.* St. Louis: Concordia.
1945   *Christ, Set the World Aright!* St. Louis: Concordia.
1946   *Jesus Christ, Our Hope.* St. Louis: Concordia.
1946   *My Suffering Redeemer.* St. Louis: Concordia.
1946   *Rebuilding with Christ.* St. Louis: Concordia.
1947   *Christ Crucified.* St. Louis: Concordia.
1947   *Let Us Return Unto the Lord.* St. Louis: Concordia.
1948   *The Airwaves Proclaim Christ.* St. Louis: Concordia.
1948   *Christ Died for Us.* St. Louis: Concordia.
1948   *He Will Abundanly Pardon.* St. Louis: Concordia.
1949   *Behold the Lamb of God.* St. Louis: Concordia.
1949   *Global Broadcasts of His Grace.* St. Louis: Concordia.
1950   *Go Quickly and Tell.* St. Louis: Concordia.
1950   *One Thousand Radio Voices for Christ.* St. Louis: Concordia.
1959   *The Book of Nahum.* Edited by George V. Schick. St. Louis: Concordia.

The list of the more than 800 periodical articles by Walter A. Maier is available from Concordia Historical Institute, St. Louis, Missouri. Cassette recordings of Maier's sermons from his last two seasons on the "Lutheran Hour" are available from Station KFUO Lutheran Radio, St. Louis, Missouri.

### Selected Studies about Walter A. Maier

*Lutheran Cyclopedia*, 2nd ed., s.v. "Maier, Walter Arthur," by Lester E. Zeitler.
Maier, Paul L. *A Man Spoke, A World Listened: The Story of Walter A. Maier and the Lutheran Hour.* New York: McGraw-Hill, 1963.
Rudnick, Milton L. *Fundamentalism and the Missouri Synod: A Historical Study of Their Interaction and Mutual Influence.* St. Louis: Concordia, 1966. See especially chapters 9 and 10.
Wolfram, Michael C. "Dr. Walter A. Maier's Use of Preventative Group Therapy in His Preaching Against Divorce." Master's thesis, Concordia Theological Seminary, 1977.
Zeitler, Lester E. "An Investigation of the Factors of Persuasion in the Sermons of Dr. Walter A. Maier." Master's thesis, Concordia Seminary, 1956.

GUY C. CARTER

# Malcolm X (Malcolm Little)

A collage outside the municipal building in Mound Bayou, Mississippi, a historically black town in the impoverished Delta region, depicts several black leaders. Alongside such figures as Martin Luther King, Jr.*, O. J. Simpson, Mary McLeod Bethune, and Jackie Robinson hangs the visage of Malcolm X, a leader of the Black Muslim movement during the fifties and early sixties. Although the pastor of Mound Bayou's African Methodist Episcopal Church

knew of no Black Muslims among Mound Bayou's 3,000 residents, Malcolm
X's influence on black consciousness was so profound that he merits inclusion
in almost anyone's pantheon of twentieth-century leaders—even in Mound
Bayou, Mississippi.

## Biography

Born in Omaha, Nebraska, on 19 May 1925, Malcolm Little later recalled
several childhood events that seared his memory and helped to shape the direction
of his life. The first, according to *The Autobiography of Malcolm X,* came on
a night in 1929 when two white men, trying to intimidate Malcolm's father, an
itinerant Baptist minister and a follower of Marcus Garvey*, set fire to the family
house outside of Lansing, Michigan. Amid pistol shots and flames and smoke,
the family stood outside and watched their home tumble down in flames. The
white policemen and firemen watched too, Malcolm recalled, and did nothing
to extinguish the blaze. The Black Legion, a white racist group Malcolm believed
was responsible for the arson, continued to hound Malcolm's father, and he died
under mysterious circumstances when Malcolm was six years old.

The second incident that Malcolm recalled from his childhood occurred while
he was in the eighth grade, when his English teacher asked what he had in mind
for a career. Malcolm, one of the top three students in his class, replied that he
wanted to be a lawyer, whereupon the teacher, whom Malcolm remembered as
a kindly, well-meaning man, suggested that a more realistic vocation for a
"nigger" was carpentry.

"It was then," Malcolm remembered, "that I began to change—inside." He
withdrew from white people, he neglected his studies, and at the end of the
eighth grade he went to Boston to live with his older sister. There, in the Roxbury
section of Boston and later in Harlem, he plunged into a world of hustling,
numbers, pimping, drugs, zoot suits, "conked" hair, and lindy-hopping. Malcolm's immersion in ghetto life soon led to narcotic dependencies and, eventually, to arrest and conviction on charges of burglary.

In 1948, while serving a ten-year sentence in the Massachusetts prison system,
Malcolm's brother wrote to him about the Nation of Islam, the "natural religion
for the black man," to which several of Malcolm's siblings had recently converted. Malcolm, known as "Satan" in the penitentiary for his vile language
and his antireligious attitudes, soon began eschewing pork and cigarettes, the
initial steps in this new religious discipline.

The theology of the Nation of Islam, propagated first by Master Wallace D.
Fard in the Detroit ghettos and later popularized by the Honorable Elijah Muhammad, struck Malcolm with the force of divine revelation. There is one god,
Malcolm learned; his name is Allah. The white man is the devil who has successfully brainwashed the black man into thinking he is inferior. The devil white
man has robbed the black man of his soul, his history, his dignity, and his true
identity as the "Original Man" and the progenitor of a glorious, ancient civilization.

History's greatest crime, the Nation of Islam taught, was the traffic in slavery, when white captors seized blacks from Africa and brought them to the West in chains. "The devil white man cut these black people off from any knowledge of their own kind," Malcolm later recounted, "and cut them off from any knowledge of their own language, religion, and past culture, until the black man in America was the earth's only race of people who had absolutely no knowledge of his true identity." In America, blacks felt the sting, the toil, and the torture of slavery. The white man convinced the black man that his native Africa was peopled with heathens and savages, and he foisted on blacks a religion of a white god, Christianity. So complete was this brainwashing that the black man in America came to believe that he was superior if he had a lighter complexion, if his blood held more of the pollution of the white slavemaster. This "Negro," so named by the white man, knew nothing of his true identity; he did not even know his true family name.

The Black Muslim account of "Yacub's History" taught a far different version of human origins than that propagated by the white man. The first beings, all black, founded the Holy City of Mecca, but about 6,600 years ago an evil man named Yacub, exiled to the island of Patmos with 59,999 other malcontents, set out to create a demon race. Through eugenics, Yacub succeeded in breeding the lighter, recessive genes until he came up with a lighter, weaker race of people who were susceptible to wickedness and evil. These blond, blue-eyed devils were exiled to Europe, whereupon Allah sent Moses to civilize them and decreed that this devil white race would rule for 6,000 years. But just as Moses the prophet was sent to civilize the white man and Jesus the prophet was sent to civilize the Jews, now the Prophet Elijah Muhammad had come to civilize blacks and lead them out of their oppression. The end of "spook civilization" was imminent and would occur sometime around the year 2000, when the white devils and their religion (Christianity) would be destroyed and blacks would reclaim their rightful place as leaders.

Malcolm recalled being "struck numb" by these teachings; he compared the force of this revelation with Paul's blinding conversion on the road to Damascus. Everything in his past—his father's death at the hands of white racists, his eighth-grade teacher's remarks about vocation, his ghetto existence, even the excruciating pain of conking his hair with lye in order to straighten it and appear more "white"—verified these teachings. Eager now to stretch his eighth-grade education, he copied every page of the dictionary, word for word, including diacritical marks. Armed with a new understanding and appreciation for words, he corresponded daily with Elijah Muhammad and read voraciously everything he could check out of the prison library. Even after lights out he would lie on the floor of his cell and read in the meager light that filtered under the door.

Malcolm began spreading the "truth" about the devil white man to his black brothers even before his release from prison, but after his parole in 1952 he became a firebrand, disseminating the teachings of Elijah Muhammad in the Detroit ghettos. At Elijah Muhammad's direction, Malcolm rejected his surname

"Little" and took the name "X" to symbolize his true African family name that he could never know. Minister Malcolm X eventually returned to Boston to help organize a temple, then went on to Philadelphia to organize another. Elijah Muhammad next appointed Malcolm as minister of Temple Seven in New York City. His organizing skills, dogged persistence, and impassioned oratory about black self-respect and the depredations of the white man soon began to win converts. Malcolm would invite blacks to assess how they and their neighbors lived and then to go across Central Park and to downtown Manhattan to see how whites lived, to see what the white man's religion had done for him, how it stripped the black man of his dignity even as it promised a better life in the hereafter.

Malcolm urged blacks to reject their ghetto mentality and lifestyle, which only perpetuated their subjection. In addition to proscriptions against pork and cigarettes, the Nation of Islam demanded abstinence from alcohol, narcotics, dancing, gambling, and fornication. Black Muslims emphasized the importance of a strong, stable family life and insisted that black men "shelter and respect" black women. After some hesitation, Malcolm himself took a wife, Sister Betty X, of the New York mosque.

As the media caught on to the Black Muslims, Malcolm, who called himself "the angriest black man in America," quickly emerged as the Nation of Islam's most forceful and effective ambassador. His command of facts and his unswerving conviction made him a formidable debater whose rhetoric frightened whites (and many blacks) while he won support among lower-class, urban blacks. Elijah Muhammad sent him to various cities around the country to organize new temples or to address great rallies of blacks, whose size and enthusiasm recalled those of Marcus Garvey decades earlier. Malcolm founded a newspaper, *Muhammad Speaks,* to disseminate news about the Nation of Islam and to propagate Black Muslim teachings. Malcolm taught that racial desegregation was still another attempt on the part of the devil white man to placate blacks while denying them any real justice, a posture that placed him at odds with Martin Luther King, Jr. Malcolm called the 1963 March on Washington a "monumental farce" and reviled the "Uncle Tom" blacks, the "house and yard Negroes," well educated and middle class, who spoke out against the separatist teachings of the Nation of Islam.

As early as 1961, Malcolm, who now held the title of National Minister, began to get wind of resentments building against him within the Nation of Islam. Although he insisted that he was always a loyal and self-effacing servant of Elijah Muhammad, rumors circulated that he had ambitions of taking over the movement. By 1962 Malcolm learned that Elijah Muhammad had violated his own teachings about marital fidelity and that he faced paternity suits brought against him by two former secretaries. Malcolm eventually—and reluctantly—confirmed these rumors, and shortly thereafter Elijah Muhammad silenced him for ninety days, ostensibly because of his highly publicized remark that John Kennedy's assassination was a case of "the chickens coming home to roost."

Malcolm became suspicious of threats to his life from within the Nation of Islam, and he began planning his own organization, Muslim Mosque, Inc., to advance the social, economic, and political agenda of black people.

In a lifetime marked by personal transformations, Malcolm's pilgrimage *(hajj)* to the Islamic holy city of Mecca ranks behind only his conversion to the Nation of Islam as the most formative. Exposed to orthodox Islam for the first time, he was overwhelmed by the hospitality he received and by the absence of any race consciousness among his fellow pilgrims. Malcolm began, he recalled, "to perceive that 'white man,' as commonly used, means complexion only second-arily; primarily it describes attitudes and actions." The color blindness of the Islamic world inspired him to renounce his blanket condemnation of all whites as devils, even as he insisted that white America had consistently denied justice to the black man. He spoke about going to the United Nations to bring charges against the United States for refusing to deal justly with American blacks. Fresh from a visit to black Africa at the conclusion of his pilgrimage, he referred to America as a colonial power because it offered blacks only second-class citizenship.

Malcolm had returned to America with the Arabic name El-Hajj Malik El-Shabazz and with a resolve to broaden his black nationalist appeal to non-Muslim blacks; the need for economic solidarity and self-sufficiency, he believed, transcended religious boundaries. Amid the uncertain climate among American blacks, heightened by the tensions between Malcolm and Elijah Muhammad, however, his Organization for Afro-American Unity foundered. Malcolm's premonitions about his own violent death at the hands of Elijah Muhammad's operatives came true on Sunday, 21 February 1965. As he addressed the Organization for Afro-American Unity rally at the Audubon Ballroom, on West 166th Street between Broadway and St. Nicholas Avenue in New York City, several gunmen stood and fired sixteen bullets into him.

The assassination of Malcolm X received press attention throughout the world. In Harlem, 22,000 people filed past the bier of this black leader, struck down three months short of his fortieth birthday, and the remains of El-Hajj Malik El-Shabazz, also known as Malcolm X and born as Malcolm Little, were interred at Ferncliff Cemetery in Ardsley, New York.

### Appraisal

Malcolm's influence on black consciousness has extended well beyond his lifetime, and his ideas have transcended racial boundaries. His autobiography alerted many whites to the rage simmering in American ghettos, and it indicted them for their continued complicity in the problem of racism. Malcolm's teachings, his self-assurance, and his personal example of renouncing the trappings of ghetto life infused a measure of hope and dignity into black America. Throughout his career as a Black Muslim minister he assailed the "magnolia myth" of black docility and inferiority and sought to replace it with the doctrine of black supremacy, a notion that, to some degree, has taken hold among blacks from

Harlem to Los Angeles to Mound Bayou, Mississippi. Even if they reject his religious views, many blacks continue to look to Malcolm X as a source of inspiration.

## Survey of Criticism

After Malcolm's death in 1965, a kind of Malcolm X cult emerged, which produced several hagiographical sketches of his life, reprinted his speeches (often in pamphlet form), and examined the circumstances surrounding his death, generally asserting that some sort of government conspiracy had slain Malcolm, not the Nation of Islam. The best inquiry into Malcolm's death, one that manages to maintain a measure of objectivity, is Peter Goldman's *The Death and Life of Malcolm X*.

In recent years two bibliographies, one selected and the other comprehensive and annotated, have appeared: Lenwood G. Davis, compiler, *Malcolm X: A Selected Bibliography*, and Timothy V. Johnson, *Malcolm X: A Comprehensive Annotated Bibliography*. The very appearance of published bibliographies suggests the volume of secondary literature that Malcolm X has inspired. The finest accounts of Malcolm X and the Black Muslims remain, however, E. U. Essien-Udom's *Black Nationalism: A Search for an Identity in America*, which examines the black nationalist impulse, and the revised edition of C. Eric Lincoln's landmark study, *The Black Muslims in America*. Although it antedates the Nation of Islam, Arthur Huff Fauset's *Black Gods of the Metropolis: Negro Religious Cults in the Urban North* provides a context for understanding the rise of the Black Muslims.

*The Autobiography of Malcolm X* is unabashedly tendentious. It also provides the best insight into the life and thought of Malcolm X.

## Bibliography

### Books by Malcolm X (Malcolm Little)

1965    *The Autobiography of Malcolm X*. With the assistance of Alex Haley. New York: Grove Press.
1965    *Malcolm X Speaks: Selected Speeches and Statements*. Edited by George Breitman. New York: Merit Publishers.
1965    *Two Speeches by Malcolm X*. New York: Pioneer Publishers.
1968    *The Speeches of Malcolm X at Harvard*. Edited by Archie Epps. New York: William Morrow.
1969    *Malcolm X and the Negro Revolution: The Speeches of Malcolm X*. Edited by Archie Epps. London: Owen.
1970    *By Any Means Necessary: Speeches, Interviews, and a Letter by Malcolm X*. Edited by George Breitman. New York: Pathfinder Books.
1970    *Malcolm X on Afro-American History*. New York: Merit Books.
1971    *The End of White World Supremacy: Four Speeches of Malcolm X*. Edited by Benjamin Goodman. New York: Merlin House.

### Selected Studies about Malcolm X (Malcolm Little)

Balk, Alfred, and Alex Haley. "Black Merchants of Hate: The Black Muslims." *Saturday Evening Post* 236 (26 January 1963): 68–74.

Breitman, George. *The Last Year of Malcolm X*. New York: Pathfinder Press, 1967.

Clarke, John Henrik. *Malcolm X: The Man and His Time*. New York: Macmillan, 1969.

Davis, Lenwood G., comp. With the assistance of Marsha L. Moore. *Malcolm X: A Selected Bibliography*. Westport, Conn.: Greenwood Press, 1984.

Essien-Udom, E. U. *Black Nationalism: A Search for an Identity in America*. Chicago: University of Chicago Press, 1962.

Fauset, Arthur. *Black Gods of the Metropolis: Negro Religious Cults in the Urban North*. Philadelphia: University of Pennsylvania Press, 1944.

Goldman, Peter. *The Death and Life of Malcolm X*. 2d ed. Urbana: University of Illinois Press, 1979.

Haley, Alex. "Playboy Interview: Malcolm X." *Playboy* 10 (May 1963): 53–54.

Johnson, Timothy V. *Malcolm X: A Comprehensive Annotated Bibliography*. New York: Garland Publishing Co., 1986.

Lincoln, C. Eric. *The Black Muslims in America*. Rev. ed. Boston: Beacon Press, 1973.

————. "The Meaning of Malcolm X." *Christian Century* 82 (7 April 1965): 431–33.

Lomax, Louis E. *When the World Is Given: A Report on Elijah Muhammad, Malcolm X, and the Black Muslim World*. Cleveland: World Publishing Co., 1963.

Marsh, Clifton E. *From Black Muslims to Muslims: The Transition from Separatism to Islam, 1930–1980*. Metuchen, N.J.: Scarecrow Press, 1984.

Parenti, Michael. "The Black Muslims: From Revolution to Institution." *Social Research* 31 (1964): 175–94.

Warren, Robert Penn. "Malcolm X: Mission and Meaning." *Yale Review* 56 (Winter 1967): 161–71.

Wolfenstein, E. Victor. *The Victims of Democracy: Malcolm X and the Black Revolution*. Berkeley and Los Angeles: University of California Press, 1981.

RANDALL BALMER

# Peter and Catherine Marshall

When Peter Marshall, beloved chaplain of the U.S. Senate, died at the age of forty-six in January 1949, few would have guessed that before very long his hitherto reserved wife, Catherine, would make both their names household words across America. That is what happened, though, with the publication later that fall of the best-selling sermon anthology *Mr. Jones, Meet the Master* and the appearance two years later of the phenomenally popular biography *A Man Called Peter*. If American society has recently been split down the middle into "Christian" and "secular humanist" camps, the spiritual climate was very different when the Marshalls' words of hope were first embraced by an entire generation, hungry for security in the wake of World War II. What exactly was going on in this national love affair between a minister's family and the American people?

## Biography

Details of the Marshalls' lives are well known to readers of Catherine's books. Peter was born in Coatbridge, Scotland, on 27 May 1902. His father was an insurance agent who died when the boy was only four. Though Mrs. Marshall soon remarried, Peter always yearned for the father he had lost, and family antagonisms coupled with a passion for the sea prompted a series of abortive adolescent attempts to join the British navy. Instead, he eventually ended up working as a machinist in a tube mill while studying at night. During this period he was greatly influenced by Olympic runner/missionary Eric Liddell. This experience, along with one dramatic incident in which God seemed to intervene miraculously to save him from a near-fatal accident, convinced Peter he was being called to Christian service. A visiting cousin suggested he would have better opportunities in America, and he left his beloved Scotland in 1927.

Soon after his arrival in the United States, Peter found himself digging ditches for public service in New Jersey, apparently no closer to his goal. His fortunes changed, though, when a boyhood friend now living in Alabama got him a job with the *Birmingham News*. He became involved with the city's First Presbyterian Church, where his gifts were soon recognized, and with the financial backing of his men's Bible study group, he began training at Columbia Seminary in Decatur, Georgia.

After graduation he served for three years as a pastor in Covington; then, in May 1933, he accepted a call to Westminster Presbyterian Church in Atlanta, where he transformed that dying body into a standing-room-only congregation. Apart from his natural talent as a preacher, the content of his message had special appeal to men and women traumatized by the Great Depression, for his faith was above all practical. He believed in his heart, as a consequence of personal experience, that God can provide daily bread for the stomach as well as for the soul.

It was during this period that Sarah Catherine Wood, then a student at Agnes Scott College in Decatur, came into Peter's life. The daughter of a Presbyterian minister, Catherine was born in Johnson City, Tennessee, on 27 September 1914 and was raised in Canton, Mississippi, and Keyser, West Virginia. Her love of privacy—often as a child she would flee up the back stairs when her father's parishioners came to call—might seem to bode ill for the highly public life she would eventually lead. But if she tended to be reserved, she also had a passion for spiritual reflection and an extraordinary capacity for growth. At the time she met Peter, Catherine was still groping for a personal experience of faith. No wonder she was so drawn by this handsome and inspiring Scotsman.

They were married on 4 November 1936. Characteristically, the very next morning Peter had to meet with the pastoral committee of the Washington, D.C., New York Avenue Church. He turned down their call at that time, only to accept it eleven months later, moving to the nation's capital in 1937, where he continued to grow as a preacher and pastor. Vocational success was nurtured by the creative partnership he and Catherine shared, and their lives were enriched by the birth of their only child, a son, Peter John, in 1940. During this time Peter also became a U.S. citizen and was awarded an honorary doctor of divinity from Presbyterian College in Clinton, South Carolina.

These years were not without crisis, however. In spite of his popularity, Peter encountered intense resistance from certain church leaders who feared his bold faith, whereas Catherine drove herself mercilessly to fulfill the staggering expectations heaped on her by her husband's congregation. In part, perhaps, because of these pressures, she contracted tuberculosis in March 1943 and was ordered to bed, where she remained for over two years. Paradoxically, this illness ultimately facilitated her breakthrough into the vital faith for which she had longed: it was on her sickbed, when she finally came to a point of complete despair and helplessly surrendered herself to God, that she experienced one night a mystical sense of Christ's healing presence and from that point on made steady progress toward recovery.

No sooner had this crisis passed, though, than a new one hit. In 1946 Peter suffered a heart attack in the pulpit, and once more the Marshalls' faith was sorely tested as a terrified Catherine enlisted the prayer support of friends and relatives in a life-and-death battle for Peter's recovery. Recover he did, entering the most fruitful phase of his ministry in January 1947, when he assumed the post of Chaplain to the U.S. Senate in addition to his New York Avenue pastorate. The reprieve, though, was temporary; on 25 January 1949, Peter Marshall suffered a second heart attack, this time fatal.

Untrained vocationally and emotionally, accustomed to a completely dependent relationship with her husband, Catherine seemed ill prepared for life as a single parent. Soon, however, an exciting opportunity presented itself in the form of an invitation from the Fleming H. Revell Co. to edit a book of her husband's sermons. The resulting volume, *Mr. Jones, Meet the Master,* was a runaway best seller following its publication in the fall of 1949, staying on the nonfiction list for close to a year. Then in 1951 came the even more popular *A Man Called Peter,* Catherine's warm, moving account of her husband's life. The reserved young girl had become a celebrity in her own right, and as if to confirm this, her next major book, *To Live Again,* published in 1957, focused on her own personal story.

Still, the heady success of these years left her with a gnawing loneliness. Despite such honors as the 1953 "Woman of the Year" award in literature, presented by the Women's National Press Club, despite all the speaking engagements and article requests and even a movie version of *A Man Called Peter,* released by Twentieth Century-Fox in 1955, Catherine felt increasingly unfulfilled. Eventually she admitted to herself how much she yearned for a second marriage, and on 14 November 1959 she became the wife of Leonard LeSourd, executive editor of *Guideposts* magazine.

This second union was to bring a whole new set of challenges—most notably in the rearing of three young children from Len's first marriage. But she continued her writing, in collaboration now with Len as a kind of "in-house" editor. Together they embarked on a remarkably creative partnership that would see the publication of numerous books including *Beyond Our Selves,* the novel *Christy, Something More, Adventures in Prayer, The Helper, My Personal Prayer Diary* (which they coauthored), *Meeting God at Every Turn,* and *Julie* (published posthumously in 1984). Together with friends John and Elizabeth Sherrill, they founded Chosen Books, a small Christian publishing house that was to distinguish itself with a number of significant titles.

During this time Catherine and Len were constantly pushing forward into new dimensions of faith. They were challenged personally by the loss of two of her grandchildren, even as America was challenged socially and politically by the turbulence in the 1960s and early 1970s. Meanwhile, on the religious front, the "Jesus people" movement, neo-Pentecostalism, and the charismatic renewal on the one hand and the proliferation of cults and Satanism on the other were shaking the churches' status quo. Under these pressures, Catherine and Len became increasingly intrigued with the powers of the Holy Spirit and intercessory prayer, establishing a prayer ministry called "The Intercessors" in 1980.

When Catherine died of an ongoing lung ailment on 18 March 1983, she had just completed a draft of the novel *Julie,* which Len was to edit for posthumous publication in 1984. In addition, she bequeathed to him a lifetime's worth of her journals, from which he selected representative entries for a second post-humous volume entitled *A Closer Walk.* Just as Catherine had expanded Peter's ministry in the wake of his death, Len was now continuing hers.

### Appraisal

Many gifts characterized Peter and Catherine Marshall's ministries. Both were remarkably able communicators, he as a preacher and she as a writer. Both offered a solidly evangelical gospel that transcended theological categories to speak to the needs of ordinary men and women, the "unchurched" as well as the "churched." Yet theirs was not merely the generalized "faith in faith" or the worship of a "man upstairs" that Sydney Ahlstrom and Martin E. Marty (in *A Religious History of the American People* and *Righteous Empire,* respectively) have described as characteristic of the "age of anxiety." Though emphasizing God's practical love and guidance, their message never degenerated into materialism. Indeed, Peter often denounced materialism from the pulpit and in his Senate prayers, just as he pleaded for justice on the national scene.

Some have suggested that Catherine never fully appreciated this dimension of her husband's faith, given her more personal focus. It is probably true that there were differences in emphasis here, but they should not be exaggerated. For Peter always believed, along with his wife, that ultimately justice must spring from the soil of regenerated hearts and could not be instituted by political means alone. In this sense, his faith was as personal as hers.

A pamphlet that the Marshalls coauthored in 1944—a study of Ephesians entitled *The Mystery of the Ages*—sheds interesting light on this question. One is impressed in perusing this little document by their concern for international cooperation in the wake of World War II. What is even more striking, though, is their commitment to Paul's vision in Ephesians of all humanity's being unified under Christ through the vehicle of the church—a church composed of biblically faithful families and spiritually transformed individuals who would help usher in the new age.

Similar themes re-echo in Peter's other writings. His sermon "The American Dream," for example, called on the nation to take seriously the covenantal character of its origins and to apply moral principles to contemporary problems, but again he ultimately laid the responsibility on individual Christians living out their personal lives. On 26 June 1947, as recorded in *The Prayers of Peter Marshall*, he prayed explicitly before the Senate: "Our Father, we are beginning to understand at last that the things that are wrong with our world are the sum total of all the things that are wrong with us as individuals." What he was calling for was the complete transformation of human nature, beginning with those who call themselves Christians. "It is the modern heresy to think that human nature cannot be changed," he said in the sermon "Disciples in Clay," as reprinted in *The Best of Peter Marshall*. It "must be changed if we are ever to have an end to war." He was deadly serious.

His genius was in communicating these challenging notions to ordinary men and women with his "pungent phrasing" and "tart morsels of thought" (to quote from an article in the 11 January 1948 *New York Times Magazine*). Then there was his remarkable ability to dramatize incidents out of the gospels, making Jesus vividly real to his listeners. And always there was his mellifluous style that, if it came in for some friendly teasing early on before he got his verbal extravagance under control, was ultimately to make him, in the words of Dr. Oscar Blackwelder (quoted in *A Man Called Peter*), "one of the most thrilling evangelical preachers" the latter had ever heard.

What, though, of Catherine herself, once she began to write of her own journey in the wake of Peter's death? Perhaps the most striking quality in her work is her capacity to give of herself so intimately, to communicate deep emotion so effectively while still maintaining her clarity, objectivity, and humor. Yet ironically, it is this very strength that has prompted some to fault her for offering an excessively personal faith.

It is undeniable that Catherine tended to focus on her own religious experiences throughout her career—occasionally with a certain amount of repetition. It is also true that she seems primarily concerned with the private realm and the nuclear family, touching on broader social issues more as they impinge on the individual rather than the other way around. One suspects, though, that she would have seen this as an appropriate feminine strength, not a limitation; and most likely Peter would have agreed. After all, he not only guided her into a highly traditional role in their marriage but also espoused and romanticized such traditionalism as an ideal for all women in his famous sermon "Keepers of the Springs."

This orientation toward hearth and home as the main context for a woman's faith journey reflected the consciousness of the fifties, a time when traditional values and family life were being glorified by society as a whole, not just by a "silent" or a "moral" majority. That Catherine was integrated into the feminine (not feminist!) consciousness of her time can be seen from the fact that much of her writing in original, revised, and excerpted form appeared during these years in mainstream women's magazines: *McCall's, Woman's Home Companion, Good Housekeeping*.

Yet Catherine was no mere spokeswoman for the suburban scene, for the faith she offered was deeply challenging. She pointed to a Jesus who wills our happiness, to be sure, but will never protect us from troubles (witness her own life!); rather, he promises to be with us in their midst, working painful circumstances out for our ultimate good if only we seek to cooperate.

What is called for, she taught, is complete submission and surrender to a situation as it actually is, thereby freeing God to work; absolute trust and relinquishment, affirming helplessness as a resource insofar as it encourages us to turn matters over to God; solid commitment to the goals that God has shown us, as we strive for obedience despite rebellious emotions, believing he will change unruly feelings over time. Certainly this was not the message of a mindlessly comforting faith.

In all of this Catherine was influenced not only by Peter but also by the nineteenth-century Quaker writer Hannah Whitall Smith, whom she first encountered on her sickbed in 1944 when she read *The Christian's Secret of a Happy Life*. Hannah Smith was such a crucial influence, with her radical, down-to-earth faith, that Catherine took her work as a model for the spiritual self-help books she herself hoped to write.

Catherine's basic themes remained constant over time, but her vision expanded in important if subtle ways with the publication of *Something More* in 1974. By now her personal world had been shaken once again with the deaths of two grandchildren, just as America's national fabric had been ravaged by protest movements, assassinations, and the Watergate scandal. Hence she seems more conscious of the active power of evil but more aware too, paradoxically, of the power of the Holy Spirit, newly unleashed into this darkness.

This emphasis on the Spirit was not a new discovery: she had first begun to study Scripture on this subject as an invalid in 1944, and the following year she and Peter coauthored a pamphlet on the third person of the Trinity which appeared as the July 1945 issue of the devotional magazine *Today*. But she writes more explicitly of the Holy Spirit in her later books than she did earlier—especially in *The Helper*, which, as a matter of fact, grew out of the 1945 *Today* devotionals.

One can detect other differences in the later work. She seems more theologically adventurous in some ways, explicitly challenging certain positions like the doctrine (which she was taught as a child) that miracles were intended for the early Church alone. As Janice Franzen has pointed out, she also dares to imply in *Something More* that in some sense the Bible is still being written today, as God teaches believers new insights. Not that she intended to undermine scriptural authority; far from it. But she did emphasize the importance of experiential learning and direct communication with the Holy Spirit. In this regard, of course, she was in tune with key trends of the 1960s revival: the "Jesus movement," neo-Pentecostalism, and the charismatic renewal.

### Survey of Criticism

Both Peter and Catherine Marshall have been largely ignored by scholars of American religious history. Their names are generally not even mentioned in standard surveys of American Protestantism, and when they are (as in Martin E. Marty's *Religious Empire* or Sydney Ahlstrom's *Religious History of the American People),* it is usually only in passing. Among the few scholarly essays that are available, Mary Elisabeth Goin's "Catherine Marshall: Three Decades of Popular Religion" assesses its subject from the perspective of the late 1970s, calling Marshall's faith an "excellent example of . . . individualistic Protestantism" with its stress on "personally experienced Christianity" but faulting her for a somewhat "utilitarian element" and for her failure to nudge readers toward greater social responsibility. More recently, Paul Boyer's study, "Minister's Wife, Widow, Reluctant Feminist: Catherine Marshall in the 1950s," has analyzed the conflict between the traditional woman's role she inherited from her husband and her emerging achievements after his death.

If scholarly books and journals have tended to ignore the Marshalls, however, the popular media have not. At the time of Peter Marshall's appointment to the Senate chaplaincy and two years later when he died, a flurry of articles in sources like *Life,* the *New York Times Magazine,* and *Time* paid tribute to his unique prayer style with its striking imagery and timely content. Shortly thereafter, when Catherine began to publish his sermons posthumously, it became clear that the American nation was embarking on a collective love affair with Peter and his widow.

*A Man Called Peter* signaled a turning point in the Marshall ministry, since it was the first work in which Catherine had a sustained opportunity to stand on her own as a writer. That book was praised by critics as an "unpretentious and infinitely touching" work (1 March 1952 *Saturday Review*) which "touches the heart and appeals to the mind" (7 October 1951 *Chicago Sunday Tribune*) thanks to Catherine's "grace and charm" (7 October 1951 *New York Times*). Reviewers were especially struck with her ability to balance emotion and self-discipline, to enlist reader sympathy without descending into sentimentality.

There were, of course, exceptions to all this goodwill. In *To Live Again* Catherine herself noted a particularly caustic review by a British critic. Closer to home, Albert N. Williams' essay "Our Prettified Prophets," in the 10 April 1954 issue of *Saturday Review,* claimed that *A Man Called Peter,* like other religious best sellers of the day, concerned itself only with "the spiritual comforts available to a Christian of sure faith, and not at all with the religious foundations of that faith."

When Catherine left Peter behind, as it were, to write of her own experiences in *To Live Again,* reviews continued to be mainly positive. The 8 December 1957 *New York Times,* for instance, noted that "she writes of her faith and what faith has done for her with a conviction that has won a response from thousands of readers, transcending barriers of creed, dogma, belief or unbelief.'' Still, more overt hostility began surfacing around this time in the liberal Christian periodicals. There was, for example, Robert H. Glauber's snide review in the 5 February 1958 issue of the *Christian Century,* accusing the book of being "slick and superficial . . . a hodgepodge of emotionalism, recipes, legal information and pseudo-religious philosophizing." Then there was William Baillie Green's essay, "Two Views of Death and Life," which appeared in the 30 March 1959 issue of *Christianity and Crisis,* strongly attacking Catherine's understanding of immortality.

Her fiction too has drawn mixed responses. Whereas the 15 October 1967 *Best Sellers* called *Christy* a "highly charming novel," and Helen K. Hosier described it in her book *Profiles* as a "brilliantly written novel," others did not agree. The 22 October 1967 *New York Times Book Review* bluntly called it "a tract instead of a novel," and *Time* (13 October 1967) noted ironically that "God and the reader will have their task cut out for them in this relentlessly uplifting honeypot." Such criticism aside, though, the sales figures of this book—nearly eight million copies sold just a decade after publication, according to Mary Elisabeth Goin—speak for themselves. If many in the literary establishment did not consider Catherine Marshall much of a novelist, the public clearly did not agree. The posthumous *Julie* was also popular, though many reviewers dubbed it a young adult title and left it at that.

It is interesting that reflections on Catherine Marshall are themselves sometimes testimonial in character. A good example is Kathryn Koob's chapter in *Bright Legacy* (edited by Ann Spangler) in which she not only discusses Catherine's life and work but also shares the impact the books had on Koob herself when she was taken hostage in Iran. This testimonial aspect is not really surprising, for in the final analysis, both Peter and Catherine can be fully appreciated only by readers eager for the faith they have to offer.

## Bibliography

### *Works by Peter and/or Catherine Marshall*

(J = coauthored; P,C = material by Peter, edited/ introduced by Catherine; P = by Peter alone; C = by Catherine alone)

1944    *The Mystery of the Ages.* Philadelphia: Westminster Press. (J)
1945    "Quicken the Spirit Within You." *Reader's Digest* 46 (January 1945): 1, 2. (P)
1949    *The Exile Heart.* Washington, D.C.: Scottish Memorial Committee. (P)
1949    *Mr. Jones, Meet the Master: Sermons and Prayers. . . .* New York: Revell. (P,C)
1951    *A Man Called Peter.* New York: McGraw-Hill. (C; includes sermons by P)
1953    *God Loves You: Our Family's Favorite Stories and Prayers.* New York: McGraw-Hill. (P,C)
1953    "I Learned to Conquer Grief." *Reader's Digest* 63 (July 1953): 17–19. (C)
1953    *Let's Keep Christmas: A Sermon by Peter Marshall.* New York: McGraw-Hill. (P,C)

1953 "My Life Since *A Man Called Peter.*" *McCall's* 80 (August 1953): 28-29, 108, 114–15. (C)
1953 "What I've Learned at Gordon Cosby's Church." *Reader's Digest* 63 (December 1953): 48–52. (C)
1954 *The Prayers of Peter Marshall.* New York: McGraw-Hill. (P,C)
1956 *Friends With God: Stories and Prayers of the Marshall Family.* New York: McGraw-Hill. (P,C)
1956 *The Heart of Peter Marshall's Faith: Two Inspirational Messages from Mr. Jones, Meet the Master.* Westwood, N.J.: Revell. (P,C)
1957 *To Live Again.* New York: McGraw-Hill. (C)
1959 *The First Easter.* New York: McGraw-Hill. (P,C)
1961 *Beyond Our Selves.* New York: McGraw-Hill. (C)
1963 *John Doe, Disciple.* New York: McGraw-Hill. (P,C)
1967 *Christy.* New York: McGraw-Hill. (C)
1968 "How I'm Raising My Second Family." *Good Housekeeping* 166 (January 1968): 76, 77, 129, 130, 132, 133, 135. (C)
1974 *Something More: In Search of a Deeper Faith.* New York: McGraw-Hill. (C)
1975 *Adventures in Prayer.* Chappaqua, N.Y.: Chosen Books. (C)
1978 *The Helper.* Lincoln, Va.: Chosen Books. (C)
1980 *Meeting God at Every Turn.* Lincoln, Va.: Chosen Books. (C)
1982 *Catherine Marshall's Story Bible.* Lincoln, Va. and New York: Chosen Books and Crossroad. (C)
1983 *The Best of Peter Marshall.* Grand Rapids: Chosen Books of the Zondervan Corp. (P,C)
1983 *My Personal Prayer Diary.* New York: Epiphany-Ballantine. Coauthored with Leonard LeSourd. (C)
1984 *Julie.* New York: McGraw-Hill. (C)
1986 *A Closer Walk: Spiritual Discoveries From Her Journals.* Edited by Leonard LeSourd. Old Tappan, N.J: Chosen-Revell. (C)

### Selected Studies about Peter and Catherine Marshall

"Author Catherine Marshall Dies." *Christianity Today* 27 (22 April 1983): 36, 38.
Balliett, Whitney. "Champion of Chaplains." *Saturday Review* 36 (10 April 1954): 28–29.
Boyer, Paul. "Minister's Wife, Widow, Reluctant Feminist: Catherine Marshall in the 1950s." *American Quarterly* 30 (Winter 1978): 703–21.
"Busy Widow of Peter." *Newsweek* 45 (4 April 1955): 60.
"*Christy.*" (Brief notice.) *Time* 90 (13 October 1967): 117, 119.
Davies, A. P. "In the Scottish Tradition." *New York Times Book Review* (7 October 1951): 30.
Eidus, Janice. Review of *Julie. New York Times Book Review,* Sec. 7 (28 October 1984): 26.
Franzen, Janice. "Something More About Catherine." *Christian Life* 36 (November 1974): 32, 33, 63.
"A Full, Religious Life." *Life* 38 (4 April 1955): 115, 116, 118, 120.
Glauber, Robert H. "Bathos." *Christian Century* 75 (5 February 1958): 169.
Goin, Mary Elisabeth. "Catherine Marshall: Three Decades of Popular Religion." *Journal of Presbyterian History* 56 (Fall 1978): 219–35.

Green, William Baillie. "Two Views of Death and Life." *Christianity and Crisis* 19 (30 March 1959): 36, 37.

Harrington, Janette T. "Chaplain of the Senate." *Presbyterian Life* 1 (27 March 1948): 12, 13, 28.

Hosier, Helen Kooiman. "Dreams Can Come True: Author Catherine Marshall LeSourd." In *Profiles: People Who Are Helping to Change the World,* Chap. 7. New York: Hawthorn Books, 1977.

Koob, Kathryn. "Catherine Marshall." In *Bright Legacy: Portraits of Ten Outstanding Christian Women,* edited by Ann Spangler, Chap. 3. Ann Arbor: Mich.: Servant Books, 1983.

LeSourd, Leonard. "Our Adventure With Intercessory Prayer." *Decision* 26 (April 1985): 15–16.

"Marshall, Peter, Rev." Entry in *Current Biography: Who's News and Why,* edited by Anna Rothe. New York: H. W. Wilson Co., 1948.

"Marshall, (Sarah) Catherine." Entry in *Contemporary Authors, New Revision Series,* vol. 8, edited by Ann Evory and Linda Metzger. Detroit: Gale Research Co. 1983.

"Marshall, (Sarah) Catherine (Wood)." Entry in *Current Biography Yearbook,* edited by Marjorie Dent Candee. New York: H. W. Wilson Co., 1955.

"Ministers to Congress." *Newsweek* 29 (13 January 1947): 72.

"Plain and Pertinent." *Time* 53 (7 February 1949): 13.

Pompea, I. N. Review of *Christy. Best Sellers* 27 (15 October 1967): 278.

Seidenspinner, Clarence. Review of *A Man Called Peter. Chicago Sunday Tribune* (7 October 1951): 3.

"Senate's Chaplain." *Life* 26 (7 February 1949): 38.

Silver, Adele. "Doing Good." *New York Times Book Review,* sec. 7 (22 October 1967): 70.

Skaggs, Peggy. "Catherine Marshall." Entry in *American Women Writers,* vol. 3, edited by Lina Mainiero. New York: Ungar, 1981.

Solons, Shepherd." *New York Times Magazine,* sec. 6 (11 January 1948): 14.

Taylor, Pamela. "Security of Faith." *Saturday Review* 35 (1 March 1952): 12.

Williams, Albert N. "Our Prettified Prophets." *Saturday Review* 36 (10 April 1954): 26–28.

Yezierska, Anzia. "With a Sense of Mission." *New York Times Book Review* 62 (8 December 1957): 10.

ELISE CHASE

# Thomas James Merton (Father M. Louis Merton)

In his book *Blue Highways,* William Least Heat Moon recalls a conversation he once had with a Trappist monk at Our Lady of the Holy Ghost, near Conyers, Georgia. "Why," he inquired, "did you give up Wall Street to become a monk?" To which Brother Pius replied, "Look—talking about the spiritual life is a lot of crap. You just live it." Had Least Heat Moon spoken with the subject of this essay, he might have received a similar response, except that for Thomas Merton, "just" living the spiritual life was a monumental, arduous task, one to which he did not appear to be particularly well suited. Yet for some fifteen years he held two of the most sensitive and influential positions, master of scholastics (1951–55) and master of novices (1955–65), at his own abbey, Our Lady of Gethsemani, near Bardstown, Kentucky, after which he retired to become the abbey's first hermit. Thus was Merton a Trappist's Trappist, an exemplar religious within the Cistercian Order of the Strict Observance. From his prodigious writing, both public and private, as well as from the offical biography by Michael Mott, we are just beginning to learn something of the complexity that was this man.

## Biography

Thomas Merton was born on 31 January 1915 in Prades, the Eastern Pyrenees, France. The son of Owen Heathcote and Ruth Jenkins Merton, both artists (he a New Zealand Anglican, she an American Episcopalian-pacifist), he had an unsteady or imbalanced childhood. In 1921, when Merton was six, his mother died. The result was an odyssey that included time with his younger brother at the home of their maternal grandparents in New York, but without their father; time with his father and his father's lover in Bermuda, but without his brother; time back in New York while his father went first to France and then to Algeria; and finally time more or less with his father in France where Merton attended school.

In 1928, when Merton was thirteen, his father announced that they were moving to England. Merton attended a private preparatory school and then public school at Oakham. His father became ill within one year and died in 1931. In his autobiography, *The Seven Storey Mountain,* Merton recalled his depression for a period. But when this left, "I found myself completely stripped of everything that impeded the movement of my will to do as I pleased. I imagined that I was free."

This was true, at least financially. The previous summer, 1930, Merton's grandfather had arranged for both grandsons to be protected, no matter what. Tom Bennett, who was a Harley Street physician, an old friend of Owen's from New Zealand, and Merton's godfather, became his guardian. This brought an additional sense of liberty. Life with Tom and Iris Bennett was an adventure. "From the first moment when I discovered that one was not only allowed to make fun of English middle-class notions and ideals but encouraged to do so . . . , I was very happy." The result was his acquisition of a critical, even caustic, attitude toward those with whom he disagreed.

After his first year at Oakham, this attitude aided Merton there as well. He was a bright student, one who was both advanced and protected by his headmaster. He moved quickly through to the sixth form within two years. As Merton was weak in mathematics, the headmaster prepared him for the Higher Certificate rather than the regular School Certificate. This was more difficult, but it allowed him more control over what he studied and led him to a scholarship examination, the Johnson Exhibition to Clare College, Cambridge, in 1932.

If the years at Oakham were successful ones for Merton, the one at Clare was not. It was in fact a disaster. There was frivolous living and lack of attention to studies. There were quarrels with the guardian and the tutor. But the oddest event occurred at a party that Merton attended. In his biography, Mott describes a drunkenness during which a "mock crucifixion came close to being a real one." The student involved may have been Merton. The autobiography says nothing. Friends believe it to be true.

In January 1935, with transfer credits from Cambridge, Merton enrolled at Columbia University. He intended to combine his studies with an internship on a New York newspaper, in preparation for a career as a journalist. That this did not happen was in large part owing to a small group of special friends. Merton put the matter forcefully in the autobiography: "God brought me and a half dozen others together at Columbia, and made us friends, in such a way that our friendship would work powerfully to rescue us from the confusion and misery in which we had come to find ourselves."

The friends included Mark Van Doren, Robert Lax, Seymour Freedgood, Robert Gibney, Robert Gerdy, Edward Rice, and (afterward) Dan Walsh. In spring 1937, Lax, Gibney, and Gerdy talked of becoming Roman Catholic, though nothing then became of it. Merton believed that Lax was the most committed of the group because he had "the deepest sense of who God was." But Lax would not act alone. As for Merton, that February he had begun to read Étienne Gilson's *The Spirit of Medieval Philosophy,* in which he found considerable merit. Perhaps the Roman Catholic understanding of God required further inquiry. Then in the fall, Lax recommended a new book, Aldous Huxley's *Ends and Means.*

Merton bought it, read it, and wrote about it for the *Columbia Review.* According to Mott, Huxley offered a "logic," or an intellectual structure, for Merton's thought. Moreover, Merton appreciated the candor of Huxley, "who admitted in print that he was still searching." In his autobiography Merton himself admitted that *Ends and Means* offered what amounted to a mystical experience. There existed a "supernatural order" that was accessible to anyone, at any time, but "most readily by prayer, detachment, [and] love." It was a "necessary source of moral vitality," and although he could not then realize it, here was the birthplace of Merton the ascetic.

In February 1938, Merton graduated from Columbia and promptly enrolled in a master's program in English. He later described this as a "first remote step of retreat" from the world. He expected now to become a college teacher, with lots of time for reading and writing but with no concern for grading and committees. To do so, he needed to select a master's topic. In the midst of his work he began reading in an area, scholastic thought, in concert with a course that, for most of the school year, had been a favorite of the group of friends, especially Gerdy.

The teacher of the course was Dan Walsh. He was a faculty member of Sacred Heart College but lectured regularly on scholastic theology, including Aquinas and Duns Scotus, at Columbia. Lax intended to enroll in the course during the next year and wondered if Merton would join him. According to the biography, Merton adamantly rejected the idea because his interests lay elsewhere. And yet within weeks Merton would discover what he termed "Scholastic philosophy," which he pursued with a passion and which led him to conclude later that much of the preparation for his conversion to Roman Catholicism was completed before he had begun writing his master's topic.

That August, Merton attended his first mass at Corpus Christi, the Roman Catholic parish near Columbia. He also began to focus his reading on Roman Catholic authors, in particular, the Jesuit Gerard Manley Hopkins. He was intrigued with what the life of a priest, or a Jesuit, entailed. Merton then went to Father George B. Ford of Corpus Christi to tell him that he wished to convert. On 16 November 1938, Merton made his first confession, received his baptism, and took his first communion. His friends were there with him: Lax, Gerdy, Rice, and Freedgood. Merton called the day his "happy execution and rebirth."

In February 1939, Merton received his master's degree in English from Columbia, intending to begin on his doctorate on Hopkins. What he really wanted, however, was to become a successful, published writer. In practice this meant that he did not pursue rigorously any Catholic piety but remained "dull" and "indifferent." Later that year he did attend a lecture by the noted Thomistic specialist Jacques Maritain, and that pleased him. But he also quarreled with Lax about what it meant to be a "good Catholic." Lax told him that he should want to be a "saint." Merton considered the idea "weird."

Merton spent the summer of 1939 in Olean, western New York, with Lax and Rice, each of them attempting to write a novel. That fall, Merton returned to Columbia, prepared to resume his work on Hopkins. Then early one afternoon, as he was sitting on the floor of his apartment, a thought came to him: he was to become a priest. He went to Walsh, who was pleased to hear the news but who also wanted to talk primarily about the Cistercians of the Strict Observance. There was a Trappist abbey in Kentucky where Walsh had visited. He wondered if Merton knew anything about them. Merton thought that he preferred the Franciscans.

So be it. With Walsh's blessing Merton went to the monastery of St. Francis of Assisi in New York to inquire about becoming a Franciscan. There seemed to be nothing to prevent his application, but he could not be accepted before August of the next year, 1940, when the new postulants would enter as a group. Until then he supported himself through part-time teaching and his grant-in-aid, although he was told that he could not write his doctoral thesis on Hopkins. However frustrating, this did allow him to concentrate on his summer novel, which had been submitted to and rejected by a series of publishing houses. This in turn led him to Naomi Burton, a literary agent who would become a friend.

In June 1940, Merton at last learned that his application to the Franciscans had been accepted. To help pass the two remaining months, he returned to Olean, this time with Lax, Rice, Gibney, and an increasing number of others. Merton moved to nearby St. Bonaventure College (now University), where he had earlier visited but where he could now practice becoming a Franciscan. Things were pleasant enough until he came to realize that he was unworthy of becoming a priest and withdrew his application. Merton did not, however, abandon the Franciscans. He accepted a teaching position in English at St. Bonaventure and intended to enter the Third Order of Franciscans, a lay order. This meant that if he would "not be a religious, a priest—that was God's affair," he would still try to approximate such a life in the lay order. For now, that would have to be enough, and it was. He even liked his students, mostly first-generation college students from ethnic-American families.

In February 1941, Merton entered the Franciscan lay order and shortly afterward wrote to the Trappist abbey in Kentucky to see if he could make a retreat during holy week. He had been talking again with Walsh, who seemed to be the only one who was informed about the Cistercians. What Merton was to learn for himself that April was the power of simplicity. He found that the monks of Gethsemani "were absorbed and transformed in the liturgy." To cite a crucial passage from the official biography: "By 1941, Merton's vocation was clear. . . . The end he sought was to be a saint."

For Merton, this meant becoming one of the monks of Gethsemani. Part of the reason for this may be gleaned from his popular *No Man Is an Island:*

> If we are called to a place in which God wills to do us the most good, it means we are called where we can best leave ourselves and find [God]. . . . If I am called to the solitary life it does not mean that I will suffer more acutely in solitude than anywhere else: but I will suffer more effectively.

On 10 December 1941, Merton entered the place where his God willed to do him the most good, and on 21 February 1942, he became a novice Trappist, with the name Brother M. Louis. It was, however, "Thomas Merton" who would be the author of poems and books under the direction of two abbots, Dom Frederick Dunne and Dom James Fox. His first volume in print was *Thirty Poems,* published in November 1944. Merton was pleased when he received his own copy. The most important volume was *The Seven Storey Mountain,* which appeared in October 1948. Merton was now famous.

On 26 May 1949, Merton was ordained at Our Lady of Gethsemani and became Father M. Louis. Once again his friends were there to celebrate with him: Walsh, Rice, Lax (now a convert himself), Freedgood, as well as his two editors, James Laughlin and Robert Giroux. In a sense, this ceremony marked the fulfillment of a ten-year dream that had begun in his apartment in New York. In another sense, this ceremony marked the beginning of a life that would be filled with tension and frustration, especially about censorship of his writing and about his vow of stability to the community. And yet there would be much writing, as Merton would publish more than fifty books and hundreds of articles within the next twenty years.

Near the end of that period, in March 1968, Merton received an invitation to attend a meeting in Bangkok, Thailand, of Asian (Benedictine and Cistercian) monastic leaders. By August, he was completing an itinerary that included stops in New Mexico, Alaska, and California, before leaving for Asia. Then would come Calcutta, Darjeeling, and Bangkok, followed perhaps by Hong Kong, Japan, and Indonesia. It was to be an ambitious undertaking for a solitary.

In September, just before leaving Gethsemani, Merton wrote friends, telling them of his plans: "Considering the crucial importance of the time, the need for monastic renewal, the isolation and helplessness of our Asian monasteries, their constant appeals for help, I feel it a duty to respond." On 10 December 1968, in a small cottage at a conference center on the outskirts of Bangkok, Thomas Merton died. The cause was most probably accidental electrocution from a large standing fan.

One week later, the body was received by the community at Gethsemani, there to be buried according to custom. Those who gathered for this ceremony "were amazed to discover that Merton had known so many and such diverse people." They need not have been, for as he had written of himself in *Faith and Violence:* "My own peculiar task in my Church and in my world has been that of a solitary explorer who . . . is bound to search the existential depths of faith in its silences, its ambiguities, and in those certainties which lie deeper than the bottom of anxiety."

### Appraisal

Even to begin a critical appraisal of the writings of Thomas Merton is to enter the realm of paradox. This is in part owing to the size of the collection. In addition to the fifty-odd books and hundreds of articles that he published in his life, there are currently some sixty-five titles in print, as well as hundreds of new or reprinted articles since his death. Moreover, the three most important posthumous volumes are not one of them small: *The Asian Journal* is 445 pages; *The Collected Poems of Thomas Merton* is 1,048 pages; and *The Literary Essays of Thomas Merton* is 549 pages. To these must be added Mott's official biography, a valuable resource for Merton's private writings (to say nothing of Merton on Merton), which is 690 pages, with heavy documentation. In the face of such voluminousness, one can feel daunted.

Nevertheless, if there is a thread that runs consistently through Merton's thought and writing at a personal level for many of these years, it may be said to concern his desire for solitude. In 1952–53, 1955, 1956–57, and 1959–60, while he fulfilled heavy responsibilities for the community, he struggled with Dom James over the possibility of becoming a hermit, whether within or outside Gethsemani. It was no small moment when, in the fall of 1960, he was able to admit in his journal, cited by Mott, that a new building at the abbey was to be "just a plain cottage with two rooms and a porch. Clearly it is a hermitage." By December, even if he could use it but a few hours each day, Merton had his place of solitude. And in August 1965, Dom James selected a new novice master, thus allowing Merton to retire to his hermitage.

At a public level, even after he had become a solitary, Merton needed people, needed the world. In one of his more obscure writings, *Cistercian Life,* he argued:

> The most effective contribution the monk can make to the apostolic activity of the Church is to be himself fully what he is intended to be: namely, a man of silence and prayer. One of the functions of the monastic life is to show, or at least to suggest, something of what all Christian life is aiming at: the ultimate goal of union with God in love.

But this man of silence and prayer did not remain silent.

In January 1966, Merton confirmed his new status as a hermit in an interview with the *New York Times.* He remarked that "he would continue to write but that he hoped 'to avoid writing about current crises in so far as I can possibly do so.' " It was not possible. That year would see published *Raids on the Unspeakable,* a "safe" work, but also *Conjectures of a Guilty Bystander,* considerably less so. *Mystics and Zen Masters* and *Zen and the Birds of Appetite,* both "safe" works that expressed his long-term interest in Eastern religion, were published in 1967–68. But 1968 would also see published *Cables to the Ace,* moderately "unsafe" and perhaps Merton's most compelling cultural criticism.

Consider, for example, these words from *Faith and Violence,* which show why Merton could not avoid addressing his world:

> Of course this monastic life does not necessarily imply a total refusal to have anything to do with the world. Such a refusal would, in any case, be illusory. It would deceive no one but the monk himself. . . . We cannot help being implicated. We can be guilty even by default.

Or consider what Merton had to say about the civil rights movement:

> It has changed its basic assumptions. It no longer takes for granted that American society is just, freedom-loving and democratic. . . . On the contrary, it takes for granted that our society is basically racist, that it is inclined toward fascism and violence, and that the rights of Negroes cannot be guaranteed without real political power.

Or, finally, consider which "side" Merton took in the war in Vietnam:

> I am on the side of the people who are being burned, cut to pieces, tortured, held as hostages, gassed, ruined, destroyed. They are the victims of both sides. To take sides with massive power is to take sides against the innocent.

Harsh words for a harsh year. Merton called 1968 "a brute of a year." But he did not always find it so. At one point, according to the essay on Merton in *Contemporary Authors,* he commented that his "early work resulted in my being classified as a 'spiritual writer,' or worse still, an 'inspirational writer,' " to which he took exception. Perhaps he had in mind here the autobiography *Seeds of Contemplation* and *The Sign of Jonas.* Each is distinct in style and subject matter, but each as well expresses an intimate tale in an affecting manner, thereby helping to change the way many Americans were to feel about monastic life, Roman Catholic Christianity, their nation, and themselves.

## Survey of Criticism

Once again, the collection of criticism of Merton's writings is vast. A good place to begin is with the quarterly the *Merton Seasonal,* edited by Robert E. Daggy, of the Thomas Merton Studies Center, Bellarmine College, Louisville, Kentucky. This lists new books and articles, sometimes up to a hundred titles in one issue, on Merton. One can also find assistance in the range of perspectives, if in excerpt form, in *Contemporary Literary Criticism,* edited by Carolyn Riles (1973, 1975) and by Dedria Bryfonski (1979), and then go read the reviews in full. Or one can consider the earliest "full-length appraisal of Thomas Merton that [had] so far been printed" by 1953, and the posthumous response to his last (and most difficult) poem.

For the first of these, Dom Aelred Graham, O.S.B., wrote for the *Atlantic* in January 1953 that "it is high time that somebody took a long steady look at Thomas Merton. From out of the silent Abbey of Our Lady of Gethsemani . . . this remarkable young man is creating no small stir among those who concern themselves with the things of the spirit." Noting that Merton had published "no fewer than eight books" in the previous "six years," Graham termed Merton "a God-intoxicated man," adding that "whatever may be thought of the content of his message or of its relevance to our times, there can be no withholding tribute to the earnestness of his convictions." Nevertheless, Graham doubted "whether his well-intentioned simplifications can serve any lasting purpose," for Merton remained "a young man in a hurry."

Merton's last poem, *The Geography of Lograire,* according to James York Glimm writing in *Renascence* in 1974, "is, in his own words, a 'wide angle mosaic' on the violence, intolerance and alienation of Western [humanity]." Its "fragmented form, fractured syntax, and multiple allusions make *Lograire* rough going, but the poem greatly increases Merton's importance as a contemporary poet." Glimm concludes that "through the ingenious use of historical facts and allusions to current events, *The Geography of Lograire* shows us that we are the victims of our myth to the extent that we do not understand it."

## Bibliography

*Selected Books by Thomas James Merton (Father M. Louis Merton)*

1948  *Guide to Cistercian Life.* Trappist, Ky.: Abbey of Our Lady of Gethsemani.
1948  *The Seven Storey Mountain.* New York: Harcourt, Brace.
1949  *Elected Silence.* Edited by Evelyn Waugh. London: Hollis and Carter.
1949  *Seeds of Contemplation.* New York: New Directions.
1949  *The Tears of the Blind Lions.* New York: New Directions.
1949  *The Waters of Siloe.* New York: Harcourt, Brace.
1953  *The Sign of Jonas.* New York: Harcourt, Brace.

1955   *No Man Is an Island.* New York: Harcourt, Brace.
1956   *Praying the Psalms.* Collegeville, Minn.: Liturgical Press.
1957   *The Tower of Babel.* New York: New Directions.
1958   *Thoughts in Solitude.* New York: New Directions.
1960   *Disputed Questions.* New York: Farrar, Straus and Cudahy.
1961   *The Behavior of the Titans.* New York: New Directions.
1962   *Breakthrough to Peace.* New York: New Directions.
1962   *The New Man.* New York: Farrar, Straus and Cudahy.
1962   *New Seeds of Contemplation.* New York: New Directions.
1963   *Embers of a Season of Fury.* New York: New Directions.
1963   *Life and Holiness.* New York: Herder and Herder.
1964   *Seeds of Destruction.* New York: Farrar, Straus and Cudahy.
1965   *Gandhi on Non-Violence.* New York: New Directions.
1965   *The Way of Chuang Tzu.* New York: New Directions.
1966   *Conjectures of a Guilty Bystander.* Garden City, N.Y.: Doubleday.
1966   *Raids on the Unspeakable.* New York: New Directions.
1966   *Redeeming the Time.* London: Burns and Oates.
1967   *Mystics and Zen Masters.* New York: Farrar, Straus and Giroux.
1968   *Cables to the Ace.* New York: New Directions.
1968   *Faith and Violence.* Notre Dame, Ind.: University of Notre Dame Press.
1968   *Zen and the Birds of Appetite.* New York: New Directions.
1969   *The Geography of Lograire.* New York: New Directions.
1969   *My Argument with the Gestapo.* Garden City, N.Y.: Doubleday.
1971   *Contemplation in A World of Action.* Garden City, N.Y.: Doubleday.
1973   *The Asian Journal of Thomas Merton.* Edited by Naomi Burton, Brother Patrick
       Hart, and James Laughlin. New York: New Directions.
1974   *Cistercian Life.* Spencer, Mass.: Cistercian Book Service.
1977   *The Collected Poems of Thomas Merton.* New York: New Directions.
1977   *The Secular Journal of Thomas Merton.* Edited by Brother Patrick Hart. New
       York: Farrar, Straus and Giroux.
1981   *The Literary Essays of Thomas Merton.* Edited by Brother Patrick Hart. New
       York: New Directions.

### Selected Studies about Thomas James Merton (Father M. Louis Merton)

Baker, James Thomas. *Thomas Merton, Social Critic.* Lexington: University Press of
    Kentucky, 1971.
Burton, Naomi. *More than Sentinels.* Garden City, N.Y.: Doubleday, 1965.
De Pinto, Basil, O.S.B. *Where Love Is, God Is.* Milwaukee: Bruce, 1953.
Finley, James. *Merton's Place of Nowhere.* Notre Dame, Ind.: Ave Maria, 1978.
Glimm, James Y. "Thomas Merton's Last Poem: The Geography of Lograire." *Re-
    nascence* 26 (Winter 1974): 95–104.
Graham, Aelred. "Thomas Merton." *Atlantic* 191 (January 1953): 70-74.
Grayston, Donald, and Michael W. Higgins, eds. *Thomas Merton.* Toronto: Griffin
    House, 1983.
Hart, Brother Patrick, O.C.S.O., ed. *Thomas Merton, Monk.* New York: Sheed and
    Ward, 1974.
Kelly, F., S.J. *Man Before God.* Garden City, N.Y.: Doubleday, 1974.
Malits, Elena, C.S.C. *The Solitary Explorer, Thomas Merton's Transforming Journey.*
    San Francisco: Harper and Row, 1980.

"Merton, Thomas (James)." In *Contemporary Authors,* first rev. ed., edited by Barbara
     Harte and Carolyn Riley, 5–8: 776–77. Detroit: Gale, 1969.
Mott, Michael. *The Seven Mountains of Thomas Merton.* Boston: Houghton, Mifflin,
     1984.
Nouwen, Henri J. M. *Thomas Merton, Contemplative Critic.* San Francisco: Harper and
     Row, 1981.
Padovano, Anthony T. *The Human Journey—Thomas Merton.* Garden City, N.Y.: Dou-
     bleday, 1982.
Patnaik, Deba Prasad, ed. *Geography of Holiness.* New York: Pilgrim, 1980.
Rice, Edward. *The Good Times and Hard Life of Thomas Merton, the Man in the Sycamore
     Tree.* Garden City, N.Y.: Doubleday, 1970.
Shannon, William H. *Thomas Merton's Dark Path.* New York: Farrar, Straus and Giroux,
     1981.
Twomey, Gerald, C.S.P. *Thomas Merton.* New York: Paulist, 1978.
Van Doren, Mark. *Autobiography.* New York: Harcourt, Brace, 1958.
Woodcock, George. *Thomas Merton, Monk and Poet.* Vancouver: Douglas and McIntyre,
     1978.

STEPHEN H. SNYDER

# John R. Mott

On a hot summer's night in the middle of July in 1886, a small gathering of
students was praying in a grove of trees behind the main assembly hall of the
Mt. Hermon Summer Conference. The students were among the 250 college
representatives that had come to Mt. Hermon in Massachusetts to sit at the feet
of the great revivalist D. L. Moody. However, the special prayer meeting in the
grove of trees was not just another expression of the piety typical at Moody's
conferences. These students were praying that the heat of the night would make
its way into the hearts of every student there, calling forth a "missionary gusher."
They were praying behind the assembly hall because there was nothing about
missions in the program for the conference that was developed by Moody. It
was his hope that the conference would teach students how they could take
revivalism back to their college campuses. Regardless of Moody's intentions,
the prayers of the small band of students appeared to have been answered. Over
the course of the next two weeks, 100 students had emerged, covenanting, "God
permitting, to become foreign missionaries." It was the goal of these visionary
students to take Moody's soul-saving message not to their college campuses but
to the whole world. The emergence of the "Mt. Hermon 100" was illustrative
of a new and important transition from nineteenth-century revivalism to the
American missionary agendas that emerged at the beginning of the twentieth
century. Among the 100 names listed at Mt. Hermon was one that emerged to
become almost synonymous with the hopes and strategies of American foreign
missions, that of John R. Mott.

## Biography

On 25 May 1865, John Stitt and Elmira Dodge Mott gave birth to their third child and only son, John R. Mott. He was born six weeks after the assassination of Abraham Lincoln. Later that year the Mott family moved to Postville, Iowa, where John Stitt Mott would for many years own and operate a retail lumber yard. The Mott family was not wealthy but certainly enjoyed a comfortable life in their small town. By all indications, young Mott seemed to have had a typical midwestern upbringing that stressed practical learning, community responsibility, and regular attendance at church.

Most of his religious education as a boy, however, came from his mother, who was deeply committed to the local Methodist Church. In his collected *Addresses and Papers,* he remembered that his mother "inculcated a genuine loyalty to the church and its institutions and activities such as the Sunday School, the midweek prayer meeting, the camp meetings in the pioneer days, and above all a reverential regard for the Christian minister." In his church, it was assumed that at an impressionable moment teenage boys and girls would undergo a conversion experience and then join the church, even if they had grown up attending its services and activities. This happened to John in February 1879, when he attended an interdenominational revival in Postville. Later in life he seldom mentioned the event, and it seems to have been more of a rite of passage for him, as he fulfilled the expectations for most Protestant boys his age.

Of far greater influence was the young pastor of his church, the Reverend Horace E. Warner, who saw great potential for leadership in Mott and encouraged him to pursue a college education. At age sixteen, Mott enrolled in the preparatory department of Upper Iowa University, but only after convincing his mother that the school did not turn out atheists. He later transferred as a sophomore to Cornell University in Ithaca, New York. It was there that he would be exposed to the influences that would propel him into his lifelong career.

Almost immediately, he became involved in the Cornell chapter of the YMCA. At one of the chapter meetings J.E.K. Studd, himself a convert through the preaching of D. L. Moody at Cambridge, brought a challenging message that struck the heart of young Mott. Studd challenged the students with "Seekest thou great things for thyself? Seek them not. But seek first the kingdom of God." It was with this challenge in mind that Mott agreed to represent the Cornell YMCA at Moody's new "College Students Summer School" at Mt. Hermon, Massachusetts. Two significant things happened to Mott that summer. The first was the decision to sign the pledge dedicating his life to foreign missions, thus joining the "Mt. Hermon 100." The second was that his leadership abilities attracted the attention of Moody and of Richard Morse, the general secretary of the YMCA. Two years later, after graduating from college, Mott was asked to serve as the general secretary of the student branch of the YMCA.

Meanwhile the "Mt. Hermon 100" had developed into the Student Volunteer Movement for Foreign Missions (SVM), and its number of volunteers had swelled in two years from 100 to 2,200. Also on his college graduation, Mott assumed the position of chairman of this new organization. Motivated initially by a concern to spread Moody's message to all the world, the SVM developed the watchword "The evangelization of the world in this generation." Although the watchword would undergo several different interpretations during its existence, at no time did the slogan imply that the students expected to convert the world to Christianity. Initially, it stood as a rallying cry to enlist students in the cause of evangelizing the world, or giving everyone the opportunity to hear the gospel. Mott maintained the position of chairman of the SVM until 1920, by which time it was responsible for sending out 8,140 foreign missionaries. Of perhaps even greater significance, during his administration the SVM grew into a significant presence on college campuses. By 1920, it had 47,666 students enrolled in 3,000 mission study groups on over 800 campuses.

In the early years of the SVM, Mott spent a great amount of time traveling across the country, meeting students, and establishing mission study groups. In fact, after marrying Lelia White on Thanksgiving of 1891, he combined their honeymoon with a tour of the western college campuses. These tours did a great deal to acquaint Mott with some of the "grass roots" of his movement. He learned a great deal in these years about the student mentality, and thus how best to motivate students into mission endeavors. The second hallmark of his leadership of the SVM was the development of large conventions called "Quadrennials." Every four years, in a different city, delegates from the different campus SVM chapters would gather for inspiring lectures on the current state of the mission field. The attendance at these grew from 600 in 1891 to 7,000 in 1920. The summers of these years were spent running Moody's Northfield and Mt. Hermon conferences. The importance of these conventions and conferences for Mott personally was that he was developing some of the skills he had learned from Moody on how to organize an effective mass assembly. This was a skill that would be crucial to his future success in the ecumenical movement.

In addition to traveling across the United States, Mott had also taken three world tours of the mission field by the First World War and a fourth soon after that. These trips gave him a better idea of the real needs of the mission field to which he was sending so many students. It also began to illustrate to him the need for some type of cooperation among the many different Protestant missionary forces from both America and Europe. By 1897 Mott had been successful in establishing the World Student Christian Federation and served as either its general secretary or chairman until 1928. The WSCF linked the missional agendas of the SVM and the YMCA in the United States with the programs of the Student Christian Movements in Europe and Great Britain. Effectively it also created a means of communication among the students of over 3,000 universities around the world.

Although Mott never left his "first love" of student work, by the first decade of the twentieth century he was beginning to get much more involved in the leadership of other types of mission endeavors. Certainly one of the great turning points for his career was the World Missionary Conference in Edinburgh in 1910. Motivated by his conviction of the need to cooperate on the mission field, Mott participated in calling together Protestant mission boards to this first authentically international missionary conference. The design of the conference created eight preparatory commissions that spent two years preparing reports for the conference on "matters of large importance and of timely interest at this stage of the missionary enterprise." In addition to leading one of the preparatory commissions, Mott served as chairman for the conference. The effect of this was to propel him from being a prominent person in American student missions to a prominent international figure. At the conclusion of the conference, his preparatory commission was turned into the Edinburgh Continuation Committee, and Mott continued to serve as its tireless chairman. This committee continued till 1921, when it became the International Missionary Council, which Mott chaired until 1941. It was through his service with the IMC that Mott became quite visible in the emerging ecumenical movement.

The years immediately following the Edinburgh conference of 1910 were exceptionally busy ones for John Mott. In addition to maintaining his involvements with such student organizations as the SVM and the YMCA, Edinburgh had opened the door to many other opportunities for leadership. In a letter dated 10 August 1915, Mott explained that he would accept the position of general secretary to the International Committee of the YMCA provided he be allowed to maintain his present responsibilities as chairman of the continuation committee of the Edinburgh World Missionary Conference, chairman of the Council of North American Student Movements, chairman of the executive committee of the SVM, general secretary of the World Student Christian Federation, chairman of the Board of Missionary Preparation for the Foreign Missions Council of North America, trustee of the governing board of the Church Peace Union, and member of the executive committee of the Layman's Missionary Movement, of the administrative council of the Federation of Churches of the USA, of the China Medical Board of the Rockefeller Foundation, and of the executive committee of the World Alliance of YMCAs. Mott was kept so busy meeting the obligations of these commitments that he had little time for other involvements. He was offered five college presidencies, including that of Princeton University, and the deanship of Yale Divinity School, but declined them all. The diplomatic skills he evidenced in bringing so many international church leaders into cooperative mission endeavors attracted the attention of President Woodrow Wilson. Although Mott became a close personal friend of the president, he also declined Wilson's offer to become the ambassador to China in 1912.

He did, however, serve on several diplomatic commissions for the U.S. government and was a special advisor to the American delegation to the Paris Peace Conference in 1919. In World War I, the bulk of ministry to Protestant soldiers was given over to the YMCA, and Mott coordinated this work as part of his contribution to the war effort. He also chaired the United War Work Campaign, which raised $200 million by 1918. However, always the peacemaker, as soon as the war was over Mott led the crusade to restore relations with the German church. Mostly for his achievements in diplomacy, Mott was awarded six honorary doctorates by 1944. However, it was a continual source of frustration to him that in the midst of all of these global concerns, there was precious little time left for traveling around America talking to college students.

As the many strands of ecumenical agencies and councils began to merge into the World Council of Churches, Mott was a natural selection for its first president in 1948. Although the position was an honorary one, it signaled an important transition in the ecumenical movement. It was as though Mott's presidency illustrated the success of his life's work in achieving cooperation among the leaders of Western Christianity. In the next chapter of the WCC, the younger churches from the mission field Mott had evangelized would be seen as partners in the uniting of Christendom, a step Mott could never quite take.

Although it appeared to many that Mott exported some Western dominance along with the gospel to third world nations, it remains that he did much to further the causes of peace, international cooperation, and diplomacy. In 1946 these efforts were acknowledged when Mott was awarded the Nobel Peace Prize. In his acceptance speech he summarized his life as "an indiscourageable effort to weave together all nations, all races, and all religious communions in friendliness, in fellowship, and in cooperation." He had certainly come a long way from the feet of D. L. Moody in Mt. Hermon.

### Appraisal

Certainly one of the most striking aspects of Mott's career is the movement from the revivalism of Moody to the presidency of the World Council of Churches. Ironically, however, much of his success in the ecumenical movement can be attributed to the lessons that he learned from Moody. Of further significance, when Mott is seen not just in isolation but as the representative leader of a large missionary enterprise, his career is illustrative of a significant popular movement linking nineteenth-century revivalism with the mission aspirations of the early twentieth century.

By the beginning of the twentieth century it was apparent that Mott had learned more from Moody than the necessity of saving souls. He had spent many years working with Moody on the organization of numerous conferences and meetings. For many years he was a cherished disciple of Moody and had even been offered the presidency of Moody's new Chicago Bible Institute. These were formative years for Mott, as he was learning the practical strategies that had made Moody so successful as a revivalist. The attempt to export American revivalism to the rest of the world may have meant that revivalism took on the new agendas of foreign missions and eventually ecumenics and may even have changed its goals, but the basic strategies of operation remained generally consistent.

In Mott's long list of credentials, what is strikingly absent is any background in theology. Although he grew up as a Methodist, that tradition seems to have had little influence on his later career, other than the maintenance of personal piety and moral character that appears above reproach. From Moody, Mott had learned that the rehearsal of theological positions was detrimental to achieving a broad base of support. On Moody's platforms there would characteristically be a great variety of theological positions among representatives. Some were socially minded progressives who liked Moody's commitment to the urban poor; others were conservative pietists who appreciated his call for individual salvation. In that Moody, in his early ministry, was a-theological, no one was theologically excluded from associating with him. The summer conferences in Northfield and Mt. Hermon boasted of such speakers as Reinhold Niebuhr, Harry Emerson Fosdick*, and Charles Brent, as well as such fundamentalists as Charles Blanchard, and J. Gresham Machen. (Later in Moody's work, much of the conservative leadership found a home in the Chicago Bible Institute, leaving the Northfield conferences to the moderate and more liberal figures. However, this factionalizing did not occur during Mott's exposure to Moody's ministry.) Mott had learned early on that unity had to come in the form of cooperation around a common commitment to a common task and that to stress theological distinctives or to work for unity of belief would only frustrate the effort of getting diverse groupings to work together.

It is thus no great surprise that the SVM was committed to being interdenominational. This allowed it to lobby for an inspiring vision of global evangelization, a vision in which all could cooperate regardless of their particular theological or ecclesiastical commitments. Thus, almost 50,000 students came together under the SVM banner without ever having to leave or discuss the theological distinctives of their home churches. This strategy is further evidenced at Edinburgh, where Mott not only believed in the necessity of bringing together every Protestant mission board but also, as chairman of the conference, resisted the efforts of some to discuss the possibilities of developing a common confessional statement. It is significant that in his later ecumenical work Mott was identified with the International Missionary Council, which served as a coordinating and central planning agency for its thirty affiliated members. He admired the efforts of those such as Charles Brent who were committed to finding an organic union of the churches by laboring through the Faith and Order Commission. However, unity for unity's sake alone was never sought by Mott, and perhaps that was one of the great secrets of his success. Of course, there were other important lessons that Mott also learned from Moody, such as the importance of the "great conferences" and the viability of college students as a missionary force, but the most productive insight he gained was how to achieve cooperation without sacrificing theological distinctiveness.

It is important to note, however, that the reasons for Mott's success as a leader in popular religion are also to be found in sources deeper than his utilization of cooperative strategies. He demonstrated a genius for reading the popular sentiment of a particular era in American religious life and was always able to reinterpret the symbols and language of a preceding era in such a way as to redeem their meaning for contemporary audiences. Thus, he remained relevant to the shifting tides of public debate for over sixty years of ministry.

This ability is best illustrated by examining the periodic reinterpretations of the SVM watchword "The evangelization of the world in this generation." Initially the watchword was used to attract as many missionaries as possible to the inspiring goal of allowing every person in every nation the opportunity of hearing the gospel as articulated by such Protestant spokesmen as D. L. Moody. By 1913, Mott had completed his third world tour and had seen a great deal of the world he sought to evangelize. He had also spent a great deal of time in conversation with the diverse leaderships of Christian movements from other nations through such conferences as that at Edinburgh in 1910. As a prolific reader, he always kept abreast of new movements in American religious life. These factors all contributed to a realization that many were attempting to apply the gospel to more than individual conversions. The tours opened his eyes to the conditions under which the evangelized lived. Leaders from other nations helped Mott to measure public sentiment in Europe and Great Britain. By keeping his fingers on the pulse of American religious life in the progressive era, he began to realize that it was necessary to accommodate his message to the changing times. During this era he seemed eager to work on issues of social concern, held conferences with such social gospel leaders as Walter Rauschenbusch, and asserted the ability of the YMCAs to work for better race relations. During this time the watchword denoted not only an inspiration to change the hearts of individuals, but an inspiration to change the world itself. It was not that Mott wanted to stop preaching to the individual, but he now hoped to address the individual in the social context, and thus he labored for the redemption of both the individual and the society in which all individuals live.

In the years following World War I, there was a great disillusionment with the progressive hopes of that earlier era. Not only was the challenge to work for a real Christendom more difficult than many had assumed, but the very concept of Christendom, where religious commitments would dominate all social, economic, and political relations, now seemed farfetched. Many evangelicals began more vehemently to renounce the world as evil and reasserted the need to focus on individual conversions. Others began to speak of the corporate sins of society in such a way as to call for a Christian realism in the political arena. Mott sought to bridge these factions by reinterpreting the watchword once again. In the late thirties, he began to speak of it as commanding a vision of a whole new world. Mott used the watchword now to motivate Christians to social action by claiming that the principles of the Kingdom provided a vantage point from which missionary forces could envision new hopes for a suffering world. Thus, evangelism became for him a commitment to laboring for the healing of the systemic sickness in society that creates a sickness in the soul of the individuals it victimizes.

With this last reinterpretation of the watchword, Mott had certainly come a long way from simply taking Moody's soul-saving message around the world.

The intent of this movement may have been to stay relevant to a populace that was constantly shifting in sentiment. However, the reinterpretations illustrate that at some point theologizing became necessary even for Mott. With this last explanation of the watchword, Mott may have redeemed his beloved symbol, but only to some. The divergent camps of factionalism were becoming too fierce to accept a common leader. Whereas some honored Mott as the father of the modern missionary movement, it appeared to others that Mott had led the movement astray and had abandoned the simplicity of a commission to go and evangelize the world. Before his death on 31 January 1955, Mott lamented this factionalization and typically called for the warring camps within the Christian community "to come under the spell of the commanding vision of the Kingdom of our Lord."

### Survey of Criticism

Surprisingly there is very little written directly about Mott that provides objective analysis of his work. Although there is some good material on such student movements as the SVM, the YMCA, and the WSCF, with which Mott was closely associated, these studies tend to concentrate more on the nature of the organizations than they do on the men and women who helped to shape them. Among the best of these is Clarence P. Shedd's *Two Generations of Student Christian Movements,* published in 1934. Similarly, William Richey Hogg provides some insights into Mott's work with the International Missionary Council in *Ecumenical Foundations: A History of the International Missionary Council and Its Nineteenth Century Background.* Some significant chapters are devoted to Mott's influence in both *A History of the Ecumenical Movement: 1517–1948* by Ruth Rouse and Stephen Neill and Stephen Neill's *History of Christian Missions.* In his massive *History of the Expansion of Christianity,* Kenneth Scott Latourette provides one of the better introductions to Mott's work in volume 4. More recently, R. Pierce Beaver has published several articles that locate Mott in the broader scheme of American mission endeavors. This is done particularly well in his "North American Thought on the Fundamental Principles of Missions During the Twentieth Century."

There have been two major biographies written on Mott. The first was by Basil Matthews, entitled *John R. Mott: World Citizen.* Though this reference is rich in anecdotes and personal history, it was written too close to Mott's life to be able to offer any historical evaluation. It is also quite obvious that Matthews was rather enamored with his subject. In 1979, a marvelous gift was given to Mott studies by C. Howard Hopkins in his biography, *John R. Mott: 1865– 1955.* This work provides a very careful reporting on the facts and details of Mott's life and career, but it seems to shy away from critical analysis as well.

What is lacking in current analysis is made up in Mott's own voluminous writings. Chief among these is his six-volume collection of *Addresses and Papers.* This collection offers the researcher a bountiful supply of primary sources, but it must be remembered that Mott himself edited this work, and thus the collection leaves one with the precise opinion of Mott that he desired to leave behind. Still these volumes serve as the best source of research among the published material. Mott's unpublished papers remain in the archives of the Yale Divinity School.

## Bibliography

### Selected Works by John R. Mott

1897   *Strategic Points In The World's Conquest*. New York: Fleming H. Revell Co.

1900   *The Evangelization of the World in This Generation*. New York: Student Volunteer Movement for Foreign Missions.

1902   *Christians of Reality*. Shanghai: National Committee College Young Men's Christian Association of China.

1904   *The Pastor and Modern Missions*. New York: Student Volunteer Movement for Foreign Missions.

1908   *The Future Leadership of the Church*. New York: Student Volunteer Movement for Foreign Missions.

1909–10   *Claims and Opportunities of the Christian Ministry*. New York: Student Young Men's Christian Association.

1910   *The Decisive Hour of Christian Missions*. New York: Student Volunteer Movement for Foreign Missions.

1914   *The Present World Situation*. New York: Student Volunteer Movement for Foreign Missions.

1920   *The World's Student Christian Student Federation: Origins, Achievements, and Forecast*. [London]: World's Student Christian Federation.

1923   *Confronting Young Men with the Living Christ*. New York: Association Press.

1925   *The Moslem World of Today*. Edited by Mott. New York: George H. Doran Co.

1931   *The Present-Day Summons to the World Mission of Christianity*. Nashville: Cokesbury Press.

1932   *Liberating the Lay Forces of Christianity*. New York: Macmillan.

1935   *Cooperation and The World Mission*. London: Student Christian Movement Press; New York: International Missionary Council.

1938   *Evangelism for the World Today*. New York: Harper and Brothers for the International Missionary Council.

1939   *Five Decades and A Forward View*. New York and London: Harper and Brothers.

1939   *Methodists United for Action*. Nashville: Department of Education & Promotion, Board of Missions, the Methodist Church.

1944   *The Larger Evangelism*. New York and Nashville: Abingdon-Cokesbury Press.

1946–47   *Addresses and Papers*. 6 vols. New York: Association Press.

### Selected Studies about John R. Mott

Beaver, R. Pierce. "North American Thought on the Fundamental Principles of Missions During the Twentieth Century." *Church History* 21 (1952): 345–64.

Hogg, William Richey. *Ecumenical Foundations: A History of the International Missionary Council and Its Nineteenth Century Background*. New York: Harper and Brothers, Publishers, 1952.

Hopkins, C. Howard. *John R. Mott: 1865–1955*. Grand Rapids, Mich.: William B. Eerdmans Publishing Company, 1979.

Latourette, Kenneth Scott. *History of the Expansion of Christianity: The Great Century, Europe and the United States*. Vol. 4. New York: Harper and Brothers, 1941.

Matthews, Basil. *John R. Mott: World Citizen*. New York: Harper Publishing Company, 1934.

Murray, William D. *Principles and Organization of the Young Men's Christian Organization*. New York: YMCA Press, 1910.

Neill, Stephen. *A History of Christian Missions*. Harmondsworth, Middlesex, England: Penguin Books, 1962.

Rouse, Ruth, and Stephen C. Neill, eds. *A History of the Ecumenical Movement: 1517–1948*. Philadelphia: Westminster Press, 1967.

Shedd, Clarence P. *A History of the World Alliance of YMCA*. London: S.P.C.K., 1934.

———. *Two Generations of Student Christian Movements*. London: S.P.C.K., 1934.

M. CRAIG BARNES

# J. Frank Norris

J. Frank Norris was many things to many people: loyal friend, caring pastor, loving relative, troublemaker, confirmed enemy. Few people who encountered him could remain indifferent to him. All of Norris' relationships were dominated by one particular aspect of his character, an energetic aggressiveness determined to pursue ends of his own choosing. Pouring himself into every undertaking with seemingly endless energy, Norris was never willing to consider retreat or accept defeat. His is the story of a confident fundamentalist who possessed a fearful compulsion to win at any cost.

### Biography

Born on a farm in Dadeville, Alabama, on 18 September 1877, J. Frank Norris was forever the country boy. Norris' father, devoted more to alcohol than to his farming responsibilities, was not much of a provider. Consequently, dire poverty and near starvation characterized the early years of Frank's life, including those following the family's move to Hubbard, Texas, in 1888. Adding to the difficulty of young Frank's childhood was a traumatic incident he experienced at the age of fifteen. Vengeful cattle thieves, convicted several years earlier on the basis of his father's testimony against them, shot and critically wounded Frank. During a three-year recuperation, two of them spent in a wheelchair, Frank's mother instilled in him a strong sense of personal worth. The confidence, determination, and stance of combative readiness resulting from these early experiences in Norris' life never left him; time served only to strengthen these attributes of his character.

In 1899, Norris entered Baylor University to study for the ministry. True to his aggressive spirit, he stood in class one day and issued the proclamation that he would some day "preach in the greatest church and pulpit in the world!" During his Baylor years, Norris became the pastor of a church in the small Texas town of Mount Calm. The setting was perfect for the country boy to ply his talents, and there Norris came to a sense of absolute confidence about his abilities in ministry.

In 1902, he married Lillian Gaddy, and together they had four children: Lillian, Jim Gaddy, J. Frank, Jr., and George Louis. After graduation from Baylor, Norris immediately enrolled in an advanced studies program at the Southern Baptist Theological Seminary in Louisville, Kentucky. Feeling the pressure of needing to support his family, he hurried through the three-year program in two years and earned, along with his master's degree, the right to deliver the valedictorian address to his class.

On graduation, Norris accepted the pastorate of the McKinney Avenue Baptist Church in Dallas, sight unseen. While busy boosting membership in the church from thirteen to well over a thousand in just three years, Norris looked for other outlets through which he could express his personal creative energies. Discovering that the main newspaper voice for Southern Baptists in Texas, the *Baptist Standard,* was for sale, Norris scraped together enough funds to acquire majority ownership. He became its editor and demonstrated his natural ability to use the pen as a weapon, a propensity he utilized throughout his colorful career.

Norris relinquished control of the *Standard* in 1909 and, shortly thereafter, accepted the call to the pastorate of the prestigious First Baptist Church in Fort Worth, Texas. With its membership seated in paid pews accented by gold-plated name tags, the church was quite unprepared for the style of ministry the new pastor would soon implement. For two years Norris behaved himself. But in 1911 he conducted a revival in Owensboro, Kentucky, which revived his own spirits as well.

On returning to Fort Worth from Kentucky, the rejuvenated minister preached a sermon entitled "If Jim Jeffries, the Chicago Cubs, and Theodore Roosevelt Can't Come Back, Who Can?" Other sensationalist sermon topics followed; among them were such topics as "Should a Prominent Fort Worth Banker Buy the High-Priced Silk Hose for Another Man's Wife?" and "The Ten Biggest Devils in Fort Worth, Names Given." Controversy rocked the rich and influential church. New members, mostly from the lower strata of society, filled the church to capacity every Sunday. Fearful of how these new converts would affect the prestige of the First Baptist Church, the board of trustees met and decided to fire the pastor before the situation got out of hand. Norris, however, dismissed the trustees and the deacons before they got the opportunity to act. In late 1911, 600 members left the church, a defection that Norris viewed as a purification process.

The staid members who fled from the Fort Worth church were not alone in their desire to see Norris leave town. For most of 1911, the feisty pastor attacked prostitution, alcohol, and municipal corruption. He spoke against these issues to large crowds gathered underneath the tent he had erected in the heart of the city. Mayor Bill Davis, often finding himself the subject of these onslaughts, decided to rid Fort Worth of the overzealous troublemaking pastor once and for all. Fire officials, acting on orders from the mayor, cut down the tent Norris was using for his meetings; merchants shunned him, and the city's newspapers refused to print his name, even in paid advertisements. Early in 1912, physical violence erupted. Fire, believed to be the work of an arsonist, totally destroyed the First Baptist Church. Norris charged that his opponents were totally responsible for the fire; Davis, in turn, hired a private detective from New York to investigate the origins of the fire, hoping to implicate Norris. Shortly after the investigation, a grand jury indicted Norris for arson. The state's case against Norris must have been weak, however, because less than a month after the indictment the jury acquitted Norris.

The events surrounding the arson trial helped persuade Norris that he was invincible. With every year that passed, he grew more dogmatic and less reserved. In the early months of 1926, Norris devoted much of his attention, once again, to exposing municipal corruption. The principal target of his criticism was H. C. Meacham, Roman Catholic department store owner and then mayor of the city. Norris accused Meacham of benefiting Roman Catholic institutions through the misapplication of city funds. Meacham responded by having the manager of his department store discharge six employees who were members of Norris' church. On the following Sunday, from the pulpit, Norris referred to the leaders of city hall as ''a two by four, simlin-headed, sawdust brained, bunch of graphers.'' Concerning the mayor specifically, in the 16 July 1926 issue of *Searchlight* Norris declared him unfit to be ''manager of a hog-pen.''

Circumstances precluded Norris' intention to see this fight against city hall through to its finish. On a Saturday in July 1926, Norris received a threatening phone call from D. E. Chipps, a hefty lumberjack friend of the mayor. Chipps, calling the church from a hotel less than a block away, allegedly told Norris that he was on his way over to the church to kill him. A few minutes after Norris hung up the phone, Chipps kicked in his office door. The two men argued bitterly; four shots rang out and Chipps, struck by three of them, lay dead on the floor. Norris, immediately indicted for murder, was tried in Austin following a change of venue. Defense attorneys, presenting an impressive case for self-defense, won an acquittal from the jury after it deliberated for less than an hour. A cheering crowd of over 8,000 greeted him on his return to Fort Worth.

Less than two years later, tragedy again confronted the Fort Worth congregation. The beautiful church building constructed following the fire of 1912 was itself completely destroyed by fire in 1929. Many difficult years followed in the wake of this calamity. The stock market crash made it extremely difficult for Norris and his parishioners to reestablish themselves. A new auditorium, equipped with only the bare essentials, was dedicated in 1932.

Norris felt a deeply rooted conviction that he had been especially called to lead a reformation movement among Southern Baptists. He might have been much more successful in this endeavor had his methods not been so vicious. Tact was never one of Norris' greatest virtues. As a result of the formation of his own newspaper in 1917, originally called the *Fence Rail* and later known as the *Searchlight* and the *Fundamentalist,* and the acquisition of radio station KFQB in 1924, Norris' tactlessness soon became a well-publicized fact. His newspaper grew to a circulation of over 80,000, and his radio station's broadcasts were picked up by more than twenty-five stations. This rather unusual media presence aided in parading the activities of J. Frank Norris before most of the rest of the country.

His desire to reform the Southern Baptist Convention (SBC) soon became the source of the longest-running controversy of his life. The original causes of the controversy have become buried under the years of charges and countercharges. For Norris, the conflict centered on two primary issues: denominational control of the local church and infiltration of modernism into the convention. A close look at the evidence, however, supports the thesis that these two issues were not the primary causes of the controversy. Denominational leaders in Texas, men like George W. Truett* (pastor of First Baptist Church in Dallas), were, contrary to Norris' accusations against them, devoted to the autonomy of the local church. Even more to the point, an examination of their ministries would reveal few, if any, modernistic tendencies. In reality, a struggle for power, not unlike the current struggles in the Southern Baptist Convention (see W. A. Criswell*), constituted the heart of the conflict between Norris and these Texas Baptist leaders.

One of Norris' major fights with the Texas Baptist leadership involved Baylor University. In 1921, Norris discovered that some of the faculty at the university were espousing evolutionary views in the classroom. Most of the Baptist leaders, Truett included, wanted to handle the problems at Baylor with as little publicity as possible. Norris, seeing the Baylor issue as one that would enable him successfully to divide the Baptist General Convention of Texas and perhaps boost him into the leadership position he had long hoped to hold, relentlessly attacked the established denominational leadership for its unwillingness to move quickly in resolving the problem. Accusing Truett and others of being under the control of modernist organizations, Norris took his fight to the people of the convention. As a result, eight Baylor faculty members were forced to resign. Norris, for the moment, emerged victorious. His temporary successes in the Baylor conflict, however, were soon offset by heavy losses in his running battle with the denominational leadership in Texas.

The first sign of trouble with the SBC came early in his ministry, even before he took the reins of the Fort Worth church. Denominational leadership quickly became unhappy with his sensationalist approach to journalism in the *Baptist Standard*. His flashy style may have increased subscriptions, but it simultaneously alienated Baptist leaders in Texas. In 1914, the Pastors Conference of Fort Worth ousted Norris for his constant criticism of other area ministers. By 1922, the Tarrant County Baptist Association had followed suit. Finally, in 1924, the Baptist General Convention of Texas formally expelled both the minister and his church from membership. The expulsion came after Lee Scarborough, president of Southwestern Baptist Theological Seminary, and S. P. Brooks, president of Baylor University, conspired and placed a spy in Norris' church. Through this process, they were able to charge Norris with various offenses, including accepting "alien immersion" and allowing non-Baptists to preach in his pulpit.

Norris realized after 1924 that he had greatly misread the measure of his support within the convention. Even though he was greatly disheartened by the fact that most denominational doors were closed to him, he still considered himself a Southern Baptist. Throughout the late 1920s, Norris maintained hopes of gaining enough grass-roots support from the membership in the convention to force Truett and Scarborough to abdicate their positions. Arguments launched against denominational programs generally took the form of diatribes aimed at discrediting convention leadership. In late 1929, Norris finally faced the fact that his campaign had failed. In the fall of 1930, the First Baptist Church of Fort Worth completely severed its relationship with the denomination, though Norris continued to be a thorn in the side of the SBC the remainder of his life.

In 1934, Norris was offered the pastorate of the Temple Baptist Church in Detroit, Michigan. In accepting it, he stipulated that he be allowed to continue his responsibilities as pastor of the Fort Worth church as well. The Detroit church agreed, and he found himself pastoring two large, successful churches at the same time. Under his energetic, caring, and autocratic leadership, the Fort Worth church grew from 1,200 members to 13,000 whereas Temple's membership ballooned from 800 to 12,000.

Having already cut the formal ties between the First Baptist Church of Fort Worth and the SBC, Norris took his first step as pastor of the Temple Baptist Church in Detroit by severing the church's relationship with the Northern Baptist Convention. By making the church independent of denominational interference, he could more completely dictate the church's policies.

After 1934, Norris formed his own denominational organization. In early 1933, he had founded a traveling Bible school which he called the Premillennial Baptist Missionary Fellowship. This ambulatory fellowship eventually enabled him to foster enough support to establish the World Fundamental Baptist Mission Fellowship (WFBMF) in 1938. Its stated purposes included support for foreign missionaries, stimulation of evangelism, training for preachers, and opposition to modernism. In order to fulfill these objectives more completely, the WFBMF founded a seminary, the Baptist Bible Institute, in Fort Worth in 1939. John R. Rice, noted fundamentalist and editor of the *Sword of the Lord* newsletter, and John Birch, namesake of the John Birch Society, both attended the seminary.

Though Norris' independent churches and his seminary both thrived for a time, they later suffered schism because of Norris' ultimate inability to share leadership responsibilities. Slowed by increasing age and deteriorating health in the late 1940s, he offered leadership that consisted more of vociferous bullying than solid administration. After meeting together briefly, WFBMF pastors decided that schism constituted the only way to nullify Norris' dictatorial influence. The major fellowship churches broke away and formed the Baptist Bible Fellowship, which later founded its own Baptist Bible College in Springfield, Missouri. The remaining churches, still loyal to Norris, renamed their group the World Baptist Fellowship and moved the seminary to Arlington, Texas, where today it is known as Arlington Baptist College.

After the schism, Norris, frustrated and desperate, instituted a vicious campaign to discredit the other group's leadership. As a result of his continued public attacks on these other fundamentalist leaders, the Temple Baptist Church voted 3,000 to 7 to discontinue Norris' pastorate there. Exhausted by a lifetime of slugging it out with his enemies, and greatly disheartened by the loss of many of his lifelong friends, Norris, seventy-four years old, died in the early hours of the morning on 8 August 1952. The *Fort Worth Star-Telegram* (21 August 1952) noted his death in the following way:

> The new generation may not fully recognize in the death of Rev. J. Frank Norris
> the passing of an unusual personality and the close of a life in which strife and
> storm and the exercise of dynamic leadership played the dominant chords. . . . He
> possessed ambition, and brilliance, and the ability to gather others to his will. The
> force of his personality was tremendous. . . . He built in beliefs, in numbers, and
> in stone. These monuments remain.

## Appraisal

The theological posture of J. Frank Norris was typical of most of those who would place themselves in the fundamentalist camp. He defended the inerrancy and verbal inspiration of the Bible with incredible passion during a time when "liberalism" seemed to be creeping in around every corner. Anyone who differed in any way with Norris immediately became a likely candidate for a tongue-lashing, if not something worse. Few respected progressive religious leaders escaped the scrutiny of his attention. A modern scholar, C. Allyn Russell of Boston University, has aptly referred to him as the "religious Joseph McCarthy of his generation."

Most political leaders also experienced the power of his pen, some positively and others negatively. Texas politicians gave Norris credit for Republican Herbert Hoover's victory over the Roman Catholic Democrat Al Smith in the largely Democratic state of Texas in the presidential election of 1928. Though such an assessment is certainly an overstatement, it still points out the public influence of the man. Hoover even invited him to the inaugural ceremonies, an invitation he quickly accepted. The next year, a member of the Texas legislature so feared Norris' political influence that he introduced a bill that, if passed, would have kept any minister from ever becoming governor of Texas.

Franklin Roosevelt and Harry S. Truman both drew Norris' ire, the first for Yalta's accommodation with the Soviets and the second for what Norris perceived as his weak policy of "containment." Anticommunism was synonymous with the gospel so far as Norris was concerned. In fact, Pope Pius XII's strong stand against communism brought warm accolades from the normally anti-Catholic fundamentalist. Norris even had a fifteen-minute audience with the pope when he visited Rome.

According to his daughter, Norris loved to be around important people. He had personal contact with each of the four American presidents who served from 1928 to the time of his death. During his travels, he had audiences with such important world leaders as David Lloyd George, Benito Mussolini, and Winston Churchill. Thus, the fact that he carried considerable influence on national and international issues can hardly be denied. His charismatic personality, carefully strategic maneuvering, and outright manipulation of people and issues guaranteed his status as a person one could simply not afford to ignore.

For the greater part of his seventy-four years, Norris was a colorful and highly controversial figure on the American religious scene. As pointed out by Russell, the career of J. Frank Norris greatly contributed to the tarnished image of the fundamentalist movement as a whole. Indeed, his career probably posed as much a threat to fundamentalism as liberalism itself did. The dissidence created by his style caused a split that hurt the movement at the very time when it needed all the unity it could muster.

Without question one of the most impressive pulpit masters of the twentieth century, Norris simultaneously ministered to two of the largest churches in the world. His ministry was one of extremism, representing the far-right sector of American life, in religion and in politics. As a champion of vituperative oratory, Norris loved a good rhetorical fight; and he loved to win. The only thing to which he was subject was his own undying passion to dominate. Few among his contemporaries could hold their own against his verbal attacks, for his conscience seemingly never interfered with his method. Any tactic was acceptable to him so long as it helped him to achieve his purposes, purposes that, to the consternation of his opponents, he sincerely viewed as synonymous with the purposes of God.

## Survey of Criticism

The life of J. Frank Norris has received a great deal of attention in the past few decades. Most of the first works to appear are uncritical and written by close associates. His close friend Louis Entzminger's book can rarely be trusted. It is often hyperbolic in its adulation. Its style so closely resembles that of Norris that the fiery pastor most likely wrote much of it himself. Two other highly sympathetic accounts were written by authors E. Ray Tatum and Roy E. Falls. Tatum's *Conquest or Failure? Biography of J. Frank Norris* addresses his work up to the acquittal of 1927. Falls' *A Biography of J. Frank Norris, 1877–1952* is a completely positive picture of the man. Neither work offers anything that could be called a scholarly account of Norris' activities.

Of the many theses at the master's and doctoral level, two studies deserve particular mention. Royce Lee Measures' work at Southwestern Baptist Theological Seminary, a 1970 master's thesis entitled "The Relationship of J. Frank Norris to the Northern Fundamentalist Movement," sheds light on his participation in the national fundamentalist movement. By far the best book-length critical study of Norris is Clovis Gwin Morris' Texas Tech University doctoral thesis, "He Changed Things: The Life and Thought of J. Frank Norris." This work is the first to use extensive primary source materials and represents a particularly reflective and helpful analysis of the whole ministry of the man, including a very good analysis of his theology.

Two more-recent books include illuminating chapters on Norris. C. Allyn Russell, a highly regarded expert on the personalities of the fundamentalist movement, includes a chapter on Norris in his *Voices of American Fundamentalism: Seven Biographical Studies*. Among the best article-length treatments of the man, it emphasizes the "violent" nature of his ministry, as well as provides insight into the psychological influences that probably helped to shape his personality. More recent is John W. Storey's treatment of Norris in his *Texas Baptist Leadership and Social Christianity: 1900–1980*. Storey, a professor at Lamar University, presents a chapter on Norris to explain the forces at work restricting the emphasis and activity of those Baptists in Texas who were interested in the Social Gospel.

Two journal articles focus on Norris and the Southern Baptists. Mark G. Toulouse's "A Case Study in Schism: J. Frank Norris and the Southern Baptist Convention" challenges traditional ideological accounts of the split between Norris and the SBC by claiming that the schism resulted primarily from a struggle for power between the two parties, in which both sides relied on less than honorable methods as they attempted to control the channels of authority among Texas Baptists. C. Gwin Morris' "J. Frank Norris and the Texas Baptist Convention" spells out in scholarly detail the relationship of Norris to Texas Baptists during the early decades of the twentieth century, up to about 1924.

## Bibliography

### Works by J. Frank Norris

1932    *Inside the Cup; or, My 21 Years in Fort Worth*. Fort Worth: Fundamentalist.
1938    *Inside History of First Baptist Church, Fort Worth; and Temple Baptist Church, Detroit: Life Story of Dr. J. Frank Norris*. Fort Worth: n. p.
1939    *Inside the Cup; or, My First 21 Years in Fort Worth*. Fort Worth: n.p.
1946    *Infidelity Among Southern Baptists Endorsed by Highest Officials: Exposed by J. Frank Norris*. Fort Worth: Bible Baptist Seminary.
1949    *Americanism: An Address to the Texas Legislature*. Fort Worth: Seminary Bible and Book House.
n.d.    *Norris Papers 1927–1952*. Southwestern Baptist Seminary, Fort Worth.
n.d.    Charles Evans Hughes and J. Frank Norris, eds. *New Dealism Exposed: Communism in Baptist Circles, Red Hot Messages*. Fort Worth: Fundamentalist.

### Periodicals Edited by J. Frank Norris

1908–9.    *Baptist Standard*.
1917–22.   *Fence Rail*.
1922–27.   *Searchlight*.
1927–52.   *Fundamentalist*.

### Selected Studies about J. Frank Norris

Entzminger, Louis. *The J. Frank Norris I Have Known for Thirty Four Years*. Fort Worth: n. p., n. d.

Falls, Roy E. *A Biography of J. Frank Norris, 1877–1952*. Euless: n. p., 1975.

Measures, Royce Lee. "The Relationship of J. Frank Norris to the Northern Fundamentalist Movement." Master's thesis, Southwestern Baptist Theological Seminary,
1970.

Morris, Clovis Gwin. "He Changed Things: The Life and Thought of J. Frank Norris."
Ph.D. diss., Texas Tech University, 1973.

Pitts, William L., ed. *Texas Baptist History: The Journal of the Texas Baptist Historical
Society*. Vol. 1, no. 1. Waco: Baylor University Press, 1981.

Russell, C. Allyn. *Voices of American Fundamentalism: Seven Biographical Studies*, 20–
46. Philadelphia: Westminster Press, 1976.

Storey, John W. *Texas Baptist Leadership and Social Christianity: 1900–1980*, 39–70.
College Station: Texas A & M University Press, 1986.

Tatum, E. Ray. *Conquest or Failure? Biography of J. Frank Norris*. Dallas: Baptist
Historical Foundation, 1966.

Toulouse, Mark G. "A Case Study in Schism: J. Frank Norris and the Southern Baptist
Convention." *Foundations* 21 (January-March 1981): 32–53.

MARK G. TOULOUSE

# Fulton Oursler, Sr.

In Oursler's posthumously published autobiography, *Behold This Dreamer!*,
Fulton Oursler, Jr., remembered his father as "a man of seemingly inexhaustible
talents and careers—a reporter, novelist, biographer, playwright, journalist and
screenwriter; an editor, critic, radio scenarist and broadcaster; a magician, de-
tective-story writer and columnist; a world-traveller, ventriloquist and psychic
investigator; a lecturer, criminologist and undercover agent for the F.B.I." During the last decade of his life Oursler also authored a number of best-selling
religious and inspirational books and was a major figure in the psychologically
oriented piety that was prominent in the postwar revival of religion in the United
States.

## Biography

Charles Fulton Oursler was born on 22 January 1893 in Baltimore, Maryland,
to Lillian Sappington Oursler and William Clarence Oursler, a horsecar driver
and later line superintendent for a transit company in the city. The Ourslers'
first child, May, had died of scarlet fever two years earlier, and a second daughter
died in 1898 at less than two years of age. In effect an only child, Oursler grew
up as a Protestant living in Catholic neighborhoods and as a member of a well-
to-do Baptist church where he was shunned by the wealthier children in the
congregation. Oursler's parents lived in ten different homes during their first
nine years of marriage, and by the time Fulton was thirteen they would have
lived in seven more.

The feelings of isolation and of being something of a misfit would appear in
a positive sense in some Oursler's later religious writings but nearly always

against a backdrop of evil. Other elements of Oursler's later religious outlook probably were influenced by his childhood as well. A half century later, powerful memories persisted: the revulsion at having to kiss the sweaty forehead of a dying uncle; the fondling and exhibitionism of a fifteen-year-old babysitter; an interest in magic, hypnotism, and the writings of Edgar Allan Poe; overhearing the beating of a cousin caught molesting his sisters; and the sound of his parents in bed. "I believe now it was this fierce internal conflict about sex and my parents that afflicted my sleep with the most hideous nightmares any child ever knew—scenes of bloody cannibalism and worse."

Family financial difficulties forced Oursler to drop out of school before completing the eighth grade. He aspired to become a writer and held a succession of part-time jobs before becoming an assistant in a law office. Two years later, after a year's persistence, Oursler was hired as a cub reporter for the *Baltimore American* at a salary of ten dollars a week. At seventeen he covered crime and wrote obituary notices, reviews of concerts, articles on unions, religious conventions, and politics, while indulging his lifelong fascination with celebrities by interviewing Sarah Bernhardt, Emma Goldman, Carry Nation, and others.

When he was eighteen he eloped with Rose Killian Karger. To supplement his income from the newspaper, Oursler sought employment as a local correspondent with various trade magazines. In 1918 he moved to New York, joining the staff of *Music Trades*. When the editor entered officer-training school three days later, Oursler became managing editor, a position he held for four years. After contributing four articles to the inaugural issue of health-faddist Bernarr Macfadden's magazine *Brain Power,* Oursler joined the staff of Macfadden Publications and in three weeks was named supervising editor. The association would last until 1942. Eventually Oursler supervised thirteen magazines, including *Physical Culture, True Story, True Detective Mysteries, True Romances, Liberty Magazine,* and *Master Detective.* When he was confronted by religious leaders who denounced *True Story* as "salacious, lewd, licentious, pornographic," Oursler shrewdly assembled a five-man review board including a Catholic priest, a rabbi, a Methodist, a Presbyterian, and a Congregationalist, making the magazine "immune from the reformers."

During these years Oursler's outlook was that of "contented agnosticism," as he would later refer to it. As an editor and as a writer he enthusiastically affirmed the liberating revolution in morals of the 1920s in which organized religion represented superstition, puritanical morality, and repressive authority, in sum, a major obstruction to self-expression and human progress.

Oursler's quasi-autobiographical first novel, *Behold This Dreamer!,* appeared in 1924, and the same year he met and fell in love with Grace Perkins, an aspiring young author and a Catholic. The next year he obtained a Mexican divorce, and he and Grace were married in Mexico within a week. During the following year a second and third novel appeared and the couple's first child, April, was born.

In 1927 the innovative, audience-participation play *The Spider* opened a year's successful run on Broadway, later appearing as a novel authored by Grace

Perkins, and as a movie. The same period saw the first of Oursler's Thatcher-Colt detective novels written under the pseudonym of (and narrated by) Anthony Abbot. The series reached eight volumes by the early 1940s.

In 1931 Macfadden purchased the financially precarious *Liberty* and named Oursler editor. Oursler used the magazine as a forum for politicians and world leaders, carrying articles by and interviews with Al Smith, Franklin Roosevelt, Churchill, Trotsky, Mussolini, and Hitler and publishing young writers such as Mackinley Cantor, Erle Stanley Gardner, and Budd Schulberg. In 1932 he moved to Hollywood to work as a screenwriter and continued to supervise Macfadden's magazines long-distance. Soon, five Oursler films were in production, three by Oursler and two by Grace Perkins. Never one to miss an opportunity, Oursler solicited stories for *Liberty* from Marie Dressler, Jean Harlow, and Charlie Chaplin.

Within a year Oursler returned east and set up residence in Cape Cod. In 1934 he entered radio broadcasting with the fifteen-minute series, "Stories That Should Be Told" and served as master of ceremonies for "Liberty's Forum of the Air." He met and formed a lasting admiration for J. Edgar Hoover and ran articles on G-Men and the FBI in *Liberty*. Oursler's penchant for transforming nearly any enterprise into one of social service led him to advertise one-hundred-dollar rewards for information leading to the capture of criminals pictured in *True Detective*.

Even though he obtained three articles from Roosevelt for *Liberty* in 1938, Oursler was becoming disenchanted with the policies of the New Deal and subsequently supported Thomas E. Dewey. Grace Perkins had entered an extensive treatment program for alcoholism, and the youngest children were away in boarding school. In 1941 Macfadden resigned over a scandal concerning the circulation figures of *True Story,* and Oursler left the next year and returned to New York. Two years later he accepted a position as senior editor of *Reader's Digest,* a post he held until his death in 1952.

The ten-year residence in Cape Cod witnessed a marked change in Oursler's writing and in his career. Recalling the pattern of another famous life, he wrote in *Behold This Dreamer!*, "I was born in Baltimore, crucified in New York, and raised from the dead in Cape Cod." He traced the turning point in his life to his first trip to the Middle East in 1935. "Almost literally on the road to Damascus I began to turn back to Christ." But it was not until after the publication of *A Skeptic in the Holy Land* in 1936, which he later called "an ignorant and impious work," that he became convinced that the "ethical statements of Christianity needed to be reemphasised in a world that became less and less attractive as Naziism offered its hand, stained with the blood of the Jews, and received the clasp of Communist Russia." He set out to write "an elevator boy's life of Christ," a task he began in earnest in 1939 after a second trip to the Middle East.

His study of the Bible and the early church led to an increasing interest in Catholicism, and he began receiving instruction in 1941, entering the church two years later. Grace Perkins, now recovered and a popular writer with twelve published novels, was hired the same year by Norman Vincent Peale* as executive editor of *Guideposts*.

In 1942 Oursler published the first of his inspirational books, *Three Things We Can Believe In*, a short collection of speeches and addresses. During the final decade of his life he completed ten books, nearly all with explicitly religious themes, partially wrote three others that appeared posthumously, and contributed more than seventy-five articles to *Reader's Digest*, some condensed or reprinted from other magazines. His newspaper column, "Modern Parables," was widely syndicated and the Sunday-evening ABC radio program "The Greatest Story Ever Told" opened in 1947 and was on the air for nearly a decade.

The topics that had fascinated Oursler throughout his career—crime, magic, politics, celebrities, law enforcement, communism, sex, and world leaders—had scarcely disappeared. Instead they were gradually sublimated into retelling the story of the most unforgettable character anyone had ever met, Jesus Christ. *The Greatest Story Ever Told* was published in 1949. The book was Oursler's crowning achievement and one of the landmarks of popular piety in America. Almost immediately it became the best-selling life of Jesus written in the English language, indeed the best-selling work of religious nonfiction ever published in the United States. Fifteen years later a Hollywood film was released. The final two works of Oursler's biblical trilogy, *The Greatest Book Ever Written* (the Old Testament) and *The Greatest Faith Ever Known* (the work of Paul), also appeared on best-seller lists.

Oursler died of a heart attack in New York on 24 May 1952. Bishop Fulton J. Sheen* led the mourners through the decades of the Rosary at his funeral.

Oursler's view of his own life as well as his portrayal of the exemplary characters in his stories and essays illustrated the familiar paradigm of the spiritual pilgrimage from sin to grace or, in more modern terms, from mental strife to peace of mind. Donald Meyer astutely observed that Oursler's life also closely paralleled a radical shift in popular Christianity in the first half of this century:

> Oursler's career sheds some light on a central problem in narrating the history of American popular culture in the twentieth century, namely, explaining how the wide-based, popular 'revolution in manners and morals' of the 1920's, presumably emancipatory and individualistic, was absorbed and socialized into a new defensive tribalism by the late 1940's. At the time of his death, Oursler was identified as an exponent of patriotic, conservative piety: his thirty years of service to the popular journalism of crime, sex, fads and public relations were forgotten.

### Appraisal

Through his newspaper column, magazine articles, religious books, and the forum of *Reader's Digest*, Oursler probably reached more readers than any other religious and inspirational writer in postwar America, with the exception of Norman Vincent Peale. Nonetheless, little has been written about Oursler's contributions. His eclecticism and his roles as editor and popularizer of the ideas of others no doubt have contributed to this neglect, as has the fact that unlike Peale, Billy Graham*, Fulton J. Sheen*, Thomas Merton*, and others, he assumed no role of public leadership in (and seldom even public identification with) any well-defined religious movement, explaining that "we should keep far away from any process of evangelization, however dignified." Fulton Oursler, Jr., wrote accurately and tellingly of his father's audience: "The majority of Fulton's readers probably never realized he was a Catholic."

Oursler is a significant figure in popular religion chiefly because he achieved an appealing synthesis of diverse and sometimes opposing currents in popular American Christianity. One measure of the inclusiveness of his thought is that a list of popular religious books by other best-selling religious authors of the period provides an accurate inventory of major themes in Oursler's own thinking. He praised the restorative effects of periodic withdrawal from society and of the contemplative life, as did Thomas Merton (*The Seven Storey Mountain*) and Anne Morrow Lindbergh (*Gift From The Sea*), and with Le Comte de Nouy (*Human Destiny*) he viewed science and religion as natural allies. Biblical religion and modern psychology confirmed one another, in the solutions they offered both for problems of worry and self-doubt (Peale, *The Power of Positive Thinking*) and for social problems, particularly those associated with adolescence (Pat Boone, *'Twixt Twelve and Twenty*). The cult of the Christian personality represented by Catherine Marshall's* inspirational *A Man Called Peter* also figured prominently in Oursler's writings, most notably as it highlighted individuals who gave totally of themselves for the good of others (Dale Evans Rogers, *Angel Unaware*). The biblical-historical romance (Lloyd C. Douglas*, *The Robe;* Thomas B. Costain, *The Silver Chalice*) and anecdotal, human-interest stories and testimonials (*Faith Made Them Champions,* ed. Norman Vincent Peale; *This I Believe,* ed. Edward P. Morgan) proved effective vehicles for communicating religious truths. Like many other popular religious leaders of the forties and fifties, Oursler set the choice confronting the modern world as that between Christianity and communism or, in his words, between "Marx and his *Manifesto*" and "the marks of the nails in His hands." Appropriately for a postwar era of rising international tensions, the greatest gift religion offered was simply "peace"—*Peace of Mind* (Joshua Loth Liebman), *Peace of Soul* (Fulton J. Sheen), *Peace With God* (Billy Graham).

Underlying Oursler's vision was a diffuse and pervasive strand of popular piety to which Sydney E. Ahlstrom, in *A Religious History of the American People,* gave the name "harmonial religion." It was represented in the last century by Mary Baker Eddy, Warren Felt Evans, and Ralph Waldo Trine, and in this century by Bruce Barton*, Anne Morrow Lindbergh, and Peale, among many others. According to Ahlstrom, harmonial religion "encompasses those forms of piety and belief in which spiritual composure, physical health, and economic well being are understood to flow from a person's rapport with the cosmos." In "What Prayer Can Do," an article in the January 1951 *Reader's Digest,* Oursler wrote that prayer brings "a continuous feeling of being in harmony with the constructive forces of the universe," and the same theme emerged in many of his stories and essays.

But Oursler's harmonialism was anything but a cheerful and world-affirming religion of healthy-mindedness. From time to time he sounded like the typical positive thinker, as he did in *Why I Know There Is a God:* "Obstacles in our path are actually and literally our greatest opportunities." More typical, however, was his tendency to point out and linger over a range of middle-class anxieties concerning unions and labor unrest, infidelity and divorce, juvenile delinquency, racial tensions, political corruption, communism, domestic subversion, an antiquated religious moralism, and an empty modernism. Worst of all was the erosion of spiritual values that produced "complete despair—the last and worst virus of all, born in the unclean quagmire of abandoned faith, of lost hope, the soul trap of atheism." In such circumstances, the most pressing questions were not those of the positive thinkers—"How To Think Your Way To Success" and "How Power and Efficiency Can Be Yours." Rather it was the simple question standing at the center of his life of Jesus, "Is life worth living?"

Usually Oursler did not promise that religious faith brought wealth, success, power, or even the avoidance of suffering. Nor did he attempt to reduce the Bible to auto-suggestive techniques that could unlock hidden powers and release inner resources. Peale sponsored a heroic therapy that would "flush out," "drive out," and "throw overboard" negative and enfeebling thoughts and worries. Oursler's was the more modest task defined by a chapter title in Billy Graham's *My Answer*—"How To Be Happy Most of the Time."

Oursler set out to make worry and despair impossible by reminding readers in anecdote after anecdote and testimonial after testimonial that the troubling dualities of success or failure, victor or victim, helping oneself or helping others were subsumed under an exemplary pattern of living, aspects of which were likely to recall moments of high moral exhilaration in the lives of his readers. Again and again Oursler eulogized those cheerful martyrs and happy victims who threw themselves totally into seemingly hopeless causes and in so doing discovered the personally therapeutic benefits coming from selfless service to others. This, in brief outline, was the greatest story ever told of the greatest lives ever lived. It was a story found in the New Testament but also in the careers of Sir Walter Scott, Marie Curie, Richard E. Byrd, Father James Keller, Bill Williams, founder of Alcoholics Anonymous, and a host of lesser-known real and fictional characters: the reclusive and pallid war veteran Pete Wakefield, in the nostalgic Christmas story "A String of Blue Beads"; or Jou-Jou, the Ziegfeld dancer who vowed to work in Brazil to discover a cure for cancer in "The Woman Who Changed Her Mind"; or Father Harold Purcell, who found personal renewal in opening a mission for black children in Montgomery, Alabama; or the elderly woman in "An Old Way To A New Life." Nearly an invalid, she stopped sending money to buy flowers for her son's grave and personally began taking flowers to hospitals and mental institutions. She recovered almost immediately. "She had discovered what most of us know and forget; that in helping others she had helped herself."

Though Oursler clearly intended his example stories as injunctions to moral behavior, the stories were constructed so that reading them was itself a therapeutic exercise. The stories and anecdotes singled out as virtues soft and passive feelings—suffering, submission, passion, sacrifice—the very things that unless freely chosen gave the sense of being victimized by a hard and uncaring world. Equally important, Oursler was careful to have his characters illustrate the wide but acceptable (at least in print) diversity among individuals. Readers were reminded over and over that a host of problems threatening peace of mind resulted from seeing distinctions where none existed and then needlessly fretting and worrying about conflicts that were only illusory.

Two distinctions, however, really did make a difference. The first was central to a century of American mind-cure thinking: the distinction between mind and matter or, put a bit differently, between bodily, animal impulses and spiritual aspirations. "Man does not represent the end of evolution but only a middle stage between the past with all the memories of the beast and the future, rich in the promise of the soul," Oursler wrote in an appreciative summary of *Human Destiny*. "From now on, our progress will not be physical but spiritual."

The second distinction was that of child/adult, reflecting a middle-class preoccupation with child and adolescent psychologies that had been growing since the turn of the century. Oursler did not employ these distinctions to define a practical, step-by-step method for self-improvement (as did the mind-cure thinkers) or to recommend programs for child rearing and education (as did the psychologists). Oursler used them as narrative devices to remind readers of the timeless models of the human personality and to plot the logical nuances of human deviancy. Thus, Nazis, unfaithful spouses, and Idumeans could be seen as having a logical affinity with one another, since all erred in indulging animal passions. Permissive parents treated their young children as adults; the Pharisees treated adults as if they were children; zealots, Communists, and juvenile delinquents shared the habit of continuing with the childish games pitting good against evil, the cowboys against the Indians.

The examples could be multiplied at length, but even a brief sample suggests that Oursler's stories and anecdotes were reassuring for three reasons. First, they reminded readers not to worry about the myriad of normal and healthy ways in which normal and healthy people differed from one another (hence Oursler's emphasis on individualism, his tolerance and liberalism). Second, they reminded readers that American democracy was the only system founded to recognize and foster the unique differences among individuals (hence his patriotism and fear of subversion). Third, they supported the familiar boundaries governing sexual behavior and rebelliousness and validated the traditional offices of authority vested in parents, schools, churches, and law-enforcement agencies (hence Oursler's conservatism). In the end, readers were reminded that whatever the power of the threats ranged against them—disease, political oppression, financial misfortune, or even the temptation to doubt and question their own beliefs and values—they possessed an inner tranquillity that could not be shaken, since it rested on the precious secret of peace of mind, namely, that they were permanently and unalterably normal.

Oursler's view of reality was neither idiosyncratic nor exclusively religious. The most popular harmonialist, peace-of-mind book ever published in the United States (and the best-selling book ever written by an American) appeared during the same period, Dr. Benjamin Spock's *Baby and Child Care* (1946). Spock viewed the world in similar terms, minus the specifically religious overtones: the present was a time of despair; human ("spiritual") values were in rapid decline because of the "focus on his crude, animal side"; self-confidence came from living in harmony with "Nature" and from people's conviction that "they are in this world not for their own satisfaction but primarily to serve others." Finally, as countless examples demonstrated, worrying about the numerous ways in which normal and healthy babies differed from one another represented the single greatest threat to self-confidence and peace of mind. Dr. Spock's advice was a fitting epigraph for Oursler's work and for "the world's most popular magazine" for which he served as senior editor. "Trust yourself," Dr. Spock advised parents in the first words of the book. "You know more than you think you do."

## Survey of Criticism

Assessments of Oursler's importance as a shaper and mirror of popular religion are limited to book reviews, obituary notices, the reminiscences of family members and friends, and a few biobibliographical entries in encyclopedias. Reviews of Oursler's religious books, and especially those of his biblical trilogy, typically praised the absence of denominational or theological bias and his ability to render the Scripture in the style of newspaper reports or in that of the *Reader's Digest* (*San Francisco Chronicle*, 17 April 1949, p. 22; *Library Journal*, 1 January 1949, p. 57; *Kirkus*, October 1951:608). Less frequent were the complaints that the books suffered from a total absence of modern historical scholarship (*Chicago Tribune*, 25 October 1953, p. 13; *Christian Century*, December 1950: 1524) and from a tendency to revise the Bible with an eye to mid-twentieth-century issues such as peace of mind, social and racial justice, and the supremacy of the individual (*New York Times*, 6 February 1949, p. 10; *Commonweal*, 25 February 1949, p. 500). As noted earlier, Donald Meyer is helpful in locating Oursler's work in the context of a pattern of change in secular popular culture.

## Bibliography

### Selected Books by Fulton Oursler, Sr.

1924  *Behold This Dreamer!* New York: Macaulay Company.
1925  *Sandalwood*. New York: Macaulay Company.
1926  *Stepchild of the Moon*. New York: Harper and Brothers.
1928  *Poor Little Fool*. New York: Harper and Brothers.

1929    *The True Story of Bernarr Macfadden.* New York: Lewis Copeland Company.
1929    *The World's Delight.* New York: Harper and Brothers.
1930    *The Great Jasper.* New York: Covici, Friede.
1935    *Joshua Todd.* New York: Farrar and Rinehart.
1936    *A Skeptic in the Holy Land.* New York: Farrar and Rinehart.
1942    *Three Things We Can Believe In: A Formula For Peace of Mind in Anxious Days.*
        New York: Fleming H. Revell Company.
1947    *The Precious Secret.* Philadelphia: J. C. Winston Co.
1948    *The Happy Grotto.* New York: D. X. Mcmullin Co.
1949    *Father Flanigan of Boys Town.* With Will Oursler. Garden City, N.Y.: Doubleday.
1949    *The Greatest Story Ever Told: A Tale of the Greatest Life Ever Lived.* Garden
        City, N.Y.: Doubleday.
1950    *Why I Know There Is a God.* Garden City, N.Y.: Doubleday.
1951    *A Child's Life of Jesus.* New York: F. Watts.
1951    *The Greatest Book Ever Written: The Old Testament Story.* Garden City, N.Y.:
        Doubleday.
1952    *Modern Parables.* Garden City, N.Y.: Doubleday.
1953    *The Greatest Faith Ever Known: The Story of the Men Who First Spread the
        Religion of Jesus and of the Momentous Times in Which They Lived.* With April
        Armstrong Oursler. Garden City, N.Y.: Doubleday.
1954    *Lights Along the Shore.* Garden City, N.Y.: Hanover House.
1956    *A String of Blue Beads.* Garden City, N.Y.: Doubleday.
1964    *Behold This Dreamer! An Autobiography by Fulton Oursler.* Edited with com-
        mentary by Fulton Oursler, Jr. Boston: Little, Brown and Company.

### Selected Studies about Fulton Oursler, Sr.

Armstrong, April Oursler, "My Friend, My Father." *Good Housekeeping* 139 (July
    1954): 54–55.
Hoehn, Matthew Anthony. *Catholic Authors: Contemporary Biographical Sketches.* New-
    ark: St. Mary's Abbey, 1957.
Meyer, Donald. "Oursler, Charles Fulton." *Dictionary of American Biography: Sup-
    plement Five, 1951–55.* New York: Charles Scribner's Sons, 1977.
O'Brien, John Anthony. *The Road to Damascus: The Spiritual Pilgrimage of Fifteen
    Converts to Catholicism.* Garden City, N.Y.: Doubleday, 1949.
Oursler, William Charles. *Family Story.* New York: Funk and Wagnalls, 1963.
———. "Oursler, Fulton." *Twentieth Century Authors: First Supplement.* Edited by
    Stanley J. Kunitz. New York: H. W. Wilson Company, 1955.
                                                                    WAYNE ELZEY

# Norman Vincent Peale

"I was honored by being born in a beautiful little American village," commented
Norman Vincent Peale in his autobiography, *The True Joy of Positive Living,*
written after a lifetime of urban church ministry, "where love of God and love
of country and Christian morality were taught and practiced by sturdy people
who were indeed the salt of the earth. To the last, at least in heart, I will always

be a country boy from Ohio.'' Indeed, although Peale was sometimes depicted by his critics as a misguided or even demonic distorter of Christian teaching, he faithfully espoused the small-town values of an older America finding its way toward new urban realities. Far from being a charlatan of capitalist values cloaked in religious piety, as his cultured despisers liked to depict him, he was simply an advocate of the science of personal and moral well-being firmly grounded in nineteenth-century thinking.

Norman Vincent Peale established himself as the chaplain of what Douglas Walrath has called the ''striver'' generation. He became pastor and preacher to white middle- and upper-middle-class Americans who struggled to survive a Depression and two world wars and who were positioned to ride the economic escalator in the new prosperity of the 1950s. He took as his mission to inspire people to strive, following the example of notable fellow citizens, toward a better life for themselves, their families, and their country. Rising to his peak of popularity in the ''can-do'' atmosphere of the Eisenhower years, Peale was most at home in the business world and the sphere of personal fulfillment. The intractable social dilemmas of an America wrenched apart by civil rights, war protest, Watergate, and the desperation of urban centers were not amenable to the Peale approach. Yet he continued to hold a sizable following on into the 1980s, as he approached his own ninetieth birthday.

### Biography

Peale was one of relatively few popular religious leaders in American history who stood firmly within a mainstream Protestant denominational tradition even while attracting a following numbered in the millions. He was born on 31 May 1898 into a devout Methodist family. His father, Charles Clifford Peale, had received medical training and was a practicing physician until his own miraculous recovery from illness, whereupon he entered the Methodist ministry. He was serving in Bowersville, Ohio, at the time of Norman's birth, under the appointment of Bishop John H. Vincent, and thus came Norman's middle name. (His first name derived from a line in Tennyson about ''Norman blood.'') Norman's mother was Anna Delaney, a bright and effervescent woman of Irish descent who later became a well-known speaker and advocate for world missions.

The senior Peale's itinerant ministerial journey took him to various small Ohio towns as well as to Cincinnati, and he eventually served First Methodist Church in Columbus and was made a district superintendent, Methodism's regional assistant to the bishop. Thus Norman became thoroughly familiar with parsonage life and entered the adolescent struggle common to ''preachers' kids'' trying to reconcile feelings of admiration and resentment of the ministry. When he finished high school in Bellefontaine, Ohio, he enrolled in Methodism's major Ohio college, Ohio Wesleyan, from which he graduated in 1920. Attracted by the excitement of national affairs in the postwar era, Norman tried his hand at journalism, first with a paper in Findlay, Ohio, where his parents were living, then in Detroit, where his father's friend Grove Patterson was a newspaper editor.

Patterson was to be one of Norman's role models, teaching him that the only worthwhile ideas are ones that can be put simply and understandably for the ordinary person. But Norman had a gnawing sense of missing his calling, and in the fall of 1921 he enrolled in the school of theology at Boston University, also a Methodist institution.

A consummate master of the anecdote, Peale developed a stock of standard tales about these first twenty-some years of his life. Sprinkled liberally through his preaching and writing, these were endearing incidents usually involving his father (the day Norman was caught with a cigar, the time his father found him preaching from the pulpit to a dark, empty sanctuary) or some other adult who was influential in his life (the man who sent him out to the farmhouses to peddle out-of-style suits). Perhaps because of his countless speeches to business people in later life, Peale also loved to tell of his early sales experiences, especially the fear of knocking on people's doors.

His adolescent struggle with shyness also was the stuff of many lessons. Peale recalled his fifth-grade teacher's philosophy that "you can if you think you can" (later the title of one of Peale's books). He remembered fondly his college professor of economics who scolded him for the egotism and self-preoccupation that made him a red-faced sputterer in front of an audience, a challenge that precipitated a religious experience for Peale, as he sought once again to commit his life to Jesus Christ on the college chapel steps. Even after thousands of speeches over the years, he insisted that this hesitancy and self-consciousness in public speaking had never entirely left him.

Yet Peale was also an aggressive and flamboyant young man, an eager member of the debate team and class president in college. On a visit to Washington, D.C., he arranged to tour the White House, meeting President Calvin Coolidge and giving him the Phi Gamma Delta fraternity handshake. Soon after that, he called on the Methodist bishop of New York without an appointment in early 1924. He asked for and received assignment to a congregation, and in May 1924 with his seminary degree in hand he began his full-time ministry.

Peale liked to say that he had always taken on churches where "there was no place to go but up." His first congregation was meeting in a run-down building in the Flatlands of Brooklyn, yet the thousands of new families moving into housing developments nearby offered a perfect opportunity for Peale to put his sales techniques to work. He obtained lists of new residents from the gas company and knocked on their doors, calling them by name and inviting them to church. He sent out postcards by the hundreds, emblazoned with the message "Why have our congregations increased until the church is crowded to capacity? . . . Come around and your questions will be answered." It wasn't true, but it was great sales strategy. By his third Easter there, Peale had attracted over 3,000 people to one of Brooklyn's theaters for worship, and with the completion of a new building, everybody in town knew where Kings Highway Methodist Church was.

In 1927 Peale took the same style to the old University Methodist Church in Syracuse. Eyeing an extension ladder laid across the balcony pews, he pledged to fill the huge gothic sanctuary every Sunday. "Why is it suddenly hard to get a seat" in University Church, his newspaper ads cried. That was the way he envisioned it, so that was the way it was. With the help of the college music department, he assembled an attractive choir, brought in guest singers and speakers of national fame, and soon enjoyed the reality of his vision.

The Syracuse years introduced three more influential persons to Peale's life. One was Harlowe B. Andrews, a businessman whom Peale and everybody else called Brother Andrews and who taught Peale how to raise money through prayer, faith, and the courage to ask people straight out for what they ought to give. Another was Hugh M. Tilroe, head of the department of speech, whom a still self-conscious Peale found threatening but who insisted that Peale simply relax and preach the gospel without any intellectual airs. A third was Ruth Stafford, on whose counsel and support Peale came increasingly to rely and who married him on 20 June 1930.

By 1932 Peale was already well established as a popular young preacher. He had turned University Church around, had started a radio ministry, and was receiving invitations to speak around the country. Two of those invitations were to mark a crossroads in his life, for they evolved into calls to assume the senior minister's position. One was at First Methodist Church of Los Angeles, then a thriving downtown congregation with thousands in worship every Sunday. The other was a historic but sadly empty church in lower Manhattan, a congregation of the Reformed Church in America with roots in the Dutch colony that had become New York City. It was named Marble Collegiate Church, being built of marble and being part of a collegium of five formerly Dutch Reformed churches in New York. It represented the greater challenge, and Peale accepted it.

He soon had misgivings, however. Depression-era New York was a dismal place, the church building was old and inadequate, the congregation was a shell, with perhaps 200 people in attendance on Sundays. After a year of struggle, Peale was discouraged. Then, while vacationing with his wife in England, he had another of his life-changing experiences of the efficacy of prayer. Surrendering himself to the Lord and declaring his weakness and inability to cope, he found himself overflowing with warmth, joy, and tears. Rushing back to New York, he tackled the situation with a new vigor that would in time bring him to national renown.

In the summer of 1933 Peale was asked to begin a radio program under the auspices of the Federal Council of Churches (later the National Council of Churches). Called "The Art of Living," the program continued on Saturdays for the next forty years. It would later be joined by a ninety-second spot feature called "The American Character" and a regular broadcast of Peale's Sunday sermon. Peale always felt that radio offered the most intimate access to people's lives, using simply the power of the human voice. He never believed that any medium was effective in getting people to join churches, but he did think he could touch lives with his message through radio. Television never had any appeal for him, partly because he did not like to see himself on screen but mainly because of its enormous expense. He could never bear to ask for money on the air. Yet two long-running syndicated television programs, "What's Your Trouble" and "Positive Thinking with Norman Vincent Peale," did become part of his ministry.

After ten years at Marble Collegiate Church, Peale was beginning to attract large crowds with his simple, personal preaching style. Two services on Sunday morning and one on Sunday evening were full most of the time. The demand for copies of his sermons was so great that Peale had to move the publication and mailing service to Pawling, New York, where he and his family had a second home. The operation soon evolved into the Foundation for Christian Living, of which his wife was primarily in charge.

By the mid-1940s, with encouragement from Lowell Thomas of radio fame and DeWitt Wallace, publisher of the new *Reader's Digest* of popular literature, Peale began a newsletter intended to find its way to homes, churches, and executive desks. Called *Guideposts,* the publication offered the anecdotes and inspirational words for which Peale was becoming so well known. After early years of struggle, *Guideposts* achieved a circulation of nearly a million.

As Arthur Gordon reported in *Norman Vincent Peale: Minister to Millions,* Peale's interest in the power of prayer for healing began with his own father's medical interests but was encouraged by physicians, such as Gordon Hoople in his Syracuse congregation who argued that "the great majority of people who come to me for help are more sick in their minds than in their bodies." In New York Peale was introduced to a psychiatrist named Smiley Blanton, who was also intrigued by the connection of faith and mental health. Together they began a clinic that soon acquired a heavy caseload. Eventually the clinic opened branches outside the city and expanded into training of pastoral counselors, under the name of the Blanton-Peale Institutes of Religion and Health. The two men also wrote books together, *Faith is the Answer* (1940) and *The Art of Real Happiness* (1950).

From his days in Syracuse Peale had found the lecture circuit exhilarating, and in New York he acquired an agent who soon arranged engagements all over the United States. His particular interest was in finding a way to reach men, a distinct minority in most congregations. He took as his task, he wrote in *The True Joy of Positive Living,* "to speak and write and present Jesus Christ and Christianity to the men of our times as the most exciting, practical, tremendous way of life available." Proud of the large numbers of men in his worship services, Peale found himself addressing mainly a male audience as he made the circuit of business conventions and motivational sales gatherings around the country. He fondly recalled the many times he was met with skepticism as a preacher in the business world yet won people over with his engaging style.

In addition to his books with Smiley Blanton, Peale had published *The Art of Living* (1937) and *A Guide to Confident Living* (1948) that established his anecdotal format for inspiration and interpretation of principles for living. But his astonishing breakthrough into the public mind came in 1952 with a manuscript that he had originally entitled "The Power of Faith." His publisher at Prentice-Hall suggested that he try to appeal more to people not connected with churches by calling it *The Power of Positive Thinking*. The book was soon on the best-seller lists, where it remained for over three years, and continued in perennial reprint editions for over thirty years thereafter.

The popularity of his best seller, along with his regular syndicated newspaper columns and numerous articles in *Reader's Digest* and elsewhere, thrust Peale into the public spotlight. He was featured by *Look* as the "Minister to Millions," selected by *Life* as one of "Twelve Great American Preachers," and joined by his wife and children for a story about their family life in *Good Housekeeping*. *Time, Newsweek, Saturday Review,* and other magazines described his activities and later the controversies surrounding him.

Peale's heavy speaking and writing schedule caused him to seek an associate at Marble Collegiate Church, and Arthur Caliandro assumed that post. In Peale's later semiretirement from church responsibilities, Caliandro became his designated successor. However, with his publication of an autobiography, *The True Joy of Positive Living,* in 1984 at age eighty-six, Peale made it clear that retirement from the excitement of his lifelong work was not in the picture.

### Appraisal

Four themes were evident throughout Peale's voluminous writings and recorded speeches. First and foremost was his stress on power. The passion of his ministry was fed by people who came to him defeated or overwhelmed by life's experiences. He wanted to offer them not only the power of positive thinking but also prayer power, spiritual power, "commanding power over life and circumstances." All authentic personal power derived from a higher power that Peale saw exhibited in Jesus Christ. "The principles of happiness and success were not created by the author, but are as old as the Bible," he wrote in *A Guide to Confident Living* (1948). "In fact, they are the simple principles taught in the Bible." He insisted that his viewpoint always represented the best interpretation of the gospel that he could effect; he was no systematic theologian, but clearly for him the freedom of a Christian meant freedom from guilt, grief, and other self-limitations (sin) and freedom for self-fulfillment and control over one's own destiny (salvation).

The means of tapping the higher power and so enhancing one's own personal power were to be found in the science of living well, a science of principles that could be mastered and followed down the road of achievement and success. In this theme Peale stood in a line stemming not so much from the arcane sciences of the mind advocated by the likes of Christian Science founder Mary Baker Eddy as from the nineteenth-century mainstream Protestant guides to moral uplift and rational living. "I've always felt that Christianity itself may be described as a science," he told a Hope College audience on the occasion of their naming the academic science building after him and his wife. "I think that Jesus lays down certain simple formulas that if you follow them precisely, you will get an equivalent result" (from *Alumni Magazine* of Hope College, Winter 1973). His principles for daily living were inspirational aphorisms ("Believe in your own God-released powers") based on his adaptations of verses from Scripture ("I can do all things through Christ working in me"). They were undergirded with homey stories from family, school, and workplace showing how their practice could bring positive, powerful results.

No doctrine or principle had a place in Peale's thinking unless it was practical and efficacious in everyday life. He particularly wanted to establish the amazing efficiency of prayer and told many stories of how solutions to nagging problems appeared to believers in the practice of prayer. Peale was convinced that the churches were empty to the extent that they failed to offer a practical message for ordinary people in daily living.

Finally, his own ministry, as well as Christian faith itself, was in the service of people, their needs, hopes, aspirations, and happiness. Peale never attempted to make a point without telling a story about a person, usually one he had known pastorally or socially, almost never someone he had not actually met. As his fame grew, his appetite for people and their stories lent an even more popular quality to his words, leading to what was tagged as a name-dropping approach. His list of characters in role model stories expanded from Grove Patterson, Hugh Tilroe, Harlowe Andrews, and his own father, to include Branch Rickey, Clement Stone, Jesse Owens, J. C. Penney, and Eddie Rickenbacker. He enshrined the Horatio Alger fable in an annual award and constantly appealed to the biographies of major industrialists of businessmen such as Justin Dart, Arthur Rubloff, J. L. Kraft, and others who rose from obscure origins to become men of forcefulness and influence.

### Survey of Criticism

As Peale became a household name in the 1950s, so also did Peale become a target of criticism and, for some, the epitome of what was shallow and false in American Protestantism. One layer of critique simply focused on his writings. "These problems seem too easily solved, the success a bit too automatic and immediate, the answers a little too pat, and the underlying theology a shade too utilitarian," wrote the 26 October 1952 *New York Times* reviewer of *Positive Thinking*. At a deeper level, William L. Miller and other critics took him to task for distorting Christianity into a gospel of success, for inverting belief in God into belief in oneself. If prayer was only an energy to get results, church going only an activity with amazing benefits, and sin only a "mental infection" in otherwise good people, Miller wrote, then what was the necessity of the whole biblical story of redemption? There was no conflict between Christ and American culture, since the former simply reinforced the purposes to which the latter was already devoted.

Yet a more vitriolic level of censure derived from Peale's association with the rich and famous, particularly with conservative politicians such as Richard Daley, Ferdinand Marcos, Dwight Eisenhower, and Richard Nixon. Peale had adamantly opposed the New Deal and warned his listeners about socialism and communism. His own family, after all, had been "good, clean, self-respecting, decent American poor" and had risen above it. When he was inadvertently caught emceeing a dinner given by opponents of John F. Kennedy's candidacy and its specter of Roman Catholicism in the White House, all Peale's professions of innocence fell on deaf ears. His very association with wealthy and powerful Americans seemed to his adversaries both uncritical and naive.

Peale was always deeply stung by the bandying about of his reputation. Of particular offense to him was the open attack in 1954 by some officers of the National Council of Churches, of which his wife was a board member. He even considered resigning from the ministry, but his congregation rallied around him, and his many defenders spoke out. "He talks to millions while scholars talk to handfuls," said one, according to Arthur Gordon. Some grudging applause even came later from the *Christian Century* magazine of liberal Protestantism when Peale, acting as president of the Protestant Council of Churches of New York, called for taking "Christianity out into the streets" in the battle against racial discrimination and injustice.

Yet the most trenchant criticism remained, coming as it did from writers who simply viewed American society from the other end of the telescope. Donald Meyer saw in Peale the pathos of a Protestant America trying to adapt to life in the city, striving to control that part of life—the self—that one can manage while remaining hopeless about the systems that ultimately would force everyone into consumerist conformity. Peale's world was "grim and merciless," a message of adjustment to a system no longer amenable to Horatio Alger stories, permitting only a nostalgia for the peace and simplicity of small-town life. Some years later Colman McCarthy would echo the same sentiment, calling Peale "one of the most doom-obsessed figures in America," offering no hope for conquering the real social and global problems confronting humanity but only a little happiness in the sphere of the individual.

Yet Peale had obviously tapped into a deep-running stream of uniquely American longings for success, optimism, and a religion to boost one up the ladder. "Today is yours—seize it," he would say, and many Americans greeted such words with a smile.

## Bibliography

### Books by Norman Vincent Peale

1937   *The Art of Living*. New York: Abingdon-Cokesbury Press.
1938   *You Can Win*. New York: Abingdon Press.
1940   *Faith is the Answer*. With Smiley Blanton. Englewood Cliffs, N.J.: Prentice-Hall.
1948   *A Guide to Confident Living*. New York: Macmillan.
1950   *The Art of Real Happiness*. With Smiley Blanton. New York: Prentice-Hall.

1952   *The Power of Positive Thinking.* New York: Prentice-Hall.
1954   *Faith Made Them Champions.* Carmel, N.Y.: Guideposts Associates.
1954   *The Power of Positive Thinking for Young People.* New York: Prentice-Hall.
1955   *Inspiring Messages for Daily Living.* Englewood Cliffs, N.J.: Prentice-Hall.
1957   *Stay Alive All Your Life.* Carmel, N.Y.: Guideposts Associates.
1959   *The Amazing Results of Positive Thinking.* Englewood Cliffs, N.J.: Prentice-Hall.
1961   *The Tough-Minded Optimist.* Englewood Cliffs, N.J.: Prentice-Hall.
1963   *Adventures in the Holy Land.* Englewood Cliffs, N.J.: Prentice-Hall.
1965   *Sin, Sex, and Self-Control.* Carmel, N.Y.: Guideposts Associates.
1967   *Enthusiasm Makes the Difference.* Englewood Cliffs, N.J.: Prentice-Hall.
1970   *Norman Vincent Peale's Treasury of Courage and Confidence.* Garden City, N.Y.:
       Doubleday.
1971   *The New Art of Living.* Pawling, N.Y.: Foundation for Christian Living.
1974   *You Can if You Think You Can.* Greenwich, Conn.: Fawcett.
1975   *Positive Thinking For a Time Like This.* Pawling, N.Y.: Foundation for Christian
       Living.
1982   *Dynamic Imaging: The Powerful Way to Change Your Life.* Old Tappan, N.J.:
       Revell.
1984   *The True Joy of Positive Living: An Autobiography.* Pawling, N.Y.: Foundation
       for Christian Living.
1987   *Power of the Plus Factor.* Old Tappan, N.J.: Revell.

**Selected Studies about Norman Vincent Peale**

Broadhurst, Allan R. *He Speaks the Word of God: A Study of the Sermons of Norman
       Vincent Peale.* Englewood Cliffs, N.J.: Prentice-Hall, 1963.
Fuller, Edmund. "Pitchmen in the Pulpit." *Saturday Review* 40 (9 March 1957): 28–
       30.
Gordon, Arthur. *Norman Vincent Peale: Minister to Millions.* Englewood Cliffs, N.J.:
       Prentice-Hall, 1958.
McCarthy, Colman. "Sunday Morning with the Rev. Dr. Peale." *New Republic* 160 (25
       January 1969): 14–15.
Meyer, Donald. "The Confidence Man." *New Republic* 133 (11 July 1955): 8–10.
Miller, William L. "The Gospel of Norman Vincent Peale." *Union Seminary Quarterly
       Review* 10 (January 1955): 15–22. Substantially the same article appeared in
       several other publications in 1954 and 1955.
"Minister to Millions." *Look* 17 (22 September 1953): 86.
Peale, Margaret, et al. "We Like Our Parents." *Good Housekeeping* 142 (January 1956):
       56–57.
Peale, Mrs. Norman Vincent (Ruth Stafford). *The Adventure of Being a Wife.* Englewood
       Cliffs, N.J.: Prentice-Hall, 1971.
"Twelve Great American Preachers." *Life* 34 (6 April 1953): 126.

                                                                              THOMAS E. FRANK

# James A. Pike

Ever since Roger Williams left the doctrinaire and repressive Puritanism of
seventeenth-century Massachusetts to engage in his own religious and theological
quest, there have always been individuals to challenge the prevailing theological

orthodoxy on the grounds of reason and conscience. Rarely, however, especially in recent years, have such people drawn much notice from the communications media or achieved widespread celebrity. An exception was James A. Pike, who for more than a decade attracted a great deal of attention from the press and generated public interest with virtually every utterance of his controversial theology and practically every turn of his controversial life.

## Biography

James Albert Pike was born on 14 February 1913, in Oklahoma City, Oklahoma, to James Albert and Pearl Agatha Wimsatt Pike. His father died of tuberculosis in 1915, and six years later his mother relocated with her "little Valentine" to Hollywood, California, where both were very active in their Roman Catholic church.

After graduation from Hollywood High School, James enrolled in the University of Santa Clara, a Jesuit school, with every intention of studying for the priesthood. He soon began to question his church's stance on birth control and papal infallibility, however, and in his sophomore year he dropped out of the university as well as the Roman Catholic church, apparently over what he perceived as the latter's authoritarianism, and spent several years of disaffection with institutional Christianity, which he later would describe as his period of "agnosticism."

In 1933, James transferred to the University of Southern California, where he earned degrees in arts and in law. Admitted to the California bar in 1936, he went on to Yale, where he received his doctor of sciences in law. He then moved to Washington, D.C., where he took the prestigious job of attorney with the Securities and Exchange Commission, cofounded a law firm, and married Jane Alvies. By 1940, he was a member of the bar of the U.S. Supreme Court, on the faculty of the George Washington University Law School, and divorced. He had also joined the Protestant Episcopal church.

During World War II, Pike served as a Navy officer in Washington, D.C., at first in Naval Intelligence and later as an attorney with the U.S. Maritime Commission and War Shipping Administration. In 1942, he married one of his students, Esther Yanovsky, and became a postulant for the Episcopal priesthood. Pike's clerical career began officially in 1944 with his ordination to the diaconate at St. John's Church, near the White House. That same year he began to study at Virginia Theological Seminary, while serving as curate at St. John's and chaplain to students at Georgetown University. In 1945, he moved to New York City to complete his theological studies at Union Theological Seminary, avoiding the "practical" courses in favor of the rigors of courses with such luminaries as Paul Tillich and Reinhold Niebuhr.

Pike was ordained priest in 1946 and the following year became rector of Christ Church, Poughkeepsie, New York, where he remained for two years, serving at the same time as chaplain to Episcopal students at Vassar College. In 1949, he became chaplain of Columbia University and chairman of the department of religion, whose curriculum, faculty, and enrollment he personally built into a first-rate program in less than two years. In 1953, he coauthored with Norman Pittenger *The Faith of the Church,* as part of a series on *The Church's Teaching* that the department of Christian education of the Episcopal church published, and it remained in print and in use for lay instruction for many years. Pike would later label the theology of this work as "smooth orthodoxy" and use it as a point of reference for his subsequent doctrinal vagaries.

In the fall of 1952, Pike became dean of the Cathedral of Saint John the Divine, the largest Episcopal church in the country, an appointment important enough to be announced in *Time* magazine. By all accounts, Pike "pumped new life" and visibility into his landmark charge: he had it legally renamed The Cathedral of New York (St. Patrick's and Cardinal Spellman notwithstanding) and attracted to it unprecedented crowds with his topical and often controversial sermons. He raised his own profile nationally by publishing articles of general interest for widely circulating popular periodicals and by hosting one of the earliest national religious television programs, "The Dean Pike Show," which ran every Sunday afternoon for six years on the ABC network. Finally, with his positions of conscience and, equally important, with his flair for rhetoric and the dramatic, he also began to evolve into a newsmaker in his own right. In 1953, for example, he refused an honorary doctor of divinity degree from the University of the South (Sewanee) on the grounds that the school was segregated, and he declared publicly that he would not accept "a degree in white divinity." All of this activity brought Pike attention and publicity, including a February 1958 article about him in the *Reader's Digest* (reprinted from a religious journal) entitled "The Joyful Dean."

That very month, Pike was elected Bishop Coadjutor of California and was consecrated in the episcopal office in May. When the ailing incumbent died the following September, Pike became Bishop of California, a position he held until 1966 and, according to statistical indicators (communicants, contributions, etc.), quite successfully. As bishop, he managed to raise some three million dollars for the completion of Grace Cathedral in San Francisco and to inaugurate a remarkably well-balanced ministry to both the "street people" and the business community. Finally, he gained a great deal of recognition in 1960 when Dr. Eugene Carson Blake, Stated Clerk of the Presbyterian Church, used the pulpit of Grace Church to announce the ecumenical plans that soon led to the founding of the Consultation on Church Union (C.O.C.U.).

But Pike also stirred up a storm of controversy and a swell of opposition during his tenure as Bishop of California, as, for example, when he had certain "secular saints"—e.g., Albert Einstein, Thurgood Marshall, and John Glenn—honored in stained glass in the cathedral windows, when he invited such controversial leaders as Martin Luther King, Jr.,* to the cathedral pulpit, and when he ordained the first woman to Episcopal ministerial status. Along with such incidents, his liberal outspokenness on social and political issues was a constant source of consternation to the more conservative Episcopalians of the diocese.

In 1960, Pike published several short essays in popular and widely read periodicals, all on rather timely and touchy topics involving religion and politics. Controversial as these were, however, none of them even hinted at the break with Christian orthodoxy and movement into theological conflict that would follow from his final article of the year, carried in the Christmas issue of the *Christian Century* (21 December 1960) as a part of its popular "How My Mind Has Changed" series. In this milestone essay, entitled "Three-Pronged Synthesis," Pike expressed disenchantment with the Trinity, the virgin birth, and Christ as the only way to salvation, setting over against these staple tenets of orthodoxy his own belief in a "big God," by which he meant "One who cannot be enclosed in a tabernacle or in a philosophical or theological concept." Throughout the article Pike asserted that he was rejecting certain traditional conceptual formulations because they did not do justice to God: "God—and God only—is final and . . . all else is in greater or lesser degree tentative." Consequently, "I don't believe as many things as I believed ten years ago, but I trust that what I do believe, I believe more deeply."

Within three weeks, an editorial in the conservative periodical *Christianity Today* denounced Pike for having doubts, and during the next six years, Pike was officially charged with heresy no fewer than three times because of that article and later elaborations on it: first, by a group of Georgia clergy (1961), then by a coalition of Arizona clergy (1965), and finally by a group of bishops led by Bishop Henry I. Louttit of Florida (1966). It was not always clear to what extent these heresy charges were actually motivated by issues other than doctrinal ones, for Pike had the ability to offend his colleagues on practical matters as well as to irritate them with his flamboyant and public style. Whatever the real root of the heresy charges, however, Pike took them seriously and responded with three major theological works that were a departure from his usual topics of ethics, politics, and church and society: *A Time for Christian Candor* (1964), *What Is This Treasure?* (1966), and *If This Be Heresy* (1967). All of these reflected an attitude similar to, and no doubt influenced by, his friend and fellow "modernizer," Anglican Bishop John A. T. Robinson, who himself was drawing fire during this period for his "radical" book *Honest to God*.

In the midst of dealing with such weighty professional controversies and conflicts, Pike was repeatedly beset with personal trauma and tragedy as well. In 1964, he joined Alcoholics Anonymous after some twelve years of debilitating drinking. He also met and began a disastrous affair with a woman, whom he supported (apparently with episcopal discretionary funds) until her suicide in 1967, in which he may have been an accomplice. In February 1966 Pike's son, Jim, committed suicide, and in the following year, he was divorced by his wife of twenty-five years, Esther, and endured the attempted suicide of his daughter.

Of all these events, the most devastating for Pike was the death of his son, and it led to yet another round of controversy and publicity when the bishop claimed to have had what seemed to be contact with his dead son "from beyond the grave." Many seances ensued, including one on television with well-known psychic Arthur Ford, and many articles appeared in the popular press. Pike himself recorded his experiences and his reflections on them in a fascinating volume, *The Other Side,* published in 1968, and even began to interpret some of the traditional Christian doctrines (e.g., the Resurrection) in light of these experiences.

Later that same year, he submitted his resignation as Bishop of California (though retaining his episcopal status) and joined the Center for the Study of Democratic Institutions in Santa Barbara, California, to pursue some long-standing scholarly interests, including study of the Dead Sea Scrolls. Later that year, under formal accusation of heresy by Bishop Louttit and others, he was censured by the House of Bishops without any consideration of theological issues whatsoever. Incensed at having been deprived of what he considered a fair hearing and due process, he startled his fellow bishops by demanding a heresy trial. The trial never materialized, for he felt sufficiently vindicated the following year when his church endorsed openness in theological inquiry and a commitment to social justice.

In 1968, the recently divorced Pike married Diane Kennedy, his former student who had helped him on *The Other Side*. Pike's episcopal successor in California, Bishop C. Kilmer Meyers, thereupon declared that he had not given his permission and sent a request to all his clergy that Pike be banned from performing any priestly functions, including preaching. This action very much disappointed and saddened Pike, and in a *Look* article (29 April 1969) he announced his and his wife's intention to leave the institutional church, to embark on "an unencumbered journey into an open future" and a nomadic trip "to the wilderness" in the style of the earliest Christians, and to form a Foundation for Religious Transition for other like-minded "church alumni."

Pike's words about the "journey" and "wilderness" proved prophetic. During a trip to Israel later that year to study the Essene communities of Jesus' day, he and his wife got hopelessly lost and finally were stranded on an ill-planned automobile excursion into the very Judaean desert where Christ was said to have fasted at the beginning of his ministry. Though his wife managed to make her way out and to find help, Pike was found dead by a search party some five days later and was buried on 8 September 1969, in Jaffa, Israel. Predictably, as he had done throughout his life, he commanded headlines all over the world even in death.

### Appraisal

It should not be surprising, perhaps, that a man who was reared in "Tinsel Town" on the West Coast and who spent most of his early professional years in "the Big Apple" became a brilliant public relations man and a public personality. Of course, it did not hurt that Pike possessed a natural charm and charisma, flamboyance and flair, energy and eloquence, or that his life seemed prone to the tragic, the bizarre, and sometimes the tragically bizarre, all of which made him "good copy." In addition, he seems to have had a natural ability to use the various popular communications media, not for personal aggrandizement but for accomplishing his goals, stating his views, confronting his critics, and even announcing major personal and professional decisions. All of this made him a "darling of the media" and a fascinating public figure.

But Pike was a very complex man who operated at a number of levels simultaneously, for the most part successfully. He was an extremely effective churchman, not only as a communicator but as an administrator as well. He was a prolific and articulate author who wrote on a variety of subjects, from theology to ethics to politics. He was a civil rights and antiwar activist, a vocal opponent of captial punishment, and an enthusiastic advocate of ecumenism. Indeed, his wide-ranging involvements and interests often made him appear unfocused. But what gave him both his focal point and his popular identity, and what constitutes his major impact in American religious history, was his theology, as well as the ecclesiastical controversies that it fomented.

Theologically, Pike was a classic liberal in his willingness to submit all religious claims to rational scrutiny. Yet, as his three specifically theological books attest, he was by no means a reductionist with respect to Christian doctrine, for he always wound up affirming much more than he rejected. His standard approach was to regard the doctrines and creeds of Christianity as important but always subject to the test of plausibility, and as expendable when they either failed to communicate or foiled communication of religious truth and meaning. In this regard, his ongoing appeal was to 2 Corinthians 4:7: "We have this treasure in earthen vessels, that the excellency of the power may be of God, and not of us." For Pike the necessary but exchangeable "vessels" were, as he put it, "Creed, Code, and Cult," but the "treasure"—faith in God—was nonnegotiable.

In retrospect, therefore, Pike's reputation as a "heretic" must be viewed as highly exaggerated. Indeed, his theology appears quite mild. He was a dedicated theist, despite the fact that he questioned many of the traditional images and formulas used for God; he had the highest regard for Christ as the definitive embodiment of divine presence, though he criticized most of the traditional Christological formulations for compromising Jesus' humanity; he even advocated the continued use of such symbols as the virgin birth, the divinity of Christ, and the Resurrection, though he refused to take them as literally or historically true. In short, he did not reject traditional Christian doctrine so much as he relativized and reinterpreted it.

Pike was by no means an original theologian and probably lacked the patience and focus to be the serious scholar he aspired to be. He was, however, a diligent and extremely intelligent reader who had an uncanny ability to absorb, analyze, and articulate even the most difficult theological principles and concepts. That trait, rather than originality, made him an effective teacher of traditional theological options, popularizer of current theological trends, and apologist of rational Christianity.

It is difficult to assess in any scientific way Pike's lasting impact. It is clear that many of the things that made him very controversial in his own day—such as civil rights and women's ordination—have become much more accepted, if not fully actualized, in his own denomination and elsewhere in church and society. It is also demonstrable that because of its struggles with Pike the Episcopal church is much more open to theological inquiry and much less likely to raise a charge of heresy than it was before his challenge. Nor is it difficult even today to find those in the church and academia who, at a formative point in their lives, were influenced back to the church and its teachings by Pike's rational approach to Christianity's more problematic doctrines.

As prominent and influential as he was in his own time, however, there is little evidence that his impact is ongoing in any direct way and little likelihood that his name (much less his work) would be widely recognized today, even in Christian circles. One reason for his apparent eclipse is that, in the years since his death, media and public attention have been seized by those at the opposite end of the theological spectrum. More than that, however, he has suffered the fate of all popularizers and public personalities: as visible and valuable as they are for their times, eventually they all become "old news."

**Survey of Criticism**

There is only a modest amount of literature on the life and work of James Pike. While he was alive, his writings received very little critical attention, especially in professional, scholarly circles. And since his death, there has been only one comprehensive, definitive biography of him published.

By far the most substantial and thorough treatment of Pike's life and work is William Stringfellow and Anthony Towne, *The Death and Life of Bishop Pike*. Though admittedly friends of Pike's and sympathetic toward him, the authors are nonetheless frank and even critical about Pike's weaknesses and failings, including his difficulties in relating personally to women, his naivete about human nature, and especially his credulity in the face of psychic "experts" and "evidence." Before Pike's death, these same authors had published an exhaustive and well-documented treatment of the heresy proceedings against Pike, *The Bishop Pike Affair*, which is also revealing, though more about ecclesiastical machinations than about Pike himself.

Also predictably sympathetic, yet remarkably balanced, is Diane Kennedy Pike's *Search: The Personal Story of a Wilderness Journey*, which focuses on the final traumatic episode in Pike's life. Her affection for her subject is nicely balanced by more objective and sometimes highly critical reviews and essays that appeared in popular periodicals both before and after Pike's death. Of virtually no worth at all is *The Psychic World of Bishop Pike*, by noted psychic Hans Holzer, which gives the most attention to what would otherwise appear to be the least consequential and most suspect part of Pike's life.

## Bibliography

### Selected Works by James A. Pike

1953  *Beyond Anxiety: The Christian Answer to Fear, Frustration, Guilt, Indecision, Inhibition, Loneliness, Despair.* New York: Scribner.
1953  *The Faith of the Church.* With Norman Pittenger. Volume 3 in *The Church's Teaching.* Greenwich, Conn.: Seabury.
1954  *If You Marry Outside Your Faith: Counsel on Mixed Marriages.* New York and Evanston: Harper and Row.
1954  *Roadblocks to Faith.* With John McG. Krumm. New York: Morehouse-Gorham Co.
1955  *The Church, Politics, and Society: Dialogues on Current Problems.* With John W. Pyle. New York: Morehouse-Gorham Co.
1955  *Doing the Truth: A Summary of Christian Ethics.* Garden City, N.Y.: Doubleday.
1957  *The Next Day.* Garden City, N.Y.: Doubleday.
1960  *A Roman Catholic in the White House.* With Richard Byfield. Garden City, N.Y.: Doubleday.
1960  "Three-Pronged Synthesis." *Christian Century* 77: 1496-1500.
1961  *A New Look in Preaching.* New York: Scribner.
1961  *Our Christmas Challenge.* New York: Sterling.
1963  *Beyond the Law: The Religious and Ethical Meaning of the Lawyer's Vocation.* Garden City, N.Y.: Doubleday.
1964  *A Time for Christian Candor.* New York: Harper and Row.
1965  *Teen-agers and Sex.* Englewood Cliffs N.J.: Prentice-Hall.
1966  *What Is This Treasure?* New York: Harper and Row
1967  *If This Be Heresy.* New York: Harper and Row.
1967  *You and the New Morality: 74 Cases.* New York: Harper and Row.
1968  *The Other Side: An Account of My Experience with Psychic Phenomena.* With Diane Kennedy. New York: Doubleday.

### Selected Studies about James A. Pike

Cogley, John. "From Pulpit to Think Tank." *New York Times Magazine* (14 August 1966): 16–17, 33–34, 36, 38, 40, 43–44, 46.
Day, Beth. "The Joyful Dean." *Reader's Digest* 72 (February 1958): 140–45.
Didion, Joan. "The Late Great Bishop of California." *Esquire* 86 (November 1976): 60–62.
Ellison, Jerome. "Battling Bishop." *Saturday Evening Post* 234 (7 October 1961): 38–42.
Hazelton, Roger. "The Bothersome Bishop." *New Republic* 157 (7 October 1967): 32–33, 36.
Holzer, Hans W. *The Psychic World of Bishop Pike.* New York: Crown, 1970.
Kinsolving, Lester. "Bishop Pike's Last Diocesan Battle." *Christian Century* 83 (1 June 1966): 726–29.
Lee, Peter James. "The Grace of Comedy." *New Republic* 161 (20 September 1969): 14–15.
Montgomery, John Warwick. "The Bishop, the Spirits, and the Word." *Christianity Today* 12 (16 February 1968): 48 [524].
Pike, Diane Kennedy. *Search: The Personal Story of a Wilderness Journey.* Garden City, N.Y.: Doubleday, 1970.

Stringfellow, William, and Anthony Towne. *The Bishop Pike Affair: Scandals of Con-
    science and Heresy, Relevance and Solemnity in the Contemporary Church*. New
    York: Harper and Row, 1967.
————. *The Death and Life of Bishop Pike*. Garden City, N.Y.: Doubleday, 1976.
Wren, Christopher S. "An American Bishop's Search for a Space-Age God." *Look* 30
    (22 February 1966): 25–29.

PAUL A. LAUGHLIN

# Oral Roberts

By the end of the first decade of the twentieth century, the United States was
being swept by a wave of Pentecostal fire. The new movement combined sharp
evangelistic fervor with an emphasis on the Holy Spirit's gifts of power, which
offended many mainline Christians. Members of older denominations mistrusted
the new emphasis on speaking in tongues and faith healing, dubbing practitioners
of this enthusiastic piety "holy rollers." By the beginning of the 1980s, however,
much of the criticism had been blunted, and Pentecostal Christianity had found
a place of respect in American life. The career of Oral Roberts began in the
faith healing tent and paralleled the rise of Pentecostalism to respectability in
American society.

### Biography

Born on 24 January 1918 to Ellis and Claudius Roberts, Granville Oral Roberts
breathed the air of Pentecostalism from his earliest years. His parents had committed themselves to the new Pentecostal movement in Arkansas and Oklahoma.
By the time of Oral's birth, Ellis Roberts was an itinerant evangelist in the local
Pentecostal orbit. Claudius was much in demand in the surrounding community
for her ability to pray for the sick. She later confessed that she believed God
had promised her that Oral was to be a preacher.

Oral's early life offered little promise of his future prominence. From early
childhood, neighborhood boys taunted him because he stuttered. By the age of
fifteen, Oral deeply resented the poverty and restrictiveness of his parents' religious commitments and left his home, against the wishes of his family, to
attend school in another town. Although the change of scenery was successful
at first, it soon turned to disaster when young Oral was stricken with tuberculosis.
After a single year of independence, Oral returned home to his family in February
1935 and took to the sickbed. Five months later he found himself traveling to
a tent revival led by George Moncey in Ada, Oklahoma. On the way to the
meeting, Oral believed that God spoke to him, promising healing. At the conclusion of the service, Moncey prayed for those in the healing line, including
Oral. In that moment Oral Roberts found himself healed of the disease and his
stammer. He began to preach that very evening.

After months of convalescence young Oral joined his father in conducting evangelistic meetings. Gradually his father introduced him to the techniques and personalities of the new movement. Within a year Oral had begun to speak in tongues, had been baptized, and had been finally ordained into the ministry of the Pentecostal Holiness church. During the same year he met and courted his future wife, Evelyn. He began to write for the *Pentecostal Holiness Advocate,* the denominational newspaper, and completed his first book, *Salvation by the Blood,* in 1938. As his abilities sharpened, so did tension with his father. The two parted company, finding it easier to remain close if they were not working so intimately together.

Oral Roberts' career can best be understood as moving through several stages. By the middle of 1938 the period of preparation was over, and Oral had entered the first phase of his evangelistic career. He was well recognized in Pentecostal Holiness circles and began to enjoy considerable popularity as an itinerant evangelist. By 1940 he had begun to travel extensively, conducting revival meetings in churches from Georgia to Canada. He continued to write, producing numerous letters and articles for denominational publications and, in 1941, his second book, *The Drama of the End Time.* All of his work was the standard fare of Pentecostal Holiness orthodoxy.

Oral's career seemed secure when, in 1941, he accepted a call to pastor a new church in Fuquay Springs, North Carolina. The next year, disappointed with his failure to induce the Fuquay Springs Church to join the Pentecostal Holiness denomination, Oral returned to Oklahoma to pastor a church in Shawnee. The pastoral phase of his ministry continued during a brief pastorate in Toccoa, Georgia, where Oral performed his first healing service. He returned to Oklahoma again in 1946 when he began a pastorate in Enid and also began to attend classes at Phillips University. By the end of that year Oral Roberts was settled in the ministry of his denomination. Slightly better off than during his childhood, Oral still lived in relative poverty with his wife and two children, Rebecca and Ronald. The scene was set for the spiritual crisis that marked the beginning of the next phase of Oral's ministry.

The crisis came in the midst of a 1947 sociology class at Phillips University when the professor began to ridicule part of the Bible. As he listened, Oral heard the same voice of God he had reported in 1935. He recalled in *My Story* that this time it commanded him not to be like other preachers but to "be like my Son, Jesus Christ, and bring healing to the people as he did." Oral was elated and immediately instituted Sunday afternoon healing services in his church. He met with such success that he took the unorthodox step of renting a hall in downtown Enid. The meeting was so successful that it marked the end of Oral's service as a local church pastor. Within a month he had resigned his pastorate to take up full-time evangelism and healing.

Oral Roberts and his family moved to Tulsa in July 1947. He began to sponsor healing services almost immediately. In November he established his own magazine, *Healing Waters,* to report the work of the ministry and to seek financial support. Impressed with the growing success of tent ministries, Roberts purchased his own tent in 1948. He soon developed the technique of the healing meeting, which was to remain virtually unchanged for twenty years. The meetings were characterized by careful advance preparations, including preliminary meetings conducted by Roberts' assistants. The service itself began with prayer and two or three songs, followed by the offering. This was followed by a long sermon, often lasting more than an hour. After the sermon, Roberts first visited the invalid tent, where the most seriously ill awaited, and then plunged into the healing line. He believed his healing power to be particularly located in his right hand and often moved through the line with a swimming motion, touching his hand to the foreheads of the supplicants while speaking a brief word of prayer for them.

The new healing ministry was widely successful. Roberts began to attract huge crowds in campaigns that rolled across the country. The successes also attracted critics, and Roberts often faced a hostile press. Criticism and occasional financial or public relations reverses seemed only to encourage Roberts. When a freak storm destroyed his tent and injured some of the faithful in 1950, Roberts ordered a larger tent and expanded the ministry. The faith healing ministry brought Roberts his first experience with national prominence and a national constituency. He continued to write for the Pentecostal Holiness press, although tensions with his denomination began to increase, perhaps because of his success. He also issued new books, including the 1947 *If You Need Healing—Do These Things* and his *Life Story* in 1952. He turned to other media as well, including radio and his first film, "Venture Into Faith," in 1952. Other efforts included his support of Demos Shakarian in founding the Full Gospel Business Men's Fellowship International in 1952.

Despite the continuing success of the tent meetings, changes were afoot in the Roberts ministry. Oral had taken the crusades abroad, including a disastrous trip to Australia in 1956. Bad publicity and growing criticism from the religious establishment seemed to encourage him to emphasize evangelism more and healing less. He initiated his first television series in 1954, the first stirrings of today's electronic church, with his series, "Your Faith is Power." The next year he began filming his tent crusades for television. His entry into the mass media produced a range of different efforts, including "Oral Roberts' True Stories," his own comic book series, which ran from 1956 to 1961. Oral Roberts the faith healer had given way to Oral Roberts the media star. The corresponding efforts to appeal to a wider audience led to a noticeable change of emphasis, if not of theology. Although Roberts insisted that he had not changed his beliefs or his message, his audience came to consist more and more of non-Pentecostals.

In 1960 Oral Roberts indicated the next focus of his ministry with the announcement of God's command to him to build a university. At first his efforts seemed to indicate the development of yet another Pentecostal Bible college. Only after several years of building was the full scope of Roberts' vision clear. As he focused his attention on the task of raising money for the college, the

crusades began to wane. They dropped from an average of ten days in length
to five. At the same time the emphasis on healing continued to diminish, both
in the crusades and on the television series still airing on Sunday mornings.

The year 1965 was of great importance for the Roberts ministry. Oral was
invited to attend the World Congress on Evangelism to be held the following
year in Berlin. Never readily accepted by the mainline churches, Roberts was
reluctant to attend but finally agreed. While there he was invited by Billy
Graham* to lead the assembly in prayer and to assist in a panel discussion on
divine healing. Roberts so won over the delegates that he became far more
acceptable to the evangelical mainliners. More important, he established a friendship with Billy Graham that seemed to blossom, as Graham participated in the
dedication of Oral Roberts University two years later.

Roberts' increasing preoccupation with the affairs of the university signaled
the decisive change that had taken place in his ministry. The crusades dwindled
until they came to an end in 1968. His Sunday morning television series had
ended in 1967, the same year that Roberts dedicated the new prayer tower in
the center of his campus. Perhaps the most profound symbol of the change in
the ministry was Roberts' decision to unite with Tulsa's Boston Avenue Methodist Church in 1968. This change signaled a decisive end to the support he had
long enjoyed among many Pentecostals. Though insisting that he had not changed
any of his beliefs about the work of the Spirit, Roberts had clearly become
respectable to mainline churches. For his part, Roberts explained the change of
denominational affiliation as an effort to return home. He claimed to have returned
to the church of his childhood and lauded the Methodist pulpit as the most free
in all the country.

Roberts' growing acceptance by mainline Christians increased in 1969 with
the first of his prime-time television specials. Sensing the value of this new
approach, Oral soon purchased production equipment and established appropriate
facilities on the campus of Oral Roberts University. Former Pentecostal associates
bitterly decried the advent of "show business" in the ministry, but audiences
grew rapidly. Indeed, the old healing message had been largely replaced by an
emphasis on evangelism and "Seed Faith." Still, Brother Oral included in every
show his admonition to "expect a miracle."

The ministry continued to grow during the 1970s and into the 1980s, but not
without signs of strain. Defections by former associates led to several unflattering
books about Roberts and his ministry. He continued to complain of unfair treatment by the press. The loss of some of his aides reflected tensions and changes
within the ministry. Some of his advisors objected strenuously to his campaign
to establish a medical school and to build the controversial hospital he calls
"The City of Faith." These difficulties were intensified by Roberts' claim, in
1980, to have seen and conversed with a 900-foot-tall Jesus.

Other crises were more personal, including the death of his daughter and son-
in-law in an airplane crash in 1977 and the suicide of his son Ron in 1982. One
of the most difficult crises for the Roberts ministry came with the failure of son

Richard's marriage to Patti in 1979 and Richard's remarriage the next year. More recently the family has had to cope with the 1984 birth and death of Oral's namesake grandson.

These many difficulties have not prevented the ministry from continuing. Indeed, Oral and Evelyn Roberts have often responded to personal tragedy by going on the air to share their suffering with the public. Personal tragedies have tended to rally the support of those who follow the Roberts ministry. Formal difficulties within the organization have proven more difficult to master but have never greatly hindered the ministry. Internal opposition to his City of Faith project, coupled with the intense objections of the local medical community in Tulsa, did not prevent the dedication of the new facility in 1981. In 1987 Oral struggled to finance teams of medical missionaries, the latest thrust in his healing ministry. Once again God appeared to Oral, warning that failure to raise the needed funds would signal the end of his usefulness and the time to "call him home." The faithful responded, and Oral's goals were met. The ministry of Oral Roberts continues on the campus of his university, through his correspondence with his "partners," and on television.

### Appraisal

Oral Roberts represents the increasing acceptability of Pentecostalism in American society. He has consistently maintained that his theology has not changed. Instead, the methods change. He continues to call for Christians to expect the goodness of God to be demonstrated through the Holy Spirit. He still speaks in tongues, believes in miracles, attributes sickness and disease to the devil, and promotes an active ministry of faith healing.

Despite these constants, Roberts has made many changes. None of these are as dramatic as the change in his healing ministry. At the beginning of his ministry he emphasized faith healing, particularly as exercised in the revival tent. With the founding of the university, he began to move in increasingly non-Pentecostal circles. His emphasis on healing was transformed into the building of a medical school and hospital where the scientific skills of doctors and nurses could be united with the power of the prayer of faith. More recently, Roberts has committed himself to supporting medical missionaries as an expression of the outreach of his healing ministry. Such an approach is, of course, far more palatable to mainline Christians than the healing line of his early crusades.

To be sure, Roberts has always insisted that he is as interested in evangelism as in healing or other miracles. Certainly his contributions in this field have been substantial. Since his rapprochement with the evangelicals at the World Congress on Evangelism in Berlin in 1966, Roberts has held a position of eminence rivaled only by Billy Graham. The founding of Oral Roberts University has ensured his place as a leader in the mainstream of American religion.

It has always been dangerous to predict the course of Oral Roberts' ministry. The combination of his broad appeal, his wide experience, and the variety of his ministry has allowed him to speak as one of the deans of American Protestantism. His persistent loyalty to a theology emphasizing the gifts of the Holy Spirit foments continuing unease among the traditional churches. Oral Roberts remains a figure who is, at one time, greatly loved and heavily criticized.

### Survey of Criticism

There is a huge body of literature about Oral Roberts. His crusades have stimulated extensive local press coverage. These stories reflect trends clearly visible in the large body of literature. Reporters tend to be either attracted to Roberts or repulsed by him. Clearly objective reports are rare. In general, Roberts is justified in complaining of the unfriendliness of the press. Recently, however, many reporters have offered more flattering interpretations of his ministry. National journals have also reported on Roberts at length. Articles appeared in *Life* and *Look* as early as 1951. Since then nearly every major national magazine has done at least one feature on Roberts or on some aspect of his ministry.

Roberts and his team have not been reluctant to contribute to the periodical literature themselves. The ministry has supported no less than fifteen different magazines, journals, comic books, or newsletters. In addition to these, Roberts and his family have issued a steady stream of tracts, pamphlets, and books. A list of publications by and about the Roberts ministry team can be obtained from the library at Oral Roberts University.

There have been many book-length studies of Roberts and his ministry. The best of these is David E. Harrell's *Oral Roberts: An American Life*, published in 1985. In addition to its balanced portrayal of Roberts, it contains an excellent bibliographical essay. No other treatments have shown such depth of research and determined fairness. Three insider treatments share the flavor of the exposé, portraying Roberts in an unflattering light. Harshest of these is *Ashes to Gold*, by Patti Roberts (divorced wife of Oral's son Richard) and Sherry Andrews. Jerry Sholes' *Give Me That Prime-Time Religion* is similarly critical of Roberts, whereas Wayne A. Robinson, a former Roberts aide, is more friendly in his *Oral: The Warm, Intimate, Unauthorized Portrait of a Man of God.*

Not surprisingly, Oral Roberts has fared more or less well in broader treatments of the Pentecostal movement, depending on the author's sympathy to the movement itself. Good sources include John R. Rice, *Four Great Heresies*, and V. E. Howard, *Fake Healers Exposed*. Less tendentious treatments of the movement include David Edwin Harrell, Jr., *All Things Are Possible* and Richard Quebedeaux, *The New Charismatics*.

### Bibliography

#### Books by Oral Roberts

1938  *Salvation by the Blood*. Franklin Springs, Ga.: Pentecostal Holiness Publishing House.
1941  *The Drama of the End Time*. Franklin Springs, Ga.: Pentecostal Holiness Publishing House.
1947  *If You Need Healing—Do These Things*. Tulsa: Standard Printing Co.

1951   *The Diary of a Hollywood Visitor*. Tulsa: Healing Waters Tract Society.
1952   *Oral Roberts' Life Story*. Tulsa: Oral Roberts.
1954   *Deliverance from Fear and Sickness*. Tulsa: Oral Roberts.
1956   *Oral Roberts' Best Sermons and Stories*. Tulsa: Oral Roberts Evangelistic Association.
1958   *The Oral Roberts Reader*. Rockville Centre, N.Y.: Zenith Books.
1960   *God Is a Good God*. New York: Bobbs-Merrill Co.
1960   *Seven Divine Aids for Your Health*. Tulsa: Oral Roberts.
1961   *My Story*. Tulsa: Summit Book Co.
1964   *The Baptism with the Holy Spirit*. Tulsa: Oral Roberts.
1964   *How God Speaks to Me*. Tulsa: Oral Roberts Evangelistic Association.
1964   *What Is a Miracle?* Tulsa: Oral Roberts.
1967   *My Twenty Years of a Miracle Ministry*. Tulsa: Oral Roberts.
1968   *My Personal Diary of Our Worldwide Ministry*. Tulsa: Oral Roberts Evangelistic Association.
1968   *101 Questions and Answers*. Tulsa: Oral Roberts Evangelistic Association.
1968   *The Teen-Age Rebel*. Tulsa: Oral Roberts Evangelistic Association.
1969   *God's Timetable for the End of Time*. Tulsa: Heliotrope Publishers.
1970   *The Miracle of Seed Faith*. Charlotte, N.C.: Commission Press.
1972   *The Call*. New York: Doubleday and Co.
1973   *The Miracle Book*. Tulsa: Pinoak Publishers.
1974   *The Holy Spirit in the Now*. 3 vols. Tulsa: Oral Roberts University.
1974   *How to Live above your Problems*. Tulsa: Pinoak Publishers.
1974   *Twelve Greatest Miracles of My Ministry*. Tulsa: Pinoak Publishers.
1975   *A Daily Guide to Miracles*. Tulsa: Oral Roberts Evangelistic Association.
1975   *The Miracles of Christ*. Tulsa: Oral Roberts Evangelistic Association.
1975   *Seed-Faith Commentary on the Holy Bible*. Tulsa: Pinoak Publishers.
1976   *Better Health and Miracle Living*. Tulsa: Oral Roberts Evangelistic Association.
1976   *Oral Roberts' Favorite Healing Scriptures*. Tulsa: Oral Roberts Evangelistic Association.
1977   *How to Get Through Your Struggles*. Tulsa: Oral Roberts Evangelistic Association.
1981   *Flood Stage*. Tulsa: Oral Roberts.
1982   *How to Know God's Will*. Tulsa: Oral Roberts Evangelistic Association.
n.d.   *It Is Later Than You Think*. Tulsa: Oral Roberts Tract Society
n.d.   *Questions and Answers About His Life and Ministry*. Tulsa: Committee on Information, Oral Roberts' Million Soul Crusade.
n.d.   *Questions and Answers on Doctrine*. Tulsa: Oral Roberts Evangelistic Association.
n.d.   *Turn Your Faith Loose!* Tulsa: Oral Roberts Tract Society.
n.d.   *Why You Must Receive the Baptism of the Holy Ghost*. Tulsa: Oral Roberts Evangelistic Association.
n.d.   *You Are What Your Believing Is*. Tulsa: Oral Roberts Tract Society.

### Selected Studies about Oral Roberts

Buursma Bruce. "Oral Roberts and His Skeptics." *Chicago Tribune Magazine* (3 January 1982), sec. 9, pp. 8–10, 14.
Corvin, Raymond O. "Religious and Educational Backgrounds in the Founding of Oral Roberts University." Ph. D. diss., University of Oklahoma, 1967.
Harrell, David E., Jr. *All Things Are Possible*. Bloomington: Indiana University Press, 1975.

————. *Oral Roberts: An American Life*. Bloomington: Indiana University Press, 1985.
Howard, V. E. *Fake Healers Exposed*. 6th rev. ed. West Monroe, La.: Central Printers
    and Publishers, 1970.
Neal, Emily Gardner. *God Can Heal You Now*. Englewood Cliffs, N.J.: Prentice-Hall,
    1958.
Oursler, Will. *The Healing Power of Faith*. New York: Hawthorn Press, 1957.
————. "Healing—with Faith." *American Weekly* (17 February 1957): 22, 25–26.
Quebedeaux, Richard. *The New Charismatics*. Garden City, N.Y.: Doubleday, 1976.
Rice, John R. *Four Great Heresies*. Murfreesboro, Tenn.: Sword of the Lord Publishers,
    1975.
Roberts, E. M., and Claudius Roberts. *Our Ministry and Our Son Oral*. Tulsa: Oral
    Roberts, 1960.
Roberts, Evelyn. *His Darling Wife, Evelyn*. New York: Dell Publishing Co., 1976.
Roberts, Patti. *Ashes to Gold*. New York: Jove Publications, 1985.
Robinson, Wayne A. *Oral: The Warm, Intimate Unauthorized Portrait of a Man of God*.
    Los Angeles: Acton House, 1976.
Sholes, Jerry. *Give Me That Prime-Time Religion*. New York: Hawthorn Press, 1979.
                                                          MICHAEL R. McCOY

# Pat Robertson

In March 1985, the *Saturday Evening Post*'s "CBN's Pat Robertson: White House Next?" focused attention on the presidential aspirations of Marion Gordon (Pat) Robertson. Regrettably, the ensuing media barrage paid only superficial attention to the most influential figure to emerge from the broad movement characterized as the "new religious right." Little attention was paid to the evolution of his coherent and controversial set of political principles and programs. Too often, episodes from Robertson's life are turned against him to "prove" that the world view of conservative evangelicalism is a profound threat to the civic health of the nation. Conversely, other episodes are used to "prove" that his vision of a reawakened America has been shaped directly by God and that his election to the presidency is the only event that can return the nation to its Christian roots and save it from the perils of secular humanism. Neither view does justice to Robertson, one of the pivotal political and religious figures in contemporary America.

### Biography

Pat Robertson was born on 22 March 1930, in Lexington, Virginia. He speaks proudly and often of his family's heritage. His mother, Gladys Churchill Willis, the daughter of a minister, was born in Switzerland and grew up in the upper strata of society in Alabama. She married a longtime friend, A. Willis Robertson, the son of a Baptist minister. He was serving in the Virginia legislature by 1916, went to Congress in 1932, and was elected to the Senate in 1946. The family tree includes President William Henry Harrison, President Benjamin Harrison, another Benjamin who signed the Declaration of Independence, and two members of colonial Virginia's House of Burgesses.

Robertson portrays his life as a three-act drama: act one reveals a "fast and loose" young man attending Washington and Lee University, followed by a brief period of study at the University of London, two years in the Marine Corps, and eventual graduation from Yale Law School. While at Yale, he met Adelia "Dede" Elmer, and they were married in 1954. Timothy, the first of four children, arrived shortly. Robertson did not pass the New York State bar examination and, disillusioned, took a job with W.R. Grace & Company. In his autobiography, *Shout It From The Housetops,* he looks back on this time as one of great "emptiness," a time when he even contemplated suicide. He decided to enter the ministry after hearing a voice that told him that "God has a purpose for your life."

The second act of the drama opens as Robertson, expecting his mother to be overjoyed at his career decision, is taken by surprise when she cautions that without being "born-again" he would be "just as spiritually empty a minister as you are a businessman." The drama of his conversion unfolded soon after as Robertson, mindful of his mother's words, ate dinner with evangelist Cornelius Vanderbreggen. During an "embarrassing" discussion about religion, Robertson sensed the intimacy of God. "Suddenly I knew him, not just as God, but as Father. And I knew him because he had come to me in Jesus Christ." Robertson entered New York Theological Seminary in 1956 and shortly thereafter was asked by Harald Bredesen, an influential figure in the charismatic movement, to join him as associate minister at the First Reformed Church in Mount Vernon, New York. Bredesen helped Robertson to appreciate the transformative power of the gifts of the Holy Spirit. In his later years, Robertson would continue to insist that it was precisely these gifts that would be the crucial element in the religious awakening that could transform the nation.

In 1959, after graduation, Robertson lived in the slums of Brooklyn for several months before buying a defunct UHF television station in Portsmouth, Virginia. He claims little credit for the astonishing success of the Christian Broadcasting Network (CBN), claiming that God has led him, like John the Baptist, to "proclaim the end of the old age and to prepare the people for the coming of Jesus Christ and the new age." Through the medium of television Robertson believes that he has been given the power for this new age, for "God has told me how to claim the world."

CBN's first broadcast took place on 1 October 1961, the same year that Robertson was ordained as a Southern Baptist minister. In order to alleviate the chronic shortage of money that plagued that station, Robertson developed the concept of "faith partners" in 1963. He asked for 700 committed people to give ten dollars a month to keep "spiritual television" alive. In 1965 he brought Jim and Tammy Bakker's* children's show, "Come On Over," to CBN. "The 700 Club" made its debut in 1966 and became the vehicle for Robertson's rapid rise as a television celebrity. In 1975, buoyed by the financial success of CBN,

Robertson bought land in Virginia Beach that would by 1978 house CBN University. By 1986, a law school was added to schools of communication, education, business, biblical studies, public policy, and journalism.

The third act in the drama does not have a precise beginning. Beginning in 1972, "The 700 Club" became a nationally syndicated program. With its talk show and news magazine format, it resembled secular television more than any other religious broadcast, and Robertson resembled an informed talk show host more than a television preacher. As CBN began utilizing satellite transmission, Robertson had a technologically advanced, well-financed base from which to develop his varied "ministries" (a nationwide telephone counseling service, literacy programs, a legal foundation, food programs, and, of course, CBN University). The secular format of "The 700 Club" allowed Robertson to develop his skills as a television social critic, and in addition to the media stars of the evangelical world, he welcomed national and foreign celebrities from every walk of life. But "The 700 Club" never became simply news and commentary. Robertson maintained an effective relationship with viewers by blending prayer, Bible instruction, and calls for revival with carefully crafted "Christian" social commentary. Using television skillfully, he has popularized his diagnosis of the ills of America and his "Biblically-based" prescriptions for the nation's recovery.

There is nothing novel about Robertson's diagnosis. He believes that the nation has turned away from the Christian principles that made its citizens virtuous and that this act has left the nation susceptible to internal rot and external enemies. Robertson adopts the language of 1950s neoevangelicalism to identify "secular humanism" as the primary internal threat. From fundamentalist traditions he adopts the rhetoric of warfare to describe the battle now being waged for the nation's soul. His Pentecostal experiences inform him that the gifts of the Holy Spirit can serve as part of the process of biblically based cultural restoration.

Robertson makes use of a rhetorical form with deep and evocative roots in American culture: the Puritan jeremiad. Like the Puritans and their evangelical offspring, Robertson warns of doom and declension but hopes for restoration and a new order. The degenerative processes began only recently. In Philadelphia's Constitution Hall in 1986, Robertson declared that "we have permitted during the past 25 years an assault on our faith and values that would have been unthinkable to past generations of Americans" (from an article by Bert Spring in *Christianity Today*). In *America's Date With Destiny* (1986), he developed his vision of the tragic process of American history. The colonial period and the nineteenth-century era of Protestant hegemony are clearly a "golden age" when Christian and democratic ideals were intertwined and embodied in the nation's daily life. Robertson looks with favor on formative manifestations of the pioneer spirit, on the ideals of national Scriptures, and on the evangelical spirit of the new nation.

The nation began to lose its way, he says, only in the twentieth century. As he wrote in *America's Date With Destiny*, new intellectual currents fostered a "disregard of [the nation's] Judeo-Christian heritage." Through the machinations of the New Deal, the American Civil Liberties Union, and the Great Society, personal rights were lost and fiscal responsibility was abandoned. As the nation turned from Christian principles, it lost the spiritual dimension of patriotism and, hence, lost the will to win the war in Vietnam. Finally, the infamous Supreme Court decision on the right to abortion revealed the nation's utter spiritual bankruptcy.

To reverse this process of civic degeneration, Robertson turns both to the language of religion and to the language of politics. Undergirding all of his policy positions is his belief that a nationwide religious revival will signal the renewal of commitment to Christian principles in public and private life. At the center of such a revival must be the belief that the "invisible world of the Spirit" can help bring about a new order. The principles that govern this world are as real as "the laws of thermodynamics or gravity," and Robertson taught the utilization of these principles in his book *The Secret Kingdom*, one of the best-selling religious books of 1983. He believes that the inauguration of Ronald Reagan on 20 January 1981 symbolized America's return to these "Kingdom Principles," as well as a return to America's pioneer spirit.

Robertson's presidential candidacy represented an articulate response to this stark "either/or" proposition. It resuscitated the political energies of a large number of conservative evangelicals and, more important, further legitimized the neoevangelical reconstruction of Western intellectual history that includes an impassioned critique of modern liberal society.

### Appraisal

Despite his failure to attract widespread support for his 1988 campaign for the Republican presidential nomination, Pat Robertson's emergence as an influential political spokesman was much more than a curious moment in American social history. Until his campaign for the nomination, conservative evangelicals had not found a voice or a comprehensive message that could potentially move beyond sectarian boundaries. Robertson's vision of a revitalized Christian commonwealth, drawn from Puritan and Whig traditions, may yet motivate all but hard-core separatist-fundamentalists into a new and enduring engagement with American political culture. Consequently, conservative evangelicals may yet have to rethink their relationship as "insiders" and "outsiders" within the culture. Robertson often uses the language of the outsider, claiming that liberals have effectively disenfranchised "real" (Christian) Americans; consequently his candidacy's purpose was to restore to their rightful place such authentic Americans and end the aberrant period of secular liberal leadership. He argues that his family heritage gives him an almost instinctive sense of what it means to be a "real" American. In response to criticism from Norman Lear, founder of People for the American Way, Robertson said, "I have a fairly good idea of what the American way is because it was my ancestors who helped make this country."

Robertson's political activity was also significant because as the campaign progressed, to solidify his position as a mainstream candidate, he had to bridge the gap between what Grant Wacker has identified as the "custodial" and the "plural" ideals in church-state relations. The custodial ideal assumes that civil leaders have a responsibility to articulate spiritual principles in the culture at large. The plural ideal holds that religion is, for the most part, a private concern, having little specific guidance to offer in public affairs. Clearly, Robertson's instincts place him within the custodial tradition, but he must make grudging accommodation with the plural ideal, since it reflects the reality of contemporary American culture. Although it is notoriously difficult to draw lasting conclusions from political rhetoric, Robertson the politican sounds quite different from Robertson the religious broadcaster. He no longer has the luxury of adopting a stance of sectarian righteousness but must recognize the reality, if not the desirability, of plural America. Recently, he has begun to modify his long-standing conviction that America was founded as a "Christian" nation. Also, his "New Vision for America" is more than restorative, although that impulse is surely a powerful one. In foreign policy, for example, Robertson's religious principles and a sense of realism have combined to shape his vision for a new cooperative venture between nations. This vision was expressed in a spring 1987 speech before the Council on Foreign Relations, "Toward a Community of Democratic Nations."

Robertson's failure to attract more voters in the 1988 presidential primaries may signify a failure in his attempt to bridge the gap between the custodial and the plural ideals. It remains to be seen, should Robertson choose to enter future political contests, whether his attempt to embrace the plural ideal will be convincing to the electorate. Certainly, breaking his ties with the Southern Baptist Convention and with CBN is meant to convey such commitment. It also remains to be seen how his longtime followers—some of whom have called his opponents "demon possessed"—will respond to even a rhetorical embrace of this plural ideal.

Robertson's vision of an America trusting in a particular relationship with God and a public policy informed by biblically based "Kingdom Principles" is part of the ever livelier debate over the role of "religion" in civil society. Opponents of Robertson have feared, with some justification, that his narrow vision of the restoration of public morality based on a sectarian style of evangelical Christianity would introduce a religious bigotry, sometimes blatant and sometimes subtle, into the life of the nation. Opponents have also questioned whether his message can ever transcend the sectarian roots that nourished it. Can Robertson recognize and respect the kind of civic virtue that has been practiced by those not associated with religious traditions but who may be motivated by the ethical imperatives of such traditions? Can he move beyond a style of religiosity that apes the worst aspect of secular American culture: the frantic desire for material success? Can he move beyond the Cold War world view that informs his foreign policy and contributes to irresponsible and alarmist statements about America's nuclear strength in relation to the Soviet Union?

And, finally, can Robertson's vision of America rely less on triumphalist recollections and sentimental nostalgias regarding American history? (When, after all, did the nation embody the ideals contained in our sacred national texts?) A dose of realism like that advanced by Reinhold Neibuhr would contribute a maturity to Robertson's message that it does not now have: a sense that America has always been both secular and religious, and a realization that irony, not victory, is the key term in the story of America.

## Survey of Criticism

Journalistic literature about Pat Robertson is vast in amount but mostly lacking in insightful analysis. For example, Hubert Morken, a political scientist at Oral Roberts University and author of *Pat Robertson: Religion and Politics in Simple Terms,* estimates that between January 1986 and August 1986 over 2,000 articles were written about Pat Robertson. Many of these dealt simply with predictions about the Robertson presidential campaign and its chances for success. Some articles fit Robertson into the Elmer Gantry category, extracting episodes from his life (testimonies of healing, prayer in the face of hurricanes, etc.) to "expose" him. The *Christian Century* began worrying about Robertson's influence in 1980, when an editorial declared that he "poisoned the air waves with right-wing views couched in biblical prophecy language." By 1985 the editors appreciated Robertson's appeal, if not his message. He was, they exclaimed, the "Jesse Jackson of the 1988 presidential campaign," able to tell stories about a particular vision of America. In a 1986 issue of the *National Review,* John McLaughlin spoke of Robertson's enduring legacy, the "deghettoizing of the Religious Right," and the pleasant prospect for new and energetic conservative Republicans. One gains little from a systematic study of such accounts. They are overwhelmingly oriented to the passion and issue of the moment and are a useful index only of the current trends of support or opposition to Robertson's message and political plans.

The most substantive interpretation of Robertson and the culture of CBN was done by Dick Dabney in a 1980 issue of *Harper's.* Dabney characterized Robertson as a "19th century entrepreneur" and, though critical of much of Robertson's message, offered that "a Pat Robertson purged of the itch for corporate expansion, self-righteousness, and the lust for political power really would be formidable."

Books about Robertson have tended to be either harsh exposés or hymns of adulation. Gerald Straub, who worked at CBN for several years, is unsparing in his criticism of Robertson in *Salvation for Sale.* Straub insists that Robertson, through his effective mix of religion, politics, and television, has formed a "holy terror with the potential to endanger freedoms we take for granted." Straub writes of his personal experiences with Robertson and concludes that Robertson practices a "spiritual bigotry that is as hateful and menacing as anything ignited by the Ku Klux Klan, Hitler or the Ayatollah Khomeini." A quite different story is told by Neil Eskelin, Robertson's first full-time employee at CBN. In *Pat*

*Robertson: A Biography,* Eskelin seems still to stand in reverential awe of Robertson. He wrote the book, he declares, because he felt the "full story of this unique American would be an inspiration to many." Eskelin says that in the process of writing, "I have become a believer, not just in Robertson, but in what he stands for."

More balanced examinations of Robertson serve as welcome correctives to these subjective portraits. Historian David E. Harrell, Jr., who has written a sensitive and insightful biography of Oral Roberts*, remarks in his recent *Pat Robertson: A Personal, Political and Religious Portrait* that "no one's life story and belief system cries more for clarification than Pat Robertson's." Harrell takes Robertson's religious identity seriously. He unravels Robertson's charismatic, evangelical, and Southern Baptist heritage and argues that this complex identity is the key to understanding the man and his message. Harrell does not treat Robertson's thought as static but as the product of a dynamic and creative mind, nurtured but never held captive by his religious roots.

Hubert Morken's aforementioned *Pat Robertson: Religion and Politics in Simple Terms* is a valuable complement to Harrell's biography because he has traced the development of Robertson's political ideas and their relationship to his faith through analysis of Robertson's unpublished speeches and interviews. At times, Morken seems to adopt too readily Robertson's assumptions, and he does admit to the reader that in the writing of the book he shifted from "total opposition" to Robertson's candidacy to "sympathetic neutrality" to "supporting him with reservations." Regrettably, Jeffrey K. Hadden and Anson Shupe's *Televangelism, Power, and Politics on God's Frontier* (published by Henry Holt in 1988) was not available for prepublication reading.

## Bibliography

### Books by Pat Robertson

1972  *Shout It From The Housetops.* With Jamie Buckingham. South Plainfield, N.J.: Bridge.
1977  *My Prayer For You.* Old Tappan, N.J.: Fleming H. Revell Company.
1983  *The Secret Kingdom.* With Bob Slosser. Nashville: Thomas Nelson.
1984  *Answers To 200 Of Life's Most Probing Questions.* Nashville: Thomas Nelson.
1984  *Beyond Reason.* New York: William Morrow and Co.
1986  *America's Date With Destiny.* Nashville: Thomas Nelson.

### Selected Studies about Pat Robertson

Dabney, Dick. "God's Own Network: The TV Kingdom of Pat Robertson," *Harper's* 261 (August 1980): 33–52.
Eskelin, Neil. *Pat Robertson: A Biography.* Lafayette, La.: Huntington House, 1987.
Frankl, Razelle. *Televangelism: The Marketing of Popular Religion.* Carbondale and Edwardsville: Southern Illinois University Press, 1986.
Hadden, Jeffrey. "Taking Stock of the New Christian Right," *Christianity Today* (13 June 1986): 38–39.
————, and Anson Shupe. *Televangelism, Power, and Politics on God's Frontier.* New York: Henry Holt, 1988.

Harrell, David E., Jr. *Pat Robertson: A Personal, Political and Religious Portrait*. San Francisco: Harper and Row, 1987.

Kramer, M. "Are You Running with Me, Jesus?" *New York* (18 August 1986): 22–29.

McLaughlin, John. "Preacher Pat." *National Review* 38 (23 May 1986): 20.

Morken, Hubert. *Pat Robertson: Religion and Politics in Simple Terms*. Old Tappan. N.J.: Fleming H. Revell Company, 1987.

Servaas, Cory, and Maynard Good Stoddard. "CBN's Pat Robertson: White House Next?" *Saturday Evening Post* (March 1985). Reprint.

Spring, Bert. "One Step Closer to a Bid for the Oval Office." *Christianity Today* (17 October 1986): 39–41, 44–45.

Straub, Gerald Thomas. *Salvation for Sale*. Buffalo, N.Y.: Prometheus Books, 1986.

Wall, James. "God's 'Piece of Cheese.' " *Christian Century* (27 February 1980): 219–20.

———. "Watch for Robertson in the 1988 Campaign." *Christian Century* (23 October 1985): 939–40.

EDWARD TABOR LINENTHAL

# John A. Ryan

The Catholic church in America emerged united from a long and sometimes bitter struggle between its conservative and liberal wings during the closing decades of the nineteenth century. At the heart of the numerous controversies that divided this church of many immigrants was the question of assimilation to the American cultural, political, and religious milieu. Pope Leo XIII's condemnation of those heresies known as "Americanism" warned Catholics in this country that too much compromise with the modern spirit, especially in regard to the church's institutions and theology, would not be tolerated by Rome. This blow was made doubly effective by the condemnation of "modernism" in 1907. Progressive Catholicism in America, as represented by prelates such as James Cardinal Gibbons, Archbishop John Ireland, Archbishop John Keane, and Bishop John Lancaster Spalding, nevertheless managed to continue its work, especially in the church's championing of social and economic justice. It was Monsignor John A. Ryan, for over twenty years the director of the social action department of the National Catholic Welfare Conference, who acted as the primary resource person, theoretician, and spokesman for the American Catholic church in the area of social reform and economic rights. As such, Msgr. Ryan was one of those leaders who kept the torch of progressive Catholicism alive during decades of profound theological and ecclesiastical conservatism in the church at large.

## Biography

John Augustine Ryan was born on 25 May 1869 on his family's farm near Vermillion, Minnesota. The oldest of the ten children of William Ryan and Maria Elizabeth Luby, both immigrants from Ireland, John was taught the importance of hard work at an early age. The Ryans practiced a fervent, typically

Irish, highly personal Catholic piety. Four of the Ryan children eventually accepted a religious vocation. Besides learning the values of faith and hard work, young John Ryan was also inculcated with the populist principles of the National Farmers' Alliance that were sweeping rural Minnesota at the time. This organization, to which the elder Ryan belonged, stood for economic justice for farmers through government regulation of prices.

John Ryan's parents prospered in farming sufficiently to send him to a Christian Brothers' high school in St. Paul. It was there that young John experienced the call to the priesthood. With a $200 gift from his grandfather Luby, John was able to enroll in the diocesan seminary in St. Paul. At the seminary, John Ryan's academic interests quickened, and he soon moved to the head of his class. He became interested in moral theology and particularly in *Rerum novarum* (1891), Pope Leo XIII's encyclical that condemned both socialism and unbridled capitalism. It was the application of traditional Catholic moral principles to the problems spawned by an industrial economy that enlivened John Ryan's imagination and helped to define his life's work.

Archbishop John Ireland of St. Paul proved to be another important influence on the young seminarian. At a time when many conservative voices in the American church were calling for caution in the assimilation of American culture and values that were perceived as being tainted by Protestantism, Archbishop Ireland was urging American Catholics to abandon their fortress mentality and splendid isolation within their own institutions and to embrace and mingle with the best that America had to offer. Inspired by the work of his first bishop, John Ryan was to remain dedicated all of his life to the idea that Americanism and Catholicism were mutually compatible.

During his seminary years, Ryan published articles in the St. Paul diocesan newspaper on the need for governmental regulation to ensure a healthy and just economy. He was ordained to the priesthood in 1898, and after one short summer spent working in a St. Paul parish, the young priest was sent by Archbishop Ireland to Catholic University in Washington, D.C., to pursue a doctorate in moral theology. There Father Ryan was able to focus his scholarly interests on the impact of Christian moral principles on the economic and social life of the nation. He became the student of Father Thomas Bouquillon, who was one of the intellectual powers behind the progressive Catholic movement known as "Americanism." Ryan would follow the example of his mentor at Catholic University in drawing on the conclusions of the social sciences to apply the Catholic moral tradition to the problems of an industrial society. Ryan's articles on the ethics of speculation and the minimum wage began to be published in national journals.

After earning his doctorate in sacred theology, Father Ryan returned to St. Paul Seminary to begin his teaching career. His doctoral dissertation was published in 1906 under the title *A Living Wage*. This inquiry into the demands that justice makes on the wage system is one of Ryan's most important theoretical works, applying the traditional canons of moral theology to a highly controversial problem of the day. Here Ryan forcefully argued that the minimum wage is a right grounded in the natural law. In his view, every society therefore is obliged to ensure that all of its citizens are making a living wage sufficient to live in "frugal comfort."

After the publication of *A Living Wage,* the invitations to write articles, give lectures, and to sit on various committees for social reform came pouring in to Father Ryan. Among the numerous organizations in which Ryan participated during his long career were the American Civil Liberties Union, American Federation of Catholic Societies, Catholic Conference on Industrial Problems, Labor Defense Council, National Child Labor Committee, National Consumers League, American Indian Defense Association, National World Court Committee, and National Council for the Prevention of War. Father Ryan's boundless energy seemed capable of taking on project after project without dissipation for over forty years. However, his goal as a social reformer was always religious: to raise the awareness of the church to its responsibilities to the poor and underprivileged.

By 1915, Father Ryan had become anxious to move to a university position that would give him more flexibility to pursue the many activities that by now were consuming so much of his time. Archbishop Ireland finally gave him permission to assume the post of professor of moral theology at Catholic University. Washington, D.C., would prove to be the perfect location for Ryan's work in social justice. In addition to his work at the university, Father Ryan also found time to teach classes at both Trinity College for women and the National Catholic School of Social Service.

Shortly after his move to Catholic University, Father Ryan published the second of his two major systematic works on the ethics of modern economic institutions. Entitled *Distributive Justice,* this book attempted to widen the scope of his thought beyond the moral position of workers to include all participants in the economic order. For Ryan, "distributive justice" meant an equitable allotment of what is realized from the sale of a finished product among all who contributed in whatever way to its production. The rights of the businessman to his profit, the capitalist to his interest, and the landowner to his rent are always modified by the right of the laborer to a living wage and by the good of society in general. For Father Ryan, the church is obliged to preach just distribution of the world's goods, and governments are obliged to enforce it through income taxes, inheritance taxes, and minimum wage legislation.

At the conclusion of World War I, the U.S. Catholic bishops adopted many of Father Ryan's ethical principles and concrete proposals for reform in their *Program for Social Reconstruction.* The bishops had decided to continue the work of the National Catholic War Council in organizing and speaking for the church to American society. The new body was called the National Catholic Welfare Conference (NCWC), and John Ryan was asked to supervise the work of the Washington office of the NCWC's Social Action Department, which was carried out through publications, lectures, workshops, correspondence, lobbying, and cooperation with non-Catholic religious bodies. With this work, Father Ryan attained national prominence as a social reformer.

Although Ryan's advocacy of the minimum wage, child labor laws, the right of labor to organize, national unemployment and old age insurance, the regulation of monopolies, a federal income tax, and similar forward-looking legislation made him appear as a radical in some eyes, he was in fact well within the principles set down by *Rerum novarum* and scholastic tradition. The issue on which his credentials as a progressive were compromised as he stood with Catholic tradition was the relationship between church and state. In a textbook that he wrote, along with Moorehouse F. X. Millar, Ryan supported the position that the state, because its most important obligation is the spiritual welfare of its citizens, should make a public profession of religion. Given a Catholic majority, a government has the obligation to recognize Catholicism as the religion of the state. Since error has not the same rights as truth, Ryan wrote, anyone who holds the truth of the Catholic faith can look at the situation in no other way. Ryan was quick to point out, however, that religious freedom is justified for expediency's sake in the United States and anywhere there is religious pluralism. Catholic church-state doctrine became a major issue in the presidential election campaign of 1928, when a Catholic for the first time was a candidate. Ryan came repeatedly to the defense of Governor Al Smith, the Catholic candidate, but was hard pressed to calm the anxiety that most progressives felt on the issue. Many assumed a Catholic president would show favoritism to his own church.

The crash of 1929 brought a new urgency to Ryan's work. Although he never blamed President Herbert Hoover for the Depression (the result, Ryan felt, of overproduction and low wages), Father Ryan did hold the administration responsible for making the situation worse through inaction. Pope Pius XI's encyclical *Quadragesimo anno* (1931), which celebrated and updated the thought of Pope Leo XIII on social justice, provided Ryan with more ammunition in his fight for economic renewal.

Ryan fully supported Franklin Roosevelt in the election of 1932 and in all subsequent elections when Roosevelt ran. Indeed, Roosevelt's New Deal represented a triumph for the program of social reform that Ryan had long advocated. Father Ryan developed a close relationship with the Roosevelt administration through an old friend, Frances Perkins, the secretary of labor. In 1934, Ryan was appointed to the three-person Industrial Appeals Board of the NRA which heard petitions for exemptions from the norms of minimum wage, working conditions, and business practices.

Although he confessed abhorrence at the public spectacle of two Catholic priests in ideological confrontation, Ryan's support for the New Deal compelled him to address the issues raised by Father Charles Coughlin, the radio priest from Royal Oak, Michigan, whose demagogic attacks against President Roosevelt had become infamous. In a famous radio broadcast of his own in 1936, Msgr. Ryan stated that Coughlin was at least 50 percent wrong in his explanation of America's economic maladies and at least 90 percent wrong in his monetary remedies. Father Coughlin's response, intended as pejorative but regarded by Ryan as complimentary, referred to the Catholic University professor as the "Right Reverend New Dealer," alluding to the papal honor Ryan had received in 1933 naming him a right reverend monsignor.

In 1939, at age seventy, Msgr. Ryan was forced to retire from his professorship at Catholic University, although he continued to teach at Trinity College and the School of Social Service and to carry out his work at the social action department of the NCWC. Much of Ryan's last years, however, was given over to the writing of his autobiography, *Social Doctrine in Action,* and to revising some of his earlier works. Although Ryan had helped to champion the cause of world peace, the victories of the fascist powers in 1939 and 1940 convinced him that democracy would have to be defended through the shedding of blood. Ryan joined the Committee to Defend America by Aiding the Allies, and in 1941 he gave a radio speech in support of the Lend Lease Bill.

Msgr. Ryan's health declined steadily during the war years. One of the last causes he took up was the international organization of nations, which he hoped would be given enough authority to override the sovereignty of nations in order to keep the peace. Ryan lived long enough to eulogize his friend President Roosevelt as a champion of social justice. The great Catholic voice for social and economic justice, of Msgr. John A. Ryan, finally fell silent on 16 September 1945. He was buried in his hometown of Vermillion, Minnesota.

## Appraisal

Although Msgr. Ryan's liberal opinions on social renewal were indeed controversial, his Catholic orthodoxy was never called into question because he did narrowly limit himself to the single field of theological and moral doctrine, in which progressive thought was tolerated. Ryan had no interest in, nor did he ever express any opinion concerning, liturgical or ecclesiastical reform or the modernist questions about the Bible, revelation, and the role of theology. Even in his own discipline of moral theology, Msgr. Ryan's progressivism began and ended with questions of social and economic justice.

In other areas, his views were in keeping with Catholic orthodoxy. In the debate over artificial contraception, for example, Ryan broke ranks with his fellow reformers by staunchly defending traditional church teaching. Artificial means of birth control, Ryan held, were not only a perversion of the God-given faculty for procreation, and thus a sin against the natural law, but also had serious adverse social consequences, namely the creation of self-indulgent instead of self-sacrificing families and the decline of national population. This position again demonstrates the conservative and traditional foundation of Ryan's moral principles, based as they were on the church's natural law doctrine that had progressive implications only in the area of social and economic justice.

Msgr. Ryan's position on church-state relations, as we have seen, faithfully followed traditional Catholic doctrine which insisted that the Catholic church be recognized as the official religion in any nation where Catholics make up a majority. This doctrine likewise denied the freedom of religion so basic to the liberal American mind because it presumed that error has not the same rights as truth. In the 1920s, John Ryan defended the Catholic doctrine on this matter, as abhorrent as it may have been, because he was genuinely convinced that the church's teaching authority was divinely inspired and was preserved against error in matters of faith and morals. To fail to understand this is to fail to understand the mind of John Ryan. Indeed, it is to fail to understand the Catholic mind during this entire period.

The terms *liberal* and *conservative* might not be that revealing when applied to the career of John A. Ryan, for he combined something from both agendas to create his own point of view. In this regard, he was a typical American. Ryan felt no conflict between, for instance, his traditional Catholic opinion on the relationship between church and state and his membership on the national board of the ACLU. He was determined that whatever disagreements he had with Roger Baldwin should not keep the two from cooperating on the goals that they held in common. Ryan's progressivism rested on his unshakable belief that Catholics must leave the splendid isolation of their own specially created world and enter the American political, social, and cultural debate. In this, Ryan could be said to have anticipated a distinctly post–Vatican II attitude in which the Catholic church finally began to perceive its role in the modern world as one of moral persuasion, not coercion. For so long, the church had refused to accept the fact that it no longer held a privileged position in society, that its voice was only one among many contending for people's loyalty. John Ryan accepted the authority of the church in his own life, but he recognized that to have its moral agenda considered in the public forum, the Catholic church would have to enter the fray of open debate and to compete as an equal. This was the source of his progressivism.

And what of the moral agenda in the field of social and economic renewal that Msgr. Ryan championed so tirelessly? To those who were convinced that laissez-faire capitalism was the best economic system from a pragmatic or even a moral viewpoint, Ryan indeed was a liberal. At the heart of both *A Living Wage* and *Distributive Justice* lies the natural law principle that the goods of creation exist to serve the basic needs of all people. If an economic system does not provide for the adequate material comfort of all in a given society, Ryan felt, then it must be either modified or discarded. In a written debate with Morris Hillquit in 1913, Ryan defended the capitalist system of private ownership as consonant with the dignity of the individual and as a practical system superior to socialism for the production and just distribution of material goods. Ryan demonstrated that a *via media,* however, between socialism and capitalism made sense from both a moral and economic point of view. Government has a moral obligation to regulate the economy to provide for a living wage for all workers while at the same time ensuring a reasonable exercise of entrepreneurial rights. But the economically powerless, Ryan asserted, have a special claim on any government's attention, since the wealthy have the resources to defend their own rights.

The goal of Msgr. Ryan's program for social renewal was greater economic democratization in which more people would enjoy a greater portion of the nation's resources through a modification of the present system. Class conflict is not necessary to achieve this end. Through legislation, the status of workers could be raised so that they are able to participate as equals in the economic life of the nation. Such a program, although far from being radical, does clearly mark its author as a Christian progressive in social and economic ethics. Ryan's genius was his ability to combine traditional Catholic doctrine on the dignity of the person and the universal destiny of the goods of creation with a typically American belief in democracy and hope in the future, thus creating an American Catholic outlook. The U.S. Catholic Bishops' 1985 pastoral letter on the nation's economy demonstrates that the legacy bequeathed by Msgr. John Ryan to American Catholics is still alive and well, for it affirmed the essentials of Ryan's position.

## Survey of Criticism

The only complete biography of Msgr. Ryan remains Francis L. Broderick's *Right Reverend New Dealer: John A Ryan*. It is a thorough, well-researched, cogently written, critical treatment of Ryan's life from childhood through his productive years to his death in 1945. Broderick is particularly to be recommended for his clear, understandable presentation of the sometimes complex economic theories that contributed to Ryan's program for social reform. Also explained here is the Catholic natural law doctrine that provided the methodology for Ryan's works. In the course of the biography, Broderick reviews the content and impact of Ryan's major books and articles, as well as providing a valuable bibliographical essay. The biography was written with a certain pre–Vatican II slant, however, in which Ryan's strict conformity to Catholic dogmatic teaching, especially in the church-state question, is taken for granted. But one senses that Broderick correctly asserts that Ryan saw himself first and foremost as a Catholic priest and an interpreter of the Catholic moral tradition to the modern world, not as a representative of any liberal or progressive point of view.

John Ryan's autobiography, *Social Doctrine in Action,* is as formal and personally unrevealing as the title suggests. Much of the book consists of exerpts and lengthy quotations from previously published material. In his businesslike approach to summarizing his career, Ryan offers us very little insight into his motivations, beliefs, or inner conflicts. His stated intention is to demonstrate the continuity and consistency of his social thought. Once again, however, one can detect that, of the many hats he wore in his lifetime, the most important to Ryan himself was that of a Catholic professor of moral theology.

Two books greatly assist the reader who is seeking background to the life of John A. Ryan in the history of American Catholicism: Thomas T. McAvoy, *The Great Crisis in American Catholic History, 1895–1900,* and Robert D. Cross,

*The Emergence of Liberal Catholicism in America.* McAvoy gives a detailed account of the several conflicts that divided American Catholics into liberal and conservative factions during Ryan's formative years. Cross brings the insight of sociological analysis to that same period of conflict that was to prove to be so stimulating for American Catholicism but that was cut off prematurely by the papal encyclicals of 1899 *(Testem benevolentiae)* and 1907 *(Pascendi gregis).*

A complete list of all of Ryan's published works is contained in Theodora E. McGill's "Bio-Bibliography of Monsignor John A. Ryan." Herein also is a short essay on the life of Msgr. Ryan, a list of the reviews of Ryan's sixteen books, and a lengthy list of articles about Ryan published through 1952.

One of the most recent works on John Ryan, and perhaps the most thoughtful analysis of Ryan as a Catholic moral theologian, is Charles E. Curran's *American Catholic Social Ethics: Twentieth Century Approaches.* In a lengthy chapter devoted to Ryan, Father Curran carefully reviews Ryan's methodology with distinctly post–Vatican II eyes and identifies the continuing sources of Ryan's relevance for modern-day readers.

## Bibliography

### Books by John A. Ryan

1906  *A Living Wage.* New York: Macmillan. Rev. ed., 1920.
1914  *Socialism: Promise or Menace?* With Morris Hillquit. New York: Macmillan.
1916  *Distributive Justice.* New York: Macmillan. Rev. eds., 1927, 1942.
1919  *The Church and Socialism and Other Essays.* Washington, D.C.: University Press.
1920  *The Church and Labor.* Edited with Joseph Husslein. New York: Macmillan.
1920  *Social Reconstruction.* New York: Macmillan.
1922  *The State and the Church.* Edited with Moorehouse F. X. Millar. New York: Macmillan.
1927  *Declining Liberty and Other Papers.* New York: Macmillan.
1928  *The Catholic Church and the Citizen.* New York: Macmillan.
1931  *Questions of the Day.* Boston: Stratford Co.
1935  *A Better Economic Order.* New York: Harper and Brothers.
1937  *Seven Troubled Years, 1930–36.* Ann Arbor: Edwards Brothers.
1940  *Catholic Principles of Politics.* Edited with Francis J. Boland. New York: Macmillan.
1941  *Social Doctrine in Action: A Personal History.* New York: Harper Brothers.
1952  *The Norm of Morality Defined and Applied to Particular Actions.* Washington, D.C.: National Catholic Welfare Conference.

### Selected Articles by John A. Ryan

1909  "The 'Perverted Faculty' Argument Against Birth Prevention." *Ecclesiastical Review* 21: 608–14.
1909  "A Program of Social Reform by Legislation." *Catholic World* 89: 433–44, 608–14.
1912  "Private Ownership and Socialism." *Catholic World* 94: 497–504.
1918  "Catholic Doctrine on the Right of Self-Government." *Catholic World* 108: 314–30.

1920   "A Democratic Transformation of Industry." *Studies* 9: 383–96.
1921   "The Moral Obligation of Civil Law." *Catholic World* 114: 73–86.
1924   "Are Our Prohibition Laws Purely Penal?" *American Ecclesiastical Review* 60: 404–11.
1925   "The Supreme Court and Child Labor." *Catholic World* 108: 213–19.
1929   "Assault Upon Democracy." *Catholic World* 128: 641–47.
1930   "Catholicism and Liberalism." *Nation* (6 August): 150–54.
1930   "The New Morality and Its Illusions." *Catholic World* 129: 129–36.
1943   "The Place of the Negro in American Society." *Catholic World* 141: 13–22.

### Selected Studies about John A. Ryan

Broderick, Francis L. "The Encyclicals and Social Action: Is John A. Ryan Typical?" *Catholic Historical Review* 55 (1969): 1–6.
———. *Right Reverend New Dealer: John A. Ryan*. New York: Macmillan, 1963.
Cerny, Karl H. "Monsignor John A. Ryan and the Social Action Department." Ph.D. diss., Yale University, 1954.
Cross, Robert D. *The Emergence of Liberal Catholicism in America*. Cambridge, Mass.: Harvard University Press, 1958.
Curran, Charles E. *American Catholic Social Ethics: Twentieth Century Approaches*. Notre Dame, Ind.: University of Notre Dame Press, 1982.
Geartz, Patrick W. "The Economic Thought of Monsignor John A. Ryan." Ph.D. diss., Catholic University of America, 1953.
Gouldrick, John W. "John A. Ryan's Theory of the State." S.T.D. diss., Catholic University of America, 1979.
Higgins, George G. "The Under Consumption Theory in the Writings of Monsignor John A. Ryan." Master's thesis, Catholic University of America, 1942.
McAvoy, Thomas T. *The Great Crisis in American Catholic History, 1895–1900*. Chicago: Henry Regnery Co., 1957.
McGill, Theodora E. "A Bio-Bibliography of Monsignor John A. Ryan." Master's thesis, Catholic University of America, 1952.

MARK B. SORVILLO

# Robert Schuller

The fertile soil of American optimism and idealism has produced a long line of popular religionists who have proclaimed a gospel of self-help through various forms of mind conditioning. Included in this lineage, which can be traced back at least to the early decades of the nineteenth century, are such diverse figures as Phineas Parkhurst Quimby, Mary Baker Eddy, Ralph Waldo Trine, and Norman Vincent Peale*. During the last half of the twentieth century the most prominent heir of these proponents of positive religion has been Robert Schuller, founding pastor of the 10,000-member Crystal Cathedral, whose message of "possibility thinking" has been widely promulgated through his popular television program "Hour of Power," numerous best-selling religious books, and a long-standing church growth institute. Considering the success and influence of his ministry, the *Christian Century,* a leading Protestant journal, in 1982

ranked Schuller among the most prominent contemporary religious figures in
America.

## Biography

Robert Harold Schuller is a genuine American farm boy. Born at Alton, Iowa,
on 16 September 1926, he was raised on a farm near the hamlet of Newkirk,
located in the northwest corner of the state where some of the country's most
productive cropland is tilled by a rather large enclave of Dutch-American farmers.
Like most of their neighbors, Jenny and Anthony Schuller (or *Skuller,* as the
folk in Iowa pronounce the name) were members of the Reformed Church in
America, a small Dutch Calvinist denomination that was organized in 1628 in
New York City but that was undergirded by a wave of Dutch Reformed immigrants who settled into pockets of the upper Midwest seeking economic security and the opportunity to establish colonies of Reformed faith. So along with
the typically agrarian qualities of industry, determination, and self-reliance,
young Robert was nurtured in the doctrine and piety of orthodox Calvinism. It
appears that Robert was destined to become a Christian minister. Anthony
Schuller had secretly dedicated his fifth child to the Lord's service, even before
he was born. Early on, Robert set his sights on such a calling, even perfecting
his skills, we are told, by preaching enthusiastically to a congregation of cows
and cornstalks.

In 1943, at the age of sixteen, Schuller graduated from high school and enrolled
at Hope College, a Reformed Church liberal arts college located in Holland,
Michigan. With his sights set firmly on the ministry, he took preseminary courses,
and on graduation he entered Western Theological Seminary, another denominational institution located next to the campus of Hope College. At both educational institutions Schuller gained a reputation for self-confidence and
determination to succeed. He was also recognized as a persuasive speaker, as
he won the preaching prize during his senior year at the seminary. Following
his ordination, Schuller became the pastor of the Ivanhoe Reformed Church, a
small and struggling congregation located near Chicago in Riverdale, Illinois.
The young pastor remained at Ivanhoe for more than four years, demonstrating
gifts in preaching and outreach that would become renowned in southern California. Under his leadership the church experienced resounding growth—its
membership multiplied from 40 to 400.

During June 1950, the very month of his ordination and of his move to suburban
Chicago, Schuller had married Arvella De Haan, whom he had met while preaching back home in Newkirk. Over the years Arvella has become an invaluable
associate in all phases of their ministry but especially in the production of "Hour
of Power." During those early years at Ivanhoe she was also busy raising Robert
A. and Sheila, the oldest of five Schuller offspring (Jeane, Carol, and Gretchen
were all born later in California). In general, the Schuller ministry has been a
family affair, as all the children, at one time or another, have been involved in
the California operation.

In 1955 Schuller was asked by denominational leaders to organize a new congregation in Garden Grove, California. Enamored with the West Coast and excited about the possibility of building a ministry from the bottom up, Schuller seized the opportunity. The church that grew out of the orange groves of Garden Grove is one of America's ecclesiastical success stories. As Schuller himself tells the saga, he arrived in California with these assets: $400, an old Chevy, an electric organ, and a dream of organizing a great church. Unable to secure a suitable building for weekly worship services in the booming southern California real estate market, Schuller received permission from the owner of a local drive-in theatre to hold services there until a congregation could be organized and a building erected. This obstacle became a great opportunity for growth, as many prospective members were attracted by Schuller's newspaper ads: "Come as you are in the family car." While Arvella played the portable organ, Robert preached and prayed from the roof of the refreshment stand at the drive-in. A congregation was quickly organized, but even when a church building was constructed, Schuller continued to carry on the successful drive-in ministry. In 1961, the Garden Grove Community Church constructed a drive-in, walk-in church, and this innovative structure first brought national attention to Schuller's ministry. The fifties and sixties were years of spectacular growth in membership for the congregation. Structuring his church programming around the needs of people, Schuller placed great stress on evangelism, education, and community building. Innovative and willing to take risks, Schuller constantly challenged the congregation with new forms of ministry, including a telephone counseling service that was put into operation around the clock and eventually reached across the nation. In addition to a large, modern steel-and-glass sanctuary that served as the drive-in, walk-in church, Schuller proposed the building of the Tower of Power, a multi-story multi-use building that was topped by a ninety-foot cross that, lighted at night, could be seen throughout Orange County.

When the sanctuary became too small to hold the thousands of people who were now attending three successive Sunday morning services, Schuller announced his dream to build a massive glass church. Phillip Johnson, one of the most respected architects in America, was secured to design the ultimate worship structure. In September 1980, the Crystal Cathedral was dedicated. Johnson produced a spectacular all glass-and-steel building. Shaped like a five-pointed star, it stretched 400 feet long and 200 feet wide, and it soared 125 feet high. The steel skeleton was wrapped by more than 10,000 windowpanes. With main floor and balconies, the structure would seat more than 3,000 people. Huge glass doors opened to those who preferred to participate from their cars. When a magnificent pipe organ was added, the total cost of the building came to nearly $20 million. Schuller was forced to defend the project against those critics who questioned the stewardship of building such an expensive edifice during an era of human want. He argued that it was a monument to God, like the great cathedrals of Europe, and that it would quickly attract revenue that could be used for mission projects. Although few of Schuller's critics were satisfied by such arguments, most agreed that it was a breathtaking worship center, one that has become a standout southern California tourist attraction, along with Disneyland and Knotts Berry Farm. When he first viewed the impressive structure, Norman Cousins, a friend of Schuller's, reportedly remarked: "This is the kind of church God would build; if he could afford it."

Success breeds imitation. The monumental growth of the Garden Grove Community Church (officially renamed the Crystal Cathedral of the Reformed Church in America in 1980) has propelled Schuller into the limelight of the contemporary church growth movement. An ecclesiastical entrepreneur and not one to hide his light under a basket, he has gone into the business of sharing his secrets of success. In 1969 he organized the Robert H. Schuller Institute for Successful Church Leadership. The four-day conferences generally have been held three times a year with an enrollment of about 200, mostly pastors, their spouses, and church lay leaders. Fees charged entitle participants to attend diagnostic clinics and how-to workshops, but the central features of the institutes have been five well-tuned and humorous presentations in which Schuller expounds the principles of church growth that he tested at Garden Grove. In general, Schuller has emphasized that church growth occurs only where there is possibility thinking, strong pastoral leadership, a needs-oriented ministry, noncontroversial preaching, and a staff ministry. Over the years thousands of church leaders have attended the institutes and imbibed Schuller's basic philosophy.

Schuller's television ministry was inaugurated in January 1970. The idea was first suggested to Schuller during the previous year by Fred Dienart, one of the producers of a Billy Graham* crusade in Anaheim. Dienart was convinced that the animated and charismatic Schuller would be an ideal television personality. From the very beginning it was apparent that Schuller was made for television. "Hour of Power" was originally tested on the West Coast, where it caught on quickly. Soon it was made available to markets across the country. For many years the program has sustained its appeal and has consistently been rated by Neilson and Arbitron as one of the top two weekly religious broadcasts in America. Appearing on more than 150 stations, "Hour of Power" has tended to do better by comparison with other television ministries in the urban Northeast and the Midwest. Like the other television ministries, "Hour of Power" is watched by a disproportionate number of women and persons over fifty years old. Schuller attributes the success of "Hour of Power" to the fact that it is "broadcasting" rather than "narrowcasting." Realizing that his audience is free to switch off the program, Schuller aims to produce a high-quality show that holds the viewer as long as possible. Hence, "Hour of Power" is good television. The tempo is fast-paced, the music is upbeat, and the mood is positive. The centerpieces of "Hour of Power" are Schuller's dynamic and dramatic messages. Whereas Schuller has been an obvious target of those critics who complain that television preaching is too unambiguous, simplistic, and self-oriented, he argues that he is actually a pre-evangelist attempting to get in contact with the cultural despisers of Christianity and, therefore, must offer a version of the gospel that is understandable, entertaining, positive, and needs-oriented. During the early days of his television ministry, Schuller discovered that ratings rose whenever recognizable guests were invited to appear on the program to reflect on what God has done for them. The long list of famous guests has included Mickey Rooney, B. J. Thomas, Steve Garvey, Chuck Colson, and Billy Graham. As costs for producing and buying air time have skyrocketed, viewers of "Hour of Power" have been subjected to an increasing number of fund-raising appeals. Still, whereas other television ministries have been damaged by revelations of financial mismanagement, "Hour of Power" generally has been given a clean bill of financial health.

The ideological trademark of Schuller's ministry has been "possibility thinking," an upbeat expression that has been stamped onto nearly every enterprise emanating from Garden Grove. In addition to his well-known Possibility Thinker's Creed ("When faced with a mountain, I will never quit, I will keep on striving, until I climb over, find a pass through, travel underneath, or simply stay and turn the mountain into a goldmine! With God's help"), there have been the "Ten Commandments of Possibility Thinking," a "Possibility Thinker's Club," and a "Possibility Thinker's Game." Three of Schuller's earlier books also carried the trademark: *Move Ahead With Possibility Thinking, Peace of Mind Through Possibility Thinking,* and *The Greatest Possibility Thinker That Ever Lived.* Possibility thinking is a message and a method of self-improvement that, when properly employed, will bring the practitioner peace of mind, happiness, and success. Convinced that our attitudes shape our lives, Schuller offers possibility thinking as a therapeutic technique for purging the mind of negative thoughts so that positive mental forces will be allowed to direct our destinies. Schuller has outlined at least three positive mind conditioners in his writings: (1) imagineering—mentally focusing on the goal sought; (2) P.T.M.—Possibility Thinking Meditation, a relaxation exercise that blocks negative thoughts; and (3) auto-suggestion—the repetition of positive words, phrases, or verses. Possibility thinking, of course, is an updated version of the positive thinking approach espoused by Norman Vincent Peale, the longtime pastor of the Marble Collegiate Church in New York City, a fellow Reformed Church pastor and friend of the Schullers'. When Schuller arrived in California, Peale's *Power of Positive Thinking* (1952) was still on the best-seller list. In an effort to grab the coattails of the famous preacher, Schuller invited Peale to speak at his drive-in church. Peale's appeal convinced Schuller that he should orient his own ministry more in the direction of positive thinking. Though Schuller has moved beyond Peale in recent years, he owes a great intellectual debt to the New Yorker.

In an effort to supply a theological framework for his ministry, Schuller in recent years has given shape to "the theology of self-esteem." His most comprehensive and substantive writing in this regard was *Self-Esteem: The New Reformation* (1982). Convinced that much of Protestant theology was archaic because it presupposed a Christian society that no longer existed in the secularized West, Schuller proposed a new reformation in theology that began with an examination of human needs rather than with God-talk. He went on to argue that the basic human need, the driving force of human nature, was that of self-esteem, or the awareness that we are worthy beings. Hence, the basic human sin, or weakness, is lack of self-esteem. The Fall of Adam and Eve resulted in a weakened self-esteem of all humans. Jesus Christ is the ultimate answer for humans because he not only forgives our sins but also restores our primal human dignity. Having been declared worthy by God through Christ and having acquired a positive self-image, we are now free to pursue our grandest personal dreams and ambitions. As Schuller puts it: "The cross sanctifies the ego trip." The theology of self-esteem, then, is directly linked to the approach of possibility thinking, for the latter is a self-help method for achieving our personal goals.

## Appraisal

Robert Schuller is an American success story, a poor farm boy from Iowa who has erected one of the great ecclesiastical empires in America. Over the years he has received strong support not only from grateful members of his own congregation but also from the millions who have been inspired by his "Hour of Power" telecasts and his possibility thinking books and from the thousands of clergy and church lay leaders who have benefited from his principles of church growth. But if success has brought praise and imitation, it has also brought reproof from both ends of the religious spectrum in this country. Like Norman Vincent Peale during an earlier era, Schuller has been the target of a withering blast of criticism over the years. Whereas some have questioned the propriety of building the multi-million dollar Crystal Cathedral in an age of material want and others have wondered why he has not taken public stands on political and social issues, most of Schuller's critics, especially those from evangelical quarters, have assailed Schuller's basic message. Deeply sensitive to such attacks, Schuller has maintained, with justification, that his critics have often misunderstood or misrepresented his thought.

Although he stresses accomplishment and achievement, it would be unfair to insist, as some have, that Schuller encourages crass materialism. Essentially Schuller is arguing that true success is building self-esteem in oneself and others. A more fundamental question to pose is whether the stress on self-esteem is compatible with the Christian faith. Certainly, in emphasizing the importance of a strong self-concept, Schuller has helped to counter unhealthy theologies of self-negation that still persist in certain corners of religion, but perhaps he has encouraged persons to focus too intently on the self. Schuller's emphasis on the self seems to be in danger of fostering a form of Christian narcissism. Traditionally Christians have argued that the gospel frees persons from the ego trip, not for the ego trip.

Schuller's doctrine of sin has also come under attack. By defining sin as lack of self-esteem, he understands it to be a condition of human weakness rather than perverse strength. Hence, Schuller never tells people they are sinners or has them repeat a prayer of confession for sin, for such would have the result of further lowering a person's self-esteem. The therapeutic approach, he insists, will be that which is always positive and affirming. This of course raises a further question. Is the Christian faith to be reduced to psychological categories? Some would insist that whereas psychology can tell us a great deal about the human condition, it does not study humanity as it relates to God.

In most respects, Schuller broadly represents evangelical American Christianity. In fact, his own Reformed heritage has had a very strong influence on his personal doctrine and piety. Moreover, his Crystal Cathedral worship services feature broadly evangelical music and guests, and some of his sermons and books urge personal commitments to Christ as Lord and Savior. Schuller's evangelicalism, however, is mediated through the "New Thought" tradition of success and self-help. Schuller seems to be a transition figure in the history of American positive thinking—a bridge across which evangelicals seem to be traversing with greater and greater frequency. The religious motivation market has been taken over by the evangelicals in the latter half of the twentieth century. Oral Roberts*, Gloria Copeland, and Zig Ziglar typify this movement. So if Schuller represents a blend of the New Thought and evangelicals, he does not stand alone.

### Survey of Criticism

Robert Schuller is a flamboyant and controversial figure in American religion. It is not surprising, therefore, that a good deal has been written about him that is both popular and scholarly, descriptive and critical. It is telling that both *Newsweek* and *Time* have devoted several articles to various aspects of Schuller and his ministry since the early sixties. Many lengthy newspaper articles have also covered the Schuller phenomenon. Although no single bibliography has systematically gathered materials about Schuller, most of the important works have been cited in Dennis N. Voskuil, *Mountains Into Goldmines: Robert Schuller and the Gospel of Success.*

Two "insider" books have been written about Robert Schuller. Sheila Schuller Coleman, his oldest child, has put together *Robert Schuller, My Father and My Friend,* a short study that, though unanalytical, provides some interesting information about the Schuller family. A more extensive account of Schuller and his ministry was written by Michael and Donna Nason, friends and associates of Schuller's in the production of "Hour of Power." *Robert Schuller: The Inside Story* is not an official biography, but the Nason book is an affectionate and positive portrait. It does not deal extensively with Schuller's thought or with the cultural ramifications of his ministry.

Voskuil's *Mountains Into Goldmines* examines various aspects of Schuller's ministry and thought and offers a rather mild critique from a broadly Reformed perspective. Two of the finest analyses of Schuller are Lloyd Billingsley's "The Gospel According to Robert Schuller" and Kenneth Kantzer's "A Theologian Looks at Schuller." Martha Solomon's "Robert Schuller: The American Dream in a Crystal Cathedral" examines the rhetorical implications of Schuller's messages.

## Bibliography

### Books by Robert Schuller

1963   *God's Way to the Good Life.* Grand Rapids: Eerdmans.
1964   *Your Future is Your Friend.* Grand Rapids: Eerdmans.
1967   *Move Ahead with Possibility Thinking.* Old Tappan, N.J.: Spire Books.
1969   *Self-Love: The Dynamic Force of Success.* New York: Hawthorn.
1973   *The Greatest Possibility Thinker That Ever Lived.* Old Tappan, N.J.: Fleming H. Revell.
1974   *Your Church Has Real Possibilities.* Glendale, Calif.: Regal Books.
1977   *Peace of Mind Through Possibility Thinking.* Garden City, N.Y.: Doubleday.
1977   *Reach Out for New Life.* New York: Hawthorn.
1978   *Discover Your Possibilities!* Irvine, Calif.: Harvest House.
1978   *Turning Your Stress Into Strength.* New York: Fawcett Gold Medal.
1980   *The Peak to Peak Principle.* Garden City, N.Y.: Doubleday.
1980   *You Can Become the Person You Want to Be.* Old Tappan, N.J.: Spire Books.
1982   *Self-Esteem: The New Reformation.* Waco, Tex.: Word Books.
1983   *Tough-Minded Faith for Tender-Hearted People.* Nashville: Thomas Nelson.
1983   *Tough Times Never Last But Tough People Do.* Nashville: Thomas Nelson.
1985   *The Be Happy Attitudes.* Waco, Tex.: Word Books.
1985   *The Power of Being Debt Free.* With Paul D. Dunn. Nashville: Thomas Nelson.
1986   *Be Happy You are Loved.* Nashville: Thomas Nelson.
1987   *Your Church Has a Fantastic Future.* Ventura, Calif.: Regal Books.

### Selected Studies about Robert Schuller

Billingsley, Lloyd. "The Gospel According to Robert Schuller." *Eternity* 34 (March 1983): 22–27.
Coleman, Sheila Schuller. *Robert Schuller, My Father and My Friend.* Milwaukee: Ideals, 1980.
Kantzer, Kenneth S. "A Theologian Looks at Schuller." *Christianity Today* 28 (10 August 1984): 22–24.
Nason, Michael, and Donna Nason. *Robert Schuller: The Inside Story.* Waco, Tex.: Word Press, 1983.
Solomon, Martha. "Robert Schuller: The American Dream in a Crystal Cathedral." *Central States Speech Journal* 34 (Fall 1983): 172–86.
Stumbo, Bella. "Schuller: The Gospel of Success." *Los Angeles Times,* 29 May 1983, pp. 1, 3, 22–24.
Voskuil, Dennis N. *Mountains Into Goldmines: Robert Schuller and the Gospel of Success.* Grand Rapids: Eerdmans, 1983.
Yates, Ronald. "From Outdoor Theatre to Cathedral—A Religious Success Story." *Chicago Tribune Magazine* (27 July 1980): 10–11, 23–24, 26.

DENNIS N. VOSKUIL

# C. I. Scofield

During the last half of the nineteenth century, John Nelson Darby (1800–1882) and the Plymouth Brethren were to alter the landscape of American religious thought. Darby's consistent application of the hermeneutical principle of literal interpretation to all of Scripture—including prophetic texts, which resulted inevitably in a distinction between Israel and the church in God's program of salvation—and his refinement of the early church's belief in millennialism and the imminent return of Christ constitute key elements in the formulation of fundamentalism in America. These doctrines, coupled with a belief in the inerrancy of the Bible that emerged in large measure from Princeton Theological Seminary, were to provide the pillars on which the prophetic and Bible conferences of the last quarter of the nineteenth century and first quarter of the twentieth would rest. And it was this theological milieu that furnished the context for the life and work of C. I. Scofield, popularizer of the theological system that has come to be known as dispensationalism.

## Biography

When attempting to decipher Scofield's past, the researcher quickly encounters troublesome lacunae and contradictions in the meager historical records and source materials currently available. Scofield himself left no written record on his activities but did cooperate in the production of a small volume entitled *The Life Story of C. I. Scofield*, written by his friend and admirer Charles G. Trumbull. All other attempts at chronicling Scofield's life were written decades after his death. With these limitations in mind, the following sketch is set forth as constituting the main features of Scofield's life.

Cyrus Ingerson Scofield (1843–1921), youngest of seven children, was born into an Episcopalian family in Lenawee County, Michigan, on 19 August 1843. At some undetermined time, perhaps in the 1840s, young Scofield was transplanted to Wilson County, Tennessee, which was to serve as his home until his seventeenth year. When the Civil War broke out, Cyrus joined the Confederate Army and participated in a number of bloody battles. As an excellent horseman, he was often called on to perform the work of an orderly. Scofield was officially discharged from the Confederate Army in September 1862; official records are silent, but it appears that he either reenlisted or stayed on as a participant in guerrilla operations until the end of the war in 1865. For distinguished service, the young cavalryman was awarded the Confederate Cross of Honor.

At the conclusion of the war, twenty-two-year-old Scofield went to St. Louis to live with his eldest sister. On 21 September 1866, the year following his arrival in that city, Scofield married Leontine Cerre, youngest daughter of one of the oldest and most prominent French Roman Catholic families in St. Louis. Three children would be born to the Scofields: Abigail (1867–1958), Marie (1869–1958), and Guy (1872–74). Under his brother-in-law's influence, Scofield was apprenticed to a local law firm. Though he lacked formal education and his plans to enter the University of Virginia had been interrupted by the war, Scofield had been substantially self-educated through intensive reading in his youth in Tennessee. Before he could pass his bar exams in St. Louis, Scofield was sent to Kansas to defend Cerre family land-holding interests against a pending lawsuit involving "squatters." After settling with his family in Atchison, Kansas, in

1869 at the age of twenty-six, Scofield passed the appropriate exams and was admitted to the bar in that state. At the invitation of John J. Ingalls, whose legal services had been enlisted in the Cerre land-dispute case, Scofield joined the Ingalls law firm.

In the political arena, Scofield served in the Kansas state legislature from 1871 until 1873 when, at the request of then U.S. Senator Ingalls, he was appointed U.S. attorney for the District of Kansas by President Grant. Not yet thirty years of age in June 1873 when he took the oath of office, Scofield was at that time the youngest U.S. district attorney in the country. After only seven months, however, Scofield resigned his new appointment. He departed the post under conditions clouded by unsubstantiated charges that he had accepted bribes not to prosecute a pending case. Scofield never sought public office again.

At this point, the movements of the Scofield family are not clear, but it appears that there was a return to St. Louis, where Scofield resumed his law practice. At some time during 1879, the reason for which is obscure, Leontine and Cyrus separated. Mrs. Scofield took the children and returned to Atchison, Kansas. Following this event a troubled Scofield, who had turned to alcohol for escape, was led by friend and business acquaintance Thomas S. McPheeters to make a commitment to Jesus Christ in September 1879. Shortly after his conversion, Scofield came under the influence of James Hall Brookes, pastor of Compton Avenue Presbyterian Church in St. Louis. Brookes was one of the most influential Christian leaders of his day. He was a leading proponent of dispensational premillennialism and the architect and helmsman—until his death in 1897—of the Niagara Bible Conference, the prototype for all such conferences to follow.

Another great influence on Scofield's life and ministry was the renowned international evangelist D. L. Moody. It was during Moody's evangelistic efforts in St. Louis that Scofield put his newfound faith to work by enlisting as a volunteer. He would later invite Moody to preach in his church in Dallas and to hold special evangelistic meetings in that area. The association between Scofield and Moody was to continue until the latter's death in 1899, when Scofield himself would officiate at the evangelist's funeral in Northfield, Massachusetts. In addition to his volunteer work with Moody, Scofield also became acting secretary of the St. Louis branch of the YMCA and organized and pastored the Hyde Park Congregational Church of North St. Louis.

In the spring of 1882, Scofield was asked by the superintendent of the Congregational Home Missions to assume the pastorate of the small and failing First Congregational Church of Dallas. It was not until some months later in 1883, after more than a year and a half of intensive personal theological study, that Scofield was ordained as a minister in the Congregational Church. Also in 1883, Leontine Scofield was granted a divorce from Cyrus. The year following the divorce, Scofield married Hettie Van Wark, a member of the Dallas church. They were to have only one child, Noel Paul (1888–1962). Scofield's tenure as pastor of the Dallas church would extend from 1882 to 1895 and witness a growth from 14 members to an aggregate for the thirteen years of over 800 members enrolled.

During the course of his local pastoral work, Scofield always maintained an interest in the broader evangelistic and missionary enterprises of the church. This was due in large measure no doubt to his association first with Moody and later with Hudson Taylor, founder of the China Inland Mission. Thus while serving in the Dallas pastorate, Scofield accepted the position of superintendent for the states of Louisiana and Texas when it was offered by the American Home Missionary Society in 1887. In 1893, he accepted the superintendence of the AHMS work in Colorado and surrounding areas. Scofield's missionary endeavors would peak in November 1890 with his founding of the Central American Mission.

In addition to his interest in missions, Scofield also became active in the Bible conference movement. He first began attending the Niagara Bible Conferences in 1887. Here Scofield would be influenced by the leading contemporary champions of the doctrines of the verbal inspiration of Scripture, the premillennial return of Christ to rapture the church, and dispensational theology generally. This influence is much in evidence in one of Scofield's best known and most influential works. During his summer vacation of 1888, as a result of what he perceived to be a real need in Bible classes that he had begun, Scofield assembled "the beginning truths" of Bible study. These were eventually published in booklet form as *Rightly Dividing the Word of Truth*. Next to the *Scofield Reference Bible,* this work has done as much as any other to propagate the dispensational approach to biblical interpretation. During this time also, Scofield started a monthly publication called the *Believer,* headed the Southwestern School of the Bible, and designed and taught a Bible correspondence course which would be taken over by Moody Bible Institute in 1914.

In 1895, Scofield was invited by D. L. Moody to pastor his home church, the Trinitarian Congregational Church in East Northfield, Massachusetts. For seven years he served this church before returning to the First Congregational Church of Dallas, where he remained until 1907. While at Northfield, Scofield served on the faculty of the Northfield Bible Training School founded by Moody and is identified by that institution's letterhead as the school's president in 1900 and 1902. Whether Scofield also headed the two preparatory schools started by Moody at Northfield, one for girls (Northfield Seminary) and one for boys (Mt. Hermon School) grades nine through twelve, is not certain. What is certain, however, is that Scofield began to take up Bible conference work in earnest during the Northfield years.

The idea for what is undeniably Scofield's most enduring and influential work, the *Scofield Reference Bible (SRB)*, came during his early days of ministry at the church in Dallas. Scofield first shared his plan and outlined the method he intended to follow with his friend and editor of *Our Hope* magazine Arno C. Gaebelein at the Seacliff (Long Island) Bible Conference in the middle of 1901. With Gaebelein's encouragement, financial support was enlisted and the project launched in 1902. After several years of labor which included consultations with Bible scholars at home and abroad, what Scofield believed would be his greatest contribution to the cause of Christ was published in 1909 by Oxford University Press.

In 1910 Scofield broke with the Congregational Church over its increasingly liberal tendencies and became a member of the U.S. Presbyterian Church (South). As a result of what was to become known as the fundamentalist-modernist controversy, the First Congregational Church of Dallas had already withdrawn from the denomination two years earlier during Scofield's absence, but with his written approval. Scofield was to remain pastor emeritus of the Dallas church until his death in 1921. Though Scofield did indeed have a role in the fundamentalist movement as a whole, and even though he contributed an essay on "The Grace of God" to the *Fundamentals,* his part in the controversy itself seems to have been minimal. In the same year that he changed denominational affiliation, Scofield accepted the chairmanship of the committee for the revision of the *King James Version (KJV)* of the Bible sponsored by the Oxford University Press. The revision was scheduled for publication in 1911 to commemorate the 300th anniversary of the 1611 *KJV.*

The year 1914 was to find Scofield and others, especially William L. Pettingill, engaged in the task of founding Philadelphia Bible Institute (PBI), now Philadelphia College of the Bible. While Scofield served as president of PBI from its inception until 1918, Pettingill managed the day-to-day operation of the school. One of Scofield's disciples since the Northfield days, Lewis Sperry Chafer, was lecturer in Bible at PBI. He held that position from 1914 until 1923, when he succeeded Scofield as pastor of the First Congregational Church in Dallas, then renamed the Scofield Memorial Church. From 1924 until his death in 1952, Chafer served as president and professor of systematic theology at what was first called the Evangelical Theological College in Dallas but later became known as Dallas Theological Seminary. Some sources trace the seminary's roots back to educational work begun in Dallas by Scofield.

Scofield's time after the publication of the *SRB* was devoted primarily to writing and public teaching. After the *SRB* made its debut in 1909, a work for which Scofield would be elected to membership in the Société Academique d'Histoire Internationale in France, no fewer than fourteen other works appeared with Scofield's name affixed either as author or as originator of materials compiled by another. Scofield continued in Bible conference work until, at the New York Prophetic Conference of 1918, the last he would attend, he was physically unable to participate. In a progressive state of poor health, C. I. Scofield, whose life had been plagued by periods of illness of an undisclosed nature, finally died on 24 July 1921 of cardiovascular renal disease, less than a month shy of his seventy-eighth birthday.

### Appraisal

In a very real sense, C. I. Scofield was a product of the Bible conference movement of the last quarter of the nineteenth century and of the forces that gave it rise. His conversion in 1879 occurred in the midst of the founding stage of the Niagara Bible Conference, the parent of all future conferences. One of the founders and the guiding force of that conference, James H. Brookes, was to become Scofield's earliest and most important Bible teacher. Through Brookes and other leaders at the Bible conferences, who themselves had profited in varying degrees from the teachings of J. N. Darby and the Plymouth Brethren, Scofield early developed a dispensational and premillennial theology.

Central to Scofield's theology is the belief that there is a system of seven "ages," or "dispensations," discernible in the gradual unfolding of the divine program for human redemption. He defines a dispensation as "a period of time during which man is tested in respect of obedience to some *specific* revelation of the will of God" (*SRB*, 5). It is Scofield's contention that ignorance of this "doctrine of ages and dispensations" results in a profitless and confused understanding of the sacred text. Scofield's approach to biblical interpretation came to be characterized by II Timothy 2:15, "Study to shew thyself approved unto God, a workman that needeth not to be ashamed, rightly dividing the word of truth" (*KJV*). The concluding phrase of this verse suggested the title for Scofield's first published work, *Rightly Dividing the Word of Truth*. Almost a century after it first appeared in print, the little booklet is still available through the Scripture Truth Book Company in Fincastle, Virginia.

Scofield was by no means the first to set forth a doctrine of ages and dispensations. Some of the earliest church fathers, like the apologist Justin Martyr (A.D. 100–165) and the polemicist Irenaeus (A.D. 120–202), were staunch premillennialists who also set forth rudimentary dispensational systems. Certainly men like Darby in his *Collected Works* (1800s), Brookes in *Maranatha* (1870), William E. Blackstone in *Jesus Is Coming* (1878), and others propounded similar teachings years before Scofield. Yet whereas the works of these men gather dust on the library shelves of the few, Scofield's work—primarily the *Scofield Reference Bible (SRB)*—has found its way into the hands and homes of the many. Why?

The work that Scofield himself believed would be his life's greatest and most lasting achievement, the *SRB*, has indeed had an impact on the American religious community surpassed by few, if any, other works in the twentieth century. Literally hundreds of thousands of people have owned and used the *SRB*, many without a knowledge of the theological system that it promotes. Ernest R. Sandeen is undoubtedly correct in saying that this study Bible "is perhaps the most influential single publication in millenarian and Fundamentalist historiography" (*The Roots of Fundamentalism*, 222). In a recent letter to this writer, the Bible editor of the Oxford University Press (New York branch) maintains that "it would be fair to say that aggregate sales of all Scofield Bibles, in all bindings and versions, have easily exceeded ten million copies since 1917." To this number would have to be added all those bindings sold between 1909 and 1917. The *SRB* has been translated into French, German, Spanish, and Portuguese, with current interest also in a Korean version.

The success of the *SRB* is no great mystery. It can be attributed, we believe, to a very simple formula, or combination of appealing ingredients, that, in retrospect, augured well for success. Scofield produced a study Bible that was attractive in appearance, readable in style, and systematic and authoritative in presentation. In large measure the genius of the *SRB*'s success was the attractiveness of its format and content. The brief introductory materials and chapter introductions, coupled with the cross-references and exercise of restraint in the appended annotations, gave the appearance of a study resource that was not formidable to use. Furthermore, owing perhaps to his legal training, Scofield had a knack for simplicity, clarity, and compactness of expression. Charles G. Trumbull quotes James M. Gray, a former president of Moody Bible Institute, as saying: "This is Dr. Scofield's richest gift. He knows how to read the Word of God, and give the sense, and cause the people to understand the reading" (*The Life Story of C. I. Scofield,* 85).

But more than any other ingredient in the *SRB*'s recipe of success, the dispensational system itself—and the authority with which Scofield presents it—has been repeatedly cited as the root cause of the drawing of the masses to this study Bible and consequently to Bible study. Whether one agrees with the dispensational system of interpretation or not, for the ordinary layman it seems to have been viewed as a key by which the mysteries of Scripture could be unlocked, a scaffolding from which an understanding of divine revelation could be constructed. Whereas Darby's wearisome repetition, carelessness in literary style, and disdain for systematic presentation have caused only the more intrepid among Bible students to wade into his works, Scofield's orderly and emanently readable presentation of dispensational theology has encouraged even the most timid of Bible students to dive into the *SRB*. Thus it is not surprising to find that for thousands, the *SRB* has become the classic expression of "orthodox" theology. Understandably, it has also become the focus of attack for all those who are opposed to the dispensationalist interpretation of the Bible.

Some critics of the *SRB* have pointed out the dearth of notes and the uneven distribution of those appended. Most modern study Bibles have annotations and explanatory notes on almost every page, whereas Scofield often leaps over scores of pages with little or no comment. But the chief concern of others is that for perhaps all too many readers, the notes in the *SRB* have become virtually synonymous with the biblical text itself. The great fear is that the user of Scofield's reference work may think he is saying, "Thus saith the Lord," when in fact he is citing a footnote and in reality saying, "Thus saith C. I. Scofield." The nondispensationalist naturally resents the very concept of fusing one theological system of interpretation with the biblical narrative to the exclusion of all others. The purist, on the other hand, rejects the whole concept of the reference Bible in principle as a perversion of the sacred text.

The *SRB* is without doubt the single most noteworthy achievement of Scofield's life, but no assessment of his influence and work would be complete without reference to his role as educator. In 1890, in response to the need for the instruction of laymen in the Bible, Scofield began work on what was to become the Scofield Correspondence Course. From 1890 to 1914, Scofield personally conducted these Bible classes. In 1914, the program was turned over to Moody Bible Institute (MBI). To date, according to MBI, there has been a total enrollment of 106,419 in the combined New Testament, Old Testament, and doctrine segments of the course. When this number is added to the total enrollments of Philadelphia College of the Bible and Dallas Theological Seminary, the former founded through Scofield's direct efforts and the latter most likely through his preliminary groundwork and influence on Chafer, the results are indeed noteworthy. As three of the leading dispensational institutions in the country, every year MBI, PCB, and Dallas Seminary train hundreds of students in the Scofield tradition. Most of the graduates of these schools go on into full-time Christian professions and in turn instruct many others in the dispensational interpretation of Scripture. The literary and academic apparatus for biblical instruction set in motion by Scofield during his lifetime shows no signs of fatigue since his death.

### Survey of Criticism

Remarkably, for a man who by all accounts has had such a tremendous impact on American religious life, there is relatively little literature about C. I. Scofield. At the time of this writing, there has been no legitimate biography of his life attempted. The reason for the literary shortfall on the life and work of Scofield is not readily apparent. But if primary works about Scofield and his legacy are scarce, secondary references are too numerous to count. The latter occur regularly both in attacks against and defenses of dispensational theology or with reference to the rise of fundamentalism, as in Ernest R. Sandeen's, *The Roots of Fundamentalism*.

Of the five primary studies on Scofield's life and work, three deal generally with the whole scope of his background and contribution to American religious life, whereas two focus specifically on the *Scofield Reference Bible*. In the first category is Charles Gallaudet Trumbull's *Life Story of C. I. Scofield*. The main strength of this biography—*tribute* or *eulogy* is perhaps a better description—is that it was written while Scofield was still living and benefited from his direct involvement. A major weakness is quickly detected, however, in that this is an uncritical account of the subject's life by an adoring disciple. A more objective interviewer could have perhaps obtained the answers to troublesome questions that have bothered the modern researcher. Joseph M. Canfield, *The Incredible Scofield and His Book,* is a masterpiece of vituperative writing. It is no more objective than Trumbull's work but for just the opposite reason. Even the most innocuous of events in the lives of Scofield and his compatriots are interpreted with a transparent presumption of perfidy. In several respects the study shows evidence of extensive research, but the many instances in which the author relies on "folk-knowledge" (64), "rumors" (66), "speculation" (109), "underlying hints" (162), and "suspicion" (169, 189) severely diminish the overall credibility of the study. Much more objective than either of the foregoing is William

A. Be Vier's M.A. thesis, "A Biographical Sketch of C. I. Scofield." The study is carefully researched, and critical questions concerning its subject are met head on. Be Vier engages neither in superfluous praise of Scofield nor in gratuitous criticism.

The two most important studies on the *Scofield Reference Bible* also represent opposite extremes. Arno C. Gaebelein, who was for many years Scofield's close friend and associate, served as a consulting editor of the *SRB*. His work, *The History of the Scofield Reference Bible,* produced in a variety of formats by different publishing agencies, furnishes an insider's account of the inception of the project and the unfolding process toward its publication. Albertus Pieters' study, *A Candid Examination of the Scofield Bible,* focuses not on the history of the *SRB* but on its theological content and interpretive approach to the Bible. As one planted firmly in the Reformed tradition, Pieters not surprisingly is highly critical of Scofield's dispensational theology. But unlike Canfield, who is critical of Scofield and his work from start to finish, Pieters uses a procedure, which has since been used by several of his Reformed colleagues, of praise followed by acrimony. Initially, Pieters affirms Scofield's personal piety and commitment to the cause of Christ and elevates the *SRB* to a place of singular significance in twentieth-century American religion. But he then goes on to accuse Scofield of intellectual inferiority and of proposing answers to questions that are unanswerable. A crucial point for Pieters is what he perceives to be the lack of Scriptural support for the basic tenets of dispensationalism.

An approach similar to that found in Pieters' work is taken by William E. Cox, another Reformed theologian. In *Why I Left Scofieldism*, Cox first acknowledges indebtedness to the *SRB* for his early Christian training, before he finally labels "Scofieldism" as "heresy." Prominent also in Cox's study is the off-treated theme that Scofield borrowed his theology wholesale from John Nelson Darby and the Plymouth Brethren. For a substantial rebuttal of this charge, see Larry V. Crutchfield's Ph.D. dissertation, "The Doctrine of Ages and Dispensations as Found in the Published Works of John Nelson Darby (1800–1882)." In this study, the areas of agreement as well as the areas of significant disagreement between the two men's dispensational systems are discussed and documented.

### Bibliography

*Books by C. I. Scofield*

1888 *Rightly Dividing the Word of Truth*. Rev. ed. Fincastle, Va.: Scripture Truth Book Co., n.d. (first published in 1888).
1890 *Scofield Bible Correspondence Course*. Rev. ed. Chicago: Moody Bible Institute, 1934 (several editions, first published in 1890).
1899 *Plain Papers on the Holy Spirit*. New York: Fleming H. Revell Co.
1903 *The Epistle to the Galatians*. New York: Publication Office of *Our Hope*.
1909 *The Scofield Reference Bible*. New York: Oxford University Press. Revised, 1917. *The New Scofield Reference Bible,* edited by E. Schuyler English, et al., 1967.

1912   *The Jewish Question*. With Arno C. Gaebelein. New York: Publication Office of *Our Hope*.
1913   *No Room In the Inn and Other Interpretations*. New York: Oxford University Press.
1913   *The World's Approaching Crisis*. Philadelphia: Philadelphia School of the Bible.
1914   *Addresses on Prophecy*. New York: Charles C. Cook. (Published in Scotland and England as *Prophecy Made Plain*. Glasgow: Pickering and Inglis; London: Alfred Holness, n.d.)
1915   *New Life in Jesus Christ*. Chicago: Bible Institute Colportage Association.
1916   *The Truth About Heaven*. Philadelphia: Philadelphia School of the Bible.
1916   *Where Faith Sees Christ*. New York: Publication Office of *Our Hope*.
1917   *Dr. C. I. Scofield's Question Box*. Compiled by Ella E. Pohle. Chicago: Bible Institute Colportage Association.
1917   *Scofield Bible Study Leaflets*. Philadelphia: Philadelphia School of the Bible.
1917   *Will the Church Pass Through the Great Tribulation?* Philadelphia: Philadelphia School of the Bible.
1918   *What Do the Prophets Say?* Philadelphia: Philadelphia School of the Bible.
1920   *Things New and Old*. Compiled and edited by Arno C. Gaebelein. New York: Publication Office of *Our Hope*.
1922   *In Many Pulpits with Dr. C. I. Scofield*. New York: Oxford University Press.
n.d.   *The Truth About Hell*. Philadelphia: Philadelphia School of the Bible.

### Selected Studies about C. I. Scofield

Albright, Raymond W. "Scofield, Cyrus Ingerson." *Twentieth Century Encyclopedia of Religious Knowledge*. 2 vols. Grand Rapids: Baker Book House, 1955.
Be Vier, William A. "A Biographical Sketch of C. I. Scofield." Master's thesis, Southern Methodist University, 1960.
————. "C. I. Scofield." *Fundamentalist Journal* 2 (October 1983): 37–39, 56. (Page 56 of this article is missing and according to the publisher is no longer available.)
Canfield, Joseph M. *The Incredible Scofield and His Book*. Asheville, N.C.: By the Author, 1984.
Chafer, Lewis Sperry. "Dr. C. I. Scofield." *Bibliotheca Sacra* 100 (January 1943): 4–6.
————. "The Scofield Bible." *Bibliotheca Sacra* 109 (April 1952): 97–99.
Cox, Willam E. *An Examination of Dispensationalism*. Phillipsburg, N.J.: Presbyterian and Reformed Publishing Co., 1963.
————. *Why I Left Scofieldism*. Phillipsburg, N.J.: Presbyterian and Reformed Publishing Co., 1978.
Crutchfield, Larry V. "The Doctrine of Ages and Dispensations as Found in the Published Works of John Nelson Darby (1800–1882)." Ph.D. diss., Drew University, 1985.
Gaebelein, Arno C. *The History of the Scofield Reference Bible*. New York: Publication Office of *Our Hope*, 1943.
————. "The Story of the *Scofield Reference Bible*." *Moody Monthly* 43 (October 1942): 65–66, 97, (November 1942): 128–29, 135, (December 1942): 202–3, 233, (January 1943): 277–79, (February 1943): 343–45, (March 1943): 400–401, 419.
Gaebelein, Frank E. *The Story of the Scofield Reference Bible*. New York: Oxford University Press, 1959.
Haldeman, I. M. *The Kingdom of God, A Review of Mr. Philip Mauro's Book "The Gospel of the Kingdom."* New York: Francis Emory Fitch, 1931.

Mauro, Philip. *The Gospel of the Kingdom*. Boston: Hamilton Brothers, 1920.

Pieters, Albertus. *A Candid Examination of the Scofield Bible*. Swengel, Pa.: Bible Truth Depot, 1938.

Sandeen, Ernest R. *The Roots of Fundamentalism*. Grand Rapids: Baker Book House, 1970.

Trumbull, Charles Gallaudet. *The Life Story of C. I. Scofield*. New York: Oxford University Press, 1920.

LARRY V. CRUTCHFIELD

# William J. Seymour

Pentecostalism, often called a third force in Christianity after Catholicism and Protestantism, may well be America's most significant religious export in the twentieth century. Doctrinally, it can be traced back to the Methodist Church, the nineteenth-century holiness movement, and the Kansas evangelist Charles Parham. But Pentecostal Christianity first attracted worldwide attention because of a 1906 revival in Los Angeles. The leader of that revival was William J. Seymour.

### Biography

Born on 2 May 1870 on the Bayou Teche in Centerville, Louisiana, William Joseph Seymour was the son of recently emancipated slaves. He grew to manhood in Centerville where, apparently, he had little schooling. He is reputed to have taught himself to read. In 1895, Seymour left the bayou country of Louisiana and moved north to Indianapolis.

A young, single black man, newly arrived from the South and unaccustomed to large cities, Seymour lived in black neighborhoods and joined Simpson Chapel, an all-black congregation of the Methodist Episcopal Church (North). He supported himself by waiting tables in a restaurant in one of the downtown hotels and was a member of a black labor union, the Association of Head and Side Waiters.

In 1899 or 1900, Seymour moved to Cincinnati where he came into contact with the Methodist evangelist Martin Wells Knapp, who preached the "apocalyptic return" of Jesus, healing by prayer, and the laying on of hands. Although a white man, Knapp included blacks in his meetings and classes and may have provided Seymour with his first exposure to a racially mixed congregation. Seymour joined the Evening Light Saints, a group affiliated with the Church of God Reformation Movement led by Daniel S. Warner, the founder of the Church of God (Anderson, Indiana). The Saints were part of the holiness movement and preached sanctification as an experience for the believer subsequent to conversion. Although he felt called to the ministry, Seymour rejected such a step. When he was stricken with smallpox and then recovered, he interpreted this as God's chastisement and accepted ordination by the Evening Light Saints.

Seymour moved to Houston in 1902 or 1903 when he was in his early thirties. He lived with relatives and carried on his ministry. In the winter of 1904–5, he visited Jackson, Mississippi, where he took counsel with Charles Price Jones, the leader of the Church of Christ (Holiness), U.S.A. In July and August 1905, Charles F. Parham, a white holiness evangelist from Topeka, Kansas, conducted a preaching campaign in Houston. When the pastor of a black holiness church went back to Kansas with Parham, she invited Seymour to take over the congregation until her return. While Seymour was serving as pastor, a visitor from Los Angeles, Mrs. Neely Terry, heard Seymour preach and was so impressed that when she returned to California she persuaded her holiness congregation to call him as pastor.

Meanwhile, in December 1905, Parham returned to Houston to conduct a short-term Bible study on speaking in tongues as a gift of God meant for all believers. The prevailing racial attitudes in Houston prevented Seymour from joining the study, but Parham left the classroom door ajar so that the black preacher might sit outside and listen. However, Parham separated the races at his meetings and would not pray with Seymour for the gift of tongues. As a seeker of tongues, Seymour had moved beyond the doctrine of the Evening Light Saints as well as of other holiness groups.

After a few weeks at most or, possibly, only a few days of listening to the teaching of Parham, Seymour accepted the call to Los Angeles and left Houston. The congregation of eight black families that he came to California to pastor had been expelled from a Baptist church the previous year for espousing holiness teachings. Although he had yet to speak in tongues, Seymour began at once to preach that it should be part of every believer's experience. After listening to Seymour preach for only four nights, the leader of the congregation locked him and those who agreed with him about speaking in tongues out of the meeting hall. Seymour and his followers moved their nightly services to a private home.

The meetings continued over the next two months with a small number of black washwomen, cooks, laborers, janitors, and railroad porters in attendance. On Monday, 9 April 1906, one of the men spoke in tongues when Seymour prayed with him. By the end of the evening, many if not all in the group were speaking in tongues. As word spread of what was happening, crowds of black and white people gathered in and around the house for the meetings. On 12 April, the first white man spoke in tongues. The growing number of visitors necessitated a larger meeting place and on 14 April, the eve of Easter, the meetings were moved to an abandoned tenement and stable at 312 Azusa Street. The building became known as the Azusa Mission, and the Azusa Street Revival was under way.

On 17 April, with a reporter for the *Los Angeles Times* present, a man prophesied "awful destruction" for the city unless it turned to God. The following day, an earthquake virtually destroyed the city of San Francisco, and the tremors were felt in Los Angeles. By the end of May, nightly throngs of a thousand and more were crowding into and around the building on Azusa Street. Missionaries began to leave for other parts of the country as well as for Europe to tell of the revival that was taking place in Los Angeles. Many others, black and white, were coming to visit the Azusa Mission, to sit under Seymour's preaching, and to receive the gift of tongues.

In August 1906, Seymour formed a board of twelve to supervise the mission, ordain candidates for the ministry, commission missionaries, and issue credentials. In September, he began publishing the *Apostolic Faith* newspaper, whose circulation jumped from 5,000 for the first issue to 40,000 by April 1907, with copies circulating all over the world.

Charles Parham arrived in Los Angeles in October 1906 and preached at the Azusa Mission at Seymour's invitation. The interracial fellowship was not to his liking, however, and he started a rival mission nearby. Other white holiness preachers, for example G. B. Cashwell, overcame their racial prejudice, were prayed with by Seymour, and returned home to promulgate speaking in tongues. Black holiness leaders, like C. H. Mason of Memphis, also came to Azusa Street to receive Seymour's ministry. The aura of growth and excitement around the Azusa Mission continued into 1907. A camp meeting in June of that year on the outskirts of Los Angeles accommodated a thousand participants.

Seymour's marriage to a coworker, Jennie Evans Moore, in May 1908 provoked the first serious setback for the revival he was leading. Clara Lum, the mission secretary, disapproved of the marriage, quit her post, and moved to Portland, Oregon, taking with her all the newspaper mailing lists except those for the Los Angeles area. She began issuing the *Apostolic Faith* from Portland, where she was associated with Florence Crawford, an Asuza disciple. Seymour refused to go to court to recover the mailing lists and thus lost control of the newspaper. Without the newspaper, the influence of Seymour and of the Azusa Mission began to decline.

A second setback occurred in 1911 when William H. Durham, a Chicago evangelist, preached at Azusa Mission in Seymour's absence and undercut the Pentecostal doctrine of three separate experiences of conversion, sanctification, and filling with the Holy Spirit by insisting that there was only one work of grace in the life of a believer. Durham's doctrine and personality split the Asuza Mission along doctrinal and racial lines and Durham opened a rival center in Los Angeles.

Although Seymour traveled widely across the country on preaching tours, the Azusa Mission declined in numbers. However, it did remain interracial. In 1915, Seymour wrote *Doctrines and Disciplines* and gave the mission a constitution providing that the leader should be a bishop and "a man of color." When he died from a heart attack on 28 September 1922, Seymour's congregation at the Azusa Mission consisted of about twenty people, largely his original prayer group and a few whites. His wife, known to their followers as Mother Seymour, continued to lead the mission until 1931 when financial difficulties and the condemnation of the building as a fire hazard by the city of Los Angeles brought about its closing and demolition. Mrs. Seymour died on 2 July 1936.

## Appraisal

Whereas Charles F. Parham is generally credited with being the first to propound the doctrinal position that gave rise to the Pentecostal movement in the twentieth century, Seymour's Azusa Street Revival was the event that brought Pentecostalism to the attention of America and the world. In spite of his central position in this revival, Seymour has remained largely unknown. Although he traveled widely in the United States on preaching tours after 1906, no sermons or sermon notes remain which might offer an insight into Seymour's message and his pulpit skills. The only writings of Seymour's that have survived are his articles in the *Apostolic Faith* (1906–8), his *Doctrines and Disciplines* (1915), and the constitution that he wrote for the Azusa Mission (1915).

Several descriptions of Seymour plus his refusal to sue for the return of his newspaper mailing lists suggest a man who may have been too self-effacing to have long continued as the leader of a movement as contentious and expansive as Pentecostalism would prove to be. In addition, neither American society nor the white leaders of the emerging Pentecostal movement in the years 1906–20 were ready to accept the leadership of a black preacher, however much they may have recognized his ministry to them personally. At the time of his death in 1922, Seymour's influence and following in the Pentecostal churches were small, even in the Los Angeles area.

## Survey of Criticism

Seymour has suffered from caricatures of himself and his work. Alma White, a holiness preacher whom he visited in Denver in January 1906 en route to Los Angeles, later described him in *Demons and Tongues* as dirty and unkempt, a description that photos do not bear out. White was hostile to Pentecostalism and a supporter of the Ku Klux Klan. Frank Bartleman, who vied with Seymour for leadership of the revival and who was so antagonistic to any form of church organization that he split with the Azusa Mission in 1906 because it chose a name, belittled Seymour's leadership of the Azusa Street Revival in *How Pentecost Came to Los Angeles,* describing it as eccentric and ineffective.

The *Los Angeles Times* reporter who wrote about the revival in April 1906 described Seymour as an old man (he was thirty-six) with a glass eye, whose preaching was emotional and who stressed speaking in tongues. Two unpublished dissertations by Charles Shumway offered a more flattering picture of Seymour and inquired into the practice of glossolalia by interviewing many of the participants in the Azusa Street Revival.

The early historians of Pentecostalism were not generous to Seymour in their appraisal of his work. Although it contains a wealth of information based on the recollections of Azusa participants, the first written history of the Pentecostal movement—by B. F. Lawrence, *The Apostolic Faith Restored*—was done by a white man who mostly interviewed other white people. Seymour is described as the catalyst in the movement, a disciple of Parham's who carried his master's teaching from Houston to Los Angeles. In her biography of her husband, *The Life of Charles F. Parham*, Parham's wife wrote of Seymour that he was a disciple who strayed, a man possessed by a spirit of leadership.

More recent historians of Pentecostalism have ascribed to Seymour a more important role in the origin of the movement. The second general history of the Pentecostal movement, Stanley Frodsham's *With Signs Following*, described Seymour as the prayerful leader of the Azusa Street Revival. Although he mentioned the racial equality at Azusa, Frodsham pointed to speaking in tongues as the central element in Seymour's preaching. Whereas Thomas R. Nickel's fiftieth anniversary volume on the Azusa revival, *Azusa Street Outpouring*, concentrated on the events surrounding Seymour, Klaude Kendrick's general history of Pentecostalism, *The Promise Fulfilled*, recognized the black preacher as the leader in the early months of the Azusa revival but described him as the disciple of Parham. Kendrick noted that the separation of the races at Azusa followed the loss of leadership by Seymour. Nils Bloch-Hoell's general history of Pentecostalism, *The Pentecostal Movement*, repeated most of the caricatures of Seymour and added that he was a primitive and powerful medium who exerted great influence on women. Although he acknowledged that Seymour was the catalyst for the Pentecostal movement, Bloch-Hoell put him down as a poor leader.

Several histories of Pentecostalism written in the 1970s repeated most of the previous assessments of Seymour without evidence of any new research. William Menzies' story of the Assemblies of God, *Anointed To Serve*, described Azusa as significant for "transforming the embryo Pentecostal outpouring into a worldwide movement." Though he noted the racial equality at Azusa, Menzies said little about the racial segregation that characterized the later development of the Pentecostal denominations in the United States. John T. Nichol's *The Pentecostals* described Seymour as the key figure in the Los Angeles revival, noted the racial unity among the early Pentecostals, and singled out the promulgation of glossolalia as central to Seymour's ministry. Vinson Synan, in *The Holiness-Pentecostal Movement in the United States*, called Seymour the "Apostle of Pentecost" and attributed the beginning of the Azusa Street Revival to his preaching.

Walter J. Hollenweger's comprehensive study of worldwide Pentecostalism, *The Pentecostals*, emphasized the black origins of the movement and saw Seymour's ministry as representing the restoration of human equality in the Body of Christ. A Ph.D. dissertation by Leonard Lovett, "Black Holiness-Pentecostalism," offered a more nuanced account of the earlier histories that saw Parham as laying the doctrinal foundations of Pentecostalism and Seymour as the catalyst who, in spite of the racism of his time, extended the Pentecostal revival to the world. Lovett regarded speaking in tongues as central to the Pentecostal movement and gave considerable attention to its black and African origins. Although Robert Mapes Anderson's *Vision of the Disinherited* described Seymour as the disciple of Parham, he acknowledged that the Azusa Mission was the center from which the Pentecostal movement spread around the world and that Seymour's newspaper, the *Apostolic Faith,* was the most influential of the many that were started in the years 1906–10. Anderson remarked on the interracial aspect of Azusa but did not regard equality in Christ as central to Seymour's message.

Douglas J. Nelson's Ph.D. dissertation, "For Such A Time As This," the most carefully researched study of Seymour to date, argued that racial unity, not speaking in tongues, was the most significant feature of Seymour's work as well as of his teaching. Since we lack a representative sample of Seymour's preaching over the years, that conclusion must remain in doubt. Clearly though, the tendency of recent scholarship has been to recognize Seymour's contribution to the Pentecostal movement and to see him as a pioneer in the struggle for racial equality.

## Bibliography

### Works by William J. Seymour

1906–8  Articles in the *Apostolic Faith,* Los Angeles, fourteen issues.

1915  *Constitution* (for the Azusa Mission).

1915  *The Doctrines and Disciplines of the Azusa Street Apostolic Faith Mission of Los Angeles, Cal., with Scripture Readings by W. J. Seymour, Its Founder and General Overseer.*

### Selected Studies about William J. Seymour

Anderson, Robert Mapes. *Vision of the Disinherited: The Making of American Pentecostalism.* New York: Oxford University Press, 1979.

Bartleman, Frank. *How Pentecost Came to Los Angeles: As It Was In The Beginning—From My Diary.* 3rd ed. Los Angeles: Privately printed, 1925.

Bloch-Hoell, Nils. *The Pentecostal Movement: Its Origin, Development and Distinctive Character.* Oslo: Universitets-forlaget, 1964.

Frodsham, Stanley. *With Signs Following: The Story of the Pentecostal Revival in the Twentieth Century.* Rev. ed. Springfield, Mo.: Gospel Publishing House, 1946.

Hollenweger, Walter J. *The Pentecostals: The Charismatic Movement in the Churches.* Minneapolis: Augsburg Publishing House, 1972.

Kendrick, Klaude. *The Promise Fulfilled: A History of the Modern Pentecostal Movement.* Springfield, Mo.: Gospel Publishing House, 1961.

Lawrence, B. F. *The Apostolic Faith Restored.* St. Louis: Gospel Publishing House, 1916.

Lovett, Leonard. "Black Holiness-Pentecostalism: Implications for Ethics and Social Transformation." Ph.D. diss., Emory University, 1978.

Menzies, William W. *Anointed To Serve: The Story of the Assemblies of God.* Springfield, Mo.: Gospel Publishing House, 1971.

Nelson, Douglas J. "For Such A Time As This: The Story of Bishop William J. Seymour and the Azusa Street Revival." Ph.D. diss., University of Birmingham, England, 1981.

Nichol, John T. *The Pentecostals.* Plainfield, N.J.: Logos International, 1971.

Nickel, Thomas R. *Azusa Street Outpouring: As Told To Me By Those Who Were There.* Hanford, Calif.: Great Commission International, 1956.

Parham, Mrs. Charles F. *The Life of Charles F. Parham, Founder of the Apostolic Faith Movement.* Baxter Springs, Kans.: Commercial Printing Company, 1930.

Shumway, Charles William. "A Critical History of Glossolalia." Ph.D. diss., Boston University, 1919.

————. "A Study of 'The Gift of Tongues.' " A.B. thesis, University of Southern California, 1914.

Synan, Vinson. *The Holiness-Pentecostal Movement in the United States.* Grand Rapids: Eerdmans, 1971.

White, Alma. *Demons and Tongues.* Zarepath, N.J.: Pillar of Fire, fourth printing, 1949 [1910].

JAMES T. CONNELLY

# Fulton J. Sheen

Archbishop Fulton J. Sheen paralleled Father Charles Coughlin as a Catholic cleric who was a master of the use of the media and in the long run was much more successful than Coughlin in making an impact on the American scene. Sheen was one of the most articulate spokesmen for Roman Catholicism in America from the 1920s through the 1960s and gave that church an unprecedented visibility and credibility through his creation of an image as apologist, prophet, scholar, and folksy conversationalist. His later career as bishop of Rochester, New York, was something of an anticlimax for a man accustomed to the national spotlight.

## Biography

Peter Fulton Sheen was born on 8 May 1895 in El Paso, Illinois, to Newton Morris Sheen and Delia Fulton Sheen, three of whose parents had been Irish-born. Fulton, who later dropped the "Peter" and adopted his confirmation name of "John" as a middle name, was raised in an atmosphere of hard-working Irish-American midwestern piety. His father was variously a farmer and small-town merchant, and Fulton's three brothers all became successful businessmen or professionals. Fulton attended parochial elementary school, the Spalding Institute, conducted by the Brothers of Mercy in Peoria, where his parents had moved; St. Viator College in Bourbonnais, Illinois; and St. Paul's Seminary in St. Paul, Minnesota. After ordination in Peoria in 1919, Sheen pursued graduate studies in philosophy first at the Catholic University of America, where he received his S.T.D. and J.C.B. in 1920, and then at the Catholic University of Louvain in Belgium, where he attained the doctorate in 1923 and then the *Agrege en Philosophie* with "very highest distinction" in 1925. (Sheen liked to recount how champagne was served at dinner on the latter occasion as a ritual recognition of the honor.) While in Europe, he also pursued studies at the Sorbonne and at the Angelicum and Gregorian in Rome and taught at St. Edmund's College in Ware, England.

After his studies had been so successfully completed, his bishop recalled him to Peoria to serve a stint in a down-at-the-heels parish as a "test of obedience." Sheen apparently satisfied his superior, for after a few months he left the parish ministry permanently to take the chair of apologetics at Catholic University in Washington, D.C. Internal politics, at which Sheen was never very apt, soon resulted in his transfer to the philosophy faculty. Here he pursued the Neo-Thomist agenda for which his studies had prepared him and which informed his first book, *God and Intelligence in Modern Philosophy: A Critical Study in the Light of the Philosophy of Saint Thomas*, published in 1925 with an introduction by Gilbert K. Chesterton (to whom he was frequently compared later in his career).

Although Sheen continued to hold a faculty position at Catholic University until 1950 and published an astonishing stream of books and other writings during the next several decades, his fame was not to lie in academics. In 1930, he began the series of "Catholic Hour" radio broadcasts on NBC that continued till 1952 and helped to propel him to the status of the best-known Roman Catholic in America until the time of John Kennedy. His radio work was augmented by regular preaching at St. Patrick's Cathedral and by courses of instruction in Catholicism for large groups of inquirers in New York and Washington and privately for prominent individuals such as Clare Booth Luce, Heywood Broun, Fritz Kreisler, Henry Ford II, and Louis Budenz, editor of the *Daily Worker*.

Sheen's reputation as a mediagenic personality and effective public spokesman for the Catholic viewpoint was by the early 1950s ripe for translation into the medium of television, which Sheen compared to the New Testament ("the Word is seen as it becomes flesh and dwells among us"), as opposed to the Old Testament character of radio. First, in 1952, on the now-defunct DuMont network, and then from 1955 to 1957 on ABC in prime-time slots opposite the celebrities Frank Sinatra and Milton Berle at 8 P.M. on Tuesdays, Sheen's "Life Is Worth Living" eventually attracted a viewing audience of some twenty million on 123 stations. A similar series, "The Bishop Sheen Program," later ran from 1961 to 1968.

Sheen's striking, deep-set eyes and high cheekbones; his episcopal robes, cape, and skull-cap; and his masterful diction and timing created a video image that stands out as one of the most memorable from television's early years. Sheen consciously avoided proselytization or even specifically Catholic instruction on these programs and instead presented an accessible, theologically informed commentary on the events of the day, especially communism, general religious questions, and perennial popular favorites such as motherhood or the Irish. Perhaps the most memorable of these programs was that on the "Death of Stalin," delivered on 24 February 1953. When Stalin actually died on the following 5 March, Sheen was regarded as a latter-day prophet by many, although he disclaimed any such gift. Contrasting with such "heavy" themes as the theological implications of the East-West confrontation were his lighthearted "signatures," such as his ongoing joke about the "angel" who erased his

chalkboard when the camera was not on it, or his tag line, "God love you."
Sheen also attributed his success to the quality of his writers: Matthew, Mark,
Luke, and John.

While carrying on his career as a television personality, Sheen also served as
auxiliary bishop of the Archdiocese of New York (1951–66) and as national
director of the Society for the Propagation of the Faith (1950–66). In this latter
capacity he coordinated fund-raising in America for Catholic missions around
the world, a cause to which he was particularly devoted and into which he
channeled virtually all of his extensive earnings from his books, the fees paid
by his sponsor (the Admiral Corporation), and various other sources. He also
traveled widely for the missions; wrote a regular newspaper column, "God Love
You," on the topic; and edited two magazines, *World Mission* and the more
popular *Mission*.

Sheen was never comfortable as an ecclesiastical poltician and, in a celebrated
televised interview with Mike Wallace on CBS's "60 Minutes" on 28 October
1969, stated that he "could have gone higher"—become a Cardinal—had he
been more willing to compromise his principles. A long-standing personality
clash with the imperious Francis Cardinal Spellman, Sheen's superior, came to
a head when Sheen allegedly caught Spellman in an untruth in a dispute that
had gone to the Vatican for arbitration. Sheen's "reward" was his appointment
in 1966 as bishop of the diocese of Rochester, New York, a post singularly
lacking in glamour.

Even in relative obscurity, however, Sheen managed to attract considerable
media attention through a number of gestures designed to illustrate his desire to
implement the spirit of Vatican II and to make Christianity relevant to the political
and social issues of the 1960s. His elevation of the age of confirmation from
the traditional ten or twelve to seventeen or eighteen was generally well received.
In more controversial gestures, however, he attempted to give an entire inner-
city parish to the federal government for use as low-income housing, an offer
he rescinded when the parishioners, who had not been previously consulted,
raised strenuous objections. He also involved himself in controversy in a racial
dispute involving Eastman-Kodak and backed away from an earlier call for
American disengagement in Vietnam. After experiencing considerable frustration
as a diocesan administrator, he eventually prevailed on Rome to accept his
resignation in 1969 and received the honorific title of archbishop. Sheen lived
in retirement in Manhattan till his death from heart disease at the age of eighty-
four on 9 December 1979. He was buried in the crypt of St. Patrick's Cathedral.

## Appraisal

Although a disappointment as a bishop—a role for which he was untrained
and unskilled, in an era he did not fully understand—Fulton Sheen was extraor-
dinarily effective as a communicator of Catholic teachings and viewpoints
through the mass media. As an author, he was learned but derivative. In such
works as *Peace of Soul* (1949) he could demonstrate a sophisticated compre-

hension of contemporary theological issues; at points he quoted Kierkegaard and Reinhold Niebuhr approvingly, and his analysis of the spiritual plight of "modern man" often resembled their own quite closely. Much of his intellectual impact, however, was blunted by his preoccupation with the twin "materialistic" evils of Marxism and Freudian psychoanalysis. In the latter case particularly, he so distorted the work of contemporary practitioners for polemical purposes that he at times caused Catholic psychiatrists to resign their church-affiliated hospital posts in anger. His critique of communism as a metaphysic was somewhat closer to the mark, and he shared with his evangelical counterpart Billy Graham* a sense of the theological burden of contemporary world history. Sheen's theology of history, which was informed by a kind of Catholic millennialism very different from Graham's, deserves further study. Unlike other anti-Communists of various stripes, he did not resort either to personal accusations of disloyalty or to an unqualified praise of American capitalism, for the materialistic, "post-Christian" dimensions of which he had harsh words as well. During the 1960s, Sheen began to perceive world problems to a greater extent in political and economic terms than previously but did not develop a consistent social ethic.

Sheen will probably be best remembered in the long run for embodying the hesitant maturity that American Catholicism had attained by the 1950s. His manner was at once sophisticated, even Old Worldly, while yet partaking of American down-home folksiness and corny humor. Though in retrospect somewhat simplistic, his theology was many cuts more complex than that of many of his popular religious contemporaries and successors of whatever theological persuasion. Though apparently somewhat self-centered, he was generous and honest beyond reproach, and he did not descend to the ecclesiastical maneuverings that brought fortune to some of his superiors. His association with celebrities, particularly the high-status converts he had privately instructed, now seems ostentatious but was typical of the Catholic desire for public respectability in that era. His devotionalism, expressed in the letters "JMJ" (Jesus, Mary, Joseph) on his television chalkboard and pervasively through his writings, was also characteristic of the era and deserves further study in the context of the history of spirituality. What Sheen did demonstrate in the longer run was that mass-media ministry could be conducted with decorum, grounded in learning, and executed without a hint of impropriety or personalized animus.

## Survey of Criticism

Secondary literature of any value dealing with Sheen is almost nonexistent. The primary source of information on Sheen's career is his own autobiography, *Treasure in Clay,* which is not well organized, often strays into homiletics, and deliberately avoids any adverse reflections on such villain-figures in Sheen's life as Cardinal Spellman. Two book-length works—*The Passion of Fulton Sheen* and the earlier *Missionary With a Mike*—by D. P. Noonan, a priest who worked with Sheen, are rambling, anecdotal, and highly personal in their reflections on Sheen's career but do provide some interesting firsthand impressions. Noonan's appraisal of Sheen as a decent man who suffered from political obliviousness and a prima donna–like character is plausible, if insufficiently developed. Brief but well-done summaries of his career are contained in the obituaries by George Dugan (*New York Times*) and Jasper Pennington (*National Catholic Reporter*). Interesting interviews with Sheen late in his career are found in *National Catholic Reporter* for 5 October 1969 ("Fulton Sheen says: 'I could have gone higher . . . ,' " an account of a televised interview with Mike Wallace), and in the 3 June 1977 issue of *Christianity Today* ("Bottom-Line Theology").

Sheen's early work as bishop of Rochester is treated in the last chapter of Robert F. McNamara's history of that diocese and in journalistic fashion in Douglas J. Roche's *The Catholic Revolution*. William M. Halsey treats Sheen's philosophical writings provocatively in *The Survival of American Innocence* in the broader context of American Neo-Thomism. Sheen's political opinions, especially his anti-Communism, are dealt with in David J. O'Brien, *American Catholics and Social Reform;* in Donald F. Crosby, S.J., *God, Church, and Flag: Senator Joseph R. McCarthy and the Catholic Church, 1950–1957;* and at greater length but without sufficient critical perspective in Kathleen Riley Fields' article, "Anti-Communism and Social Justice." Most histories of television and TV reference books include brief mention of Sheen.

Clearly, an authoritative and comprehensive study of Sheen's life and work would be a welcome and significant addition to scholarship. No doctoral dissertations are listed through 1985 in *Dissertation Abstracts;* a graduate student who approached Sheen in the late 1960s about such a project was discouraged by the bishop, who reportedly remarked that his life had been a failure and he did not wish it to be studied. The principal source for such a study is the Sheen archives at St. Bernard's Seminary in Rochester; its special collections room contains videotapes and cassettes as well as books, correspondence, and clippings. (Videocassettes of some of Sheen's television programs are available through Trinity Communications, P.O. Box 3610, Manassas, VA 22110–0973). The *New York Times Index* is also useful for following Sheen's career in New York City, on which the *Times* reported extensively.

### Bibliography

*Books by Fulton J. Sheen*

The following list is of Sheen's major hardback publications and does not include picture books, articles in periodicals, pamphlets, hardcover or paperback reprints, translations into foreign languages, and brief items. See Jasper G. Pennington's *Chronology and Bibliography* as well as the *Catholic Periodical Index, Guide to Catholic Literature, Reader's Guide to Periodical Literature,* and *Cumulative Book Index* for more extensive citations, as well as for articles about Sheen in the religious and secular press.

1925  *God and Intelligence in Modern Philosophy: A Critical Study in the Light of the Philosophy of Saint Thomas.* London and New York: Longmans.
1928  *Religion Without God.* London and New York: Longmans.
1929  *The Life of All Living.* New York and London: Century Co.

1930    *The Divine Romance*. New York and London: Century Co.
1931    *Old Errors and New Labels*. New York and London: Century Co.
1932    *Moods and Truths*. New York and London: Century Co.
1932    *Way of the Cross*. Garden City, N.Y.: Garden City Books.
1933    *Seven Last Words*. New York and London: Century Co.
1934    *The Eternal Galilean*. New York and London: D. Appleton-Century.
1934    *Philosophy of Science*. Milwaukee: Bruce.
1935    *The Mystical Body of Christ*. New York: Sheed and Ward.
1936    *Calvary and the Mass*. New York: P. J. Kenedy and Sons.
1936    *The Moral Universe: A Preface to Christian Living*. Milwaukee: Bruce.
1937    *The Cross and the Beatitudes*. New York: P. J. Kenedy and Sons.
1938    *The Cross and the Crisis*. Milwaukee: Bruce.
1938    *Liberty, Equality and Fraternity*. New York: Macmillan.
1938    *The Rainbow of Sorrow*. New York: P. J. Kenedy and Sons.
1939    *Victory Over Vice*. New York: P. J. Kenedy and Sons.
1940    *Freedom Under God*. Milwaukee: Bruce.
1940    *The Seven Virtues*. New York: P. J. Kenedy and Sons.
1940    *Whence Come Wars*. New York: Sheed and Ward.
1941    *A Declaration of Dependence*. Milwaukee: Bruce.
1941    *For God and Country*. New York: P. J. Kenedy and Sons.
1942    *God and War*. New York: P. J. Kenedy and Sons.
1943    *The Armor of God: Reflections and Prayers for Wartime*. New York: P. J. Kenedy
        and Sons.
1943    *The Divine Verdict*. New York: P. J. Kenedy and Sons.
1943    *Philosophies at War*. New York: Scribners.
1943    *Seven Words to the Cross*. New York: P. J. Kenedy and Sons.
1944    *Love One Another*. P. J. Kenedy and Sons.
1944    *Seven Pillars of Peace*. New York: Scribners.
1945    *Seven Words of Jesus and Mary*. New York: P. J. Kenedy and Sons.
1946    *Preface to Religion*. New York: P. J. Kenedy and Sons.
1947    *Characters of the Passion*. New York: P. J. Kenedy and Sons.
1947    *Jesus. Son of Mary*. New York: D. X. McMullen.
1948    *Communism and the Conscience of the West*. Indianapolis: Bobbs-Merrill.
1948    *Philosophy of Religion*. New York: Appleton-Century-Crofts.
1949    *Peace of Soul*. New York: Whittlesey.
1950    *Lift Up Your Heart*. New York: McGraw-Hill.
1951    *Three to Get Married*. New York: Appleton-Century-Crofts.
1952    *The World's First Love*. New York: McGraw-Hill.
1953    *Life is Worth Living*. New York: McGraw Hill.
1954    *Life is Worth Living*. 2nd series. New York: McGraw-Hill.
1954    *The Life of Christ*. New York: Maco.
1954    *Way to Happiness*. Garden City, N.Y.: Garden City Books.
1954    *Way to Inner Peace*. New York: Maco.
1955    *God Love You*. Garden City, N.Y.: Garden City Books.
1955    *Life is Worth Living*. 3rd series. New York: McGraw-Hill.
1955    *Thinking Life Through*. New York: McGraw-Hill.
1956    *Life is Worth Living*. 4th series. New York: McGraw-Hill.
1956    *Thoughts for Daily Living*. Garden City, N.Y.: Garden City Books.

1957  *Life is Worth Living.* 5th series. New York: McGraw-Hill.
1960  *Go to Heaven.* New York: McGraw-Hill.
1962  *These Are the Sacraments.* New York: Hawthorn.
1963  *Missions and the World Crisis.* Milwaukee: Bruce.
1963  *The Priest Is Not His Own.* New York: McGraw-Hill.
1965  *The Power of Love.* New York: Simon and Schuster.
1965  *Walk With God.* New York: Maco.
1966  *Christmas Inspirations.* New York: Maco.
1967  *Footprints in a Darkened Forest.* New York: Meredith.
1967  *Fulton J. Sheen's Guide to Contentment.* New York: Simon and Schuster.
1970  *Children and Parents.* New York: Simon and Schuster.
1974  *Those Mysterious Priests.* Garden City, N.Y.: Doubleday.
1979  *The Electronic Christian: 105 Readings.* New York: Macmillan.
1979  *A Fulton Sheen Reader.* St. Paul, Minn.: Carillon.
1980  *Treasure in Clay.* Garden City, N.Y.: Doubleday.

### Selected Studies about Fulton J. Sheen

Crosby, Donald F. *God, Church, and Flag: Senator Joseph R. McCarthy and the Catholic Church, 1950–1957.* Chapel Hill: University of North Carolina Press, 1967.
Dugan, George. "Archbishop Sheen, Who Preached to Millions Over TV, Is Dead at 84." *New York Times,* 10 December 1979, A1, D13.
Fields, Kathleen Riley. "Anti-Communism and Social Justice: The Double-Edged Sword of Fulton Sheen." *Records of the American Catholic Historical Society of Philadelphia* 96 (1986): 83–91.
Halsey, William M. *The Survival of American Innocence.* Notre Dame, Ind., and London: University of Notre Dame Press, 1980.
McNamara, Robert F. *The Diocese of Rochester 1868–1968.* Rochester, N.Y.: Diocese of Rochester, 1968.
Noonan, D. P. *Missionary With a Mike: The Bishop Sheen Story.* New York: Pageant Press, 1968.
———. *The Passion of Fulton Sheen.* New York: Dodd, Mead, 1972.
O'Brien, David J. *American Catholics and Social Reform.* New York: Oxford University Press, 1968.
Pennington, Jasper G. *Fulton John Sheen: A Chronology and Bibliography.* Rochester, N.Y.: St. Bernard's Seminary Library, 1976.
———."Media Missionary Sheen Dead at 84." *National Catholic Reporter* 16 (21 February 1979): 18.
Roche, Douglas J. *The Catholic Revolution.* New York: David McKay, 1968. Chapter 3, "The Post-conciliar Sheen."
Williams, Peter W. "Perceptions of Time in American Catholicism." *Journal of Religious Studies* 11 (1983): 1–13.

                                                              PETER W. WILLIAMS

# Thomas Todhunter Shields

Church historians may debate definitions of fundamentalism, but standing squarely in the middle of anyone's definition is Canada's best-known and most influential fundamentalist, Thomas Todhunter Shields, D.D. (1873–1955).

## Biography

Shields was born in Bristol, England, the fifth of eight children. His father, formerly an Anglican priest and later a Primitive Methodist, was a Baptist preacher when he moved the family to Canada in 1888 to pastor a church in southwestern Ontario. Under his father's tutelage and example, T. T. Shields grew up with the ambition to be the Canadian equivalent of Charles H. Spurgeon, England's best-known evangelical. Indeed, he hoped to preach at Spurgeon's own London Tabernacle and to pastor the preeminent church of his denomination, Jarvis Street, Toronto.

Shields was to realize these ambitions after a pastoral career in several southwestern Ontario towns. Following his father's advice to write his sermons longhand and in full, using simple, clear language and without relying on commentaries or the "opinions of others," he had prepared over 1,100 sermons by the time he was called to the Jarvis Street pastrorate in 1910. In another respect as well 1910 marked a turning point for the tall, heavy-set preacher with the deep voice. The Baptist Convention of Ontario and Quebec that year heard pastor Elmore Harris repeat charges he had raised in 1908 questioning the orthodoxy of a professor at the denominational school, McMaster University, located in Hamilton, Ontario. In response, the board of governors of the university presented the report of its theological faculty affirming the orthodox doctrinal statement in McMaster's trust deeds and the professor's agreement with it.

Harris and his friends pressed the matter. John J. McNeill, eminent pastor of Walmer Road Church in Toronto, responded by asking Shields to sponsor a motion to clear the air and cut off debate. Shields agreed, and the motion passed, putting the convention on record as approving the statement of the board and relying on it to ensure that McMaster's teaching was in accord with the doctrine of the trust deeds. No doubt Shields was swayed by the fact that the doctrinal statement in question was identical to that in the trust deed of his own Jarvis Street Church, of which Senator William McMaster had been a member. Shields believed that the university's apparently genuine affirmation of what was an obviously orthodox document would be the end of the matter.

With World War I came both a rest from theological controversy and several honors. Shields preached at Spurgeon's Tabernacle in 1915 and again in 1918. Back in Toronto, he received word in 1917 that Temple University would award him the D.D. degree at its June convocation. Shields, a man who respected higher education even though he himself had not attended college, expressed his reluctance to accept it, since he thought that preachers often hid their true ability behind honorary degrees. But his friend Russell H. Conwell*, president of the school, surprised him while visiting Toronto with an impromptu presentation at an evening service. McMaster needed no such subterfuge to award him its D.D. the next year.

One wartime issue did arouse Shields: conscription, especially justified, he thought, in the defense of his beloved England. He vehemently championed it and denounced the Roman Catholic church in Quebec for its reluctance to endorse the Allied cause. This conflict with the Roman Catholics over politics would arise again with wider implications in Shields' future.

Following the war, however, the battle that Baptists in Ontario and Quebec call "the great controversy" began in earnest. In the autumn of 1919, two editorials in the *Canadian Baptist* defended liberal views of the Bible. Addressing the annual convention in Ottawa less than a month later, Shields threatened that if the convention supported the views of the editorials, he and others would leave. He did believe, however, that the majority of the convention in fact disagreed with these views and that the *Canadian Baptist* should hew to the orthodox line of this majority. A proposed amendment, a typical Baptist response, affirmed the Bible as the word of God, the right of the individual to private interpretation, and the evil of controversy arising from excessive doctrinal precision. But this apparently generic Baptist position was shouted down from the floor, and once Shields had concluded his hour-and-a-half-long speech, the convention voted with him and rapped the knuckles of the *Canadian Baptist*.

Shields returned, flushed with his victory, to encounter dissension in his own ranks. A dispute over the church organist's playing too much music in the services to suit Shields was the occasion for deeper differences in the congregation to surface, and soon the church was embroiled in a full-scale battle between Shields and a number of disaffected members. A committee of such members drafted a letter, published in a Toronto newspaper, that asked the deacons to take action toward Shields' resignation. The letter explicitly denied any theological difference with Shields, stating that "it is the man in whom the fault lies." Shields, they said, "has assumed the position of a dictator, and a self-appointed Bishop of the Baptist Church of Ontario and Quebec."

Shields resorted to the ultimatum, calling a church meeting and polling the church as to whether they wanted to keep him or not. He agreed that he would submit his resignation should less than two-thirds of the vote be cast in his favor. At the meeting itself, however, the congregation repealed the "two-thirds" agreement (it is not clear how the congregation saw itself as the authority to repeal such an apparently private agreement) and voted to retain Shields. It did so, however, by a 284–199 count, or a 58 percent majority. Shields did not resign. The next regular business meeting in June called for him to resign by a count of 204–176. Shields replied that he had no intention of resigning for the sake of a 28-vote majority, and both sides looked to the final showdown in September.

Coincidentally, perhaps, Shields invited John Roach Straton of New York to conduct an evangelistic campaign in the intervening summer months. The September business meeting then sustained Shields by a 351–310 count, significantly with the votes of forty-six members added to the church rolls that summer as converts from the campaign but without the customary interviews by the deacons. (And Shields never did receive his two-thirds of the vote.) The aroused congregational majority voted to discipline the leaders of the minority, who responded ultimately by leaving the church with 341 members to found Park Road Baptist Church. This schism, rather than Shields' success at the Ottawa convention, set the pattern for the results of Shields' subsequent efforts to lead pure, orthodox institutions.

Things got a little better, however, before they got worse. In August 1924 Shields hosted his friend J. Frank Norris*, the American fundamentalist, as Norris preached an evangelistic campaign at Massey Hall, Toronto. Shields' biographer reports that over 50,000 people attended sometime during the month-long campaign. With this kind of verification of the rightness of his cause, Shields protested when McMaster awarded an honorary degree to W.H.P. Faunce, president of Brown University and defender of Harry Emerson Fosdick*. His alliance with Fosdick was enough to damn him in conservative eyes, but Faunce also had published several books that placed him squarely in the liberal camp. McMaster's board, of which Shields himself had been a member appointed by the convention a few years before, denounced Shields as a meddler with whom they could no longer work. The 1924 convention, however, agreed with Shields and instructed McMaster to award degrees in the future only to those whose views were in accord with evangelical principles.

McMaster, though, had had enough of Shields and his friends. After the sudden death of J. L. Gilmour, professor of practical theology, late in 1924, McMaster appointed L. H. Marshall of Coventry, England, to replace him. There is some evidence that Marshall held liberal views at least later in life, but Marshall at the time made no obviously liberal pronouncements and seemed basically sound, as the university claimed he was. An English pastor in Liverpool, however, who apparently himself had no direct contact with Marshall, accused him of modernism in two letters to Shields. Shields asked the board to hold back on the appointment until the charges could be investigated. The board, understandably anxious to fill the vacancy, if a little cavalier about how Shields and others of his views might respond to their decision, went ahead with the appointment. The 1925 convention upheld the appointment by the necessary two-thirds majority but only after an eight-hour debate. This was the shape of things to come.

Shields refused to yield. Over and over in the widely read pages of his house organ, the *Gospel Witness,* Shields denounced the man who he believed doubted the verbal inerrancy of the Scriptures, the vicarious atonement and bodily resurrection of Jesus, and the total depravity of man. At the 1926 convention he repeated his charges. Marshall would not roll over either. Stung by Shields' accusations of dissembling, Marshall replied:

> Calmly and deliberately, and without malice [!], I take all those suggestions and thrust them down Dr. Shields's throat, and I say to him, 'Thou liest.' The phial of poison of which you have heard so much is not in my hands, it is in his. And I commend Dr. Shields to this text—I know that it deals with the most elementary morality—'Thou shalt not bear false witness against thy neighbour.'

Shields defended his charges, but the convention was tired of controversy and particularly, it seems, of Shields. It offered Shields the opportunity to apologize to the convention or to resign from McMaster's board of governors and to be barred from future conventions. Shields characteristically declared that he counted it an honor to be opposed by such a spirit and left the hall. Shields left, in fact, to set up the Regular Baptist Missionary and Education Society of Canada early in 1927, a channel for missionary funds that were to be diverted from the normal giving to the Baptist Convention of Ontario and Quebec. The convention responded by securing the power to expel any member churches that it deemed were out of harmony with the convention. Shields, seeing the crisis coming, fought this action but in the end fell victim to its success. Jarvis Street Church and other like-minded participants in the Regular Baptist society were read out of the convention in 1927.

These churches and some others (thirty in all) formed a new denomination, the Union of Regular Baptist Churches of Ontario and Quebec, and elected Shields as its first president. Shields' church formed a Bible college, Toronto Baptist Seminary, that served as the denomination's training school. His own church's membership had increased to 2,219, almost twice that of the church before the 1921 split. Surely a new era was at hand. Shields saw hope in other projects too. He helped form the Baptist Bible Union with like-minded American fundamentalists in 1923 and was elected its president. Shields then became chairman of the board and acting president of the Baptist Bible Union's newly purchased Des Moines University in 1927. With this new role, however, Shields' fortunes began to reverse.

The faculty in the departments of chemistry, biology, physics, and mathematics left almost immediately. They objected to the Baptist Bible Union's statement of faith, which all faculty members were required to sign, since it included a highly articulated clause on creation that stipulated belief in the direct creation not only of human but also of vegetable and animal life. Within two years, other faculty were joined by students in their resentment of what they saw to be Shields' regimentation of college life: he insisted that the students, most of them American, sing "God Save the King" at assemblies; he suspended fraternities and sororities; and he openly questioned the Christian commitment and orthodoxy of members of the faculty, including the president he himself had appointed. When Shields proved resistant to dialogue, a number of students rioted, and in 1929 the school closed. As Billy Vick Bartlett unkindly put it in *A History of Baptist Separatism,* "The two-year history of Des Moines University is a history of the blunders of Shields."

But Shields soon encountered further trouble. He held to a view of eschatology (the doctrine of "last things") that did not entirely square with the premillennialism of his fellow fundamentalists. Allowances were made in the Baptist Bible Union and other fundamentalist groups for Shields, but in his own Union of Regular Baptists he encountered militant premillennialists of the dispensational sort. This was difficult enough, but when Shields attempted to bring under control of the union two independent fellowships—one for women and the other for youth—a number of these premillennialists resisted. These incorrigible "Scofieldites'' (so named after their adherence to the ideas of C. I. Scofield*, one of the founders of Dallas Theological Seminary and editor of the widely popular *Scofield Reference Bible*) Shields expelled in 1931. In 1933, those expelled formed the Fellowship of Independent Baptist Churches of Canada.

Shields weathered the rest of the 1930s, enjoying preaching in London at the celebration of the centenary of Spurgeon's birth in 1934, enduring a heart attack in 1937, and seeing Jarvis Street Church burn in 1938. When war came, Shields once again enthusiastically represented England's cause and once again attacked the Roman Catholic hierarchy in Quebec for its opposition to conscription.

In 1941, however, several incidents coincided to prompt Shields to take more than verbal action against Catholicism. With traditional Baptist antipathy toward linkage of church and state, Shields opposed the saying of a Roman Catholic Mass for peace on Parliament Hill in September 1941. He had also heard of a Toronto Protestant bookstore that had had its mail service suspended because it was judged to have distributed anti-Catholic literature—a charge apparently unfounded. A meeting of disaffected Toronto clergymen established the Canadian Protestant League and elected Shields as president.

This league, which included several prominent evangelical laymen and clergy of Baptist, Anglican, Presbyterian, United, and Salvationist churches, had a threefold object, according to its constitution: to defend ''the traditional, civil, and religious liberties of British subjects,'' to believe in and propagate ''the great doctrines and principles of the Protestant Reformation'' (orthodox doctrines of the Trinity, Christology, soteriology, and Scripture were spelled out), and to resist the religious authority of Rome and its ''political methods of propagating its tenets, and of extending and exercising this illegitimate authority.''

By December 1941 the league had over 1,800 members, and this number more than tripled following Shields' tour of the West. Support came in from across the country, although national membership rarely exceeded 6,000, but most activity centered in Toronto. The league held mass rallies, distributed anti-Catholic literature, and supported political candidates favorable to its cause. In 1945 a ''Protestant Party'' was formed to oppose the Ontario premier's proposal to introduce religious education into the schools and to increase support for Catholic separate schools: three candidates ran and were all badly defeated.

The league attracted the attention of members of Parliament, who denounced Shields and the *Gospel Witness* (as of October 1942 the *Gospel Witness and Protestant Advocate*) on the floor of the Commons. In 1943 a resolution to muzzle Shields was actually debated, with the measure failing only when Prime Minister W.L.M. King opposed it on the grounds that he wanted to avoid religious controversy in wartime and to avoid making a martyr of a man for whom he had nothing but ''utter contempt.''

Prominent Canadian historians have lent credence to the league's fears that King's wartime policies threatened the unity of Canada and the freedom of Canadians. And the league's publications were joined by the *United Church Observer* and the *Presbyterian Record* in expressing concern over Roman Catholic doctrine and political influence. What is not clear, however, is what difference, if any, the league made in Canadian politics. And some Protestant missionaries in Quebec denounced the league as making evangelicalism seem anti-Catholic. With peace came the waning of interest in perpetuating quarrels that seemed more important in wartime and the waxing of interest in reuniting the country. The league protested the official welcome afforded a Roman Catholic cardinal by the City of Toronto and the Province of Ontario in 1946, the Marian Congress in Ottawa in 1947, and the arrest of Protestant street preachers in Rouyn, Quebec, in 1947. But the league faded; by 1949 there were just over 2,000 members. With Shields out of the country in much of 1948 and 1949, and then with his ouster from the presidency of the Union of Regular Baptists in 1949, the league lost much of the impetus it had owed to his leadership. Shields resigned the presidency in 1950, and the league carried on only in drastically attenuated form.

Shields not only lost influence in Canadian cultural and political life with the wane of the Protestant League's questionable influence but also lost influence in his own denomination. Having forced a large number out in 1931, he himself was forced out of the presidency in 1949 after firing W. Gordon Brown from the deanship of Toronto Baptist Seminary. Brown promptly led the disaffected students and faculty (and chef!) with him to form Central Baptist Seminary. The union, out of patience with Shields' autocratic manner, removed him from the presidency. Shields promptly withdrew his church, with several others following suit, to form a new, tiny denomination known as the Association of Regular Baptist Churches of Canada.

By 1950, Shields had isolated himself from all but a few Baptists and fundamentalists of other denominations. He had joined with American fundamentalist Carl McIntire* to form the International Council of Christian Churches in 1948 as a counterpart to the World Council of Churches and was head of its small Canadian chapter. Besides the circulation of the *Gospel Witness* and the enrollment in his dwindling seminary, Shields enjoyed no other links, no other fellowship, no other influence. He died in 1955, deeply loved by his church and honored by other fundamentalists, but well outside the mainstream of Canadian evangelicalism.

### Appraisal

T. T. Shields had a remarkable career, one noted by the Canadian edition of *Who's Who*. He pastored one of Canada's largest churches for forty-five years; edited a newspaper that reached 30,000 subscribers in sixty different countries; served on the board of governors of McMaster University; received two honorary degrees of doctor of divinity; was the major cause in the split of three denominations; founded the Toronto Baptist Seminary and the Canadian Protestant League; presided over Des Moines University and its parent organization, the Baptist Bible Union; wrote the doctrinal statement of the International Council of Christian Churches; and fascinated several generations of historians of Canadian religion and culture. Above all, perhaps, Christians on both sides of the Atlantic—and certainly not all of them fundamentalist—recognized him to be a preacher of extraordinary power.

Like his fundamentalist colleagues and counterparts in the United States, however, Shields enjoyed prominence only for a short while. The militancy that brought him to the attention of the nation as he provoked the most important schism on the Canadian side of the fundamentalist-modernist controversy also prevented him from forming lasting alliances that would give him enduring influence on Canadian religion. Most of the organizations he headed, with the conspicuous exception of Jarvis Street Church itself, enjoyed at best only modest support, if widespread notoriety, and then faded into insignificance.

Shields commented in the 22 June 1939 issue of *Gospel Witness*, "I find myself referred to in the press as 'the militant Pastor of Jarvis Street Church.' I should like to enquire, what other sort of Pastor is of any use to anyone?" It is clear that many Baptists in Ontario and Quebec found Shields' combination of principle and pugnacity of significant use in the struggles over theological pluralism in the denomination in the 1920s. So did other Protestants in the reaction to Roman Catholicism in Canada during World War II. But it is also clear that most Canadian Christians, even those of evangelical convictions, viewed the militancy of the "battling Baptist" as dogmatism, if not sheer arrogance, in the years that followed. Most Christians, that is, sooner or later decided to separate from the most prominent ecclesiastical separatist in Canada, T. T. Shields.

## Survey of Criticism

The literature about Shields, as the reaction by most Canadians in his own day, tends to divide almost entirely into two types: patronizingly critical or hagiographically uncritical. With a few important exceptions, almost all of the studies that originated in the academy are of the first sort; Leslie K. Tarr's *Shields of Canada* is the most prominent example of the second.

Other studies, however, have attempted a more balanced view. C. Allyn Russell's biographical sketch of Shields, "Thomas Todhunter Shields, Canadian Fundamentalist," tries to present Shields fairly, if without apparent sympathy. Walter E. Ellis' work adds sociological depth to the understanding of the Baptist schism without thereby reducing the conflict to class struggle (Mary Bulmer Reid Hill's study suffers in this regard). G. Gerald Harrop describes Shields as one of three "great preachers" among Canadian Baptists of the time, even as he acknowledges Shields' inclination toward controversy that in some respects lessened his impact as a biblical expositor. And two articles, one by Clark H. Pinnock and the other by Tarr, have tried to show that Shields was not reacting hysterically to mere hints of liberal theology at McMaster but was instead reacting, albeit passionately, to a real presence of liberal theology that threatened traditional, orthodox Christianity.

A full-scale study that takes Shields' measure in Canadian religion while appreciating the broad range of his pastoral interests, however, remains to be attempted.

## Bibliography

### Selected Works by Thomas Todhunter Shields

1921 *The Inside of the Cup*. Toronto: Jarvis Street Baptist Church.
1937 *The Plot That Failed*. Toronto: Gospel Witness.
1942 *Premier King's Plebiscite Speech in Commons Analyzed*. Toronto: Gospel Witness.
1943 *Canadians Losing at Home the Freedom for Which They Are Fighting Abroad*. Toronto: Gospel Witness.
1943 *Three Addresses: I. A Challenging Answer to Premier W. L. M. King and Other Parliamentary Critics; II. Shall the Dominion of Canada Be Mortgaged for the Church of Rome?: The Religious Aspects of the Sirois Report as Symptomatic of Dangerous Trends in Canadian Life; III. An Answer to the Roman Hierarchy's Attempted Refutation of Life's Article on Quebec*. Toronto: Canadian Protestant League.
1952 *Will Manitoba Taxpayers Consent to Pay for Roman Catholic Separate Schools*. Toronto: Gospel Witness.
1972 *Christ in the Old Testament*. Toronto: Gospel Witness.
n.d. *The Papacy in the Light of Scripture*. Toronto: Canadian Protestant League.

### Selected Studies about Thomas Todhunter Shields

Bartlett, Billy Vick. *A History of Baptist Separatism*. Springfield, Mo.: Roark & Son, 1972.
Carder, W. G. "Controversy in the Baptist Convention of Ontario and Quebec, 1908–1929." B.D. thesis, McMaster Divinity College, 1950.
———. "Controversy in the Baptist Convention of Ontario and Quebec, 1908–1928." *Foundations* 16 (1973): 355–76.
Dozois, John Donald Egide. "Dr. Thomas Todhunter Shields (1873–1955) in the Stream of Fundamentalism." B.D. thesis, McMaster University, 1963.
Ellis, Walter E. "Gilboa to Ichabod: Social and Religious Factors in the Fundamentalist-Modernist Schisms among Canadian Baptists, 1895–1934." *Foundations* 20 (1977): 109–26.
———. "Social and Religious Factors in the Fundamentalist-Modernist Schisms among Baptists in North America, 1895–1934." Ph.D. diss., University of Pittsburgh, 1974.
Harrop, G. Gerald. "The Era of the 'Great Preacher' among Canadian Baptists." *Foundations* 23 (1980): 57–70.
Hill, Mary Bulmer Reid. "From Sect to Denomination in the Baptist Church in Canada." Ph.D. diss., State University of New York at Buffalo, 1971.
May, George S. "Des Moines University and Dr. T. T. Shields." *Iowa Journal of History* 54 (July 1956): 193–232.
Pinnock, Clark H. "The Modernist Impulse at McMaster University, 1887–1927." In *Baptists in Canada: Search for Identity amidst Diversity*, 193–207. Edited by Jarold K. Zeman. Burlington, Ont.: G. R. Welch, 1980.

Russell, C. Allyn. "Thomas Todhunter Shields, Canadian Fundamentalist." *Ontario History* 70 (1978): 263–80.

Stackhouse, John G., Jr. "Proclaiming the Word: Canadian Evangelicalism since World War I." Ph.D. diss., University of Chicago, 1987.

Tarr, Leslie K. "Another Perspective on T. T. Shields and Fundamentalism." In *Baptists in Canada: Search for Indentity amidst Diversity,* 209–24. Edited by Jarold K. Zeman. Burlington, Ont.: G. R. Welch, 1980.

————. *Shields of Canada.* Grand Rapids: Baker Book House, 1967.

Wicks, Donald A. "T. T. Shields and the Canadian Protestant League, 1941–59." Master's thesis, University of Guelph, 1971.

JOHN G. STACKHOUSE, JR.

# Ralph Washington Sockman

In the fall of 1914, a student at Union Theological Seminary in New York enrolled in his first preaching class. The instructor, Harry Emerson Fosdick*, was immediately impressed with the pulpit presence of the young man. His first student sermon "exhibited such mature ability and skill that I told the class he acted as though he had twenty years of experience behind him," Fosdick wrote in his own autobiography *(The Living of These Days),* "and I doubted whether even a homiletical professor could spoil him."

This prize pupil was Ralph Washington Sockman, who had originally come to New York seeking neither a theological education nor a career in the ministry. But the gifts so evident to his teacher were soon noticed by others, and by the time his active service drew to a close, Sockman had developed an immense public following. Pastor of one Manhattan congregation for forty-four years and the regular weekly preacher on "The National Radio Pulpit" for twenty-five years, he was respected among peers as well as the populace. When professors of homiletics were polled in 1950, they ranked him second only to Fosdick as the leading Protestant preacher in the United States. *Life* magazine featured him in 1953 among the dozen preachers responsible for a "great religious upsurge" in the nation. The *New York Times* of 30 August 1970 judged that his "was a household name throughout the world."

Yet, since his death in 1970, that popular acclaim has almost entirely disappeared. Few scholars have shown interest in his work. Contemporary preachers rarely cite his words or emulate his style. His books go unsold. The public scarcely knows his name. And the congregation he served for forty-four years has suffered a noticeable decline. Sockman has joined the roster of many popular religious leaders whose fame faded with the silencing of their voices.

## Biography

Ralph Sockman was born on 1 October 1889 and raised on a farm in Knox County, Ohio. He attended Mount Vernon schools near his home and enrolled in Fredericktown High School, from which he was graduated in 1960 as valedictorian; at age sixteen, he was the youngest graduate ever in the history of the school.

For a year he taught grades one through eight in the local schools and helped on the family farm while his father started a construction business. In 1907, Sockman entered Ohio Wesleyan University, returning to the family enterprises each summer and earning additional income by selling aluminum ware. While on campus, he engaged in so many activities that he was nicknamed "Octopus." But he excelled as a member of the debating team and in the classroom. In 1911, he received his degree, was elected to Phi Beta Kappa, and entered graduate school at Columbia University, studying law and political science.

Always resourceful and hard-working, Sockman financed his graduate studies with a position as intercollegiate secretary for the YMCA from 1911 through 1913 and with odd jobs at the Physicians and Surgeons Club of New York, a residence for medical students. One Sunday in 1911, a group of these students asked him to accompany them to worship. They attended Madison Avenue Methodist Episcopal Church, and later that year Sockman joined the congregation.

Meanwhile his studies led to a master's degree in political science from Columbia in 1913. Under the influence of the renowned historian Charles Beard, he considered preparing himself for a career as a history professor. But, encouraged by the Madison Avenue pastors, he chose instead to enter Union Theological Seminary. He joined the staff of the church as a part-time assistant minister. As his senior year closed, he was retained full time. On receiving his bachelor of divinity degree in 1916, he decided to pursue one more academic goal, a Ph.D. from Columbia. While writing his dissertation, he was asked to become the senior pastor of the Madison Avenue Church. He accepted the appointment with the stipulations that he would preach only on Sunday mornings, not at the evening services, and that his freedom to complete the dissertation would be respected. The conditions were met, and he assumed the post in the same year he was awarded the doctorate, 1917.

His life was not all work and study, however. On the campus at Ohio Wesleyan, he had renewed his acquaintance with Zellah Endly, whose father had been the pastor of the Mount Vernon Methodist Church in the 1890s. The childhood friendship between Ralph and Zellah blossomed into romance during their college years, and they were married on 16 June 1916, just after his graduation from Union. Two children followed, William and Elizabeth.

Ralph Sockman's ministry at the Madison Avenue Church was hardly an overnight success. Several pastors prior to Sockman had served there briefly and moved elsewhere. The membership stood at 450 and was declining. The building was crumbling. The neighborhood was disintegrating. But within the ensuing decade, circumstances improved. Prosperous economic conditions enhanced the value of the property. A merger with the East Sixty-First Street M. E. Church strengthened the institution. And the newly formed congregation committed itself to selling the existing properties and constructing a new edifice at the northwest corner of Park Avenue and Sixtieth Street in 1929.

That was in April. The following October, the stock market crashed, sending the nation's economy into a tailspin. At the time, however, Sockman was among those not prescient enough to appreciate the depths of the crisis. Plans for the building program proceeded. Renowned architect Ralph Adams Cram traveled to Europe and Asia, returning with ideas for an "early church" style of architecture that incorporated the art and imagery of the Eastern heritage of Christianity. Italian marble, Byzantine mosaics, and a sixteenth-century reredos from an old czarist church in Russia were to be imported and installed. The eventual cost approached three million dollars.

Two years after the building opened, Sockman admitted that the plans would never have been pursued had the enormity of the Depression been understood earlier. Many doubted that millions should be spent on stone and stained glass at a time of such hardship. The irony of religious elegance amid great suffering troubled Sockman, but he took comfort from the words of Bishop Francis J. McConnell, who said in the dedicatory sermon in November 1933 "that the beauty of the building would go on feeding the souls of men down the decades long after people would have forgotten the food which could have been bought with the money spent on the building." The structure was not completed until 1949. Along the way were major administrative problems, not least being the difficulties of importing materials during a world war. Some of those challenges were addressed by Sockman personally; most were met by a building committee.

Sockman was never known as an administrator. His gift was preaching, and his fame was a product of the pulpit. In 1924 he published his first book, a collection of sermons from the previous two years titled *The Suburbs of Christianity*. His theme, expressed in a preface, was that "many areas of life are lying close to, but just outside, the corporation line of true Christianity." This broader landscape included the "inquisitiveness of our young people regarding the truths of religion . . . the growing regard for Jesus' teachings in matters of health and happiness, the sharpening hunger for human brotherhood in industrial and international relations" and more. He wanted the church to increase its impact by extending "the boundaries of Christ's rule" into such surroundings of the Christian faith. It became the agenda for his entire ministry. His preaching never stressed the narrow concerns of Christian doctrine; rather, he sought the widest possible outreach to annex into the city of God those who dwelled on the periphery of the faith.

Meanwhile, Sockman's own ministry was reaching beyond the bounds of his Manhattan parish. In the summer of 1928, he began an eight-year assignment as the summer vacation replacement for S. Parkes Cadman on NBC's "National Radio Pulpit." When Cadman retired in 1936, Sockman was chosen to replace him. For the next twenty-five years, Sockman preached each week to an audience in the millions. Several hundred letters a week arrived in response to his messages. And on Sundays at Christ Church, Methodist, nearly half of the worshippers who packed the pews for each service were visitors, many of whom came to see the preacher whose radio voice they heard regularly at home.

Sockman's many other involvements included two terms as president of the Protestant Council of Churches of the City of New York. In 1928 he became president of the Methodist Board of World Peace, a post he retained for thirty-two years. He served a term as president of the Federal Council of Churches. He wrote a weekly newspaper column. He was a member of the boards of trustees at Syracuse University, Ohio Wesleyan, Drew, and New York University, where he was also senior chaplain. He published twenty books and wrote a score of articles for periodicals ranging from the scholarly *Religion in Life* to the popular *Parade* Sunday supplement.

He also traveled extensively. His personal vacations included cruises to Hawaii, Europe, Asia, and the Middle East. A man without hobbies, he once said that his preferred form of relaxation was to sit in a deck chair aboard ship reading a mystery novel. But more than his personal leisure took him across the country and abroad. His growing popularity fostered invitations to preach and lecture widely, and he embraced every opportunity possible. During some of his busiest weeks, notably in Lent, he would leave Manhattan on Monday or early Tuesday and travel all week, preaching each evening in communities across the country. Returning to the city on Friday, he would then prepare himself to preach on Sunday, possibly to repeat the same schedule in the following week.

This life-style took its toll. Sometimes his sermons had to be prepared on the run. His manuscript notes, housed in the archives at Syracuse University, are often made on an assortment of stationery from hotel rooms and railroad cars that track his itinerary for the week. His Sunday morning sermons were always prepared in complete manuscript, written in longhand from the accumulated notes of the previous week, drawing on his reading, personal reflection, and firsthand experience. He wrote the finished product in his study at home, a parsonage apartment on Park Avenue. Entering the study in mid-afternoon on Saturday, he would work late into the night, generally retiring around 2:00 A.M. On Sunday morning, he usually arose around 7:00, reviewed the manuscript written the night before, prepared for the radio broadcast, and then made ready for the pulpit, where he rarely used a note.

The content of his sermons fit the style generally known as "life situation preaching." Pioneered by Henry Ward Beecher in the nineteenth century and polished by Harry Emerson Fosdick in the twentieth, this approach focused on a circumstance, dilemma, issue, or need in human life and then brought the biblical word and the Christian tradition to bear on it. Sockman's manuscripts invariably started with a biblical text at the head of the first page. But his style was not textual exposition. In his 1931 book on ethics called *The Morals of Tomorrow,* Sockman declared that the pulpiteer can be a convincing moral guide "not on the ground that he is sent from God but that he knows how to get to people." He dealt with personal and social issues in his sermons. Sometimes he offered a prophetic word: pleading for the social relief of poverty, proposing the construction of low-cost housing, addressing the phenomenon of racial prejudice, complaining about the spending habits of consumers who indulge themselves too frivolously in personal luxuries, pointing to the cult of prosperity that too often identifies itself with godliness, or promoting efforts at international peace. Yet he resisted the technique of attacking sinners who are outside a preacher's own congregation. A sermon in Christ Church against powerful labor leaders, for instance, would be inappropriate, he said, for no labor leaders worshipped there.

In fact, his was a church of the wealthy and well placed. Among his parishioners were Alfred P. Sloan, the chairman of General Motors; Herbert Brownell, the successful Republican lawyer who served as Eisenhower's attorney general; and J. C. Penney. Impeccably dressed, Sockman looked like the bankers and businessmen who belonged to his church. He knew those with whom he could share a cocktail and those who required temperance. He knew when to light up a cigar and when to abstain. In his view, all this was part of being a successful pastor. "The preacher must gain the confidence of his congregation through personal friendship, if he would win the acceptance of his message," he wrote in his 1938 volume *Recoveries in Religion*. For this reason, he believed that the pastor/preacher was far more effective than the "radio pulpiteer" or the "travelling evangelist." His pulpit ministry, by every practical measurement, was extremely effective. As he approached his twenty-fifth year at Christ Church, the membership had grown from 450 to 2,000, and the budget had increased tenfold.

In that silver anniversary year, 1942, he published *The Highway of God,* his Lyman Beecher Lectures on Preaching delivered the previous year at Yale. He dedicated the book to his son, William, whose story was certainly the most profound tragedy that Sockman had ever faced. William had been a brilliant student who had had trouble finding a fitting place for himself in the world. A poet and Latin scholar, William had been educated at the Hill School, a prestigious academy in New Jersey, and then at Harvard and Columbia. In the spring of 1941, while Sockman was in Houston, William apparently took his own life, plunging to the pavement below the family apartment. The bereaved father expressed his grief in a mixture of anger, hurt, and a renewed commitment to work harder. He lamented the young man's expensive education that was now wasted. He and his wife sought counseling from a colleague. He sat in his dentist's chair and wept. And he resolved to double his work efforts, as if to fulfill his own calling and also that of his deceased son.

By this time, of course, others' sons were going to war. There were ninety young men from Christ Church in uniform by October 1942. His work with various peace groups notwithstanding, he began to adjust his pacifist inclinations. In an August 1981 interview one of his coworkers said, "Ralph was a pacifist until war came; then he was a patriot." In the postwar period, Sockman joined his voice with those who were alarmed about the spread of communism. Some found him not sufficiently alarmed. When he traveled to the Soviet Union in

July 1946 as president of the Federal Council of Churches, the American Council of Christian Laymen accused him of harboring Communist sympathies. In response, he contacted one of his regular radio listeners, J. Edgar Hoover, and suggested that the FBI might investigate the lies being spread about him. The criticism quickly subsided. When Americans again faced combat during the late forties and early fifties in Korea, Sockman praised the effort to devise a "police action" rather than a "war system" to contain communism.

By the mid 1950s Sockman was the senior active figure among popular religious leaders in the land. His fellow Methodists had elected him delegate to their general conference nine times. They had (without success) pressed him three times to accept a nomination for the office of bishop. He had taught preaching at Yale Divinity School (1947–49) and Union Theological Seminary (1949–57) and had served on the board of preachers at Harvard (1944–48). He received twenty-one honorary degrees. He held membership on the central committee of the World Council of Churches. His ministry brought him fame and a modest fortune.

After forty-four years as pastor of Christ Church, Sockman retired at the end of 1961. In all those years, he never once missed a scheduled preaching assignment because of illness. A dinner was held in his honor at the Waldorf Astoria, and 2,000 persons attended. The president of the United States, his predecessor, and the governor of New York were among those who sent greetings. In one of the testimonials, he was praised by David Sarnoff of RCA, the parent of NBC, as "broadcasting's most durable celebrity." In retirement, he continued to travel, lecture, preach, write, and publish. He remained active on boards and committees and as director of the Hall of Fame for Great Americans.

On 26 July 1970, he preached for the last time at Christ Church. Five weeks later, on 29 August, he died quietly at his Park Avenue apartment, with Zellah at his side.

### Appraisal

Ralph Sockman was a product of late-nineteenth- and early-twentieth-century liberalism in America. He shared its optimism, cherished its confidence in human reason, and celebrated its commitment to human freedom. In keeping with classical liberalism, he saw a basic continuity between humanity and divinity. He believed that the task of the church was to capture the imagination of humanity with a vision of the will of God and then to align human will with God's will.

During his career, he was often criticized for being too optimistic. There is no doubt that he tended to see the sunnier side of things. Sometimes this optimism made him merely sentimental, as when, in *Date with Destiny,* he appealed for his audience "to see the tree in the apple, to catch the scent of spring in the winds of winter." Other times it kept him from fully understanding the pervasive power of evil. "Evil is the absence of God," he wrote in *The Higher Happiness;* it is merely the consequence of free choice. That Jane Addams and Al Capone lived in the same Chicago slum was proof enough to him that the human will was free to claim promise and hope for itself. Besides, he said, it was easier to account for evil in God's world than it was to account for good in a godless world. He believed that there was too much focus on wickedness and not enough on healing and that Jesus stressed not human depravity but human redemption. At his retirement dinner, he appealed for fewer cries of alarm over the infiltration of communism and for moving the church to do more infiltrating of godliness.

Though Sockman understood himself to be a preacher who drew life situations and the Scripture together, there is doubt about whether his pulpit authority grew out of the Bible. Every sermon had a text, and he insisted that the Bible provided a basic skeletal framework on which he built a contemporary message. Yet his pursuit of credibility in the pulpit depended not on Scripture but on the power of reason and personal experience. When he listed his reasons for believing in immortality, for example, he identified the integrity of the human personality, the universe, and Jesus, and the conviction that it would be true even if Christ's career had ended on the cross.

If anything, the real authority for Sockman's ministry was his pastoral relationships with people. He was accessible to persons in all sorts of situations, and he cultivated many personal contacts. His ability to remember names was legendary. Yet the strength of these personal links bound him to the culture of his congregation, basically the white upper-class echelon of business and political leadership. On occasion, that led to some unfortunate statements. In the 21 November 1932 *New York Times,* he noted the gravity of the economic crisis by saying, "It is one thing for a nation to have a few million ignorant idle; it is quite another to have several million educated idle." In 1945 in a sermon titled "My Place in God's Family" he dismissed the notion that Americans in general were responsible for racism in Harlem or Detroit, saying only that "each of us is responsible for his own heart." And in a 1950 sermon, "Our Mother Country," he drew a distinction between the quality of life in the two Americas: North America was founded by people looking for God; South America, by people looking for gold. The United States of America, he said, was based on "the union between Father God and Mother Country."

This tendency toward a kind of privileged-class civil religion, always an element of his ministry, surfaced more clearly in his later years. He wrote in *How to Believe* that he considered it "no accident that Christian lands have produced the Magna Carta, the Declaration of Independence, the Bill of Rights, and the largest laboratories." He saw a direct line from Luther's reform movement in sixteenth-century Germany to the American democracy in "the greatest nation in the world." It becomes a legitimate question to ask whether Sockman developed from a preacher to the culture to become a pastor of the culture.

His rhetorical flourishes were memorable: "The problem of Christianity is not the wolfishness of the wolves, but the sheepishness of the sheep"; "Beatitudes cannot stop a blitzkrieg"; "We are the salt not the sugar of the earth." Yet there was more form than substance to his message. Avoiding any identification of his ministry with a specific doctrine, emphasis, mission, or objective, he tried to claim the broad middle of religious sensibilities in the culture as his terrain. In an interview with Robert Bruce Hibbard he described himself as "halfway between the intellectualism of a Reinhold Niebuhr and the comforting nature of a Norman Vincent Peale.*" On another occasion, he defined his ministry as a middle ground between defeatism and saying that all is sweetness and light. Such broad strokes left him without focus. When his work was done, when death stilled his remarkable personality, he left little that could confront the world with the claims of the gospel.

## Survey of Criticism

Published material about Sockman is meager. Robert Bruce Hibbard has produced the only significant study of Sockman's life and work, "The Life and Ministry of Ralph Washington Sockman," a doctoral dissertation completed in 1957 at Boston University. Unpublished, it was researched and written while Sockman was still at Christ Church, and it includes data compiled from interviews with him. Though not uniformly laudatory, Hibbard's work draws favorable conclusions about Sockman's ministry in general and his status as a biblical preacher in particular. Merrill R. Abbey, *The Epic of United Methodist Preaching: A Profile in American Social History,* gives attention to Sockman's Beecher lectures, his theological tendencies, his radio ministry, and his concerns for peace. It is essentially a narrative identifying his historical place.

Brief articles in general-circulation magazines over the years praised Sockman's radio ministry and the construction of Christ Church. An article by Kyle Haselden places Sockman's preaching style in line with that of Beecher, Fosdick, and others. Dissertations by William McLeister and William B. Lawrence locate Sockman in the context of his pulpit contemporaries; the latter addresses also the cultural context and theological orientation of their work. The only recently published article on Sockman appeared in *Quarterly Review.* Written by William B. Lawrence, "Ralph Sockman: The Compleat Methodist" demonstrates Sockman's style as representative of his denomination.

## Bibliography

### Books by Ralph Washington Sockman

1924  *The Suburbs of Christianity.* New York: Abingdon.
1927  *Men of the Mysteries.* New York: Abingdon.
1931  *The Morals of Tomorrow.* New York: Harper.
1933  *The Unemployed Carpenter.* New York: Harper.
1936  *The Paradoxes of Jesus.* New York: Abingdon.
1938  *Recoveries in Religion.* Nashville: Cokesbury.
1939  *Live for Tomorrow.* New York: Macmillan.
1942  *The Highway of God.* New York: Macmillan.
1944  *Date with Destiny: A Preamble to Christian Culture.* New York and Nashville: Abingdon-Cokesbury.

1946   *The Fine Art of Using*. New York: Joint Division of Education and Cultivation, Board of Missions and Church Extension, the Methodist Church.
1946   *Now to Live*. New York and Nashville: Abingdon-Cokesbury.
1947   *The Lord's Prayer: An Interpretation*. Boston: Pilgrim Press.
1950   *The Higher Happiness*. New York: Abingdon-Cokesbury.
1953   *How to Believe: The Questions That Challenge Man's Faith Answered in the Light of the Apostles' Creed*. Garden City, N.Y.: Doubleday.
1955   *The Whole Armor of God*. New York: Abingdon.
1956   *The Lift for Living*. New York: Abingdon.
1958   *Man's First Love: The Great Commandment*. Garden City, N.Y.: Doubleday.
1961   *The Meaning of Suffering*. New York: Abingdon.
1963   *Whom Christ Commended*. New York: Abingdon.
1966   *The Easter Story for Children*. New York: Abingdon.

### Studies about Ralph Washington Sockman

Abbey, Merrill R. *The Epic of United Methodist Preaching: A Profile in American Social History*. Lanham, Md.: University Press of America, 1984.
Haselden, Kyle. "An Honor Roll of American Preachers." *Pulpit* 35 (1964): 3ff.
Hibbard, Robert B. "The Life and Ministry of Ralph Washington Sockman." Ph.D. diss., Boston University, 1957.
Lawrence, William B. "Ralph Sockman: The Compleat Methodist." *Quarterly Review* 5 (1985): 27ff.
————. "Sundays in New York: Directions in Pulpit Theology, 1930–1955." Ph.D. diss., Drew University, 1984.
McLeister, William. "The Use of the Bible in the Sermons of Selected Protestant Preachers in the United States from 1925–1950." Ph.D. diss., University of Pittsburgh, 1957.

WILLIAM B. LAWRENCE

# Billy Sunday

When Billy Sunday died in November 1935 the *Christian Century* remembered him as "the last of his line." Sunday's sensational urban revivals during the second decade of the twentieth century had been merely "signs of the desperate and hopeless condition of the evangelical type of piety." Revivalism—the tradition in which Sunday stood—"had been running down by progressive stages since the great days of Finney. . . . In Billy Sunday it exhausted itself."

The *Christian Century* was, in this one rare case, somewhat off the mark. Billy Sunday was very much the product of his generation, and in this sense his impact was definitely limited. But insofar as Sunday represented revivalism and "the evangelical type of piety," he contributed, for better and worse, to the preservation and adaptation of that tradition. For a few years, Sunday was a wildly popular shaper of rural nineteenth-century evangelicalism by contorting that piety into the idioms, modes of organization, and ethos of progressive, urbanizing America.

## Biography

William Ashley ("Billy") Sunday was born on 19 November 1862. His father had enlisted in the Union Army in August and died of pneumonia two days before Christmas, leaving behind, in a small log house near Ames, Iowa, his wife and three sons—Billy, Albert (age four), and Edward (age two). The family was poor and struggled to stay together until 1874 when, after some more family troubles, Sunday and his brother Edward were sent to the Soldiers' Orphan Home at Glenwood, Iowa. After 1877, Billy was on his own. There is little evidence of extensive religious influence on Sunday either from his extended family or at the orphanage. Billy's education generally was haphazard. He never finished high school, although he did in later life take a few courses at Evanston Academy, the prep school for Northwestern University.

Sunday's earliest passion was apparently athletics. He won several local running races in Iowa and eventually joined the Marshalltown baseball team, for whom he starred. He was "discovered" there in 1883 and began a professional baseball career with the Chicago Whitestockings (and later with Pittsburgh and Philadelphia) that was to last until 1891. After becoming an evangelist, Sunday often drew on the name recognition his baseball career afforded him, and he peppered his sermons with the imagery of athletics. He was known, early in his preaching days especially, simply as "The Baseball Evangelist."

The story of Sunday's conversion to Christianity is the source of some controversy. What is clear is that he was converted around 1885 at the famous Pacific Garden Mission in Chicago. Sunday's earliest biographer, however, hinted strongly that Sunday converted in order to woo the devout Presbyterian, Helen A. ("Nell") Thompson, the daughter of a prominent Chicago business man. Sunday understandably preferred to emphasize other motives for his conversion, and his authorized biographies stated that he in fact met Nell only after his choice of Christianity. Sunday did admit, however, that he joined the Presbyterian Church solely because of Nell: "If she had been a Catholic I would have been a Catholic," he once said, according to biographer William McLoughlin. In any event, religion undeniably was becoming a priority in Sunday's life around this time, and the trend was not discouraged when Nell became Mrs. Sunday in 1888.

Aside from his marriage, the most notable by-product of Sunday's conversion was that he began to work for the YMCA. Sunday began with the "Y" as an occasional lecturer and eventually left baseball in 1891 to become assistant secretary in the religion department of the Chicago Association. Sunday put in long hours at a meager salary, distributing tracts in saloons or on street corners, arranging speakers for prayer meetings, carrying out office chores, and occasionally also speaking. The job, carried out in the "manly" but nurturing Christian ethos of the association, was undoubtedly a primary influence on Sunday's developing theological perspective.

Even more influential was Sunday's affiliation from 1893 through 1895 with the Presbyterian itinerant evangelist J. Wilbur Chapman (1859–1918). Chapman introduced Sunday to the possibilities, and the details, of the revivalist's trade. Sunday usually served as Chapman's "advance man," responsible for making all the technical arrangements in a town prior to Chapman's arrival. Sunday handled finances for the rental of an arena, organized a choir from local talent, soothed egos of local ministers, conducted prayer meetings, set up coordinating committees, occasionally preached, served as usher, and generally made sure that the entire revival machinery was working smoothly. During these years, Chapman usually visited small- to medium-sized towns such as Peoria, Illinois; Evansville, Indiana; and Oskaloosa, Iowa. The contacts Sunday made among the midwestern clergy were to prove indispensable.

In 1895 Chapman suddenly decided to settle in his Philadelphia parish. Sunday, now the father of two children, was out of a job. He and Nell took it as providential when he received an invitation to hold a revival on his own in Garner, Iowa. In fact, Chapman had asked the Garner ministers to extend the invitation. The revival began on 9 January 1896, lasting for a week, and Sunday never lacked work thereafter.

Throughout the years 1896 to 1907 or so, Sunday worked at developing his own style, mostly by visiting small, rural midwestern towns. Initially, he preached sermons from outlines Chapman had lent him, but very early he added new material while dramatically simplifying Chapman's somewhat staid rhetoric. The reviews in the Iowa papers were good. "Fiery," "forcible," "clear," "magnetic," and "outspoken" were typical descriptions. Even more impressive were the reports of the results. More than one paper could headline "Largest congregation ever assembled," or "Church people aroused as never before." Sunday was becoming a civic asset. His ordination by the Chicago Presbytery in 1903 only added to his credentials.

The story of Sunday's increasing success after 1907 has often been told through statistics. In 1907 the average population of the towns that he visited was 10,000. By 1913, that number had risen to 76,000. And by 1917, the year Sunday campaigned in New York City, the figure shot up to 1,750,000, according to William McLoughlin. After 1911 or so, Sunday was clearly a national figure, and from 1912 to 1918 he was probably the most popular preacher in America. In 1914 the *American Magazine* polled its readers on the question, "Who is the greatest man in the U.S.?" and Sunday placed eighth, tied with Andrew Carnegie and Judge Ben Lindsey. No other preacher made the list.

With success came refinements in the revival apparatus and further development of Sunday's characteristic style. After a revival tent collapsed from the weight of snow in 1905, Sunday demanded the construction of a large, temporary wood tabernacle with sawdust floors in every town he visited. "Hitting the sawdust trail" became a synonym for "converting" at a Sunday meeting. The smallest of these tabernacles sat 1,500; the largest, in New York and Chicago, held 22,000. Homer Rodeheaver was hired in 1910 as choir leader, musician, and cheerleader, and he served to warm up crowds for Sunday's sermons for twenty years. As the revivals moved to larger cities, Sunday developed a precinct system of revival planning, by means of which he would partition the city into numerous districts with designated leaders and would target publicity for each. Covering all the ground was not difficult. At its peak the "Sunday party" had a full-time staff of twenty and was aided by countless volunteers.

The atmosphere at a Sunday revival was raucous without being emotional. Sunday intentionally downplayed the enthusiasm traditionally associated with revivalistic conversion. He appealed more to group than to individual psychology. This was accomplished especially through the "delegation system," whereby groups from shops, factories, churches, lodges, and so on would be seated together in the tabernacle. Rodeheaver would draw these delegations into competition with one another through hymn sings or cheers, and Sunday would appeal through his sermon for the delegations to lead the way down the sawdust trail to shake his hand. And Sunday's sermon was always the highlight of the meeting. In his prime, he could be heard without electronic amplification in a tabernacle of 22,000. His pulpit methods, or antics, such as jumping, sliding across the floor of the speaker's platform, whirling a chair over his head, or doing handsprings, were legendary. His use of slang to tell Bible stories made many Christians irate. Sunday claimed simply to be "acting out" his sermons. His critics accused him of debasing the gospel with vaudeville.

After 1918, Sunday's popularity declined dramatically. He had been judged from the outset by the number of converts he could add to local churches, and though there were numerous "trail-hitters" recorded at every revival, more often than not these people were already church members or showed no interest in joining any one church after being contacted by local ministers. Sunday's somewhat callous refusal even to consider questions on the lasting effects of his revivals did not help his credibility.

That credibility was further damaged in 1918 after Sunday issued what he called "the first book appearing under my authorship," *Great Love Stories of the Bible*. Shortly after the book's release, Hugh A. Weir sued Sunday for breach of contract, claiming he had ghostwritten the book and had not been remunerated as promised. Sunday had been accused of plagiarism before, but the Weir case, and another suit in the same year brought by Sidney C. Tapp, came when Sunday was being most closely scrutinized by the national press and undoubtedly damaged his reputation with that influential group.

A lack of financial accountability was another cause for Sunday's decline. Initially, it was customary for Sunday to accept as payment only the "free will" offering collected on the last day of a revival. Sunday's staff, however, utilized a "hard-sell" auction format to create a competitive spirit among the givers. Later, a local "offering committee" was established prior to revivals, and this group encouraged giving by prominent area residents. By 1920 Dun and Bradstreet listed Sunday's net worth at $1.5 million. Questions about fiscal ethics were rebuffed by Sunday as "nobody's business."

From 1920 until his death in 1935 Sunday continued to conduct revivals, but mostly in the South and, once again, in the Midwest. He also visited smaller towns than during his peak years. Sunday had managed to appeal to many "progressives" during the teens, but when the fundamentalist-modernist controversy became cultural warfare in the 1920s and when Sunday sided clearly with the fundamentalists, he was branded "old-time" or "the last of his line." He suffered a first heart attack in 1933 and died from another on 6 November 1935. He had conducted more than 300 revivals in his career, had dined with presidents, and had pushed evangelism further down the road toward business and entertainment.

### Appraisal

Sunday is perhaps the first figure in the history of American religion for whom the label *star* is not anachronistic. In other words, the print medium played a major role in making, and to a degree in unmaking, Billy Sunday. During the revivalist's heyday, newspapers and popular magazines printed full transcripts of his sermons, published "box scores" of the number of trail-hitters at each meeting, and generally provided sensational, free publicity for the evangelist. After 1918, the publicity was no longer forthcoming. Sunday himself had alienated the press in part, but the national mood had also changed after the war, and Sunday simply no longer sold newspapers. He virtually disappeared from popular magazines after 1918.

But of course Sunday's success was also the result of the intrinsic relevance of his message, which was a complex blending of traditional evangelical and village values with progressivist and urban rhetoric and methods. It was a message that tried to bridge Protestant and secular America, and for a few years it succeeded. Sunday himself called his theology "progressive orthodoxy," and the Janus-like label is illustrative.

On the progressive side, Sunday dressed stylishly, used contemporary language and street-slang in his sermons, stressed effectiveness over ideology, and sometimes spoke out against graft, vice, inadequate living and working conditions, and monopolies. Sunday went beyond even the progressives in support of the war effort, and he frequently made nativist-sounding statements that should have grated on any liberally tuned ears. But some progressives managed to hear what they wanted to hear in Sunday's sermons, and the revivalist undoubtedly drew some early support from them.

On the orthodox side, which was always the more prominent, Sunday supported what were to become the traditional five points of fundamentalism (inerrancy of Scripture, virgin birth, substitutionary atonement, bodily resurrection, and premillennial eschatology), but during his popular days few of his sermons were doctrinal in character. Individual conversion was the focus of most of Sunday's rhetorical attention but without, again, the emphasis on "conviction" or emotionalism common to previous revivalists. Sunday preached against personal "sins," such as drinking, dancing, theater-going, smoking, adultery, and fornication. He promoted traditional, hierarchical sex roles and generally condemned labor unrest. He was frequently criticized later in his career for being a "stooge" of big business, and it is hard not to draw the conclusion from his sermons that he believed in "clean living" according to village values as the cure for both individual and social unrest. Sunday's "Booze Sermon" was perhaps his most famous, and the issue of Prohibition is the perfect analogue on the social plane to Sunday's impact on the spiritual. His influence was dramatic but not long lasting.

At root, Billy Sunday offered worldly and eternal success through belief in Jesus and individual moral improvement to an audience who wanted to believe it was true but already half-doubted that it was. Sunday was a transitional figure during what Robert T. Handy has called "the second disestablishment" of Protestantism. In other words, Sunday's heritage was evangelical and mainstream, his legacy was fundamentalist and marginal, and for a few years, roughly 1912 to 1918, Sunday managed uneasily to straddle the two camps.

Billy Sunday was never deep. To an extraordinary degree, his rhetoric had to carry him. In light of this, his physical gyrations and contortions while preaching can be seen as the visible expression of the intellectual contradictions plaguing not only the evangelical but also the Protestant mind of his era. Sunday could not cognitively pinpoint the religious tensions of his time, so he acted them out. His performance appealed to many in the American middle class who were similarly mute, or undecided, before the substantive challenges of modernity.

## Survey of Criticism

The place to begin the study of Billy Sunday is with William G. McLoughlin's definitive biography, *Billy Sunday Was His Real Name*. This work is excellent for relating Sunday to early-twentieth-century American social history, and especially to topics such as progressivism, World War I, temperance, liberalism, evolution, and fundamentalism. McLoughlin more critically evaluates Sunday in light of the evangelical tradition in *Modern Revivalism: Charles Grandison Finney to Billy Graham,* as does Bernard A. Weisberger, *They Gathered At The River*. Lee Thomas' biography, *The Billy Sunday Story*, is a simple, uncritical narrative, and McLoughlin's section on Sunday in his *Revivals, Awakenings and Reform* perhaps stresses too heavily Sunday's nationalism and political involvement.

Sunday was the subject of several biographies while he was still living, and these remain useful for general information, anecdotes, or sermon transcripts. Three of these are generally available: Theodore Thomas Frankenberg, *The Spectacular Career of Rev. Billy Sunday* (revised under the title *Billy Sunday: His Tabernacles and Sawdust Trails*); Elijah P. Brown, *The Real Billy Sunday*; and William T. Ellis, *"Billy" Sunday: The Man and His Message*. An earlier monograph published by the Herman, Poole Co. in 1908 was suppressed by Sunday, and only one known copy exists in the Library of Congress, according to McLoughlin. The Brown and Ellis books are authorized and adulatory biographies but contain significant sermon excerpts.

Recent studies of Sunday in scholarly journals or monographs are relatively scant. David T. Morgan has traced "The Revivalist as Patriot: Billy Sunday and World War I," and Joseph H. Hall contributed "Sunday in St. Louis: The Anatomy and Anomaly of a Large-Scale Billy Sunday Revival." Neither of these offers new perspectives on Sunday's significance. McLoughlin, however, offered "Billy Sunday and the Working Girl of 1915," which hints at how an innovative approach to Sunday, along the lines of feminist and/or mentalité studies, might work. And Razelle Frankl has clarified the connection of Sunday to the popular television preachers of the 1980s in *Televangelism: The Marketing of Popular Religion*.

## Bibliography

### Works by Billy Sunday

1913    "My All-Star Nine." *Collier's* 52 (October): 19ff.

1915    "Why of My Methods." Interview. *Ladies Home Journal* 32 (April): 13, 82–83.

1917    *Great Love Stories of the Bible*. New York: Putnam.

1932–33    "Autobiography." *Ladies Home Journal* 49 (September-December; February-April): 4–5ff.; 12–13ff.; 17ff.; 16ff.; 87ff.; 60–61ff.

1940    *Wonderful, and Other Sermons*. Grand Rapids: Zondervan.

1970    *Billy Sunday Speaks*. Introduction by Oral Roberts. Edited by Karen Gullen. New York: Chelsea House.

Wheaton, Illinois. Archives of the Billy Graham Center. Billy Sunday Papers. Complete microfilm set.

### Studies about Billy Sunday

Betts, Frederick W. *Billy Sunday: The Man and Method*. Boston: Murray, 1916.

"Billy Sunday." *Commonweal* 23 (22 November 1935): 103–4.

"Billy Sunday, the Last of His Line." *Christian Century* 52 (20 November 1935): 1,476.

Brown, Elijah P. *The Real Billy Sunday*. New York: Revell, 1914.

Coleman, William L. "Billy Sunday: A Style Meant for His Time and Place." *Christianity Today* 21 (17 December 1976): 14–17.

Denison, L. "Sunday and His War on the Devil." *American Magazine* 64 (September 1907): 451–68.

Ellis, William T. *"Billy" Sunday: The Man and His Message*. New York: L. T. Myers, 1914.

Frankenberg, Theodore Thomas. *Billy Sunday: His Tabernacles and Sawdust Trails*. Columbus, Ohio: F. J. Heer, 1917.

———. *The Spectacular Career of Rev. Billy Sunday*. Columbus, Ohio: McClelland, 1913.

Frankl, Razelle. *Televangelism: The Marketing of Popular Religion*. Carbondale: Southern Illinois University, 1987.

Hall, Joseph H. "Sunday in St. Louis: The Anatomy and Anomaly of a Large-Scale Billy Sunday Revival." *Presbyterian* 10 (Spring-Fall 1984): 99–110.

Marsden, George M. *Fundamentalism and American Culture: The Shaping of Twentieth-Century Evangelicalism: 1870–1925*. New York: Oxford University Press, 1980.

McLoughlin, William G., Jr. "Billy Sunday and the Working Girl of 1915." *Journal of Presbyterian History* 54 (Fall 1976): 376–84.

————. *Billy Sunday Was His Real Name*. Chicago: University of Chicago Press, 1955.

————. *Modern Revivalism: Charles Grandison Finney to Billy Graham*. New York: Ronald Press, 1959.

————. *Revivals, Awakenings, and Reform: An Essay on Religion and Social Change in America, 1607–1977*. Chicago: University of Chicago Press, 1978.

Morgan, David T. "The Revivalist as Patriot: Billy Sunday and World War I." *Journal of Presbyterian History* 51 (Summer 1973): 199–215.

Rodeheaver, Homer. *Twenty Years with Billy Sunday*. Nashville: Cokesbury, 1936.

Sizer, Sandra S. *Gospel Hymns and Social Religion: The Rhetoric of Nineteenth-Century Revivalism*. Philadelphia: Temple University Press, 1978.

Szasz, Ferenc Morton. *The Divided Mind of Protestant America, 1880–1930*. University: University of Alabama Press, 1982.

Thomas, Lee. *The Billy Sunday Story: The Life and Times of William Ashley Sunday*. Grand Rapids: Zondervan, 1961.

Weisberger, Bernard. *They Gathered at the River: The Story of the Great Revivalists and Their Impact upon Religion in America*. Boston: Little, Brown, 1958.

JON PAHL

# Jimmy Swaggart

By the late 1950s and early 1960s most Americans recognized that the great healing revival of the post–World War II era was drawing to a close. The crowds were dwindling, and the finances were becoming more difficult to obtain for even the best evangelists. By the sixties only a handful of the great independent healing revivalists who had influenced a generation of Americans remained national figures. Yet as the older ministries were fading, a new group of more sophisticated deliverance revivalists were coming to the forefront as the powerful charismatic revival swept the nation in the late sixties and the seventies.

One of the most impressive new evangelistic ministries to emerge to national prominence in the seventies was that of Jimmy Swaggart of Baton Rouge, Louisiana, an ordained Assemblies of God minister. He was the cousin of the famed recording artist Jerry Lee Lewis and was himself one of the nation's top gospel recording stars. Swaggart combined old-fashioned revivalism with a solid Pentecostal emphasis and flavored this with an appeal that extended his outreach into the charismatic movement. His ministry offered a new era of cooperative revivalism that brought together classical Pentecostals and charismatics.

### Biography

Jimmy Lee Swaggart was born on 15 March 1935, eighty-five miles northwest of Baton Rouge, Louisiana, in the small town of Ferriday. His father, Willie Leon Swaggart, and mother, Minnie Bell Herron, were married in their teens and lived in deep poverty during the Depression era. Throughout the early years of their marriage, Father Swaggart eked out a living by fishing, trapping, bootlegging, and fiddle playing. During these hard years, their oldest son died of pneumonia, and the resulting trauma caused severe strains and tensions within the family for years.

In 1942 Father Swaggart accepted Christ, and the family environment changed for the better. Becoming active members of the Assemblies of God church, the family accepted the strict moral and personal standards of Pentecostalism. During his adolescent years, Jimmy was to struggle with these standards, but maintaining them became especially important by the late forties when his father became a pioneering preacher with the Assemblies of God and traveled to small towns throughout Louisiana planting "full gospel" churches. It was at one such church in Wisner, Louisiana, that Jimmy met and married Frances Anderson. Within two years the young couple had their only child, whom they named Donnie after Jimmy's older brother who had died.

As a seventeen-year-old high school dropout, Jimmy had a difficult time providing a living for his new wife. While maintaining only miscellaneous jobs during the first five years of marriage, he began conducting street meetings in nearby towns in January 1953. His first meeting was held in Mangham, a town of 200, and his audience consisted of less than twenty people. During this period Swaggart studied the great deliverance evangelists of the fifties. He was especially influenced by the healing evangelists that were publicized by Gordon Lindsay's *Voice of Healing* magazine. These included such figures as William Branham*, Jack Coe, Raymond Richey, W. V. Grant, and Jack Moore, pastor of a Pentecostal church in Shreveport. It was Lindsay's popular book on the life of William Branham, *A Man Sent from God,* that convinced Swaggart that he could succeed in the ministry even without a formal education. On 1 January 1958 he entered evangelistic work on a full-time basis.

In the early years of his evangelistic meetings, Swaggart quickly discovered that he could draw notoriety and large crowds by publicly identifying with his cousin, Jerry Lee Lewis. By 1958 Jerry Lee had become a national celebrity and had sold over twenty-five million copies of his first record. When Swaggart applied for ordination with the Louisiana District of the Assemblies of God in 1959, he was initially rejected because of his relationship to Jerry Lee and the opposition of many local pastors to his own rhythmic piano playing and singing that was similar to that of his cousin. The following year he was ordained, but pastoral criticism continued to plague his ministry as he traveled throughout the Southeast ministering in small Assemblies of God churches.

Swaggart began recording gospel albums in 1959. His toe-tapping, hand-clapping piano playing and singing was an immediate favorite with church folks. When Jerry Lee arranged for Swaggart to record his third album in the Sun Records Studio in Memphis, where the greatest rock and roll hits of the fifties were recorded, his record sales skyrocketed. As his record sales increased, the attendance at his evangelistic meetings significantly increased also. In turn, this produced invitations to larger churches. By 1968 he was preaching some of the longest revivals (six to eight weeks) in some of the largest Assemblies of God churches in the country. So successful were his record sales and their influence on his popularity that Swaggart has produced at least one album every year since his first. By 1988 he had produced fifty-four albums and sold over fifteen million records. His record and tape sales by this date exceeded $200 million. The recording industry has crowned him "the best-selling gospel artist in record history."

On 1 January 1969, Swaggart began what was to become his greatest success, ministering through the mass media. On that date he began his radio broadcast, "The Campmeeting Hour," on stations in Atlanta, Houston, and St. Paul. So successful was the program that within five years he had built one of the largest networks of stations in the world. By 1977 his daily program was heard on 600 stations, with the broadcast being repeated as many as 15,000 times a month. As the radio audience grew, his record sales mushroomed, with his albums frequently becoming the top-ranked gospel albums in the nation. With this increased popularity, attendance at his revivals surged, and he was forced out of church buildings and into city auditoriums and coliseums. It was at this time that he changed his revival tactics and began conducting crusades for three-day weekends only.

With momentum on his side, Swaggart quickly moved to start a weekly television program in 1972, and by 1977 he was on over one hundred stations. With finances beginning to flow abundantly, $600,000 to $700,000 per month, he purchased WLUX, Baton Rouge's all-gospel radio station. He was later to purchase radio stations in such cities as Dallas, Houston, Oklahoma City, Pensacola, Florida, and Bowling Green, Ohio. Today his ministry owns and operates eight stations. In May 1981 Swaggart started a daily thirty-minute television program, "A Study of the Word."

By July 1983 Swaggart's weekly television program had become the number one syndicated religious program in America according to the Arbitron ratings and maintained that position until 1988. His daily program had also ascended into the top-ten religious programs by November 1987. In the late 1980s, throughout the United States Swaggart's programs were viewed weekly by an audience of ten to fifteen million, and his worldwide audience was approximately 300 million. His network of over 3,200 television stations in 145 countries was larger than CBS, NBC, and ABC combined. Writing for *Religious Broadcasting* magazine, Swaggart proclaimed his strong belief that the "greatest propagation tool" for world evangelization is television.

With his mushrooming national audience, Swaggart's monthly mail increased from 5,000 letters in 1977 to over 100,000 in 1988. He has had over one million financial contributors, and 500,000 of these support him on a monthly basis. His ministry's yearly income exceeded $150 million. With his income escalating in the 1980s, he built a new $30-million headquarters, including his own television production center and recording studio, located on a 300-acre site in Baton Rouge. In addition, he added a 7,500-seat Family Worship Center, an elementary and secondary academy, and a Bible college with an enrollment in 1988 of

1,500. His new theological seminary opened in the fall of 1988, with plans for a retirement center in the future.

Swaggart has also established Child Care International, the largest parachurch children's ministry in the world, providing basic essentials for more than 450,000 children and their families in fifty countries. It operates sixty-six mobile medical vans or stationary clinics in twenty-six countries servicing over 150,000 people a month. This ministry supports 610 missionaries in 117 countries and also supports 110 Bible colleges. At least six million dollars of his mission support is channeled through the General Council of the Assemblies of God. An integral part of his worldwide outreach in the past decade has been international crusades, the number of which continues to increase.

Over the years a vital part of Swaggart's ministry has been his magazine, the *Evangelist*. Started in 1970 as a flimsy four-page newsletter to advertise his meetings, it has slowly evolved into a high-quality, sixty-four-page monthly publication. It is one of the largest monthly publications produced by any tel-evangelist today. The magazine is presently sent to more than one million homes.

Even with its expanded outreaches, the Swaggart ministry continued in the late 1980s to be built on "old fashioned" Pentecostal revivalism. The crusade meetings have remained the backbone of the ministry, as they also serve as the source for the weekly television programs. Until early 1988 when Swaggart ad-mitted to a "moral lapse" with a prostitute, it would have been safe to assume that his crusade outreach would remain the foundation of his ministry in the short term. However, the historical pattern of televangelists indicates that studio tele-vision productions, the educational enterprise, and missionary endeavors will gradually take center stage as Swaggart ages, if he is successful in maintaining a pub-lic ministry after being disciplined by the Assemblies of God for his "moral lapse."

Whether he can be successful remains an open question. When the denomi-nation's sanctions against Swaggart proved more stringent than what the evan-gelist expected, he announced his intention to ignore them and return to his television ministry after a three month absence. In the meantime, however, the Assemblies of God had taken moves to discipline other of its ordained clergy who remained part of the Swaggart operation. Faced with staff defections, a decline in viewing audience, and a catastrophic drop in contributions, Swaggart faced an uphill struggle to regain his position of prominence at a time when the public itself was increasingly suspicious of the motives and morality of all televangelists. Nevertheless, Swaggart has already achieved a significant place in the history of American revivalism and Pentecostalism.

### Appraisal

Sociologist Jeffrey Hadden and Charles E. Swann, coauthors of *Prime Time Preachers,* claim that the Christian right, powered by TV evangelism, is "des-tined to become the major social movement in America" during the late twentieth century. Agreeing with this assessment, the Reverend Ben Armstrong, president of the National Religious Broadcasters, argues in *The Electric Church* that grass-roots people are "dying for personal religion and traditional values," both of which they feel are received from televangelists. Through the medium of television, Swaggart is perceived by millions of Americans to meet these needs. His expanding audience and growing acceptance are enabling him to influence a significant segment of American Christianity both spiritually and socially.

Swaggart is a fundamentalist Pentecostal who accepts the Bible as the inerrant and infallible Word of God. As a Pentecostal he accepts the spiritual gifts of the New Testament for today and as an Assemblies of God minister adheres to their Articles of Faith, which include an emphasis on holiness of life and pre-millennialism. As an "old-fashioned" Pentecostal evangelist, Swaggart preaches a strict Pentecostal message that focuses primarily on personal holiness/righteousness and worldwide evangelism.

From its inception in 1914, the Assemblies of God as well as most Pentecostals have anticipated Christ's imminent return and have thus maintained that they have little stake in society. Their unique theological distinctive was the baptism in the Holy Spirit, evidenced by speaking in tongues. This baptism, or "enduement with power for service," was closely related to a spirituality that demanded particular expressions of holiness and separation. This relationship with culture is best described in H. Richard Niebuhr's phrase that understood Christ to be "against culture." Swaggart, despite his personal prosperity, represents those who continue to understand Pentecostalism in this eschatological context. These Pentecostals generally identify with traditional concerns for holiness, evangelism, and spirituality.

Like first-generation Pentecostals, Swaggart insists that "separation from the world" is a prerequisite to a valid experience of the Spirit. As a result of this theological position, Swaggart preaches against movies, rock-and-roll music, pornography, drugs, alcohol, smoking, dancing, and most leisurely pursuits. He strongly denounces homosexuality, abortion, and divorce. Using his vast audience, he has even led letter-writing campaigns for specific purposes, such as a campaign against Circle K convenience stores for selling pornographic literature. Swaggart's positions on most social/moral issues are the same as those of the general holiness, fundamentalist, and Pentecostal movements.

Although Swaggart's ministry reaches out to more people in America than does his denomination, the Assemblies of God, with its 2.7 million adherents, he has maintained excellent relations with them. He is deeply loyal to what he perceives its founders intended the Assemblies of God to be. Not since the early 1950s has that denomination embraced a parachurch ministry as it has Swaggart's. Over the years, Swaggart has been very careful to cultivate a warm relation with its leadership and funnels millions of dollars of his missions money through the denomination. The leadership of the Assemblies has acknowledged his influence in their midst by having him as a keynote speaker at their general council. Clearly, no Assemblies of God minister in history has achieved the outreach or prominence of Jimmy Swaggart, and as such, he is an honored son.

It is noteworthy to observe that most of Swaggart's audience is Pentecostal. Jamie Buckingham evaluates his followers as being mostly blue-collar folks who enjoy a bluegrass beat. They are people trapped in the daily confines of work and financial woes, desperately needing someone who comes from where they are and who, they feel, can understand their circumstances. They believe that Swaggart could have been as big as Elvis Presley or the Beatles, but he chose to be a minister. They are proud of him and feel a deep personal loyalty to him.

But that loyalty was challenged after Swaggart confessed his "moral lapse" in the spring of 1988 and was formally disciplined by the Assemblies of God. Swaggart acceded to a three-month period during which he would not appear on his television program or preach in public. Although he, like his fellow televangelists Jim and Tammy Bakker, asked for public forgiveness, he did not immediately regain his former following on his return. It is safe to say that Swaggart will be numbered among the most influential Pentecostal evangelists of the twentieth century, one whose ministry brought much social respectability to the Assemblies of God. But how much greater his influence might have been had he not suffered a "moral lapse" can be a cause only for speculation.

### Survey of Criticism

Viewed by more than ten million Americans a week, Jimmy Swaggart is television's most popular evangelist. Yet as *Time* magazine reports, he is the "most controversial" of all televangelists. Swaggart's frequent outspokenness and condemnation of other religious groups in America have increasingly aroused the criticism of both the national media and church officials. Charges of religious intolerance and bigotry are continuously being leveled at his ministry. John Garvey, in *Commonweal,* expressed alarm at Swaggart's condescending attitude toward those who disagree with his brand of Christianity, especially his lambasting of Jews and mainstream Christians. *Newsweek* magazine headlined an article with the title "Swaggart's One-Edged Sword." The author noted that for Swaggart "the Bible is a one-edged sword designed to smite any religious tradition that does not square with his own brand of Christian fundamentalism." Seldom in the short but influential history of religious broadcasting has a top-ranked televangelist struck out so harshly against other elements of the Christian church, or the religious community of the nation, on a syndicated program.

In an article entitled "King of Honky-Tonk Heaven," *Newsweek* charged Swaggart with being contemptuous of "liturgical religious monstrosities," as he refers to the Roman Catholic Mass and the services of most Protestant denominations. He demeans Catholics as "poor pitiful individuals who think they have enriched themselves spiritually by kissing the pope's ring," and he urges born-again Catholics to leave the church, which he calls a false cult. On one of his recent broadcasts, he declared that Mother Teresa of Calcutta is going to hell unless she has a born-again experience. On another, he flashed gruesome pictures of the Nazis' extermination of the Jews on the television screen and suggested that the Holocaust was caused by the Jews' nonacceptance of Christ.

Swaggart also has reached out to condemn his own Pentecostal brethren by voicing his skepticism about those who claim healings in public meetings. He loudly announces his belief that, according to Kenneth Woodward in *Newsweek,* "most of the time it's not real." Recently a national conference of charismatic Pentecostal leaders gathered, and many of the prominent leaders present shared the supernatural happenings that have occurred in their ministries. Swaggart responded on national television by declaring that most of them had never even seen a miracle. As he wrote in *Evangelus* in September 1987, one of his frequent themes is "that most ministers preach little of the Gospel anymore; they preach some form of humanistic religion."

The contemporary church is not the only part of the Body of Christ that has received condemnation from Swaggart's one-edged sword. He has reached back into the history of the church to claim that, as Kenneth Woodward reported, Augustine "came up with doctrines that cause millions to be lost." He attacks John Calvin as saying "God's foreknowledge is based on predestination and God's will is the cause of all evil."

Several television stations have reacted to Swaggart's attacks. In Boston, Atlanta, and Miami, stations have canceled his programs. In Atlanta even a station owned by fellow television celebrity Pat Robertson* dropped Swaggart's program after he persisted in criticizing Roman Catholics. Church historian Martin Marty, in the *Christian Century,* announced that his response to Swaggart was "an impulse to throw up."

At present, literature that analyzes Swaggart's ministry is scarce. However, as the premier Pentecostal evangelist of the eighties, Swaggart may be forging a constituency that will assure him that position for the remainder of the century. Through the powerful medium of television, he influenced a large audience. For many, Jimmy Swaggart symbolized the strength and vitality of American Pentecostalism in the latter part of the twentieth century.

## Bibliography

### Books by Jimmy Swaggart

(All volumes are published by the Jimmy Swaggart Ministries in Baton Rouge, Louisiana, unless otherwise indicated.)

1976   *The Campmeeting Hour: The Radio Miracle of the 20th Century.*
1977   *To Cross a River.* Plainfield, N.J.: Logos International.
1978   *There's A New Name Written Down in Glory.*
1978   *To the Point.*
1979   *The Great White Throne Judgment.*
1980   *Christ the King: The Life of Christ . . . Four Gospels.*
1980   *Praying in the Spirit.*
1980   *Sinless Perfection.*
1981   *The Balanced Faith Life.*
1981   *The Baptism in the Holy Ghost.*
1981   *The Confession Principle and the Course of Nature.*

1981  *Ere the Lamp Went Out.*
1981  *Four Conditions for Being Included in the Rapture.*
1981  *Paul's Thorn in the Flesh.*
1981  *That Thing.*
1981  *What Satan Can and Cannot Do.*
1981  *Will the Church Go Through the Great Tribulation Period?*
1981  *The Word, the Will, and the Wisdom.*
1982  *Authority of the Believer.*
1982  *Blessed is the Man Who Passeth Through . . . Baca.*
1982  *Dieting, Fasting, Prayer and Exercise.*
1982  *The Future of Planet Earth.*
1982  *God's Plan for You.*
1982  *God's Psychiatry.*
1982  *How to Receive the Baptism in the Holy Spirit.*
1982  *Hyper-Faith: A New Gnosticism?*
1982  *Is Speaking in Tongues Scriptural and Relevant to This Day and Age?*
1982  *Rebellion, Retribution and Redemption.*
1982  *What is the Doctrine of Unconditional Eternal Security?*
1983  *The Prayer of Paul in Prison.*
1983  *Questions and Answers.*
1983  *A Rhetorical Analysis of Selected Television Sermons.*
1984  *Cults.*
1984  *Sodom and Gomorrah.*
1985  *Rape of a Nation.*
1986  *Catholicism and Christianity.*
1987  *Religious Rock 'n Roll.*
1987  *Spiritual High Treason.*
1987  *Straight Answers to Tough Questions.* Brentwood, Tenn.: Wolgemuth and Hyatt.

### Selected Studies about Jimmy Swaggart

Blumhofer, Edith L. "Divided Pentecostals: Bakker vs. Swaggart."*Christian Century,* 103 (6 May 1987): 430–31.

Buckingham, Jamie. "He Points 'em to Heaven." *Logos* 8 (September 1987): 16–20.

———. "Jimmy Swaggart, the Best of Gospel Music and Country Preaching." *Logos* 8 (October 1978): 16–20.

Franzen, J. "Jimmy Swaggart Tops the Charts." *Christian Life* 41 (June 1979): 24–25ff.

Garvey, John. "Truth Flashes: What's Right About Jimmy Swaggart." *Commonweal* 113 (26 December 1986): 677–78.

Lamb, Robert Paul. "Jimmy Swaggart's Ministry." *Charisma* 3 (March 1977): 17–20.

Marty, Martin E. "Onward, Christian Shoulders." *Christian Century* 102 (10 December 1986): 1,135.

Ostling, Richard N. "Offering the Hope of Heaven." *Time* 129 (16 March 1987): 69.

———. "Power, Glory—and Politics." *Time* 127 (17 February 1986): 62–69.

———. "TV's Unholy Row." *Time* 128 (6 April 1987): 60–67.

Woodward, Kenneth L. "King of Honky-Tonk Heaven." *Newsweek* 101 (30 May 1983): 89ff.

———. "Swaggart's One-Edged Sword." *Newsweek* 103 (9 January 1984): 65.

                                                        PAUL G. CHAPPELL

# George W. Truett

George W. Truett was a Southern Baptist preacher. As the minister at First Baptist Church, Dallas, Texas, for forty-seven years, he epitomized both parts of that descriptive phrase. Whereas *preacher* is perhaps the term that best describes what Truett did, *Southern Baptist* most adequately describes what he was. He was a man who saw his life as a calling to preach the gospel, a calling that he originally resisted yet eventually accepted. Truett was a man who avoided controversy and theological argument, yet spoke with a most compelling passion and conviction. It is fitting that a biography of this man is entitled *Prince of the Pulpit* and that in his obituary the *Christian Century* called him a major actor in unifying the Southern Baptist Convention.

## Biography

George W. Truett was born in Hayesville, North Carolina, in May 1867. Along with many of his peers in the Southern Baptist Convention, he was born into a poor farming family. As did the children of most families in the area not in dire poverty, George Truett attended a small private academy in his hometown. Hayesville Academy, under the direction of John Hicks, provided most of the children in the community with their education, for North Carolina in the late 1800s, like most of the South, had a very weak public education system. In fact, Truett's first job on graduation from high school was as a teacher in a one-room public school just across the state line in Towns County, Georgia. The entire school year at this educational establishment, entrusted to the care of an eighteen year old just out of high school, was three months. A private academy was not, therefore, a luxury but a necessity for those families seriously interested in their children's education.

It was during his time teaching in Towns County that Truett was converted. The conversion, which occurred in 1886 in the church he had attended all of his life, did not produce a tremendous change in the life of the nineteen-year-old Truett. It did not mean a turning away from a dissolute life, for his life had not been of that nature. During a revival, Truett felt moved by the Scripture reading for one sermon, which was "the just shall live by faith; and if any man draw back, my soul shall have no pleasure in him." Truett was struck by both the promise and the judgment in the text. He felt truly called by God, yet wondered about his willingness not to draw back. The day following the service Truett spent the morning cross-examining himself as to whether he was willing to allow Christ to have complete control over his life. As he answered "yes" to each question he addressed to himself, he felt able to respond to the call that night.

Shortly after his conversion, Truett had the first opportunity to exercise publicly those gifts that made him a renowned preacher. At the Wednesday night prayer meeting following his baptism, Truett was surprised to hear the minister call on him to exhort the congregation to turn to Christ. Despite his surprise, Truett took up the challenge and began to exhort the members of the congregation, moving up and down the aisles. Suddenly he felt that he was making a spectacle of himself and sat down feeling humiliated and ashamed. Despite his perception of his behavior, however, for months afterward those who had been in the church that day would turn to him with the question, "Oughtn't you give yourself to the preaching of the Gospel?"

At that time in his life Truett did not intend to do so. His desire was to become a lawyer. However, his immediate goal was the founding of a private academy in north Georgia in order to educate the poor mountain children of the area. With the encouragement of his cousin Fernando C. McConnell, the Baptist minister in Towns County, Truett founded Hiawassee Academy in 1887 and served as its principal until 1889. By that time the school had grown to 300 students and had been incorporated into the Georgia Baptist Convention as part of its work among the state's highlanders.

It was at a meeting of the Georgia Baptist Convention that Truett's speaking ability first was likened to Charles Haddon Spurgeon's—a comparison that others would make throughout his life. At that meeting McConnell, who was speaking about the impact Mercer University was having on the state and on education in the state, called on Truett to speak on the work that several Mercer graduates were undertaking at Hiawassee Academy. Truett's talk not only spurred the convention in its support of the mountain schools but also led a wealthy layman to offer to pay Truett's expenses to attend Mercer University.

Truett, however, never attended Mercer University. In the summer of 1889 he left Georgia to be with his family, which had moved to a farm in Texas. In the fall of that year he finally started his college education at Grayson Junior College in Whitewright, Texas. Truett also took an active role in the Baptist Church of Whitewright, where he served as superintendent of the Sunday School and occasionally preached on Sundays when the pastor was away. Although Truett enjoyed these duties and felt they were part of his Christian obligation, he retained his desire to enter the law. These plans were radically altered on a Saturday in 1890 when during a church conference—which Truett admitted to having been surprisingly well attended—the eldest deacon moved that the church call a presbytery to ordain George W. Truett as a gospel minister. Truett was shocked by this event and resisted the call. The congregation unanimously approved the motion, however, along with another calling for Truett to be examined the next morning and to receive his ordination at the Sunday service. Through the entire day and night, Truett struggled with this occurrence and—aided by the advice of his mother, who reminded him that they were godly people who had seen fit to call him—became convinced that it was indeed the will of God that he be ordained. Accepting this call, George W. Truett received his ordination to the ministry from the Baptist Church of Whitewright, Texas. Following his ordination, Truett continued in his studies at Grayson Junior College and served as a supply preacher at churches throughout the area. These activities ended abruptly when Truett was called to an important task—one most surprising to be handed to one so young.

Baylor University, the first college chartered in the state of Texas and the pride of the Texas Baptist Convention, was heavily in debt. At the convention's annual meeting in 1890 it became necessary to find a new financial agent for the university, one who, it was hoped, could free Baylor from this crushing debt. At the close of the convention all those in attendance were charged to pray that God would lead them to the right man to guide Baylor out of its financial straits. One of those present was R. F. Jenkins, Truett's pastor at Whitewright Baptist Church. Throughout all of his prayers it seemed to Jenkins that the face of Truett constantly came before him. Soon he became convinced that Truett was the man to raise the funds, despite the fact that he was only twenty-three years old and practically unknown in the Texas Baptist Convention. Jenkins wrote to Dr. B. H. Carroll, who had been commissioned to find the new financial agent, suggesting that Truett was the man for whom they were looking. In his letter he stated, "There is one thing I know about George W. Truett—wherever he speaks the people do what he asks them to do." Carroll, evidently moved by the letter, wrote Truett asking for a meeting. At that meeting he asked Truett to take the position. Truett requested time to consider the matter and returned home. On returning home Truett fell seriously ill, and it was feared he would die. It was nearly two months after his interview with Carroll that he finally was able to accept the position, pending approval by the university's trustees.

Truett traveled to Waco to meet with Carroll and the trustees, who were surprised to see the new financial agent as a youngster of twenty-three still showing the effects of his illness. Before anyone could raise strenuous objections to his appointment, Truett asked them to hear him out. He stated that he had first rejected the position but that after taking the offer under prayerful consideration became convinced that it was God's will that he accept this obligation. The trustees, evidently impressed by the young man's words, approved his appointment and ended the meeting with prayerful support of Truett in this endeavor. He did not disappoint them. Less than two years after he began as financial agent for Baylor University the debt was retired. Truett's speaking was such that the people did indeed do what he asked them.

It is strange that the savior of a college should next enroll there as a student, but that was what George Truett did. In September 1893 he entered Baylor University as a freshman. While at Baylor, Truett served as pastor at East Waco Baptist Church. He also married. His wife was Josephine Jenkins, the daughter of a judge and trustee of the university. It was a most fortuitous match for Truett. Mrs. Truett's intelligence and capabilities made it possible for him to become the denominational and religious leader that he was. Her organizational abilities freed Truett to devote his time and effort to his professional work.

On graduation from Baylor, Truett took over as full-time pastor at East Waco Church. Many other churches had offered him a position on graduation, but he refused all of them. The people in Waco had supported the Truetts during his college years, he and his wife had many attachments to the community, and they desired to remain where they were. It was, however, not to be. In the summer following his graduation, against his objections, Truett received a call from the First Baptist Church of Dallas. After meeting with the congregation and the deacons, he eventually agreed to accept the position. Truett remained there as pastor until his death in 1944. For forty-seven years he ministered to that church. During that time he emerged as one of the great preachers of the day and was compared to such orators as William Jennings Bryan*, Harry Emerson Fosdick*, and Charles Haddon Spurgeon.

During his long tenure in Dallas, Truett probably filled the pulpit only half the time. He was under constant demand as an evangelist and speaker. Every summer he spent several weeks ministering to the cowboys of West Texas. During World War I he spent six months preaching to the soldiers of the American Expeditionary Force in Europe. He served three terms as president of the Southern Baptist Convention, guiding the denomination after the collapse of a major fund-raising drive, the defalcation of the treasurer of the Home Mission Board, and the struggles over evolution, modernism, and biblical criticism. Truett, in his position as vice-president of the Baptist World Alliance, replaced the ailing Edgar Y. Mullins when the alliance met in Toronto in 1929, and he was elected to its presidency at its meeting in Berlin in 1934. Because of the obligations resulting from this position, he spent six months visiting Baptists around the world in 1935.

Truett was a man of peace and presided over the 1939 meeting of the Baptist World Alliance when it held its quadrennial meeting in Atlanta. He not only presided over a racially integrated conference but also led the alliance in expressing a wish for world peace. Peace, however, was not in the air, and his commitment to the Baptist principles of soul freedom and liberty of conscience led Truett to be quite vocal in his opposition to Hitler's Germany and in his support for England.

## Appraisal

In many ways it is difficult to speak of any substantive appraisal of George Truett. He was rare among men of action in that his work and struggles achieved results without creating enemies and critics. At most it might be said that he was disliked by J. Frank Norris*, who once called him a modernist, although this hostility was probably engendered as much by Truett's commitment to the Southern Baptist Convention and his continued support for Baylor University than by any substantive reasons. One might even suggest that Norris' attacks on Truett—a man universally liked and admired—helped to bring about Norris' downfall.

Truett should be remembered as a pastor and preacher, for that is what he indeed was. He ministered to his congregation, to his denomination, and to the world. He did not claim to be a theologian and published no books on religious topics beyond collections of his sermons and talks. He was not a controversialist, feeling as he said in one sermon that religious debates were "pesky and inexcusable." Truett had a compassion and sincerity that made him a great pastor, and an ability to communicate that sincerity that made him a great preacher. Many stories about Truett dwell on his constant attempts to minister to his fellow human beings. This element of his life often is ignored because of his preaching ability and his denominational leadership. It is also a very interesting element of a man who was quite reserved in his demeanor—there was a rumor that he never smiled. Though Truett thought that a minister should not spend his time running all over town making social calls when he should be in his study preparing his sermons, he also felt that the preacher should go whenever and wherever he was needed.

Truett's sincerity and decency also served him well as a denominational leader. When he was elected president of the Southern Baptist Convention in 1927 many doubted his ability to control the unruly denomination. Yet it was indeed his fairness and decency that enabled him to do so, with less than the usual number of disagreements and conflicts. Truett's ability as a presiding officer rested not in any mastery of the rules of order—which he lacked—but in the fact that everyone assumed that his decisions were fair and honest. His success as president is attested to by the fact that he was reelected to the position in 1928 and again in 1929. It was this spirit, along with his preaching ability, that led to Truett's election to the presidency of the Baptist World Alliance in 1934.

Truett must also be remembered for his steadfast belief in the principles of religious liberty and the freedom of conscience. Although Truett spoke on the importance of the separation of church and state throughout his career, his most important address on the subject was delivered in Washington, D.C., in May 1920 during the annual meeting of the Southern Baptist Convention. An estimated 15,000 people heard Truett give his address, "Baptists and Religious Liberty," from the east steps of the Capitol. Along with his friend and colleague Joseph Martin Dawson, Truett was a leader in preaching the gospel of religious liberty and in proclaiming the importance of the Baptist genius of soul freedom. Simultaneously, however, Truett remained uniquely and unashamedly a Baptist and wished that all would become Baptists. This intense religious passion and sincerity, combined with an unbroken decency and concern for people, are what fundamentally set Truett apart. It was this decency and concern that drew people to him and that made them receptive to his message, whether he was preaching, raising funds, or consoling the bereaved.

Perhaps Truett's most important activity was his opposition to the fundamentalist forces in the Texas Baptist Convention. Whereas Truett believed in the virgin birth, God's creation of Adam, and a literal resurrection, he refused to support attempts to pass laws prohibiting the teaching of evolution in Texas schools as well as attempts to purge Baylor University of so-called modernists and evolutionists. This opposition was what led Frank Norris to claim that Truett was a "modernist" himself. Truett's commitment to the denomination throughout this period, both in Texas and nationally, helped the Southern Baptist Convention to survive without a schism the conflicts over the issues of evolution, biblical criticism, and modernism.

## Survey of Criticism

About George W. Truett one can honestly say that when it comes to criticism, there is nothing to survey. Nearly everything written about Truett both during his life and after is favorable. He was a very popular figure during his time. Articles about him appeared in *Collier's, American Review of Reviews, Time,* and *Newsweek.* He was a man about whom people wrote using anecdotes, consisting of stories of sinners saved, talks delivered, or condolences offered. Both magazine writers and his biographers were especially intrigued by his yearly sojourn among the West Texas cowboys, who during the annual cattle roundup became Truett's congregation.

The major biography of Truett was written by his son-in-law Powhatan W. James. Entitled simply *George W. Truett: A Biography,* it supplies all the anecdotal information that appears in other articles and books. Whereas it and Joe W. Burton's *Prince of the Pulpit* are filled with praise for Truett, so are all the contemporary magazine articles about him. Even Edgar DeWitt Jones, in his *American Preachers of Today,* remarked that there were practically no critical opinions of Truett, with the exception of that offered by Frank Norris. He wrote this with a tone of surprise, for though he evidently admired all of the subjects of his book, he was quite aware that they all had their share of detractors.

Truett's books are all collections of sermons or talks he delivered in the course of his career. The two most important of these are probably *A Quest for Souls* and *God's Call to America.* The former, consisting of a series of revival sermons, provides a fine example of Truett's sermon style. The latter, which includes Truett's "Baptists and Religious Liberty," illustrates his attitudes toward political and social issues.

All of the books are derived from shorthand accounts of his sermons, for Truett did not preach from prepared manuscripts. Read, they are good sermons but not great ones. Heard from the lips of Truett, they are transformed into greatness. Many of Truett's sermons exist on record, and to listen to the man preach is an exciting and illuminating experience. The written word cannot and does not convey the power of his sermonizing. His sermons lack the cadences and rhythms of those of Billy Graham* or Oral Roberts*. They draw the hearer in, rather than overwhelming the listener with passion, and soon the hearer is immersed in a sermonic experience very different from the norm. It is only by hearing Truett that one can truly understand the source of his reputation as a preacher.

## Bibliography

### Books by George W. Truett

1913   *The Supper of Our Lord.* Dallas: B. J. Robert Book Company
1915   *We Would See Jesus, and Other Sermons.* New York: Fleming H. Revell.

1920   *Baptists and Religious Liberty*. Nashville: Sunday School Board of the Southern Baptist Convention.

1923   *God's Call to America and Other Addresses Comprising Special Orations Delivered on Widely Varying Occasions*. Philadelphia: Judson Press.

1929   *These Gracious Years*. New York: R. R. Smith.

1939   *The Baptist Message and Mission for the World Today*. Nashville: Sunday School Board of the Southern Baptist Convention.

1944   *Follow Thou Me*. Nashville: Broadman Press.

1945   *Christmas Messages*. Chicago: Moody Press.

1945   *A Quest for Souls*. Nashville: Broadman Press.

1946   *Some Vital Questions*. Grand Rapids: Eerdmans.

1947   *Sermons from Paul*. Grand Rapids: Eerdmans.

1948   *The Prophet's Mantle*. Grand Rapids: Eerdmans.

1950   *The Inspiration of Ideals*. Grand Rapids: Eerdmans.

1952   *Who is Jesus?* Grand Rapids: Eerdmans.

1953   *On Eagle Wings*. Grand Rapids: Eerdmans.

1954   *After His Likeness*. Grand Rapids: Eerdmans.

1957   *The Salt of the Earth*. Grand Rapids: Eerdmans.

1959   *Revival Sermons*. Dallas: Evangel Press.

1969   *Fifty Years of Preaching at the Palace*. Grand Rapids: Zondervan.

n.d.   *The Leaf and the Life, an Address Delivered at St. Paul, Minn., May 23, 1902*. Philadelphia: American Baptist Publication Society.

### Selected Studies about George W. Truett

Brannon, Richard S. "George W. Truett and His Preaching." Th.D. diss., Southwestern Baptist Theological Seminary, 1956.

————. "George W. Truett: Evangelist." Master's thesis, Southern Baptist Theological Seminary, 1954.

Burton, Joe. *Prince of the Pulpit: A Pen Picture of George W. Truett at Work*. Grand Rapids: Zondervan Publishing House, 1946.

James, Powhatan W. *George W. Truett: A Biography*. New York: Macmillan, 1939.

Jones, Edgar Dewitt. *American Preachers of To-Day*. Indianapolis: Bobbs-Merrill, 1933.

EDWARD L. QUEEN II

# Jim Wallis

Since the early 1970s, in an era characterized by the identification of evangelicals with the political Right, Jim Wallis, a leader of the Sojourners community in Washington, D.C., and editor of a magazine by the same name, has sought to dispel the notion that conservative evangelical faith leads ineluctably to conservative politics. Wallis sees himself in what he called in *Revive Us Again* "the historical stream of radical Christian orthodoxy," a tradition that places him at odds with most American evangelicals.

## Biography

Jim Wallis was born on 4 June 1948 into a Plymouth Brethren household in Redford Township, Michigan, just outside of Detroit. In his autobiography,

*Revive Us Again: A Sojourner's Story,* Wallis recalls the childhood influences
of church, summer Bible camp, and an itinerant evangelist, A. P. Gibbs, who
taught him the value of studying the Scriptures. Wallis was "saved" at age six,
and until the age of thirteen he was the perfect son—an athlete, Boy Scout,
leader in student government and in church activities—a child who reflected his
parents' deeply held beliefs in God and in the goodness and righteousness of
America.

At thirteen, as he wrote in *Revive Us Again,* "the world I had grown up in
went sour on me." His family moved to Southfield, an upper-middle-class suburb
of Detroit. Wallis became sullen and withdrawn. He grew cynical and disre-
spectful of teachers and all authority figures; he dropped out of the Boy Scouts
just short of attaining the rank of Eagle Scout; he quit organized sports, allowed
his hair to grow long, and attended dances, thereby violating one of the taboos
of his religious upbringing. Although he eventually grew out of his overt rebelliousness, he remained introverted and vaguely discomfited by the appurte-
nances of his upper-middle-class surroundings.

In 1967, the summer of racial disturbances in Detroit, Wallis' uneasiness
focused on the problem of racism. He began to ask questions of his parents, his
church, and his faith: Why were whites rich and blacks poor? Why did the white
Christians he knew have so little to do with blacks, despite their dedication to
sending missionaries to darkest Africa? Wallis ventured into Detroit's inner city
and found, to his surprise, black congregations of Plymouth Brethren. He read
such books as *My Friend, the Enemy* by William Pannell, a young leader in
black Plymouth Brethren assemblies, Charles Silberman's *Crisis in Black and
White,* and *The Autobiography of Malcolm X.* "I was beginning to see," he
wrote later in *Revive Us Again,* "that to stand with those who suffered I would
have to shed myself of the assumptions of privilege and comfort on which I had
been raised." When he took his concerns to his church, however, Wallis met
with defensiveness, resistance, or worse, indifference.

Wallis' growing impatience with what he considered the hypocrisy of evangelicalism on the issue of racism led to a total rupture with the church over the
Vietnam War, which he regarded as merely an extension of America's racism
and callousness toward the poor. He believed that the United States, he wrote
in *Revive Us Again,* was "a large and powerful nation trying to impose its control
over the destiny of a small nation, and falling into the unspeakable brutality of
attempting to destroy a people it could not master." As a student at Michigan
State University, Wallis became a leader in protests against American policies
in Southeast Asia, the "search and destroy" missions, the My Lai massacre,
and the invasion of Cambodia.

What were evangelicals doing in the face of an ignominious war abroad and
repression at home, symbolized in the killing of four students at Kent State
University? Nothing, Wallis concluded. Campus Crusade leaders at Michigan
State believed that the Communists should be blown off the map, and the representatives from InterVarsity Christian Fellowship, Wallis says, never could

make up their minds. On the other hand, Wallis found that some of the more liberal campus ministers expressed sympathy for the protests, but he sensed that their faith did not really inform their views, that opposition to the war, as he recalled in *Revive Us Again*, "seemed more a student activity to be involved in than a clear and public demonstration of Christian conscience."

By 1968, after the assassinations of Martin Luther King, Jr.*, whom Wallis considered "probably the greatest political leader produced by America in the twentieth century," and Robert F. Kennedy, "the only elected official in whom I placed any hope," Wallis was "ready to commit the rest of my life to resisting the system that oppressed the poor at home and killed them in Vietnam," he wrote in *Revive Us Again*. As the fervor of the student movement dissipated in the early seventies, Wallis turned back to the New Testament, particularly to the Sermon on the Mount, and found there a biblical warrant for his own concerns about justice. The twenty-fifth chapter of Matthew prompted his real religious conversion, he insists. "I was deeply struck by a God who had taken up residence among the poor, the oppressed, the outcasts," Wallis wrote. "How much we love Jesus, this passage tells us, is determined by how much we serve those who are at the bottom of society."

He wanted to learn more about the Bible, so in the fall of 1970 he enrolled at Trinity Evangelical Divinity School, a conservative evangelical seminary in the affluent Bannockburn section of Deerfield, Illinois. At Trinity, he recalled in *Revive Us Again,* Wallis found a handful of kindred spirits interested in "recovering the prophetic biblical tradition, the authentic evangelical message, and applying it to our historical situation." This group organized itself as the People's Christian Coalition, which in turn formed the core of what would eventually become Sojourners Fellowship. At the seminary, however, their call for "radical discipleship," based on intensive study of the New Testament, met with resistance from administration, faculty, and even fellow students. Wallis and his radical confreres quickly became known as the Bannockburn Seven; they passed out leaflets on the campus, conducted various demonstrations, and held a forum each week on such issues as the war, militarism, discrimination against women, and racism.

They survived various attempts by the seminary to expel or silence them, and Wallis and his friends soon found that their message of radical Christian discipleship resonated with other evangelicals far beyond Deerfield, Illinois. During the summer of 1971 they began work on the first issue of the *Post-American*, a magazine that propagated their understanding of the New Testament, so named, Wallis noted in *Revive Us Again,* because it "tried to put forward a Christian faith that broke free of the prevailing American civil religion." The *Post-American,* a sixteen-page tabloid, rolled off the presses in August, advertising an annual subscription price of "two dollars or whatever you can afford." As the *Post-American* began to appear quarterly, the sense of cohesion and shared interests among the people who published it evolved into a Christian community among the poor in the Rogers Park section of Chicago.

Although that initial community dissolved within two years, Wallis and a handful of others regrouped and moved to Washington, D.C., not, he insists, to be near the center of political power, but because of friends already there and the opportunity the city offered to live among the poor. With that relocation in the fall of 1975, the magazine changed its name from *Post-American* to *Sojourners,* and the community of eighteen adults and two children took the name Sojourners Fellowship. In the years since, Sojourners Fellowship has addressed the needs of the poor in its neighborhood for housing, health and child care, and resistance to gentrification.

From his base in the Sojourners Fellowship, Wallis maintains an exacting regimen of writing, travel, and speaking engagements. His casual, almost phlegmatic demeanor belies his intensity and a determination born of self-assurance. Yet, amid the demands of his schedule and an ascetic lifestyle (Wallis did not marry until he was nearly forty), he insists that the community in Washington provides him both intellectual stimulation and spiritual sustenance.

*Sojourners* magazine, under Wallis' direction, reflects the concerns of the community that produces it. Though it retains much of the fervor and criticism of American culture found in the *Post-American, Sojourners* has propounded a rather eclectic mix of Christian spirituality and activism. Influences on Wallis and *Sojourners* include figures as diverse as St. Francis of Assisi, Dorothy Day*, Dietrich Bonhoeffer, Thomas Merton*, Clarence Jordan, William Stringfellow, Jacques Ellul, John R. W. Stott, Henri Nouwen, John Howard Yoder, and liberation theologians such as Gustavo Gutierrez.

*Sojourners,* with a circulation in excess of 50,000, carries articles about political issues that, the editors believe, merit the attention and involvement of evangelical Christians. Repressive regimes in South Korea, the Philippines, South Africa, and elsewhere regularly receive notice in the magazine. *Sojourners* has decried U.S. policies in Central America, corporate exploitation of third world nations, and American complicity in supporting right-wing dictators. Wallis acknowledges a personal debt to Dorothy Day and the Catholic Worker movement, and the magazine occasionally carries articles about labor issues, such as the struggle to organize textile workers in the South or in developing countries. World hunger, Wallis believes, represents an affront to the gospel and a rebuke to Christians, particularly to American Christians in their comfortable complacency.

One of the primary issues to engage Wallis' attention in recent years has been nuclear proliferation and U.S. defense spending. Wallis and the Sojourners community often demonstrate against the arms race, and they have prepared various study guides to apprise American Christians about the issue. Each spring as the income tax deadline approaches, *Sojourners* runs an article that urges resistance or civil disobedience on the "war tax," the percentage of an individual's income tax that goes toward defense spending. *Sojourners* also carried an interview with Billy Graham*, in the course of which he effectively recanted the Cold War rhetoric that had characterized his early career as an evangelist and called for nuclear disarmament.

Although Wallis' politics generally place him at odds with the religious Right—Jerry Falwell* once likened him to Adolf Hitler—Wallis rejects political labels, insisting that his ideas are shaped by his understanding of the New Testament rather than by political ideologies. Senator Mark O. Hatfield (R.–Oreg.) was an early supporter of Wallis and remains a contributing editor to *Sojourners,* as does Daniel Berrigan*, a Catholic priest and antiwar activist. One example of Wallis' political unorthodoxy centers on abortion. When *Sojourners* addressed the question, the editors agreed with the religious Right that abortion was morally reprehensible, but they urged a closer look at some of the ghetto conditions that give rise to abortions and sought to link opposition to abortion to such other issues that undermine human dignity as capital punishment, poverty, and nuclear proliferation. (Joseph Cardinal Bernardin, archbishop of Chicago, advocated this notion of linkage some time later.)

### Appraisal

Despite general agreement with the religious Right on the matter of abortion, Jim Wallis, whom *Time* once numbered among a select group of young leaders in America, has been swimming against the stream of popular evangelicalism for all of his adult life. His own spiritual pilgrimage took him from "cultural evangelicalism" to antiwar activism to a mature faith that blends fidelity to conservative orthodoxy with a genuine compassion mandated by his understanding of the New Testament. Such advocacy has placed him at odds with Protestant liberals, who distrust his evangelical theology, and with many evangelicals, who abhor his willingness to use Marxist categories of analysis and who feel threatened by Wallis' condemnation of an evangelical theology skewed by American consumerism and white, upper-middle-class sensibilities.

But Wallis, standing, he believes, in the tradition of the Hebrew prophets, has reached beyond the condemnations that characterized the early years of the *Post-American.* He has leavened his calls for social justice with invitations for renewal within the church; indeed, he sees the two as inseparable, and he has drawn increasingly on Catholic spirituality in recent years as a source of his own spiritual inspiration. Such eclecticism has deepened the suspicions that many evangelicals already harbored about him and his radical views, but although Wallis represents a minority impulse in American evangelicalism, he and the Sojourners community have attracted a substantial following of evangelical Christians chary about the easy identification of Christianity with American culture.

### Survey of Criticism

Little has been written about Wallis. In his book *The Young Evangelicals: Revolution in Orthodoxy,* however, Richard Quebedeaux identified Jim Wallis and the People's Christian Coalition as part of an emerging cadre of what he called young evangelicals. Quebedeaux cited Wallis' efforts to disassociate true, biblical Christianity from American civil religion. In a subsequent work, *The Worldly Evangelicals,* Quebedeaux labeled Wallis "the most eminent young evangelical leader."

In a profile of *Sojourners* in *Religious Periodicals of the United States: Academic and Scholarly Journals,* David Kling emphasized the magazine's assault on establishment Protestantism, both liberal and conservative, and its search for a "transcendent vision" that restored the prophetic dimension to Christian theology. Kling also cited the magazine's financial independence from any constituency other than its readers as a measure of its theological integrity.

### Bibliography

#### Books by Jim Wallis

1976    *Agenda for Biblical People.* San Francisco: Harper and Row.
1981    *The Call to Conversion.* San Francisco: Harper and Row.
1982    *Waging Peace: A Handbook for the Struggle to Abolish Nuclear Weapons.* San Francisco: Harper and Row.
1983    *Peacemakers: Christian Voices from the New Abolitionist Movement.* San Francisco: Harper and Row.
1983    *Revive Us Again: A Sojourner's Story.* Nashville: Abingdon Press.
1984    *Agenda for Biblical People.* New ed. San Francisco: Harper and Row.

#### Selected Studies about Jim Wallis

Kling, David. *"Sojourners."* In *Religious Periodicals of the United States: Academic and Scholarly Journals,* edited by Charles H. Lippy. Westport, Conn.: Greenwood Press, 1986.
Quebedeaux, Richard. *The Worldly Evangelicals.* New York: Harper and Row, 1978.
————. *The Young Evangelicals: Revolution in Orthodoxy.* New York: Harper and Row, 1974.

RANDALL BALMER

# Alan Watts

From Puritanism to such homegrown groups as Mormonism and Christian Science, dissident religions have always found a refuge and breeding ground in the United States. For the most part, the dissidents have belonged to the wider family of Christianity, but shortly after World War II a dramatic shift occurred as Oriental religions began to deeply penetrate the native culture. The war had fostered interest in the East, and with Mao Tse-tung's conquest of China and the later Indo-Chinese conflicts, the East became firmly rooted in the American sphere of influence and consciousness. A fascinating aspect of this expansion of horizons was the burgeoning interest in Taoism and Zen Buddhism. First catching seed among the beatniks of the fifties, by the early seventies these faiths had become pervasive cultural influences, figuring in everything from the Human Potential Movement to Robert Pirsig's best-selling *Zen and the Art of Motorcycle*

*Maintenance* (1974). Arguably, the key person in this popularization of Zen and Taoism was Alan Watts, a guru to the counterculture of the fifties and sixties and a man who made a career out of lecturing and writing on these two faiths.

## Biography

Alan Watts was born on 6 January 1915 in Chislehurst, a rural town on the outskirts of London. A precocious child with a taste for the mysterious, he early on showed a love for the "exotic" Orient that was to characterize his whole life. As a boy he was enamored of the Orientalia with which his mother had decorated their home, and by age eleven he was stoking his imagination on such tales as Sax Rohmer's thrillers about the inscrutable Dr. Fu Manchu. Increasingly bored with what he later labeled, in *In My Own Way,* "the boiled beef culture of England" and feeling oppressed by his mother's strict fundamentalism, he next began to explore Eastern religion as an alternative approach to life. It was not long before he took to the practice of yoga and meditation; and two years before graduating from King's College, Canterbury—one of England's premier public schools—he even took the step of declaring himself a Buddhist. About the same time he started frequently to visit London, where he was taken under the wing of Christmas Humphreys, the director of the London Buddhist Lodge— the center of Buddhism in England. As an adolescent, Watts was sophisticated and cosmopolitan beyond his years.

On completion of his schooling in 1932, Watts took a job as a fund-raiser for a group of London hospitals and threw himself into the life of the lodge. Soon he was moving in the circles of England's elite Buddhists and Theosophists and meeting such international luminaries as Krishnamurti and D. T. Suzuki. By 1936, after the publication of a number of pamphlets and articles, Watts had become so well respected that he was appointed an editor of the journal of the lodge. Next came two books, *The Spirit of Zen* (1936) and *The Legacy of Asia and Western Man* (1937), which set forth the Taoist and Zen principles that were to form the core of his mature thought. These two faiths hold that the apprehension of ultimate reality and the experience of mystical insight lie in surrendering the ego, with its disruptive passions and fears and its propensity to interpret existence through the categories of discursive thought. Whereas each also stresses the practice of quiet meditation, Taoism held an additional appeal for Watts in its doctrine of yin-yang—that there are two opposite and comple- mentary forces in nature, with spiritual and physical health to be won by living in a state of balance between them. With these beliefs Watts thought he had found a remedy for the alienation of modern man who, he judged, had fallen out of harmony with his subjective and spiritual depths.

In 1938 Watts married Eleanor Everett, an American Buddhist who along with her mother had studied Zen in Japan. The daughter of a wealthy lawyer, Eleanor was easily able to support her husband in a very comfortable manner, as well as to finance the move they made to New York later the same year. There Watts studied for a time with Sokei-an Sasaki, a leading missionary for

Rinzai, and was soon enjoying the company of some of New York's more impressive intellectuals, musicians, and artists. He also published *The Meaning of Happiness* (1940), a work that made clear the panentheism he had learned from Hinduism and that argued that happiness is not a future and heavenly reward for the good, but a present reality for those who spiritualize their lives and live in harmony with nature. Meanwhile Watts' wife, paradoxically, had become severely depressed, and he decided that a career and a more conventional lifestyle might help matters. He settled on the priesthood and entered the Episcopalian seminary of Seabury-Western in Chicago, where he experimented with what he called the "square" life of middle-class America. Ordained to the ministry in 1945, he was assigned to the chaplaincy at Northwestern University, where he became an immediate cult figure with the students, largely because he enlivened the liturgy with such exotic features as Gregorian chant and Renaissance polyphony and made his home and hospitality easily available to all. Watts also entered into a phase of energetically trying to synthesize his Oriental beliefs with his Christian vocation. The result, in *Behold the Spirit* (1947) and *The Supreme Identity* (1950), was a turn to the "Philosophia Perennis," the view of Aldous Huxley and others that Christianity, as all religions, is but one cultural adaptation of a universal set of spiritual insights and convictions.

This mood of reconciliation began to crack when in 1950 Watts' wife had their marriage annulled and reported to his bishop that her husband was an adulterer. His career severely hurt, Watts resigned his ministry and retreated to a farm in New York. There he went to work on *The Wisdom of Insecurity* (1951), a book that reflected a turn against organized religion and propounded the Taoist paradox that the realities of religion could be discovered only in the immediacy of experience, after the abandonment of any effort to fix them in creeds. Watts was entering a more militantly Eastern period of his life, and in 1951, after remarrying, he moved to San Francisco, where he had been offered a job at the newly founded American Academy of Asian Studies. There he found a ready audience for his philosophy and did well enough that in 1953 the financially troubled academy gave him the institution's main administrative responsibilities. The same year also saw the appearance of *Myth and Ritual in Christianity* which, influenced by the thoughts of Jung and Coomaraswamy, presented a mythological interpretation of Christianity that set aside the religion's historical claims as irrelevant.

Fatiguing of the responsibilities of his job, in 1956 Watts retired from the AAAS to devote himself to the life of what in *In My Own Way* he called a "philosophical entertainer," a free-lance speaker and writer. The time was ripe, for America was going through what *Time* on 4 February 1957 referred to as a "Buddhist boomlet." The roots of this boomlet lay with the beats who, in their rebellion against middle-class conformism, had turned to Zen as a legitimation for their seemingly natural and spontaneous lifestyle. Soon it had become a full-scale movement as, from the nightclubs of Greenwich Village to the coffee-houses of Venice West, the new ideas began to percolate up into mainstream society, along with bongos, jazz and talk of "hepcats." Even the comic strip "Popeye" gained a Zen-like beat character, as did the popular radio soap opera "Helen Trent." On a more literary level, fame was being won by poets and writers such as Allen Ginsberg, Lawrence Ferlinghetti, and Jack Kerouac, who were developing improvisational styles of writing that, they hoped, would be intuitive and unmediated by reason.

Although Watts himself was not a beat, he rode this Zen wave to the heights of popularity. By the late fifties he had a radio program in five cities, was lecturing in about one hundred cities a year, and, in addition to his many individual appearances on television, had put together a twenty-six-program series for National Educational Television titled "Eastern Wisdom and Modern Life." He also came out with the most sophisticated of his introductions to Zen and Taoism, *The Way of Zen* (1957), and an extremely influential article, "Beat Zen, Square Zen, and Zen" (1958), in which he dissociated himself from the more frivolous Zen of the beats. Here he warned that before converting to Zen, a westerner had to come to terms with the dictatorial Christian God, otherwise his Zen risked turning into either petulant rebellion or a new form of disciplined religion. This rebellion Watts labeled "Beat Zen," which he identified with shiftlessness and laziness in conduct and such caprice in art as John Cage's silent piano recitals and Jack Kerouac's "spontaneous prose." The disciplined alternative he labeled "Square Zen," because it bypassed the liberating aspect of Zen in imitation of the Japanese monastic tradition with its highly regimented search for enlightenment. For his own part Watts proposed the Zen of "No Fuss," an accepting approach to existence that is free from the anxieties, roles, and fears of conventional life. This would be, as the philosopher William Barrett judged in an 18 December 1960 *New York Times* book review, "a tranquilizing doctrine if one could master it." Watts believed that one could, and in *Nature, Man, and Woman* (1958) and in later books that evinced a strengthening Taoist streak, he further elaborated the view that one should live in harmony with the underlying rhythm of nature and in tune with one's tastes, moods, and sexual urges.

Watts' own mood by the beginning of the sixties had become one of dissatisfaction. He was increasingly unhappy with his wife, drinking heavily, and feeling suffocated by what in *In My Own Way* he parodied as "suburban dormitory culture." Consequently in 1961 he left his wife for his mistress, Jano Yates, whom he soon married, and he moved with her to the more exotic home of the decommissioned ferryboat the SS *Vallejo* in Sausalito. He also took a new turn with his work. Since the late fifties Watts had been experimenting with psychedelic drugs, at first under the supervision of a psychiatrist and then with Richard Alpert and Timothy Leary at Harvard. He came to see drugs as a means of expanding the consciousness and of liberating the self from socially generated patterns of thought and awareness. The result of these insights was *The Joyous Cosmology* (1962), which continued the endeavor of Aldous Huxley's *The Doors of Perception* by describing the psychedelic experience in bright colors and by drawing an analogy between it and the Zen experience of satori.

The book was to become a bible to the hippies, who were to provide the next groundswell of disciples for Watts. Alongside the resistance movement, the sexual revolution, and the acid rock music, the sixties were also a period of spiritual renewal and of unprecedented interest in Asian religions. These were the years of the Maharishi Mahesh Yogi and "bliss consciousness"; of Yogi Bhajan's Healthy-Happy-Holy movement; and of the Divine Light Mission of the "Perfect Master," the boy-guru Maharaj Ji. It was also the time when Taoism and Zen became firmly embedded in popular culture, as the *I Ching* became a top-selling book and Zen centers cropped up from San Francisco at Boston. Watts, ever in love with the role of guru, quickly became the charismatic leader to a new generation of the spiritually disaffected. By the "Summer of Love" of 1967, he had turned into a colorful flower-child, complete with long flowing hair and frequently decked out in a sarong or kimono. And he became a major influence in the widespread turn to the practice of meditation while also developing into one of the main spokesmen for free love. At a more conventional religious level, he was being taken as a guide by a number of Christian leaders who were trying to open doors to the East—men such as the American Trappist and poet Thomas Merton* and the English Benedictine and author of *Zen Catholicism,* Dom Aelred Graham. At a more secular level, he had a profound impact on the Human Potential Movement, with its interest in consciousness raising, encounter groups, and self-realization. The Esalen Institute at Big Sur, where Watts often ran workshops, was founded by two of his pupils from his days at the AAAS, Michael Murphy and Richard Price. And Werner Erhard, the founder of EST, incorporated much of Watts and Zen into his mind-improvement training program.

For all his influence, Watts' own views were evolving little, though in emphasis his discontent with Christianity was becoming more blatant and his love for Taoism deeper. In *The Two Hands of God* (1963) he launched into an attack on Christian dualism, arguing against a division of nature into the good and the evil, saying that each should be seen as an integral part of one whole, the one being the condition of the other. He had always felt ill at ease with the tendency of Christianity to consign self-interest, sex, and pleasure to an independent realm of the devil, shame, and guilt. Repression, he warned, would lead only to the projection of our devils onto others. Watts returned to the attack the following year with *Beyond Theology,* where he formally broke with the "Philosophia Perennis" and concluded that there was no evidence that Christian leaders had ever considered their faith as but one line of transmission of a universal spiritual insight. The stumbling block was Christianity's imperialistic historical claims, and Watts now lashed into his old religion as "uncompromising, ornery, militant, rigorous, . . . and invincibly self-righteous."

On a more irenic note, Watts took to reflecting more on the quietistic and easy-going Taoist approach to life. In *Cloud-hidden, Whereabouts Unknown*

(1968), he likened the spiritual life to a watercourse gently flowing down its natural path and suggested that we too should surrender the effort to control our lives and simply let our thoughts, feelings, and experiences run where they might. It was a message that fit well with the "go with the flow" mood of the times. And it was a message that he repeated in the beautiful and scholarly *Tao: The Watercourse Way* (1975), which was published posthumously with the collaboration of his friend, Al Chung-Liang Huang.

By the early seventies, Watts was at the pinnacle of his fame, widely greeted as a mystic of great charisma and vision. This image, however, was deceptive; in his own personal life Watts was in a steep decline. An alcoholic for much of his life, he could now easily drink as much as a quart of vodka a day, a practice that often led to confused ramblings during his speaking engagements—ramblings that, fortunately, his followers tended to take as the musings of genius. He was pressed financially by alimony payments, the support of some of his seven children, and the responsibilities he felt toward his menagerie of hangers-on. The hectic demands of free-lance writing and speaking were taking a toll on his health. He was unhappy with his wife. And he was so pestered by religious seekers at his boat in Sausalito that in 1969 he made his main home an isolated cottage on Mount Tamalpais. Despite the peace this offered, the end was closing in on Watts, and on 16 November 1973, after returning from an exhausting lecture tour in Europe, he died in his sleep of heart failure. Watts was only fifty-eight, but he had looked old, tired, and weak for years.

### Appraisal

Watts has been widely condemned, both in his own days and at present, by many academic Orientalists and numbers of the more formal students of Zen. They tend to see him as a charlatan who got lost in the acclaim of his role as guru and as a man who had a distorted vision of Zen and Taoism. There is certainly some evidence for this judgment. Watts very rarely practiced the disciplined za-zen meditation of Zen, and he had little patience for working on koans. He did not even travel to Japan until 1960, and aside from Mandarin, his knowledge of Eastern languages was poor. He was adulterous and hedonistic, hardly qualities many would associate with a mystic or a visionary. He ran short of creative insights early on in life, for the most part limiting himself to the refinement of a stockpile of ideas he had learned as a young man. And he was sometimes unsophisticated in his assaults on Christianity, frequently seeming to assume it could be identified with the fundamentalism of his mother. Watts himself responded to many of these criticisms in his autobiography, *In My Own Way* (1972), which was published the year before his death; and though his detractors must be granted a hearing, there is much to be said on his behalf.

On the issue of Watts' understanding of Zen and Taoism, it would be rash to condemn him out of hand. He did not have the erudition of an academic Orientalist, but he had learned most of his Zen from D. T. Suzuki, who was unmistakably the premier expositor of Japanese religion to the West in the twentieth century. In any event, he must be forgiven the expected lapses of a groundbreaking figure. With a few exceptions, it was only after World War II that American universities began to build up their Oriental studies programs, and it was not until the sixties that there were a large number of serious scholars at work in the field. This was also the time when Zen centers began to become widely established in America, and many students of Zen turned to this religion as a formal discipline; some, like Gary Snyder and Philip Kapleau, even went to Japan for monastic training. But it is uncharitable for the more disciplined devotees of Zen to fault Watts for the lacks in his formal training and to criticize his understanding as a result. Watts repeatedly denied that he was a partisan of any sect or doctrine, including Zen. Zen and Taoism, for Watts, were not traditions that he wanted to transplant in the West, and he had little patience for the "skinheaded military zip" of the Japanese monks. Watts' concern was to mine these traditions to creatively transform and use them in ways suited to Western culture and his own needs. He should be judged on the basis of his thought, not by the standard of adherence to any of the various orthodoxies of the East.

The criticism of Watts that possibly has proved more damagingly tenacious is that he was a charlatan of too dissolute a character to be capable of any great spiritual insight. In his own words in *In My Own Way,* he was "an unrepentant sensualist . . . an immoderate lover of women and the delights of sexuality." He was also, again by his own words, "a shameless egoist" who enjoyed being the center of attention—and he did in fact cherish the role of guru. With his sandaled feet, beads, long hair, and beard, it was, moreover, a role that he played very well. It would be presumptuous, however, to discard Watts as spiritually shallow because he had strong tastes for life's pleasures and the accolades of his admirers. It would also be unjust to characterize him as a charlatan, for he did not pretend to be anything other than what he was. His was a wayward spirit, and he loved to wear different and exotic masks, if for no other reason than that he found release from boredom in the sheer art and game of it. He was quite ready to admit that "I am unashamedly in 'show-biz.' "

It is unfortunate that Watts' character has become a bone of contention in the literature, and in fairness to him it should at least be kept in mind that he saw no clash between sensuality, egoism, and religion. As a lover of Taoism he accepted the natural state as a harmonious counterpart to the spiritual. The world-denying ethic of much of Christian theology and the doctrine of original sin never held any appeal for him. Instead of fighting nature, he believed we should spiritualize it, even in the depths of its seeming weaknesses and flaws. And if this attitude does not meet the Western image of a mystic, it is in keeping with a number of the strands of Eastern thought that Watts was enamored of. In many respects he was like the eccentric hermits, poets, and mystics of Zen—men who had experienced liberation from the ego, only to feel free to return to ordinary life with greater insight and to enjoy the pleasures of food, drink, and good company and the physical comfort of women.

Watts was a complex man, and for all his failings, he was brilliant, literate, possessed of an innate sensitivity for religion, and superb and spellbinding as a speaker. If many devotees and scholars of Oriental religions now look down on him, it would be wise to remember that his popular appeal was immense. It is difficult to imagine the spread of Eastern religions in the modern United States without him.

### Survey of Criticism

For all the celebrity Watts enjoyed while alive, he has been poorly covered by scholars since his death, largely because the study of Eastern spirituality in the United States remains a young field. There are, however, three excellent histories of Buddhism in North America, two of which pay him some note. Charles Prebish's *American Buddhism,* a specialized study of eight Buddhist traditions, approaches Watts as a popularizer who was extremely influential in the spread of Zen but who misrepresented Zen because of his seeming shallowness of personal experience and his lack of intellectual rigor. Somewhat kinder is Rick Fields' *How the Swans Came to the Lake,* which portrays Watts as an important bulwark against the fanciful Zen of the beats and of the pseudointellectuals of the fifties.

Watts appears in many works of the growing genre of literature that deals with popular religious movements in postwar United States. But many of the books here are somewhat journalistic and impressionistic in style. Among the better ones, for both an introduction to Watts as well as his times, are *Understanding the New Religions,* which is a collection of papers from a conference held at Berkeley in 1977 edited by Jacob Needleman and George Baker; Robert Ellwood's *Alternative Altars,* which offers a brief exposition of Watts and a helpful appraisal of Zen as both a cultural influence and a formal religion; and Theodore Roszak's classic, *The Making of a Counter Culture,* which devotes a chapter to Watts and Allen Ginsberg, two men whom he judges fundamental to the growth of Eastern spirituality in America.

There is only a handful of published works dedicated solely to Watts. David Stuart's *Alan Watts* is an enjoyably written but uneven book that hangs Watts' biography on the history of his writings and that has a propensity for pop-psychological and astrological reflections on its hero. But Stuart paints a fair portrait and acknowledges Watts' hedonistic showman streak as well as his more serious contributions to religious thought. At the other extreme is David Clark, *The Pantheism of Alan Watts,* a defense of traditional Christian theism in opposition to Watts's Orientalism and seeming anti-intellectualism. As an American who grew up in Japan, Clark offers the promise of being a helpful bridge between the East and the West, but his conservative theology often seems to interfere with his understanding of Watts. The most entertaining and illuminating of the biographies is Monica Furlong's *Genuine Fake.* Furlong is a British free-lance writer of considerable ability, and in this, the authorized biography, she explores Watts' life with a thoroughness and detail not accessible elsewhere. The only disappointment is that she is much less interested in Watts' ideas than she is in Watts the man, from his drinking habits to his romantic life.

## Bibliography

### Books by Alan Watts

1932   *An Outline of Zen Buddhism.* London: Golden Vista Press.
1936   *The Spirit of Zen: A Way of Life, Work and Art in the Far East.* London: John Murray.
1937   *The Legacy of Asia and Western Man: A Study of the Middle Way.* London: John Murray.
1940   *The Meaning of Happiness.* New York: Harper and Brothers.
1947   *Behold the Spirit: A Study in the Necessity of Mystical Religion.* New York: Pantheon.
1947   *Zen Buddhism: A New Outline and Introduction.* London: Buddhist Society.
1948   *Zen.* Stanford: James Ladd Delkin.
1950   *The Supreme Identity: An Essay on Oriental Metaphysic and the Christian Religion.* New York: Pantheon.
1951   *The Wisdom of Insecurity.* New York: Pantheon.
1953   *Myth and Ritual in Christianity.* London: Thames and Hudson.
1955   *The Way of Liberation in Zen Buddhism.* San Francisco: American Academy of Asian Studies.
1957   *The Way of Zen.* New York: Vintage Books.
1958   *Easter: Its Story and Meaning.* London: Abelard-Schuman.
1958   *Nature, Man, and Woman.* New York: Pantheon.
1958   *This Is It and Other Essays on Zen and Spiritual Experience.* New York: Pantheon.
1959   *Beat Zen, Square Zen, and Zen.* San Francisco: City Lights Books.
1961   *Psychotherapy East and West.* New York: Pantheon.
1962   *The Joyous Cosmology: Adventures in the Chemistry of Consciousness.* New York: Pantheon.
1963   *The Two Hands of God: The Myths of Polarity.* New York: George Braziller.
1964   *Beyond Theology: The Art of Godmanship.* New York: Pantheon.
1966   *The Book on the Taboo against Knowing Who You Are.* New York: Pantheon.
1968   *Cloud-hidden, Whereabouts Unknown: A Mountain Journal.* New York: Random House.
1971   *Erotic Spirituality: The Vision of Konarak.* With Eliot Elisofon. New York: Macmillan.
1972   *Does It Matter? Essays on Man's Relation to Materiality.* New York: Pantheon.
1972   *In My Own Way: An Autobiography, 1915–1965.* New York: Pantheon.
1975   *Tao: The Watercourse Way.* With Al Chung-Liang Huang. New York: Pantheon.

### Selected Studies about Alan Watts

Clark, David. *The Pantheism of Alan Watts.* Downers Grove, Ill.: InterVarsity Press, 1978.
"Eager Exponent of Zen." *Life* 50 (21 April 1961): 88A–93.
Ellwood, Robert S. *Alternative Altars: Unconventional and Eastern Spirituality in America.* Chicago: University of Chicago Press, 1979.

Fields, Rick. *How the Swans Came to the Lake: A Narrative History of Buddhism in America*. Boulder: Shambhala, 1981.

Furlong, Monica. *Genuine Fake: A Biography of Alan Watts*. London: Heinemann, 1986.

Mahoney, Stephen. "The Prevalence of Zen." *Nation* 187 (1 November 1958): 311–15.

Needleman, Jacob, and George Baker, eds. *Understanding the New Religions*. New York: Seabury Press, 1978.

Prebish, Charles. *American Buddhism*. North Scituate, Mass.: Duxbury Press, 1979.

Roszak, Theodore. *The Making of a Counter Culture: Reflections on the Technocratic Culture and Its Youthful Opposition*. Garden City, N.Y.: Doubleday, 1968.

Stuart, David. *Alan Watts*. Radnor, Pa.: Chilton Book Co., 1976.

Wheelwright, Philip. "The Philosophy of Alan Watts." *Sewanee Review* 61 (1953): 493–500.

"Zen." *Time* 91 (4 February 1957): 65–66.

EDMUND C. BALLANTYNE

# Morris L. West

In his book *Making Peace in the Global Village,* Robert McAfee Brown describes the Hebrew word for "peace," *shalom*, or what one might call "spiritual well-being." Brown says that it is "almost shockingly materialistic." He then emphasizes the collective or social aspect of spiritual well-being:

> It also involves seeing to it that people have enough to eat; that they are not undernourished or malnourished; that they can go to bed at night without fear . . . ; that the politics of the country (and of the world) are so arranged that everybody's basic needs are met.

To put the issue bluntly, spiritual well-being has no currency, is a null category, amounts to nothing, if there is materialistic want.

Morris L. West is an Australian author, journalist, and playwright of considerable popular success in the United States whose work raises concern for this kind of spiritual well-being. West is as well a committed, postinstitutional Roman Catholic layperson who has, over a forty-year period, written more than twenty books, the most important of which have treated difficult moral issues and recurrent ethical problems.

There are adventure/moral tales: *Gallows on the Sand* (1955), *Summer of the Red Wolf* (1971), and *Cassidy* (1986). There are sociopsychological cases: *Children of the Shadows* (1957), *Daughter of Silence* (1961), and *The World Is Made of Glass* (1983). And there are Roman Catholic church tales: *Moon in My Pocket* (1945), *The Devil's Advocate* (1959), *The Shoes of the Fisherman* (1963), *Scandal in the Assembly* (with Robert Francis, 1970), and *The Clowns of God* (1981). In this last group West has been concerned with Roman Catholic spiritual well-being. But he has done more. For our purposes, let us examine in particular three West novels that are in part character studies and in part harsh ethical indictments of a broader collective spiritual responsibility. The three are *The Ambassador* (1965), *The Tower of Babel* (1968), and *Proteus* (1979).

## Biography

Morris Langlo West was born on 26 April 1916 in St. Kilda, Melbourne, Australia. The son of Charles Langlo and Florence Guilfoyle West, Morris West had an awkward and unhappy childhood. According to the largely autobiographical *Moon in My Pocket,* a monastery of the Christian Brothers, a lay teaching order, became for him "a symbol of fixity, a centre of balance in the chaos of his world," promising him the "solitude and peace of the cloister." West joined the order at fourteen, was a teacher in the order's schools from 1933 to 1939, received his baccalaureate from the University of Melbourne in 1937, and left the order in 1939 after declining to take final vows.

During World War II, West served from 1939 to 1943 in the Australian Imperial Force, achieving the rank of lieutenant. He left the service to become personal secretary to and biographer of former Australian Prime Minister William Morris Hughes. Much later, in an interview published in the *New York Times* on 9 August 1981, West recalled this brief career: "What I didn't know was that I was one of a long line of his secretaries, which at the time numbered 72. The old man would in furious anger sweep his desk clear of papers and say pick them up. I survived three months."

West spent one year as publicity director of a newspaper radio network, after which he became an independent writer and producer with his own company, Australasian Radio Productions. For a decade he had great success, until one day he became very ill and could not walk. His doctors could discern "no physical cause for his illness" and suggested psychiatric care. West refused. Instead he passed one year in a hospital "analyzing his own illness, which he called a 'psycho-somatic job.' " What he discovered was that he preferred to write for himself rather than for his "radio sponsors." As the *Current Biography Yearbook* noted in 1967, this meant selling his business and retiring "to a cottage near Sydney to test his ability to make a living as a writer."

It was not an easy living, but with proceeds from a play for Australian radio and from two modest novels, West was able to move to Europe. There something changed, if not in West himself, then clearly in his writing. The occasion for the change was his experience with the wretchedly poor street children of Naples, Italy, and the work done on their behalf by Father Mario Borelli. West could not find a publisher in Italy, but *Children of the Shadows* was successful in Great Britain where it became a best seller, as it did in the United States as *Children of the Sun*. As *Current Biography Yearbook* noted, West later remarked that he had discovered that it was his obligation "to affirm constantly . . . [one's] right to the minimal dignity, the minimal possession, the minimal care without which [one] cannot function as a responsible human being." It was this obligation that would mark West's most important future writing.

In 1958 West served six months as Vatican correspondent for the *Daily Mail* of London. While in this position he "absorbed much of the technical background" for three novels: *The Devil's Advocate, Daughter of Silence,* and *The Shoes of the Fisherman.* The first and second were adapted for Broadway, the first and third for motion pictures. At a time when the United States was crossing a most tangible barrier to elect its first Roman Catholic as president, West was likewise helping the nation to explore the possibility that issues involving the Roman Catholic church might be catholic in the more general sense.

As if to underscore the point, in 1963 West traveled to Japan, Thailand, and Vietnam in an effort to study Buddhism. He did so in part because, as he said in *Life* magazine, "I realized that I, as a Christian, am a member of the minority in the world. I had strong curiosity about a completely different religious viewpoint." One religious viewpoint that was unexpectedly different was that of his own tradition in South Vietnam. West found that "the whole policy of South Vietnam's Catholics was wrong. I felt . . . they were Catholics out of the Middle Ages who were abrogating what there is of Christian charity." While on the other side, he discovered that "the terrible thing about Vietnamese Buddhists is that they can lend themselves to violence which ends up with a schoolboy with a meat cleaver in his hand." West would pursue further this Vietnamese "Buddhist-Catholic controversy" in *The Ambassador,* the first of his topical novels to be examined below.

Three years later, in 1968, West offered a second topical novel. *The Tower of Babel* describes events in the Middle East during the period approximately six months before the outbreak of the Six Day War of 1967. Although the main characters and the overall tone of the novel favor the Israeli position, the leadership and policies of the state of Israel (and implicitly, its overseas supporters) do not escape West's criticism. It is as though West had made another change, had broadened his perspective, and would now challenge any significant threat to worldwide spiritual well-being, Roman Catholic, Christian, or not. In many ways, and especially given the continued turmoil in the Israeli-occupied territories, this remains West's most disturbing book.

In 1970 West published two works, both highly critical of the Roman Catholic church. The first is a play in blank verse, *The Heretic,* that concerns the life and work of Giordano Bruno, a sixteenth-century Italian scientist and philosopher who was condemned for heresy and executed in Rome in 1600. The second is *Scandal in the Assembly,* an extended "bill of complaints" directed against the official Roman Catholic position on marriage laws. In the mid-seventies West wrote a quartet of stories of mixed attention. *Summer of the Red Wolf* (1971) is a mid-life male adventure set in the Outer Hebrides and is West's least satisfying novel. *The Salamander* (1973) returns to the intrigue and danger of postwar Italian politics, with the integrity of the main character subject to threat from both the Right and the Left. With *Harlequin* (1974) West again broadens his perspective to examine the machinations and duplicity of international business and finance. Indeed, one may fairly ascribe to this novel a sense of cynical despair. And perhaps in response to this, *The Navigator* (1976) presents an antiworldly quest for a sacred Pacific island, with an attendant reordering of society into a type of tribalism.

By the late seventies West had lived in Europe for more than a decade, including seven years in Rome, after which he moved to England. One may infer that a primary reason for the move was the increased sophistication of "professional terrorists" who had become, according to a report on the growth of terrorist groups in the 23 July 1976 *New York Times*, "expert in coordinating and executing such operations as airplane hijacking, the massacre of civilians and the holding of government officials as hostages." The matter of such terrorism led West to decline an opportunity to return to Rome to work on a film. Insurance was exorbitant, and "besides," West noted in an interview appearing in 1979 in the *New York Times*, "kidnappers do not provide guarantees of returning their victims in one piece." West did respond to the threat of terrorism with *Proteus* (1979), his third topical novel to be examined below.

In 1981 West published *The Clowns of God*, his fourth Roman Catholic church tale, and *A West Quartet*, a collection of his earlier and more obscure "novels of intrigue and high adventure." Despite the ambitions of his publisher, these four stories remain unremarkable. *Clowns*, however, merits attention for two reasons. It is based on the premise of the forced abdication and seclusion of a Roman pontiff. It has as a major character an aging German scholar, Carl Mendelius, who is arguably West's best creation. Unhappily, the good professor is assassinated at about the midpoint of the novel, after which the story deteriorates rapidly. The other notable event of 1981 was that West planned to return to Australia after a fifteen-year absence. It was time to go home.

West's homecoming present, dedicated to his wife, Joyce Lawford West, was *The World Is Made of Glass* (1983). This is the story of a six-hour-long, one-day visit of a patient, Magda Liliane Kardoss von Gamsfeld, with Swiss analyst C. G. Jung. Set in Europe just before the outset of World War I, it is based primarily on an enigmatic entry in Jung's papers but includes other entries as well. Whatever else its merit, the novel elicited from a critic in the *Christian Century* the curious observation that it demonstrated "the important Jungian insight that religion, sex and suffering make up the most constant trinity of human experiences."

*Cassidy* (1986) is West's latest novel, the only major piece by West that is set in Australia. Since West once said that he would not write about Australia, this may mean a significant change for him. In any case, West here brings home the unsavory legacy of an Irish politico that must somehow overcome or be overcome by his morally upright son-in-law without losing either his ethics or his life.

### Appraisal

The *Ambassador, The Tower of Babel*, and *Proteus* are three novels that are in part character studies and in part ethical indictments of our collective responsibility for spiritual well-being. As such they best represent Morris L. West as a shaper of American popular religion, for in the manner of an Amos or a Jeremiah, the rectitude of the cultural criticism at the heart of these works becomes increasingly acute as we become distanced from the events West describes. And, one hopes, it is not merely a matter of hindsight or of a change of political fashion but is a matter of increased ethical sensitivity to and awareness of the extent of implications from our simplest decisions.

The ambassador is Maxwell Gordon Amberley, a fifty-eight-year-old widower who accepts a special request from the secretary of state and from the president to move from his comfortable post in Tokyo, Japan, to one in Saigon, South Vietnam. The year is 1963. There is a Vietnam "crisis." According to the man who gives Amberley his instructions:

It's a mess, Max. A bloody, thankless mess. We call it a subversive war, but at bottom it's a civil war as well. . . . We've committed thirty thousand men and God knows how many millions of dollars and we're still "advisors" with no final voice in the conduct of operations.

The fictional president of South Vietnam, Phung Van Cung, and his family, whom the United States had heretofore supported as "the best and strongest administrators available," were now "out of control." Whereas Amberley's predecessor had been instructed to work with Cung "by persuasion and charm," this was no longer possible:

We can't work like that anymore. We have to play rough and tough and bring the Administration to heel with financial sanctions. . . . [Y]ou'll see why we need a strong man for this assignment, Max. There are no Oscars in it. Win [lose] or draw, it's still a bloody mess. . . . Everyone at home hopes you'll take it.

Amberley does. On the day he arrives in Saigon, to a full military honor guard reception, he is greeted in the city streets by the self-immolation of an old Buddhist monk to protest Cung's policies. This is only the beginning. There are quarrels and disagreements within and between Amberley's staff and advisors. The first secretary wants one thing, the Central Intelligence Agency station chief wants another, and the commander of the army wants something else again. As for President Cung, he and Amberley, though nearly very fond of one another, find that they have profound, irreconcilable differences. Finally, Amberley and the station chief signal a group of four South Vietnamese generals that the United States would accept a coup (not a "revolution"), but with the stipulation that Cung and his family be protected, if at all possible, from physical danger.

The coup takes place. Cung is executed, though at his own behest. A young junior officer, dear to Amberley, very nearly a son, is killed. A military junta is installed, but with the inclusion of the seed of its own destruction. Amberley collapses into a state of depression and guilt, from which he is rescued at last by his old Zen master at the Temple of the Heavenly Dragon, near Kyoto, Japan.

This is no grand resolution. Things are not tidy. They are, however, very human. One critic, Robert Trumbull, "whose profession for many years [was] to interpret Asian affairs," first in South Vietnam and then as bureau chief for the *New York Times* in Tokyo, wrote: "At another time when the events here recounted have become a recitation from the forgotten past, the book may achieve recognition as a sensitive account of one man's inner conflict as he faces a hateful duty in the service of his ideology."

Maxwell Gordon Amberley may not have been Henry Cabot Lodge, Jr. Phung Van Cung may not have been Ngo Dinh Diem. And certainly the "events here recounted" in this novel have not "become a recitation from the forgotten past." Nevertheless, Trumbull's assessment of Amberley's condition well illustrates the absence of spiritual well-being so troubling to West and to which he spoke with stunning effect in *The Ambassador*. One may add only that on the day that this novel was reviewed in the *New York Times,* 25 April 1965, on the front page of that newspaper was the report:

> Vietcong guerrillas overwhelmed two United States Marine outposts near the vital air base at Danang today, killing two Americans and wounding four others. It was the first conventional military attack against United States combat troops in South Vietnam . . . and the first in which United States Marines were known to have been killed by the Vietcong.

There is, so far as this writer can determine, no tower in *The Tower of Babel*. There is, however, considerable babel. One main character is Adam Ronen, an Iraqi Jew who is masquerading in Damascus, Syria, as a merchant named Selim Fathalla. He is also an advisor to Colonel Omar Safreddin, director of public security and strongman for Syria, who is also in the closet. There is Nuri Chakry, a Lebanese banker, with "an empire that stretched from Beirut to Fifth Avenue, from Brazil to Nigeria to Qatar." Unfortunately for Chakry, most of that empire is based on dubious paper at best. This perilous situation does not, however, preclude Chakry's misleading and lying to control his young American assistant, Mark Matheson. There is Idris Jarrah, a spy and an agent for the Palestine Liberation Organization. Jarrah makes a deal of sorts with Chakry and attempts to flee to Paris with P.L.O. money but is captured and tortured. And there is General Jakov Baratz, who is the control for spy Ronen-Fathalla, in love with Yehudith Ronen (who is abandoned by, but still married to, Ronen-Fathalla), and is himself yet connected to his own wife, Hannah Baratz, who is quite mad.

At base, *The Tower of Babel* is about raiding, retaliation, and preparation for war. Syria and Egypt publicly, but also with Iraq secretly, are conspiring to provoke and eventually to wage war against the state of Israel. Conversely, Israel is attempting to decide whether or not it is in its best interest to wage a "fast war" against Syria, Egypt, and Jordan, but not Iraq. According to the best thinking of the Israeli leadership, such a military undertaking would require "the first air strike [to take] out every aircraft [of the Arab states] on the ground."

For our purposes, there are two sets of consequences that derive from this Israeli planning. The first comes in response to a question raised by the foreign minister early in the discussions. "Given a fast and successful campaign," he asks, "what does it get us?" The defense minister answers, "In terms of territories? All of Sinai at least. It could get us all of West Jordan, the Bethlehem-Hebron bulge, old Jerusalem and the hills of Western Galilee. Maybe a little more." To which the chief of staff adds: "A lot more. A million and a half Arabs against our own population of two and three-quarters millions. A social problem, a food problem and a police problem of the first magnitude."

With respect to this last problem, that of policing, one may well raise the question of policing whom? In a report from the village of Qalqilya, in the Israeli-occupied territories, Thomas Friedman wrote in the 13 April 1987 *New York Times:*

> The Israeli Army bulldozed several rows of Arab-owned orange trees outside this village today, a day after an Israeli woman was burned to death by a firebomb tossed into her car from the edge of the citrus grove. Dozens of West Bank Jewish settlers rampaged through Qalqilya. . . . The settlers ran through the warren of houses, smashed car windows with guns and steel pipes, set vehicles ablaze and tried to set fire to Arab-owned fields and orchards.

To consider the second set of consequences that derives from Israeli planning in the novel, at the close of West's story, presumably just before the outset of the Six Day War on 5 June 1967, General Baratz is worried about "stockpiles" of weaponry. They are "down below the agreed minimum of six month's reserves." He is questioned by his commander, "What happens next and when?" Baratz replies:

> I don't like guessing games. . . . But there is one foregone conclusion. The Syrians will keep hacking away at us in Galilee until they force us into a confrontation. Then they'll yell for the Egyptians. If the Egyptians move troops into the Sinai, the game is on. When? Who the hell knows? How *can* you know? You read the files. You read the daily news. It's a mad world—a tower of babel, where we all shout gibberish and die in a wilderness of apes.

To return to the report by Friedman from the village of Qalqilya:

> The army imposed a curfew. . . . Residents of Qalqilya shuttered their windows and locked themselves in their homes today, apparently welcoming the curfew and the hundreds of Israeli troops who circled the village, as much to keep the residents in as to keep potential vigilantes out. . . . As often happens after such violent incidents, Israeli politicians and parties of widely different views cited it as proof why Israel must or must not negotiate peace with the Arabs.

This is a different geography from Vietnam, with different peoples, and (perhaps) a different war. Nonetheless, it is the same absence of spiritual well-being and the same critical, ethical indictment of our collective responsibility for that absence. To repeat, *The Tower of Babel* remains West's most disturbing book.

In *Proteus* West turns from a consideration of particular trouble spots in the world to a trouble that has become virtually worldwide. In Homer's *Odyssey* Proteus is, according to the *Oxford Companion to Classical Literature*, "an 'ancient one of the sea,' who herds the seals, knows all things, and has the power of assuming different shapes in order to escape being questioned." In West's book Proteus is the pseudonym of John Spada, a wealthy and powerful New York capitalist, in his role as head of a secret international organization designed to build "bridges of benevolence" in the world. Proteus is as well the name of that secret organization. Thus, while Spada, Inc., makes its millions where it may, Spada-Proteus fights international terrorism where he can.

Then Spada's daughter and son-in-law are captured and tortured by forces of the government of Argentina, the country where they live. The daughter is a physician who treats a politically incorrect patient; the son-in-law is the editor of a "liberal" newspaper. They are rescued and returned by Proteus to a familial estate in New York where they slowly begin to heal. Then the Argentine government retaliates by assassinating the daughter and son-in-law and Anna Spada, Spada's wife. When Spada begins to prepare his own response, he is accused by his attorney and longtime friend of seeking vengeance.

This, Spada denies:

> You're a million miles off the mark! I always thought vendetta was a wasteful cult anyway. But I want an accounting for my dead! And, by the living God, I'm going to get it! And it isn't only with the hired killers, it's with every goddam group and system that make such horror possible! . . . I'm a civilized man, for Christ's sake, and in half a year they've stripped me naked, back to barbarism. Now they'll contend with the beast they've made!

That beast steals from one of his own companies vials containing Boise Type A botulinus. "Its toxic effect was high. The mortality rate was more than 50 per cent and the incubation period minimal." And so, with assistance from Proteus volunteers, Spada secretly spreads the toxin throughout the world. He then requests and is granted permission to address the General Assembly of the United Nations. There he offers "a schedule, necessarily incomplete, of those places of detention where men and women are confined, interrogated, [and] tortured, in defiance of every principle of humanity." He demands that the doors of such places be opened and their prisoners returned home within twenty-one days.

To make certain that compliance be full and safe, Spada would have the rescue procedure "supervised and confirmed by observers from international agencies appointed by the United Nations." He receives, however, little help, as the nations have indeed become united, but against him as the greatest of all international terrorists. Spada's attorney offers his assessment of the situation:

> Against the assembled nations, their vast aggregates of population and resources, your power is inadequate and temporary. . . . My conclusion is that they will com-

promise and that you must compromise. . . . You will have to capitulate first, not they.

Spada does so. In a second appearance before the General Assembly he instructs Proteus to surrender the toxin and then commits suicide with a cyanide capsule. From his last testament we learn that this is not an act of "despair" but "a religious act, a donation" to his colleagues whom he could betray were he tortured, what he termed would be the "ultimate debasement." And so, this life, those lives, reflect as close to an absence of spiritual well-being as I am aware. Once again West has acted as a shaper of American popular religion if we understand his indictment of our collective responsibility for allowing that ultimate debasement to continue.

## Survey of Criticism

There is no great body of literary criticism of the work of Morris L. West. His novels are regularly reviewed in newspapers such as the *New York Times* and in journals such as the *Christian Century,* and elsewhere. Those reviews are occasionally collated in volumes such as *Contemporary Authors, Contemporary Literary Criticism,* and *Current Biography Yearbook.*

This is so because West has given us, especially in the three novels here examined, popular literature, fast reads, summertime semipulp. And the topics, if anything, are especially mundane. Yet herein lies West's worth for us: a dirty little war, in an obscure land, for purposes that we cannot grasp. What other dirty little wars, in other obscure lands (if in this hemisphere), for other purposes that we cannot grasp, is our government waging? Or consider the Israeli-occupied territories, where 800,000 Palestinians now refer to 60,000 Israelis as "Jews," in response to the systematic and long-standing Israeli policy of calling Palestinians "Arabs," thereby making the land mutually invisible and incapable of being claimed.

Or consider the multifaceted, anyone-can-have-one terrorisms that have been, until the immediate past, devouring Lebanon, especially its once most gracious city. In early 1987 the *National Public Radio* news program, "All Things Considered," had Noah Adams, then one of the cohosts, speaking with Nora Boustany, a *Washington Post* correspondent and regular contributor to the program. Boustany described the starvation in the Palestinian refugee settlement of Bourj el-Barajneh (held under siege for months by Shiite militia), the activities of other militia groups in and around the city, and so on.

Only her report was interrupted, and for long moments, by the noise of automatic weapons fire that was, in her words, "just outside my window." When there was a break in the firing, Adams asked Boustany if she ought not move from where she was, perhaps go down to the basement of her building to find a more secure location. Her response: "Oh, no. I am sitting under my table. I am on the fifth floor." And she completed her report. In her own way, Boustany was pursuing West's obligation to affirm constantly the right to minimal dignity, possession, and care, without which we cannot function as responsible human beings.

## Bibliography

### Books by Morris L. West

1945    [Julian Morris, pseud.]. *Moon in My Pocket*. Sydney: Australasian.
1955    *Gallows on the Sand*. North Ryde, Australia: Angus.
1956    *Kundu*. North Ryde, Australia: Angus.
1957    *The Big Story*. London: Heinemann.
1957    *Children of the Sun*. London: Heinemann.
1958    [Michael East, pseud.]. *McCreary Moves In*. London: Heinemann.
1958    *Second Victory*. London Heinemann.
1959    *The Devil's Advocate*. London: Heinemann; New York: Morrow.
1960    [Michael East, pseud.]. *The Naked Country*. London: Heinemann.
1961    *Daughter of Silence*. London: Heinemann; New York: Morrow.
1963    *The Shoes of the Fisherman*. New York: Morrow.
1965    *The Ambassador*. New York: Morrow.
1968    *The Tower of Babel*. New York: Morrow.
1970    *The Heretic; A Play in Three Acts*. New York: Morrow.
1970    *Scandal in the Assembly*. With Robert Francis. New York: Morrow.
1971    *Summer of the Red Wolf*. New York: Morrow.
1973    *The Salamander*. New York: Morrow.
1974    *Harlequin*. New York: Morrow.
1976    *The Navigator*. New York: Morrow.
1979    *Proteus*. New York: Morrow.
1981    *The Clowns of God*. New York: Morrow.
1981    *A West Quartet*. New York: Morrow.
1983    *The World Is Made of Glass*. New York: Morrow.
1986    *Cassidy*. New York: Doubleday.

### Selected Studies about Morris L. West

Ethridge, James M., ed. *Contemporary Authors*. Detroit: Gale Research Corp., 1963.
Moritz, Charles, ed. *Current Biography Yearbook*. New York: Wilson, 1966, 1967.
"A Novelist Named West Faces East." *Life* 58 (19 March 1965): 79–80ff.
Olson, Patricia. Review of *The World Is Made of Glass*. *Christian Century* 100 (1983): 914.
Riley, Carolyn, and Phyllis Carmel, eds. *Contemporary Literary Criticism*. Detroit: Gale Research Corp., 1976, 1983.
Trumbull, Robert. Review of *The Ambassador*. *New York Times*, 25 April 1965, sec. 7, p. 5.

STEPHEN H. SNYDER

# Wovoka

Since aboriginal times, the Northern Paiute people have hunted, fished, and gathered piñon nuts along the range from Oregon's Blue Mountains south to the Sierra Nevada crest. The area is a virtual picture—snow-capped peaks, volcanic ridges, and dark piñon trees. Canopied by an infinite blue sky, it seems set apart from the world. Save for a few excursions as a young man, the Paiute known as Wovoka would never depart from the Walker River Valley of western Nevada. Here he would continue the prophetic tradition of his father, Tavibo, who was regarded as a great shaman and medicine man among the Paiute. In time he would be identified with that outbreak of popular religion known as the Ghost Dance. In the words of ethnographer James Mooney, whose study of Wovoka and the Ghost Dance has become a classic, the son of Tavibo was uniquely born to "see visions and hear still voices."

## Biography

Wovoka was born sometime between 1856 and 1858. His spiritual pilgrimage was shaped while straddling the harsh tensions between whites and Indians. He was first and foremost a Paiute. As a contemplative boy he perhaps accepted a unique role in reviving the spiritual heritage of his people. He was only fourteen when his father died, but he was taught to seek spiritual visions, and he learned the Paiute creation myth that described the sick being healed, the dead brought back to life, and the desert one day returned to lavish abundance. His father, Tavibo, had been a close disciple of the Wodziwob, the prophet of the 1870 Ghost Dance movement that spread through parts of California, Nevada, and Oregon. The Paiutes, along with other tribes, performed the ancient round dance with new vigor, prompted by visions of impending earthquakes and catastrophic change; the Great Spirit would counteract the dominance of the white man while dead ancestors would return to live in a new world.

Wovoka also learned the ways of the white Americans. After his father's death he was taken in by the David Wilson family, ranchers whose hard work and devout Christian behavior gave acceptance and security to this Indian lad, adopted as "Jack" Wilson. He became a blood brother to the Wilsons' son, Bill, and proved dependable as a worker, moving with ease among the ranches and farms scattered up and down the valley. He was also included in the family Bible readings. Wovoka marveled at stories describing a wondrous creation filled with abundant game and fish—a place called Paradise. He listened intently to the story of the miracle worker Jesus, who was able to change water to wine and feed thousands with just a few fish and bread. He absorbed Jesus' moral teachings about peace and love and was amazed at this savior's ability to heal others while accepting suffering and death, only to rise again promising a new age of bliss.

Though drawn to the Christian messiah, Wovoka could not square this faith with white behavior. The Wilsons treated him fairly, but he entered adulthood fully conscious of the corrosive effects of white encroachment on his native people. As early as the 1832 Walker Expedition, Paiutes had been indiscriminately slaughtered. After 1849 the area was a virtual highway for the California gold rush. Then came Virginia City and the Comstock Lode; Nevada achieved statehood in 1864; and the transcontinental railroad was completed in 1873, with homesteads and landgrants enticing thousands of settlers. Chief Winnemucca kept up the fight until the 1860s, but the hearts of the people prepared for defeat. The Paiute women were abused, the men became hirelings on the migrant trails, and the hunting and fishing ceased as land-hungry settlers spilled out of the valleys. Alcohol, disease, and depression had taken the fight out of this once proud people. Wovoka shared the belief, as did many, that only a new revelation from the Great Spirit would provide an answer.

As a young adult Wovoka traveled the migrant circuit through Oregon and Washington, coming into contact with disciples of a spiritual high priest called John Slocum ("Squ-sacht-un") of the Squaxin tribe. Slocum founded a religious group near Puget Sound known as the Shakers. Though he mixed elements from Catholic, Protestant, and native sources, he gained the approval of Presbyterian missionaries for stressing moral discipline. Wovoka was impressed that each believer could hear the voice of God through a hypnotic-like trance induced by rapid and rhythmic "shaking." He also learned of Slocum's miraculous death and rebirth. Slocum had seen heaven, returning with a message that God would restore his people if they practiced moral purity and rejected white vices like alcohol and greed. Wovoka became adept as an apostle precisely when white officials persecuted the movement. He would soon experience his own epiphany.

Back in his valley home, Wovoka may well have undergone a period of deep soul-searching and mystical contemplation. While cutting wood for the Wilsons in the mountains, he claimed that God "took him to heaven" where he saw a beautiful land filled with game. He remained in a state of death for two days, unable to breathe or eat. He then shared his revelation. All Indians would be united with one another and their friends in the other world. They must not lie, steal, or quarrel. They must love one another and live at peace with the whites. Wovoka also told his people to dance. For five days straight, the "Ghost Dance" was performed as male and female together shuffled in clockwise fashion while singing songs that evoked hopes of deliverance. The dance spread throughout Paiute country and was picked up by neighboring tribes. Often, after dancing, believers would dip themselves into the river for spiritual cleansing and then share in feasting.

Wovoka's reputation was growing, and he was increasingly touted as a great medicine man in the tradition of the ancestors. He perhaps copied the techniques of shaman "tricksters" to perform a variety of miracles, though followers were convinced of his power to heal the sick and to control the forces of nature. He was afflicted with the dreaded scarlet fever in late 1888, and although few survived, Wovoka's recovery occurred precisely in tune with a total eclipse of the sun on 1 January 1889. Many followers would remember "the day the sun died" and the new revelation delivered by the prophet who again proved victorious over death.

Wovoka's new vision achieved the status of doctrine, though varying from tribe to tribe. Indians everywhere should dance and seek visions. The Great Spirit would soon send a messiah to his people. Earthquakes would usher in a millennium of peace and bliss, as the dead would be restored. Drought, disease, and famine would disappear. At first many white observers were encouraged that the emphasis on moral discipline and brotherly love would hasten Indian acculturation. Yet tribes to the East would emphasize Indian renewal at the *expense* of the white man and his culture. Disciples like Porcupine of the Cheyenne repeated the belief that a great flood of mud and water would wipe away the whites while Indians long dead would come alive to hunt replenished herds of buffalo.

It was the Sioux of the western Dakotas who embraced the Ghost Dance with the most zeal. Many believed that an Indian millennium would arrive by the summer of 1891 and that even the white man's bullets would prove harmless to the "ghost shirts" worn by the Sioux. The rapid deterioration experienced by the Sioux made them desperate for a miracle. Once more than 20,000 strong, they no longer roamed the high plains as proud, free warriors and hunters of countless buffalo. The heroics of Sitting Bull and Red Cloud had been overshadowed by a combination of depression, disease, and the inept mismanagement by the federal government. In less than fifteen years, millions of acres of Sioux land from northern Montana to Nebraska were snatched for American settlement. The sacred Black Hills were overrun. Promised rations never came to the ever shrinking reservations. In 1889, North and South Dakota, Montana, and Washington became states, with Idaho and Wyoming following in 1890. Settlers and immigrants poured into the area in increasing numbers. Convinced that the "Indian problem" was largely solved, many grew uneasy as thousands of Sioux took to dancing and singing, ignoring the white road to civilization. Late in 1890 regional newspapers in Rapid City, South Dakota, and Bismarck, North Dakota, often carried daily reports of rumored Indian "atrocities" and wondered when these "exciteable" Indians would turn vicious. Fervent disciples like Kicking Bear and Short Bull made harsh statements that seemed to justify such fears. Snippets of Short Bull's impassioned speech at the Pine Ridge agency of South Dakota were reprinted in many newspapers. He believed the new messianic age to be only months away. It would include only the sacred Indians. The faithful were to keep dancing and to ignore the soldiers, as they and their horses would sink into the earth. "Now you must know this, that all soldiers and that race will be dead." The *Bismarck Daily Tribune* was convinced that the Sioux nation was plotting a major uprising. "It is positively stated that the Wounded Knee Indian fanatics threaten to shoot anyone who interferes with the dance," it editorialized on 23 November 1890.

Events were ripe for tragedy. Kicking Bear had encouraged the old mystic Sitting Bull to take up the dance. Sitting Bull was a symbol of unyielding resistance on the Standing Rock reservation in southern North Dakota. When 200 of his braves started dancing, he was arrested and killed while his followers joined hundreds of others who were converging on Pine Ridge and the Rosebud reservation near the Black Hills. The U.S. Army was preparing for the worst. A cabinet meeting at the White House authorized troops from California to Texas to reinforce the Dakota agencies through the winter of 1890–91. On 29 December

1890, hundreds of hungry and desperate Sioux were rounded up near Wounded Knee Creek at Pine Ridge. After they were checked for firearms, a shot was heard, with the medicine man Yellow Bird screaming that the ghost shirts would block the white bullets. The army responded with an avalanche of fire, including four Hotchkiss guns. Mooney quotes an eyewitness: "The guns poured in two-inch shells at the rate of nearly fifty per minute, mowing down everything alive." Nearly 300 bodies of men, women, and children were counted. Many were left to freeze into grotesque figures, shot as far as two miles from the initial encounter. Infants were seen sucking the breasts of their dead mothers.

When Wovoka heard of the massacre at Wounded Knee, his spirit was broken, as he grieved for the dead. Interviewed a year later by James Mooney, he claimed that many had distorted his message. He rejected the notion that he had portrayed himself as "Christ." He insisted that he had taught his disciples to live with whites in peace and be morally pure. Most, like biographer Paul Bailey, concluded that the Paiute prophet was soon forgotten. "Wovoka, as far as the world at large was concerned, was as dead as Sitting Bull." Yet Omer Stewart has argued that Wovoka kept in contact with many disciples well into the twentieth century. He lived out his life on the Walker River reservation with his family. Wovoka died with little notice in 1932 and was buried as Jack Wilson. Yet his windswept grave at Shurz, Nevada, still bears fresh offerings from those who honor him.

### Appraisal

Early criticism of Wovoka and the Ghost Dance movement came from both Indian and white sources. Not all Indian tribes embraced Wovoka or the Ghost Dance movement. James Mooney, a government ethnologist, traveled more than 30,000 miles to interview participants, including Wovoka. His brilliant study, "The Ghost-Dance Religion and the Sioux Outbreak of 1890," published in 1896, noted that tribes like the Ute and Navajo ridiculed the notion of the dead returning to earth. Tribes east of Oklahoma ignored it because, reasoned Mooney, they had successfully accepted white culture.

For whites in the late nineteenth century, the Indian was a "problem" to be solved through acculturation (usually including "Christianization") or extermination. Mooney's quote of one missionary illustrated initial enthusiasm for Wovoka's doctrine: "He has given these people a better religion than they ever had before, taught them precepts which, if faithfully carried out, will bring them into better accord with their white neighbors." This reflected the progressive hope of many eastern Protestant reformers, such as Helen Hunt Jackson, whose *A Century of Dishonor* was an impassioned plea for humane policies that might civilize the Indian and redeem the white culture from its sin of genocide. But even progressives found little of indigenous value in Indian spirituality. In an address to the 1890 meeting of the American Folklore Society, Alice Fletcher admitted the devastation caused by whites. "The conviction that ours is a cruel and unjust race has been seared into the Indian mind in many ways." Yet she dismissed the Ghost Dance as a "pathetic" and aboriginal response, claiming that the more enlightened Indians had been overcome by the "nonprogressive and turbulent elements."

President James Garfield accomplished little in his six-month presidency of 1881, but he did manage a despairing comment supporting the notion of extermination, thinking it best, as Martin E. Marty quoted him in *Pilgrims in Their Own Land,* "to let the Indian races sink as gently and easily as possible in oblivion, for there they will go in spite of all efforts." The slaughter at Wounded Knee seemed stark confirmation of this policy. Agent James McLaughlin of the Standing Rock Sioux reservation concluded that Indians who followed such "absurd nonsense" as the Ghost Dance were utterly unfit for civilization. At Pine Ridge, medals were given to the soldiers for bravery, but no dignity was wasted on the Indian dead. Frozen bodies were piled in a pit "like so much cordwood," according to James Mooney. Even the missionaries offered no protest. "It is a commentary on our boasted Christian civilization that although there were two or three salaried missionaries at the agency not one went out to say a prayer over the poor mangled bodies of these victims of war."

James Mooney's pioneering work in ethnology paved the way for later scholarly appreciation of the Ghost Dance by anthropologists and historians of religion. Mooney attempted to use a more objective methodology in recognizing the social and cultural framework of religious behavior. He noted a diversity of religious practices among Indian tribes similar to the varying denominations and sects within Christianity. He saw pan-human characteristics at work in the nativistic renewal movements, suggesting that forces driving the Ghost Dance were common to primitive and civilized societies throughout history.

By the 1930s scholars began to examine the Ghost Dance as a recurring type of "crisis cult." Most concluded that the apocalyptic and messianic elements were nontraditional features of Indian religion that helped to facilitate adaptation in times of extreme cultural deprivation. Scholars gave sympathetic analysis to the dramatic loss of land, buffalo, and tribal population in the face of an overwhelmingly dominant Euro-American culture. Scholars like Weston La Barre and Anthony F. C. Wallace saw the Ghost Dance phenomenon as a generic type—a "crisis cult" or "revitalization movement"—that behaved as a predictable social-cultural organism in reaction to various kinds of stress or change.

More recent appreciation of the Ghost Dance has come from those in the Indian community and from religious history scholars who argue that the religion (and "the religious") of any people deserves study on its own merit. Indian spirituality has achieved greater consideration for its emphasis on the wholeness of life. The "holy" is seen to impinge on everyday life. There is no radical dualism that separates "spirit" from "nature" or contrasts the human with the divine. The Ghost Dance had its roots in the ancient round dance as an experience of "being centered." Historian Catherine Albanese reflects this view: "Religion became a centering process in which the Native American learned to maintain harmony by living equidistant from all the boundaries. Life blossomed not on

460

WOVOKA

the edges of society, as transformation had hinted, but in the middle.'' The dance in fact symbolized the cosmos, and the circle was a key religious symbol and pattern governing architecture, time, and the "reciprocal" notion about property. Land, horses, and "things" were not to be owned but were to be used and then passed on to others in concert with the reciprocal rhythms of life. Whereas the Ghost Dance contained many adaptive elements, it also continued ancient themes, as myth and history came together in the drama of cosmic rebirth and renewal.

**Survey of Criticism**

An excellent sample of regional public opinion characterizing the Ghost Dance as the "messiah craze" is found in the *Bismarck Daily Tribune,* November and December 1890. Lieutenant Marion P. Maus' "The New Indian Messiah" appearing in *Harper's Weekly* was typical of the impressions received by easterners in 1890. Alice Fletcher's "The Indian Messiah" hints at the quandary of progressives in the 1890s—committed to reform yet unsure of their own convictions about the meaning of civilization.

James Mooney's "The Ghost-Dance Religion and the Sioux Outbreak of 1890" remains the classic resource for material on Wovoka and the Ghost Dance. Though some errors have needed correction and Mooney made unwarranted judgments about cultural factors influencing the acceptance and spread of the movement, his study shaped the trajectory for a whole generation of scholarship. The only detailed biography of Wovoka is Paul Bailey's *Wovoka: The Indian Messiah,* which is very readable and based on firsthand accounts. Bailey can be faulted for too easily dismissing the depth and persistence of Indian spirituality, at times giving the impression that Wovoka was a mere charlatan. David H. Miller's *Ghost Dance* treats the movement from the perspective of the final days of despair experienced by the Sioux nation. He journalistically weaves interview data into a lively narrative. Dee Brown's *Bury My Heart at Wounded Knee* is a passionate history told from the Indians' perspective. She is not always objective with the Ghost Dance data. A well-researched treatment of the Sioux Ghost Dance is Robert M. Utley's *Last Days of the Sioux Nation.* In "Jack Wilson and the Indian Service: The Response of the BIA to the Ghost Dance Prophet," L. G. Moses argues that white Indian agents acted with uncompromising indifference and blatant cultural insensitivity to the spiritual elements of the Ghost Dance, perpetuating misunderstanding and tragedy.

The interest in the Ghost Dance from sociological and anthropological perspectives has produced extensive literature. Themes of acculturation and deprivation can be explored in Bernard Barber's "Acculturation and Messianic Movements" and David Aberle's "The Prophet Dance and Reactions to White Contact," an important article that illuminates the concept of relative deprivation. Anthony F. C. Wallace's 1956 article "Revitalization Movements" has become something of a classic, treating a phenomenon like the Ghost Dance as a conscious attempt by a culture system to achieve a more satisfying existence. Weston

La Barre has concluded that the Ghost Dance is a phenomenon whose essential elements—messianic hope, myth-dream, nativistic return to paradise, revitalization—recur with the birth of all new religions. See his "Materials for a History of Studies of Crisis Cults: A Bibliographic Essay" for a good introduction to this scholarship.

Catherine Albanese's chapter "Original Manyness: Native American Traditions" in *America: Religions and Religion* is a capable introduction to Indian spirituality from the perspective of the history of religions. Likewise, Ake Hultkrantz's chapter "The Changing Meaning of the Ghost Dance" in *Belief and Worship in Native North America* levels criticism at the socioanthropological bias that usually treats Indian spirituality and oral traditions as "primitive."

The Sioux holy man Black Elk was a contemporary of Wovoka and witnessed the events before, during, and after Wounded Knee. *Black Elk Speaks,* recorded by John Niehardt, portrays the strength and pathos of the Indian spiritual journey in coming to terms with cultural death. Black Elk captures the intense sadness after the dancing stopped: "The nation's hoop is broken and scattered. There is no center any longer, and the sacred tree is dead." A marvelous collection of essays, edited by Walter H. Capps, is *Seeing With A Native Eye*. The writers, many from within the Indian community, share the conviction that Indian spirituality offers positive alternatives to the isolation and anomie experienced by a rootless, technocratic society.

## Bibliography

### Studies about Wovoka and the Ghost Dance

Aberle, David F. "The Prophet Dance and Reactions to White Contact." *Southwestern Journal of Anthropology* 15 (1959): 75–83.

Albanese, Catherine L. *America: Religions and Religion*. Belmont, Calif.: Wadsworth Publishing Co., 1981.

Bailey, Paul. *Wovoka: The Indian Messiah*. Los Angeles: Westernlore Press, 1957.

Barber, Bernard. "Acculturation and Messianic Movements." *American Sociological Review* 6:5 (October 1941): 663–69.

*Bismarck Daily Tribune* (November, December 1890).

Brown, Dee. *Bury My Heart at Wounded Knee: An Indian History of the American West*. New York: Bantam Books, 1973.

Brown, Joseph Eppes. *The Sacred Pipe*. Norman: University of Oklahoma Press, 1970.

Capps, Walter Holden, ed. *Seeing With A Native Eye*. New York: Harper and Row, 1976.

Fletcher, Alice C. "The Indian Messiah." *Journal of American Folk-Lore* 4 (1891): 57–60.

Grinnell, George Bird. "The Messiah Superstition." *Journal of American Folk-Lore* 4 (1891): 61–68.

Hittman, Michael. "The 1870 Ghost Dance at the Walker River Reservation: A Reconstruction." *Ethnohistory* 20:3 (Summer 1973): 247–78.

Hultkrantz, Ake. *Belief and Worship in Native North America*. Syracuse, N.Y.: Syracuse University Press, 1981.

Knack, Martha C. "A Short Resource History of Pyramid Lake, Nevada." *Ethnohistory* 24:1 (Winter 1977): 47–63.

La Barre, Weston. *The Ghost Dance: Origins of Religion*. New York: Doubleday, 1970.

———. "Materials for a History of Studies of Crisis Cults: A Bibliographic Essay." *Current Anthropology* 12:1 (February 1971): 3–44.

Maus, Lt. Marion P. "The New Indian Messiah." *Harper's Weekly* (6 December 1890).

Miller, David H. *Ghost Dance*. New York: Doubleday, 1970.

Mooney, James. "The Ghost-Dance Religion and the Sioux Outbreak of 1890." *Bureau of American Ethnology, Annual Report, Part II* 14 (1896): 645–1136.

Moses, L. G. "Jack Wilson and the Indian Service: The Response of the BIA to the Ghost Dance Prophet." *American Indian Quarterly* 5:4 (November 1979): 295–316.

Moses, L. G., and Margaret C. Szasz. "My Father, Have Pity on Me: Indian Revitalization Movements of the Late-Nineteenth Century." *Journal of the West* 23 (January 1984): 5–15.

Niehardt, John G., ed. *Black Elk Speaks*. Lincoln: University of Nebraska Press, 1961.

Overholt, Thomas W. "The Ghost Dance of 1890 and the Nature of the Prophetic Process." *Ethnohistory* 21:1 (Winter 1974): 37–63.

Stewart, Omer C. "Contemporary Document on Wovoka (Jack Wilson), Prophet of the Ghost Dance in 1890." *Ethnohistory* 24:3 (Summer 1977): 219–22.

Utley, Robert M. *The Last Days of the Sioux Nation*. New Haven: Yale University Press, 1963.

Wallace, Anthony F. C. "Revitalization Movements: Some Theoretical Considerations for Their Comparative Study." *American Anthropologist* 58:2 (April 1956): 264–81.

JOEL SHERER

# Index

Brooks, S. P., 313
Broun, Heywood, 388
Brown, Dee, 460
Brown, Elijah P., 415
Brown, John, 80
Brown, Robert McAfee, 445
Brown, W. Gordon, 399
*Brown* v. *Board of Education*, 66
Brownell, Herbert, 406
Brunner, Emil, 145
Bruno, Gilbert, 447
Bryan, Mary Baird, 63
Bryan, William Jennings, 20, 83, 86,
    127, 144, 428; appraisal of, 62–63; life
    of, 57–61; works about, 63–64
Bryant, William Cullen, 80
Bryfonski, Dedria, 299
Bucco, Martin, 245
Buckingham, Jamie, 231, 422
Buddhism, 447. *See also* Zen Buddhism
Budenz, Louis, 388
Bundy, Edgar C., 260
Burkett, Randall, 169
Burnham, Kenneth E., 112, 117
Burton, Joe W., 430
Burton, Naomi, 295
Burton, Richard, 118
Business of Christ, 23
Byrd, Richard E., 323

Cadman, S. Parkes, 154, 404
Cage, John, 439
Calgary Prophetic Bible Institue, 3–4, 5
Caliandro, Arthur, 331
Callahan, Daniel, 94
Calvin, John, 423
Calvinism, 131, 141–42, 365
Camp meetings, xxi, 187
Campbell, Debra, 109
Campbell, Robert, 200
Campbell, Will D.: appraisal of, 69–71;
    life of, 65–69; works about, 71
"Campmeeting Hour," 419
Campus Crusade for Christ, 48–55, 248–
    50
*Canadian Baptist*, 395
Canadian Protestant League, 398
Canfield, Joseph M., 378, 379

Cannon, James, Jr.: appraisal of, 77–79;
    life of, 72–77; works about, 79
Cannon, Lydia Primrose, 73
Cantor, Mackinley, 320
Capitalism, 49, 52, 53, 85, 100, 208,
    259, 261, 357, 361, 390; Christian,
    25; corporate, 24, 28
Capone, Al, 407
Capps, Charles, 188
Carmichael, Stokely, 220
Carnegie, Andrew, 53, 83, 412
Carroll, B. H., 427
Carson, Clayborne, 223
Carter, Jimmy, 235, 237
Carter, Joseph C., 87
Carter, Paul, 63
Carver, W. O., 97
Casdorph, H. Richard, 231
Casey, Phil, 178
Casey, William Van Etten, 30, 36
Cash, Johnny, 51
Cashwell, G. B., 383
Caste system, xix
Catholic Conference on Industrial Prob-
    lems, 358
"Catholic Hour," 388
Catholic Interracial Council, 30
Catholic Left, 36
Catholic Peace Fellowship, 33
*Catholic Worker*, 104
Catholic Worker movement, 30, 32, 106–
    9, 434
Catonsville Nine, 34, 36
Cauthen, Kenneth, 147
CBN University, 351
Center for Intercultural Documentation,
    90
Center for the Study of Democratic Insti-
    tutions, 38
Central American Mission, 374
Cerre, Leontine, 372, 373
Chafer, Lewis Sperry, 375, 378
Chafin, Kenneth, 53
Chandler, Russel, 254
Chaplin, Charlie, 320
Chapman, J. Wilbur, 411–12
Charismatic movement, 44, 46, 186,

Ethics, 214; Christian, 320; economic, 358; fiscal, 413; personal, 414, 421
Eugenics, 147, 279
European Economic Community (Common Market), 249, 251
Evangelical Church Alliance, 227
Evangelical Lutheran Synod. *See* Missouri Synod
Evangelical Orthodox Church, 53
Evangelicalism, 54, 55, 94, 102, 144, 181–82, 183, 207, 262, 286, 349–54, 410–15, 432–35; nineteenth-century, 73
Evangelism, 52, 98, 150, 160, 180–81, 187, 197–98, 204, 208, 264–65, 267, 275, 303, 307, 314, 434–44, 346, 366, 374, 395, 396, 399, 411–15, 417–22
*Evangelist*, 420
Evangelization, 322
Evans, Dale, 52
Evans, Warren Felt, 322
Evening Light Saints, 381, 382
Everett, Eleanor, 437–38
*Every Week*, 23
Evil, view of, 407–8
Evolution, 61, 144, 213, 313, 415, 428, 429
Executive Seminars, 51, 53
Experience, Jewish, 211–12
Explo '72, 52; '74, 52; '85, 52; '90, 52
Extremism, 262, 316

Fairclough, Adam, 223
Faith and Order Commission, 306
Faith movement, 186, 188
Faith partners, 350
"Faith Seminar of the Air," 187
"Faith That Lives," 188
Falls, Roy E., 316
Falwell, Jerry, 16–17, 19, 54, 154, 182, 183, 200, 235, 260, 262, 435; appraisal of, 137–39; life of, 133–37; works about, 139–40
Family, view of, 234, 238, 287
Family Life Seminars, 235
Farah, Charles, 189
Fard, Wallace D., 278
Farmer's Alliance, 59, 197, 357

Fascism, 130, 274
Fast, Howard, 66
Faunce, W.H.P., 396
Fauset, Arthur H., 117, 172, 173, 178, 282
Federal Bureau of Investigation, 165, 166, 318, 320, 407
Federal Communications Commission, 18
Federal Council of Churches, 127–29, 147, 151, 257, 258, 273, 329, 405, 407
Fee, Gordon, 190
Fellowship of Independent Baptist Churches of Canada, 398
Fellowship of Reconciliation, 41
Feminism, 35, 136, 268
*Fence Rail*, 312
Ferlinghetti, Lawrence, 439
Ferreira, James, 28
Ferris, William, 167
Feuchtwanger, Lion, 123
Fickett, John, 190
Fields, Kathleen Riley, 391
Fields, Rick, 443
Film, 121–23; use of, 180, 200, 285, 344
Finkelstein, Louis, 213
Finney, Charles, 49, 51, 73, 182, 230, 410
Fisher, Brenda, 66
Fiske, Edward, 53
Fitzgerald, Frances, 139
Flake, Carol, 19, 55
Fleming, Esther, 245
Fleming, Robert E., 245
Fletcher, Alice, 458, 460
Ford, Betty, 99
Ford, George B., 295
Ford, Gerald, 99
Ford, Henry, 27
Ford, Henry II, 388
Forster, Arnold, 195
Fosdick, Harry Emerson, 39, 127, 128, 154, 206, 237, 306, 396, 402, 405, 409, 428; appraisal of, 145–47; life of, 141–45; works about, 147
Foundation for Christian Living, 330
Foundation for Religious Transition, 338
Four Spiritual Laws, 49, 50–51, 52, 54

Walrath, Douglas, 327
Walsh, Dan, 294, 295, 296
Walters, Ray, 254
Walters, Stanley D., 254
Walther League, 271, 273, 275
Walton, Hanes, 223
Walton, Samuel B., 161
Waltrip, Burroughs A., 227
Wanamaker, John, 73
War: Civil, 80, 81, 372; Cold, 38, 49,
  130, 131, 132, 179, 181, 193, 435;
  First World, 80, 85, 120, 127, 162,
  170, 271, 274, 303, 304–5, 307, 358,
  394–95, 415, 428; just, 128; Korean,
  26, 141, 247, 407; Middle East, 451;
  nuclear, 259; Second World, 27, 31,
  44, 49, 88, 122, 129, 130, 145, 147,
  151, 179, 186, 193, 206, 225, 233,
  239, 258–59, 275, 283, 286, 335, 398,
  400, 406, 417, 436, 442, 446; Six
  Day, 447, 451; Spanish-American, 59;
  Vietnam, 38, 90, 93, 135, 141, 221,
  260, 298, 352, 389, 432, 433, 449–50
Ward, Ralph, 42
Warfield, Benjamin B., 73
Warner, Daniel S., 381
Warner, Horace E., 302
Washington, Booker T., 162, 163, 164,
  166
Washington, James, 223
Washington, Joseph, 177
Watergate, 93, 288, 327
Watts, Alan: appraisal of, 441–43; life
  of, 437–41; works about, 443–44
Wayland, Francis, 80
Wealth, 58, 69, 81, 83, 253; Gospel of,
  83
Weaver, Douglas, 46
Weber, Timothy, 254
Weisberger, Bernard A., 415
Weisbrot, Robert, 116
Weiss, Ellen, xxi
Welfare, 137
Welk, Lawrence, 156
Well-being, spiritual, 445, 447, 449,
  450, 453
Welles, Orson, 249

Welles, Sumner, 128
Wells, Rufus, 172
West, Morris L., xiii; appraisal of, 448–
  53; life of, 446–48; works about, 453–
  54
West, Rebecca, 245
Westbourne Baptist Church, 2
Westminster Confession, 257
"What's Your Trouble," 330
Wheeler, Wayne, 76
White, Alma, 384
White, Lelia, 303
White, Ronald Moran, 117
Whitehead, Alfred North, 39
Whiting, Albert, 178
Whitney, Florence, 146
Wieman, Henry N., 39, 215
Wier, Hugh A., 413
Wigglesworth, Smith, 188
Wilburn, Gary, 254
Wilkerson, Ralph, 229
Wilkins, Roy, 220
Willard, Frances, 78
Williams, Albert N., 289
Williams, Bill, 323
Williams, Hosea, 220
Williams, Peter, xx
Williams, Roger, 334
Williams, Samuel, 222
Williams, Wayne, 63
Willkie, Wendell, 26
Wills, Garry, 36
Wilson, Betty Douglas, 120, 123
Wilson, David, 455
Wilson, Jack. See Wovoka
Wilson, Woodrow, 56, 60–61, 304
Wimberly, Ronald C., 184
Winnemucca, 455–56
Winona Lake Bible Conference, 198
Wodziwob, 455
Wolfram, Michael C., 276
Wolin, Sheldon, 139–40
Women: discrimination against, 433; or-
  dination of, 336, 340; role of, 287–88,
  289
Women in Communication, 158

# About the Contributors

R. SCOTT APPLEBY (Ph.D., Chicago), is assistant professor of religious studies at St. Xavier College, Chicago. Specializing in the impact of theological modernism on Roman Catholicism, he is currently working on a study of the historical roots of the contemporary Roman Catholic parish. He is a contributor to *Religious Periodicals of the United States*.

EDMUND C. BALLANTYNE holds the doctorate from the Divinity School of the University of Chicago. His main academic interests are the history of modern religious thought and the relations between science and religion.

RANDALL BALMER received his Ph.D. from Princeton University. On the faculty of Columbia University, he has had articles appear in *Church History, Methodist History,* and the *Journal of Presbyterian History,* and also contributed to *Religious Periodicals of the United States*.

SHELLEY BARANOWSKI (Ph.D., Princeton) teaches in the history department and program in the humanities at Kenyon College. A specialist in the history of Christianity, she is currently engaged in a comparative study of radicalism in the United States and Germany.

M. CRAIG BARNES has pursued his doctoral studies in the history of Christianity at the University of Chicago. He is currently teaching pastor of the First Presbyterian Church in Colorado Springs.

GUY C. CARTER received the Ph.D. in religious studies from Marquette University in Chicago. Presently pastor of Faith Lutheran Church in Sault Ste. Marie, Michigan, he is a contributor to *Religious Periodicals of the United States*.

PAUL G. CHAPPELL is dean of the School of Theology and Missions at Oral Roberts University in Oklahoma. He received his Ph.D. degree from Drew University. He contributed to *Religious Periodicals of the United States*.

ELISE CHASE, who holds masters degrees in English literature and pastoral ministry in addition to a degree in library science, is a reference librarian in Northampton, Massachusetts. She compiled *Healing Faith: An Annotated Bibliography of Christian Self-Help Books* for Greenwood Press.

THE REV. JAMES T. CONNELLY, C.S.C., is archivist for the Congregation of Holy Cross, Indiana Province, in Notre Dame. His Ph.D. dissertation at the University of Chicago studied the charismatic movement in U.S. mainline denominations. He contributed to *Religious Periodicals of the United States*.

LARRY V. CRUTCHFIELD is a free-lance writer and public affairs specialist living in Baumholder, West Germany. He received his Ph.D. from Drew University. Crutchfield's scholarly work has appeared in the *Journal of the Evangelical Theological Society* and *Biblical Illustrator*.

BARBARA RITTER DAILEY holds a doctorate in American history from Boston University. She has taught at Tufts University and Wellesley College. Currently Dailey is editor of the *Working Papers* for the Nuclear Age History and Humanities Center at Tufts.

WAYNE ELZEY, associate professor of religion at Miami University, received his doctorate from the University of Chicago. He has written numerous articles on popular Christianity in the United States and on the religions of Mesoamerica.

CRAIG A. FORNEY pursued his doctoral studies in the history of Christianity at the University of Chicago. His work focuses on the history of religion in the United States, ethics, and the thought of W.E.B. Du Bois.

THOMAS E. FRANK is assistant professor of congregational life and director of the Rollins Center for Church Ministries at Candler School of Theology, Emory University, where he received his Ph.D. A former United Methodist pastor, he is a contributor to *Religious Periodicals of the United States*.

DAVID GARRISON, after doctoral studies in the history of Christianity at the University of Chicago, is presently research associate at the Foreign Mission Board of the Southern Baptist Convention in Richmond. He formerly taught at Hong Kong Baptist College.

STEPHEN R. GRAHAM did doctoral studies at the University of Chicago where his dissertation dealt with Philip Schaff's analysis of the religious situation in the nineteenth-century United States. He is presently on the faculty of North Park Theological Seminary in Illinois.

MICHAEL HARRIS received the Ph.D. in music and American church history from Harvard University. Currently on the faculty of Wesleyan University, he has taught at the University of Tennessee in Knoxville and been a visiting scholar at Temple University. Harris is completing a book on the development of gospel blues music in Afro-American churches.

JOHN O. HODGES teaches cultural studies and religious studies at the University of Tennessee in Knoxville. He received the Ph.D. from the University of Chicago. His writing has appeared in the *College Language Association Journal,* the *Langston Hughes Review,* and the *Journal of Religion.*

THOMAS D. KENNEDY received the Ph.D. in religious studies from the University of Virginia. He is currently teaching philosophy and religious studies at Austin Peay State University in Tennessee.

L. DeANE LAGERQUIST received her graduate training at Luther Theological Seminary and the University of Chicago. Currently assistant professor of theology at Valparaiso University, she is author of *From Our Mothers' Arms: A History of Women in the American Lutheran Church.*

PAUL A. LAUGHLIN received the M.Div. and Ph.D. degrees from Emory University. He is assistant professor of religion and philosophy at Otterbein College in Ohio, author of *Lectionary Worship Aids, Series II,* and a contributor to *Religious Periodicals of the United States.*

WILLIAM B. LAWRENCE, senior pastor of Owego (New York) United Methodist Church, received the Ph.D. with special distinction from Drew University. He has been an adjunct professor at Lycoming College and teaching fellow at Drew.

L. DAVID LEWIS is associate professor of history at Anderson University in Indiana. He earned the Ph.D. in the history of Christianity from the University of Chicago. Lewis is a contributor to *Religious Periodicals of the United States.*

EDWARD TABOR LINENTHAL is associate professor of religion and American culture at the University of Wisconsin-Oshkosh. A contributor to *Religious Periodicals of the United States,* he is currently completing a book on the cultural significance of battlefields in American life.

CHARLES H. LIPPY (Ph.D., Princeton) is professor of religion at Clemson University. The author of books on religion in the South and on Charles Chauncy, he is, with Peter Williams, editor of the *Encyclopedia of the American Religious*

*Experience*. Lippy edited *Religious Periodicals of the United States* for Green-wood Press.

EUGENE Y. LOWE, JR., received his Ph.D. from Union Theological Seminary in New York. Presently dean of students and member of the religion faculty at Princeton University, he is a contributor to *Religious Periodicals of the United States*.

RALPH E. LUKER, who received his Ph.D. from the University of North Carolina in Chapel Hill, is associate editor of the Martin Luther King papers and author of *A Southern Tradition in Theology and Social Criticism*. His articles have appeared in numerous scholarly journals.

DEBORAH VANSAU McCAULEY received degrees from Harvard and Columbia universities before beginning doctoral work in American religious history at Columbia. Her major interest is Appalachian mountain religion.

MICHAEL R. McCOY is head of the department of philosophy and religion at Union College in Kentucky. He holds degrees from Emory and Henry College and Princeton Theological Seminary. McCoy, a contributor to *Religious Periodicals of the United States,* received the Ph.D. from Emory University.

JON PAHL received degrees from Valparaiso University and Trinity Lutheran Seminary before undertaking doctoral studies in the history of Christianity and American religion at the University of Chicago. His special interest is the impact of the doctrine of free will on the American character in the nineteenth century.

D. G. PAZ, a contributor to *Religious Periodicals of the United States,* is associate professor of history at Clemson University. His next book is a study of anti-Catholicism in Victorian England.

EDWARD L. QUEEN II received his Ph.D. from the Divinity School of the University of Chicago. With special interests in American religion, he currently lives and writes in Chicago.

JOEL SHERER is campus minister at Bismarck State College in North Dakota. A Lutheran clergyman, he pursued doctoral studies in American religions at the University of Chicago.

GERALD L. SITTSER received degrees from Hope College and Fuller Theological Seminary. After a career as a pastor, chaplain, and teacher, he undertook Ph.D. studies at the University of Chicago. He is the author of *The Adventure*.

STEPHEN H. SNYDER is associate professor and head of the department of religious studies at Linfield College. He is a contributor to *Religious Periodicals of the United States*.

MARK B. SORVILLO is a priest of the Roman Catholic Archdiocese of Chicago. He serves as instructor in church history at the University of St. Mary of the Lake in Mundelein, Illinois, and lecturer at the Institute of Pastoral Studies at Loyola University of Chicago.

JOHN G. STACKHOUSE, JR. (Ph.D., University of Chicago) is assistant professor of history at Northwestern College in Iowa. The author of several articles on Christianity in Canada, he wrote his dissertation on Canadian evangelicalism since World War I.

DANIEL SWINSON is a United Methodist pastor of a rural parish in western Illinois. His doctoral studies at the University of Chicago specialized in nineteenth- and early-twentieth century religious reform movements in the United States. He contributed to *Religious Periodicals of the United States*.

MARK G. TOULOUSE received the Ph.D. from the University of Chicago. On the faculty of Brite Divinity School at Texas Christian University, he is the author of *The Transformation of John Foster Dulles* and a contributor to *Religious Periodicals of the United States*.

DENNIS N. VOSKUIL (Ph.D., Harvard) is professor and chair of the department of religion at Hope College in Michigan. He is the author of *Mountains into Goldmines: Robert Schuller and the Gospel of Success* and numerous scholarly articles.

CECILE HOLMES WHITE is religion writer for the *Houston Chronicle* in Texas. A graduate of the University of South Carolina, she was a fellow in the Program in Religious Studies for Journalists at the University of North Carolina at Chapel Hill.

PETER W. WILLIAMS received the Ph.D. from Yale. Author of *Popular Religion in America*, he edited the three-volume *Encyclopedia of the American Religious Experience* with Charles H. Lippy. He is currently completing books on American religious architecture and the history of religion in the United States. Williams also contributed to *Religious Periodicals of the United States*.

ROBERT J. WILLIAMS is pastor of the First United Methodist Church in Pennington, New Jersey, and visiting lecturer at Princeton Theological Seminary. Holder of the Ph.D. degree from Drew University, he contributed to *Religious Periodicals of the United States*.

JOHN R. WIMMER graduated from the University of Indianapolis and the Duke University Divinity School. He pursued his doctoral studies in American religion at the University of Chicago Divinity School.

3